To Joi
Keep naviga
love & truth.
& your family



# ONE FAITH—MANY TRANSITIONS

# One Faith—Many Transitions

## Worldviews in Church History

(Second Edition)

By K.G. Powderly Jr

Printed in the United States of America

# DEDICATION

*For my beautiful Bride, Cheryl; Lord, please give us many happy hears together*

*For the pastors and people of Calvary Rio Rancho; who believed God's work in me even when I did not fit the standard molds*

# ACKNOWLEDGEMENTS

- All Bible quotations not from the ***King James Version*** **(KJV)** or ***Revised Standard Version*** **(RSV)** come from any of the following versions and will be identified accordingly:
    - ***New International Version*** **(NIV)** © 1973 by New York Bible Society International
    - ***New American Standard Bible*** **(NASB)** © 1960, 1962, 1963, 1968, 1971, 1972, 1973, 1975 and 1977 by The Lockman Foundation, La Habra, Ca.
    - ***New King James Version*** **(NKJV)** © 1982 by Thomas Nelson, Inc.
    - ***Holman Christian Standard Bible*** **(HCSB)** © 2003 by Holman
    - ***Bible in Basic English*** **(BBE)** © 1949

# Table of Contents

# INTRODUCTION:

The Bible meshes with history to a level no other body of sacred books can claim. Christian Theology began to develop a little later; when the historical and prophetic significance of events recorded in the New Testament books became plain. I do not mean much later—only about the generation's distance between the ministry of Jesus and writings of the Apostle Paul. Paul put the life of Jesus and other early events in the Christian movement into a theological context. Later generations of believers then built upon that foundation. The Holy Spirit designed it that way. This makes Christian history significant.

> **For we are God's fellow workers; you are God's field, you are God's building. According to the grace of God which was given to me, as a wise master builder I have laid the foundation, and another builds on it. But let each one take heed how he builds on it. For no other foundation can anyone lay than that which is laid, which is Jesus Christ. *1 Corinthians* 3:9-11 NKJV**

Learning from history sharpens our awareness of the patterns in Bible prophecy. Bible prophecy is not just about the prediction of future events, with the fulfilment simply being how and when those events happen. It includes that, but there is much more. Prophecy unveils repeating patterns in the flow of human events. So does history. The difference is that Bible prophecy has its source in the Divine, while history is a collective work of humanity. Appreciating one sharpens our understanding of the other, if only because God created humanity in His own image. Humanity will make mistakes in its studies of both prophecy and history. That does not make either subject useless to the Christian Faith.

The worth of this new edition of *One Faith – Many Transitions* reflects several things. One is that the trends in immediate future history projected by the conclusion of the 1st edition, nearly a decade and half ago, have unfolded as predicted. I would have rather been wrong about many of those. Since the Lord graced it otherwise, it seemed best to follow up in a sharper, easier to read version, with some new material.

Another reason for writing a new edition is to clarify my use of the ***Inductive Bible Study*** (IBS) method where appropriate in the biblical analysis dimension of this book.

**INDUCTIVE BIBLE STUDY -- STAGE 1**

| Inductive Bible Study Chart for Any Given Scriptural Book/Passage | | |
|---|---|---|
| Observation | Interpretation | Application |
| **What does the text say?** | **What does the text *mean by* what it says?** | **How do *I apply that meaning to my life* in this day & age?** |

Biblical analysis of Christian history takes an active role in *One Faith – Many Transitions*. Inductive logic reasons from particulars toward universals; in the case of studying the Bible, from particular books and passages toward universal questions like, *"What does God's word teach about marriage?"* A ***particular*** is an isolated object. A ***universal*** is that which connects the dots between the particulars to reveal patterns and establish their meaning. Inductive Bible Study emphasizes the distinctions between observing a biblical text, interpreting it, and then applying it. The figure below gives a more detailed look at the sort of questions that go into observation, interpretation, and application.

**INDUCTIVE BIBLE STUDY -- STAGE 1**

| Inductive Bible Study Chart for Any Given Scriptural Book/Passage | | |
|---|---|---|
| Observation | Interpretation | Application |
| **Who, what, when, where, & how many? What the text *explicitly* says as raw data, with <u>no talk</u> of interpretation or "what it means to me." Take time to notice details that seem odd or significant.** | **Drawing valid *inferences* by "if-then" logic statements to determine *implications & meaning*. What did the text mean to the original writers & readers? Historic context** | **What does the text mean to me today? How can I apply it personally to my life, philo-sophically to my culture, communally to my family and church (if in leadership),** etc. |

The reader will also notice some words in ***bold italics***. These terms are in the glossary at the end of this book. We live at a time when language—including that by which we access Scripture—is collapsing. These terms expand our ability to discuss history, and the worldviews that have affected it. Teachers of the word in particular will find them useful.

Since *One Faith—Many Transitions* attempts to shine the Bible as a light on Christian history, it is important that the reader understand this interpretive approach. *One Faith—Many Transitions* is not a Bible study as such, but it does bring Scripture to bear regularly, to add perspective. It also tries to sensitize the reader to assumptions that believers in past eras made in their views of Scripture. In so doing, we can gain insight on some of the unconscious assumptions we might be making, as we seek to apply the word for today.

This is an important clarification, especially for a pastorally driven study of church history, and worldviews. A student of history would add in the Application Column; *how is the given Bible text applicable to the analysis of a particular historical period?* Were Christians in parts of church history really "ignoring God's word" or did they just apply its truths differently than we would, in another historical situation? One might also ask that question in reverse. Are we really so sensitive to God's word that we always apply it wisely to our own historical situation? Is it possible that not considering the significance of our own history to the issues we face today can lead us to shallow views of Scripture?

It is important to stress that we should not look to church history as the ideal for how Christianity should function. That ideal foundation place belongs uniquely to Scripture. We can, however save ourselves much time and hassle by having a working knowledge of worldviews in church history. It keeps us from the waste of reinventing the wheel every generation, and gives us insight into the origin of ideas. We also find good models of what is likely to work or not, as we build in the superstructure toward the end of the age. This study also sensitizes us to the fact that universal truths never change, though the best ways to apply them in differing historical periods likely will.

It is not about the past, but the future.

# 1

# First Century Origins: New Testament Faith from a Jewish Worldview

## Why Study Worldviews in Church History?

The history of Christianity often reads like a wartime romance, when reduced to its basic plot and theme. This is thought provoking, considering that the New Testament refers to the church as the *bride of Christ.* (Eph. 5:25-32, Rev. 21:9)

The heroine Bride waits for her nobleman fiancée to come for her during intense wartime challenges in a battle-torn countryside. Partisan factions pull her in opposing directions, tempting her, and threatening her life. At times, they cleverly try to slander her fiancé, or else they falsely claim to be his messengers to her. Behind these factions lurk her fiancée's enemy, an evil manipulator of nations working by multiple intrigues and assassinations to subvert her fiancée, and to bring ruin to the Bride.

The war soon presents the Bride with confusing moral choices, some with no good options, where she must choose whatever does the least amount of damage. Sometimes, she fails to do the right thing, or even the least damaging thing. A few of her failures become so shameful that she feels she cannot face the horror of them, and so on those issues, she begins to live in denial.

Rival men in her life seem useful to give her security for the moment, so she convinces herself that leading them on is necessary for her to survive dangerous times. Deep down inside, she really wants to be true to her groom, and tries to be, but there are now so many complications.

Nevertheless, her fiancée knows her plight, and forgives her weaknesses. He sends trusted soldiers to help her through the enemy lines so they can be together. Unfortunately, the Bride is wounded and shell-shocked. After so many conflicting experiences, some of them brought on by her compromises, she is not always certain which side everyone is on anymore. She does not always see her fiancé's emissaries for what they are.

She is still at least partly in denial.

The Bride follows some of her fiancé's guides willingly, others with great reluctance. Still others, she treats as enemies, because they confront her directly about her compromises. She cannot believe that any friend of her Intended would say such hard things to her. It rarely occurs to her that they might do so because they are his friends—and hers too.

Christian history seems dark and disappointing to many Christians. It sometimes resembles tiny islands of integrity in a bloody ocean of incompetence, corruption, and fanaticism. The epic is both uplifting and discouraging. It sinks into pits of human cruelty and weakness, while all too few mountains of spiritual power, clarity, and compassion appear. Of course, that is just *how it seems.*

In reality, this is not a balanced picture, despite the very real low points. To some extent, secularist media and academics have conditioned us to focus on these. Sometimes we really should focus there, but not to the point where we get a tunnel vision that leaves us blind to the vast civilizing influence Christian thought has had in our history. Almost 300 years ago, Christians painted too rosy a picture of church history. Then another ideology rose to power in Western education, which focused only on the low points, and sought to make low points of the high ones. Neither approach is honest.

Monty Python has hilariously conditioned us "not to expect the Spanish Inquisition" since 1970. Witch-hunts real and imagined are a regular part of our cultural story-telling landscape, where church history is concerned. I love the Python skits with Cardinals Fang and Biggles. Aside from their usefulness at inducing a belly laugh, they remind us that Christians have not always taken the moral high ground in history. Still, there are more high points than we think. We just don't always know where to look for them.

To have a balanced historical picture, we need to compare the Christian story to what went on in places with little or no Christian influence during the same era. The key idea is *during the same era*. Usually, we only have so dismal a view of church history because we compare it with good things we take for granted today, without asking how those good things got there. Either that or we compare it to an unrealistic view of the Book of Acts. We take the miracles from the 35 to 40 years covered by Luke as if they happened every day in that era. This affects our assumptions about spiritual power and relationships.

We forget that the church of the 1st century had as many problems as we face today, as shown by situations described in 1 Corinthians, Jude, and Galatians. The Apostolic Era was the Foundational Age, not the Golden Age. We should not look through rose-colored glasses. Church history is also the story of people who perverted God's work, some even with good intentions, and others for power and misguided zeal. Rogues sincerely convinced themselves (and most everyone else at the time) that they were doing the right thing. The heroes were sometimes those that nobody thought would amount to much.

The Christian faith has several times stood at the verge of extinction in its long history. Whenever the world thought Christianity obsolete as a spiritual and intellectual force, Christians rose from the ashes. They reshaped both themselves, and their societies, by radical new applications of ancient and timeless Bible truths. They made comebacks by embracing in new ways the same scriptural principles that seemed so hopelessly outmoded to their critics. At such times, they did what appeared to be the very opposite of what conventional wisdom dictated, and history proved them right.

At other times, Christian movements bent to popular culture, only to hamstring their own influence. Either that or they walled themselves off into spiritual, intellectual, and sometimes even physical ghettos. They kept their most visible practices intact, only to stagnate in isolation. In either case, history marginalized their churches into cultural relics—the opposite of what those movements expected. Then, God worked later through new spiritual movements.

If the Lord waits, this Arthurian cycle will go on until our own cherished spiritual forms and traditions become the relics of another era. God will then again revitalize His church. We may already be there. Yet history shows that revitalization does not always come from the direction we anticipate. It is not always with the "cutting edge," seeking "relevance." Nor is it always with those forces trying to cling to tradition or a formulaic approach to an established systematic theology. It will however, involve a return to the Bible and a movement of the Holy Spirit in some way.

The present stage of American Evangelical Christianity often seems neat and functional each Sunday. It seldom occurs to us that the long haul of getting there was a sloppy, often bloody business. After searching the records to ask what our spiritual forebears might have done differently, all too often no easy answers arise; sometimes no answers at all.

At first, we have an easy time comparing Scripture with what happened in church history, and pointing out the unbiblical flaws. (There are often many.) Then, closer inspection of historical records show that many such Christians, who seemed so easy to criticize, actually wrestled to obey God's word diligently against huge obstacles; often more diligently than we do. Like us, they also missed stuff. This challenges our assumptions, and forces us to refine our understanding. Church history seems to scare many Christians for this very reason—even some pastors. (I have had some pastors actually tell me this, and heard others who seemed to imply it.)

Yet, the adage is true that those who do not learn from history are doomed to repeat it. If history is any gauge, the worst spiritual dangers facing us, as Christians, today will likewise come screaming at us from out of our blind spots. Our biggest blind spots usually hide in the shadows of our greatest strengths.

I did not explore history because I am a scholar, but because I wanted to know how and why my church family developed as they did. For years, I had little clue about the transitions Christianity suffered over the millennia. I did not know what they meant for us today or why believers had to endure them "back in the day." I had a huge gap in my picture of how the church got from its apostolic infancy to the varied forms it takes today. While there will always be gaps in history, some are too big to ignore, and should be filled.

I began my search for answers, using the Bible as my spiritual compass. I started from the assumption that God would be faithful to reveal His work in history, if not with absolute clarity, than at least with adequate clues. As I interact with my brothers and sisters in the faith, I see that many are as I was. They have questions about why different churches believe different things, how that started, and even why their own churches may teach a certain position. These questions go beyond *"how did this happen?"* or *"who started this teaching?"* They go right to the core of *why?*

Those who take the Bible seriously, often do as I did. They read up on church history, learn what happened, who made it happen, and when and where it happened. Yet many, like me, come away afterward even more confused. Church history often seems so unbalanced to American Christians that we feel the need to ask of our spiritual forebears, *"What were you thinking?"* Sometimes past Christianity really was unbalanced, just as today's Christianity can be. At other times, we may need to question our own assumptions a little more rigorously. I'm hoping we can learn to do the latter before we conclude the former.

Answers here do not come only from reading about what happened in church history. One must ask what ***worldviews*** drove the thinking of people behind the historical events, and how. A worldview is not a philosophy, but something more basic, like a grid. It is how people see reality at the bottom line, in terms they often take for granted in ways that "go without saying." We do not often think about our worldviews consciously. Nevertheless, our worldviews shape our impressions and beliefs about virtually everything.

In analyzing the impact of worldviews on church history, many questions need asking. Those of pastoral calling, who care about the cause-and-effect of how ideas have consequences, might ask; *how have major non-Christian worldviews of the past and present influenced the development of Christian thought and practice both positively and negatively?*

Can a non-Christian worldview positively affect the faith?

It can if some part of it is consistent with biblical truth, and if the Holy Spirit uses that part of it redemptively. God can bring good out of evil, despite evil's intent. That means He is quite capable of redeeming a thought-form, reasoning tool, or an art form or music and literary style from a non-Christian source. The God of the Bible is the God of reality.

Of course, that does not mean we should be sloppy, or unrealistic in examining worldviews. Our civilization dies from lack of discernment over the liabilities some worldviews can carry. Not all of them fit the human condition equally well. Not all worldviews lead to equally benevolent or realistic ideas about justice. Not all have a sound basis for ethics. This is not a racial or nationalistic issue, but rather a matter of ideas and the assumptions that undergird them.

It is historically self-evident that majorities in any given people group sometimes accept bad ideas from worldviews that do not fit the human condition terribly well. This disproves the false idea of racism. There are always those from that same people group who reject the bad ideas and the faulty aspects of the worldviews producing them. This is true whether we speak of Nazism in Germany or human sacrifice among the Aztecs. Truth is not about racial or cultural identity, it is about ideas that fit reality.

The now dominant Western worldview of ***Postmodernism*** tells us, "All truth is relative," that all we can really have are "truth claims." It essentially would have us think that *all ideas are equally good*, if enough people sincerely believe them.

Really?

One thing history reveals clearly about the human social condition is how frequently popular consensus turns out to be wrong in the end. Ask Late Medieval scientists and churchmen, both Catholic and Reformed, who were so sure that the Bible taught that the earth was the absolute center of the universe. Ask George Washington, whose doctor followed the prevailing medical assumptions of his day, and bled him to death. Ask chemical evolution pioneer Dean Kenyon if he still thinks that complex amino acids and DNA molecules can "self-organize."

Consensus theology works about as well in the end as consensus science, or whenever people view consensus as the bottom-line way of knowing if something is true. "All those people couldn't be wrong," is the motto of Lemmings.

A recent Gallop Poll showed that many Americans today look upon religion as a kind of spiritual smorgasbord. They choose their beliefs to fit their personal lifestyle tastes. This has filtered into churches. Many people increasingly view religious doctrine as rigid and outdated, and "faith" as something disconnected from the realm of reason.

Though the poll revealed more than 80% of Americans want to grow spiritually, it also showed rampant illiteracy of the Bible and church history. This is a tragedy of immense magnitude.

One gets the sense that many people think that too much focus on the doctrines of the church is what caused all the trouble in church history. This simplistic, inaccurate assumption does not stand up to scrutiny, but it is certainly a "consensus view." It assumes the foundational human problem is one of intellectual focus on an emotional subject that naturally leads to argument. What if that assumption is wrong; what if, instead, the fundamental human problem is that we have a sin-warped **"heart that is deceitful and desperately wicked?"** (Jer. 17:9)

The first assumption only evades the issue. The second touches on something universal to the human condition. Consequently, people often have many questions, but seem to also have that ingrained fear of seeking answers, mentioned earlier. Faith only matures when things challenge it.

One of my biggest questions concerned the nature of the "true church." Was it an organism or an organization, an institution or a group of people?

The teaching that there is always a "faithful remnant," whether of Israel or the Church, is biblical. That historical reality did not often resemble the naïve picture of it I had as a young believer, however. The "true church" throughout history was not some tiny, shadowy circle who thought pretty much like American Fundamentalists did, all the way back to the Apostles. How could any group of people be faithful to the calling of Christ to go into the world, and yet remain invisible to history? Nevertheless, a faithful remnant was present in history. It just did not often take the form I had expected in my youthful over-simplification of the ***Doctrine of the Remnant***.

This was an area where my preconceptions had me looking for the wrong things. I do not mean my biblical assumptions, but those I unconsciously took into both the Bible and history from my background culture. The discovery that I had those surprised me, too. My study of worldviews in church history shattered such false confidence, and replaced it with a richer understanding of God's grace and providence. It also gave me deeper trust in God's word.

Another challenge came when church history occasionally showed me people who found salvation in spite of what they believed, as well as because of it. Their conversion did not come by a different gospel—anyone truly saved got that way because of the work of Christ, through their faith in him. Yet their faith sometimes took very different forms than ours does, in the way they applied it to the issues of their day. Those differences of form arose out of different worldviews and different challenges to the Faith than those we face. The essential truth remained the same, even if we had to look more deeply to recognize it.

Many believers out of church history accepted things that would be unthinkable to us. Many even believed things that are rankly unbiblical by any objective standard. Yet they trusted the Bible's Jesus as best they had the tools to understand Him. This is not to say that having a biblical understanding of the gospel is not important—far from it! Such periods characterized by this pattern were also rife with unchallenged religious corruption, or social breakdown, or both. Then there were those disturbing times when the doctrine looked good, but Christians still did ugly things to one another, and society broke down just as quickly. Sometimes, too, Christians remained faithful, and the culture just did not want to hear it.

The discovery that people who had little in the line of good teaching were sometimes the most faithful people of their era forced me to pause and think. It made an important category. Does salvation come by faith in Christ's work or by an ability to have a precise knowledge of Christ's work by 21st century American Conservative Evangelical standards? If by the latter, we are all in trouble. If by the former, then there is hope.

This is not an apologetic for sloppy doctrine, or some kind of "Big Tent" ecumenicalism that ignores Scripture. It is a simple recognition that there are limits to what we can all know, observe, and apply even from the same Bible. Not everyone in every age received the same tools to work with, except for the Holy Spirit, and He is far more than a mere tool. He does not often pass out information the same way to everyone.

Conservative biblical faith has nothing real to fear from church history. Once equipped to question the foundational assumptions of Modernist, and Postmodernist academics, believers find that they have sure footing. Liberal scholars often seem threatened today by where the evidence is leading on many intellectual and spiritual fronts. I know this because they respond so often by political methods instead of by those of reason.

Another good reason to learn about worldviews in church history is that we, as servants of Christ, are in a spiritual war. We need to study this for the same reason midshipmen must study military history at the naval academy. We don't want to make the same mistakes made in past battles.

We also do not want to "reinvent the wheel" in our attempts to deal with today's spiritual and ethical problems. There is a developing pattern to the enemy's tactics. Satan learns. He is not all knowing or all-powerful, nor is he everywhere at once. He modifies his tactical attack patterns. Still, he never leaves his strategic objectives and basic military doctrines. These he designed to appeal to us through the world, the flesh, and the power of the demonic through the lust of the flesh, the lust of the eyes, and the pride of life.

## How Does History Relate to the Divine Inspiration of Scripture?

Having established why it is a good idea to study church history with a worldview perspective, maybe we should briefly look at what church history actually is.

This book does not pretend to be an in-depth analysis or even a historical overview, though it might be closer to the latter. It zeroes in on the roles major worldviews of the past and present played in shaping the history of Christian thought and practice. Think broad brushstrokes.

We have many ways of knowing history, each with differing "mechanics." History can be a view of the past taken directly from the written and oral testimonies of those who actually lived through the events. Here, "the people who were there" wrote about their own experiences. Historians call such writings *source documents*. Usually, younger writers later interviewed the eyewitnesses after the meaning of the events became clearer. This, too, might be a source document, because eyewitnesses are still involved. It also describes a *secondary source* that interviews, records, collates, edits, and sometimes comments. The first scenario describes how the Gospel of Matthew came to be, the second how Luke wrote his Gospel and much of Acts.

History also involves inferences made by those who lived long after the fact, and have the benefit of hindsight. For this reason, history has both an ***objective*** and ***subjective*** element to it. It analyzes objective records and artifacts that speak of happenings from times before people living today could directly know. Yet records come through the subjective viewpoint of whoever wrote them. Even authors that valued objectivity, and practiced it in what they wrote, show some subjective element.

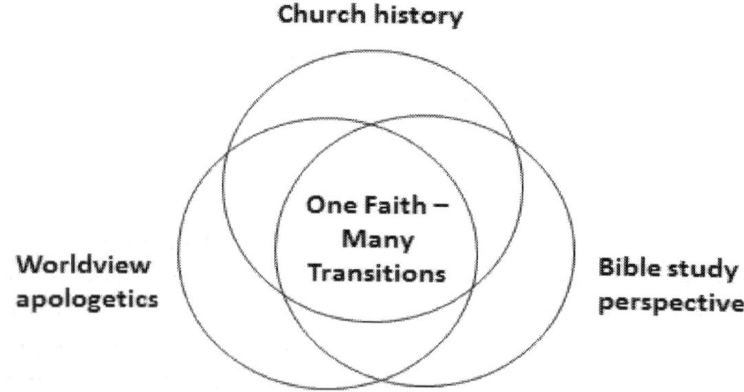


**Where *One Faith—Many Transitions* fits into the "big picture" as an aid to Christian ministry and education**

The ***legal-historic method*** of knowing the past involves recording, and harmonizing many testimonies. It is ultimately our only way to know that history even happened. Yet it is quite different from the scientific method. No one can reproduce History in the laboratory. It can only be re-enacted. All re-enactments rely on accurate records, with only the most limited help from forensics. Any interpretation of forensic evidence, in fact, demands a grid of starting assumptions. Only rarely will "CSI" crime shows reveal that on television, and then only as if it were an oddball occurrence. In reality, interpretive assumptions break down far more often.

The truth is, that both forensic and testimonial evidence can and have been "gamed" by clever enough people, and misread by accident. Nevertheless, the logical fallacies of ***Postmodernist*** views of history are still fallacies. Just because it is impossible to know the past perfectly, does not mean it is impossible to know it substantially and truly. There are honest methods of analysis.

Yet because history is partly subjective, it also involves making value judgments about the past. That does not mean morality and ethics are mere subjective matters of opinion, only that the act of making ***values*** is. People do not always create values on a moral basis, or in relation to an ***ethic***. It is possible to make values based on political or some other kind of preference. Often, people make values on an arbitrary emotional basis. It is common today, as it was in the Greek-Roman world, to make values based upon ***pragmatism*** (what seems to work). Others make them based on ***hedonism*** (what brings pleasure), or in order to please the powerful and service their agendas (***political correctness***).

None of that makes it irrational to form values based on well-reasoned moral absolutes that self-evidently fit the observed human condition. Western Common Law and the Eastern Tao both did this. [1] People can also base values on Divine revelation. Doing both of the latter well involves reasoning with moral and intellectual integrity. One recognizes integrity when people making such values "swear to their own hurt," as Psalm 15:4 put it. Of course, church history shows many times when Christians failed to do that. It also shows quite a number of other times when it happened well enough to shape the best of Western Civilization. [2]

Morality and ethics are not the same things as "values." People who make values based on morality and ethics must often do so *against their natural inclinations and desires*. They make such values regardless of whether the outcomes are pleasurable, pragmatic, or politically convenient for them. *Morals, values,* and *ethics* are not different words for the same thing, and never truly have been. While Postmodernist academics insist on equating the three, they have consistently failed to prove this equation by ignoring evidence, which brings us back to their key logical fallacy.

Postmodernism's moral and cultural ***Relativism*** demands we treat their faith-assumption that "moral absolutes don't exist" as if it were the only moral absolute. They gain ground by pretending that moral absolutes cannot exist, and then repeat this idea through popular media. It seems so superficially convenient, that many people jump on the bandwagon. Soon however, demands pop up for everyone else to either conform to this view or face ugly consequences. Sound familiar? Moral relativism is not honest or terribly smart. Yet it has become foundational to today's academic humanities, politics, entertainment, and the arts.

While history cannot be absolutely objective, that does not mean that it is totally subjective, either. Just because no human form of analysis works with absolute objectivity, does not mean that substantial objectivity is not attainable or desirable. Try switching out the value of *objectivity* with some other value, like *selflessness*, and see if the idea holds up. Just because human beings lack the ability to be absolutely selfless, does not mean that selflessness is an illusion, and should not be valued. Nor does it mean that selflessness is just a mask to cover "the true selfish motive." Such cynicism is the faith-assumption of a dull and dismal myth.

There is a difference between educated, morally honest points-of-view, and self-serving spin. Point-of-view is relevant to the study of history, but so is the fact that not all points-of-view are equally honest or well informed.

Some attempts to revere "historic objectivity" proved just as phony as Postmodernism's fanaticism to discredit it. A hundred years ago, idealist progressives duped academics into the myth that the Catholic Church taught that the earth was flat before Columbus' voyage. ***Positivist*** ideologue Andrew Dickson White started this trend, hoping to demonize Christianity as an "enemy of objective science," and of "objective history." [3] The idea resonated with the rising popularity of Darwinism at the time, so few checked White's sources for nearly a century. Once historians looked more closely, they stopped taking White seriously. I am, however, old enough to remember having White's myth taught to me in elementary school as "historical fact."

It should have been easy to see through ideologues like White. Art from circa 800 to 1300 AD often depicted both Charlemagne and the Roman Popes holding a ball, sometimes with a cross sticking out of it. This was the *royal orb*. It signified that the one holding it was the rightful *ruler of the world*. The orb was a stylized globe, showing that most Europeans before Columbus (1492 AD) knew the earth was round. Today, media and academics routinely present ideas as proven facts that are no more than assumptions. Worldviews of the past and present often rest on far less than we think. We can train ourselves to notice the differences between a faith-assumption, a piece of objective evidence or common human experience, and a conclusion or "fact." It is not "rocket science," but it does require a willingness to learn.

***Worldview apologetics*** is the defense of the Faith using knowledge of worldviews from the past and present. This has fast become a basic survival skill for Information Age Christians. For me, only a working understanding and personal application of the Bible is more important, at this time in history. Pastors and leaders need it now more than ever.

Yet how do we really get to the worldview of peoples who lived thousands of years ago? Honestly, we can't, always. Even when we can, we cannot do so completely. Still, we can piece together the major working parts of ancient worldviews by examining common perceptions expressed in their records. The ancient authors may not even have been conscious of some of these perceptions, but they stick out like sore thumbs to us because of their seeming oddity. We do not make the same assumptions about reality that people made a thousand or even a hundred years ago.

Ancient writers, like those of today, assumed that their readers would intuitively pick up at least some of what they meant by what they wrote. The communication medium also affects the message. Some media, like clay tablets, demanded a form of writing that maximized cultural assumptions. Those using it wrote as if the reader would already carry most of the information needed to understand the writing in their own minds. Clay tablets took up a lot of space, and thus could not indulge a writing style that required space for the easy explanation of terms, such as we can do today. By New Testament times, the writing medium was mostly vellum and papyrus, which allowed more space for detail, but still had other limitations we do not often think of.

Even today, we still write in ways that assume the reader and the author already share common knowledge. For example, I don't have to explain what the Internet is if I mention it when I write. This is why 19th century novels are sometimes hard to understand for 21st century readers. Many household items in the 19th century are foreign to us today. If I said that *I had vouchsafed my portmanteau against my journey on the proverbial iron horse*, how many readers today would know what I meant? (I stored my luggage in a safe place for my train trip.)

Worldview ideas of the past often seem even weirder than mere terms for items we no longer use. That is part of where this book comes in. It brings out some of the common worldview perceptions that influenced the church in the past. These include the ideas that seemed thinkable or unthinkable at the time, and what questions were considered worth asking or not, and why. Such things would not be the focus in history books that did not explore worldviews.

The primary documents written by the Apostles (or those who knew and worked with the Apostles, including Paul), are found in the New Testament. Divine revelation happened within the backdrop of history. We all encounter half-truths about how the Bible developed, and what "Divine inspiration" even means, as we grow in faith. Some stem from innocent oversimplifications of well-meaning believers. Others are hostile attempts to twist the idea of "Divine inspiration" itself. Perhaps the most misleading idea is that there is a hard dividing line between "regular history" and historical books found in the Bible. All histories written by peoples of the ancient world, like those of today, reflect the writer's worldviews.

It helps to remember that the Christianity of the 1st century arose out of a Jewish worldview. In fact, people in the 1st century saw Christianity as a small, often vocal sect of Judaism. As an example of seeing New Testament Christianity through a Jewish worldview, look at one of the Kingdom Parables in Luke 13:20-21; **"And again he** (Jesus) **said, 'To what shall I compare the kingdom of God? It is like leaven which a woman took and hid in three measures of flour, till it was all leavened.'" (RSV)**

We often hear pastors teach that the leaven is the spread of the gospel. This may be partly true, but the parable's Jewish culture reveals another, earlier context than the one often assumed by later Gentile Christians. Three measures of grain were the standard "fellowship offering" of the Torah. Jews often used the idea of leaven as a type for spiritual or ceremonial contamination. There are exceptions to this, but Jesus' use of the fellowship offering measurements adds clarity in two ways:

The word, *church,* in Greek means the *gathering* of that which God has separated out from the world for a specific purpose. In the case of the church, the primary purpose of gathering is that of *fellowship* in the worship of God through Christ. The Jewish worldview background adds clarity in a couple of possible ways. The first is as a prophecy that the Gentiles would become God's main instrument for furthering His kingdom—in which case the Gentile spread of the gospel makes sense.

There is a second, negative dimension revealed by a Jewish framework that we cannot discount. Jesus and the Apostles also warned that corrupting influences would find their way into the expression of God's kingdom here on earth in this present age—the church. Wheat and tares would grow together. The tiny mustard seed would grow incredibly, but house "birds of the air," which is often parable-speak for demonic influences. Jesus expressed uncertainty as to whether He would find "faith alive on the earth" at His Second Coming. The Jewish worldview of the parable lends insight to both interpretive shades, making it a proverbial "double-edged sword." Church history is also consistent with both pictures.

Because we Christians believe the New Testament books to be the inspired word of God, we need to understand how they came into being, and how they came to be recognized. We also need to know what it is we mean when we say that the New Testament books are *historical* in nature. Why are these books ***God-breathed*** and other church historical records not? What does Divine inspiration even mean?

To eliminate the misconceptions, I will summarize from *The Words of Jesus in the Gospels: Live, Jive, or Memorex?* by Darrell L. Bock (Ph.D.), Professor of New Testament Studies at Dallas Theological Seminary. This paper belongs to a volume of related articles by conservative biblical scholars titled, *Jesus Under Fire,* which shows how modern liberal scholarship has reinvented a "historical Jesus"' to fit their ideological prejudices.

The first misconception about Divine inspiration is that because Scripture is the word of God, then there can be no real human authors as such. Imagine the biblical authors "channeling the Holy Spirit," bypassing their own thoughts, to leave no human element, except the handwriting style. This error might appeal to some who truly "want it to be all about God, and not about us," as humans. Yet it does not fit the facts of what we find in the Bible or what Scripture says of itself.

Other well-meaning believers seem to have a related notion that Divine inspiration means, "God gave dictation." Young believers sometimes want to remove the human element because it makes them feel safe. They are so freshly out of the darkness that they want God, and not the human, so badly that they do not consider the implications. The idea of God taking over the inspired writers' hands, to make them write things that did not spring from their own minds and hearts, may seem attractive superficially. Yet it does not stand up to scrutiny. We can observe wildly differing writing styles in the Bible.

In order to remove the possibility of error, those who hold such views have removed the human element. They imagine that anything human must contaminate Divine inspiration. Such views embrace a serious error, despite their intention to honor God over man. As Christ is the living Word of God in the form of a real man, so the Scriptures are the written word of God, developed and authored through real human writers.

Inspired authors showed real human viewpoints, reasoning, and writing styles. The Holy Spirit breathed into the process in a variety of ways to produce texts that ultimately came about according to God's will. It was not either/or, it was and/both, under the sovereign hand and breath of God. Some (though clearly not most) of the writers may even have been unaware that they were writing God's word at the time.

Paul's thoughts were truly Paul's thoughts. They just happened also to be God's thoughts, who had orchestrated Paul's life and gifting in such a way that those thoughts expressed exactly what God wanted to say. For example, in his First Epistle to the Corinthians, Paul answered a list of questions that came to him in a letter we no longer have. Here God prompted the Apostle to answer the issues of other writers who were not inspired themselves, but part of a complex process of events. Paul was not just a mindless pen. He was a living, thinking, and creative instrument, fearfully and wonderfully made!

The second major misconception on Divine inspiration is that it simply means having an extraordinary spiritual motivation. Here, the words of Scripture are merely human words motivated by a love for God at best, and religious manipulation at worst. This removes the Divine element. At best, the Scriptures become only devotional in nature, at worst they become fallible compilations of self-seeking men who often resorted to pious fraud to reinforce their teachings. Those with this misconception are often at the opposite end of the theological spectrum from those who have the first two.

A third oversimplification is perhaps a subset of the first, which applies only to the New Testament. It assumes that the Bible passages printed in red are an exact transcript of the very words Jesus used. The idea is that inerrancy demands we think of the words of Jesus as if a tape recorder had recorded them. Those with this view often feel that they hold the highest view of inspiration. Yet they ignore the nature of what history is, and how it is recorded—even when done through the leading of the Holy Spirit. They also ignore important details in the Gospel texts.

Does this mean that knowing history diminishes confidence in Divine inspiration? No. It can and should make it stronger!

A robust view of Divine inspiration accounts for all relevant text and historical evidences. It also remains faithful to the orthodox doctrine of biblical inerrancy. God providentially used the normal processes of historical record to set down in the Scriptures exactly what He wanted to say to us for all time, in exactly the words He wanted used. This involved a wide variety of methods on God's part, as the Scripture says:

> **God, who at various times and in various ways spoke in time past to the fathers by the prophets... Hebrews 1:1 (NKJV)**

Historic recording works through the memories of eyewitnesses, and interviewing, documenting, and editing of their recollections. It may infuriate some well-meaning people to think of the biblical writers *editing* God's word. Yet that anger only assumes one or more of the inspiration misconceptions. Editing is an important part of any writing procedure. Working with imperfect human authors, God would especially want to guide the editorial process to give his fallible human instruments the grace needed to get it right.

Others object that fallible humans are incapable instruments to write and edit infallible Divine Scripture. This is a logical fallacy, however. Fallible humans write accurate manuals on how to assemble and maintain complex equipment all the time. Such manuals are often error-free, though they come from fallible human writers and editors. In the 1st century, authors often edited their own work, if they could. There are rare cases in Scripture of "Divine dictation" such as Revelation, Chapters 2 and 3, where Jesus had John write out his messages to the seven churches of Asia Minor. These are exceptions however.

Likewise, we do not often have a word-for-word transcript of Jesus' exact words in the red letters of the Gospels. We actually have something better! The Gospels not only give us the accurate content of Jesus' teachings and life events, but the Holy Spirit-guided impressions of many witnesses to those things. Some remembered things that others missed. The words of Jesus often affected people in a variety of ways; choreographed by the Holy Spirit using varied impressions to weave a pattern of history that is multi-layered and rich.

If we merely had a word-for-word transcript of Jesus' exact words, then we would not have the multi-textured tapestry of the Holy Spirit expressing himself through many witnesses. The account would be one-dimensional. All three members of the Godhead worked together in the task of inspiring Scripture, just as they worked together in the creation of the universe. [4]

The next question is about how churches recognized the Scriptures as God's word. Two extreme positions exist on how this happened. Biblically and historically under-literate Evangelicals often hold to one fringe, while the other comes from similarly afflicted Roman Catholics. Both positions are oversimplifications, which have produced errors.

Some Evangelicals mistakenly believe Christians recognized all the books of the New Testament as Canonic Scripture by the time the last Apostle died. This half-truth is also half-false. It is true that all the books that later became part of the New Testament were written by that time, as we shall see presently.

Roman Catholics hold that there are two equally authoritative sources of apostolic teaching, Tradition and Scripture. In this view, the tradition of the church produced Scripture. This eliminates Scripture as the measuring stick to determine what beliefs qualify as having apostolic character. [5] Conflicts of church authority in the 1st century took different forms than in later eras for one simple reason; the Apostles or their immediate disciples were still alive.

Scriptural support for "two equal ultimate church authority sources" is extremely weak. The interpretation it appeals to effectively redefines the two nouns of the last phrase of 2 Thessalonians 2:15:

> **Therefore, brethren, stand fast, and hold the traditions which ye have been taught, whether by word, or our epistle.**

The assumption is that Paul wrote of two separate bodies of authority: *epistles* and *oral tradition.* This reads something back into the text from much later in history, when Roman Catholic scholars reacted to the Reformation. [6] Some in this camp go as far as saying that the church had no New Testament Scripture for 400 years. That is blatantly not true.

Taking 2 Thessalonians in historical context considers that Paul wrote during the lifetime of the Apostles. The New Testament, as inspired Scripture, was still in the process of being written and recognized. Not everything was as clear then as it is to us after 2000 years of hindsight. Nor is it good for us to read our 21st century assumptions and desires back into that text, any more than it would have been for readers in the 1500s. When Paul wrote to the Thessalonians, not all inspired apostolic teaching had yet crystalized into what would become the New Testament.

The Apostles were living oracles of God's word, unique in that sense to their generation. In their day, it was possible to have both inspired written epistles and inspired oral apostolic teaching (*inspired* in the 2 Timothy 3:16 sense of "directly *God-breathed*"—Greek *theopneustos*). Even toward the end of the 1st century, that was changing however.

"False apostles," as the New Testament called them, were on the rise well before the death of Paul. This made oral authority less and less reliable as time went on. The early Church Fathers saw this. By the 4th Century, uncertainty even arose in discerning if some of the written sources were genuinely apostolic. Most books that ended up in the New Testament were never in question, as we shall see. Yet others were. Since that was true of certain written sources after less than three centuries, how much more of a hazard existed with orally transmitted traditions? The worldview shift from Hebrew to Greek-Roman would also need scrutiny.

Which brings us to the questions of how were New Testament writings recognized as God-breathed, and how did they end up grouped into the canon we know today?

While it is mistaken to say that Christians knew all the New Testament books were inspired before the death of the last Apostle, they saw that quality in many of those books almost from the start. We know this because of what Peter said in 2 Peter 3:15b-16:

> **...just as our dear brother Paul also wrote you with the wisdom that God gave him. He writes the same way *in all his letters*, speaking in them of these matters. His letters contain some things that are hard to understand, which ignorant and unstable people distort, as they do *all other Scriptures*.**

Peter used the word *Scriptures* here as he would for the Jewish Scriptures, to mean authoritative, divinely inspired writings. This is a historical statement that the 1st Century church saw Paul's letters, at least, as being authoritative as Jewish Scripture.

It was not always so clear-cut with some of the other New Testament books. For example, some churches accepted the Epistle of Jude, while others rejected it for almost 200 years. The same was true with James, Hebrews, Revelation, and 2 Peter. (Though not all churches accepted 2 Peter as Scripture at first, they accepted it as an accurate reflection of real late 1st century Christian beliefs.)

For a couple centuries, some churches had slightly different lists of which books they considered "God-breathed." Some accepted a few books that later became rejected as Scripture universally; *The Shepherd of Hermas*, the *Didache*, and the *Epistles of Clement*, for example. [7] They still respected such books, just not as God-breathed Scripture.

Several trends forced early Christians to research which books showed genuine connection to one or more of the Apostles. The most compelling was the rise of heretics who tried to redefine the Faith to conform to the dominant worldviews and popular thought of the times.

In addition to the influx of false teachings toward the end of the 1st Century, Christianity experienced a major cultural shift. Growing numbers of Gentile converts pulled the church from its Jewish roots toward a Gentile, Greco-Roman worldview. This broadened the gospel's outreach. It also injected Greek-Roman thought patterns into how Christians viewed their Faith, even among orthodox believers.

One heretic, who forced the hand of 2nd century churches toward drawing up lists of approved canonical books, was a rogue bishop named Marcion of Sinope. Marcion rejected all but Luke and Paul's writings because he said that the God of the Old Testament was different from the God of Jesus. He wanted to get rid of all things Jewish from a movement that arose out of a Jewish worldview. That is a bit like trying to invent "powdered water" for people who hate carrying that sloshing wet stuff.

A slightly later heretic, Montanus, preached ecstatic revelations he claimed came from the Holy Spirit. His "revelations" distorted and contradicted the apostolic message more as time went on. By the end of the 3rd century, such characters made one thing increasingly evident. Christians needed a universal standard of apostolic teaching for a future when memory of the Apostles' worldview, doctrine, and ethics faded. "Spiritual spontaneity" was not enough. The Holy Spirit was also rational.

The Councils of Hippo and Carthage, in 393 and 397 AD, eventually agreed upon a final canon list of both Old and New Testament Scripture. Yet long before that, churches used earlier, non-universal canons, like the middle 2nd Century "Muratorian Canon." Church leaders in the 2nd century commonly cited books from such lists, which always included the same four Gospels we have today, Paul's epistles, and most of the other books. These "early canons" served effectively as New Testament Scripture, and each was nearly as complete as the list our Bible's feature today. [8]

## AN APOSTOLIC ERA SNAPSHOT

In discussing documents and worldviews, we must not forget how church history really began. Though foreshadowed by the teachings of Jesus in the Gospels, the church started with the baptism of the Holy Spirit, described in Acts, Chapters 1 and 2. To get the most out of *One Faith – Many Transitions*, one should really pause here, and read the entire Book of the Acts of the Apostles.

The Book of Acts essentially frames the rest of church history. In it, God's Spirit empowered a small group of men and women to be Christ's **"witnesses in Jerusalem and in all Judea and Samaria and to the end of the earth." (Acts 1:8)** The power of the Holy Spirit given human hands, mouths, and feet is at the core of what the church really is supposed to be. This element was missing until the power of the Spirit fell upon the disciples. Only then did a fearful crew of followers transform into a circle of dynamic leaders. These men gave their lives to spread the good news of Jesus Christ in the face of powerful, often terrifying, opposition. People will not willingly die for something they do not think is true in the real world!

What was the world they faced really like?

While a complete description of 1st century Roman society is too in-depth for this book, two words sum things up—*regimented* and *brutal*. Roman peace rested on Roman military power, as is true with any major civilization. Roman legions provided security to keep an elaborate road system safe enough for commerce and missionaries like the Apostle Paul. People could walk from North Africa through Egypt, Jerusalem, into Asia Minor, and cross at the Dardanelles into Europe. From there they might continue walking all the way to the English Channel, and cross to Britain, all without leaving Roman rule.

In each city along those roads, Jewish communities with copies of the Old Testament, awaited their Messiah. These and other historical forces staged the Christian faith to spread rapidly throughout the Roman Empire in only one generation.

Nevertheless, the regimentation of the Roman world was not always good. Roman law permitted a Roman man to kill his wife or slave, often without penalty. Although without life or death authority, Jewish men of that era could divorce their wives on any pretext, and leave them destitute. (Like lawyers today, their legal scholars found inventive ways to weasel around the firewall of Mosaic laws designed to prevent such abuse.) Unlike the Jews, Greek women could divorce their men, but that option often proved even less attractive than enduring the abuse.

Greek-Roman culture of the 1st Century gave little protection to widows or young divorced women. The latter could expect no more than a social environment of chummed waters where the sharks at feeding frenzy were in total control. Under such harsh conditions, the relative stability of a bad marriage or even slavery was often more desirable for a woman than life on her own. There were exceptions, but that was the rule. In that era, men of moderate means had wives to bear legitimate children, mistresses to share their interests, and concubines or prostitutes for sexual fantasies. Centuries earlier, the Greek poetess Sapho formed an insular female dominated society on the Island of Lesbos. We get the word *Lesbian* from that name. [9] In practice, such experiments provided no real shelter from the "sexploitation." They failed to fit the human condition, merely exchanging one form of systematic abuse for another.

It was only with the advent of Christianity that women and slaves began to slowly (often far too slowly) gain some respect. Radical new ideas of social justice began a long infusion into the bloodstream of Western Civilization from Paul's writings. Laws based on such ideas would take centuries to gain a foothold, and permeate Europe in different forms, and they never would do so perfectly. Nevertheless, they would transform the West from Roman despotism to a place where the "unalienable rights" we take for granted at least became thinkable.

> **There is neither Jew nor Greek, there is neither bond nor free, there is neither male nor female: for ye are all one in Christ."** ***Galatians*** **3:28 KJV**

Today's pop-culture fiction that patriarchal 1st Century Christian churches oppressed women because of Paul's theology shows staggering ignorance of both Paul's words and history. While Paul taught that male and female social roles differed, he gave history the first lasting concept of gender equality before God. The New Testament records the works of deaconesses, like Phoebe and Lydia; prophetesses, like the daughters of Philip; and teachers like Priscilla, who instructed a variety of new believers. In the 1st Century church, submission to God's word of was for everyone—not just women in their role as wives (though that was included).

That does not mean early Christians permitted women or men to adopt just any social role they pleased in the church. While our present "politically correct" culture may not like it, Scripture does not allow women pastoral teaching authority over the men of the church. The earliest Christians understood this as a God-ordained role issue. Female teachers, prophetesses, and deacons in the New Testament showed that early Christians nevertheless valued women even for many leadership roles.

While men had more authority, women often had great influence. For example, whenever the New Testament mentioned the renowned married ministry team of Priscilla and Aquila, Priscilla's name usually came first. That was no trifle. Custom in that era always placed the man's name in front. Paul listened to women, such as Chloe of Corinth. This no-nonsense lady had initiative to inform the Apostle of a dangerous situation in the church. (1 Cor. 1:10-13) Because Paul trusted Chloe's integrity, it is possible that the pastor and elders of the church at Corinth rose and fell at her word.

Controversial passages, like 1 Corinthians 14:24, commanded women to be silent in Corinth's church services. We know from other New Testament scripture that this was not a universal stifling of female contribution even to many key roles. 1 Corinthians 14 also tells us that prophecy was a gift designed to "edify" the church gathering, in verses 22-32. Acts 21:8-9 calls Philip's daughters "prophetesses"—you all can "do the math."

Paul's command in 1 Corinthians 14 spoke to a well-known disorder in the Corinthian church services. This came from boisterous women interrupting the teaching. It happened because many early churches followed the Jewish synagogue pattern, where men and women sat apart from each other. Wives (frequently uneducated in that culture) would yell across the room to their husbands to ask questions and make comments.

This leads us to another reason why a working knowledge of church history is helpful. It prevents half-baked and provincial applications of the Scripture. Misapplying even otherwise correct interpretations of God's word sidetracks the church into needless controversies. These put obstacles in front of those who are honestly seeking truth, and whom God is drawing to Himself.

For the first couple of centuries, the church often operated more spontaneously than it did later on. One might say it functioned more as an organism than as an organization. Teaching standards did not look nearly as uniform as we often see them in denominations today. Although a variety of worship and teaching styles developed, content remained in reasonable harmony for a long time. This does not mean serious conflicts never arose over secondary issues—like when to celebrate holy days. When it came to primary teachings however, like the Deity and Humanity of Christ, churches rejected those (like the Gnostics) who held straying views.

God used a "perfect storm" of historical forces to set Christianity up to spread rapidly. In addition to Jewish communities spread along well-patrolled Roman roads, Gentile admirers of Jewish customs clustered around each enclave. History calls these admirers the ***God-fearers***.

The God-fearers saw common sense in the morality of the Jewish God. They wanted to honor Him, but were not quite willing to become circumcised Jews themselves. We see one of these God-fearers in Acts 10, Cornelius the Centurion. God-fearers quickly became the first Christian disciples because the gospel gave them a way to come to God without complex and burdensome Jewish laws.

Paul and Peter envisioned a church where Jewish and non-Jewish believers lived in harmony. Sadly, this was one of the first New Testament principles to disappear. Entrenched Jewish prejudice against Gentiles, magnified by Roman domination, drove a growing rift between Jewish and Gentile believers.

In 70 AD, the Roman general Titus, son of Emperor Vespasian, laid siege to Jerusalem, and slaughtered over a million Jews. His soldiers accidentally destroyed the Second Temple, when they tried to burn out the zealots that had taken refuge there. The heat turned the structure into a giant kiln that melted the gold and silver down into the cracks between the stones. In order to get at it afterward, the Roman soldiers had to tear the temple down stone by stone.

> **And Jesus went out from the temple, and was going on his way; and his disciples came to him to show him the buildings of the temple. But he answered and said unto them, "See ye not all these things? verily I say unto you, There shall not be left here one stone upon another, that shall not be thrown down."**
>
> ***Matthew* 24:1-2 ASV**

This prophecy of Jesus, recorded in Matthew 24, Mark 13, and Luke 21, had warned the Christians. They escaped well beforehand. This pivotal event helped dislodge Christianity from its Jewish roots, sending it into a Greco-Roman orbit. It also alienated many Jews, who may have thought wrongly that the Christians were co-belligerents with the Romans.

People continued to view Christians as a Jewish sect for some decades yet, but the formal division between Jew and Christian had begun in the eyes of the world. Not much else had formalized yet in the expanding movement that followed the teachings of Jesus and His Apostles, however.

As far as church authority, administration, and formal services went, 1st century Christians operated on a mostly local level. They met in homes, and sometimes in synagogues, but only rarely in rented amphitheaters such as the School of Tyrannus, described in Acts 19:9. The Greek word for *church*, *ekklesia* simply means *gathering*. Leadership structure supported practical individual and communal spiritual growth. Christians gathered to worship, pray, share fellowship and food, to partake in communion, and for the teaching of the Apostles. The Book of Acts reflects this pattern.

> **And they continued steadfastly in the apostles' doctrine and fellowship, and in breaking of bread, and in prayers. *Acts* 2:42 (KJV)**

Each congregation had ***elders*** or ***presbyters*** for leadership and the service of communion. Many gatherings also had a primary teaching elder, called a *pastor* or ***bishop*** in the Timothy Epistles. The word for *shepherd* and *pastor* is the same in New Testament Greek, *poimen*. *Bishop* is a different word, *episcopae*, which means *overseer—epi*, being *over*, and *scopae* being root of the English *scope*, as in *microscope* or to *scope out*. It is a term for a servant who had oversight of other servants.

At first, the only difference between a bishop and other presbyters or elders was in function, not rank. The words for *bishop* and *pastor* were essentially synonymous, being the presbyters or elders concerned with teaching the Scriptures. The other elders handled the service of communion and government in the practical affairs of the local church. Any sense of hierarchy between bishops and elders developed later, mainly in larger urban churches.

Helping the pastor-bishops and elder-presbyters in practical matters, like feeding the poor, and caring for the sick, were the ***deacons***. Originally, these servant-hearted men and women freed the elders up to teach and train people in the Faith.

Most of the larger early churches followed the pattern in Acts 7, appointing seven deacons to be the direct assistants of the bishop. None of these officers dressed any differently from any other member of the congregation. Bishops, elders, and deacons were free to marry and raise families. According to 1 Timothy 3, the best way churches had of telling if a man would make a good pastor, elder, or deacon was whether he managed his wife and children in a loving, responsible, and orderly way.

Today's churches do well in trying to return, as much as reality permits, to the simplicity of this structure. As we shall see, learning the lesson that simpler is often better, where church leadership is concerned, has taken the greater part of 2000 years.

## BIBLIOGRAPHY

1. C.S. Lewis, ***The Abolition of Man***, 1943, Harper San Francisco edition, 2001
2. Vincent Carroll and David Shiflett, ***Christianity on Trial: Arguments Against Anti-Religious Bigotry***, Encounter Books, 2002
3. Andrew Dickson White, ***A History of the Warfare of Science with Theology in Christendom***, Cornell University, 1896
4. Bock, Darrel L. ***The Words of Jesus in the Gospels: Live, Jive or Memorex?*** from ***Jesus Under Fire***, Micheal J. Wilkins & J.P. Moreland, 1995, Zondervan Publishing House, Grand Rapids, Mich. 49530
5. Kreeft, Peter. ***Fundamentals of the Faith***, pp. 274-275, 1988, Ignatius Press, San Francisco
6. Geisler, Norman L. & MacKenzie, Ralph E. ***Roman Catholics and Evangelicals – Agreements and Differences***, pp.180-181, 1995, Baker Books, , Grand Rapids, Mich. 49516
7. Shelley, Bruce L. ***Church History in Plain Language*** (2nd Edition), p.67, 1995, Word Publishing, Dallas, Tx.
8. Ibid. pp. 65-68
9. ***Online Etymology Dictionary***: *Lesbian*, http://etymonline.com

# 2

# When Worldviews Collide: The Greek-Roman Challenge

## Greek Heresies to the Left, Judaic on the Right

The Apostle Paul warned the Corinthian church about false teachers, who would seek to move the faith away from its simplicity in Christ.

> **But I am afraid, lest as the serpent deceived Eve by his craftiness, your minds should be led astray from the simplicity and purity of devotion to Christ. 2 *Corinthians* 11:3 (NASB)**

Of course, there is a difference between child-like simplicity of faith, and a childish refusal to deal with important, complex issues. Unfortunately, one can sometimes come wrapped in the other.

As the church entered the 2nd century, its composition shifted toward fewer Jewish and more Gentile converts. Christianity soon faced thorny new forms of opposition, across a wide spectrum of belief and practice. They could not ignore these without sacrificing their effectiveness for Christ in the society of that day. The influx of non-Jewish disciples forced churches to think more clearly about defining themselves in the face of Greek-Roman worldview questions. This demographic shift came on like the tilt of a giant seesaw. Gentiles quickly became leaders in the churches of the early 2nd century. By the middle of that century, Jewish Christians dwindled to near non-existence in the wake of the Bar Kochba Revolt.

Judean rabbi Akiva of Yavneh (or *Jamnia*) tried to engineer the fall of both Roman rule and the last Jewish sect to accept Jesus as Messiah. He, or his near predecessors, distorted the Book of Daniel's Messianic timeline in his oral teaching. Though he could never get away with altering the text, he could still exert local control over who read it directly, and how those rabbis interpreted it. [1]

In 132 AD, Akiva declared zealot leader Shimon bar Kochba "Messiah," lending his support to the Bar Kochba Revolt. Akiva gambled on nobody noticing that he had to "cook the books" to make it work. He apparently did this by applying the principle of "those who control the present control the past, and whoever controls the past, controls the future."

Most Jews in Judea at the time did not have a precise concept of timing historical events, unless they were formally educated. Akiva controlled the Academy of Yavneh, which was the principle Judean school after the sack of Jerusalem in 70 AD. It was also the only one using Hebrew texts of the Old Testament, rather than the Greek translations used by Jews and Christians elsewhere. Akiva subtracted years from recorded Jewish history, some here some there. This had the effect of adding 100 years to the 483 given in the prophecy of Daniel 9. The timespan began with the rebuilding of Jerusalem as a walled city, and ended with the coming of Messiah (62 plus 7 weeks, or 69).

> **"Know therefore and understand, That from the going forth of the command To restore and build Jerusalem until Messiah the Prince, There shall be seven weeks and sixty-two weeks; The street shall be built again, and the wall, Even in troublesome times. And after the sixty-two weeks Messiah shall be cut off, but not for Himself; And the people of the prince who is to come shall destroy the city and**

**the sanctuary. The end of it shall be with a flood, And till the end of the war desolations are determined." Daniel 9:25-26 (NKJV)**

Before the days of the printing press and rapid communications, such slight-of-hand was sometimes possible on a local level. Akiva's trickery did not fly universally, however. The "weeks" in the prophecy is the Hebrew word for "sevens," in this case, sets of seven-year periods. Only *years* makes sense historically or prophetically. Some Bible translations, like the Revised Standard Version (RSV), render the Daniel 9 prophecy as "70 weeks of years..."

The Yavneh School sought a new, Hebrew version of Scripture because by this time, Christians used the Greek ***Septuagint*** to show easily that Jesus was the Messiah. Shimon bar Kochba was a "messiah" under Akiva's control, but that only lasted until 135 AD. The Roman Emperor Hadrian then crushed the revolt, killed bar Kochba, deported the Jews from Judea, and had Akiva tortured to death. This was a little over a hundred years after the death and Resurrection of Jesus.

Had Shimon succeeded, Akiva could then have believably claimed that the Septuagint was "corrupted by Gentiles" to further his fabrication. With bar Kochba on David's Throne, and Akiva's monopoly on Hebrew texts, no 2nd century rabbi would have likely argued with him about Daniel. Fortunately, custody of the Hebrew texts went to others, and Daniel's prophecy remained un-doctored. Akiva's influence was powerful, nonetheless. Modern Judaism reveres him as a "founding father," though it admits he was deceived in his acceptance of bar Kochba as Messiah.

This fulfilled the prophecy of Jesus. Sadly, it will happen again.

**"I have come in My Father's name, and you do not receive Me; if another comes in his own name, him you will receive." John 5:43 (NKJV)**

The Gentile side of the tracks presented other problems for the Faith. Greek and Roman Gentiles had a worldview radically different in key ways from the Jewish one. Christianity effectively bridged that gap and adapted. The church gained many spiritual victories in the process, but also absorbed a few warped perceptions. Ideas still had consequences. These hurt the faith later, after they embedded into Christian thought.

Many of the historical church's concepts about its own identity did not come directly from anything said in God word. Rather, some came in the wake of distorting influences that forced Christians to define themselves biblically in response. Sometimes believers responded well, other times, not. Christians caught in the throes of this spiritual warfare had to think about and answer questions like; *what do we mean when we say that Jesus is the Son of God? In what sense was he was raised from the dead? What do we mean when we refer to the followers of Christ as his* church?

Some framed their questions in an honest search for truth, trying to reason through the issues. Others turned questions into prideful challenges. They merely took their old pagan ideas, and stated them again in 2nd century "Christianese." It matters how we frame our questions. The God of the Bible has always met honest seekers (like the Ethiopian Eunuch of Acts 8, Cornelius the Centurion in Acts 10, Dionysus with Damaris at Athens in Acts 17, and Apollos in Acts 18 and 19). Problems arise only when people demand that God form-fit Himself and His truth to their assumptions and opinions. This is as true now as in the 2nd Century.

Ultimatums for churches to tolerate Pagan thinking dressed in vaguely Christian jargon drove many early false teachings. Pride often reared its head. Such belief systems either denied or added to one or more of the basic premises of the Apostolic Faith. Each of these false ideas needed rebutting in concise statements (if possible) that were consistent with Scripture. This forced Christians to think more clearly about who God is, and what having a relationship with Him in Christ meant. It also opened the door to bunny trails away from the simplicity of the 1st century Apostolic Church.

The early Christians had to engage the culture around them by answering these distortions because souls were at stake. In this sense, many of the complications that followed were unavoidable. Bunny trails were the lesser of two evils when compared to failure at being "the salt of the earth." (Matt. 5:13) Without answering the issues of the day, Christians run the risk of making the gospel seem unreal to those with whom they interacted. Therefore, we need to understand the challenges to the Faith made by the major early heresies. Virtually all modern false teachings are simply a rehashing of one or more of them.

The list given here is not exhaustive, but covers the main bases.

## The Ebionites

The earliest false teachings sprang from conflicts the Apostles dealt with in both the Epistles and the Book of Acts. Galatians recounts Paul's debate with other Jewish believers who told Gentile converts that they must become circumcised Jews to find salvation. Bible commentators often call these New Testament Era troublemakers the ***Judaizers***.

The ***Ebionites*** were a sect of late 1st to early 2nd century successors to the Judaizers. They believed one had to become a Jew first in order to become a Christian.

We saw that, in the 1st century, people viewed Christianity more as another Jewish sect than as a religion in its own right. The Ebionites wanted to keep it that way. They separated themselves from the Gentile churches, and emphasized the epistles and teachings of James, Peter, and Jude. To them, Paul the Apostle was a heretic who corrupted the original teachings of Jesus. They also believed that Jesus was only a man, much as most Jews today believe that Messiah, when he comes, will be a man and not God.

Regrettably, some sects on the fringe of modern Messianic Judaism have become "Neo-Ebionites" or new Ebionites. They hold many, if not all, of the old Ebionite heresies. This does not describe modern Messianic Judaism in general, which is a very good movement, just the divergent sects. While there was much more to the 2nd Century Ebionites, our purpose is just to view their place in the big picture.

Legalistic, exclusively Judaic demands from this sect alienated non-Jewish converts. Its denial of Christ's deity likewise divided it from mainstream churches, Jew and Gentile alike. The Ebionites forced Christians to ask and answer the question: *What do we mean when we say that Jesus is the Messiah?*

What we should mean is the very specific answer that *Jesus is the Jewish Messiah of both Old Testament prophecy and history*. Ebionite heresies, followed by the Bar Kochba Revolt, became nails in the coffin of the apostolic vision of a church where both Jews and Gentiles lived harmoniously in Christ.

## The Gnostics

***Gnostics*** belonged to a variety of religious movements that, in one way or another, believed in the superiority of mystical knowledge over love. Their name is drawn from a Greek word for *knowledge, gnosis*. These groups earned the name because they each emphasized salvation through some form of secret knowledge.

As the church jumped from Judean to Greek and Roman culture, converts who simply expressed their old Greek worldview in new Christian terms drifted into Gnosticism. Their belief systems redefined key words in Scripture about Jesus, and about the nature of the spiritual and material worlds. Sometimes they did this unconsciously. Everyone goes through a phase where they must learn that the Word converts them, not the other way around. At other times, this redefinition came as prideful reaction against correction, prompted and fed by the demonic. Redefining the words used in a discussion is a dishonest way to manipulate the outcome. That is why heresy is bad, not just something that church leaders look down upon because they are "fussy and judgmental."

It is a bad idea to let too much of a worldview that is foreign to the Bible, or to the influences that gave us the Bible, define how we interpret Scripture. It involves mismatched faith-assumptions about truth, which makes for bad presuppositions about what Scripture might mean by what it says. Since the Bible is about reality, it is important we know its meaning. While it is impossible for us to eliminate all cultural assumptions from our thinking, we want to minimize their effect on interpretation. We want Scripture to judge our cultural assumptions as much as possible, not the other way around.

A ***presupposition*** is an idea at the foundation of a person's thinking processes or view of reality. It is a concept that "goes without saying" and cannot be proved or disproved. To *suppose* is to think on something. *Pre* is a prefix that means *before*. Hence, a presupposition is assumed to be true before thinking. That just plain sounds like a bad idea.

Actually, presuppositions of some sort are necessary because we must start somewhere in our thinking. Since only God knows everything, the only way finite beings can begin to think at all is by assuming that certain basic things must already be true; though we cannot prove them. This would logically be true even in a world that never fell. Angels and humanity would still need to assume that God told them the truth about anything unknowable to a finite being. They would need to trust, just as we do.

Usually presuppositions are not things that people consciously think of when they express their ideas. Bad presuppositions can embed themselves deep in our reasoning methods, almost like a computer virus of the mind. Good ones guard our thinking in ways that we often do not realize. People groups will intuitively arrange related presuppositions together into worldviews; networked assumptions that work as grids through which they interpret reality.

People often accept beliefs from others without exploring the faith-assumptions holding those ideas up. Sometimes, presuppositions are obvious and seem quite sensible. Others are subtle, difficult to see, and may even violate reason. Often, people are not aware of the starting assumptions that rest beneath many of their own beliefs for this very reason. Sometimes, people even believe ideas that start from faith-assumptions they would never knowingly agree with.

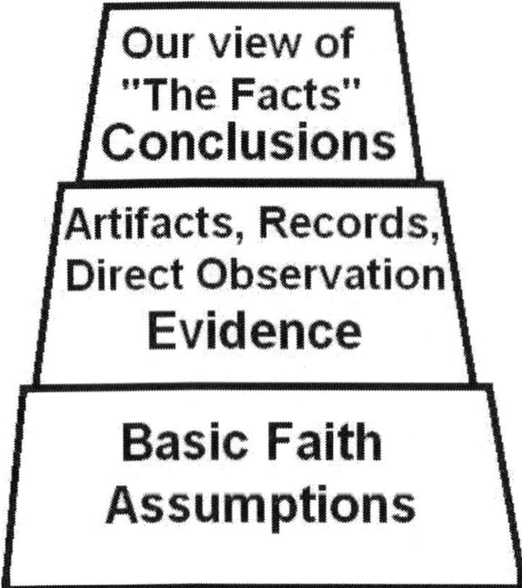


*This basic pyramid can map any worldview, or worldview portion, no matter what the given worldview believes. All worldviews have foundational assumptions. These guide the interpretation of evidence and experience, from which people draw their conclusions. The denial of the existence of foundational faith-assumptions is itself an assumption one must accept by faith.*

Influential 2nd century philosophies like ***Stoicism, Platonism,*** and ***Epicureanism*** grew from Greek worldview presuppositions. Although different in their responses to those assumptions, these philosophies all assumed that matter was evil, and spirit was pure and good. This assumption made the ideas that Christ came in the flesh, and was bodily raised from the dead, unthinkable to many Greek minds. Their kneejerk reaction was to "spiritualize" the Gospels, and other apostolic writings, to make them mean something other than what they plainly said.

The reason these orthodox teachings seemed so "unthinkable" to them was that if matter was evil, and the human body was physical, then it must also be evil *just because it was material.* In their minds, the good, holy, and pure Son of God could not have possibly come in such a form. To suggest otherwise felt "blasphemous" to the Greek mind. Put simply, matter was heavy. Heavy stuff sank to the lowest places. Evil is low. Therefore, the earth is the center of the universe because the garbage sinks, and we are walking on it, and it is a part of us. Of course, this also shifts the blame for sin away from the human spirit and onto matter.

The ancient Greeks, (excepting Plato, who was a rebel with a sun-centered cosmos), did not put the earth at the center of the universe because they thought humanity was special. They did so because they thought matter was inherently corrupt, and they saw humanity as partly made of matter, and partly of air or spirit. (The Greek word *pneuma* means both *air* and *spirit.*) Humans were spiritual bottom-feeders to them.

## The World-view Pyramid

### How We Know What We Think We Know

**Conclusions - Our Beliefs**

1- What we think we know - Our view of "the facts".
2- Principles we base our choices on - Our morality and values.
3- How we see truth in the real world - Our sense of what is real.

**Records, Artifacts & Other Evidence**

1- Objects that tell us something has happened, like fossils, ruins & forensic evidence.
2- Records that tell a story from various points of view - like manuscripts or clay tablets.
3- Observed phenomena & patterns - controlled experiments & the data gathered from them. Includes other forms of direct observation.

**Basic Faith-Assumptions & Presuppositions**

1- Ideas we must accept on faith that can't be proved.
2- Unconscious assumptions we all take for granted.
3- Cultural assumptions of religion, philosophy & ideology.
4- Family relationship assumptions that affect our perception of ourselves & others.

**Nobody can avoid having faith-assumptions no matter how skeptical or objective they try to be. All reasoning systems can be peeled back to reveal their faith-held foundations - even scientific forms of reasoning. There is no escape from it.**

*Above is a more detailed worldview pyramid map that gives examples of what sort of ideas go into which of the 3 layers. The following page has a map of how conflicting worldview assumptions can alter meaning.*

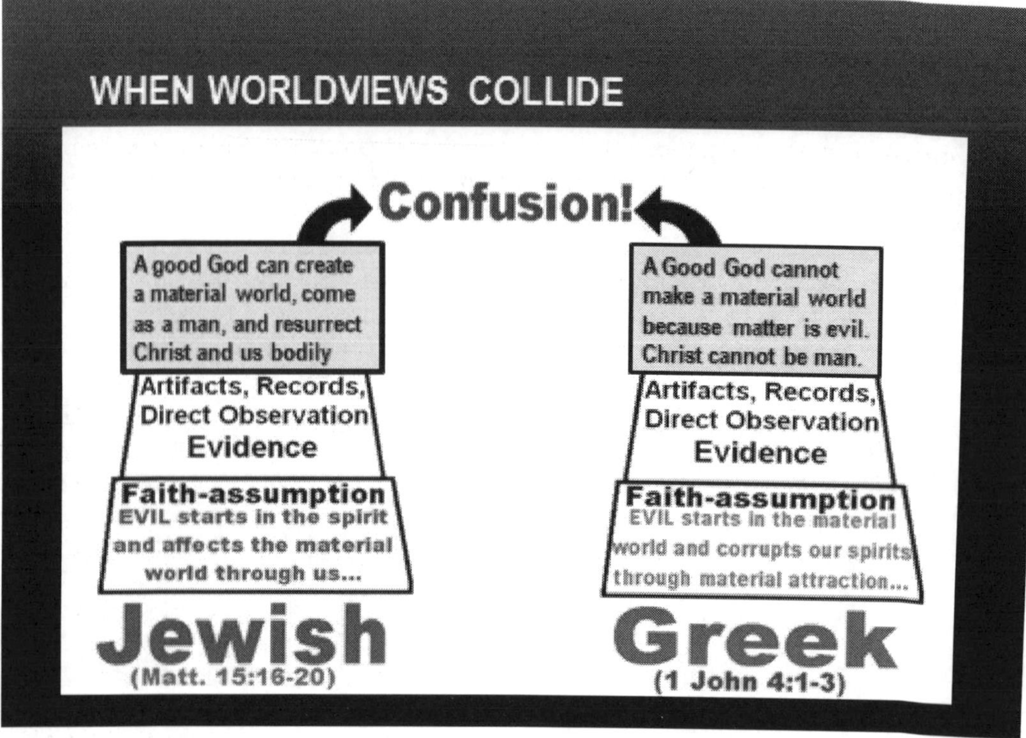


Saying that *the material world is innately evil* is different from saying that *the Genesis Curse universally affected the material world*. A purely Hebrew worldview would say the latter, but never the former. In the Hebrew worldview, things were not corrupt simply because they were material. God had created a material as well as spiritual reality.

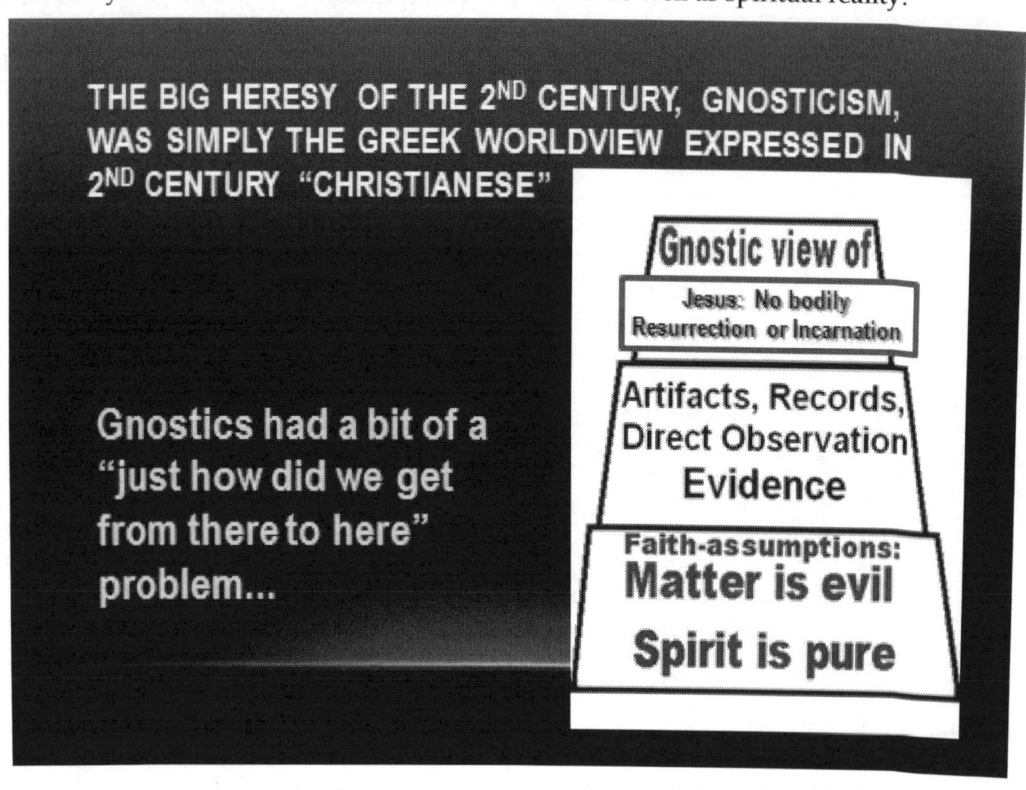

In Hebraic thought, material things became agents of evil only when used contrary to God's design or purposes. Genesis 2:12 tells us that the gold in the land of Havilah was good. Only after the Fall did men use the gold in evil and power-hungry ways. To Hebrew thought, sexual pleasure was holy in its place—as an expression of affection between a man and a woman within the legal, cultural, and spiritual boundaries of marriage. The Song of Solomon has many erotic themes for a man and wife. God created sex and marriage before humanity fell.

Gnostic minds, building from Greek faith-assumptions with mismatched Hebrew terms, never connected these dots. It was not possible to connect them coherently starting from Greek assumptions. Yet these very "dots" described self-evident things about the human condition. An arrogant background culture ensured that few Gnostics would ever become teachable enough to notice what should have been obvious. Behind this worked spiritual forces that were hardly "pure and good." The Apostle John spoke of such teachers in 1 John.

> **Dear friends, do not believe every spirit, but test the spirits to see whether they are from God, because many false prophets have gone out into the world. This is how you can recognize the Spirit of God: Every spirit that acknowledges that Jesus Christ has come in the flesh is from God, but every spirit that does not acknowledge Jesus is not from God. This is the spirit of the antichrist, which you have heard is coming and even now is already in the world. *1 John* 4:1-3 (NIV)**

Though worldviews are not the same as philosophies, philosophies always rest on some kind of worldview. Gnosticism is also an example of what happens when people make a worldly philosophy or theory the guideline by which they interpret Scripture. Francis Schaeffer said in his book *How Should We Then Live? "We will be more faithful to our presuppositions than even we ourselves realize."* [2]

The Gnostics could not conceive that a holy God could create a material world. They believed that the original God created another god, who created another god, who created yet another god, and on and on it went. Each carbon copy "god" or ***emanation*** grew more corrupt as the process went on. Finally along came a god-copy corrupt enough to create a material universe. [3] This was the God of the Old Testament, in Gnostic thinking.

Jesus, to the Gnostic, was a new spiritual emanation designed to bring us back to the original, pure proto-god. The "proto-god" differed from what they called the ***demiurge***, or "craftsman," which was supposed to have created the material world. This view allowed heretics, like Marcion (who drew from Gnosticism), to imagine that the God of the Old Testament was a different being from that of the New.

Pagan Greeks often reacted to their worldview assumptions about evil with a sense of helplessness before the pull of material desires. They lived licentious lives because they thought it was inevitable. They might have thought, "Well, we're all made of this material meaty stuff, and we can't help how we feel, and the drives we have, so why worry?" They would have fit well in the 21st century. This describes the ***Epicureans***.

The ***Stoics***, on the other hand, felt that "the sage" could control the material and live above it. They tried to avoid the emotional pull of fear and lust over carnal things like food and sexual desire. On the surface that might sound good. Yet they did not know when to stop. In today's words, it would go, "Mind over matter! What's that, dinner with friends? No! I'm going to sit in this giant birdcage and eat grass! Pain, heartbreak, and empathy are for softies! Marriage is for you spiritually second-string folks! We're doing celibacy because no one can 'have God first' and enjoy sexual relations with a spouse! In fact, you can't have God first and enjoy anything. So, get with the program, forget human emotions and needs."

This mindset strongly tempted Christians who wanted to please God in the midst of a corrupt world filled with every sort of sensual indulgence. It created for committed believers the perfect illusion. It felt right, if one did not look too deeply, yet it was not the genuine *spirit versus flesh* warfare described in apostolic teaching. The Hebrew-worldview of the Apostles did not believe that material things were corrupt of themselves.

The Apostles also warned us that not all spiritual things were good. Satan is a spirit and, **"we fight not against flesh and blood, but against spiritual wickedness in high places."** (Eph. 6:12) Yet certain Scriptures, when popped out of their context, and interpreted according to Greek assumptions, could be made to sound like they supported a Gnostic view of *all matter is bad, and all spirit is pure*—whether passages on liberty from the law or passages on the spiritual disciplines.

The Gnostics were not a single sect. A wide range of groups held this faith-assumption about materiality versus spirituality. They tended to react to this general belief system in two widely opposite ways in how they lived. The ***Antinomian*** or "anti-law" Gnostics followed a large part of Greek culture into a fatalistic view. Since they saw "the flesh" as trashed-out anyway, it did not really matter to them what one did sexually in their material bodies. They felt that the "gospel" (their gospel) gave them the mystic knowledge needed to get back to spiritual purity in the end. Antinomian Gnostics believed this "purity" was entirely divorced from what they did in their physical lives. Paul spoke out against the beginnings of this distorted view of grace in Romans 3.

> **But if our unrighteousness brings out God's righteousness more clearly, what shall we say? That God is unjust in bringing his wrath on us? (I am using a human argument.) Certainly not! If that were so, how could God judge the world? Someone might argue, 'If my falsehood enhances God's truthfulness and so increases his glory, why am I still condemned as a sinner?' Why not say – *as we are being slanderously reported and as some claim that we say* – 'Let us do evil that good may result?' Their condemnation is deserved. Romans 3:5-8 (NIV)**

***Docetic*** Gnostics, on the other hand, reacted to their Greek presuppositions more like the pagan Stoics. The term ***Docetism*** comes from the Greek word *dokei*, meaning, *in the appearance of*. Because matter was evil, Christ, in their view, only came *in the appearance of* a physical body, not a true one. They also believed that since all material things were bad, they should avoid all pleasures derived from material and bodily things. They even felt compelled to shun pleasures that God designed us to enjoy in their proper place.

This distortion struck a chord even in orthodox churches. It left a lasting influence even among those who rejected the grosser, Docetic heresies about Christ's nature. The reason this view took hold was that it was easy to express in subtly redefined biblical words. As Christians, we all have a genuine internal conflict spiritually with our "flesh" or "old man." For the undiscerning, this seemed like a difference that made no difference. It even resembled holiness, superficially.

If we fail to distinguish Greek definitions on this topic from Hebrew ones, we can make the same Scriptures give two entirely different messages. People popped apostolic writings out of their spiritual and cultural context to fit them into the Gnostic position. They gave less flexible passages "allegorical" meanings. This happened even when making it an ***allegory*** violated the literary style of the text. Eventually, when the Gospels and epistles proved too inflexible, Gnostic gospels like that of Thomas and Philip began to appear. These works date into the 3rd century by the idioms they use. That same method can tell us that Jane Austen's *Pride and Prejudice* is a work of the 19th century, not the 21st, just by how the book uses language.

When people interpreted Scripture from Greek rather than Hebrew presuppositions too much however, it warped the message. Married sex seemed just as "filthy" as sex outside marriage, and even sexual perversions, because it involved bodily pleasure. Fasting became no longer just a spiritual discipline, but a way of making oneself holy through a method of "mind over matter." Nor did it stop there.

Adjustments seemed necessary to make Jesus' early family life more-than-human. This was the essence of the first big heresy about Christ. Unlike today, nobody back then, except the Jews, had trouble with Christ's divinity. His full humanity and full deity together threw them into fits. The Gospel texts insisted on both. Yet, even for many orthodox Christians, it could not be "that human kind of humanity." Mary and Joseph, after the birth of Jesus, could not possibly have had normal marital relations, resulting in other children. How could the "blessed virgin who bore God in her womb" ever defile that womb afterward with an act involving bodily pleasure?

This, despite the fact that the Gospels mention Jesus' siblings repeatedly, and that Luke 2:7 calls him Mary's *firstborn* son, not Mary's *only* son. Matthew 1:25 also tells us that Joseph, **"did not know her *till* she had brought forth her firstborn Son. And he called His name JESUS."** The word *till* or *until* says that Joseph "knew" Mary afterward sexually.

The same worldview that shaped Gnosticism tugged at orthodox Gentile and even Hellenistic Jewish believers. They still lived in a Greco-Roman culture. Paul wrote of these root assumptions in Colossians, calling them the **"rudiments"** or **"basic principles"** of the world.

> **Do not let anyone who delights in false humility and the worship of angels disqualify you for the prize. Such a person goes into great detail about what he has seen, and his unspiritual mind puffs him up with idle notions. He has lost connection with the Head, from whom the whole body, supported and held together by its ligaments and sinews, grows as God causes it to grow. If you died with Christ to the *basic principles* of this world, why, as though you still belonged to it, do you submit to its rules: 'Do not handle! Do not taste! Do not touch!?' These are all destined to perish with use, because they are based on human commands and teachings. Such regulations indeed have an appearance of wisdom, with their self-imposed worship, their false humility and their harsh treatment of the body, but they lack any value in restraining sensual indulgence. Colossians 2:18-23 NIV**

A Greek view of the material world enabled later systemic hypocrisy in the church. It eventually created an outward religion, under which human nature strained; fallen human nature seeking sinful license and redeemed human nature seeking genuine spiritual life, alike. It is ironic that it should work that way. The Greek worldview simply did not fit the human condition, in either its fallen or redeemed forms.

Earlier, in Colossians 2:8, Paul warned, **"See to it that no one takes you captive through hollow and deceptive philosophy, which depends on human tradition and *the basic principles of this world* rather than on Christ."** Another irony is that, historically, this is more likely to happen during times when Christians are under pressure, and truly desire to be set apart from the world. Paul wrote this warning in such a time.

Docetic Gnosticism was like a demonic, stinging insect that attached itself to the body of Christ. It stung, and left its stinger to pump poison for centuries after the insect itself was brushed away and crushed underfoot. Many of the early church fathers effectively refuted the heresies about Christ's nature. Yet they accepted subtle, "tolerable," distortions about holiness under their "spiritual radar." This later made holiness seem less like something normal people could really have. It started to warp perceptions about spiritual war against our old carnal man. Gnosticism forced Christians to ask and answer: *What is the nature of Christ's Incarnation, and what are its implications for holiness in our current human condition?*

Unfortunately, Greek-Roman believers of the 2nd century were more faithful to their cultural presuppositions than they realized. Before we judge the post-Apostolic church fathers too harshly, we need to remember that we likely make new and different mistakes, stemming from cultural assumptions of our own age.

Sometimes we just adopt the old assumptions by new names.

**Greek and Gnostic World-view Pyramid**
**Different Gnostic groups reacted to this world-view differently.**

**Beliefs & Conclusions**
1- A holy God could not create a material universe.
2- Christ did not come in a physical form and was not bodily raised from the dead because matter is evil.
3- All human physical drives are evil.

**Observations & Records (Evidence)**
1- People have physical appetites - food & sex.
2- People who follow their physical appetites with no self-restraint usually come to miserable and degrading self-destructive ends.
3- Disciplined people have limited control.
4- All physical creatures deteriorate and die.

**Presuppositions or Basic Faith-Assumptions**
1- Physical things are corrupt because they are material.
2- Only unseen spiritual realities are pure and perfect.
3- The gods (or emanations) are capricious and unreliable - they are bound by forces higher than they are.
4- The basic human problem is not sin but being hopelessly mired in the material realm.

*__Right__ is a simple Gnostic pyramid map. __Above__, a more detailed one shows how the Gnostics followed the "conventional wisdom" of their day, denying the humanity and resurrection of Jesus. Orthodox Christians raised in a Greek worldview also struggled with reconciling the New Testament to prevailing cultural ideas. They accepted the Incarnation and Resurrection, but often saw even God-given human desires as inherently evil. This distorted later views in the church about creation, sex in marriage, holiness, and spirituality.*

**Gnostic view of "The Facts" Conclusions**

**Artifacts, Records, Direct Observation Evidence**

**Faith-assumptions: Matter is evil Spirit is pure**

## MARCIONISM

Marcion of Sinope appeared in the last chapter as an early catalyst who made it necessary for early Christians to think in ways that would later lead to a *New Testament Canon*. His heresy taught that the Old Testament Jewish God was a "God of wrath and justice," completely different from the New Testament "God of love." Marcion's hatred for Jewish Scripture, and rejection of all things Jewish, became a trend in some 2nd century Gentile fellowships. The bitter fruit of anti-Semitism would culminate in the Middle Ages, on into the Reformation Era, and beyond.

The pendulum of history swings wide between each human extreme. The self-righteous Judaizers of Paul's day had alienated Gentile churches. The Ebionites separated themselves from a church free of bondage to the Jewish law. Yet the Gentile church also reacted against this hyper-Jewish element. Marcion swung at the far end of that reaction. Regrettably, hatred for the Jews would magnify later, through far more "orthodox" sources.

Ironically, Marcion formed the first known "sealed New Testament canon," or holy books list. His reason was to exclude the most Jewish apostolic writers like Matthew, John, James, Peter, and Jude. His list included only Paul's letters, Luke, and Acts. Churches reacted to Marcion by beginning to produce canon lists of their own, to prevent the gutting of content from the Faith. The process finally ended with the Councils of Carthage and Hippo at the end of the 4th Century, and the New Testament list still used today. Citations of period writings show substantial informal agreement with that list from at least the middle of the 2nd century on.

Marcion and his followers forced Christians to ask: *What relationship does the Church of Jesus Christ have to the Old Testament Jewish religion and its Scriptures?*

## MONTANISM

Late 2nd century churches encountered a spiritual movement coming out of Asia Minor that called itself the "New Prophecy." It emphasized continued revelation through gifts of the Holy Spirit, and even seemed to have an orthodox view of the nature of Christ. History knows it by the name of its founder. A mystic named Montanus started travelling with two women, Priscilla and Maximilla, who had left their husbands to be "prophetesses." This threesome claimed direct descent of office from Agabus and the Daughters of Philip the Evangelist from the Book of Acts.

They wrote their prophecies down into collections of sayings that Montanists treated as Scripture, about twenty of which have survived to this day. Despite this, some Church historians debate whether we should view the Montanists as heretics. Some believe they were a misunderstood orthodox sect who valued spiritual spontaneity, but had bad PR at a time when "spontaneity" had given rise to suspicion.

On the one hand, a few prominent orthodox sources of the day, mainly Tertullian, claimed they had a correct view of Christ. On the other, Montanus and his dancing prophetesses used induced trances and hypnotic suggestion to reach altered states of consciousness. Their methods were identical to the Cybeline Cult that Montanus had supposedly left behind at his conversion. This set them far apart from other Christians of the era who still practiced the charisma gifts listed in 1 Corinthians 12 through 14.

Montanus, like the Stoics, and the Docetic Gnostics, taught that physical pleasures of any sort were inherently evil. The "New Prophecy" openly renounced marriage as sinful. They idolized personal perpetual virginity like the Docetic Gnostics. One should side with Scripture on this one:

> **Now the Spirit expressly says that in latter times some will depart from the faith, giving heed to deceiving spirits and doctrines of demons, speaking lies in hypocrisy, having their own conscience seared with a hot iron, *forbidding to marry*, and commanding to abstain from foods which God created to be received with thanksgiving by those who believe and know the truth. *1 Timothy* 4:1-3 (NKJV)**

Unlike the Docetists, the Montanists rejected secret mystical knowledge as the basis for salvation. Nor do I know of any evidence that Montanus, Priscilla, and Maximilla were ever sexually involved with each other, despite their odd companionship. Often a thin line divides "spiritual spontaneity" from arbitrary, manipulative, and controlling behavior. Church history bears this pattern out more often than not.

Montanus believed that he was "the harp upon which the new wind of the Holy Spirit was blowing" to vibrate the chords. He emphasized experience with the Holy Spirit in ecstatic trances, and dissertations in unknown tongues. Trouble started when his followers began to proclaim that "New Prophecy" superseded even the old apostolic revelations. [4]

At first, many Christians welcomed Montanus, for he seemed to usher in a return to the power of the Apostles' miracles. Yet many such miracles had never really departed. Ample evidence of their continuance exists in the writings of the church fathers from that period, and much later.

The 3rd century apologist, Tertullian, thought that churches relied too much on bickering human bishops, at the expense of a living relationship with the Holy Spirit. This motivated his support for Montanus. While a valid concern, Montanus clearly did not hold real answers. Using the methods of Pagan Cybeline oracles showed ***syncretism***, not redemptive adaptation. Syncretism is the practice of mixing belief systems that would not naturally have an affinity toward each other. The Holy Spirit did not need to adopt Cybeline methods to make Christ known in Asia Minor. People had known Christ there for over two hundred years.

When Montanists claimed first that their prophecies were on par with the Apostles', and then that they superseded them, warning flags went up. "Charismania" is not new.

The Montanists also pushed the church toward closing out a list of recognized apostolic New Testament manuscripts. Tertullian feared that this was *"chasing the Holy Spirit into a book,"* [5] and good men spoke on both sides of the dispute. We can say this of Tertullian because it takes time for things to become clear in the course of events. Even Christians who accepted the Divine inspiration of the Gospels and the epistles of Paul, James, John, and Peter were not yet thinking in terms of a closed canon list of recognized books.

Yet accumulating incidents with the likes of Marcion and Montanus made an objective standard of apostolic truth necessary. Christians needed objective truth to gauge their spiritual experiences against. Rather than "chasing the Holy Spirit into a book," a canon list actually ensured the potential to continue having a vital experience of the Holy Spirit. It protected Christians from the bizarre distortions of Montanus and his spiritual descendants by giving them a way to sanity check their spiritual experiences.

*Montanism forced believers to ask what it really means to be led and empowered by the Holy Spirit.*

Tertullian's fear was not entirely groundless, however.

It is unreasonable to suppose that believers of the 3rd century could individually study Scripture the way we can today, not when a complete Bible cost the life-savings of a wealthy man. Nevertheless, a historical principle is still just as true with spiritual things as in the political realm. In times of growing instability, people often surrender their rights and responsibilities to elites that promise them order.

Once that happens, people become used to having that elite think for them. An old American proverb says, *"Give a man a fish and he will eat for a day; teach a man to fish and he will eat for a lifetime."* The teaching ministry of the church slowly drifted away from learning "how to fish" through the word of God, toward dependency on an authorized "fish soup line." It was a slow creep, and perhaps in some parts, inevitable.

Tertullian, though wrong about Montanus, was right to fear what was coming.

## MONARCHIANISM

A coherent ***Doctrine of the Trinity*** is a logical necessity for making sense of all that the Scriptures say about the nature of God. It is also essential to understanding the relationship of Jesus Christ to the Father, and the Holy Spirit. Likewise, the Trinity gives us great insight into the meaning of a humanity created in God's image, both socially and individually. Nobody comes to the Doctrine of the Trinity by understanding how it meshes. We get there because we assume that all Scripture has equal authoritative weight as God's word. This will become increasingly evident as we cover the next couple centuries of Christian thought.

***Monarchianism*** emphasized God's "oneness" at the expense of the scriptural distinctions between the Father, Son, and later the Holy Spirit

The two widest propagators of this heresy were Paul of Samosata, and a shadowy figure named Sabellius. ***Sabellian*** became the bad name to call a teacher in the Eastern churches of the dawn of the 4th century, if one wanted to demonize the fellow. Using this name associated the target with everything thought most hateful in a heretical teacher. Unfortunately, it is not always clear why. Other heresies were equally disturbing, (some even seemed more so,) and we know little of Sabellius.

This is not to give readers the impression that Monarchianism was a "heresy-lite." Like most heresies, the problems were in the implications—what we today might think of as, "the fine print." Teachers building from Monarchian ideas had trouble accepting the full humanity of Christ, which caused many problems later on.

Monarchianism in its most common form was strikingly similar to the modern United Pentecostal "Oneness" doctrine. This teaches that Jesus is simply the Father manifesting himself as the Son; a mask that the Father wears, rather than a person in the Godhead. Why is this important? Why is this idea so destructively wrong? It comes down to common sense.

If the humanity of Jesus is diminished, then so is his eligibility to die for human sin, if we carry things to their logical conclusion. A sinless human is needed as a substitute to pay for human sin. Animal sacrifices from the Mosaic Law could picture that, but only a sinless human could actually *be* that. If Jesus was not fully human, he could not be "tempted in all points as we are," and he would bear no kinship to us.

It is irrelevant what someone's intentions are, who hold this, or any other erroneous view of Christ. Sincerity and "heart attitude" are irrelevant here, because it is the idea itself that is destructive. In the real world, decisions made on bad information do not end well. Bad information about who Jesus is, and what he did for us, is damaging because our eternal destiny before God is at stake. To blow that off is to treat Jesus as just another religious figment of the human imagination—as something unreal.

Monarchianism forced the church to begin to ask, *what do we mean when we say that the Father is God, the Son is God, and the Holy Spirit is God?*

***

Other heretical groups and ideas helped shape the first 300 years of church history, but these all fell within the major categories just covered. The Ante-Nicene Church Fathers and martyrs distinguished themselves by defending the Faith against these false teachings, and then often paying with their lives. Their contributions shaped the next major phase of church history.

## BIBLIOGRAPHY

1. Daniel Gruber, ***Rabbi Akiva's Messiah***, 1999 Elijah Press; see also, ***Seder Olam—Revisited, Generation 33, Year 3870 - 110 CE - The Targum of Onkelos the Proselyte***, *http://www.seder-olam.info/seder-olam-g33-bar-kochba.html*. (Note: *Seder Olam* is an ancient anthology compiled in Hebrew by Babylonian Talmudists circa 160 AD. It gives a chronology of the history of the Jewish people, and of the world, from Adam until the Bar Kochba Revolt against the Romans. This "revisited" version is an English translation at the Jewish history site above, by Albert Benhamou; see also, ***Jesus ...the Jewish Messiah***, *Why do Modern Jewish People Reject Jesus?* Light of Messiah Ministries: http://www.lightofmessiah.org/resources/articles/the_jewish_messiah.php, See block quote of latter below:

   > ***Why do Modern Jewish People Reject Jesus? (Author: Murray Tilles—L.M.M.)***
   >
   > *I wish that I could say that the reason is because, having examined the evidence, most Jewish people have decided that Jesus cannot be the Messiah. But this is not the case at all. By the way, the same thing could be said for non-Jewish people. Relatively few people who reject the claim that Jesus is the Messiah and Savior do so on the basis of an informed search of the evidence.*
   >
   > *To find the answer to the question, "Why do Jewish people reject Jesus?" one need only look at Jewish history. The earliest followers of Jesus were all Jewish and worshipped in the synagogues alongside those who did not follow Jesus. Tensions gradually increased between the groups. A final blow to the relationship between these two groups within Judaism was the Bar Kochva rebellion in 132 CE.*
   >
   > *Bar Kochva was a revolutionary who received the approval of Rabbi Akiva, who in many ways is the founder of modern Judaism. Messianic Jewish believers, that is Jewish believers in Jesus, fought alongside their Jewish brethren during the first year of the revolt. But then, Rabbi Akiva declared Bar Kochva the Messiah. The Jewish believers in Jesus could no longer support this war since it would involve denying Jesus as Messiah. This was the last straw in a gradual growing apart of these two groups within Judaism.*
   >
   > *Alongside this split within Judaism over Jesus, there was also a trend in the congregations of more and more Gentiles coming in and less and less Jewish people. It is a shameful fact of Christian history that even by the beginning of the second century, believers in Jesus were forgetting their Jewish roots and the Jewishness of their Messiah…*

2. Schaeffer, Francis A. ***How Should We Then Live? The Rise and Decline of Western Thought and Culture***, p.19, 1976, Fleming H. Revell Co. Old Tappan, NJ.
3. Shelley, Bruce L. ***Church History in Plain Language*** (2nd Edition), pp.51-52, 1995, Word Publishing, Dallas, Tx.
4. Placher, William C. ***A History of Christian Theology: An Introduction***. Westminster John Knox Press, 1983, p. 50; see also, Chapman, John (1911), *"Montanists,"* ***The Catholic Encyclopedia 10***. Robert Appleton, Retrieved 27 June 2011,
5. Walker, Williston. ***A History of the Christian Church*** (4th Edition), pp. 69-70, 1st Edition, 1918, 4th Edition 1946, Charles Scribner's Sons, New York, NY.
6. Op cit. Shelley, Bruce L. p.64

# 3

# WORLDVIEW OF THE ANTE-NICENE CHURCH FATHERS: A CHRISTIAN VIEW OF MARTYRDOM

## GRECO-ROMAN COLLISION DENTS

Christianity moved out of Judea in its first century on collision course with the popular culture of the Roman Empire. A subtle change of presuppositions in the way believers saw both themselves and God accompanied this move. The formal truths of the New Testament did not change, but Greeks accessed those truths differently. At first, Greeks had a hard time accessing them at all, given some of their cultural assumptions.

The Hebrew-based thought of the Apostles started from different assumptions on the nature of Divinity and creation than those of the pagan Greek-Romans. The church collided with the Greco-Roman world, and turned it upside down in a massive rollover. This radical shift in the culture of an empire is unparalleled in history. The true miracle is that the biblical belief system not only survived this collision, it flourished in its wake.

It was not only that Christianity changed the world, however. Some cultural imprint of the Greco-Roman worldview remained indelibly on the "front fenders" of the church's developing sense of identity. Up-and-coming church leadership forms also reflected this collision. The Ante-Nicene Church Fathers hammered straight the grosser dents, those major heresies of the "Catholic Age." (*Ante-Nicene* is a term for the period after the Apostles, but before the Nicene Council of 325 AD, a major landmark in church history.)

Nevertheless, an accretion of smaller dents, and the "sprung frame" that comes with any collision also had future consequences that only time would reveal. God used this worldview collision to refine the church's understanding of Jesus' nature. The Greco-Roman worldview also left marks on the church that the church fathers did not intend or anticipate.

One mark was the popularization of allegorical over natural literal methods for interpreting Scripture. Allegorical interpretation is not bad, any more than a contrived, wooden literal interpretation is good. Language breathes. It is not always either/or. Genuine allegory and a naturally literal interpretation often dovetail with each other. It all depends on the text's literary, thematic, grammatical, and historical context. Is the genre of the Bible book history, poetry, apocalypse, epistle, or is it proverb or law? One does not read a parable quite the same way as a history narrative. The Bible contains all of the above, so genre is important when interpreting its texts.

Hellenistic Jewish philosophers, like Philo of Alexandria, effectively gave Greek steroids to allegories drawn from Scripture. ***Hermeneutics*** is the science of text interpretation. A good hermeneutic fits the language of the text as the author used it. It might allow one to make an allegory of a normally non-allegorical passage to illustrate something. Yet that would never be to the exclusion of the passage's primary meaning. For example, Paul justifiably used the history of Ishmael and Isaac as an allegory of the flesh and the Spirit, to illustrate his point in Galatians 4:21-31. He did not deny the historical nature of Genesis to establish the symbolism, however. Nor did Paul exaggerate to type Ishmael and Isaac this way—they remained true to character.

Over-allegorization dismissed reasonable literal meanings in a text as if they were less important. Often this happened without any attempt to deceive. Nevertheless, the system had a blind spot that sometimes obscured what it tried to illustrate. The problem was that it over-indulged Greek philosophy, and imitated Stoic allegorization of the *Homer Epics.* [1] A

Greek hermeneutic was also incompatible with the Hebraic worldview framework of the subject texts. Imagine trying to hammer in a nail with the butt end of a screwdriver. The nail may go in okay sometimes, but someone designed the tool for turning screws.

Paul and the other Apostles found many allegoric types of Christ in the Old Testament. By contrast, the Greek concept of interpretation allowed for foreign presuppositions. These were alien to the worldview of the inspired authors.

For many centuries, Greek philosophers had tooled this allegorical hermeneutic to get deeper meaning from myths and fables. Virtually everyone at the time knew those stories were too fantastic to take literally. This was how the Greeks and Romans viewed the record of their gods—as often-contradictory fables and allegories. They made no bones about it, though some had more respect for the ethics of their mythology than others did.

By contrast, the Old and New Testaments contained no fables, but accounts of real people, who in various historical situations encountered a real God in the real world. Bible characters were not larger-than-life, semi-divine heroes, nor were the extraordinary events they witnessed understood as mere fable (though they might serve similar moral purposes). The Jews culturally understood their sacred texts to be accurate accounts of people and events that really happened. Jesus spoke as if he understood them that way.

The early Christians preached a Christ who died and rose again at a certain time and place in history. They understood the difference between myth, fable, and historical record.

> **For we have not followed cunningly devised fables, when we made known unto you the power and coming of our Lord Jesus Christ, but were eyewitnesses of his majesty.** 2 *Peter* **1:16 KJV**

The Jews had never been a society of simpletons that could not tell literal from figurative writing. Their literature had a sophisticated system of allegory, poetry, and history with clearly marked contexts. Nobody who has ever read Solomon could honestly draw the conclusion that Hebrews were simply more gullible than the Greeks were. The writing styles of the two bodies of literature are different in their approach to their subjects, rising out of different worldviews. Therefore, a method of interpretation designed for Greek myth would ultimately be mismatched when applied to books of the Hebrew Bible.

The Ante-Nicene Fathers were not equipped to notice the problem described above. The intellectual tools for that level of textual analysis had not yet developed. The reader should not take my commentary as a doctrinal criticism of the Fathers. It merely shows what led to what, and possibly why. Blind spots are not sins, but Satan can still exploit them. It would be arrogant of us to expect 2nd century pastors, who were often running for their lives, to write with 20th century expository precision. Nor is it wise to suppose 21st century "intellectual tools" are therefore of little use, since the Holy Spirit did not see fit to bless us with them in the 2nd century. Today's inductive and deductive study methods grew in an incubator defined by a biblical concept of truth. The Lord took great care cultivating them in the church for our benefit.

The Ante-Nicene Church Fathers performed two essential services to the growing church in the early centuries. They first served as apologists, then often as martyrs. The word ***apologist*** means *one who rationally and systematically defends the faith.* The term comes from the Greek word, *apologia,* which means *to offer a reasoned defense.*

A ***martyr*** originally was a term that meant more than *someone killed for the Faith.* Certainly, Christians never used the word to describe a person who murdered their religious enemies to cow others into accepting Christianity. The word meant *witness.* Martyrs had witnessed the power of God in their lives in a transformative way. They were prepared to die rather than change their testimony. Only after Rome had coerced many into changing their stories did the word become associated with killing. The idea of martyrs killing others to become "the martyr" is foreign to Christian thought and history. Misguided crusaders were never revered as martyrs.

The first major group the church needed to offer a reasoned defense of the faith against was the 1st century Jewish religious leaders. We can see the martyr Stephen doing this in Acts Chapter 7. As the church moved into the Gentile world, the second group it needed to defend itself against was the Greco Roman Pagans. As the Gnostics and other heretical groups grew, apologists turned their attentions on them. The threat here often came from inside the church itself.

Historians called this sort of apologist a ***polemicist***. Polemicists wrote against spiritually and morally destructive trends inside the Christian community. That word has taken on negative shades in recent years, and people do not often used it anymore. Unfortunately, just because careless polemics degenerate into mere demonization does not mean that actual spiritual dangers never arise from inside the church. Nor does it mean that "loving Christians" should leave such dangers unconfronted. Paul had to engage in polemics often in the New Testament. The Epistle of Jude is entirely polemical. As seen with Stephen, apologetics often led to martyrdom in the early days. Later on, so did polemics.

It would be impossible in this brief a work to cover all the important Pre-Nicene Church Fathers and their contributions. My purpose is to show the big-picture role these church fathers played, both wittingly and unwittingly. We will use these people as "test samples" for reading the mood of the age in a general sort of way.

## SNAPSHOTS OF THE ANTE-NICENE CHURCH FATHERS

A shadowy figure named **Barnabas of Alexandria** taught during the late 1st to early 2nd centuries, at the large urban church founded by Apollos, fifty years earlier. He was not the Barnabas of the Book of Acts, but a later convert from Hellenized Judaism. ***Hellenized*** is a historical term meaning that Greek ideas shaped his thinking as much or more than Jewish ones did. He wrote the *Epistle of Barnabas*, which Orthodox Christians and Gnostics both revered for its allegorical approach to Scripture.

Barnabas was not a Gnostic however, because he rejected the Gnostic heresies about Christ's nature. Greek thought influenced all the Ante-Nicene Fathers to some degree without making them heretical. Philo's methods heavily influenced Barnabas, who probably first used them to interpret Scripture in a Christian church setting.

Although Greek allegorical method had great power of illustration, it stressed looking for "mystical deeper truths" in Scripture. This sometimes happened at the expense of the text's common-sense meaning. Deep meanings that need more than superficial analysis intertwine throughout the Bible. That does not imply such meanings supersede the natural literary, thematic, grammatical, historical, understanding of the text. Genuine deeper meaning compliments rather than contradicts what the text plainly says.

The authors of the New Testament wrote in the common ***Koinae Greek*** of the marketplace for average people on the street. Yet, Greek philosophical speculation in Bible interpretation sometimes fostered an environment that impaired down-to-earth application of scriptural principles. Historical examples of how this impediment played out are many. The scriptural principles ranged from how to keep holy days, to modes of church government, and on rare instances, even touched on tests for an "orthodox" belief or practice. The "problem areas" were not so much about interpretation as application. No ambiguity existed over core issues.

The post-apostolic fathers had a viscerally real concept of Christ's lordship. In today's language, we might say that they believed that Christ was Lord and God of the real world. We could also safely say that they put their spiritual descendants of today to shame by their sense of Christ's lordship over reality.

It is an odd paradox. Some issues that we would consider straightforward and obvious applications of Bible teaching seemed lost on them, through the influence of Greek thinking. Of course, sometimes things were not as simple as we like to think. For example, Genuine Christians in both East and West were already comfortably using the pagan name *Easter* for Christ's Resurrection day in the early 2nd century, over 200 years before the reign of Constantine (more on him later).

I suggest that this sort of thing can sometimes happen because of worldview blind spots—a number of which have shaped the landscape of church history. This is where the historical *Law of Unintended Consequences* comes into play. Church history often shows that the Holy Spirit allows us to stumble over our worldview blind spots, sometimes for centuries. It also shows how the Spirit orchestrates the natural growth of intellectual tools, both in churches and in the world. Believers then redemptively use these tools to shed light in ways that help us interpret and apply God's word with greater precision to new situations.

We will see, as time goes on, that every hostile worldview the church encountered eventually gave Christianity tools, which God's Spirit used in this redemptive way. Often Christians used these tools to defeat the opposing worldview they came from, almost as spiritual antibodies fighting disease in the body of Christ!

As the popularity of Greek allegoric interpretation models grew in the church, teachers began to seem elite. They were not often arrogant men who deliberately looked for that—not at this early date. The drift in that direction was an inevitable side effect of Greek-styled Bible interpretation and assumptions. If the average person could not understand what the Scriptures said, and deeper meanings sometimes trumped surface ones, then what other answer was there?

The idea that the basic meaning of Scripture is shadowy, even to literate believers, opens the door to religious manipulation. Greek-Roman believers were often literate, as are today's Christians. The main difference between their ability to study Scripture and ours was the availability of the texts. From the 2nd century until the invention of the printing press, it took the life savings of a wealthy man to purchase a set of books the size of the Bible. This may explain why God waited so long to bring the Reformation. He would not hold church leaders who *could not* make the Scriptures easily accessible to the same level of accountability as church leaders who could. This was a formidable economic hurdle.

Nevertheless, the writings of the Apostles and other late 1st century sources show a major false teaching crisis by the latter half of the 1st century and early 2nd. This was due to more than mere cultural blind spots, but these often created openings for Satan to work if believers did not respond well to their discovery. [2] Most everybody sensed that something was going wrong. The question was what to do about it.

**Clement of Rome** naturally stressed ***apostolic succession*** as the test of spiritual integrity for an individual teacher or church. The Apostle Paul mentioned Clement, at the time a young man, in Philippians 4:3. Roman Catholics consider him the 4th Pope. Whether a church could trace its teaching authority back to an Apostle became a litmus test for truth beginning in the early 2nd century.

Apostolic succession worked well enough in early centuries, when traceability and transmission of truth was straightforward. Everyone still spoke Greek, the language of the New Testament. Nevertheless, it is fair to ask, some 2000 years later, "What happened when bishop seats that could trace their office back to an Apostle slowly moved away from truth? How and when did that happen?" It is difficult to study church history honestly without concluding that it happened.

Gross departures easily revealed themselves as heresies. Yet, what of the slower buildup of smaller mistakes, not attributable to any single source, which take centuries to warp a religious system? How did these turn the vibrant relationship with Christ in apostolic Christianity into the oppressive state religion of late medieval times?

It did not happen overnight. Nor was it always a deliberate departure—in fact, more often than not, it wasn't. Frequently it came as dominant ideas in the church swung between various extremes, over time. This left a historical wake, like that of large ships passing on waterways made of thought, faith, and practice. There are rarely simple answers to such questions, but history sheds light.

Clement was martyred under the Roman Emperor Domitian. Even if he had lived to a ripe old age, it would not have allowed him to see that he had established only a relatively short-term solution. One can hardly fault him for that. The solution was sufficient for his day. Although the individual New Testament books had all been written by now, many of them were still in the process of being recognized for what they were. Such things took time on the human level.

The early 2nd century church father, **Ignatius of Antioch**, became one of the first apologists against Gnosticism. He wrote a series of letters while *en route* to martyrdom under the Emperor Trajan at Rome. He was the first to make a real distinction in the authority rank of bishops over elders (presbyters) as church officers. [3] Many church historians think that the distinction had only been functional before that.

The distinction of authority that placed bishops over other elders came as a natural, even practical development. By the early 2nd century, larger urban churches began to take leadership over nearby smaller rural ones. The equation was simple; bigger churches had more resources to support smaller ones. It was only good stewardship if the smaller churches must account for how they used those resources. This developed into the ***diocese*** and archdiocese regional church government of Roman Catholicism and Eastern Orthodoxy.

The early 2nd century was an era when the immediate students of Apostles themselves still had much influence. This tended to reinforce enough of the Hebraic worldview to establish the essentials of the Faith for later times. **Papias** and **Polycarp** had both been disciples of the aged Apostle John in their youth. Since the 1st century church had lived in the expectancy of Christ's return, early 2nd century believers often focused on prophecy. They considered the Lord's Coming to be all the nearer.

Papias held a ***Pre-millennial*** view of end-time prophecy. That is, he did not consider the Millennium of John's Revelation to be an allegory of the church age. Papias' epistles show that he believed the Millennium would actually happen in future history, after Christ's literal and bodily return. Since he studied under the man, he probably knew how John himself understood his Apocalypse. Sadly, Papias' straightforward approach to prophecy did not seem long for the world.

Polycarp was Bishop of Smyrna—a contemporary of the heretic Marcion, mentioned in the last chapter. Records have him confronting Marcion, and calling him the "firstborn of Satan" to his face. This feisty bishop was martyred at age 86, during the imperial reign of Antoninus Pius. The *Letter to the Church of Smyrna*, written in the Revelation of Polycarp's mentor, must have held special meaning to him toward the end of his life.

> **And to the angel of the church in Smyrna write... 'Do not fear any of those things which you are about to suffer. Indeed the devil is about to throw some of you into prison, that you may be tested, and you will have tribulation ten days. Be faithful until death, and I will give you the crown of life.' *Revelation* 2:8a & 10 NKJV**

Polycarp did not live to see that there would indeed be ten periods of Roman persecution against the church. But he did see the prophecy's immediate fulfillment in his own life.

Trouble for Christians increased with the Roman Empire in the early 2nd century. Rabbinical leaders systematically expelled Christians from synagogues by then. The Jews had an understanding with Rome, exempting them from adding praises and oaths to Caesar to their religious ceremonies. Rome found it easier to give them a "get out of jail free card" than face Empire-wide riots. Jews outside of Judea generally kept to themselves, and did not actively seek converts the way Christians did. Another reason giving the Jews a "conscience exception" was easier for Rome was that Jewish communities rarely grew.

Most other religions at the time worshipped many gods. ***Polytheistic*** religions had no spiritual problem adding Caesar as a minor deity to be appeased. Rome only sporadically enforced this requirement against other cults, and the Christians, before the middle 3rd century. At first, not even many emperors took the cult of emperor worship seriously. Claudius refused to allow people to make sacrifices to him because he did not want to seem obnoxious.

As long as the imperium perceived Christians as a Jewish sect, they also usually enjoyed this protection. When Jewish leaders began in the 2nd century to insist that they had nothing to do with the Christians, churches began to lose this security. This often happened according to the whims of a local mob. Enter Polycarp, whose church was denounced by the synagogue at a time when the pagan temples were also losing worshippers to Christianity.

When arrested by Roman troopers, Polycarp asked the arresting officer for a brief time of prayer to prepare for his ordeal. The troopers allowed it. He also used that time to cook a meal for his arresting officers, and to share his faith with them. When asked by the crowd-pleasing magistrate to renounce Christ and swear by Caesar, Polycarp said, "These past eighty-six years my Lord has been faithful to me. How can I now prove unfaithful to him who has showed me such kindness all my life?" [4]

People abuse the word *martyr* today, especially since the events of 9-11. Polycarp bore witness to the life changing power of Jesus, and died rather than change his story. Jesus, for Polycarp, was Lord of reality.

The next few "snapshots" are of church fathers that lived about a generation later, in the middle 2nd century. They are not so far ahead that their lives did not overlap with some of the men mentioned before.

**Justin Martyr** developed the ***"Logos Theology"*** of Christ as the "living word of God," building from John's writings. He wrote primarily in response to heretics. His most notable work took Marcion apart, whom he debated personally and possibly more effectively than did Polycarp. Justin trained in classical oratory, which enabled him to frame his arguments in ways that reached both philosophers and churchmen. His arguments for Christ centered on fulfilled prophecy, documented miracles, and ethics. He usually avoided spiritually loaded name-calling (even if the names tended to fit). That did not prevent his beheading in Rome. Satan fears a well-reasoned defense of the Faith more than he does a merely emotional one.

Justin's student, **Tatian**, wrote the *Diatessaron*, which was the first known harmony of the four Gospels. For a while, Tatian showed all the signs of being a great apologist like his mentor, but later in life, he fell into Gnosticism. This illustrates just how seductive Gnostic ideas and Greek presuppositions were to thinkers of that time. Popular culture exerts incredible pressure on people. They are sometimes unaware that ideas can feel terribly real even without proof, if repeated often enough. Nobody is immune to conditioning, even those who understand how it works. Worldview analysis is a relatively recent "intellectual tool" that can help us discern popular assumptions from genuine evidence-based reason.

It would not have occurred to 2nd century people to ask if the worldview assumptions of the Apostles and those of Greek philosophers led to the same conclusions, given the same evidence. They faced an intellectual struggle similar to that faced by many of today's Christians. People often do not understand or else underestimate the influence worldview assumptions have had on popular science. Popular science and the scientific method are two different things. Thus, Christians can feel compelled to try to harmonize Genesis with the Theory of Evolution or some of its resulting ideas. Christians who do not understand how worldview assumptions drive the interpretation of evidence feel backed into two unnecessary corners. Either they feel they must explain away parts of the Bible or they feel uncomfortable applying their minds to origins-related subjects. Later, we will explore a better option.

Tatian did not examine the foundations of his own thinking, or that of the popular trends in the world around him. He did not see how the theological and lifestyle conclusions drawn by the Gnostics came not by genuine intellectual proofs. Rather, they came by interpreting the evidence according to anti-biblical assumptions based on nothing but faith.

The danger exists more intensely for us today, although we have many more tools to work with. Even without our tools, Tatian still had enough information to conclude that Jesus was who the Gospel accounts portrayed him to be. Nor did eighty contradictory Gospel narratives exist to make a choice other than Tatian's arbitrary, as claimed by novelist Dan Brown's fictional "historian" in *The DaVinci Code*. Not only is the novel fiction, but its "history," also.

By the early middle 2nd century, the writings that later became New Testament canon were already widely circulated, and being called "New Testament Scripture." Thousands of manuscripts were available for 2nd century apologists to cite and quote. No other work claiming to be a 1st century Gospel had near that kind of circulation, and history has the paper trail to prove it. [5] In fact, obvious late 2nd, 3rd, and 4th century language use discredits the nearest contenders. The 2nd century *Muratorian Canon*, a list of books then considered Scripture by many churches, was nearly as complete as the canon universally adopted, later.

Tatian's mentor and other orthodox thinkers were no intellectual slouches. They usually thought clearly and honestly in their responses to opposing ideas. Even if some indulged in what we today might call "demonization" of their opponents, their opponents often stooped far lower. They incited mobs, using false accusations that got people killed.

**Irenaeus, Bishop of Lyons**, who lived in the late 2nd Century, maintained apostolic starting assumptions more effectively than Tatian. Irenaeus was the student of Polycarp, and a strong opponent of Gnosticism, as shown by his most famous writing, *Against Heresies*. He is the one who coined the word ***orthodoxy***, which means *right-thinking regarding the things of God*. Tradition says he was martyred at Lyons, in what is now France.

We have already talked about **Tertullian**, who also lived in the late 2nd and early 3rd centuries. In contrast to his sympathy for the Montanists, his writings clarified the ***Doctrine of the Trinity***, working from the Logos Theology of Justin Martyr. He also wrote a dissertation, ***Against Marcion***. (Marcion was, by this time, quite old or possibly even dead, but his followers still hung on.) Despite Tertullian's misguided support of Montanus, his writings built up the church far more than this one mistaken impression tore it down.

**Hippolytus**, student of Irenaeus, made a historical footprint, though not always in ways that Evangelicals would find biblical. I mention him here to glean information about developments in the state of church leadership of the time. His teacher, Irenaeus, wrote in glowing terms about the example and leadership of the church at Rome in the 2nd century. Nevertheless, Irenaeus was not afraid to disagree with the Bishop of Rome in the Dating of Easter Controversy. He told Victor, Pope of Rome, that differences in minor matters like the dating of holy days were not essential, and should not divide the church. He wrote that such uniformity was insufficient reason to excommunicate whole churches in distant lands, as Victor tried to do. [6]

Hippolytus later found even more occasion to disagree with Rome than his mentor had. He opposed what he called the "moral laxity" of Callistus, Bishop of Rome, whom the Roman Catholic Church considers one of its Popes. Callistus was the slave of a Christian advisor to the Emperor, who had pastoral authority over his earthly master. The term *Papa* or ***Pope*** had become a popular title for bishops of large metropolitan districts like Rome, Alexandria, and Antioch. The term of affection meant *dear father*.

A prelude to the idea of Roman primacy had already begun to develop by the end of the 2nd Century. Yet, when Pope Victor of Rome tried to excommunicate prominent churches in Asia Minor over when to celebrate Easter, it backfired in his face. It never occurred to him to obey Colossians 2:16, **"So let no one judge you in food or in drink, or regarding a festival or a new moon or sabbaths."**

Irenaeus made a straightforward application of this passage in his dissent with Victor. The Pope of Rome's decree had no binding power on these churches, beyond the city of Rome. All other congregations and bishops throughout the church still respected the "excommunicated fellowships." It suggests that imperialistic notions began to grow from Clement's apostolic succession. [7] If so, however, Irenaeus and the majority of churches showed that it was by no means an idea held by the universal church.

The Dating of Easter Controversy is also important because it helps us track the extent that pagan names and ideas had infiltrated Christianity. Evangelical pastors have often blamed the acceptance of pagan worship forms into the church on the emperor Constantine, the subject of the next chapters. They frequently cite calling Christ's Resurrection Day *Easter* as an example. They are correct that the term comes from the Babylonian goddess Ishtar through its Phoenician pronunciation, *Aestarte*.

Easter's emphasis on bunnies and eggs all came from pagan symbols of the fertility worship associated with this goddess. The problem for this Evangelical claim is that the Dating of Easter Controversy happened over a century before Constantine. That means one of two things; either the fusion of pagan with Christian worship forms began far earlier than is often supposed, or compromise is not the earliest cause of what happened. The purity of faith found in the great apologists and martyrs would belie the idea that such a universal apostasy could happen so soon. Even Irenaeus comfortably referred to the day as *Easter*, as did even earlier Christians.

This forced me to question whether use of the name *Easter* really began as a spiritual compromise at all. It is possible that another reason makes more sense, given the timing of events. Pagan forms later entered Christian worship to distort some of the customs the Church developed. History documents this. A clearer, stronger historical apologetic clarified itself through my asking two questions. The first was whether past worldviews may have played a quiet role. The second involved asking what the practical obstacles to sharing the Christian faith in a Greek-Roman world actually were in the 2nd century.

A far more realistic way to explain how pagan ideas and customs began to find their way into Christianity began to take shape. I became convinced that it is best to avoid simplistic, single-cause answers that invoke conspiracy theories centered on Constantine. While conspiracies likely happened, and Constantine had problems, the original causes likely had more to do with the underlying worldview shift already discussed. Conspiracy theories rarely explain history well. There were also some aggravating factors.

As Jews vocally distanced themselves from Christianity, it sometimes caused persecution to fall on the Christians. It is not surprising that Christians of that period reacted by distancing themselves from Jews, especially as Christians came to see themselves as what historian Bruce Shelley called an "army of martyrs." Gentile believers (illustrated by Pope Victor) also wanted a uniquely Gentile way to celebrate the Resurrection. Thus, they sanitized the name *Easter* with its fertility emphasis on rebirth. Yet that explanation, too, is overly simplistic. Why would Christians dying for their faith want to use a term from one of the most perverse forms of idolatry they knew?

It just makes no sense to see bitterness and compromise as the origin of this trend, despite what happened later. Many 2nd century Gentile converts came from families that worshipped Aestarte in one form or another. Since the spiritual themes of the Aestarte fertility cults were rebirth and renewal, it made sense for 2nd and 3rd century Christians to show unbelieving loved ones how Christ gave what Aestarte falsely promised. Imagine them saying something like, "You want rebirth? I'll show you some rebirth! You talk about Easter, I'll show you the real 'Easter' in the resurrection of Jesus!" They were not afraid of names.

These were the same Christians dying bloody deaths rather than denying Christ. This model makes more historical sense than saying that these same martyrs were actually "compromisers" willing to water down the gospel. It even makes more sense, despite growing tensions between Jews and Christians that drove a desire to celebrate the Resurrection with a Gentile flavor.

Most Evangelicals today agree that this "uniquely Gentile" flavor was not a very good idea in the end. Eventually, traditions like eating an Easter ham developed that showed a petty anti-Jewish rancor to them. Pope Victor wanted to detach the dating of Easter from that of Passover. Eastern churches (who also called it Easter) wished to keep celebrating the Resurrection on Passover as they always had. Christians of the 1st century celebrated a Jewish Passover enhanced by the significance of the empty tomb.

We should consider other dimensions, if we are to have a balanced understanding of the worldview shift Christianity underwent in the early 2nd century. One is that the shift was never total. This was generally true during all the later worldview transitions as well. The essentials of faith needed for salvation and discipleship managed to survive through many struggles. They expressed themselves differently in whatever cultural transition Christians went through—most of the time—but they did express themselves.

When those essentials began to fade from the church's culture, the Holy Spirit would stir the pot, and bring them back somehow to the surface. It also helps to remember that not all results from worldview shifts, and the transitions they brought to the Faith, were necessarily bad. The gospel of Jesus Christ not only answered the cultural questions and needs of the Hebrew worldview, but also of Gentile peoples.

Don Richardson's book, *Eternity in Their Hearts*, documents how even isolated pagan societies had some aspect in their mythology recalling the true Creator God. Though often oblique, distorted, and even morally debased, the human soul still reflects something of the image of God. The human need for redemption rears its head in the most unlikely places. Wise and discerning missionaries often discovered these cultural elements, and showed how Jesus Christ gave answers for them. We see the Apostle Paul doing this in Acts 17 at Athens. He spoke to the Greeks on Mars Hill in their own cultural language about the "Unknown God," quoting their own philosopher-poets rather than the Hebrew prophets. [8]

It also helps to remember that, at one point, there were eight people on this planet, and they all knew God. I speak of Noah and his family as a historical reality. If the reader finds that incredulous, I humbly ask that they suspend judgment until they have followed this book through to its logical conclusion. I give reasons later on why it is not a blind leap of faith to trust the Genesis record as history. My point here, however, is to demonstrate that even pagans had some memory of God, as the first two chapters of the Book of Romans maintain.

Other worldviews would soon bring further challenges to Christian belief, and yield tools for believers to redeem and use. The Celts, for example, found in Christ the fulfillment of the main theme in their mythology of a "Once and Future King." They were fiercely independent, but often divided by their own cultural distrust of authority.

Consequently, no matter how bravely Celtic tribes fought against more organized enemies, they often went down in a kind of glorious defeat. They kept their dignity alive through stories, in a rich mythical tradition that sometimes crisscrossed actual history. Despite or perhaps because of their distrust of authority, they yearned for a strong and kindly king that would come and unite them. Hence, their mythology is filled with such lordly figures as Bran the Blessed, Tristan, Aurelius, and King Arthur.

Christ became the ultimate High King for the fragmented Celts, who had no cultural concept of sin in the Semitic sense. (They only developed that after they became Christians). They flocked to receive the gospel, and serve a true monarch who would not ever fail them. The Celts were not alone. The yearning for resurrection in the cults of Egypt found answer in the bodily resurrection of believers promised in Judeo-Christian prophecy. Even the need for rebirth and renewal men searched for in the perverse fertility rites of Aestarte found satisfaction in the Resurrection Christians celebrated at Easter.

It is unjust to accuse 2nd century Christians of simply caving in to Paganism. This happens in some sects of Evangelical Protestantism. Rather, 2nd century believers recognized that the legitimate questions posed in part by their old Pagan religions found answers in the Virgin Birth and Resurrection of Christ. We Evangelicals sometimes seem to forget that the Mother and Child religious motif did not appear first at the Tower of Babel. It originated in God's promise of Genesis 3:15 that the woman's seed would crush the serpent's head. These Pagan elements sometimes implied legitimate cultural questions that found their true answer in Christ, even as Christ fulfilled the Law and the Prophets for the Jew. Therefore, to some extent, it was only natural for these religious motifs to slide over into Gentile churches.

This does not excuse later tendencies for Christian worship to take on overt Pagan characteristics. These eventually distorted the church's understanding of Christ's work. Satan always seeks to corrupt innocent things into something destructive. There is a difference between celebrating the answering of basic Pagan questions in Christ, and establishing Pagan-like worship forms as a way to govern church culture. Whatever happened to begin this trend in the 2nd century was likely innocent enough to the Ante-Nicene Church Fathers that they focused on more immediate things. We do the same today with our own cultural and spiritual blind spots, which often involve far more dangerous attacks on the Faith than those faced in the 2nd century.

The last church father snapshots come from the early to mid-3rd Century. **Origen** was the student of **Clement of Alexandria** (a different Clement, who lived a century later than Clement of Rome). This Clement converted to Christ as an adult, already trained in Greek philosophy. While he held to orthodox Logos Theology on the nature of Christ, he taught Origen the Greek allegorical model for interpreting Scripture.

Origen was the son of a Christian martyr named Leonidas. He was extremely ***ascetic***—that is, he held to the idea that all pleasure was evil because of its material nature, especially sexual pleasure, even in marriage. So extreme were his views on this matter that he castrated himself not long after his conversion to Christ. His ideas on the nature of human sexuality typified a growing trouble in church culture by the 3rd century. The West would not begin to correct this problem until the Reformation. Mainstream Christians had come to confuse asceticism for spiritual vitality.

This confusion became a repeating trend even after the Reformation, though on a smaller scale. This usually happened whenever secular culture and even much of the church became inordinately self-focused and ***hedonistic***. The ascetic trap always begins amid legitimate responses to counteract self-focus and pleasure worship. Yet it quickly morphs into something the Bible also reveals as carnal. (Col. 2:16-23, 1 Tim. 4:1-5, Heb. 13:4, Rom. 14:1-10) The problem with asceticism was that it viewed even redeemed human nature as "unholy." It improperly blurred distinctions between sinfulness and humanness; the pathology or damage caused by sin, and God-engineered human nature.

Christians became reactionary. They embraced unrealistic standards, which in practice pretended to be higher even than God's revealed word. The false standards of asceticism ruled out positive human enjoyment of things like courtship and marriage, the fruit of one's labor, and acceptable worship. The focus went so heavily onto the "thou shalt nots," that clear or healthy ideas of how such relationships should look withered and died. It did not happen suddenly, but slowly, as an inordinate fear grew in church culture. Unrestrained sinful behavior always creates fear. What is not always so clear is the fear's object.

Neither our humanity nor our materiality makes us sinful. Sin, rather, defaces our humanity, which has material effects. God made us human and in His own image in the beginning, before the Fall and the Curse. God is a spirit, but He created a reality that is both material and spiritual. God identifies Himself gender-specifically as male, even though He is not biologically sexual like humans. The Holy Spirit, as the *Paraclete*, or *Helper* (John 14:16), takes an implicit female role analogous to "helpmeet" or "helper" (Genesis 2:18-25). Proverbs 8 also personifies the "Spirit of Wisdom" as a woman.

Scripture does not explicitly teach that the Holy Spirit is female, nor should we. It does however describe elements of the Holy Spirit's work in distinctly feminine roles. Father and Son are explicitly male by gender in a way that transcends human biological sexuality. This strongly implies that sexuality was not merely for procreation. We reflect God, not the other way around. Genesis 2:18-25 predominately expresses the purpose given for woman as that of complimentary companionship. To reduce the purpose of human sexuality only to procreation is not as bad as reducing it to mere recreation, but it still makes it into less than what Scripture reveals. This will become evident as the centuries passed.

In fact, human sexuality is also a reflection of creation in God's image, stated as such in the first chapter of Genesis.

> **So God created man in His own image; *in the image of God He created him; male and female He created them. Genesis* 1:27 NKJV**

Human sexuality is a product of Creation, not of the Curse. The Curse negatively affected human sexuality deeply, but it was not the origin of human sexual desire and behavior of itself. We reflect God's image not only as individuals, but also as married couples, families, and as social beings. This is another reason the Doctrine of the Trinity is so essential. God is a Trinity of Father, Son, and Holy Spirit, a social Being, by nature. Families (and other basic human social units) are also structurally triune. This is why man-woman marriage is the essential shape for human sexual behavior. Human nature and biology reflects this design.

Sin, and the pathologies it caused, broke this design in an expanding pattern of individual, relational, and social wreckage.

While Origen was orthodox in his view of Christ, one can easily see how much Greek thought had influenced his thinking from the way he described creation. This fed into his asceticism. Greek-styled allegorical Scripture interpretation reached new extremes in how he understood early parts of Genesis. In Origen's view, God created spirits that later became both men and angels in a totally non-material realm. The Garden of Eden became for him allegory rather than history, despite the Hebrew genre of Genesis. These pre-existing spirits then fell away from God. Only after that fall did the material universe form—already corrupted by sin—to reenact what had already happened in spirit.

This enabled Origen to take the Pagan Stoic view that human sexuality, even in marriage, was a "necessary evil," rather than a gift from God. If material creation came already fallen, then no aspect of that reality was good. Jesus Christ was the one great exception to that, in Origen's mind. Yet his exception defied logic.

Here we see a near-total abandonment of the Hebrew worldview. Only by the fact that Origen insisted on Christ's bodily Incarnation, death, and Resurrection mitigated this view. Ironically, the Holy Spirit used a product of the Greek worldview here to rescue orthodoxy. Aristotle's Dictum states that the benefit of the doubt must go to a document that claimed to tell a history of real events, and not to the philosophy of the critic. We could have no real knowledge of history apart from this principle.

The Gospels presented a Jesus who was in every way both God and man, who died and rose bodily from the dead. The resurrected Jesus invited Thomas to put his hands on his bodily wounds. This same Jesus ate with them after the Resurrection. Genuine love of Jesus, bolstered by the redemptive use of Aristotle's Dictum by the Holy Spirit, braced Christian thinkers for the next few centuries. The influence of the Greek worldview had yet to reach its high water mark.

Origen also saw interesting things in 1 Corinthians 15:28.

> **Now when all things are made subject to Him** (God)**, then the Son Himself will also be subject to Him who put all things under Him, that God may be all in all. (NKJV)**

Origen speculated that there might be a basis here for the idea that God would eventually restore all men, and even fallen angels, to eternal fellowship. He reasoned quite loosely that God could not be **"all in all"** if anything in creation was excluded.

While that may sound comforting, his overly allegorical approach to Scripture lacked the logical coherence needed to hold this "comfort" up against scrutiny. Origen failed to balance this one passage rationally with the many Scriptures that clearly speak of eternal torment and separation from God for demons and Christ-rejecting men. [9] (Is. 66:24, Mt. 8:29, Mt. 25:46, Mark 9:42-48, John 3:36, Rev. 14:11.) The stakes in life are too high for such selective speculation. The Bible often speaks more clearly on this subject than we might wish it to. Not liking the implications of something is a foolish reason to deny that thing, by itself. Reality demands the full counsel of God, even when it is not pleasant.

Remember however, that Origen did not have all of the interpretive tools we enjoy today. Scripture includes allegory, even if the Greek method for it better fit other forms of literature. God also used Origen to clarify one of the most important tools for understanding Scripture's role in the life of the church.

It is ironic that Origen first introduced the idea of ***Sola Scriptura***, in its classical sense, to Christian theology. There is something humbling about it for those of us today, like me, who view this as foundational to church authority. *Sola Scriptura* is the principle that only Scripture is the ultimate authority for the church. Scripture is also the only reliable measure for apostolic teaching. Bible-centered churches still operate under this principle today, but without Origen's shakier interpretations.

Origen died soon after being tortured during the First Universal Persecution. Nothing I have written in my all-too-simplified review of this man's speculations calls into question his faith in Christ. Origen accomplished much in a desperate time of unspeakable cruelty. He did not write, as I do, from the comfort of a reclining chair. It is unlikely he often had time to follow the logic of all his speculations out to their conclusions over espresso.

The final Ante-Nicene father snapshot is that of Cyprian, Bishop of Carthage. He ministered during the first two Universal Persecutions, and played a major role in how the church came to deal with those who lapsed under the pressure. For these reasons, Cyprian figures prominently in the following chapter.

## BIBLIOGRAPHY

1. Walker, Williston. ***A History of the Christian Church*** (4th Edition), pp. 90-91, 1st Edition, 1918, 4th Edition 1946, Charles Scribner's Sons, New York, NY.
2. Ibid. p. 43
3. Ibid. p. 48
4. John Foxe, ***Foxe's Book of Martyrs*** (Updated through to the 21st century), Ch. 2, *The Fourth Persecution, Under Marcus Aurelius*, Polycarp, pp. 13-14, updated edition, 2001 by Bridge-Logos original 1563
5. F.F. Bruce, J. I Packer, Philip Comfort, Carl F.H. Henry, ***The Origin of the Bible***, pp. 188-189, 2012, Tyndale, see also section of ***The Origin of the Bible***, *The Canon of the New Testament*, by Milton Fisher, pp. 65-78; see also, ***Kenyon, Frederic G., Our Bible and the Ancient Manuscripts*** (revised), 1958
6. Davis, Glenn. ***Irenaeus of Lyons***, from ***The Development of the Canon of the New Testament*** web page, 1997 **http://shell5.ba.best.com/~gdavis/ntcanon/index.shtml** *"In many cases Irenaeus acted as mediator between various contending factions. The churches of Asia Minor (where he was probably born) continued to celebrate Easter on the same date (the 14th of Nisan) as the Jews celebrated Passover, whereas the Roman Church maintained that Easter should always be celebrated on a Sunday (the day of the Resurrection). Mediating between the parties, Irenaeus stated that differences in external factors, such as dates of festivals, need not be so serious as to destroy church unity."*
7. Walker, Williston. ***A History of the Christian Church*** (4th Edition), pp. 77, 1st Edition 1918, 4th Edition 1946, Charles Scribner's Sons, New York, NY.
8. Richardson, Don. ***Eternity in Their Hearts***, 1981, Regal Books, Ventura, Ca.
9. Shelley, Bruce L. ***Church History in Plain Language*** (2nd Edition), pp.86-87, 1995, Word Publishing, Dallas, Tx.

# 4

# The Universal Roman Persecutions and the Problem of the Lapsed

## What Made the Universal Persecutions Different?

Ten periods of church persecution happened under the Roman Empire; the "ten days of tribulation" predicted in the letter to the church at Smyrna, in Revelation Chapter 2. Each produced martyrs, who gave powerful testimony to the life-changing power of Christ under violent pressure. The first seven periods however were local, relatively brief, and limited in scope. Historians call the last three the "Universal Persecutions." Unlike the others, these affected every church in the Roman Empire.

Many believers today assume that the Romans persecuted Christians simply because they worshipped Christ. That is not true in the direct sense. Like most historic persecutions, the Roman incidents arose from ethical and cultural disputes that went political. Christians had to stand apart from society in areas where society demanded they treat the lordship of Christ as functionally unreal. They took no part in public feasts, which happened at the Pagan temples after a sacrifice. They declined dinner invitations from non-Christian acquaintances because such parties began with wine spilled as an offering to the household god.

Christians spoke out against popular entertainment at coliseums because it violated human dignity. Like today, they opposed the practice of abortion and infanticide. They combed city dumps, where parents left unwanted girl infants to die because they wanted sons. Christians raised those babies themselves. On top of that, Christians insisted they knew the Creator God of all reality, and that all other gods were, by definition, false. Christians often met secretly because they held the ordinance of communion off-limits to outsiders. People called them antisocial, and intolerant. Conversely, non-Christian records also show that many average Romans admired their integrity.

The Universal Persecutions had another dimension. They came at the orders of three Roman Emperors, who each had similar political and social agendas. Decius ordered the first, Valerian the second, and a later, much worse suppression came under Diocletian, at the dawn of the 4th century. Each was a political attempt to impose cultural unity from the top down where none existed at the ***grassroots*** of Roman society. (*Grassroots* is a historical term for things driven by large numbers of everyday people.)

As multi-cultural as Rome had become, no one belief system united people any longer as in the glory days of the Roman Republic. People remembered even the expansionist times of the early Imperium as stable compared to 3rd century decay. The *Pax Romana*, or "peace of Rome," tolerated religious diversity more than any other government in the ancient world. Part of the empire's program for keeping this peace was to allow its conquered peoples to keep their own culture and religion intact. *Pax Romana* sounds good, and in many ways, it was. However, it leaves us asking the question of; *how did Christians run afoul of such political tolerance?* It also begs the question of; *under what terms did this tolerance really exist?*

The Roman idea of religious tolerance said, *Worship whatever or whomever you like, as long as you recognize Caesar is lord over all in the "real world."* In other words, the State, not God, is the ultimate authority that determines what is right and wrong.

We need to ask ourselves, in what ways has the American concept of religious freedom shifted from a Judeo-Christian one back to the Roman? As today, the Christians in ancient Rome believed in obeying governmental authorities, just not as arbiters over the true God.

This is the fundamental difference between "freedom of religion" and "freedom of worship." Freedom of religion recognizes genuine rights of free thought and conscience. "Freedom of worship" merely allows people license to indulge any fantasy they want inside their place of worship. They must accept State-defined morality and thought outside, in "the real world."

Things did not get out of hand until Roman emperors began to demand visible demonstrations reaffirming this authority over the lives of citizens.

Why did such demands arise?

Several reasons intersected as a "perfect storm," many having little or nothing to do with what Christians taught about Jesus. One factor involved the wars Rome fought with a barbarian tribe called the Goths on its long northeastern Rhine-Danube River frontiers. This situation was complicated by the rise of the Sassanid Dynasty along Rome's equally lengthy southeast flank, in the year 235. The Sassanids were a line of Persian kings bent on retaking the old territories of Xerxes and Darius. With the empire continually at war on its long northeastern and southeastern flanks, the government needed internal unity. The center had to hold. Insurrection in poorly assimilated provinces became a clear and present danger.

The Emperor Decius ordered the first empire-wide persecution of the Christians in 249 AD. He wanted to inspire an "enthusiastic" return to the Paganism he felt had first made Rome great. Nothing fuels outward enthusiasm like inward terror. All citizens were required yearly to offer a pinch of incense at the altar of the emperor and declare, "Caesar is Lord." Then the magistrate would issue them a *libellus*, which was a paper certifying that the citizen had offered to Caesar his allegiance.

Although this was sometimes more of a political statement than a religious one, Christians could not ignore the implications. The language of these ceremonies toward the emperor often mirrored catacomb engravings of praise psalms and doxologies of worship to Christ. Beyond that, reality includes the spiritual as well as the physical. Christians would gladly pray *for* Caesar, and recognize him as political ruler of the Roman Empire. They could never pray *to* him as lord of reality nor accept him as such.

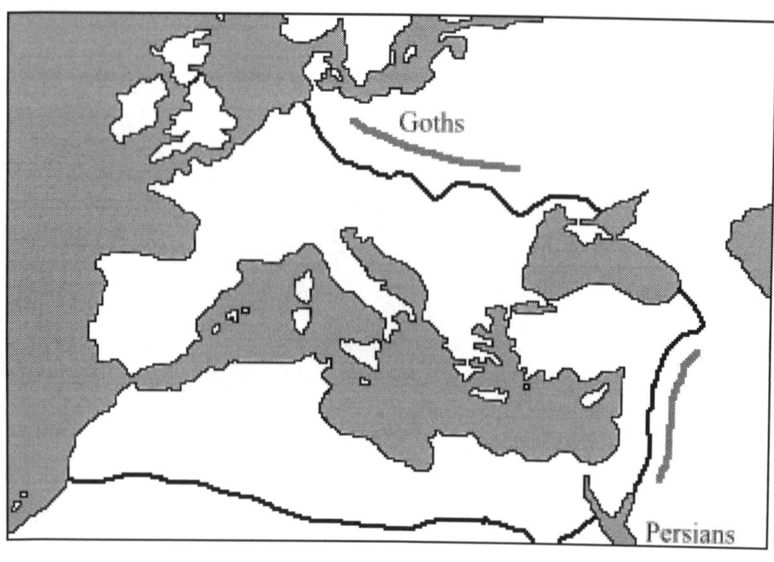


*Approximate Roman war fronts at the time of the First Universal Persecution under Decius*

The cult of emperor worship grew more powerful as time went on. Eventually, Caesar (the State) became the bottom line in the public mind over what was true and false, right and wrong. [1]

That was farther than any genuine Christian could go. It still is.

## What about Those Who Caved?

Christians had been somewhat comfortable in the relative tolerance of the first half of the 3rd Century. Stories of the martyrs had helped fuel their faith, but until now, persecutions had only affected certain regions here and there. [2] Christianity as a whole had never faced such terror simultaneously in so widespread a way before. Many in the church now rushed to sacrifice to Caesar or to purchase forged *libelli* by the thousands. This created a problem for churches on a previously unheard of scale. The reality of the Faith itself seemed in question.

The problem of dealing with "the lapsed" had no simple solution. Cyprian, Bishop of Carthage faced multitudes who had denied Christ in the 1st Universal Persecution that now wanted restoration. The brief respite between the years 252 and 257 was hardly stable. Emperor Valerian, Decius' successor a couple times removed, was no friend to the faithful either. Another large-scale persecution loomed on the horizon. Aside from the spiritual issues surrounding the denial of Christ, how could the lapsed be trusted in life-or-death situations when push came to shove?

Opinions raged from all extremes over what to do. Most of the bishops, along with Cyprian, took a hard line: No mercy to those who had denied Christ. By contrast, the ***Confessors***—those who had suffered imprisonment, torture, and other persecution short of death—favored re-admitting the lapsed. Suffering with Christ breeds mercy, any way we cut it. The Confessors held that it was not always belief in God's applied grace that had failed; merely human courage along the principle described in Romans 7:14-25.

We are all on a spiritual growth curve, after all. No Confessor dared claim that they had fully eradicated all sin from their hearts. They, in effect, argued that any sin on the part of a redeemed, though imperfect, believer was in some sense a denial of Christ's power in the present world. Since nobody could claim to have overcome sin completely in this life, it made no sense to treat this particular sin as if it were unforgivable.

I imagine the Confessors had John 8:2-11 in mind. This is the account of the woman caught in adultery that ends with Jesus saying, "Let he that is without sin cast the first stone." It is also not hard to imagine the Confessors themselves going through severe doubts and weaknesses during their ordeals. They knew it was by God's grace that their situations never came to a head as an active denial of Christ, with libellus in hand. It is one thing to admire God's strength in the Martyrs and Confessors. It is quite another to romanticize them. One invokes reality, the other fantasy.

Some believers began to claim that these Confessors had the authority on earth to forgive the lapsed based on their own merit in having suffered for Christ. The Bishop of Rome, Callistus, took this position. In fact, he even claimed that same power for himself over other sins. That was what caused Irenaeus' student, Hippolytus, to speak out against the Pope of Rome, as mentioned in the previous chapter. The church at Rome itself even split for a long while over this issue.

It would be hard to support either side in their extremes. On the one hand, Pope Callistus was taking too much on himself. On the other, Hippolytus seemed to reject any kind of restoration for the lapsed whatsoever. A natural application of Paul's teaching on how and when to restore sinning believers, in 2nd Corinthians, might have helped. Yet somehow, Christ's words against those who denied Him before men seemed to put this sin in a class by itself in the minds of the Bishops. (Matt. 10:33, Luke 12:9.) Jesus never said that caving under such pressure was unforgivable, however. In fact, He said that words spoken against the Son of Man were forgivable. (Matt. 12:32, Luke 12:10.)

Of course, this is all easy for me to say 1850 years after the fact. Inside the cauldron, the issues are rarely so clear, as today's believers in Sudan, Iran, and China know well. Callistus may have inflated his power with the situation, but that was not likely his intent. At least his way offered some sort of hospital for sinners, who really wanted another chance, and were willing to prove their sincerity.

Other churches also split over this issue, some because they felt the leaders too harsh on the lapsed, others because they believed them too lenient. This raised the additional question of, *which of the divided churches were really "the Church" when both were theologically orthodox?* It did not seem that simple fidelity to the gospel was enough anymore to establish a person or fellowship as "orthodox."

It rarely occurs to people that the Holy Spirit might guide church leaders to respond differently to different people. The crisis may affect many, but individuals with different backgrounds and responses might need different handling. Nor do Christians relish the fact that often the only solutions God places within in our reach at such times are imperfect ones. We often assume that a perfect God must always offer perfect solutions. We forget that few things work perfectly in an imperfect, fallen world, when executed by, at best, only partly perfected people.

Is that terribly realistic of us? Is it realistic to expect to see such solutions in church history when even the history of the Bible does not show such perfection, except in the life of Christ?

A practical application of the tiny Epistle of Jude might have been helpful at this point, but note that it, too, describes a messy set of options.

> **And have mercy on some, who are doubting; save others, snatching them out of the fire; and on some have mercy with fear, hating even the garment polluted by the flesh. *Jude* 1:22-23 NASB**

In other words, churches had to deal with the lapsed as with sinners newly won to Christ, on an individual basis. Some needed a gentle approach that did not rebuke, but reasoned and restored with mercy. Some of the lapsed were already sensitive to the Holy Spirit's conviction in their hearts. Others needed a sharper form of mercy that stabbed at their weakness a little more painfully. These still played games on themselves to defend their sin on some level. Still others needed to have the tar scared out of them in a devastating wake-up call on the level of Ebenezer Scrooge.

To deal with the church splits, Cyprian emphasized the authority of the bishops through succession from the Apostles again. This precedent now seemed forged in steel, despite the growing blind spot it would one day create. For the day would come, centuries later, when churches would be forced to ask the question of what made a church authority truly "apostolic" in character? Would the standard be man-to-man succession through centuries of distorting influences or the only remaining artifact of apostolic thought, Scripture? That would not be the issue of the day for a long while yet. Cyprian had no way to predict this.

Eventually, the Confessors with the bishops of Pope Callistus' view won out. Cyprian came to an uneasy compromise with these men through the adoption of a system for re-admitting the lapsed only after a period of penitential proof. Yet, the view that Confessors, and now bishops, could actually remit sins on earth by way of a sacramental ritual took hold. Eventually, this went not only for serious cases like lapsing during persecution, but everyday sins of the flesh. Some ideas, once they take hold, have no logical limits built in. Nobody at the time plotted to open a theological Pandora's Box. Nevertheless, ideas lead to other "if-then" conclusions, all having consequences spreading out like ripples in a pond.

The scriptural basis given for this procedure (much of which developed over time) was John 20:23. Here Jesus said to his disciples (not just the Apostles): **"If you forgive anyone his**

**sins, they are forgiven; if you do not forgive them, they are not forgiven." (NIV)** Jesus said this concerning the Great Commission, when He sent the disciples out to preach the gospel of salvation. Any Christian could spread the gospel to people who either accepted or rejected it. Some people were so abusive in their rejection that it sometimes made more sense not to **"cast your pearls before swine,"** as Jesus once put it in Matthew 7:6. Of course, sometimes the loudest dog is the one that is struck by your cane—as in the case of Saul of Tarsus, who became the Apostle Paul.

Christians could judge in certain evangelism situations the risk of violent reaction against God's word. In some reactionary cases, it made more sense to remain silent and try to reach somebody more open to the gospel. Jesus' words (Matt. 7:6) imply that this is not always a choice between courage and cowardice. Sometimes wisdom dictates that we let people alone to their own devices or the Spirit's.

This had application in some church discipline situations, too. We find in 1 Corinthians 5 that openly sinning, unrepentant people were to be put out of the fellowship or *excommunicated*. For all practical purposes, Scripture commanded the church to deal with such people as if they were a "heathen," or non-believing Gentile. In the case of a Jewish context, the idiom was to treat them as a Jewish "tax-collector" for Rome, a byword for betrayal in Judea. (Matt. 18:17)

The hope in church discipline, no matter how extreme, was for the sinner to repent and rejoin fellowship. Of course, church leaders always have the practical problem of telling a manipulative troublemaker from a struggling believer with a difficult besetting sin. In a certain narrow sense, a Christian can effectively regulate who benefits from God's forgiveness, and who does not. If believers evangelize only in "safe" situations, they effectively decide who enjoys a chance at forgiveness and who does not. Likewise, if leaders create either too lax or unapproachable a standard for re-admittance, they determine who benefits from the practical life of the church. God will hold us accountable in either case.

This has real consequences for the people who do not hear the gospel, for the erring believer, as well as for the Christians who evangelize or lead the church in such ways. My observation is not intended to deny the elective work of God's grace, or to give us the inside scoop on "who is really saved." Ultimately, those are things only God can determine with absolute accuracy. It only addresses the practical problems Christians face as finite people living in community.

For this reason, John 20:23 has a church discipline application. Christians must respond against members of their congregations who continue flagrantly in sin lifestyles, bringing dishonor to God and the local fellowship. No man is an island. Everything we do affects others. As in dealing with the lapsed, this needed case-by-case evaluation by people committed to God and to fairness with the people in question. It required that people take the time to know each situation, not a mechanical ritual.

Scripture teaches that God supports the Holy Spirit-led, scripturally prescribed discipline of errant believers by church officers. (Matt. 18, John 20:23, 1 Cor. 5.) Such passages were not a directive for a standardized, one-size-fits-all system operating by ritual priest-craft. Of course, the sheer numbers involved with restoring the lapsed, likely fostered a form of pastoral burnout. People being what they are, the situation spiraled toward a penitential rite, regardless of what Cyprian and the Confessors expected. Either that, or a "penitential rite" seemed for them to solve the problem, and they did not see the damaging long-term effects.

Churches maintained some case-by-case individuality in that church officers tried to mete out penances to fit the level of the lapse. Still, the whole flow of ideas became distorted by the premise that the lapsed could be restored based on the merit of a Confessor transferred to a bishop. Records of the period do not speak in terms of personal renewal of a direct spiritual relationship with Christ through repentance. There is a difference between *penance* and *repentance*. Penance focuses on temporal punishment. Repentance is a Spirit-empowered change of heart that restores a broken relationship. While one might include the other, they are really two different things.

It was commonly believed even by some church fathers at that time that Christ's death only paid for sins committed up until the time of a person's conversion. A spiritualized view of Scripture had produced an incomplete view of grace. An incomplete concept of grace gave the impression of a "need" on top of Christ's work and repentance. In the minds of many believers at the time, something more was required when spiritual power seemed to be waning. A massive shadow of post-conversion sin guilt seemed to hover over people's heads.

Too many believing people now collapsed under pressure. The courage and holiness Christians had almost taken for granted, not just in easier times but during earlier, less widespread persecutions, seemed to fade. They needed to know that God was a God of second and even many subsequent chances. Believers have always needed this. Many bishops verbally scourged their congregations. Others had the wisdom not to. The only apparent answer at the time came in a method that suffered from an undeveloped view of God's grace.

The degree to which this resulted from immature tools for Scripture exposition, and "worldview blind spots," is impossible to say. It is hard to imagine they had nothing to do with it. Satan learns to exploit whatever landscape history affords him. Either way, the stage was set for a sequence of ideas that eventually reduced penance to something even worse than priest-craft and ritual formula. Centuries later, it led to the corrupt teaching of ***indulgences***. This doctrine claimed the Roman Pope had a treasury of divine merit from the suffering of the saints, which he could dole out to people as he pleased. In time, Rome even peddled and sold indulgences.

The practice of penance solved some of Cyprian's immediate troubles. Like other short-term fixes of that period however, it would create other problems down the line. Penance eventually evolved into one of the Seven Sacraments of Roman Catholicism. The idea that Confessors had transferable virtue from their own suffering for Christ set a bad precedent. Only the sinless Savior can impute righteousness to sinners. Human merit began to encroach upon the sovereign territory of God's grace.

Cyprian could not have foreseen where this would lead, but there was now some "death in the pot" cooking on the church's stove. (2 Kings 4:40)

Rome martyred Cyprian in 258 AD, during Valerian's expected 2nd Universal Persecution.

## PERSECUTION IN OVERDRIVE

The worst of all the Roman persecutions came at the dawn of the 4th century, under the emperor Diocletian.

It is often said from the pulpit that persecution only strengthens and purifies the church. This is true on many deep and practical levels that we should never forget. It weeds out the half-hearted, and the mere cultural hangers-on. It can strengthen individual faith by forcing believers to rely solely on God. Accounts of those who overcome persecution through their faith encourage others to hold on to Christ in their difficulties. Yet if persecution of the church were truly as simple as only that, we would expect to see things in Scripture that we do not see there. History would also have unfolded differently than it did.

Persecution in real life is not that simple. There are also certain conditions under which it does not strengthen the church, but can actually damage it, even spiritually. Like many strong medicines, too big a dose can actually kill the patient, or at least produce another illness as a side effect. The value derived in some spiritual organs can come at a risk to others that are equally important. Only God, the Great Physician, knows when the dosage limits of this peculiar therapy are reached.

The New Testament never tells us to pray for persecution to come so that the church can be strengthened. It in fact tells us to pray for the opposite so the knowledge of the truth can freely be spread.

> **First of all, then, I urge that supplications, prayers, intercessions, and thanksgivings be made for all men, for kings and all who are in high positions, *that we may lead a quiet and peaceable life*, godly and respectful in every way. This is good, and it is acceptable in the sight of God our Savior, who desires all men to be saved and to come to the knowledge of the truth. *1 Timothy* 2:1-4 (RSV)**

The 3rd Universal Persecution lasted more than twice as long as the previous ones. It presented all of the same problems and divisions concerning the lapsed, and then some. It also went further than the others did. It suspended all civil rights for Christians. Roman soldiers systematically burned Bibles, empire-wide, for the first time. Thoughtful, genuine believers remained in almost all factions of the church splits. Even the fixes were failing. Penitential practices seemed more mechanical, ineffective, and at times even silly.

Zeal that had flamed bright during earlier local persecutions, and even in Cyprian's day 50 years ago, now rang a bit hollow even in faithful ears. It was not that Christians lost hope. The church had simply reached a crossroad where things needed to happen that could only happen in an open and free setting, without fear of suppression. One also gets the sense that fatigue had set in, even among those who did not deny the Faith or give Scriptures for burning. Neither the human condition nor God's plan called for an "Army of Martyrs" style of Christian identity indefinitely.

One of the bitterest church divisions of Diocletian's persecution never healed. Donatus, a North African bishop, would not recognize the ordination of men by pastors who had surrendered Scripture copies for burning. The Donatist Church split away, believing itself to be the true church against a corrupted ***Catholic***, or "Universal" Church. We might be tempted to imagine that Donatus was right because of what we know happened to the church later. However, that would be superficial, and ignore more immediate concerns.

The Donatists were an extreme sect characterized by a despicable, self-righteousness. They habitually burned farms and villages of their Catholic victims without regard for life or property. Catholic communities would then call upon the authorities to restore order. Donatists also worshipped relics and the dead body parts of martyrs in fanatical displays of pageantry and superstition.

Witch hunt-style accusations haunted many bishops during this time, concerning the surrender of Scripture copies to be burned. Many such men had given only old and rotting copies to the authorities, in order to save their lives, and often those of their congregations. The very people whose lives they saved sometimes harassed these pastors, who usually were not guilty of denying Christ. [3] Bullying from the Donatists, and even from some inside their own congregations, often forced them to move on and find work elsewhere. Most often, the leaders of the Catholic churches had mercy on them, and helped them to make new starts.

Persecution did not always bring out the best in Christians who "stayed firm under fire," sometimes just the opposite. Paul, who knew a bit more about persecution than we do, warned as much.

> **And though I have the gift of prophecy, and understand all mysteries and all knowledge, and though I have all faith, so that I could remove mountains, but have not love, I am nothing. And though I bestow all my goods to feed the poor, and *though I give my body to be burned, but have not love, it profits me nothing*. Love suffers long and is kind; love does not envy; love does not parade itself, is**

**not puffed up; does not behave rudely, does not seek its own, is not provoked, thinks no evil; does not rejoice in iniquity, but rejoices in the truth; bears all things, believes all things, hopes all things, endures all things.**

***1 Corinthians* 13:2-7 (NKJV)**

The Donatist Church lasted right up until the invasion of Islam swept them away into history, almost 400 years later.

When I use the term ***Catholic*** to describe the churches of the first four centuries, I do not mean ***Roman Catholic***, as people understand that name today. Rather, it means *universal* in the sense that churches everywhere still had a basic kinship with one another. The term *Catholic* also distinguished orthodox churches from Gnostic and Marcionist sects.

Events at the dawn of the 4th Century made it clear that both the church and the empire approached a turning point they both desperately needed. Both suffered great stresses against their internal unity for many reasons too complicated to fully cover here. This turning point began on the island province of Britannium, with a Roman governor whom the native Celts called Custennin. History would remember the Latin version of his name, Constantius Chlorus. After the death of Diocletian, he issued the first Edict of Toleration for the Christians under his jurisdiction in the Western Empire. Constantius was, like many people, sickened by the excesses of his predecessors.

Constantius had a son who would carry on this tradition of tolerance, and take it a step farther. Soon after he took over from his father in the West, Flavius Constantine won a pivotal military victory that would re-unify the Roman Empire. It would also shift the fortunes of the Christian Church forever.

The year was 312 AD, by the Christian reckoning. In a dream, just before the showdown with his eastern rival at the Battle of the Milvian Bridge, Constantine saw a cross in the heavens. He heard a voice speak to him, saying, *"In this sign conquer."* His army won the campaign against all odds. He became the first Christian emperor, re-uniting the Roman Empire after nearly two centuries of breakdown.

Christians today often doubt the authenticity of Constantine's conversion. I don't know. I wasn't there. Traditional Evangelicals accuse him of deliberately mixing Paganism with Christianity. While such a mixture did slowly come, it is clear that the beginnings of this process long pre-dated Constantine. Nor did it accelerate to absurd lengths until after his death. Few would dispute that Constantine contributed to the trend. I merely point out that it is unfair to blame him for starting it. Effects do not precede their own cause.

There were real changes in Constantine's life after his encounter at the Milvian Bridge. There were also some glaring flaws. Popular conspiracy theories abound, but conspiracy theories rarely provide good models for historical events. The reasons for that are simple. Conspiracies are only as strong as their weakest links. Once three or more people are involved, the chances of a successful conspiracy drop exponentially. Another reason is that conspiracy theories very rarely explain most of the facts. Their tendency, rather, is to ignore data that does not fit the theory's model. The whole approach usually has ideological, rather than rationally compelling starting assumptions. They generate heat rather than shed light.

Constantine had no theological agenda any serious historian has been able to identify. He had some genuine political concerns, such as any good leader might, but that is not the same as having a spiritual agenda. We know this because he often "shot himself in the foot" in his political and religious choices made to stabilize those genuine concerns. Nor did he make Christianity the state religion—that would not come until the reign of his grandson, Theodosius. Constantine seemed to have a real desire to please the God of the Christians. While he tolerated the Pagans in his realm, he desired more than anything to see unity in the church. Some of his reasons for that desire involved political stability, but that did not make him "false" in itself. That's just common sense for any political leader. It's their job.

The ironic truth was that Constantine built up the church for the same reason that Diocletian, Valerian, and Decius had persecuted it. He wanted grassroots unity in his realm. What the persecuting emperors could not force on their kingdom from the top down, the spread of the faith had caused to grow from the ground up. By now, the splintering of the Empire under the self-serving reigns of its last few Pagan emperors had magnified the integrity of Christians in the minds of the Roman people.

A new generation of immediate post-Persecution Christians even felt that Christ's ***Millennial Kingdom*** on earth had dawned. The joys of a wedding feast had suddenly enveloped a weary, battered, and flinching Bride of Christ. Constantine pulled the unity of Catholic Christianity, cracked at the seams by impossible stresses, from the cauldron just in time under the aegis of a believing king.

There were many benefits to this, and many problems. One benefit was that Constantine encouraged greater church unity, and helped it to heal its wounds by calling church councils to iron out and seal the fractures. It would be shortsighted to underestimate the damage caused by these growing fractures. One of the largest involved an inability to agree on the very nature of Christ Himself. If Christians could not know who Christ really was, then how could they know anything? One problem caused by the church gaining imperial favor appeared to be that many believers now celebrated the wedding day of Christ prematurely. This would become an intermittently waxing and waning crisis as time went on, though not as serious as that faced if the church could not agree on the nature of Christ.

For once Constantine was gone, the tired and long-harassed Bride would wake up inside a new nightmare. In her attempt to find some rest while waiting for her husband, she had half-sleepily moved in with someone that would soon demand the rights of another lover—the State.

## BIBLIOGRAPHY

1. Shelley, Bruce L. ***Church History in Plain Language*** (2nd Edition), pp.43-45, 1995, Word Publishing, Dallas, Tx.
2. Walker, Williston. ***A History of the Christian Church*** (4th Edition), p. 96, 1st Edition, 1918, 4th Edition 1946, Charles Scribner's Sons, New York, NY.
3. Smith, M.A. ***The Church Under Siege***, pp. 25-26, 1976, Inter-Varsity Press, Leicester, England.

# 5

# THE COUNCIL OF NICEA

## THE ARIAN REDEFINITION OF CHRIST

The new emperor, Constantine, found himself instantly beset with unforeseen problems once he supported the Christian church. Bitter conflicts with roots in the last Universal Persecution had Catholic Christianity coming apart in both the East and West. This happened at a time when many new converts wanted to join the Faith, now that it would not literally cost them their lives.

Older believers who had lived through the persecution often looked down on these new believers when acceptance might have helped them ground such converts in the Faith. Few churches seemed equipped to disciple such numbers. Those that readily received such new believers became embroiled in the unsettled church divisions.

Some bishops genuinely attempted to rise above the sectarianism. Others took the opportunity to engrave their own peculiar stamp onto the new converts, turning them against others in the body of Christ for political reasons. Now that Christianity had imperial favor, attempts to gain the positive attentions of the emperor seized all church factions. The largest of these attempts centered on the dispute over Arianism, which involved no less than the central question of the very nature of Christ. This was by no means the only question that fractured the Faith at this time.

Until now, an idea of doctrinal orthodoxy centered on the Scripture expositions of Logos Theology, the works of Irenaeus, and of other church fathers. Orthodoxy matured in Origen's Schools at Alexandria and Antioch, and at other Christian centers like Rome and Carthage. Nothing near a universal "systematic theology" existed in today's sense. Christians all agreed that Christ had died for our sins, was buried, had risen from the dead, that He was the Son of God, and that He would return; the central message of the gospel summarized in 1 Corinthians 15:1-8.

The Popes of Antioch, Alexandria, Rome, and Jerusalem all generally respected each other. They could not enact doctrinal standards on churches beyond their own regions, and usually would not do so within without calling a council. Pope Victor's failed attempt to impose a new universal date for Easter showed a limit most Christians understood to the power of their highest bishops. Irenaeus' criticism of Victor revealed that Western bishops felt free to correct the Pope of Rome if they thought it necessary.

Churches at this point did not even agree 100% on which New Testament era books held the authority of Scripture. An overwhelming majority had formed long ago favoring the current list, or most of it, but it was not yet absolute. All agreed on the Gospels, and Paul's Epistles, while some of John's short writings, 2 Peter, Jude, and Hebrews were still questioned in some places. A few fellowships accepted the Jewish ***Apocrypha*** as Scripture, while most (including Rome, at the time) did not. By now, different major churches had marched for a long time in divergent directions on what would prove some basic issues.

For example, the Eastern Church saw the Trinity as God existing in three distinct persons, each in a graded hierarchy. Western Christians tended to view the Trinity with more emphasis on the unity of the Godhead. East and West alike rejected the Monarchian heresies of ***Sabellianism*** and Paul of Samosata. Easterners often mistook the Western view for Monarchianism because of growing language differences. The West spoke Latin while the East spoke Greek.

In addition, Easterners did not always express their views on the Trinity with adequate safeguards. That is, they often made it sound as if they worshipped three different gods without clarifying their terminology. [1] By the time Constantine embraced the church, bishops drew contradictory conclusions even about the nature of Christ. This should not surprise us, considering the length and scope of Diocletian's persecution of the church. Christians had no workable way to address the problems they now faced, as long as they remained in a situation defined by universal oppression. The reason was simple. Persecution severely hinders the exchange of ideas. It chills communication. The only way to solve these problems demanded open interaction between churches.

The most serious dispute centered on the teachings of a certain Alexandrian elder named Arius. Arius started as a hardline anti-Gnostic conservative—the kind of guy orthodox churchmen liked. The first big heresy on the nature of Christ had always been Gnosticism, in its denial of Christ's humanity. Arius got as far as he did because he was big on Christ's humanity. He concluded that because Scripture referred to Jesus as the "only *begotten* Son of God," it must mean that Christ had a beginning. Therefore, in Arius' mind, Christ could not be co-eternal with the Father. Christ had a divine side in Arian theology, but not in the same sense as God the Father.

Some argued that earlier Christians failed to be clear on the subject. Use of the term *"only begotten Son"* is central to the theology of John the Apostle, and appears in most of his New Testament writings. Many Christians had connected it to the beginning of Christ's human incarnation, to His conception by the Holy Spirit. To *beget* is to *conceive* in the reproductive sense. Many had also used Christ being "God's only begotten" to show that Jesus had a Divine nature. Until now, nobody saw any conflict in using the term both ways. People use words in different senses without violating their meaning. It was a contrast, not a contradiction. Scripture refers clearly to Christ's pre-existence in eternity past. (John 1:1, 17:5, 17:24, Col. 1:17, Heb. 13:8, 1 Pet. 1:20, 1 John 1:1-2, and Rev. 1:8-18.)

Arius forced Christians to ask and clarify their answer to the question; *what do we really mean when we call Christ "Divine"?*

Historic Christianity holds that the term *begotten* describes Christ's Divine nature in a way that makes Him "of the same substance" as God the Father. This is like saying that a human son consists of the same human stuff as his father. It does not mean that God's Son initially became that way the same as a human son would. God is a spirit. (John 4:23-24) Nor does this word imply that Christ had a beginning. He could not be "of the same stuff" as the Father without sharing the Father's eternal attributes. In human terms, the sameness of a son to his father comes by the father begetting the son. Today, we would correctly think of this in genetic terms. The human son of a human father is genetically human because his father and mother were. Our human substance is coded in our DNA.

It is different when we speak of God, who is an eternal rather than reproductive Being. We can only use human analogies to describe how God the Father is of the same substance as God the Son—hence the term *begotten*. Back at the beginning of the 4th century, nobody had fully developed this line of reasoning yet. Believers just saw some Scriptures calling Christ, **"the only begotten Son of God,"** while others showed His existence as a Divine person, with the Father, in eternity past. We know Christ was a Divine Person before the beginning because Scripture describes Him doing something only a Divine Person can do, before His Incarnation.

> **Let this mind be in you *which was also in Christ Jesus*, who, being in the form of God, did not consider it robbery to be equal with God, *but made Himself of no reputation, taking the form of a bondservant, and coming in the likeness of men.* And being found in appearance as a man, He humbled Himself and became obedient to the point of death, even the death of the cross. *Philippians* 2:5-8 (NKJV)**

Christ made Himself of no reputation and came in the likeness of men. The Father did not choose for Him, as a baby has no choice in where, or how, or to whom it is born. Christ chose to obey and empty Himself, and the Father sent. It never occurred to the early church that anyone might construe this as a contradiction. Then, Arius came along and emphasized one set of Scriptures, while downplaying the other set.

To Arius, Jesus was a created being—a lesser god, or demigod, much as the Greek Hercules; only fathered by Yahweh instead of Zeus. Jesus was more than a man in this view, but not fully God in substance or attributes.

Despite Arius' strong rejection of Gnosticism, his thinking proved just as much driven by Greek worldview assumptions. The same old heresy model was at work here that had influenced the Gnostic teachings. It just pushed in the opposite direction, as if curing the problem was simply a matter of "reversing the polarity." Arius insisted that he was merely being biblical; that his teaching represented a "conservative argument" against Gnostic thinking, which had so much trouble with the humanity of Christ. In reality, the assumptions of Neo-Platonic Greek philosophy guided his views. The Gnostics saw Christ as fully God, with only an appearance of humanity. Arius thought he had solved the problem by making Christ into a semi-divine superman.

This inverted the dynamic that produced the Docetic Gnostic interpretations of Scripture, but it did not answer it. Neo-Platonists had the same Greek worldview problems uniting the material and spiritual as the Stoics and Epicureans. The Gnostics defended Christ's divinity by tossing out His humanity. Arius upheld Christ's humanity by making Him a superhuman "lesser god." One could not accept either approach without denying or downplaying part of what the Scriptures said. Nor did these ideas go extinct with the ancient Greek worldview.

The modern Jehovah's Witness view of Christ is nothing more than Arianism re-packaged. For they deny that Christ is fully God in the same sense that Yahweh is. Joseph Smith made a form of the Gnostic theology of "gods creating other gods to people the heavens" intrinsic to Mormonism. Smith's disciple, Brigham Young, said, "As God is, Man may become; as Man is, God once was." [2] Satan recycles his arsenal of lies every few centuries.

When Alexander, Pope of Alexandria, found that Arius taught this, he called the rest of his presbyters and bishops in to debate the issue. The council condemned Arius' theology. Arius had ignored key Scriptures (like John 1:1-14 and Phil. 2:5-8) that describe the eternal pre-existence of Christ with God, as God; something made coherent by the Trinity view.

That should have ended things, but Arius had friends in high places outside of Egypt, in the churches of the East. Eusebius, Bishop of Nicomedia, a slimy political exploiter, as churchmen of the day went, raised support for the heretic in Asia Minor. One should not confuse Eusebius of Nicomedia with the church historian, Eusebius of Caesarea (whom Arius also knew). By the time Constantine took notice, the whole affair threatened to split the church wide open.

Why were Arius' teachings so destructive? Why couldn't Alexander and the other bishops just agree to disagree in a friendly way, and leave it at that? For that matter, why can't we just do that over such things today? First, because ideas have consequences—they shape actions and attitudes in the real world. These teachings had serious implications. Arius, like most false teachers, failed to carry his own ideas through to their logical conclusions. He complained with emotion and bewilderment about all the fuss against him, but he would not answer with more than superficial responses. Arius did not seem to understand the stakes.

This was about cause-and-effect reality.

Arius did not see that if Jesus was not fully God, then there was reason to call his revelation of God the Father into question. If Jesus only carried the best reflection of God's image, he was still imperfect because of his *physical* incarnation (notice the Greek assumption). How then could we have reliable knowledge of God through him at the bottom line? More seriously, if Jesus was not fully God, then how could anyone be sure that he was in any position to save humanity?

Arius himself would not likely have raised these doubts. Yet, if the churches let his view of Christ stand, someone would eventually raise them. The effectiveness of the Christian worldview ties to its applicability in the real world. If the foundation of that worldview proved insufficient to support the claims of Christ, then eventually everything about the Faith must also collapse. This is still the strategy of Satan; to cast doubt on the reality of what Scripture claims is true. That includes ethics, a basis for knowing God, then knowing what we need rescuing from, and how Christ saves us from that thing.

This is what most of today's world thinks has happened; that "science" has already proved the Bible a fantasy. People think this for different—but just as poorly thought-out—reasons as in the days of Arius. Then, as now, real souls were at stake.

Constantine only knew that the grassroots cement of his empire—Christianity—seemed to be cracking. He understood nothing of theology, and frankly admitted his ignorance. The Emperor relied on the guidance of his elderly advisor, Hosius, Bishop of Cordova Spain. This was a good thing. Hosius was a godly man who wanted harmony in the church, but who would not sacrifice truth for the sake of a shallow form of unity.

Constantine sent Hosius to Antioch, where another council met to examine Arius' teachings against Scripture. Again, Arius' views were rejected. The council declared Christ to be *of the same substance* as the Father. Some of the Eastern bishops had trouble with this definition however, because they thought it might open the door for Sabellianism.

The church historian, Eusebius of Caesarea, was one of the dissenters. This created a political problem because Eusebius had written a glowing history crowned by the rise of Constantine at the end. People knew him to be such a close friend of the Emperor that they feared that not even Hosius could tip the scales against him. Eusebius the historian also encouraged an allegorized view of the Book of Revelation. This interpreted the Millennium as the reign of Constantine, and the ***Great Tribulation*** as the persecutions before. Anyone with an ear to the ground could hear the muffled sound of Papias, the Apostle John's student, spinning in his grave.

The council placed Eusebius of Caesarea under a kind of temporary excommunication pending another review. This would happen at an all-new universal church council the bishops wanted held at Ancyra.

Constantine may not have known much about theology, but he knew politics. He realized that his friend Eusebius was in trouble. Ancyra was home of the most zealously anti-Arian bishop in the East—Marcellus. Many Easterners even accused him of being a hated Sabellian. To avoid the roasting of Eusebius of Caesarea, who was not truly pro-Arian, Constantine ordered the council's location switched to Nicea.

## THE FIRST ECUMENICAL COUNCIL OF NICEA

Historians call the Council of Nicea the first ***ecumenical*** or universal council because Constantine invited bishops from all parts of the empire, and beyond, to attend. The Emperor made no pretenses about what he wanted, nothing short of a universal statement on what the church believed about Christ. He was fed up with all the bickering. Who could blame him for that? He did not care which position became the official Orthodox one, just that the church define some standard. The Emperor's lack of theological understanding would soon become evident.

That it took the State to force the Church to make a concise statement about what it believed on something as fundamental as Christ's nature showed that Christianity had been in deep trouble. Nor can we, today, fairly blame this on Constantine, as if he somehow schemed to replace early Christianity with something corrupt. Corruption came, but the universal church councils were a natural and necessary stage if the church expected to continue. One mark of the Holy Spirit on Nicea was that the bishops began the council divided, but ended with direction, though not always a popular one.

It likely never occurred to anyone to think in terms of simply "going back to the Bible" to solve the issues. Greek, Latin, Ethiopic, Coptic, and Syriac speaking churches were all trying to do just that, but in different languages. They each had somewhat different assumptions about word meanings and the literary structure of the Gospel texts. Nevertheless, they went "back to the Bible" in treating the Gospels and Epistles as authoritative documents on Christ's nature.

Nor was it as simple as "trying to be sensitive to the Spirit's lead," though prayer went out for God's guidance. A historical, grammatical, thematic, contextual interpretation of Scripture likewise did not show up in the records in those terms (though they did their best). While only some of the intellectual tools the Holy Spirit has since given us to interpret Scripture had been invented, logic likely was the first of these. The bishops used a logical approach to the issue, while the Emperor allowed them freedom to do so. It soon became apparent that the Holy Spirit providentially brought the council together through historical forces not even Constantine could control.

The Council of Nicea became part of both the Trinitarian and Christology Controversies, since the subjects overlapped. Christ is also a member of what Christian theology calls the ***Godhead*** of Father, Son, and Holy Spirit—the Holy Trinity. At Nicea, the Holy Spirit redemptively used Greek logic to clarify, analyze, and harmonize what Scripture teaches about the most basic ideas in the Faith. Christians tackled nothing less than the question of; *how does Christ's nature relate to that of both God and humanity?*

Everyone at the council agreed the Old Testament, the four Gospels, and almost all of the New Testament Epistles were God's Word. Honest historians dismiss nonsensical claims that Constantine decided which books went into the New Testament. We base this on thousands of late 1st, 2nd, 3rd, and early 4th century New Testament texts, and quotes from those texts. Such a huge number of texts demonstrate wide circulation in the middle 2nd century, long before Constantine. In addition, the language usage is often time-stamped to the late 1st century. [3]

The circulation issue is comparable to that of a newspaper. For a 2nd century fabricator to alter the text for posterity, they would need to gather every copy. The fact that so many copies still exist after so long shows the texts were widely accepted in the churches. Copying texts did not come cheaply back then. Thus, the sheer number of copies as early as the mid-2nd century demonstrates that New Testament texts already represented a well-established authority. Most New Testament variant manuscripts were mere misspellings, with only a few containing actual differences of missing or added content—too few to be significant.

An example of what I call "time-stamping" would be if a document claiming to be from the Civil War era used a term like *user-friendly* in it. This expression comes from the late 20th and 21st centuries, and would instantly show the "Civil War document" up as a fake. The Gnostic gospels, such as *Philip* and the *Trimorphic Protennoia*, have later time-stamped language usage in them than the four New Testament Gospels; expressions from the late 2nd through 4th centuries. [4] By contrast, the four Gospels date well within the latter half of the 1st century by their language use.

Nicea accepted the authority of the New Testament texts, but it did not officially canonize them. That was not what the council was about. It was about the nature of Christ. Most everyone agreed by this time what was and was not Scripture. Formalization of the fact came a few decades later, but as an afterthought, to counteract the growing Gnostic trend to try to forge new "gospels."

Nobody at Nicea pretended to understand how the Trinity actually works. It is not necessary to understand how it all works to accept that it does. Nobody understands how gravity works, but we accept it and build on it. The bishops at Nicea had one key thing going for them. They knew that thorough research had already shown the four Gospels were authoritative Divine revelation and history about Christ. None of the competing Gnostic works fit the profile of well-documented connection to either an apostle or a close associate.

From this basis, the Council of Nicea used a prayerful and redemptive application of logic to answer another seminal question; *why should Christianity accept the Doctrine of the Trinity when the term that describes the concept does not appear in God's word?* The answer to this complex question is remarkably simple. *When we consider all Scriptures that refer to the Father, the Son, and the Holy Spirit, **giving all passages equal authoritative weight**, only one conclusion is possible. The idea that God exists as three persons in a single Godhead is the only logical conclusion that fits all the biblical facts.*

As Christians, the bishops at Nicea were bound to accept all of the statements of God's Word as authoritative. They all agreed on that. They were, therefore, not free to favor some passages over others just to fit pet theories, or a desire for simplicity. This conviction should drive us today. The nature of Divine revelation demanded they reason from Scripture's varied claims by assuming that the data would harmonize into logical teachings. This is because, "God is not the author of confusion," nor is He "a man that he should lie." (1 Cor. 14:33, Nu. 23:19)

The reasoning process that led to a concise doctrine of God's triune nature arose from a number of simple biblical premises. Awareness of these long pre-dated the Council of Nicea. As we saw with other aspects of Christian theology, it fell out as it did because certain people tried to redefine God, and the claims of Jesus. Christians responded by observing Scripture's content, interpreting it in the faith-assumptions that God is not contradictory, communicates ideas through words, and speaks truth. The observations can be expressed in 5 statements, each derived from multiple passages in the New Testament.

1. *Scripture calls God the Father "God" or at least treats Him as such.* (Matthew 5:16, 5:45, 5:48, 6:1, 6:9, 7:21, Mark 11:25, Luke 11:2)
2. *Jesus, or the Son of God, is also called "God" in Scripture.* (Titus 2:13, 2 Peter 1:1, Philippians 2:5-11, John 8:52-59)
3. *The Holy Spirit is called "God" in Scripture, and treated as a person rather than an impersonal force.* (Acts 5:1-4, Acts 13:2, Ephesians 4:30, Genesis 1:2)
4. *Scripture narratives describe the Father, Son, and Holy Spirit behaving as distinct persons, simultaneously in front of witnesses, and in different roles in both heavenly and earthly scenes.* (Matthew 3:13-17, 17:1-8, 18:19, Mark 1:9-12, 9:7, Luke 3:21-22, John 1:1-3, 8:13-18, Acts 7:54-56, Revelation 5:1-8, Genesis 1:26-27)
5. *Scripture declares that there is only one true God.* (Isaiah 43:10-13, Deuteronomy 6:4, Mark 12:29, John 10:30-33, 1 Timothy 2:5)

The First Point, that *Scripture calls God the Father "God" or at least treats Him as such,* would seem to be a no-brainer. Jesus refers repeatedly to His "Father in Heaven." I know of no example in church history where Christians ever questioned the deity of God the Father.

The Second Point that *Jesus, or the Son of God, is also called "God" in Scripture,* has not always received such universal agreement. Nevertheless, it has been a fundamental doctrine of Christianity since its inception that Jesus has the full rights and attributes of God. While this has stirred considerable controversy at times, there is a wealth of biblical statements to support the idea, as sampled above.

The Third Point—that *Scripture calls the Holy Spirit "God" and treats Him as a person*—has also been controversial at times, but is also easily provable. Some people want to describe the Holy Spirit in terms of being an impersonal "force" that emanates from God, rather than as a person. There are some biblical problems with that.

> ***Acts* 5:1-4 1 But a certain man named Ananias, with Sapphira his wife, sold a possession. 2 And he kept back part of the proceeds, his wife also being aware of it, and brought a certain part and laid it at the apostles' feet. 3 But Peter said, "Ananias, *why has Satan filled your heart to lie to the Holy Spirit* and keep back part of the price of the land for yourself? 4 "While it remained, was it not your own? And after it was sold, was it not in your own control? Why have you conceived this thing in your heart? *You have not lied to men but to God.*" (NKJV)**

By equating lying to the Holy Spirit with lying to God, Peter makes the Holy Spirit equivalent to God.

> **Ephesians 4:30 And *grieve not the Holy Spirit of God,* whereby ye are sealed unto the day of redemption. (KJV)**

The ability to grieve is an emotional and personal attribute. One cannot cause sadness in a "force" or an impersonal emanation (like electricity or magnetism). Impersonal forces cannot speak in words as the Holy Spirit does in Acts 13:2. The only rational inference here is that the Holy Spirit is a person, and that he is God.

Point Four is more complex, but also self-evident from all the listed passages above. *Scripture narratives describe the Father, Son, and Holy Spirit behaving as distinct persons, simultaneously in front of witnesses, in both heavenly and earthly scenes.* The bishops at Nicea had to deal with the fact that Scripture portrayed Jesus, the Father, and the Holy Spirit as different persons in relation to each other. There are good reasons to take these depictions at face value. The Gospels' language did not describe appearances of one infinite person wearing three "masks," as the Monarchian heresy portrayed God. These reasons are central to the person and work of Christ, as we shall soon see.

The Gospel passages listed along with Point 4 do not portray Jesus and God the Father acting in a mere time-space driven convenience. The infinite God does not simply poke his head into space-time to speak to his own alter ego (Jesus) on earth. The Gospels and Revelation describe the distinct person-hood of Father and Son in exclusively heaven-based scenes as well.

> ***Acts* 7:54-56 When they** (the Jewish religious authorities) **heard these things they were cut to the heart, and they gnashed at him** (Stephen) **with their teeth. But he, *being full of the Holy Spirit,* gazed into heaven and saw the glory of God, *and Jesus standing at the right hand of God,* and said, "Look! *I see the heavens opened and the Son of Man standing at the right hand of God!*"**

> ***Revelation* 5:1-7 And I saw in the right hand of Him who sat on the throne a scroll written inside and on the back, sealed with seven seals... But one of the elders said to me, "Do not weep. Behold, the Lion of the tribe of Judah, the Root of David, has prevailed to open the scroll and to loose its seven seals." And I looked, and behold, in the midst of the throne and of the four living creatures, and in the midst of the elders, *stood a Lamb as though it had been slain, having seven horns***

*and seven eyes, which are the seven Spirits of God sent out into all the earth. Then He came and took the scroll out of the right hand of Him who sat on the throne.*

*John* 1:1-3 **In the beginning was the Word, and** ***the Word was with God, and the Word was God. He was in the beginning with God.*** **All things were made through Him, and without Him nothing was made that was made.**

The language conventions of the Gospel narratives explicitly describe differing persons within the Trinity.

*Matthew* **18:19 "Again** *I* (Jesus) ***say to you*** **that if two of you agree on earth concerning anything that they ask, it will be done for them** ***by My Father in heaven."***

The straightforward language of Jesus' words here, and in other passages, makes a distinction-of-person between Himself and the Father.

Nevertheless, Scripture makes clear, in the Fifth Point, that *there is only one God.*

*Isaiah* **43:10-11 "You are My witnesses," says the LORD, "And My servant whom I have chosen, That you may know and believe Me, And understand that I am He.** ***Before Me there was no God formed, nor shall there be after Me. I, even I, am the LORD, And besides Me there is no savior.***

*Deuteronomy* **6:4 ¶ "Hear, O Israel: The LORD our God,** ***the LORD is one!"***

*Mark* **12:29 And Jesus answered him, "The first of all the commandments is, Hear, O Israel;** ***The Lord our God is one Lord:"***

*John* **10:30-33** ***"I and My Father are one."*** **Then the Jews took up stones again to stone Him. Jesus answered them, "Many good works I have shown you from My Father. For which of those works do you stone Me?" The Jews answered Him, saying, "For a good work we do not stone You, but for blasphemy, and** ***because You, being a Man, make Yourself God."***

*1 Timothy* **2:5** ***For there is one God,*** **and one mediator between God and men, the man Christ Jesus; (KJV)**

This presented the bishops at Nicea, and Christians before and since, with a puzzle. What Scripture revealed in its many statements required logical harmonization. We have no liberty to downplay or ignore some passages in order to emphasize others. Our doctrine has to fit all of the Scriptural facts, not just some, or most of them. Otherwise, it is pointless.

Before one throws up ones hands and claims, "The Bible just contradicts itself," consider the following. The same Hebrew word for *one*, in Deuteronomy 6:4, "the LORD is *one*!" appears in Genesis 2:24 describing a man and wife as "*one* flesh."

*Genesis* **2:24 Therefore a man shall leave his father and mother and be joined to his wife,** ***and they shall become one flesh.***

We do not surgically attach Husbands to their wives at weddings. Nor does either spouse lose their individuality, when they marry. "If-then" logic shows us something here. Since husbands and wives are one flesh, yet remain distinct persons within the marriage; use of the word *one* in the Old and New Testaments to say "one God" does not rule out the Trinity. In the language used in Scripture, it is not doubletalk to say that there is one God, and that this God consists of three persons. Contrast is not Contradiction.

This is not just a logic game to balance off all the scriptural statements about the relationship between the Father, the Son, and the Holy Spirit. There are real-world implications involved with denying the Trinity. If the bishops at Nicea viewed God as a single person, who manifested himself three ways, or as a single person wearing three masks for three roles, as the Monarchian heretics did in the 2nd–4th centuries; *they would have actually complicated rather than simplified matters.*

To deny the Trinity, they must first assume the language structure of the Gospels is misleading, since the language presents a Jesus personally distinct from his Father. Second, it created many obstacles to presenting Jesus as truly human if they reduced him to a role that the Father played during an incarnation. If Jesus did not actually become fully human, but merely seemed to, then swarms of problems erupt.

This is important, because if Jesus was not fully human as well as fully God, He was logically in no position to die for human sin. Such a work required a perfect human to pay the price as "kinsman redeemer." If Jesus was not also fully God, then how could anyone have any assurance that He was not bound by space, time, or some other constraint? How could we be sure He was in a position to save anyone?

These logical implications all exist once we fog-out the distinctions between the biblically described persons of the Godhead. Arius may not have wished for these implications, but they would enter the picture regardless, because ideas have consequences in the real world.

At the Council of Nicea, Constantine got a first-hand look at what he was really up against. It was not always pretty. If the Emperor came into the chamber ambivalent about who was right and who was wrong, he did not leave that way. All that needed to happen was for Arius to give his own account of his teachings.

One of the reasons Arianism spread so rapidly was the appeal its teacher had with ordinary people. We are used to thinking of that as the paramount sign of a good teacher. Often, it is, but it is unwise to make that the litmus test. Arius communicated his theology through repetitive popular music, and easy-to-remember little jingles. These resonated in the marketplaces of every Eastern city like mindless pep songs from a demented motivational seminar. Repetition has great value if one intends to indoctrinate rather than educate. It is useful for new believers, but if relied on for too long, it can keep people infantile.

The masses may have found the ditties catchy, but the Emperor was not amused. Arius gave much of his dissertation by reciting his annoying little sing-songy sound bites. I have often pictured it as coming off like watching an irritating street mime trying to impress a convention of intellectual bikers—it just didn't fly.

Nevertheless, the Council of Nicea proved the most essential meeting of post-Apostolic history. It produced what eventually became the ***Nicene Creed***, the basis for all other Orthodox creeds to follow in all branches of Christianity. This declaration described God, who Jesus and the Holy Spirit are in relation to God, and the gospel in a few, easily remembered lines.

A ***creed*** is a concise recitation of statements designed to reveal briefly the biblical belief system of those who hold to it. Creeds were extremely valuable because they allowed bishops at these councils to cut through the red tape and get to the heart of matters. The first order of business at Nicea was restoring Eusebius of Caesarea from his "temporary excommunication." The bishops called upon Eusebius to recite the creed he had learned at Antioch. Everybody agreed that it was orthodox, and Constantine ordered him re-instated without debate.

Nevertheless, there was still a problem. Eusebius' creed did not say anything unscriptural; *its weakness lay in what it left unsaid*. One line referred to Christ as being, *"God from God."* While nobody could object to that statement, it left the door open for Arius to come along and redefine its meaning. Arius taught that Christ was a lesser god who came from the Father, a greater God of similar, but not the same substance. I guess simpler is not always better.[5] At least truth sometimes demands that we can speak it with enough precision to prevent the erasure of important distinctions.

One of the Egyptian Pope Alexander's assistants showed a gift for carefully wording things so as not to invite redefinition. His name was Athanasius. He would soon become the main champion of biblical orthodoxy against Arianism. He, more than any other, called attention to the fact that Christians needed a more explicit creed that ruled out Arian redefinition. Athanasius worked tirelessly to that end.

Nicea established a creed that declared clearly that Christ was fully God *in substance*, not merely a lesser deity, or demigod. But if Constantine thought that would be the end of it, he was tragically mistaken.

The worm-tongued Eusebius of Nicomedia launched an aggressive pro-Arius PR campaign to Eastern Christians. He did this by playing on their legitimate fears of Sabellian Monarchianism—the heresy that God was a single divine person who merely revealed himself three ways. It went something like this; "Arianism may not be true, but it is an effective counter-balance against Sabellianism." In other words, "Let's fight one lie with another at the opposite end of the idea spectrum. Then things will balance out in a happy middle for most people."

German philosopher Georg Hegel promoted a similar fallacy thirteen centuries later; not Arianism, but the idea that "truth always sits in the middle between extremes." This took root after Hegel, and helped shape today's moral and cultural relativism. The problem is, while it may sensibly moderate extremes sometimes, not all (or even most) conflicts involve arbitrary extremes. The method, if treated as a universal truism, assumes by faith that objective truth does not exist. What happens when the conflict is between good and evil, truth versus a falsehood? At the bottom line, there will always be ideas that fit reality, and those that do not. Basing key decisions on ideas that do not fit reality leads to disaster in the real world.

Eusebius of Nicomedia's "PR campaign" trashed key Eastern bishops who understood Latin enough to know that Western Christians were not pro-Sabellian. Chief of these was Marcellus of Ancyra. The Bishop of Nicomedia's ultimate goal was to gain the Emperor's full backing. This might have seemed an impossible dream, considering first impressions at Nicea. Yet, Eusebius of Nicomedia never underestimated the power of stupidity. Constantine did not have the theological savvy to know his friends from his enemies.

Another intrigue also distracted the Emperor. History does not know all the details, but soon after Nicea, Constantine had his eldest son, Crispus, executed. The scandal spiraled out of control, when the Emperor also put to death his second wife, Fausta, shortly thereafter. Rumors of treachery and sexual immorality spread like plague. This stain on Constantine's name decimated his family and empire even long after his death with an infamy only King David could appreciate.

All this worked to the advantage of the weasel-bishop from Nicomedia, and his cronies. The reception of the Nicene Creed proved lukewarm at best in much of the East. Only three church leaders there strongly stood in favor of it; Marcellus, Eustathius the Pope of Antioch, and Athanasius, who had just succeeded Alexander as the Pope of Alexandria. Consequently, the churches of the East gave Constantine trouble.

Satan soon knocked Eustathius out of the picture. Constantine's mother, Helena, visited Antioch during her famous tour of the Holy Lands. The plainspoken Pope made a few disapproving remarks about the overblown ceremony surrounding her every movement. Helena "felt the Spirit leading her" to "discover" holy site after holy site, many of which she got historically wrong. Eusebius of Caesarea, the historian, was still not wholeheartedly in favor of the decisions at Nicea. He therefore tried to score brownie points with the Emperor by suggesting Eustathius be punished for such insolence.

Constantine, unaware the Pope of Antioch was his chief theological ally in the region, allowed a synod to be convened controlled by the other, slimier, Eusebius. Eusebius of

Nicomedia used Eusebius of Caesaria this way as his "useful idiot." Tragic, considering that the gullible historian wrote the landmark history of the church's first four centuries. Intelligence has never been the same as wisdom. This synod deposed the venerable Asian Pope in favor of a pro-Arian bishop. Eustathius became the first of what history calls *The Exile Martyrs*. These godly men suffered exile due to the duplicity of fellow churchmen. [6]

Eusebius of Nicomedia's next victim was Marcellus. Since Easterners already widely hated his views, it did not take long to engineer his fall. Now, only Athanasius stood in the way of Arius' bulldog.

Athanasius had already ticked off Constantine over his refusal to re-admit Arius even if the latter renounced his heresy. The new Pope of Alexandria was not merely being difficult here. He knew personally how squirmy Arius could be and, like Hosius of Cordova, was not willing to sacrifice truth for a superficial unity. But Athanasius had one major character flaw that Hosius didn't. He was a hot head. He was known to have used strong-arm tactics to get his way on a few occasions, and this marred his reputation.

All it took was a muck viper like the Bishop of Nicomedia to send a lying message to the Emperor. He claimed Athanasius had threatened to have the Alexandrian dockworkers strike. This would cut off wheat shipments to the Empire's new capital of Constantinople, what is now Istanbul, Turkey. After all, the Egyptian Pope had flexed his muscle just to demonstrate his power with the people before, why not now?

The Emperor reacted swiftly, and exiled Athanasius to Gaul for the first of many such forced excursions. The Arians eventually put their own toadies into leadership positions to fill the void in Egypt. Constantine never quite realized that he had been duped into undoing his best work to further church unity. It was about to get much worse. There would be no time for the Emperor to rectify his bad judgment. Within a year, he would be dead.

Flavius Constantine put off baptism until just before his death, fearful he might commit a heinous transgression after having his sins washed away. In a diabolical irony, Eusebius of Nicomedia, archenemy of the Nicene Creed, baptized him on his deathbed. It seems the infamous weasel-bishop had successfully slinked his way into the imperial court. Unlike the 4th century Machiavelli of so many historically half-baked conspiracy theories, Constantine stayed dim to the end. Yet his desire to please God often seemed quite sincere, even if equally half-baked.

It is easy for us to accuse him of superstition, treachery, and mismanagement of church affairs that he, by rights, should have never meddled in. Yet that would forget how much God used him providentially to bring about the universal church councils. Through those, the church stabilized its teachings about the nature of Christ into a durable, coherent body of doctrines. Constantine also showed evidence of humane, God-fearing leadership by the standards of his day. He abolished crucifixion, and made it a law that all prisoners were to be taken out into the sunlight at least once a day. His penalties for murder, rape, and kidnapping, however, remained rightfully severe. He also declared Sunday a weekly holiday, but stipulated that necessary work could still be done on it.

Constantine usually treated fairly those small groups within the church, which, for varied reasons, were unpopular. His failure with Eustathius, Marcellus, and Athanasius was an exception rather than the rule—a strategically damaging one, but an exception nonetheless. He usually issued edicts to protect such people from over-zealous clerics. [7] Nor did he make harassing laws against Pagans, except in extreme cases of public sexual immorality.

He kept the title of ***Pontifex Maximus***, or "High Priest of the Imperial Cult" up to the very end, however. There is a puzzling mix of both good and bad found in the life of Constantine. It is easy to point out his flaws.

His successors, however, were about to do much worse.

## BIBLIOGRAPHY

1. Smith, M.A. ***The Church Under Siege***, pp. 37-38, 1976, Inter-Varsity Press, Leicester, England.
2. Joseph Smith, Jr., ***King Follett Discourse, Journal of Discourses***, v. 6, pp. 3-4, also in ***Teachings of the Prophet of Joseph Smith***, pp. 345-346, Brigham Young, ***Journal of Discourses***, v. 7, p. 333
3. Norman Geisler & William E. Nix, ***A General Introduction to the Bible***, Moody Press, 2008, (Note: *Geisler and Nix estimate over 36,000 citations to the New Testament in 2nd and 3rd century works indicates by its circulation clear 1st century New Testament authorship.*), see also, Harold Greenlee, ***Introduction to New Testament Textual Criticism***, p. 54, Eerdman's, 1964, (Greenlee writes on noted page: *"These quotations are so extensive that the New Testament could be virtually reconstructed from them without the use of New Testament Manuscripts."*)
4. Some gnostic gospels (example ***Trimorphic Protennoia***) use the terminology of a fully developed Neoplatonism, and must, therefore, be dated after Plotinus, in the 3rd century. *Plotinus, a native of Lycopolis in Egypt, who lived from 205 to 270 was the first systematic philosopher of [Neo-Platonism]*, ***Catholic Encyclopedia***. Retrieved 12 April 2009. See also, Harold W. Attridge and George W. MacRae, *Introduction: The Gospel of Truth*, in James M. Robinson, ed., ***The Nag Hammadi Library*** (San Francisco: Harper and Row, 1988), p. 38, see also Douglas Groothuis, ***The Gnostic Gospels: Are They Authentic?***, http://www.equip.org/article/the-gnostic-gospels-are-they-authentic/
5. Op cite, Smith, M.A. pp. 40-42
6. Op cite, Smith, M.A. pp. 43-44
7. Op cite, Smith, M.A. pp. 47-48

# 6

# The Christian Roman Empire: Part 1

## Arian Antics and "Imperial Team Sport" Theology

Constantine died without naming his successor. One gets the impression that very little trust existed in the imperial family. Likely, this resulted from the execution of son, Crispus, and wife, Fausta, and whatever conditions prompted it. Such things can create hard feelings in families.

Whatever the reason, Constantine's dark puddle flooded into a crimson ocean through his sons. Three of the competing heirs came out on top, after slaughtering the rest of the family, except for one obscure nephew who we will discuss later. The sons divided the empire amongst themselves. Constantine II controlled Spain, Gaul, and Britannium, while Constans seized the center, with the Balkans and Northwest Africa. Constantius II received the lion's share, ruling Constantinople, Egypt, and the East.

If their father's interest in the church proved a bungling, but well-intended attempt to manage a crisis that providentially helped Christianity recover and adapt; the sons' looked like three gamers gambling on a theological spectator sport. Constantius II began to support the Arians. Because of this, Constans and Constantine II rooted for the Orthodox. All of them had even less grasp of the theological issues than their father, and none of Constantine's sincerity, questionable or otherwise.

The Arian Controversy exploded with new vigor when Constantine II pardoned the exiles from his father's edicts. Athanasius returned to an adoring throng in Egypt to take up his cause again. Eastern bishops, fearful of a Monarchianism defeated generations ago, teamed up with the Arians to combat the Nicene Creed. This did not mean the Eastern Church actually supported Arianism as orthodox doctrine. It was more an alliance of two differing parties against a common foe. The Eastern Orthodox simply did not consider who "their enemy" or "the enemy of their enemy" really was.

By acting on bad information about what Latin bishops taught, the East allied itself with a heresy they also rejected, to defeat a creed that preserved their own Faith. The Eastern bishops feared the Nicene Creed's wording might enable new Monarchian Heresies like that of Sabellius. Latin-speaking Western bishops rejected those heresies with equal, if more well-balanced, vigor. Yet the wormy whispers of Eusebius of Nicomedia assured Constantius II that Athanasius threatened the peace. Again, the young Pope of Alexandria went into exile.

This sort of thing was regrettably common not only in church history, but in any history. People are always perfectly prepared to fight the previous war. The problem is that the "previous war" always took place a generation or more before the present one. Christians often do the same thing today; we man the ramparts against the thing our parents already defeated, while what is attacking us now pushes in almost unopposed around our spiritual "Maginot Lines." The Maginot Line was a fortressed wall on the French-German border, built to stop the Germans invading France as they had in the 19th century Franco-Prussian War. In the 20th century World Wars, a mechanized Germany simply went through Belgium, by two routes, around the Maginot Line, to attack from behind. Satan is smarter than Hitler.

The Eastern bishops had so demonized Sabellianism's ghost that they underestimated the clear and present dangers of Arianism. Both distortions of Christ's nature were equally bad. Yet Arianism had the additional menace of imperial backing in the East. Sabellius never imagined such a power advantage possible in his day.

## The Roman Empire as Divided by Constantine's Sons

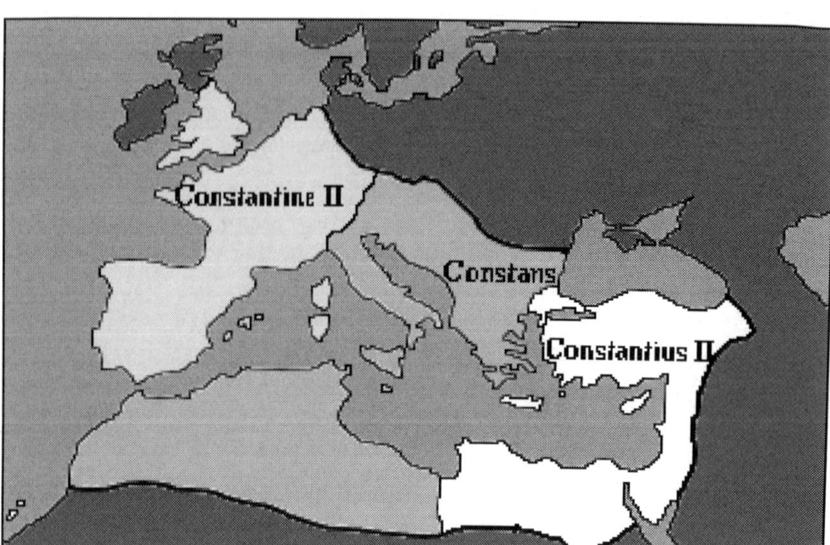


In the course of time, Eusebius of Nicomedia died, and another bishop became the chief bulldog of Arianism. Valens of Mursa (in the Balkans), proved slimier than even his predecessor. History first noticed him at the abortive Council of Sardica, which broke down into a childish name-calling fest. This, of course, did nothing to solve the Arian Crisis. The Eastern bishops marched out when Athanasius and Marcellus of Ancyra showed up under the sponsorship of Julius, Pope of Rome.

The Eastern bishops retreated over the nearby border to hold a council of their own. Then the Western and Eastern prelates slung acidic, but impotent, *anathemas* at one another over the frontier. *Anathema* is Greek for *curse* that, when used by church leaders, represented a curse to the lowest hell on those who would spread a soul-damning teaching.

The Apostle Paul issued the first known genuine anathema in Galatians Chapter 1:8: **"But even though we, or an angel from heaven, should preach to you a gospel contrary to that which we have preached to you, let him be *accursed*."** (NASB) The word translated as *accursed* in the text is the Greek word ***anathema***.

The leadership style of the Apostles contrasts with that of some church synods, and later, the Medieval Roman Popes. Anathemas were rare in apostolic writings. Some church councils hurled them around like mashed potatoes in a college fraternity food fight. Many Roman Popes seemed to use them as personal cruise missiles of the Spirit. Maybe I am too distant from such events to take them seriously, but sometimes distance is good.

It would be worse than foolish however, to trivialize Galatians 1:8. It is equally bad to imagine that today's churches are above censure. Still, it is hard to take some of church history's anathemas too seriously after reading about the Council of Sardica. If every anathema thundered by church council or pope had actual divine force, the body of Christ would have been wiped from the faces of heaven and earth long ago. Nevertheless, denial of pastoral authority, and fear even of its proper use, has led to worse than the ridiculous in our own day, as we shall see later.

The Council of Sardica—not one of church history's more dignified synods—bears mentioning for one reason. A precedent was set there that heavily affected the development of later church government. After Athanasius' second exile, a council of Eastern bishops at Tyre had deposed him as Pope of Alexandria. He appealed this decision to Julius, Pope of Rome. There was no known reason why he should do this, from a universally accepted church government standpoint. Pulling in a pope of equal authority against the spiritual *coup de'tat* at Alexandria made sense. Julius was also a Latin speaker of the West, and the church seemed ready to split along a growing East-West language barrier.

Julius seemed to think it followed some earlier precedent. The Council of Sardica afterwards passed a canon, or ruling, that gave the Bishop of Rome the right to hear appeals from regional, but not universal church synods. Had Julius' perceived precedent been more than a local one, this would not have been necessary. Even so, it had little force in the East since their bishops had already walked out. [1]

One might think that this signaled the split of the church, Greek speaking East from Latin West. That would not come for another 600 or so years yet, however. Once everybody vented their spleens, bishops from both sides made a new attempt at reconciliation. This came at the price of smearing the unfortunate Marcellus of Ancyra. Although not a Monarchian in doctrine, some of his language seemed to come close. Julius and Athanasius distanced themselves from their old ally, and joined the Eastern bishops in a condemnation of his views. This was a bitter betrayal. Yet throwing Marcellus under the chariot opened the door for Athanasius to regain his bishop seat. It also enabled the East and West to come together again against Arianism.

Victory appeared to be in sight.

Then, in 350 AD, everything changed.

Another political crisis gripped the empire, which led to civil war. Constantine II had tried to get rid of his brother Constans, who then went to war, defeating and killing him. The unsavory Constans became sole Emperor of the West. He quickly fell victim to an army uprising under a rogue general named Magnentius. Magnentius then turned on Constantius, and marched east. The two armies clashed outside the Balkan town of Mursa, home of the new Arian bulldog, Valens.

This unscrupulous Arian bishop knew the lay of the land better than the Eastern Emperor did. He stationed his clerics as watchers and runners so that he got the fastest, most up to date intelligence on the fighting. The runners of Constantius II used the winding established roads, while Valens' men went over hill. Valens made a big show about going in to seek the Lord about the course of the battle. Meanwhile, Constantius' army had defeated the forces of Magnentius.

When the Arian runners came in to their bishop with the news, Valens went to the Emperor. He announced that God had prophetically revealed to him His favor of Constantius by defeating the usurper. When the Emperor's own messengers arrived some time later with the same news, the superstitious Constantius began to eat out of Valens' hand. Soon, he became sole Emperor of an again united Rome.

Constantius, already favoring the Arians, now came to see Valens as the very mouthpiece of God on earth. Prodded by this corrupt bishop, the half-witted Emperor made Arianism the universal state Cult. Bishops in the West, who had always hated this heresy, were rounded up and forced to sign documents in agreement to it.

Most Westerners did not cave like the Eastern bishops, who had already join forces with this heresy, fearing the unlikely comeback of a different false teaching. Forcing Arian heresy from the top down on Orthodox Christians created more political trouble than it was worth. Valens and his pet Emperor silenced opposition by exiling non-compliant bishops to the East. This only allowed the strong black coffee of orthodox teachers from the West to meet their slowly awakening Eastern counterparts, and join forces to meet the new day. The day eventually would not end well for the Arians or the emperors who patronized them.

For a while, the powerful Pope of Alexandria managed to hold out. But he knew the Emperor's forces were coming. When they came, the soldiers marched in on him while church was in session. Because Athanasius dressed no differently than any other member of his congregation, however, he escaped into the crowds. His people soon spirited him from there into the desert. [2] Athanasius did much of the writing by which we now know so much about him while he hid in the North African sands.

State mandated Arianism finally fell because of yet another of history's great ironies. This brings us back to the obscure nephew of Constantine that narrowly missed being slaughtered with the rest of the clan by Constantine's sons. Constantius II now called on him to lead an army against advancing barbarians along the Rhine Frontier. The Nephew's forces were victorious, but when the Emperor called them south to a desert campaign against the Persians, they mutinied. The army demanded that this Nephew move against Constantius, and make himself the new Emperor. It turned out, he didn't have to.

Before the Nephew could bring his troops all the way south, whether in compliance or mutiny, word came to him that Constantius II had died of a sudden fever. Without a blood heir, the nearest kin inherited. The Nephew marched into Constantinople the undisputed Emperor of a still united Roman Empire. History remembers him as Julian the Apostate.

In addition to escaping death from Constantine's "Christian" sons, Julian saw a church at war with itself during his childhood. If that were not bad enough, he suffered an education under his imperial cousin's toad-like Arian court bishops. One can understand why he wanted to rid the empire of Christianity, considering the example of Christianity he saw in his youth. The superstitious, Gumby-like Constantius II, his sycophantic court clergy, sectarian strife; all salted thirst in Julian for a more dignified state cult.

Julian diagnosed the disease perfectly, only to prescribe a remedy even worse than the sickness. Once he became Emperor, he sought to restore Hellenistic Paganism to its former glory. He also granted amnesty to all religious exiles in the hope that the Christians would renew their fight over Arianism. The young Emperor expected that strife to ruin Christianity as a belief system from within, given its claim to Divine brotherly love. Julian did not understand that the root of the dispute was not hatred, but the fact that genuine love is based on, and "rejoices in," truth. (1 Cor. 13:6)

His general amnesty was just what Popes Athanasius and Julius, with their new Eastern allies, needed. They quickly re-asserted their leadership of the churches, to win a decisive victory over Arianism at the grassroots level. Arius maybe could capture the crowds with easy-to-remember, entertaining jingles; but real life eventually demanded a faith with depth and content. Reducing Jesus to less than He really is in His Divinity was just as vapid as reducing Him to less than He is in His humanity. Even the most rabid Eastern Orthodox opponent of the Nicene Creed loathed state enforced Arianism, once they saw where it led.

While the conflict went on—one Eastern Emperor after Constantius briefly backed Arianism—the tide had turned. This victory eventually led to the death of that heresy inside the Empire. Beyond Roman territory, it was another matter. The Goths and Vandals had already converted to Arianism, taking it to be normative Christianity. That did not become troublesome to Orthodox Christians again until the Western Empire started crumbling, and these tribes began to invade.

Julian the Apostate did not reign long. His aims were frustrated, both for engineering the fall of the church and for his reformed Hellenism. He could not artificially create morally sound social institutions by his Pagan ideals from the top down. Christianity, when left alone, created these things naturally through individual conversions from the ground up. Julian's repaired Pagan altars languished in city after city, while Christian churches continued to grow.

Any government—even imperial despotism—tends toward justice when people accept an unchanging moral ethic bearing the stamp of the Creator God. This was especially so when those who governed remembered that God will judge even emperors, and to a higher standard. While nothing guaranteed emperors would remember that, a thing must be a potential before it becomes an actuality. Even with growing vice in urban church politics, generations of common Christian ethics had embedded by this time in Roman culture. Julian learned that this was still a force more powerful than the will of any single emperor. It would never be perfect, but that did not mean it could not be real.

Julian soon died in battle on the Persian frontier he had before tried to avoid. It is said that his last words were, "*You have conquered, O Galilean, and the world withers gray at your breath.*" Whether he really said this or not, it is a good reflection of the dead Christianity Julian saw in his upper-class life. This was not the vital faith of the Apostles and Church Fathers, but the corrupt wheedling of men like Eusebius of Nicomedia, Valens, and the sons of Constantine.

From here on out, one thing would become increasingly apparent. It would not take long for churches that did not learn from history to repeat it.

## The Orthodox Christian Dictatorship

Not long after Julian, Constantine's grandson, Theodosius, rose to power. It was he, not Constantine, who finally made Catholic Christianity the state religion of the Roman Empire. He became the first emperor to outlaw Paganism so that non-Christians were systematically harassed for the first time. The church had come full circle. No longer the persecuted, it now became the persecutor for the first time in history on any large-scale. Even so, compared to the spectacles of Diocletian, Pagans rarely lost their lives.

Much of the grosser paganization of Christian rites and traditions accelerated during this time. Perhaps we might say the "Christianization" of Pagan rites and traditions, to make them "acceptable." What seemed like the former, eventually, often became the latter. No matter which way we put it, however, the long-term results were the same. Patron gods became patron saints. [3] The Pagan temple of Mars became the Church of St. Martin. [4] The statue of Jupiter became St. Peter, and so on and so forth. Multitudes of Pagan priests went through rubber-stamp "conversions," and learned how to be Christian presbyters. This word, by now, held virtually the same meaning as ***priest*** in common language usage.

Semi-Docetic ideas warped the correct view that Jesus fulfilled the "woman's seed" prophecy of Genesis 3:15. None could deny that Mary was the "woman" part of that picture, which intensified an already popular veneration of the Virgin. ***Semi-Docetic*** means *ideas affected by the same Greek worldview that produced Docetic Gnosticism, but which fell short of saying anything unorthodox about the nature of Christ.* This popular mother-child cult before had been denounced for its extremes by bishops at different locales. Now it further fused itself with the still totally Pagan mother-child cults of Isis and Horus, or Venus and Adonis. [5] Historians and theologians call the mixing of conflicting belief systems ***syncretism***. The biblical history of Israel and prophetic warnings to the church in Scripture call it "bad news."

Theodosius wanted to create an empire purified of Paganism. All he did was to force active Paganism underground into the very church itself. That was likely not the emperor's goal. Nevertheless, Pagans opportunistically bent whatever they could to preserve their own ways. Most Pagan cults had little trouble with the imposition of new names for their objects of worship, as long as they could keep the substance of what their objects represented. Such had always been true of Near East and Mediterranean polytheistic sects. The church seriously underestimated this, just as the Pre-Exile Jews had done so during the times of Isaiah and Jeremiah.

In social effect, one can compare Theodosius' policy to a "spiritual Prohibition." As Prohibition in 1920-30s America, this edict, intended to purify the church, instead, accelerated its decay. The near impossibility of enforcing it fatigued state officials. This made low-level officials cobelligerents against the Emperor with the Pagan holdouts. Such policies, by their over-reach, encourage bureaucratic graft. Enforcement drew limited resources away from fighting crime and keeping the peace, as we shall see in Chapter 8. Enforcers ultimately had no way to know *in the short term* if the "Church of Saint Martin" were complying with, or redefining, the spirit of the law.

One might complain that the idols would be a dead giveaway, and ultimately, they were. Yet, that only projects our 20/20 hindsight back to a time when nobody really knew where any of this would lead. Christians had distanced themselves three centuries ago from the Jewish experience needed to see the bad potentials here for what they were. Icons had earlier helped Greek minds grasp the Incarnation—an idea that the Greco-Roman worldview originally found unthinkable. That was how icons became associated with something good at first, stead of something idolatrous. At first, there had been safeguards. Only the human nature of Christ had been a legitimate subject for art.

We will cover the rise of icon use later. Those who enforced Theodosius' policies could not see the future, could not read minds, had no theology training, and thought mainly in terms of keeping order. For them, the situation was not as clear as it is to we who enjoy the benefit of Reformation-based hindsight. There is a reason the adjective *Byzantine* is a byword for low-level bureaucratic corruption. Byzantium was the original name of Constantinople, from where Theodosius ruled. In faraway Rome, rich senate families were an influential Pagan holdout capable of buying their way around the law's letter.

I describe the period of Theodosius I, through the fall of the Western Roman Empire, as the "Christian Dictatorship" for many reasons. For one, it sought to enforce from the top down what grassroots Christianity had already proven it could provide from the ground up. The problem was that grassroots faith had, by now, retreated largely into the countryside—to what used to be the old holdout places of Paganism.

While Christian influence on culture was still strong, the urban church, as an institution, had often become as politically corrupt as the state. It began to lose some of its moral and spiritual power to affect grassroots culture. The church of Theodosius became an artificial religious machine that needed imperial backing to enforce its will. Whenever the church loses its vitality to influence a voluntary society, through the arts, literature, business, and the market of ideas; Christian cultural leadership is already gone. It is only a matter of time before the society and its laws become openly hostile to a biblical Faith.

Whenever Christians have co-opted the state to enforce the church's theology *from the top down*, it has only produced ugliness in the name of Christ. A moral basis for law is not the same as theology, even if the two have a relationship. In America, churches have historically been society's heart and conscience, not its executive. The secular state likewise has no right excluding Christians from presenting ideas in the discourse of forming public policy. This is so for any other people group with a legitimate stake in outcomes. Encouraging Christian cultural and political engagement is not the same as "preaching a salvation by politics." It is a natural side effect of discipleship.

Christian faith and a nation can only go so far with one another, however. At the time of Theodosius, Christians had just discovered they could be both patriots and prophets if the circumstances were right. They had not yet developed clear ideas of the implications of being able to be both. Nor did they understand that their blind spots hid in shadows made by their imagined strengths. In America, we may soon discover the limits to this situation that we have always taken for granted. It may not always take the form we think.

Ambrose, Bishop of Milan got one of the first direct tastes of what this might mean. Imperial authorities arrested a popular Thessalonikan chariot racer for homosexual behavior just before the big races. Predictably, the mobs of race fans called for his release. This was like having a star quarterback on a Super-bowl team arrested the night before the big game for some infraction most people just didn't care about. When the Roman authorities refused to give in to the mobs, the race fans rioted, and an army officer was killed.

Theodosius overreacted with self-righteous fury. His troops massacred 6000 race fans in response. A Christian culture should always care about sexual immorality. Law reflects ethics. It is often true that in times of spiritual decay however, even Christian cultures do not care. This sometimes can lead to reactionary zeal by those who care, or at least claim to.

As the "American Culture Wars" escalate, everyone seems to expect that Christians will over-react. That does not seem to be happening—rather the opposite, at this point. It is cautionary to point out that, at this time in Roman history, the population of the Empire was almost evenly split between Christians and non-Christians. Readers can do the "sociological math" as to how long any civilization can **"halt between two opinions"** on such basic human realities. (1 Kings 18:21)

Nobody questioned the nature of *family* at the time of Theodosius, not even the Pagans or the homosexual charioteer. When Ambrose, Bishop of Milan got wind of this massacre, he refused to allow Theodosius to take communion until the Emperor did public penance for his over-reaction. Ambrose had no tolerance for homosexual behavior. He simply recognized that unbridled fanaticism and massacre did not reflect Christ. History has many examples of bishops acting to curb overzealous Christian political leaders from violence; but we rarely hear of them, despite ample documentation. [6] Ambrose had the pastoral right to rebuke the Emperor. Later however, defenders of papal meddling in state affairs stretched this event into a precedent (though Ambrose was Bishop of Milan, not Rome).

Despite many bishops who resisted the vices of power, state-enforced Christianity formed a shell of hypocrisy around the church, over time. Enough did not resist. Society had already begun to grow repulsed by the degeneration of what the name of Christ had begun to stand for. Fear came to rule the faithful more than love. It might have preserved the mechanics of the church, as a political and religious system, but it did nothing to add life. Quite the opposite, in practical terms, little difference existed between state imposed Orthodoxy and state backed Arianism. Both turned out ugly.

Orthodoxy could at least claim the doctrinal potential for enabling an encounter with Christ as Scripture revealed Him in all of its parts. We should neither forget that nor think of it as some sort of justification for the ugliness. After two generations of government assisted Christianity, and now state mandated Orthodoxy, people saw the church in a radical new way. Today, we usually use phrases like "radical new way" to mean something good. However, *radical* and *new* do not always equal *good*. Most often, they don't. Grandparents of late 4th century believers would not have recognized what the church had become.

Something had definitely changed, and folk almost everywhere were keenly aware that the change was increasingly not good. Nobody wanted to go back to where the state constantly persecuted believers. Scripture never commanded us to pray for such a thing. Christians searched for contemporary faith heroes to replace the martyrs that so many now found too super-human to relate to personally. So great became the distance that folk could not imagine the martyrs going through the same kind of life struggles other people went through. Nobody dared even consider it. The church even cultivated this.

The stage was set for the dawn of Monasticism.

## BIBLIOGRAPHY

1. Smith, M.A. ***The Church Under Siege***, pp. 56-58, 1976, Inter-Varsity Press, Leicester, England
2. Ibid. p. 62
3. Smith, Homer, ***Man and His Gods***, p. 227, and Durant, Will, ***Story of Civilization***, p. 745, Simon and Schuster Inc. New York
4. Doane, T.W. ***Bible Myths***, p. 396, and Woodrow, Ralph, ***Babylon Mystery Religion***, pp. 31-35
5. Woodrow, Ralph, ***Babylon Mystery Religion***, pp. 13-20
6. Vincent Carroll and David Shiflett, ***Christianity on Trial: Arguments Against Anti-Religious Bigotry***, Encounter Books, 2002

# 7

# THE CHRISTIAN ROMAN EMPIRE: PART 2

## THE LATER TRINITARIAN AND CHRISTOLOGY CONTROVERSIES

The Arian Dispute was just one in a campaign of battles on the nature of Christ and the Holy Trinity during the Christian Roman Empire. Picture the history of this campaign as the pendulum of a huge grandfather clock swinging back and forth, from one extreme to the next. Ideas bring actions, and then reactions push back. New terminology and modifications fit new generations, as the monstrous thing swings on each arc. Every new pivot refines our thinking, but also raises new questions and new problems.

Questions raised by Gnosticism, and then Arianism, over Christ's nature, caused the "idea pendulum" to swing incessantly for a long time. This was needful. Who and what God is, and who and what Jesus is in relationship to that, are of central importance to the Christian faith. It would be unrealistic and unreasonable to expect it to be any other way.

A series of universal church councils resulted over the next century and a half to wrestle with what all this meant. They were not mere intellectual debates (though intellectual debate was involved). These councils served to clarify Christian thinking by defining essential terms for the long haul. The Holy Spirit calls the teaching of Jesus to our remembrance, according to John 14:26. This entails a rational process, not just one of spontaneous intuition. The councils followed what the Scriptures taught on the subject—both explicitly and implicitly—to their logical conclusions.

This set needed limits for basic orthodoxy, within which future teachers might build on the foundation of Christ to their generations. The only alternative was redefinition and erosion of the very meanings of the words used to communicate the Faith. People express ideas using words that have both ***definitive*** and ***connotative*** meaning. Without that, there is no basis for communication, let alone truth. A biblical orthodoxy is not an arbitrary shackle on free thought in Christianity. Genuinely free thought retains truthful character, so it can have a basis for liberty. A rational biblical orthodoxy gives the Faith necessary structure and content. Without it, we have no way to sanity-check our personal religious experiences.

The second ***Christology*** Debate came as the "idea pendulum" swung away from Arius, back to its opposite extreme. Gnosticism had occupied this place before, but Christians had eliminated it as a truthful option. The force of the swing still pushed ideas toward putting Christ's deity over His humanity, just not in the same way. As Arius began all his nonsense in a crude attempt to crush Gnosticism, so the next conflict began as a half-baked "final blow" to Arianism. Apollinaris, an immature disciple of Athanasius, began to teach a sloppy view of Christ's Incarnation. He imagined he had the ability to define the limit to Christ's humanity, in a way that more people might easily understand.

The ***Incarnation***, for those new to Christian theology, is the teaching that God became human flesh in Jesus Christ. The word, based on the Latin *carnos*, which means *flesh* or *meat*, describes the *enfleshment* of God the Son. Apollinaris in effect taught that *since Christ was fully God, then the human part of Jesus amounted only to his physical human body*. To Apollinaris, the consciousness and personality of Christ were divine only, and not at all human.

At this point, I can see many believers today shrugging their shoulders and saying, "So what? At least it's easy to understand." Yet once again, it was an issue of carrying this idea about our Savior out to its logical conclusion. Firstly, the Gospels show a Jesus who is fully human, not only in physical body, but in personality. He grew tired. He did not know the time of his own Second Coming (Mk. 13:32). He got hungry and thirsty. He experienced temptation to sin. He suffered human pain and severe anxiety at Gethsemane, sweating blood through His skin. (20th century army doctors listed this as a symptom of extreme combat stress, as can happen during constant mechanized warfare.)

Jesus died as a man, not as an all-powerful God who was simply resident in a human flesh receptacle. In fact, if Jesus were not also fully human, then how could he be eligible to die for human sin? For that matter, if Christ's humanity consisted only of His human body, then it robs His sacrificial death of its meaning.

God is ***omnipotent***, or all-powerful. If Christ died as the all-powerful God simply wearing a human body, with no human nature and temperament, then how is that a sacrifice? He's God; diverting ample energy from an infinite reserve to rise above the situation would, by definition, be effortless for him, and therefore, trivial. On the other hand, Jesus dying as a man, with a human nature subject to the same mortality and temptation that we experience from the Fall and Curse of Genesis 3, only without actual sin; that is an entirely different story! That can lay valid and believable claim to being the Ultimate Sacrifice. It also conforms to all the details in Scripture, instead of just some.

> **For the law of the Spirit of life in Christ Jesus has made me free from the law of sin and death. For what the law could not do in that it was weak through the flesh, God did by sending His own Son in the likeness of sinful flesh, on account of sin: He condemned sin in the flesh... *Romans* 8:2-3 (NKJV)**

Notice that Jesus came not simply in a material form or even in a human form untouched by the Curse, as Adam was at creation. He came **"in the likeness of sinful flesh."** This is why the Virgin Birth is so important. In Mosaic Law, inheritance legally passed from father to son. So did debt and curses, under certain conditions. The Fall is what Adam did when he originally sinned. The Curse is how God responded to man's Fall (Genesis Ch. 3). The Virgin Birth gave Christ the legal ability to avoid the inherited Curse as a son of Adam. Christ, in the Incarnation, had a nature subject to mortality and temptation, however. His body, born of Mary, still consisted of matter like any other matter—affected by the Curse. The difference is that Christ resisted all of life's temptations and never sinned personally.

Apollinaris never considered the implications of his over-simplified view of the Incarnation. We live in an age when Christians want to make the Bible as simple as possible, so it is more accessible to people. A good intention, but we can only go so far with that. There is such a thing as simplifying something past coherence. It is like what happens when we take a digital photograph and turn down the resolution to make the file smaller for easier upload. You can do it only so far before the image becomes pixelated and distorted. Bible teaching can be like that sometimes. We should all have the simplicity of a childlike relationship with Christ, but the same passage also tells us to reason as adults.

> **Brethren, do not be children in understanding; however, in malice be babes, but in understanding be mature. *1 Corinthians* 14:20 (NKJV)**

The Apollinarian Controversy soon created the need for another universal church council. This time the bishops met at Constantinople, in the year 381. Research in Scripture, using the logic summed up above, refuted Apollinaris' teachings. Biblically orthodox Christianity taught that Jesus was not merely fully God in substance, but fully human in the Incarnation. Not half-God half-man, not fully God living in a human body with its human nature scooped out of it like a spiritual melon, but fully divine and fully human. These distinctions have real world implications.

After history's "idea pendulum" swung away from Apollinaris, it once again carried new corrections. It could not swing back to Arius because previous biblical exploration had logically ruled out his errors. Yet, the idea that Christ was fully human and fully God seemed self-contradictory to some. Greek minds still had a hard time uniting the spiritual and material as different, but related parts of a single created reality. The assumption that matter was inherently evil did not die easily.

The fourth Christology crisis came some decades later. Nestorius, Patriarch of Constantinople, described Christ's Divine and human natures as two personalities swimming around in a human body. Of course, this is an oversimplification of Nestorius' position, but when spread through popular teaching, it amounted to that. It certainly took that form in the minds of his followers. One gets the impression some of these guys had slowly started basing their theology on their own sermon illustrations, rather than the reverse. Their followers certainly saw no difference. That's a recipe for half-baked disciples even today.

Instead of seeing Christ as a whole person, Nestorius presented him as having two wills living in harmony inside one body. This made Christ sound schizoid. A later form of Nestorianism, which Nestorius himself probably did not teach, had the "nature of God" descending on the man Jesus when John the Baptist baptized him. Scripture says that the Holy Spirit rested on Jesus in the form of a dove, not that Jesus took on a Divine nature that he never had before. That would demand we read something into the text that is not there.

Here we see the Greek aversion to uniting the spiritual with the material expressed in yet another form. Let Christ be fully God and fully man, but Nestorius must at all costs maintain his conceptual barriers as if they were realities outside of his own head. For him, the two natures of Christ must remain separated into two personas. This contrived tension placed on Christ's personality looked more like divine spirit possession than God becoming man. While some historians think that Nestorius did not carry his views to this extreme, later, less educated teachers did. Some went even further.

Churches of the day fervently hated Nestorius after he condemned the, by now, popular veneration of Mary as *theotokos* – "Mother of God." One of his reasons for doing this actually made a certain amount of sense. Mary did not precede God; not even God the Son, who showed up in pre-incarnate forms in the Old Testament. Nor did she have the goddess-like powers that people, by this time, attributed to her.

Nestorius' other reasons were warped by Semi-Docetic assumptions wrapped in false piety. In his mind, calling Mary "Mother of God" was tantamount to saying that God was at one time three days old, and in need of a diaper change. Of course, common sense must concede that since Jesus is God in human flesh, born as a baby, and babies lack bodily control until nerves and muscles develop; then God the Son would temporarily have needed diaper changes.

I'm not trying to be snarky or sacrilegious here. We usually only think of Christ's humbling of Himself in connection with His death. That Nestorius felt natural birth and early childhood needs so defiling that God could not go there showed he did not understand the implications of the Incarnation. Infant necessities would be an obvious part of Christ humbling Himself, according to Scripture. The fact that some Christians today might find this paragraph over the top reveals just how much we still have not thought things through.

> **Therefore, *in all things* He (Christ) had to be made like His brethren, that He might be a merciful and faithful High Priest in things pertaining to God, to make propitiation for the sins of the people. *Hebrews* 2:17 (NKJV)**

This is perhaps one reason why bad theology about Mary went virtually unchallenged. It may even be why it began not to occur to believers that anything was wrong with it, at that time. Nestorius' discussion of Mary was just one more way he had of making too much over separating Christ's human nature from His Divine one. Christians could not accept his objection simply because it came from him, to advance a false view of Christ. It is possible for an individual to be correct about a particular detail, while dead wrong about the bigger picture. Though this does not excuse the paganized worship of Mary, there is such a thing as the lesser of two evils. Christians needed a coherent view of Jesus before they could adequately address the issue of where Mary stands in relation to Him. [1]

The historical "bigger picture" sometimes demands we keep things in perspective. Before Christians could argue the issue of "Christ being the only mediator," they needed clarity on "Christ's nature, and what qualifies Him to mediate." History must often defer to "the issue of the day" to fairly characterize the work of a person in a given era. This is true regardless of what seem to be the issues of our own day, in our own minds.

In 431 AD, Emperor Theodosius II called a universal church council over the new crisis, this time at Ephesus. Cyril, Pope of Alexandria, led the charge against Nestorius. Cyril had political reasons as well as doctrinal ones for going after Nestorius. In the century since the imperial seat had moved to Constantinople (formerly Byzantium), the Patriarchs there began to grow in power. Sometimes this came at the expense of the other popes. After Nestorius became Patriarch, he meddled in the Pope of Alexandria's affairs. He undercut Cyril's authority by restoring several Alexandrian presbyters whom Cyril had disciplined.

We will see in more detail, later in the chapter, how the Council condemned Nestorius' teachings. The doctrinal reasoning proved sound, but some of the behavior among the orthodox was not. After the Council of Ephesus, believers could state biblically orthodox truth on Jesus' nature thusly; *Christ is fully divine, fully human, and a unified person in the normal sense of the word "person."* Even so, this did not end things.

Before covering the end of the Christology Controversies, let us shift back to the subject we introduced it at the end of Chapter 6. This will add important perspective to understanding the later universal church councils. The reason for presenting things this way is that some of the machinations of the later councils came riddled with human pride and compromise.

Some believers have questioned the spiritual validity of the councils because of this. While the moral admonitions are sound, this is still a mistake. Such reasoning, if taken down to the level of individual Christian lives (including those of the objectors), would push things toward the absurd. It would force us to conclude that people with the Holy Spirit cannot reach true knowledge about God (and the nature of Christ) until they are morally perfect. Yet, how can people experience sanctification unless they can know the gospel, and the Savior it proclaims?

Objections to the validity of the early universal councils also fail the test of comparing them only to available alternatives of the day. Such protests involve using present-day 20/20 hindsight improperly. They assume we can merely second guess how past Christians set their priorities by citing a few Scripture verses, hundreds, even thousands of years removed from the issues they actually faced. There is more to understanding our history, and applying the Bible to our understanding, than that.

The problem is not that we cannot ever use focused parts of Scripture to address the sins of the past. I do that quite a lot in this book. The problem is that we often do this under the assumption that we have no real need to understand the times and peoples in question to do this properly. (We're going to live with some of these people for all eternity, after all. There is also the danger of coming away learning the wrong things from history.) Even with that understanding, there is still much we cannot know, simply because not all of the information has survived.

The Bible presupposes that we can know truth about the nature of Christ before reaching an ability to act on that truth perfectly. It depicts even its holy Apostles in moments of pride and compromise. Therefore, we do well to abide by the major findings of these councils. Their findings are not Scripture, but they are logically and prayerfully reasoned webs of biblical truth on Christ's nature that have stood the test of time. Realizing the era's tensions gives insight into how God uses flawed men to build from the foundation of Christ to make stable platforms for future works of the Spirit.

## EARLY MONASTICISM—HOLINESS, ACCOUNTABILITY, AND INTERMITTENT MADNESS

Let us move backward just a little, and place ourselves in the later decades of the 4th century again. Less than seventy-five years ago from this time, being a church leader had meant danger to life and liberty, or at least strong political disfavor. Now, within a few generations, it suddenly became one of the surest tracks to high political office in both church and empire. This situation sometimes attracted men of lower character to ministry than before, especially in major urban churches.

If many others still entered leadership for the right reasons, they had no automatic immunity to the temptations of wealth and leisure; any more than American pastors do today. The changing church culture fostered political posturing, personality cultism, and hobnobbing funds from rich patrons. This eroded pastoral ethics then as now, to the varied levels it happened. Only a short time ago, political and living conditions had repelled the self-centered from ministry. The "new normal" of imperial favor changed all that; case in point, Damasus, Pope of Rome.

In 366 AD, Damasus and his hired street gangs slaughtered one hundred and thirty seven followers of his rival, Ursinus, in a bid to become Bishop of Rome. The violence was so bad that civil order in the city collapsed, and the prefect had to flee for fear of his safety. A murder charge even hung over the head of the new Pope for the next ten years. [2]

Old "Damage-control Damasus" then went to work repairing his reputation by adorning the tombs of the martyrs. One wonders from this if he had even read the Gospels. Jesus had said, **"Woe unto you, scribes and Pharisees, hypocrites! Because ye build the tombs of the prophets and garnish the sepulchers of the righteous, And say, 'If we had been in the days of our fathers, we would not have been partakers with them in the blood of the prophets.'"** (Matt. 23:29-30 KJV) Even scarier, fewer and fewer men serving in church leadership seemed to connect those dots.

They may have felt some reason to look the other way, in this case.

Damasus and his rival, Ursinus, had been deacons of the preceding Pope Liberius. Both had served in the Church of Rome for a long time. Damasus came from what is now Portugal, where he had been a crony of then future Emperor Theodosius I, Constantine's grandson. During the reign of Constantius II, Damasus had followed Pope Liberius into exile when sent to Berea for refusing to support Arianism. He had that going for him. Unlike Liberius however, the Emperor permitted Damasus to return to Rome almost immediately. We do not know why for sure.

Future rival, Ursinus, had stayed in Rome, having collaborated with the Arians during Constantius' reign. It seemed that both of these men were trouble. Despite Ursinus' squishiness, Damasus' slaughter of fellow churchmen for political gain shocked Christians everywhere. The world saw this go on in what was then reputed to be the "church of churches," and began to wonder. Damasus had the support of the wealthy, and his friendship with Theodosius soon made him a central figure in the "Orthodox Dictatorship." Another factor also loomed in the background; one that not even friendship with the Emperor could assuage.

When Constantine had moved the imperial capital to Constantinople, power began bleeding slowly away from Old Rome. This continued until the Western Empire collapsed in 451 AD. Damasus noted this bleeding with alarm, though Rome remained capital of the

Western Empire until almost seventy years after his death. In this context, Pope Damasus formally developed the doctrine that the Popes of Rome were exclusive successors to the Apostle Peter. He infused his writings with this idea, though it likely originated in popular legends local to Rome.

One can fairly question if either he or his opponent grasped Peter's concept of church leadership, however. (See 1 Peter 5:1-4) While Damasus could claim a hollow orthodoxy over Ursinus, this travesty paraded the decay and unrest of the urban churches. Spiritually minded Christians everywhere felt a sense of revulsion. Many sought escape from the worldly cancer engulfing the body of Christ. This trend became a driving force behind early monasticism. The monastics hoped that seclusion would grant them distance to pursue holiness unhindered by the world. That was how it was supposed to work in theory, at least.

Despite flaws of concept and practice, monasticism had many positive effects on Christianity, and the Western Civilization it nurtured. Many benefits we think basic to civilization—localized hospitals, free education, most social services to the poor—began in monasteries. [3] As imperfect solutions do, monasticism also sometimes fell short. Most of its problems stemmed from acceptance of a Semi-Docetic view of the human condition. Monasticism tended to reinforce, rather than counter, confusion of asceticism with spiritual life. This had the bizarre effect of fostering a spiritual pride that all-too-often expressed itself in the language of humility. (Col. 2:16-23)

The most harmful long-term confusion of asceticism with spiritual life involved celibacy vows. This would have been fitting for singles, but a majority of monastics thought marriage incompatible with holiness from the start. Soon, this false view of holiness became universal in the monastic movements. We already covered the origin of this perception. Only monastic orders demanded celibacy at this point. It would take a few centuries to make this into a pastoral requirement in the West. It would happen through another "lesser of two evils" trade-off, covered in a later chapter. Though sometimes inescapable, one cannot expect any accumulation of such trade-offs not to produce bad things. (1 Tim. 4:1-3)

Nevertheless, for the next thousand years, any hope or actuality of church reform came from the monastic orders. This happened even during the faltering baby-steps of the movement's beginnings. Even Pope Damasus had a monastic-minded friend who "connected the dots," at least to the extent that he encouraged the Pope toward reform. Unfortunately, this friend characterized some of the weaknesses of monasticism, too. His name was Jerome. He had strong ascetic leanings that were about to get him in trouble, and would cost an innocent life.

Troubled by the worldliness infiltrating the Church at Rome, Jerome tried to use his influence as well as he might. He urged the wealthy prelates in Pope Damasus' circle toward personal holiness. Yet in an age of foppish clerics in tawdry finery (as in any other), those with so fiery a zeal can still sabotage their own ministries. Fire that warms can easily become fire that burns houses down. Even sympathetic coworkers wrote of Jerome in pitying terms, as if he suffered from a malady that today might be called O.P.D. by some well-meaning therapist; Obnoxious Personality Disorder. People found him abrasive and disagreeable to be around.

Things unraveled for Jerome after his exhortations on fasting resulted in the fervent daughter of a wealthy patron starving herself to death. Poor Jerome had even hoped to affect the church for the better if chosen as Pope Damasus' successor. When that fell through in 389 AD, he retreated to seclusion in the Holy Lands, where he gave himself fully to his studies. History remembers Jerome not so much for his clumsy monasticism, as for his skill as a Bible translator.

Jerome made the first standardized Latin version of Scripture. This became the basis for the ***Latin Vulgate*** or Common Latin Bible that would be the prototype for most Roman Catholic translations to come.

Monasticism did not start with full-blown orders and communities. It began with the hermits. These individuals retreated from worldliness in the church by going out alone into the desert to pray, and to put to death the passions of the flesh. Before Constantine, the heroes of the faith had been the martyrs, who had stood under persecution. The hermit provided a new hero model, albeit a more mystical and abstract one. People envisioned them as spiritual warriors who went out into the wastelands "to do single combat" with Satan—no fodder for embellishment there.

Later Medieval literature teemed with such figures, often greatly embellished by ***hagiographers***. These were the storytellers of the saints, who often devoted themselves individually to a particular saint. They were forerunners of historical fantasy novelists at best, and purveyors of fraud and pagan myth in Christian garb at worst. I feel badly saying this, since I am probably their literary descendant, at least as far as my novels go (hopefully not in this history.) Either way, the hermits provided far more room for creative license than the martyrs did. Martyrs usually had verifiable records as to the times, places, and manner of their deaths. Doing single combat with Satan was likely a little harder to document.

Still, it would be a mistake to write all the hermits off as a fad—though many likely deserved that fate. (One might even say the same for a few hagiographers; an unknown statistical sampling of whom must have researched as carefully as limited Dark Age source availability allowed.)

The best-known early hermit was Antony, an Egyptian who grew up during the days of the last universal persecution. He mentored Athanasius, Pope of Alexandria, who wrote the hermit's biography; the source of virtually all we know about him. An aged Antony lent his popular spiritual support to Athanasius in the fight against Arianism. There is reason to suppose him a godly man, who truly looked for ways to live above the world at a time when the church, as an institution, had begun to erode.

The "Hermit Approach" to holiness had some real problems as a spiritual movement, however. The intrusion of human merit into the realm of Divine grace, which began in the popular way people viewed martyrs and confessors; now found a new vehicle in the perceived super-holiness of the hermits. Their often "flamboyant humility" gave believers a new way to confuse asceticism with spiritual life.

Another trouble with many of the hermits, as time went on, was that there was no accountability. They became eccentric and erratic in their behavior extremes. Documentation from this period tells how some lived in giant cages, on top of pillars, or ate nothing but grass. Extreme Pagan Stoicism had now become a "Christian" ideal. In the end, hermitage proved a dead end. The human spiritual needs of community, nurture, and accountability not only were missing, but also discouraged.[4] God knew what He was talking about when He said, **"It is not good for the man to be alone..."** (Gen. 2:18) While He does not call everyone to be married, it is generally true of the human condition.

Things improved when Pachomius, a converted Roman soldier in Egypt, founded a hermit community under a rule. His was a step in the right direction, as far as accountability went. His harsh discipline however, overshadowed human needs like nurture and fellowship. The confusion of asceticism with spiritual vitality ensured that the Pachomian Order deserved its reputation for a "spiritual storm-trooper" mentality. This would cause trouble in a few short generations.

All of the monastics suffered from an unbiblical Semi-Docetic view of humanity, which confused humanness with sinfulness. God created Adam and Eve human. He did not create them sinful. Sin came only when Adam chose to disobey God. (Gen. 3) This choice had unravelling consequences on all of Adam's offspring, corrupting their future ability to choose rightly. Once men committed sin, the guilty could not repair it. Sin affected the nature of our humanity. It added something monstrous. God then cursed creation, which He had created "good," so that it would fit the divided nature of those whom He made to manage it—humanity. This was mercy, not spite. Sin really is that serious.

God, as a sovereign act, created us in His image. His image has intrinsic value, even though vandalized by sin. God's love fits both His Law and His creation in such a way that made us redeemable in our mortal state. (Rom. 8:18-25, Matt. 6:10b, Heb. 9:27-28) A logical implication of this is that every present-day human trait results from either Creation or the Fall and its Curse. We have qualities that God created in us at the beginning, but also damages done by the sins of past generations, those around us, and which we have done to ourselves. Because reality is a system of interlaced cause and effect, we observe this spiritually, morally, genetically, and historically. Collectively, we call this *the human condition*.

As in every other Christian movement, the monastics did well when their walk with Christ fit both Scripture and the realities of the human condition. The various orders eventually stabilized as balanced leaders took the helm. Others also founded new orders that learned from the mistakes of earlier ones, and matured. Basil the Great, a contemporary of Athanasius' old age, established his order in the East. The Order of Basil built hospitals and homes for the elderly, with many other social services for the poor that no civilization had ever seen before on such a scale. [5]

It is impossible to overstate the positive social changes that such advancements brought. Even the remotely situated Greek temples to Aesculapius had nothing to compare. I have explored the ruins of Aesculapian temples. I have walked the ducted corridors where Pagan priests hid, as they siphoned mildly hallucinogenic cannabis smoke over the sick. The priests hid inside the walls, pretending to be gods that whispered healing words. Since most sick people died walking the long distances to these temples, the stronger ones who made it, tended to recover. Aesculapian priests then took the bows.

By contrast, the hospitals of the Basilian Order used no such chicanery. Their monks set up operation near populated areas, where they were easily accessible to those most in need.

The monastic rule that came closest in the West to providing balance between distance from the world, and compassion for the human condition, was that of Benedict of Nursia. Benedict applied much wisdom in learning from his past mistakes. He made many of them to learn from, as he did not begin as someone sensitive to the differences between humanity and sin. A casual read of Benedict's Rule—written later—reveals what might seem to us an oppressive regimentation. He was a bit of a control freak by temperament. He also came several generations later than the others did, in far tougher times, after the Western Roman Empire fell.

During Benedict's first stint as an abbot, he regulated the lives of the monks under him so harshly that they tried to poison him just to get rid of him. After fleeing his abbey, Benedict learned that people needed satisfying physical and intellectual work, on a reasonably paced schedule, in order to function properly. While Christians needed to take sin seriously, the image and gifts of God bestowed on our redeemed humanity required cultivation. Benedict repented from being a hard case that redefined freedom as slavery, and beat rather fed the sheep. His repentance came out more as a "work in progress" over the remainder of his life, but that's likely true of us also in most things.

After beginning to learn from his mistakes, Benedict wrote his *Rule*, which became the prototype for almost all monastic communities since. It may read harshly to us in parts, but it also comes across as remarkably tender in some of the most surprising places. It gave the monks daily time for projects of personal interest, to develop the gifts God gave them. This allowed a healthy individuality that focused on service, but still forbade selfishness. Some of Benedict's harsher regulations were likely necessary, given the times. A literate civilization had crumbled, leaving illiterate tribal gangs to scuffle for turf in its ruins.

The abbeys of Benedict, and other monastics in the West, also served as fortresses to protect faith and knowledge from the chaos outside the walls. God may call Christians to do this again, in larger scale, should our hope of Jesus' return wait another generation or more. Such a hope should never divert energy from preparing following generations to face dark times. While not a scholar, Benedict committed himself to the intellectual life of monks who had such gifts. He saw their value not only as teachers of the Word, but also as preservers of history, literature, and the advance of knowledge. He placed libraries and scriptoriums in all abbeys under his Rule. Benedict encouraged monks of scholarly or artistic nature to study, copy, and preserve the records of more civilized times. We can thank Benedictine monks for preserving not only the writings of the early church, but that of classical antiquity as well. [6]

If Basil and Benedict typified nobility in the monastics, others showed how demonically exploited blind spots could make the truth seem false. The pressures of spiritual leadership—as with any leadership—during chaotic times, are vast. It is easy to get tunnel vision that focuses on some noble goal, or on an essential truth that must not be lost. Other principles quietly take a back seat at such times—principles that may be just as essential for the long term, but in ways that are not quite so apparent. Fast-moving events can leave leaders focused on firefighting against the short-term tyranny of the urgent. In times like these, Satan more easily exploits the worldview blind spots of Christians. Even the godliest people, when forced to think and move too quickly, for too long, miss important details going on around them.

Whether we look at the Christian emperors, the popes and patriarchs of major churches, or the new monastic leaders, the late 4th through middle 6th centuries fit this profile. The infused principles of Christianity late in Roman history delayed the collapse of the Empire. It gave it two more centuries to the West, and almost ten to the East. Nevertheless, the Christian emperors had co-opted the Faith into a decaying system. Greco-Roman society had never fully abandoned its old principles to let the Judeo-Christian worldview become a new foundation. Perhaps it never could. A biblically consistent worldview itself is transcultural, not a mere add-on. It is too large to limit itself to any one human system. Jesus said that His kingdom was not of this world. Roman culture, by contrast, was the epitome of this world.

Even in its Christianized form, almost half the population of the Roman Empire remained Pagan. Many Christians had taken Pagan views and practices into their Christianity with them. Church leaders faced a world system that had co-opted the church almost as much as the church had moderated Rome. Now the corruption grew systemic. At best, only a few began to grasp the enormity of what confronted them, and then only as "through a glass darkly" (1 Cor. 13:12). None grasped it with the 20/20 biblical hindsight that Christians could only develop after the Reformation. Nor was Paganism the biggest problem here. The declining integrity of orthodoxy was. It would be, off and on, for the rest of history.

After jumping back in time to Antony the Hermit, and then ahead to Benedict, let us return to 431 AD, before Rome's fall in the West, to the Council of Ephesus. In contrast to Basil, an Egyptian monastic, named Schnoudi, pressed his nose onto the stage of history as a troublemaker. Schnoudi had all of Pachomius' militancy but none of the wisdom. This bizarre fanatic and his followers, although orthodox in their doctrine, terrorized the Egyptian countryside. They came across as an army of mad monks, bent on enforcing orthodoxy by mob violence. When Schnoudi's henchmen murdered a Pagan woman philosopher in Alexandria, even the civil authorities feared to get involved.

Schnoudi was at the Council of Ephesus, which Cyril, Pope of Alexandria, used as a weapon in his power struggle against the Patriarchy of Constantinople. Nestorius' heresy gave Cyril opportunity to kill two birds with one stone. It seemed that popes of Rome were not the only popes to feel insecure about the rise of Constantinople. For this reason, Cyril often went too far, despite his doctrinally correct conclusions on Christ's nature, which the council also reached. He convicted Nestorius on evidence, but also went after people who had any past with the erring Patriarch. He defamed Nestorius' teacher, Theodore of Mopsuestia (by then, deceased), on little more than association. The venerable Eastern evangelist, John Chrysostom, with other bishops who had known Theodore, defended his orthodoxy.

Theodore should interest us because he pioneered a grammatical-historical exegesis of Scripture a thousand years before the Reformation. ***Exegesis*** means to "draw meaning from a text," as opposed to reading ideas into it. He also wrote against the Arian, Apollinarian, and Pelagian heresies (we will cover Pelagianism in Ch. 8). For these reasons, historians doubt that Theodore shared his student's heresy. [7] Time and logic would prove historical-grammatical exegesis the most honest method for interpreting the Bible. Many would later call this the normative literal interpretation. *Normative* simply means we understand words literally in a normal sense; according to the text's theme and historical-grammatical context; where we allow history to be history, poetry to be poetry, and see allegory as allegory, and so on.

Cyril seemed to read Nestorius' heresy back into Theodore's writings, as if on a witch-hunt for other heresies. Other bishops then followed his lead. Theodore had wrestled with semantics, trying to develop precise terms to clarify for Greek thinkers how Christ's Divine and human natures meshed. This idea still sounded like a contradiction to the Greek mindset. [8] Imagine the difficulty many might face today if they had to study only from Scripture translations made in 1500s English. Also, imagine that the issues dealt with something which, although agreed to (that Christ was fully God and fully human); still felt like a contradiction due to entrenched worldview assumptions that nobody yet realized were only assumptions.

Worldview blind spots often "go without saying," which means they can be hard to notice from inside the culture that has them. It is what puts the whole *blind* thing into a *blind spot*. The Holy Spirit is always able to shine light on them, but that does not mean He always does so, or that when He does, He always does so quickly. He might want men to explore certain things by a guided "trial and error" process so that deeper understanding increases along the way. Nothing quite deepens understanding like learning from painful mistakes. It can take generations to work through such things.

Whether Theodore was mistaken in some of his speculations is not the point. The point is that people need space to explore and discover. Fear of having any offhand comment turned around and treated like a major conviction or doctrine chills the learning atmosphere. Liars can warp any man's honest attempt to deal with a biblical issue by misusing his words. Others may then find it easier to mischaracterize the honest man by lumping him in with the liar, rather than deal with what he actually said, in its context. Who speaks "idle words" (Matt. 12:36), one who tries a few speculations to explore a difficult Scripture, or those too impatient for that, who carelessly slander him? Many historians think that Theodore, at worst, had some of his terms misused by Nestorius.

If Cyril was the prototype master inquisitor, his leading hit man expressed things more physically. Schnoudi distinguished himself by hurling a huge codex book at Nestorius, to silence him, after the council called upon Nestorius to defend himself. [9] Worse, Cyril behaved as if this was appropriate procedure.

There seemed to be a "henchmen mentality" embedded in Egyptian monasticism from early on. Pope Cyril used his "hospital deacons" as a private army against heretics, Pagans, and even other orthodox. They still kept their day jobs running the hospital, though the night work made for a church culture that had become a tad schizoid. Athanasius, generations before, had also stooped to this kind of thing to a lesser degree, early in his career. He matured out of it, unlike later Popes of Alexandria—like Cyril and Dioscorus—who expanded the practice. Schnoudi's antics, likewise, molded the following generation.

This undercurrent makes it easier to see how the climax of the Christology Controversies, though reinforcing biblical truth on Christ's nature; also led to the eventual breakdown and isolation of the Church at Alexandria. For just as Athanasius had his Apollinaris, so Cyril had his own reckless young fan riding "the pendulum's" next devastating swing.

## The Council of Chalcedon

The Mafia godfather-like Pope Cyril fostered a bad atmosphere at the Council of Ephesus. His behavior at times seemed that of a paranoid don wanting extra insurance that everyone would reach the correct conclusions. Trying to rig the game is never a good idea, even when the stakes are high, as unfolding events would soon prove. The council rightly rejected Nestorius' unnatural division of Christ's personality, but it did not need coercion to do that. By the grace of God, bishops drew logical conclusions; something faith-filled reason could have done without extra "help" from Cyril, and definitely without any from Schnoudi.

As anything trying to perfect in the flesh what began in the Spirit, theology at Alexandria now flew not after truth, but toward a new and different error. A repeating pattern in church history surprised me when I first began to notice it. I had expected instability to be the result of false teaching. I found that more often than not, the opposite was true. False teaching was the result of instability. We fight a spiritual war, but the battlefield is intellectual, emotional, and moral. The results of the Council of Ephesus are an example of this pattern in action. The Orthodox Pope of Alexandria, despite his leadership style, also performed many good works. I cannot say with certainty that he is not among the elect. It would be especially foolish of me to say it without certainty. His strong-arm tactics involved misapplying Scriptures about zeal, which helped create instability. That we can say! (Matt. 11:12)

False prophets seem more believable to people after genuine, or at least doctrinally orthodox, believers do stuff like this in a big way. Nestorius the heretic came off looking like the martyr. Many bishops followed in smearing an orthodox Theodore, which was a disaster to more than just a man's reputation. Theodore wrote on interpreting Scripture in its grammatical and historical context a thousand years before the Reformation! One can hardly imagine the positive influence of God's word on church and general culture had his school been allowed to develop. Instead, Theodore's writings stayed in near obscurity, despite reliable defenses from those who knew him. Worse, the approaching new deviance lurked with open arms at the opposite end of the pendulum's arc from Nestorius. Instability had ripened, as the Church at Alexandria zealously coddled it.

Soon after the First Council of Ephesus, a student of Cyril's, Eutychus, began teaching an idea that sounded like it might have dripped from the lyric of some modern praise song. (I like most modern praise music, but I have also noticed too much of it that has too little content and too much repetition; as if worship was supposed to create an altered state of consciousness.) Eutychus taught that although Christ has two natures, Divine and human, His human one was *"absorbed by the Divine as a drop of honey is dissolved in an ocean."* [10]

It sounded poetic, even infused with a heart of worship. The problem was it unraveled the very fabric of biblical theology about Christ. In Eutychus' thinking, human and Divine natures came together to form something else, which was "uniquely Christ." Theologians call this the ***Monophysite Heresy***; *mono* meaning *one* and *physite* (we get *physical* from the same root) meant *the nature of something*.

This was the extreme opposite of Nestorius' heresy, and far more of a problem. It made Christ neither God nor man anymore, but something altogether different, once one carried it out to its logical conclusion. Like the other purveyors of half-baked teachings, Eutychus failed to consider the implications of his own ideas. Patriarch Flavian of Constantinople saw where this teaching would lead, however, and called on Eutychus to repent from it. When Eutychus refused, Flavian deposed him as a heretic.

When Cyril, Pope of Alexandria died, one of his main cronies succeeded him—a rather oily character named Dioscorus. His name sounds like some sort of noxious skin condition, but his thinking and behavior were even worse. At least Cyril had put his conniving nature to work in the cause of a scripturally supportable truth. Dioscorus was about to do so for a warped man with a warped idea. Eutychus secured the Alexandrian Pope's support, who wheedled Emperor Theodosius II into calling a new universal church council. This synod also met at Ephesus, in 449 AD, but it would not go as the others before it had.

Serious problems came with redefining Christ into a new class of being, even under the pretense of worshipping Christ's "uniqueness." Pope Leo the Great saw these problems, and sent a delegation from Rome with a doctrinal paper siding with Patriarch Flavian. The council ignored Leo's emissaries, and refused his letter. Pope Dioscorus had flooded the place with his rowdy henchmen, each a spiritual clone of Schnoudi. The Second Council of Ephesus restored Eutychus and condemned Flavian. Not content with that, the fanatical mob then beat Patriarch Flavian to death.

Leo the Great, the newly elected Pope of Rome, was righteously outraged, and referred to this council as *"The Robber Synod."* He refused to recognize its doctrinal decisions in favor of Eutychus. With the Patriarch of Constantinople dead at the hands of Pope Dioscorus, Pope Leo stood virtually alone. He was the only major bishop left capable of keeping the lie that had consumed the Alexandrian Church from spreading to all the others. With Flavian gone, the Monophysites quickly penetrated churches as far away as Armenia and Syria. Leo also faced down another catastrophic threat. The Empire was collapsing in the West.

If ever Christians needed a "But God…" moment, this was it.

God providentially thwarted Pope Dioscorus and Eutychus—a pair that deserved each other. Eutychus soon proved too unstable even for Dioscorus, who deposed him as a heretic over another issue. Alexandria's Pope then nonsensically continued to teach the Monophysite Heresy even after he had sacked its source!

God also intervened, soon after the Robber Synod, in another way. Theodosius II died in a horse-riding accident. The more even-handed Marcian became Emperor in his place. This gave Pope Leo's emissaries a fair hearing. Marcian called a new council, across the channel from Constantinople, at the tiny Bosporus villa of Chalcedon.

The Council of Chalcedon in 451 AD did many things, not the least of which was to vindicate Pope Leo the Great doctrinally. It rejected Eutychus and the Monophysite Heresy, and stripped Dioscorus of his office. Unfortunately, this Heresy had already devoured the Coptic Church, as well as many in Armenia and Syria. Several more councils over the next few centuries tried to reconcile the Monophysites. Yet these merely offered strained and illogical compromises on an issue that proved too important for ambiguity: Christ's nature.

New Testament Scripture calls both Christ and the Apostles the Church's foundation. (1 Cor. 3:10-12, Eph. 2:20) We can compare the Ante-Nicene Fathers and the Trinitarian and Christology Universal Councils to reinforced bottom floors. Subsequent "universal" councils became less universal in practice. Chalcedon gave us a concise definition of Christ's nature that finally fit all the biblical data. After Chalcedon, one could state orthodox truth about the Savior thusly; *Christ is fully human, fully divine, and fully a single person, with his Divine and human natures still fully intact.*

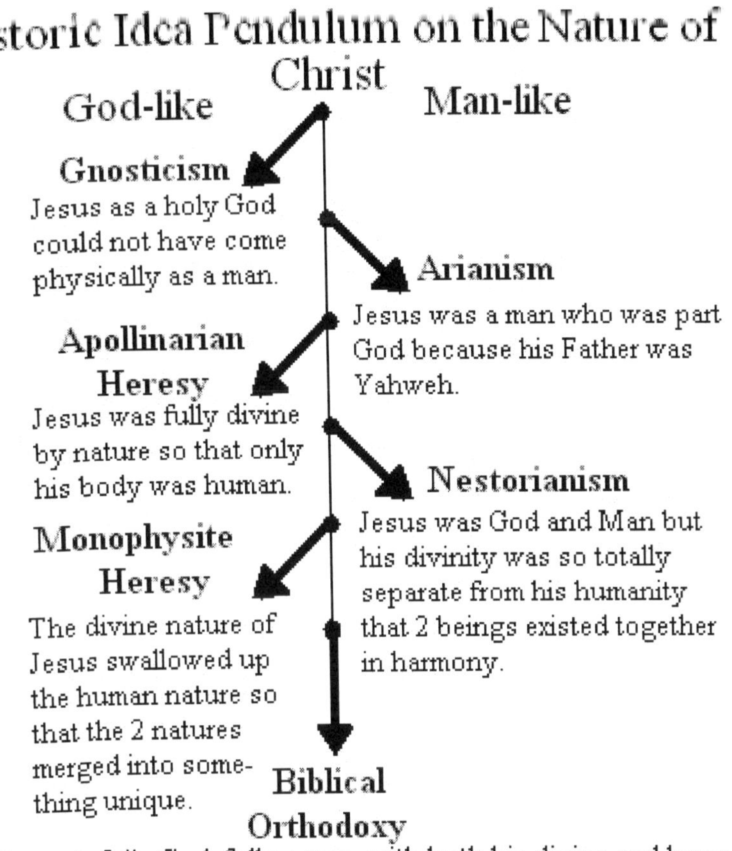


So popular was Pope Leo's doctrinal clarity—sent by emissaries—that both Easterners and Westerners said, *"Yes. This is the faith of the Fathers. Peter has spoken through Leo."* [11] Roman Catholics point to this statement as if it proved the entire church had once recognized the Pope of Rome's universal primacy. Yet if that were so, all of this would have been a moot point, and the Council of Chalcedon would have been equally clear in its second-most important ruling. Indeed, the ruling would have been unnecessary. This canon defined the structure of church leadership after the isolation of the Monophysite Alexandrian church.

The Popes of both Rome and Alexandria had watched with alarm the growing power of the Patriarchy of Constantinople since the imperial capital had moved there. It is easy to see, based on events like the Robber Synod, why God might have favored the papacy of Rome over that of Alexandria at this time. The council delegates were glad for Leo's doctrinal clarity at a time that needed clarity. Also by now, so many political rifts existed between bishops that speech at councils often came laced with flattery to ease rival tempers. Put simply, the bishops often buttered each other up to get what they wanted from each other.

In the case of Pope Leo and the Council of Chalcedon, the bishops loved Leo's refutation of the Monophysites. Nevertheless, many took serious issue with Rome's emerging ideas on its own role in church leadership. The second-most important ruling of the Council of Chalcedon made the Patriarch of Constantinople and Pope of Rome equals in authority. The Patriarch had jurisdiction over the Eastern Church and Rome's Pope over the West.

The church of Antioch had suffered many divisions in the last century. Stubborn Monophysite leadership had hopelessly estranged the Coptic Church from the rest of Christianity. This eliminated the influence of the Popes of Antioch and Alexandria in the Church-at-large. The Pope of Jerusalem had been an honorary office that had never had much influence.

While Leo rejected *Canon 28* of Chalcedon, which rendered this decision, most of the church ratified it.

> *The fathers rightly accorded prerogatives to the see of older Rome, since that is an imperial city; and moved by the same purpose the 150 most devout bishops apportioned equal prerogatives to the most holy see of new Rome, reasonably judging that the city which is honored by the imperial power and senate and enjoying privileges equaling older imperial Rome, should also be elevated to her level in ecclesiastical affairs and take second place after her. –Chalcedon Canon 28*

While vindicating Leo doctrinally on the nature of Christ, Chalcedon did not side with him in terms of the Roman Church's leadership ambitions. For while the East remained relatively stable, the empire was crumbling the West.

It was Pope Leo's intention to build a spiritual empire in its place that would not crumble.

## BIBLIOGRAPHY


1. Shelley, Bruce L. ***Church History in Plain Language*** (2nd Edition), p.112, 1995, Word Publishing, Dallas, Tx.
2. Smith, M.A. ***The Church Under Siege***, p. 22 & p. 77, 1976, Inter-Varsity Press, Leicester, England, and Stevenson, J. ***Creeds, Councils and Controversies***, pp. 86-87, 1966, SPCK, for a contemporary account of the incident given by Ammianus Marcellinus. See also, Kelly, J. N. D., *The Oxford Dictionary of Popes*. USA: Oxford University Press, (1989). pp. 32, 34.
3. Vincent Carroll and David Shiflett, *Christianity on Trial: Arguments Against Anti-Religious Bigotry* is a fair, detailed, and well-sourced analysis on the subject. While Carroll and Shiflett do not shy away from the ugly sides of monasticism—or any other part of church history—they show how the positives far outweighed the negatives.)
4. Op cit. Smith, M.A., pp. 99-101
5. Ibid. pp. 103-105
6. Baur, on ***Chrysostom, Theodore of Mopsuestia;*** *The Catholic Encyclopedia*. Vol. 14. New York: Robert Appleton Company, 1912. 18 Apr. 2014, *<http://www.newadvent.org/cathen/14571b.htm>*
7. Cyril of Alexandria, ***Second Book Against the Words of Theodore***, (Translated by P. E. Pusey)
8. Op cit. Smith, M.A., pp. 115-116
9. Ibid. pp. 122-123
10. Op cit. Shelley, Bruce L., pp.113-114.
11. Labbe and Cossart, ***Concilia***, Tom. IV, col. 562, *The Fourth Ecumenical Council, The Council Of Chalcedon*, A.D. 451, *The Definition Of Faith Of The Council Of Chalcedon. And Notes;* See also, Shelley, Bruce L., ***Church History in Plain Language*** (2nd Edition), pp. 138-139, 1995, Word Publishing, Dallas, Tx.

# 8

# The Rise of the Roman Papacy in the Fall of the Western Roman Empire

## A Star Rises as a Nation Falls

Many Protestant and Eastern Orthodox scholars consider Leo the Great the first Roman Catholic Pope, by the definition used during the rest of church history. Roman Catholics disagree vehemently. Actually, there is a sense in which Leo was the first real Pope, by any substantial post-Roman Empire definition. There is also another sense in which the Roman Papacy had incubated for centuries. Its embryo had formed around bones of expedience, using tissues of popular custom. We cannot be accurate by describing it as if it had just exploded onto the scene with Leo.

The apostolic succession principle took hold early in the 2nd century, to ensure smooth flow of authority to new generations of bishops. By the end of that century, people called the bishops of large metropolitan areas like Rome, Antioch, and Alexandria *popes*. About a century and a half after that, the Bishop of Rome in particular became an arbiter of disputes between other churches. This status seemed associated with Rome's distinction as the imperial city.

*Canon 28 of Chalcedon* reveals that the other churches saw the Popes of Rome in this way because of the city's secular imperial status. Popular legends about Peter being Rome's first bishop held little weight beyond the city of Rome. No one disputed that Peter died there, and had influenced that church. It just did not seem evident that this was the reason for Rome's special place in the reckoning of the rest of the churches.

The Gospels did not objectively teach Peter's primacy over the other Apostles. They certainly did not teach that this unique primacy was transferrable to future generations. It is, however, likely that the idea had blossomed in the minds of local Roman Christians well before the 5th century, who read that meaning into the texts.

Near the end of the 2nd century, Pope Victor tried to excommunicate several Eastern churches that disagreed with him over when to celebrate Easter. These excommunications had no effect beyond the environs of the city of Rome. Time went on, and despite Victor's arrogance, the reputation of the Church at Rome, in general, remained excellent. Then something very important changed. Constantine moved the capital of the empire east, to Constantinople, and the city of Rome began losing its former prestige.

This had bad political ramifications for the Popes of Rome.

By 366 AD, we saw how Pope Damasus opportunistically attained his *see*. It took no great insight to notice the power of the Roman Pope shrinking, along with the city of Rome's political prominence. Damasus responded by developing a theological pretense for a Roman Church primacy unattached to Rome's secular political fortunes. Yet even in Damasus' day, the city of Rome still enjoyed relative prosperity, even if people knew it as a fading glory. The city still had distinction as the capital of the Western Empire.

Pope Damasus distinguished himself as a shrewd politician, and a canny manipulator, who could read the writing on the wall. He saw the natural progression of things better than most. Since Constantinople became the new imperial seat, the Patriarch of Constantinople had taken on growing prominence that would soon outstrip that of the other popes. The Patriarchy could trace its apostolic succession back through the Pope of Antioch and Bishop of Ephesus, to the Apostles Paul and John, at least as clearly as Rome could to Peter.

Eastern Orthodoxy still claims today that their line of apostolic succession is clearer and less bumpy historically than Rome's. It often seems though that a little less rides on the matter for them than for Roman Catholicism. Damasus based his claims on the popular local folk legend that Peter was the first Bishop of Rome. He looked to a provincially colored slant on the Gospel of Matthew for a biblical pretext. [1] Of course, folklore tends to exaggerate things. It is doubtful that Peter could have been the first Bishop of Rome simply because the Church at Rome long pre-existed his arrival there at the end of his life.

Paul's Epistle to the Romans lists the church's elders in its salutation, along with many other people known to him personally. Peter's name is conspicuous by its absence. Someone pastored the church, likely Linus, whom Irenaeus, in the middle 2nd century, listed as the church's first bishop. Since Peter had not arrived in Rome as of the time Paul wrote Romans—a letter to an already established church—it is most unlikely that he could have been the bishop.

Even church tradition does not place Peter at Rome until after the second incarceration of Paul there. At best, Peter may have given some personal apostolic instructions to the elders at Rome in the brief time before he, too, was martyred. He likely also confirmed Linus as bishop there just before his death. Roman Catholics consider Linus to be the 2nd Pope. He appears in the greeting at the end of 2 Timothy, written from Rome just before Paul's martyrdom, but before Peter's arrival. Irenaeus also mentions that Peter appointed him as bishop to the Roman church. [2]

Roman Christians seemed to have sentimentally made Peter their shepherd. Nobody else in the churches all over the empire saw this as a universal authority given to the Bishop of Rome over all other churches, however. No records speak of such an office, and the conduct of the early church councils shows no recognition of a universal pontiff. The idea, like many in history, seems to have grown from small beginnings, and fought its way up the ideological food chain, sometimes, regrettably, with "tooth and claw."

Pope Damasus was too much the political climber for the whole church to take him too seriously, though his writings show he took himself that way. Leo the Great, successor of Damasus a few generations removed, was not so easy to dismiss. A theological genius of higher character than his tomb-adorning forerunner, Leo earned a respect almost fit for what Damasus had concocted. If Damasus contrived a theological pretense for Roman primacy, Leo first applied it on a sweeping scale. God even seemed to bless it at the time.

To be fair, Leo lived in an era of much greater need, and had far better leadership motives than Damasus. The Western Roman Empire had reached a state of imminent collapse. As interdependent with the state as the church had become, Leo faced the prospect of having Western Christianity collapse along with it.

We can hardly conceive the immediate pressures this Pope faced on a personal and administrative level. Barbarian invaders swept through the West. Leo could not attend the Council of Chalcedon because Attila the Hun was bearing down on Rome. What little government remained operated out of Ravenna, in the North. Leo rallied both the church and a Roman people deserted by their civil government. He went out with a small procession of priests to meet Attila near the Po River, where he convinced the barbarian chieftain to turn back.

Actually, Attila had force-marched his army too far, stretching his supply line past sane limits. Many of his men were sick. Leo pleaded before a warlord who was already more than half convinced that he had to turn back anyway. Still, think of how it must have looked to the citizens of Rome, who knew nothing of Attila's logistical problems! It seemed that Leo had just performed a miracle! Nor was it exaggerating to say that God had worked providentially in Leo's favor to preserve Western Christianity.

Our prosperous American Christianity has little clue of what those times must have been like for a church leader in Leo's position. Rome, as a civilization, was in many ways a prototype of our own. Western Europe and the Americas grew within a Roman form of law and culture on many levels. American pastors may soon experience a civilization-wide crisis with similarities to Leo's trial. Even if not, it is still instructive to place ourselves in Leo's toga to understand his times.

Pretend that North Korea and Iran detonated a coordinated high altitude nuclear electromagnetic pulse (EMP) strike, 300 miles over the western and eastern USA. The strike kills nobody and destroys nothing immediately. Instead, the EMP fuses almost every electronic device on the continent. First responders can't respond because emergency vehicles won't start. The economy collapses in a way that makes the 2008 crash look tame. Imagine that police and military become like those in Russia a few years back, unpaid for more than a year during a time of triple-digit inflation. Add to that the terror of 9-11 multiplied by a thousand. Even more, a top-heavy government bureaucracy flounders; so cut off from the real world in its policy-making that effective responses become impossible, even once replacement computers come on line.

With the unpaid military spread too thin, engaged in multiple foreign wars, order breaks down at home. Well-armed street gangs and Jihadist cells, with their own ready-made social infrastructures, rove the cities and countryside as modern techno-barbarian hordes. Gangs seize control of several major urban centers, and militias, large tracks of rural land. Starvation, riots, and terror attacks grow rampant. Plague churns in the wake of the breakdown of technology-dependent, bureaucratically dysfunctional medical systems. Mutiny in the military and police, with other apocalyptic nightmares, ravage what was once the most powerful civilization on Earth. Imagine that, and we can begin to grasp the emotional equivalent of what Pope Leo faced on a less sophisticated scale. We might even begin to understand why succeeding generations called him "the Great."

Not long after Attila, Gaiseric and the Vandals also sacked Rome. We get our word *vandalism* from the name of this Germanic tribe. They came into city after city, looting, burning, pillaging, and destroying everything in their path, as they raped women and took slaves. Terror went before the Vandals, and stripped, smoking cities languished in their wake. Rather than face Gaiseric, the last Western Emperor tried to abandon Rome, only to get himself trampled to death by his own panicking soldiers.

Again, Pope Leo stepped out to act as a negotiator. (This was actually Rome's third sacking, but the first, by Alaric the Visigoth, had happened a little before Leo's time.) When the Pope finished pleading for Rome's people, Gaiseric agreed to fourteen days of looting only, with no burnings, and no rapes of anyone taking shelter inside a church. The Vandal chieftain, being an Arian, had a respect of sorts for churches, and left most of these un-pillaged, as well. Afterward, Rome had parades in the streets to celebrate their deliverance with newfound humility and gratitude. Could any American city do the same under those conditions?

We may find out.

Civilization in the West had fallen far. The systems of education and trade unraveled, as people returned to mere subsistence living. The imperial government at Ravenna, such as it was, conferred on Pope Leo such civil powers as they could still enforce. It compelled all bishops in the Western churches to submit to Leo's authority in hope that some form of government might be preserved. To reinforce his position, Leo magnified the canon of the chaotic Council of Sardica, which had granted the Bishop of Rome status to judge in local church disputes. He tried to pass it off as a decision made at the more universally recognized Council of Nicea. While many churchmen saw through this, the dire situation in the West insured that there was little dissent. The Council of Chalcedon also cemented this with Canon 28.

This new papal power first flexed its muscles when Leo went over the head of Hilary, Bishop of Arles. The Pope reinstated certain unruly bishops, whom Hilary had deposed, after those bishops appealed to Rome. Hilary claimed that Leo had exceeded his authority; that the traditional Metropolitan Bishop over Gaul (where Arles was the major city) had corrective authority over his own flock. Sadly, for Hilary, historical gravity from a falling civilization, and a rising star, flowed in the direction of bolstering the Roman Papacy. Despite all that followed in later centuries, this outcome likely did the least amount of damage at an unstable time in an imperfect world. [3]

Leo faced the collapse of a society with Christianity as its formal state cult, which still had a large population of pagans. Pagans did not just suddenly go away. Leo hoped to reach these for Christ by demonstrating how Christianity had power to keep order by nonviolent means. The contrast of how Pagan (not to mention Christianized) Rome kept power was still a fresh enough violent memory to make his point. One may question some of his solutions, several of which set the stage for later problems. Yet, it is doubtful, faced with similar circumstances, if Leo's critics—ancient or modern—could have done much better. History is not what either Protestant anti-Papist or Roman Catholic polemics say it is. The issues of the most recent five centuries were not the issues of Leo's day.

For generations before Leo, the Bishops of Rome had feared and fought growing civil disorder in the West. This meant keeping civil order between Pagans and Christians, both major groups of which had smaller subgroups, each with varied agendas. One can argue fairly that "keeping civil order" was not the church's job. Under normal conditions, that is true. Pope Leo did not face normal conditions. Nobody else was going to do it, and the price of abandoning civil order was too high for any sane person to contemplate.

The fact that some of Leo's solutions grew from wrong assumptions, and produced bad consequences, centuries later, makes him no different from any of us. Speaking as an Evangelical Christian unwilling to sacrifice truth for a warm fuzzy ecumenical feeling, I will go on record. Some of our popular "solutions" are likely to go sour much more quickly than Leo's did, and far more predictably, based on what is knowable to us right now. This will become more apparent when we cover the 20th century and beyond.

Pope Leo's main solution made wider practical use of the Pagan title *Pontifex Maximus*, which meant "High Bridge-Builder Priest of the Imperial Cult." He did not establish the association of that title with the Papacy, however. Over seventy years before, Pope Damasus had accepted the title *Pontifex Maximus*, when the Emperor had offered it to him. Before that, the Emperor had been the *Pontifex Maximus*. Other Christians had sarcastically called two Roman popes by this title prior to then, after those popes had behaved imperiously. No surprise, they were Popes Calistus and Victor. Christians only formally applied the title to the Bishops of Rome after Damasus, but it did not carry more than honorary force until Leo.

Pope Damasus came by the title after the Emperor, Gratian, disowned it because of its strong Pagan connotation. [4] Gratian possibly understood that a Christian state cult must operate differently from a Pagan one. He abolished state funding of the imperial cult at this time. Gratian then faced a precursor to what Leo eventually faced full-blown, once the ability to enforce order collapsed. Pagans still made up a sizable portion of the population during both times, but Gratian had no fear of total collapse, just riots in the city of Rome. As a compromise, he offered the office of *Pontifex Maximus* to Pope Damasus. This Pope seemed to think the church could simply absorb the old Pagan forms and rites of the state cult, and perhaps sanctify them.

In reality, however, use of new forms actually shapes the substance. The effect may be great or negligible, but there is an effect. The medium that a message comes to us in can profoundly affect—even change—the message itself. One can endlessly speculate on Leo's reasons for boosting his title of *Pontifex Maximus*, and arrive at theories both pragmatic and sinister. There were likely a mixture of reasons, some defensible on "a lesser of several evils, to keep order" basis, others less so.

On the practical side, the imperial government gave a vast amount of civil authority to Leo. It only made sense for him to assure the public that he had a legitimate claim to that kind of authority, beyond a panicking emperor's whim. It is also possible that, by this time, the title *Pontifex Maximus* was largely a relic term of an earlier era. Many Christians of the day may even have seen it as a sign that Christ had now conquered the core of the very imperial cult that had once persecuted His sheep.

On the shadier side, it was still only a little over a century after the dawn of state enforced Christianity. People also still spoke Latin. Likely, some "Christianized" Pagan holdouts needed to be pacified to keep them from reverting to open Paganism. This would break the West culturally, as well as politically. It reinforces the hypothesis that Leo faced a "lesser of two evils" scenario. The Pope had to keep the church together. A glaring logical problem existed with this tactic, however—one that would take centuries to unfold.

Use of the title *Pontifex Maximus* made Leo as much a successor to the Pagan Caesars as it did to any of the previous Bishops of Rome. It is clear from his writings that Leo really believed the title was his right, arising as he did out of a Christian Roman Empire. Roman Catholic Popes have kept it ever since. The title illustrates the distinction between a previous universal *Catholic* Christianity, and the *Roman* Catholicism rising in the West.

A sticky question remains. Why should temporal political power from a dying earthly government be a basis for universal spiritual authority? Likely, people did not yet know to make a distinction between spiritual and earthly authority. Those categories just did not occur to them sharply, as they do to us today. History, gradual and sometimes dark, still had many lessons to teach the Christian West. Many of them would be harsh.

## AUGUSTINE: LAST LIGHT OF THE FADING ROMAN WEST

Shortly before Leo's Papacy, an African bishop watched the collapse of imperial government with a troubled spirit and agile mind. This pastor would leave his mark indelibly on Christian thought and culture. He shaped how Western Civilization would view philosophy, the human condition, banking, theology, even the waging of war.

Aurelius Augustinus—better known to us as Augustine of Hippo—welcomed refugees off the swamped and overloaded ships from pillaged Rome. His proved one of the greatest theological minds of the age. Reformation-based or *Protestant* Christians appeal to Augustine as the classical teacher of salvation by grace alone through faith. Roman Catholics revere him for teaching that the church should have a visible universal earthly leadership system. More than anything else, Augustine put the fall of the Western Empire into theological context. [5]

Rome's fall shocked Augustine's generation because it seemed so implausible to them. In many ways, it reminds me of America's failure to grasp the fragility of our own, far more complex, society. The very things sustaining the earthly power of both civilizations became the means that hastened their end. The worldview of Augustine and Leo's generation also had a religious dimension to it that made collapse unthinkable. This, too, resembles America.

Imagine a continuation of the scenario I described earlier, where North Korea launched a successful EMP strike. The detonation did no damage on the ground; it simply fried every electronic device. Coordinated terrorist attacks then set off crude suitcase-sized radioactive dirty bombs, crippling major East Coast and Central US cities. This all happens by rather low-tech means. Radiation sickness, famine, gang wars, government collapse, and sporadic martial law follow. No power, no cars, no public transit, no food—this is a disaster on a scale that many Christians did not imagine could come until after the ***Rapture,*** before the Great Tribulation of Bible prophecy; yet the Christians are still around! This gives an idea how Roman Christians felt in the Western Empire, only their event was smaller scale.

Popular allegorical interpretation of the Book of Revelation since Constantine's day had left believers unprepared for what they saw. For well over a century, priests had taught believers that the Christian Empire was Christ's Millennial Kingdom on earth! The church historian, Eusebius of Caesarea, had zealously promoted this view. Most church teachers now viewed those few who still believed that the Millennium came only after Christ's bodily return as heretics. They called this "literalist heresy" ***Chiliasm,*** and saw it as a crass belief held only by the philosophically ignorant. It seemed that Papias, the faithful student of the Apostle John, had become "crass and ignorant" to the Greek philosophy-leavened church scholars of the day. People went just as wrong by overcomplicating things as by oversimplifying them.

Eusebius' prophetic school seemed to hold up, if one did not analyze life or Scripture too closely—until the Western Empire collapsed. Then Alaric the Visigoth sacked Rome. The city of Rome had stood militarily untouched by enemies for over six centuries. Many Christians viewed it now as the new "City of God." This shook Roman faith comparably to if Fundamentalist Christians suffered nuclear war, famine, and social collapse before the Rapture; potentials that would not disrupt a "Pre-Tribulation" view of Bible prophecy, by the way. (I write from a "Pre-Trib" view.) Such was the seductiveness and comfort of both Roman and American civilization.

Augustine saw the dangers of uniting too closely the fortunes of the church with Rome. By contrast, the church had become a mere tool of the state in the East. The two realms had become so intertwined there that evangelism beyond the empire became all but impossible. Neighboring Pagan tribes saw through the politics of this relationship. It had even become hard for Easterners to imagine a Christianity without the empire to keep it socially erect.

A century after Augustine, the Eastern Emperor Justinian planned a society with church and state so intermeshed that the distinction almost dissolved. Justinian built the fabulous Hagia Sophia or "Church of Holy Wisdom" at Constantinople. When outsiders managed to convert, as Bulgar and Muschovite tribes did eventually, it was as much for love of Byzantine opulence as the gospel. While educated grasp of Christian theological concepts lasted longer in the East's upper class, it did so mainly by cultural inertia.

Hard times in the West, for a while, helped cultivate some spiritual revitalization, even if understanding often got lost. The last flower of the West, Augustine wrote a volume of books called *City of God,* warning of the dangers of mistaking Rome, or any earthly city, for God's true city of faith. He pointed out in his sermons that, whereas God destroyed Sodom, He had simply chastised Rome and given opportunity to repent. [6]

*City of God* essentially became the blueprint for Medieval European Civilization, the lens through which it saw history, all the way back to Creation. My education had conditioned me to expect *City of God* would be a hopelessly myopic diatribe. It was anything but. In it, I saw a divinely illuminated mind putting his times into historical perspective. I saw a mind I could relate to and respect. I had expected to find many extremes, and found very few. Those few were mostly in places where Augustine plainly said that he speculated to make a point.

The exercise reaffirmed for me how out-of-touch and dishonest much of today's scholarship and prevailing worldview is. To my on-the-job called and trained pastor friends, I recommend they make Augustine's *City of God* part of their educational reading. It breaks human history down into a fundamental battle between two cities, that of God and that of man. This is not only of profound pastoral import. Augustine also gives detailed historical perspective, citing many ancient sources no longer available to us.

Augustine's other major contributions included writings against three major heresies that, in varied forms, still plague churches today: ***Donatism***, ***Pelagianism***, and ***Semi-Pelagianism***.

*Justinian's Hagia Sophia basilica at Constantinople, modern Istanbul*

## AUGUSTINE VERSUS DONATISM

To understand Donatism, we must skip back to the end of the last universal persecution. In Chapter 4, we saw their origins in North Africa as a schismatic sect reacting against what they wrongly judged as spiritual compromise. Normally, we might be tempted to sympathize; Donatists were generally as orthodox in their theology of Christ as Catholic churches. Unfortunately, by this time, that might not always be the same as saying that they had a genuinely Bible-based view of the Savior.

Donatism was a leftover movement of the church splits after the 3rd Universal Persecution under Diocletian. They felt Catholic churches were too lenient on the lapsed, and refused to recognize bishops ordained by men who had turned over Scripture manuscripts for burning. That may make them sound like a "righteous remnant," but it is important to look at the whole picture before making such determinations. Most of the men who angered them had only turned over copies that were old and falling apart, keeping safe those copies still usable.

Donatism superstitiously worshipped the martyrs and their relics, even by the standards of the time. Not long before Augustine, another African Bishop named Caecilian had corrected a Catholic woman for this. She had habitually kissed the dried-out finger of a dead martyr whenever she took communion. [7] Augustine's main concern over the Donatists was their fanaticism and mob violence.

Unfortunately, Augustine faced another of those "lesser of two evils" choices in this controversy. Before the Donatist Riots, he had always opposed bringing military force to bear on spiritual problems. Of course, once there are riots and terrorism, and innocent people are murdered, and churches burned, the issues cease to be exclusively spiritual. It is always easy to "take the high road" when no blood has been shed. Augustine favored order, and called on the imperial government to send troops to put down the Donatist attacks. Centuries later, the Roman Catholic Church would justify the Inquisition based on Augustine's action, though with less provocation.

As for the real spiritual issues, Donatism forced believers to ask the questions; *what is the true church? Is it only those who have totally kept themselves pure or is it a hospital for sinners needing forgiveness even after conversion and baptism?*

The solution that came at the time, as to the nature of the "true church," in part, proved overly simplistic, but Augustine was not to blame for that. Our questions of today were not their questions. Donatist violence created so tense an atmosphere that our answer of, "those who know Jesus through the gospel," could not sensibly be part of the discussion. It did not seem to be about that. It is unfortunate that the outcome focused more on the religious system people belonged to than on spiritual relationship and transformation. Before we look back on Augustine and the church of his day unfavorably, however, we should ask ourselves a question. *How would it go if a present-day Christian sect that taught superficially correct salvation doctrine started attacking other churches Taliban style?*

We must not indulge the fantasy that such a thing could never happen today or that the issues are always so simple. Augustine responded to the Donatists because of ongoing threats to the lives and property of his flock, not because he wanted to suppress their beliefs by force. This boiled down to a matter of the very rule of law itself.

Each era of church history had its signature issues, which needed addressing in order of the priority presented at the time. We might never have become aware that individual relationship with God was so important, if earlier Christians had not first dealt with other issues. As we slide into desperate times, it is good to remember that most generations of Christians did not have the luxuries afforded us to think things out. Augustine did not exactly leave the foundation of Divine relationship based on grace uncovered. We know this because of how he dealt with the Pelagians.

## AUGUSTINE VERSUS PELAGIANISM

By Augustine's time, Britannic, Gallic, and Irish Celts enjoyed a robust Christianity. Celtic monks like Patrick, Columba (Colm Kille), and Columbanus combed savage-infested ruins of the Western Roman Empire, preaching the gospel. Great abbeys sprang up in Britain and Ireland, such as Llandaff, Iona, Bangor, and Lindesfarne. Here, Christian Celts preserved the intellectual and moral seeds of civilization against the Dark Ages. They saved records not only from early Christianity, but also from classical pre-Christian antiquity. [8]

Some historians like to say today that there really were no "Dark Ages." I get the impression they are thinking only along some narrow technological lines, like weaponry advancements, such as chain mail. I write in terms of a population's ratio of literacy to illiteracy, also law and order, and regional stability. It may be that the Dark Ages were not completely dark, but it is still safe to say they generally were, compared to what went before, and what came after. Exceptions exist for most things.

Some believers today, seeing the rise of Paganism, may belittle Christians for keeping histories of Pagan cultures. These believers might appeal to God's commands to the Israelites to wipe out the practices of Canaan. That would be shortsighted, since history—

even that of evil ideas, people, and events—has value, if only as a cautionary tale. It also ignores the fact that God prefers to operate redemptively, rather than punitively.

There is also a difference between God's work in founding Israel as a nation, and His work in spreading the gospel and making disciples of "all nations." Founding Israel was a work of protective isolation to form a single ethnic identity. Making disciples from all nations adds a spiritually active element. It works out first a personal, then a social redemption for any ethnic identity. One work involved military conquest, the other spreading a message of hope and reconciliation. The same God with the same ethics is doing different works that require different methods of operation. The comparison of the church's work with that of Israel, in this case, is invalid. God called both to be a light to the world in somewhat different ways. That does not make the church and Israel the same.

The Holy Spirit redemptively used the fierce independence of the Celtic worldview to restart the evangelization of a barbarian Europe. Celtic monks thought nothing of travelling great distances in harsh conditions to share the Faith. Those of other cultures often seemed to need more motivation and organized support, due to the collapse of order on the continent. Innovative Celtic art, storytelling, poetry, and music transformed Christian worship and literature; giving it new and vibrant color.

The Romanized Celtic Christians of Britain and Armorica (modern Brittany, France) needed hope and strength to endure the regular raids of Germanic barbarians. Newly converted Irish Celts, farther from the action, offered refuge. Only a generation before, they had been Druidic Pagan marauders known to Britannic and Gallic Celts as the "Sea Wolves." That was, until a captive Britannic slave known to the Irish as Qatrikias returned to his former captors with the gospel of Christ. We remember him as "Saint Patrick."

Roman military protection of Britannium vanished late in the 4$^{th}$ century, after the departure of the legions under Magnus Maximus. Emperor Gratian called Maximus home to quell unrest closer to Rome. A Romanized Celt, Aurelius Ambrosius, then rose under a Christian banner, to fight back invasions into Britain by the Pagan Angli and Saxon. These Germanic tribes had been hired a generation before as mercenaries against the even more savage Scoti and Picti, which were unconverted Celts in the north highlands. Blue woad-painted Picti hordes swooped down on the Christian towns each year from north of Hadrian's Wall. Their topless women fought alongside the men, just as the ancestors of the Christian Celts before their conquest by the Romans. The success of Aurelius Ambrosius lasted only a generation. Many identify either he or his son as the historic King Arthur.

If Celtic independence and initiative gave strength in some ways, it also had its blind spots. Pre-Christian Celtic culture had no understanding of sin in any Semitic sense. They only saw the concept of *sins* as being individual acts of wrongdoing. Of course, it is self-evident that bad choices made in the past affect generations born into the present. It is equally self-evident that everyone, at times, fails to act according to conscience, indicating something defective in our nature. We need strong childhood training to reinforce and obey our consciences. We need no training at all to be dishonest and selfish. That comes naturally. Nevertheless, the idea that we are born with sin by nature, resulting from a past choice made by Adam, was culturally unthinkable to many Celts. This meant they had extra trouble grasping the essential truths of ***Original Sin,*** and the ***Doctrine of the Fall and Genesis Curse***.

Even after centuries of Christianity, Celtic dislike for views of sin fully reflecting Genesis 3 and Romans 8:18-25 hung on. A British monk named Pelagius taught against the doctrine of Original Sin. He believed that men were not sinful through being born with a fallen nature transmitted through the Curse-affected matter of our flesh from Adam. He said people became sinful only after they each individually chose to commit a sin. In some ways, the Celtic worldview was the polar opposite of the Greek one. Celts, like the Hebrews, correctly saw a choice made by a non-material will, other than God's, as the origin of evil. The worldview went wrong by underrating how spiritual evil affects the material realm in ways that can further transmit sin through other material means. They saw sin only in terms of individual choice, and missed how it affected a larger cycle of cause-and-effect.

Just because our material bodies are not innately evil by being material, does not mean they do not transmit and retain evil desires. Nor does it mean that damage done to them by the Curse after Original Sin, and by subsequent sins, does not leave a mark. That mark is a resident nature in our bodies that reinforces a tendency toward sin. New Testament Scripture often calls this the *flesh.* (Rom. 7:7-25, Gal. 5:16-17) God did not originally create Adam's material body with a nature that wanted to sin. That would be unkind and unjust. God is neither of those things. Only after Adam fell, through an act of his own choice, did the desire to rebel against God fester and grow bigger than the unaided human will.

The Genesis text says that God pronounced His creation "Good" before the Curse (Gen 1:4, 10, 12, 18, 21, 25, and 31). God's creation reflected His own good character until Adam sinned, and no longer fit into that environment. God, knowing that this would happen, outfitted His creation from the start with what an engineer might call a "back-up mode." Think of your computer's "safety mode," where some capabilities are closed off to the user because something is wrong. Revelation 13:8 references Christ as **"the Lamb slain from the foundation of the world"** for a reason. God built redemption into the system before saying, **"Let there be light!"** It was His plan all along.

After Adam sinned, death became imminent. He and his descendants could not long survive in a cosmos that consistently reflected God's goodness (Gen. 2:17). A complete view of goodness also includes righteousness and justice. God cursed the cosmos in a judicial response, changing some of its material properties, to make it compatible with Adam's fallen mortal state. Though many of God's attributes are still evident in creation (Rom. 1:18-32), God's goodness and merciful character are not consistently visible in Nature. We need God's word to reveal to us His character. (Gen. 2:12, 2:16-17, 3:14-19 [Note that all the changes of the Curse are material ones], Matt. 6:10, Rom. 8:20-22)

Pelagius assumed there could be no real Genesis Curse. In his mind, a fair God would never punish all humanity for the sin of one man, even the father of humanity. Thus, he also thought men could please God by their own good works, and gain merit toward salvation if they simply chose not to sin. When they sinned, in his view, they could obtain priestly absolution, working off the new debt through penance.

Pelagius taught that the physical death of humans came before Adam's Fall, having been God's design from the beginning. Here, even Augustine had problems. He did not always clearly distinguish between Original Sin (Adam's fall) and the Curse (God's judicial response to Adam's fall). Augustine seemed also at one point to allow for a possibility that physical death might precede the Curse. He occasionally judged supposed allegorical meanings (largely read in to the text) more important than its natural historical implications.

Augustine only did this as a speculation, suggesting that pre-Fall conditions were largely unknowable. Most pre-Curse conditions are unknowable, but not those that are inferable from what the text reveals. Augustine also focused mostly on Adam and Eve's change of moral perception after their Original Sin (Gen. 3:7-12), not on changes God made to the natural world; the Curse in response to that sin (Gen. 3:14-19). The non-Hebrew interpretive assumptions of his day treated Genesis more as an allegory than a historical text. The Hebrew genre of the Book of Genesis is historical narrative. Augustine did better than most, but he was still a man of his times. For instance, he saw no need to think the Curse required outward changes to how the cosmos worked, though Genesis

3:14-19 lists several. This oversight weakened his otherwise ironclad case against Pelagius.

Before we knock Augustine too badly, we should remember why this was. The popular "extended metaphor" view of the Old Testament influenced his thinking because it influenced everyone's thinking, back then. We should also remember that the Old Testament often is an extended metaphor about Christ, *but that is not all it is*. The lazy thinking of a dying civilization often reduced it only to that in the Gentile church, however. Reading *City of God* showed me that Augustine saw the importance of the Old Testament as history far more than most others in his day. That he thought in terms of the unknowability of many *conditions before* the Curse shows that he had a historical concept of the Fall/Curse. It just needed further development. He also had a firm concept of just how much history had passed since creation through what Scripture's historical books revealed on the subject.

> ***They are deceived, too, by those highly mendacious documents which profess to give the history of many thousand years, though, reckoning by the sacred writings, we find that not 6000 years have yet passed.*** **Augustine of Hippo, *City of God*, Book VII, Chapter 10**

Though unlike Jesus and the New Testament writers, Augustine at times underestimated the importance of historical details, he was still on the right track. A Hebrew worldview, displayed in the words of Christ and the Apostles, saw the historical nature of Genesis without dismissing allegorical meanings. Jesus spoke of Adam, Noah, and Lot as real people who lived at real places, in real times. (Mt. 24:37-39, Lk. 3:23-38, 17:26-32, Ro. 5:14, 1 Ti. 2:13-14, He. 11:7, 1 Pe. 3:20, 2 Pe. 2:4-9) Orthodox Christians agreed such figures were real historical men. They just did not always write as clearly as Augustine did on the implications of that. Theodore of Mopsuestia would be an exception; but he and Augustine did not see eye to eye on other issues—one of Theodore's students (not Nestorius) actually supported the Pelagians.

Pelagius was even less consistent about details. To him, any "Genesis Curse" was only about "spiritual death" for people who sinned. He saw little or no cause-and-effect chain reaction in history, where sin affected everything downstream of it. In his mind, one man could not cause another to sin. Augustine argued against this more effectively on the moral side than on the historical one. Genesis also refutes Pelagius, as do the words of Jesus:

> **"But whoever *causes one of these little ones who believe in Me to sin*, it would be better for him if a millstone were hung around his neck, and he were drowned in the depth of the sea. Woe to the world because of offenses! For offenses must come, but woe to that man by whom the offense comes!" *Matthew* 18:6-7 (NKJV)**

Both Augustine and the Pope of Rome condemned the views of Pelagius. In *City of God*, Augustine even saw clearly the logical fallacy of the Greek worldview regarding the nature of evil. This was evident, despite his sometimes odd comments about sexual pleasure even in marriage; likely reactions to his pre-conversion sexual addiction, influenced by the church culture of his day. Both factors prevented him from always carrying his insight to its logical conclusion. [9] Former addicts are often the most susceptible to the temptations of asceticism. They legitimately must abstain from the things to which they were formerly addicted.

Of course, sexuality is a divinely created part of being human, not an artifact of the Curse in itself. It is at least as likely that a sexual addict can find healing in the disciplines of a biblical marriage as in those of celibacy. The testimony of those who have done so bucks much conventional wisdom on the nature of addiction, but God cares squat for our conventional wisdom. Augustine stated the problem with asceticism plainly, even pointing to its Stoic Pagan origins. Defining a problem is always the first step to discovering solutions. Unlike most of the church in his time, Augustine was heading in the right direction.

> ***For the corruption of the body, which is a burden on the soul, is not the cause but the punishment of Adam's first sin.*** **Augustine of Hippo, *City of God*, Book XIV, Ch. 3** [10]
>
> ***Anyone, then, who extols the nature of the soul as the highest good and condemns the nature of the flesh as evil is as carnal in his love for the soul as he is in his hatred for the flesh, because his thoughts flow from human vanity and not from divine Truth.*** **Augustine of Hippo, *City of God*, Book XIV, Ch. 5** [11] (Augustine refers here to the Stoics, and to Christians, like Origen, who accommodated their asceticism too much.)

Though Augustine did not argue the following position completely, underestimating some points, he helped set Christians on the road to seeing God's word more clearly on the subject. We, too, can only "see through a glass darkly," and not "face to face" (1 Cor. 13: 12). This involves the nature of Divine grace and human sin, subjects not isolated only to theology. God has woven them into history in the real world.

What Genesis describes in its first three chapters is the foundation for all that follows in the Bible and human history. How we see it affects the degree of reality with which we see Christ's work of redemption. We live in a time when even much of the church has lost track of the fact that the God of the Bible is the God of reality. If Christians lose track of that, then everything downstream of it, including the gospel, fades in terms of how real it seems to those in the Faith, and to those entering it. This is why what we believe about origins is not just a side issue. It may not be necessary to attaining salvation, but it sure becomes reasonable and important once one enters the Faith.

There is little more real to life than death. Genesis 3 describes physical death (labor pains, frustration in work, thorns, and rotting to dust) as the result of Adam and Eve's disobedience. Modern Progressive Creationists, Theistic Evolutionists, and others who think the Genesis creation days actually represent periods similar to supposed geologic ages; try to appeal to Augustine, in spite of most of what he wrote. They do so because he sometimes took a non-literal view of the creation week in his writings.

Augustine, by rejecting Pelagianism, also excluded much else, if we take that rejection to its logical conclusion. Augustine may not have always done so, but that does not make it a bad idea. Replacing "physical death" with "spiritual death" as Original Sin's only consequence, finds little defense in him. Both deaths are in view. In *City of God*, the two forms of death, though not identical, still had a clear relationship to Original Sin. [12] Augustine, unfortunately, did not always deal with this subject consistently. He often dealt with Genesis as history, as in *City of God*, and at other times as extended metaphor. Likely, he saw it as both.

More attention might have been paid to the Curse as God's prepared response to Adam's Fall, in terms of the material changes it brought, and their nature. This logically ties even the idea of soulish animal death to a historic Curse event that, in some ways, altered how the cosmos functioned. Augustine sometimes seemed unsure if the Curse changed things physically, though Genesis 3 plainly revealed some physical changes. The point here is not that there are no distinctions between physical death and "spiritual death." It is that the death revealed in Genesis 2 and 3 includes all death-related categories; defined within a Hebrew worldview, not by current popular thought.

Augustine did not have a Hebrew worldview. Nor did he have the intellectual tools yet to think in such terms. He was part of a centuries-long process the Holy Spirit opted to use that, among many other things, brought about the growth of such tools. Today, we understand that languages have histories, which track with those of the peoples that speak them. In addition, each word of each language has its own individual history. The new field of linguistic archaeology studies this phenomenon, and recently traced the heretofore-unknown origin of the Gypsies to India. It also means that often the process of translation is not as simple as just finding a plug and replace word in another language. This is especially so in the translation of books dealing with subjects that require abstract thought.

Before we start to pontificate on what kind of "death" Genesis 3 speaks about, one should find out how the ancient Hebrews normally defined *life* and *death*. Did they think of these concepts exactly as we do? If not, in what ways were their ideas different, and if different; was it because of a false belief in something that did not fit reality or was it simply a matter of how they classified things? The second kind of difference might well fit reality if we account for ancient Hebrew language conventions.

The problem with both the Pelagian and Modernist approaches to interpreting Genesis is that they do not deal with language conventions and worldviews. Not even all Creationists do this well. Yet, most seem to understand that Genesis fits the Hebraic genre of historical narrative. The Pelagians read Celtic cultural assumptions into the text. Modernist detractors do the same with materialistic assumptions. Consequently, one finds in both views an attempt to explain away the text's details rather than to expose and explain them. (We all pull our own perspectives into the text somewhat, but we want to do this as little as possible so the text can instruct our worldview instead of the reverse.)

The word-for-word Hebrew of God's warning to Adam about the Tree of the Knowledge of Good and Evil reads, **"In the day you eat of it, *dying*, you shall die."** While this is a Hebraism, many linguistic "isms" came into vogue by way of a pattern that reflected a literal meaning at some early point. The Bible often defines death in terms of a separation. (Phil. 1:23, 2 Cor. 5:6-9) Dying, Adam would begin to age and wear down, until he died physically. This fits what we see in the real world regarding human and higher animal death. Later Scripture describes the eternal dimensions of spiritual death. Romans 8 shows that the entire cosmos, not just the human spirit, **"groans and travails"** because of the Curse. There are natural disasters and diseases; even stars decay and die after a form.

People often object, "What about plants? They die when eaten, so how could there be no death before the Fall?" Here is where we need to examine an ancient Hebraic concept of what *life* means. Death is not the only topic where we must watch our assumptions. The Hebraic definition of *life* is not exactly the same as the modern biological one, though there is a huge overlap of common meaning. It is not so much a question of having the right or wrong definition, but of historical, worldview, and cultural context. Three Hebrew words (and their varied forms) are relevant to grasping how Genesis deals with the idea of life, and therefore, death: *chay*, *nephesh*, and *neshawmah* or the "breath of God" as used in Genesis. 2:7.

Ancient Hebrews had a three level understanding of *life*, functionally speaking. At the bottom, *chay* applied to all things that grew—plants, animals, and human. On top of, and including that, the Hebrew word *nephesh* refers to the kind of life found in higher creatures, including man, created on days five and six of the creation week. These are creatures with "the breath of life," able to move and show at least some personality or soul. On creation day 5, *chay nephesh* is translated "living creature."

Plants, fungi, bacteria, viruses, and some lower animals, although alive in the biological sense; are not "living" in the *nephesh* sense of a Hebrew Genesis-based worldview. *Nephesh* means *soul*, or *personality*. It refers to creatures with the ability to move, breathe, and show emotion, based on its usage in Scripture. [13] *Nephesh* is not limited to humanity. It describes all animate creatures, including humans. Humanity also has a unique spiritual life direct from God's breath (Hebrew *neshawmah* as used by Gen. 2:7), in addition to *nephesh*.

Humanity, when God originally created Adam and Eve, possessed spiritual life, *nephesh* (animal life), and *chay* (met qualifications for being biologically *alive*). As for animals, it is fair to say that not all *chay* have *nephesh*, though all *nephesh* have *chay*. Death, in the worldview of Scripture, refers only to loss of the *nephesh* and/or spiritual kinds of life in creatures created with those capacities. Life forms created only with *chay*, but not *nephesh* and/or spiritual life, were always capable of dying in the biological sense, even before the Curse. God and the Hebrews never defined that as "death" in any meaningful way. God made plants to be food in the beginning. This is where the Hebraic worldview idea of *death* differs from the modern biological one.

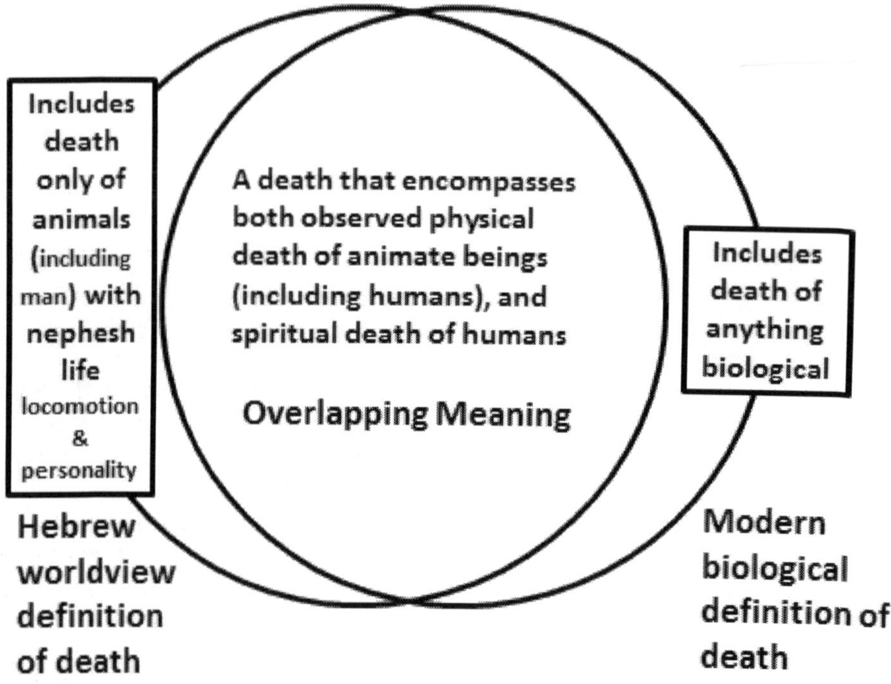


*A comparison of the worldview concepts of death (above): Ancient Hebrew versus Modern Biological – both are true, allowing for language conventions. Corresponding Hebrew idea of life (below)*

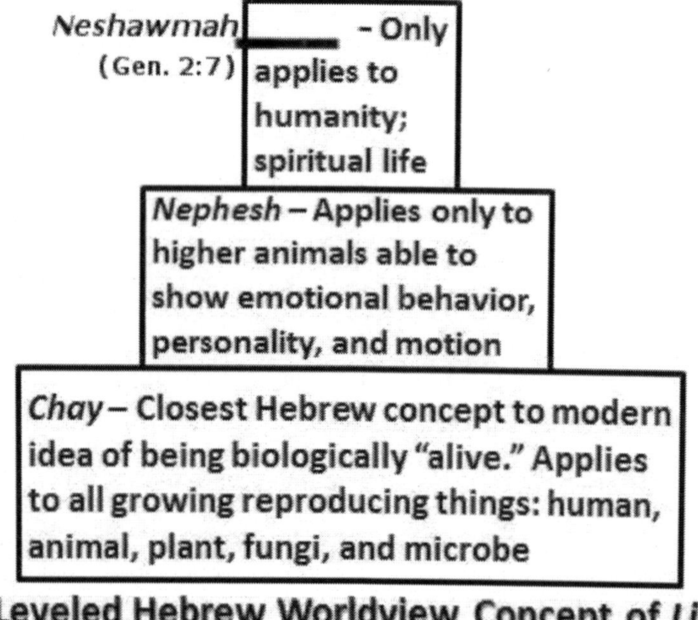

To simplify this; it all goes to purpose. Why is it wrong for God to create two classes of living things—one with varied levels of self-awareness, and the other completely non-self-aware, to serve as food for the first class? Death is a curse for the higher classification, while consumption is the normal purpose of the non-aware class. Later forces, after the Curse, modified this as need arose, like eating meat after the Flood. Yet, why should this initial state be a problem? Except for those emotionally inclined to make it one, it fits reality quite well.

While Hebrew concepts of life and death make distinctions not made by biological definitions, this does not make the Hebrew concepts wrong, and the modern, right. Nor does it mean that the reverse is true. Both fit reality, even if the exact borderline between "just *chay*" creatures and those called "*chay nephesh*" is not always clearly knowable to us. For example, ants and bees have a "hive mind" behavior. They clearly qualify as *nephesh*, but is the "unit of the living being" the individual ant/bee or the hive? We should not pretend to know such things, just because some people want to make the idea of a pre-Curse creation without death look silly. Nor should we pretend to know based only on convenience or assumption alone.

Neither should we assume the Hebrew notions mean the same as the modern theological division between physical and spiritual life and death. Saying that the death promised in Genesis resulting from sin is just "spiritual death" undercuts the meaning of the text. Every curse in Genesis 3 involves a material change in nature. Labor pains, death/decay (returning to dust), bodily changes to the serpent/thorns, and greater struggles farming each involve physical alterations. Such changes likely imply deeper adjustments made by God to creation, possibly at the sub-atomic level. The changes mentioned in Genesis 3 need not be an exhaustive list. One thing is certain. Nature now reflects the conflict within fallen humanity. Although we still see God's power, intelligence, and majesty in nature, as Romans 1:18-32 reveals; we cannot see God's loving character in Nature *consistently*.

Augustine's non-literal view of the creation week fit the Neo-Platonic belief that God made the cosmos as a system of perfect, interrelated geometries, some with spirits; functioning as a vast living organism. He sometimes taught the sudden creation of a world of interdependent prototypes, none able to operate without the others. Augustine found the entire cosmos "irreducibly complex." It was impossible, in his mind, for the things created on day 2 to exist even briefly without those things created on days 3, 4, 5, and 6. Though ***irreducible complexity*** exists in nature, it does not logically follow that all nature is therefore irreducibly complex. One cannot eliminate the possibility of a staged creation sequence.

Augustine proposed that God made perfect spiritual prototypes of all things in the beginning, from which present things then arose. The creation days were non-literal in his view because he believed they happened instantaneously. He did not imagine non-literal creation days to pigeonhole God's creative acts into a long, gradual timeframe. Rather, he did the opposite. Augustine outdid the brevity of even the literal week of today's Young Earth Creationist! He also viewed the subsequent events in Genesis as historical.

Still, Augustine made the mistake of letting part of a still influential Greek worldview guide his interpretation of Scripture. Progressive Creationists, Theistic Evolutionists, and Framework Hypothesis advocates do the same sort of thing today with more damaging results. The worldview of Augustine's time had a crucial difference from that of today. He made room for an anti-materialist philosophy that accepted an intelligent designer; an idea that at least had something in common with Genesis, even if not in the details.

By contrast, Christian promoters of non-historical views of Genesis accept beliefs built from materialistic presuppositions hostile to their own confessions of faith. They do so without serious critique or even, it seems awareness of how those assumptions hold their own position up; assumptions they must accept on faith were they to analyze them. This creates theological and scientific incoherence the more one examines it, which we will do in Chapters 18 through 24. For now, this makes appeals to Augustine invalid in their defense.

The worldview holding up Augustine's Neo-Platonism did not deny the supernatural creation of the cosmos by a personal God or a historic Genesis Curse. That Curse changed the good world God had created into one balanced by death and decay. Augustine's condemnation of Pelagius' views unfortunately did not also clearly reject the idea of death as part of God's pre-Fall creative method. Both Progressive Creationism and Theistic Evolution require this concept. Christians only later accepted that kind of thinking because academics had led them to believe that evidence demanded it. Actually, only the materialistic faith-assumption grid used to interpret the evidence, and filter the questions asked of it, demanded it. There is a huge difference.

Pelagius found some sympathy for his views in the Eastern Church. The long habit of over-allegorizing the Scriptures had muddied the waters for many teachers.

*Pelagianism should have forced Christians to think more clearly about the nature of the Genesis Curse; as to how far it has affected the human condition – body and soul.*

Stagnation in the East and oversimplification in the West ensured that this did not happen nearly as much as later events would prove it needed to. Augustine raised such questions, and more, but time was running out for civilization in the West.

Barbarians were coming across the Mediterranean.

## AUGUSTINE VERSUS SEMI-PELAGIANISM

Semi-Pelagianism, as the prefix implies, taught that salvation resulted from a mixture of good human works plus grace through faith. Paul demolished this mutually exclusive idea in Romans Chapter 4.

> **For if Abraham was justified by works, he has something to boast about;** ***but not before God.*** **For what does the Scripture say? "And Abraham believed God, and it was reckoned to him as righteousness."** ***Now to the one who works, his wage is not reckoned as a favor, but as what is due. But to the one who does not work, but believes in Him who justifies the ungodly, his faith is reckoned as righteousness,*** **Just as David also speaks of the blessing upon the man to whom God reckons righteousness apart from works: "Blessed are those whose lawless deeds have been forgiven, and whose sins have been covered. Blessed is the man whose sin the LORD will not take into account."** ***Romans*** **4:2-8 (NASB)**

It is important we ask in what sense Paul used the word *justification* here.

We should not confuse the Semi-Pelagian heresy with the biblical teaching that genuine faith *produces* godly works. James 2:14-26 tells us that people cannot tell we have faith unless they can see it by our deeds. In contrast to Paul, James speaks of how we are justified before other men when we call ourselves Christians. In Romans 4, Paul speaks of how people are justified before God in terms of redemption. God knows our hearts. Other people cannot tell who we are except by what we do, and even that is often an imperfect indicator.

Semi-Pelagianism made the mistake of applying James as if it spoke of justification before God rather than man. The Pope of Rome and Augustine also condemned this teaching during that generation.

*The only thing Semi-Pelagianism forced the church to ask itself was; how far can people make opposing ideas sound compatible just to keep other people from arguing about them?* Sadly, some 1100 years later, the Roman Catholic Council of Trent would resurrect a form of Semi-Pelagianism. This it would do in reaction against Martin Luther.

Martin Luther would begin as an Augustinian monk.

***

Augustine and his contributions to the church were too voluminous to do justice to here. His conversion and deliverance from sexual addiction is awe inspiring, even if some of his views on sexuality lack biblical perspective. (When one reads Augustine, it is surprising how rarely this is actually the case.) This came in part from his background, but mostly from the prevailing presuppositions of his period. He, nevertheless, began to confront those faulty assumptions clearly. In doing so, Augustine set the stage for later teachers to restore the biblical dignity that sexual enjoyment within marriage deserves. His conversion experience was powerful and stood out in bold contrast to the graying of white and black that so characterized most of the rest of the church in that era.

Augustine of Hippo died in 430 AD, while the Vandals besieged his city. They soon after burned it. Only Augustine's church, and the people huddled inside, remained untouched by the flames.

As with Constantine, we might target Augustine's mistakes and his few half-baked conceptions, though we would have far less justification. Some of his development of the Doctrine of Predestination seems to some Christians rather extreme. Both he and his ideas were works in process. Are not those of today's Christians in that category still?

And, like Constantine, Augustine's spiritual successors were about to do far worse.

## Bibliography

1. Shelley, Bruce L. ***Church History in Plain Language*** (2nd Edition), pp.135-137, 1995, Word Publishing, Dallas, Tx.
2. Irenaeus, ***Adversus Haereses (Against Heresies)***, circa 180 AD
3. Smith, M.A. ***The Church Under Siege***, p. 164, 1976, Inter-Varsity Press, Leicester, England
4. Woodrow, Ralph, ***Babylon Mystery Religion***, p. 81, 1966
5. Op cit. Shelley, Bruce L., pp.124-125
6. Ibid. pp.130-131
7. Op cit. Smith, M.A., p. 26
8. Cahill, Thomas, ***How the Irish Saved Civilization***, Bantam Doubleday Dell, 1996
9. Augustine of Hippo, ***City of God***, Book XIV, Ch. 16, pg 315, Ch. 26, p. 318, translated by Walsh, Gerald G. S.J., Zema, Demetrius B. S.J., Monahan, Grace O.S.U., and Honan, Daniel J., 1958, Image Books: A Division of Doubleday & Co. Inc. See also: Schmitt, É. (1983). *Le mariage chrétien dans l'oeuvre de Saint Augustin. Une théologie baptismale de la vie conjugale*. Études Augustiniennes. Paris. p. 97. See also Augustine's: ***De continentia***, 8.21; PL 40, 363; ***Contra Iulianum*** VI, 19.60; PL 44, 859; ibid. IV, 14.65, z.2, s. 62; PL 44, 770; ***De Trinitate***, XII, 9. 14; CCL 50, 368 [verse: IX 1-8]; ***De Genesi contra Manicheos***, II, 9.12, s. 60; ***Corpus Scriptorum Ecclesiasticorum Latinorum*** (CSEL) 91, 133 [v. 31-35]).
10. Augustine of Hippo, ***City of God***, Book XIV, Ch. 3 p. 298
11. Ibid. p. 303
12. Ibid. p. For Augustine's speculation on death before the curse: see Augustine of Hippo, *De Genesi ad literam 1:19-20*, Chapt. 19 [408], *De Genesi ad literam*, 2:9
13. Strong's Exhaustive Concordance Hebrew Lexicon: Compare the words *nephesh* and *chay* (Strong's numbers 5315 and 2416). Consider how these words are used, assuming the reality and integrity of their various contexts in the Old Testament.

# 9

# The Middle Ages, Part 1: Decline in the East and West

## Opposite Forms of Decline that Led to the Same Place

Despite gains in the evangelization of the Germanic tribes, churches of both the East and West declined steeply in the late 1st millennium. The forces of spiritual decay dragged both branches of Christianity along opposite routes to the same decrepit destination.

The West saw a breakdown of education with further incursions of Pagan superstition into the beliefs and practices of the church. The idea of "patron saints" advanced to new heights with the influx of Germanic folklore that took on Christian names and symbols. Devotion to these local patrons often eclipsed that given to Christ. Jesus even seemed to become a divine Germanic warlord who bore little resemblance to the biblical Savior. Widespread illiteracy impedes the spread of the Faith, and distorts it like nothing else. Even where the Faith spreads under such conditions, it does so in an adulterated form. The degree of adulteration varies, and God's word still penetrates, but that is not the same as saying the situation is harmless.

The above is perhaps an over-generalization, but not an empty one. It is hard for us today to imagine a world where only a tiny minority knew how to read, and not often well. Human progress is not the linear ramp that people today seem to imagine. Even now, tribes in places like Papua New Guinea and the Amazon rainforest still live as Stone Age hunter-gatherers. In many other parts of the world, whole societies are barely one or two generations removed from that. Civilizations do not advance without a worldview that makes progress seem thinkable, do-able, and desirable. Nor is "progress" merely a matter of superior technology. Human history is not as some 20th century science fiction movies paint things. In the real world, erudite academics who claim, "Any race so advanced must have evolved beyond such atrocities as war and conquest," end up conquered. Progress, if it happens at all, is uneven.

Throughout history, the most technologically advanced civilizations have often been the cruelest. In fact, most worldviews in history had stubborn barriers to progress and reaching general literacy. People did not just "get smarter" over time. Knowledge accumulated, but not evenly, and not easily. Civilizations sometimes lost advanced knowledge because something shifted in their worldviews that made them underestimate its worth.

Christianity met the genuine needs and questions of tribal Germanic societies, as it had the Greco-Roman and Celtic ones. Unfortunately, accumulating Pagan influences on the church's popular religion, by this time, had taken a toll. Historians call this type of thing, still observed today, *folk-Christianity,* or *folk-religion.* In it, superstitions from a buried Paganism gain acceptance in the church by taking on "Christianese" jargon. A pattern I call "magical thinking" also over-simplified some Christian theological concepts in the late 1st millennium. This often began as honest attempts to make Christian truths more reachable to people, but ended by changing those truths into cartoon versions of what they had once been. Many barbarian kings in the West belittled literacy, despite some notable exceptions. Yet, even the exceptions often seemed caught in an undertow of cultural habit.

The Holy Spirit often works providentially. One way He does this, which we will see repeatedly, is by helping people form intellectual tools that build ideas from God's word into the challenges of their times. At this point, tools had not yet matured that could always distinguish biblical ideas of the supernatural from functionally magical ones. A clear concept of such categories did not yet even exist, at least nowhere near what we can now see with present-day 20/20 hindsight. Some key words in Christian belief also underwent a subtle "definition blur" from the general loss of reading comprehension in the West. Just the normal language changes over time can do this, especially when worldviews are over-simplified compared to what they were when the key word was first defined.

Linguistically, all of this is comparable to what happens when one decreases the resolution of a digital photograph. One might turn down the resolution to make the file size smaller, for easier upload (to make it more accessible). Turn it down too far however, and the picture becomes pixelated. It is no longer a fully accurate image. The same thing can happen with the transmission of ideas. One can only simplify a message so far to adapt it to cultural norms before it ceases to be an accurate representation. Christians face a similar phenomenon today, only on a far more sophisticated scale.

After the collapse of Rome in the West, church culture reverted from literary-based thought forms to image-based ones. This caused some biblical ideas to lose shape in the minds of new converts from illiterate Germanic tribes. The Jewish and Greco-Roman cultures had both been largely literate. Romanized Celts also had a comparatively literate society. The Germanic tribes generally did not. They reserved writing for arcane religious purposes, more as a secret code or for recording royal genealogies. Their runes were not always a proper alphabet in the sense that people would think of one today.

This explains why languages like Old English used Latin letters. As in many primitive societies, they understood oral stories and images better than the written word. Christians who wanted to evangelize these tribes often had to communicate accordingly. This often-unavoidable accommodation had a hidden danger, however. Any time a message system converts its medium of communication from written words to pictures or ritual drama, important ideas get lost in the process. While Christianity slowly raised the literacy of these tribes, it also absorbed some of their illiterate habits. Distinctions between ritual imagery and spiritual reality blurred; abstract mental boundaries even under the best conditions. Idea limits naturally assumed by literate believers, crumbled in cultures without the vocabulary to discuss them. Categories became confused and dissolved.

It is good to want to make the Bible more accessible to people's understanding. There are limits even here, however. We want to "put the cookies on the lower shelf" for people. Yet, if our teaching methods cater too much to a falling level of functional literacy, we can accidentally make the gospel less accessible, instead. Forms of magical Pagan thinking still assail the church today. Even highly educated people are not immune to the seduction. Images, icons, and ritual are simpler to deal with intellectually, but they cannot express complex spiritual truths as well as literature can. A retired literature professor I bumped into at my health spa once gave me some practical wisdom in this area. He told me to give special attention to both ends of my student's ability spectrum, to focus on the gifted students as much as on those who struggled. If I worked both ends diligently, the majority in the middle would learn just fine.

It would seem in the latter half of the 1st millennium that the church in the West felt forced to cater too often to the lower end of the literacy spectrum. Hot-tempered barbarian chieftains needed careful handling in wild settings where the church often found itself caught between clashing tribes speaking many languages. Misunderstandings easily led to bloodshed. The scattered abbeys of the monastic orders provided the only real streamlet of literacy at this time. It may have seemed that there just were not enough people at the upper end of the literacy spectrum to demand much attention.

Of course, at no time was that ever true. People do not just lose intellectual potential, even if forces in their societies are "dumbing them down." That refers only to a loss of educational opportunity or to an education system that deliberately does not educate. The monasteries usually did their best with what they had, so here we see an opportunity loss.

The storyteller took on great importance in this environment. A well-told story could reach both readers and non-readers alike around the campfire. Unfortunately, people easily garble oral stories in the retelling, unless a disciplined regimen of memorization exists. By the latter half of the 1st Millennium, the age of the hagiographer had descended in force upon the church. Athanasius' account of Antony came from an earlier time of greater general literacy. By contrast, early medieval hagiographers often exaggerated their tales without even knowing it. They even considered it an act of faith and reverence to do so. Many such yarns merely retold Pagan folklore with the names of the characters changed to sound vaguely Christian.

The spread of these stories further shifted how Christians viewed the meaning of the word *saint*. Saints became magical super-humans of unapproachable holiness rather than believers who had simply received God's Grace. The power of a well-told story can either help or hurt the spiritual climate of the church. Here is, perhaps, another case for ministry that aims at the gifted as well as the struggling. Hagiographers often worked outside recognized church channels. They drummed up local devotion for obscure and sometimes fictional saints through their gifted storytelling. The church would then feel pressure from popular culture to recognize these saints and their shrines.

The church sometimes gave into this pressure, at first, to make hard times easier in the short run. Of course, the loss of literacy was never truly complete. Still, the scholar monk felt pressured to survive by appeasing the illiterate popular culture. Later, the standards for the "canonization of saints" became more rigorous—pendulums again.

Even modest church buildings took on a special status among the newly Christianized Germanic tribes. They symbolized a remnant of an advanced Roman civilization that the barbarians looked back to with religious awe. Roman ruins peppered Western Europe, outlasting tribal villages and feudal townships by centuries, even to this day. People lacked the skills to reproduce most of the highly developed technology of fallen Rome, except for some of the weaponry, which some Germanic tribes actually improved on. They still looked backward to Rome's glory as a time of great magic, however. The idea of one empire ruling the entire known world seemed inconceivable to them, yet they knew it had happened. Barbarian chieftains ardently desired the glory that was old Rome, and Christianity, in their eyes, was the religion of the Romans. In their minds, one thing must have led to the other.

Despite the hagiography, magical thinking, and superstitious lust for things Roman, the Holy Spirit guided ambassadors of Christ even in this decrepit time. A core of truth-seeking and spiritual power often remained, despite the embellishment and cultural myth. Evangelist monks of that day still demonstrated the reality of Christ in ways Germanic tribes understood. We would be starting well if people could say the same of us in Post-Christian America.

Stories abounded like that of the English monk, who took the name Boniface. He went into the heart of Germanic territory on the continent to win the barbarians to Christ, as his own tribe had been, not long before. Boniface once took an ax to a huge oak tree sacred to the thunder god Thor, in order to prove that the Christian God was mightier. Feats of strength went a long way with tribal warrior chieftains. After a single stroke, a great wind blasted the tree down, uprooting it. When lightning did not strike Boniface, he ordered the wood trimmed, and used to build a chapel dedicated to St. Peter on that same spot. Events like this brought the Germanic peoples to their knees, though often in lieu of a full comprehension of the actual gospel message. At least such things got their attention, enabling later development.

In the cultured East, causes for church decay were often the opposite, though the outcome seemed strangely the same, if on a more sophisticated level. It could be said that here, the church made the opposite mistake of its Western counterpart. Bishops catered too much in their teaching toward the intellectuals. The prolongation of Constantine's Christian Empire lurched toward its logical endgame, as an almost Christianized emperor worship took hold. Eastern Orthodoxy saw the Emperor Justinian I and his successors as God's hand on earth. This had the practical effect of making the emperor into a little god of sorts.

Theology became an intellectual team sport, greatly refined; but so dry and mixed with Roman law and Greek philosophy that it became impossible to tell where one of these elements ended and the others began. The highly educated seemed to thrive in this environment, if only intellectually. The average person, however, shriveled up spiritually, indulging much the same sort of superstitions as found in the West.

A heavily regulated society resulted, where each hydra head of ***Byzantine*** bureaucracy had little clue of what the others were doing. Accountability often died. At the top sat the Emperor, often clueless, or at best, only half-aware of what went on around him. Church and state fused together, such that few could imagine one without the other. The whole idea that Roman state and Christian church existed as separate entities virtually disappeared, except for rare instances. [1] Idyllic but sterile, Christian religion in the East often died slowly under its own political weight. Form took priority over spiritual substance. Historians have coined the adjective *byzantine* from this; to refer to any unaccountable, compartmentalized bureaucracy where corruption grows unchecked.

Through its political complications, the Eastern Church mirrored imperial government and thought forms. Greek folk ideas of "divine gateways" bred iconography that tended to compartmentalize the sacred from the world of everyday life. Icons first gained acceptance in the 2nd through 4th centuries, as a way to help support the truth of the Incarnation against a hostile Greek worldview. Some bishops cautioned against them as late as the 4th century, however.

The humanity of Christ, like the humanity of anyone else, was a legitimate subject for art. The Greek worldview, however, left its imprint even on methods used to defeat its negative side effects. *Byzantine* art, though eye-catching, became more and more symbolic. It reduced its subject almost to pictographs in an icon-based language system. (History calls what has to do with the Eastern Roman Empire "Byzantine." The original name of Constantinople was Byzantium and many people find that easier to pronounce.)

This pictorial "language" separated the Faith into a higher realm. Most people even in the Greek-speaking church could not easily understand the nuances without specialized education. This furthered the folk idea that icons were gateways into the spiritual realm. [2] Reinforcing teaching on Christ's humanity by artistically portraying it is not the same thing as having a gateway to His Divinity, however. As time went on, boundaries clear in a Hebrew mindset blurred in a Greek one. Some of the categories made in the history of what followed may well have been real in the minds of Byzantine believers. Still, there is a tendency common to both military and church history. Everyone is always perfectly prepared to fight the war of the previous generation, but barely aware of their own current tactical situation. Complacency can easily set in after a great victory.

Once upon a time, the church had seen itself as a community of believers incompatible with any national system. Now the church was the national system. Byzantine culture viewed people as part of it simply because they were a part of Eastern Roman society. This also affected the West because, for a time, Old Rome had a form of "outpost status" after the fall of the Western Empire. Before the imperial state church, people were ***born again*** into the kingdom of God. They saw themselves as "called out" of the world system. Now they were simply born and baptized as infants into the church, which effectively was the world system.

*Byzantine styled ceiling iconography at Basilica of Saint Polycarp, at Izmir, Turkey*

Spiritual erosion resulted. Few made any *effective* difference between those born naturally and those born again spiritually. Intellectuals discussed abstract distinctions between the baptized and unbaptized, but these did not touch the real world or the average person.

Orthodox clerics assumed that the rite of infant water baptism conferred the second birth. This meant they had to make many assumptions to explain why so many people given the "second birth" in infancy showed so little sign of it in adulthood. Most such assumptions did not stand up to scrutiny even on the intellectual level. They were unprovable. Some of them even led to conclusions that we could not know things that the Scriptures say we can and should know.

Nevertheless, it would not be entirely fair to project our 20/20 hindsight of where this would lead back onto believers of that day, as if they could know as we do. They could not own personal Bibles—that would be economically out of reach until the 16th century. Consequently, people depended on the teaching of priests and other clerics.

There is still a mechanics to ideas, especially once people apply them to the real world on a large scale. There is also that "Law of Unintended Consequences," where side effects of those ideas produce collateral damage. This is a statement about mechanics, not so much about the intentions of hearts. While God considers our heart, a level still exists where it does not matter what our intentions are. Poorly conceived ideas still have bad effects even when applied for the best of intentions. The American proverb, "Good intentions pave the road to hell," has some truth in it—sometimes, quite a lot of truth. I am speaking here of the many historical side effects of pervasively modelling the church after the Roman Empire.

God may have used some Roman features redemptively while the Roman Empire existed in its Christian form, and perhaps even for some time after. There were also dangers involved in that. One of the most serious concerned the way Christians came to view salvation. In the imperial state-church, people viewed the "second birth" as an automatic given by the virtue of infant baptism. This created a need to explain later evidence of conversion or the lack of it in a person's life; a distinction once so plainly visible in the lives of people in New Testament times. The logical consequence of this was the devaluation of the meaning of "conversion" in actual experience. This led to an evaporation of any biblical concept of assurance of salvation, as described in 1 John 5.

> **These things I have written to you who believe in the name of the Son of God, *in order that you may KNOW that you HAVE eternal life. 1 John* 5:13 (NASB)**

While this also affected the Western Church, the full illusion of God's political kingdom on earth as a "Christian empire" went on a thousand years longer in the East. Civilizational stagnation, deterioration, and breakdown took its full course in the Byzantine Empire, until Constantinople fell to the Ottoman Turks in the spring of 1453. In the West, this illusion did not linger. Rather, the "Christian empire" kept reincarnating itself into new forms. A positive side was that this allowed more potential for political and spiritual renewals up to and including the Reformation.

The first renewal happened under Charlemagne, which birthed the pattern of the European monarchies. In the end, "Christian empire" gasped its rattling last breaths as the Catholic dual-monarchy of Austria-Hungary and the Lutheran Empire of Kaisers Wilhelm I and II. The down side was that a potential for renewal did not guarantee it would always happen. The same spiritual torpor engulfed each imperial clone in the end.

Beyond the New Testament showing water baptism as the response from people who knew and believed the gospel; adopting the Roman model demanded a new spiritual mechanics. If we make everyone "special" as babies, then effectively nobody is. Giving everyone the status of "regenerate" through infant baptism devalued the meaning of spiritual regeneration. It may not have occurred to anyone yet to ask; *what distinctions are there between a ritual and the reality it pictures?* The church was about to find out the long, hard way that differences do exist between the two, despite any similarities.

Spiritual power and holiness had become rare in the lifestyles of bishops, popes, and patriarchs, let alone common people. Not that people who had conversion experiences have ever been perfect, even in New Testament times. Yet, an extraordinary love and grace has always marked those touched by the gospel of Jesus Christ, and regenerated through the Holy Spirit. How could an opulent society explain such a lack where everyone had "spiritual regeneration" from the cradle? For that matter, how can we believably explain such a lack today, in churches with such easy access to God's word, where multitudes "get saved" every day? We are not immune to gaping worldview blind spots any more than Byzantium. We just don't always have the same ones.

One logical side effect came from this "regeneration deficit" in Roman Christianity, *once a Roman social-religious system became the imperative*. People might express it in different words, but it boiled down to the idea that spiritual regeneration was fragile and easy to lose. If that were the case, then it was simply impossible to have any functional assurance of salvation. The sacrament of communion *effectively* became less and less a celebration of thanksgiving; and increasingly a rite perceived to perpetuate the effects of Christ's sacrifice in the lives of believers who were not often experiencing them. Religion and faith became more symbolic and removed from the reality of everyday life. People did not intend this, nor reason things out like this philosophically—not at first. Yet that was how it eventually played out in the real world. In history, heart intentions are not as relevant as mechanics.

Liturgical worship forms saw elaborate embellishment during Roman and Byzantine times. Bishops, musicians, and artists introduced great pageantry into formal worship in both the East and West. Liturgies had existed in the church since early times, evolving out of the order of worship used in the communion service. In the West, they took on importance as a teaching tool among non-literate peoples as a means of acting out the sacrifice of Christ in a way that folk could follow. In the East, they became a form of high artistic expression. People called the central liturgy the ***Mass***.

Unfortunately, by now, Christianity in both the East and West had absorbed Pagan mystery-cult ideas into their worship. What works well in Paganism does not often work well in Christianity. Such forms served to dilute the teaching power of the liturgy, and to shroud it in mysticism. In the magical thinking of the times, people confused ritual with reality even further, just when tools were surfacing to enable them to begin to see a difference. Fear and political power-hunger in the church would later perpetuate this problem. Later still, the Roman Catholic Council of Trent would sadly reinforce the matter far past its season. There, bloated views of liturgy would have "the perpetual sacrifice of the Mass" declared "one and the same as" Christ's "once for all" death on the cross.

Ritual and metaphor, however helpful as guides, are not the same as historic spiritual reality. The Letter to the Hebrews preluded God's view on this long before it ever became an issue in history.

> **He (Christ) has no need, like those high priests, to offer sacrifices daily, first for his own sins and then for those of the people; he did this *once for all* when he offered up himself. *Hebrews* 7:27 RSV**

Trent was still many centuries off yet, despite my little preview of where things headed. Today we face the far end of the reaction to all that—a transition that in our own time has become just as damaging in its own way, which we will get to later. While liturgical worship is not wrong of itself, no real need ever existed for the church to establish its own form of daily ritual sacrifice. That only impeded the efficiency of Christianity by reinventing the law.

Another factor also served quietly to pull East and West apart, which we touched on earlier. Language and thought form differences now accelerated, even if many of the outer worship forms seemed similar. The church remained organizationally unified at this time in name only. Even that dissolved after the dawn of the 2nd millennium.

Central to so much of the spiritual decay in the church of both East and West was the increasingly idolatrous use of icons. In Eastern theory, a way existed for non-idolatrous use of icons in worship. This theory did not often translate well into practice over time, however. Originally, an icon was supposed to point the believer to the real spiritual object it represented. In the Greek mind, so resistant to the idea of the Incarnation, icons had reinforced the fact that God had become man in every real physical sense in Christ. At first, no one tolerated making any icon of God's Divine nature, as evidenced by the Synod of Elvira, Spain just before Constantine came to power in the early 4th century. Canon 36 states, *"Pictures are not to be placed in churches, so that they do not become objects of worship and adoration."* [3] Only Christ's humanity was a legitimate subject matter for art. Subtle distinctions have a way of eroding as language shifts over time.

That is exactly what tended to happen at this time in both the East and West, though in slightly different ways. Eastern iconography avoided statues in favor of tile mosaics or paintings. The folk religion of both Germanic and Celtic tribes in the West drove a worship use of statues that exploded without restraint. At first, icons of Jesus, Mary, and the saints represented human ideals centered on these persons, not attempts to picture the Divine nature. Later, people slowly shifted toward viewing icons as spiritual contact points or gateways in their own right. This shift in perception entered a Gentile church culture from the Greco-Roman world.

In theory, worshippers aimed a special form of veneration at an icon much as a military salute goes to a superior officer. One is not saluting the man, but rather the rank authority vested upon the man. In the same way, one technically respected not the icon, but the value of the saint or Savior the icon represented. Eastern Orthodox and Roman Catholic theology call this kind of veneration by the Greek words ***hyperdoulia*** and ***doulia***. The worship reserved only for God in this system is ***latreia***. In English, Roman Catholic and Eastern Orthodox translate this distinction as *veneration* versus *worship*. Only worship is for God, in that view.

Unfortunately, this became an artificial distinction of words, which, if ever valid, was only so as a matter of degree. It flew out of control in the minds of all but the most subtle among the educated. In the hands of the masses, it degenerated into rank idolatry even in the more sophisticated East. For the heart condition and attitude toward Mary, the Saints or God is identical, whether one calls it *hyperdoulia* or *latreia*, or veneration or worship.

One fundamental difference between Christian thinking of East and West was in the emphasis on our relationship to God at creation. Eastern Orthodoxy gave more emphasis on humanity's creation in the Divine Image. In the West, man's legal relationship to God was more prominent. The Eastern Church saw sin as the defacing of God's image in man, while Westerners viewed it more as the breaking of God's law. Both these understandings are biblical. That does not mean every application made from them by the Eastern or Western Churches in history were necessarily sound. The Eastern emphasis on man's creation in God's image (ikonos), when mixed with Neo-Platonism and folk religion, led to an increasingly careless use of icons. This also affected the West, in which a law-centered emphasis led to a form of legalism where practical grace eventually shriveled on the vine.

By the 8th and 9th centuries, some believers in the East sensed that things had gotten out of control. History calls them the ***Iconoclasts***, or icon smashers. By the 7th century AD, Byzantine worship had developed an unhealthy hierarchy in how it viewed people's access to God in prayer. This reflected the "Christianized emperor worship" mentioned earlier. The emperor sat atop an elaborate hierarchy of bureaucrats and bishops, so it only seemed natural to Byzantines that God should operate the same way. In this system, people accessed God the Father through the Son, and the Son through the "*Theotokos*" (Mary), whom people accessed through a plethora of lesser saints.

While no one intended this to slight God's power, rather to honor His holiness, the mechanics of it nevertheless shot good intentions in the foot. It also diminished honor to God's holiness, in spite of any good intentions. This is because it effectively reduced God to less than who He is. Danger looms whenever a worldly model trumps what Scripture teaches about our access to God as His children.

Our inability to always see and hear clearly is *our inability*—not God's inaccessibility. He may allow seasons where we feel distant without actually being distant, but that does not mean we should pray with any less boldness of direct access. As for church leaders and prayer models, sometimes people's heart intentions are not as relevant as the consequences their actions and methods unleash. Here the church effectively portrayed God as distant and uncaring, imitating the limits and persona of an earthly emperor.

This was a recipe for stagnation and worse.

> **14 Seeing then that we have a great high priest, that is passed into the heavens, Jesus the Son of God, let us hold fast our profession. 15 For we have not an high priest which cannot be touched with the feeling of our infirmities; but was in all points tempted like as we are, yet without sin. 16 Let us therefore come boldly unto the throne of grace, that we may obtain mercy, and find grace to help in time of need. *Hebrews* 4:14-16 (KJV)**

Iconoclast emperors came to power at Constantinople several times, with help from bishops concerned by careless icon use. The first major incidents of Byzantine Iconoclasm began in the Aegean coastal provinces. In 726 AD, a submarine volcanic event off Santorini Island sent tsunamis into coastlands all around the Aegean Sea. Several bishops in the region took this as God's judgment of the empire against idolatry through abuse of icons. Emperor Leo III the Isaurian thought the provincial bishops had a point. He took down an image of Christ from the Bronze Gate of the Great Palace at Constantinople, circa 730 AD, replacing it with a simple cross. [4] Outraged by what they thought "sacrilege," a mob murdered several of the workers who took down the icon.

Historian Henry Chadwick captured the pro-icon character of the folk religion well:

> *The representations of Christ as the Almighty Lord on his judgment throne owed something to pictures of Zeus. Portraits of the Mother of God were not wholly independent of a pagan past of venerated mother-goddesses. In the popular mind the saints had come to fill a role that had been played by heroes and deities.* [5]

From what history now knows of him, Leo III the Isaurian likely had neither the heart nor zeal of a fanatic. The pro-icon Patriarch of Constantinople, Germanos I, even described him in one of his letters as a friend of icons. This makes traditional Eastern Orthodox portrayals of him as the ultimate Iconoclast puzzling. Likely, Emperor Leo's convictions grew over time; expressed as measured responses, which only inflated to "fanaticism" after the fact in later, pro-icon, Byzantine memory. Unfortunately, all we know of the Iconoclasts comes filtered through their pro-icon adversaries, who eventually won the controversy on earth. It was the classical "history is written by the winners" model, though that model itself is frequently an overgeneralization.

The late 6th through 8th centuries was a time of crisis for the Byzantine Empire for reasons we will cover presently. The shift toward a superstitious view of icons came in part as a byproduct of the sense of insecurity that comes in such times. Superstition assigns spiritual meanings to material objects, and then looks to those objects for comfort. It is a false comfort, but one that is difficult to break people of even in the 21st century. Iconoclasm came as an attempt to rectify evils that had crept into the Byzantine church, which Christians saw as the cause of God's punishments against their civilization. One aspect of this conflict still confused the Greek mind because of lingering problems relating the spiritual with the material.

The Iconoclasts believed it wrong even to depict Christ's humanity in art. They thought that to do so automatically denied His Deity, which does not logically follow. Early Christians had believed it idolatrous to portray the Divine nature in art, but had allowed that Christ's human nature was a legitimate subject matter; even that it could reinforce understanding of the Incarnation to a Greek mind so resistant to the idea.

After the Nestorian and Monophysite heresies, people seemed to want things to be simpler than they really were. Iconoclasts correctly believed it impossible to represent Christ's Divine and human natures together in art. They believed it wrong to try to portray the Divine nature ever. They incorrectly reasoned that to depict Christ's human nature in art automatically denied His Divine one. Another Iconoclast argument went that to portray Christ in art (with the haloes, etc.) was tantamount to Monophysitism because it mixed the natures; and to portray Him as a man in art was Nestorianism because it separated the natures. None of these arguments held water since both Iconoclasts and pro-icon positions rejected both these heresies. It was also faulty logic. A better argument would have been to appeal to the similarities such iconography had in form and use to earlier Pagan religious art.

The Iconoclasts appealed to the 2nd Commandment, but seemed to make few other direct Scriptural arguments. It may be their enemies never cited most of their biblical arguments, using the tactic of pretending an opponent had no good arguments. We should reserve judgment on that one, since we cannot know if it happened. One Scripture sheds much light:

> **1 Now it came to pass in the third year of Hoshea the son of Elah, king of Israel, that Hezekiah the son of Ahaz, king of Judah, began to reign... 3 And he did what was right in the sight of the LORD, according to all that his father David had done. 4 He removed the high places and broke the sacred pillars, cut down the wooden image *and broke in pieces the bronze serpent that Moses had made; for until those days the children of Israel burned incense to it, and called it Nehushtan.* 5 He trusted in the LORD God of Israel, so that after him was none like him among all the kings of Judah, nor who were before him. 6 For he held fast to the LORD; he did not depart from following Him, but kept His commandments, which the LORD had commanded Moses. *2 Kings* 18:1, 3-6 NKJV**

Here we have the account of Hezekiah destroying the bronze serpent made by Moses during the plague of serpents in Numbers 21. Of course, Moses never used the bronze serpent as an idol. It was a unique event, where God told him to hold it up, and that anyone who looked at it would find healing from the serpent bites. Over time, the bronze serpent ceased to be a memorial and degenerated into an idol in the way the people used it. This represents a similar shift to that in Byzantine Christianity's view of icons. Some objects may begin with a holy use, but a people can degenerate into superstition and change them into idols.

Leo III banned all icons from Constantinople in 730, but allowed for cross symbols to replace them. Riots immediately erupted, and the Emperor (by some accounts) seemed surprised by the reaction. [6] The pro-icon Patriarch Germanos resigned or else Leo had him sacked. History does not know which. As the Iconoclast controversies grew, so did the ***straw-man*** arguments made on both sides. While knowledge of the Iconoclasts comes filtered through their enemies, we do have many quotations from their writings used by their opponents. When read apart from the hostile commentary, we can get an accurate view of at least some of their beliefs.

Emperor Leo III died in 741. His son, Constantine V succeeded him, continuing his father's Iconoclast policies. As Emperor, Constantine V called the 7th Universal Church Council of Hieria in 754 AD, where the 340 attending bishops favored the Iconoclasts. Unfortunately, the Pope of Rome and none of the Patriarchs sent delegates, and considered it invalid. Constantine V ratcheted up persecutions against pro-icon monks and bishops, which resulted in the martyrdom of Stephen the Younger. Popularity of icons plus a martyr for the icon cause gave the pro-icon side powerful momentum.

When Constantine V died in 775, his son, Leo IV took the throne and loosened the reins on icons. When Leo died five years later, his wife, Irene, became regent for their minor son, Constantine VI. She called another Universal Church Council in 786-787, which the Patriarchies and the Pope of Rome recognized. This became known as the 7th General Council, also called the 2nd Council of Nicea. It voided the Council of Hieria, and declared Iconoclasm heretical. This synod was comprised mainly of Eastern bishops, except for the Papal representative. Another movement between 814 and 842 AD led to a second series of Iconoclast emperors all with nearly identical issues and motives. A regent mother of another minor emperor even brought the period to a close in a similar manner. This time, however, Iconoclasm in the Eastern Church never rose again.

Evangelicals often portray the Iconoclasts as "pre-Reformation reformers." Perhaps they had an element of that. While they often showed a biblical view of the 2nd Commandment, they still believed in praying to saints and Mary without images. In any event, the Byzantine church quashed the Iconoclast movements, and villainized the Iconoclastic emperors to the point where it is sometimes hard to know what is truth or slander.

It seemed that from early on in the Byzantine mind, icons were just too closely associated with the validity of the Incarnation to mess with. To destroy them, in their mind, was tantamount to denying that Christ had become a man. The presuppositions involved in this perception are more Neo-Platonic than biblical, however. American Evangelicals may not be able to understand the connection, but to the Greek mind, it was and may still be very real. Sadly, by then, in trying to man the walls against an unlikely attack on the Incarnation, the Eastern Church left the gateway to idolatry unguarded.

The Byzantines, like so many others in history, had pumped themselves up to fight a war already won by their grandparents, only to toss the fight of their own time.

## The Mass Conversions of Barbarian Kings and Their Tribes in the West

For the first few centuries after Rome fell in the West, Byzantium (Constantinople) became the center of Christianity. The Roman Popes had their hands full managing evangelism and negotiating peace with tribal warlords in their immediate vicinity. Often the two acts became the same thing, and left scars because of it. As time passed, however, Rome found advantages to being an outpost, instead of the creamy imperial center. By contrast, Eastern evangelism suffered near paralysis, with only a few exceptions. Surrounding nations had come to view Christianity as the political tool of the Byzantine Empire, and not without just cause.

A popular evangelistic trend grew in the West, which historians call "the mass conversion," although often, it had more *mass* than *conversion* to it. Evangelistic monks working among the Germanic tribes found that converting the chieftain caused the entire tribe to follow their king into baptism. This created a safer social setting to preach and teach in, but it had a deadly blind spot. If the rite of baptism regenerated the soul, instead of believing the gospel, it left people with their spiritual carts before their horses, so to speak. While God surely had ways of compensating for this, such that some people still found a genuine faith in Christ, ideas still had consequences. At a time when many priests and monks could barely read, the method of mass conversion created false expectations and an unrealistic sense of accomplishment.

Despite all that, real accomplishments still advanced God's kingdom in this era. In the 6th century, well-educated Celtic monks like Columba and Columbanus crossed the English Channel and preached across Europe, even as far as Byzantium. They successfully evangelized the kings of many Frankish, Frisian, Pictish, and Saxon tribes by mass conversion. In the next few centuries however, under-educated imitators often simply admitted clans of barely Christianized Pagans into the church. With them, came their traditions and superstitions. [7] While this is a bit of an overgeneralization, it is fair as a broad brush-stroke statement.

One should again recall how severely limited the access to Scripture was for most believers of this period. Here is another shocker, likely to anger some who hold to the same positions I hold to; this was not because the Catholic Church had restricted the Bible from laypersons. That would eventually come, but only much later, after the invention of the printing press. God did not hold the church accountable for things He had not yet enabled it to do. Lawlessness and inter-tribal warfare in Western Europe amplified the economic impossibility of circulating hand-written copies to many laypersons under the harsh conditions of the day. Not even many churches and clergy had their own Bibles. Monks and priests had to memorize the Gospels and parts of the Epistles, as education and occasions to visit monasteries allowed.

Even so, many monks sought to teach the gospel, as best they understood it, amid all the distorted hagiography. These showed remarkable piety; men like Boniface, and a Celtic monk named Caedmon, who translated Scriptures into Gaelic and put them to music. In a few generations, Judeo-Christian legal ideas penetrated into the varied barbarian tribes through the conversion of their kings. It was rickety and imperfect, often riddled with cracks and hypocrisies, but it created a foundation for small-scale law and order that expanded across the landscape. Such expansions met and merged with other similar efforts in time. Others did not.

The mechanics of cause-and-effect were (and still are) relentless, however. Ideas still had consequences. Common Pagan superstitions often penetrated even to the highest levels of church leadership. What intellectual tools developed in the late Roman Era seemed to die on the vine in the Early Middle Ages. Their dried-out seeds waited for another day, over half a millennium off, for rejuvenation.

What seems straightforward to us in God's word sometimes seemed obscure to the early medieval mind, even invisible. Should that really surprise us? The best teachers of that era could not even clearly discern the difference between a supernaturalism born from Pagan folklore, and one that came from a biblical worldview. The tools to do that had not sufficiently developed yet, beyond knowing basic moral differences between angels and demons. Significant as that distinction is in explaining a biblical view of the supernatural, it seemed to have taken a back seat in the Holy Spirit's agenda for that period. Raw survival of even the most essential truths often seemed in jeopardy.

Whereas in the past, grassroots people usually comprised the purer element in the church; now they became as much a source of corruption as the political power seats had been. The fact that this new corruption was more a matter of content than of intent did not change the negative impact it had on Christianity's maturity. Even more than in the East, superstition became the norm in the ruins of Western Roman civilization. People saw things like baptism in magical terms that were quite Pagan in character, even if not always in origin. Instead of a public declaration of an evident spiritual rebirth in Christ, baptism became the ritual that magically regenerated the recipient.

Semi-illiterate priests came to see themselves as bearers of the magic power to bring people into God's kingdom. They did not call it "magic," but what they often practiced came to function as a sort of Christianized sorcery. Pagan tribes, still mesmerized by the fading glory of Rome preserved in the holy litanies and colorful priestly vestments, wanted to capture the power and make it their own. Abbeys and cloisters existed to occupy the "true believers." Clerics used the same memorized words as their more literate forefathers to describe Christian practices like the *Eucharist* and baptism. Yet, the literacy breakdown poured superstitious connotations over those words, accreting around their meanings like a poisoned candy shell. The process often came inadvertently, rather than by cunning. It was a natural result of the slow paganizing of Christianity into a "mystery religion" format.

Christianity and Europe experienced great transitions in the early Middle Ages. During such transitions, old things tend to be lost and new ones gained. Hopefully new gains prove better than the losses, as people productively integrate them into what still remains. Hopefully. Unfortunately, this optimism did not often reflect reality in the churches of the late 1st Millennium. Even so, God was still in control and still at work. To understand what happened at this time in history, we need to look past many of the decay factors just mentioned, without denying their impact. We see what happened through the lens of a history marked by the losses. Yet we also benefit from the gains without recognizing them.

Despite spiritual stagnation in the West, isolated Celtic and Roman monasteries kept the seeds of civilization for future germination. Monks and Abbesses passed knowledge on even when they could not understand or apply it consistently. The monasteries held both theological and technical depth from a more advanced Roman culture in trust. Future generations were coming that could begin to re-assimilate that depth through Scholasticism, and go beyond it in the Reformation and Renaissance.

## Pope Gregory the Great

If any figure could be said to represent the transition between the Roman and Medieval church periods, Pope Gregory the Great would be him. Educated as a Benedictine monk, few in the churches of his time had a more honest missionary zeal. One day, as he walked past a slave auction in Rome, Gregory saw some blond haired boys in their teens sold on the block. He thought they looked angelic (in a good way), and asked what tribe they came from. The auctioneer told him that they were Angli barbarians. Gregory asked where the Angli lived. He decided instantly that this angelic people should no longer remain without the gospel.

This encounter launched one of the greatest missionary movements in history. It would evangelize a people who would launch the most widespread evangelistic efforts of later church history. The Angli became the *English*. Gregory, after he became Pope, sent a Greek monk named Augustine to Britain (not to be confused with Augustine of Hippo) in 596 AD. There, the Angli and the Saxons had gained a permanent foothold at the expense of the original Celtic Britons. The Christian Celts had sporadically tried to evangelize the Angli, but there was still quite a bit of bad blood between them. Fierce Angli, Saxon, and Jute hordes had forced Romanized Christian Celts to retreat westward, calling them the *Wealas*, meaning *foreigner*, in their very own land. The names *Wales* and *Welch* come from this Old English word. These Britannic Celts called themselves the Cymru.

Consequently, the main drive for evangelizing the English came not from local churches, but faraway Rome. Pope Gregory the Great was the human vehicle behind the conversion of many of our ancestors, for those of white Anglo-Saxon descent. In a few generations, the gospel changed warring savages, who drank enemy blood from human skulls, into English town folk, living under rule of law. There is no other civilizing phenomenon like this in all of history. Even so, it came imperfectly, and at a steep price.

Augustine the Greek used mass conversion to win Angli chieftains, though wandering Celtic evangelists had already done some of the foundational work. When Augustine called for help from the Christian Cymru, they refused him because they demanded that the Angli retreat from their lands as a sign of repentance. With many of the Angli chieftains still Pagan, none would agree to that. While Pope Gregory and Augustine lived, the violent conflict on the horizon remained at bay, but they did not live long. Both died about a year apart from each other, Gregory in 605 and Augustine in 606 AD.

Aggravating the tensions was a desire to bring the Celtic church under the power of Rome. Fiercely independent Celtic monks used a different, far older, ritual order for their liturgies than did the Papacy. These followed an earlier method of dating Easter than currently used in Rome. The Celts did not always seem to trust the recent absorption of mainland Western churches under Rome's See, which had been going on for 150 years. Debate exists as to how deep this distrust went. Certainly, a scarcity of surviving records leaves the question partly unknowable. English and Celtic Rites coexisted well enough at first. Pope Gregory had counseled Augustine to choose good things out of both rites and use them together. This quickly dissolved after Gregory and then Augustine died. History considers Augustine the Greek the first Archbishop of Canterbury, the head of the Church of England.

Eventually, the Synod of Whitby in 664 AD settled conflicts between the Celts and Romans in England. Unfortunately, it did so only in favor of Rome. In Wales, the controversy led to the massacre of some 1200 Celtic monks at the monastery of Bangor-on-Dee sometime between 607 and 613 AD. Bangor had a library of records from pre-Roman Celtic times reaching back into pre-history. [8] The independent Celts were by no means pre-Reformation reformers, though some Evangelicals have tried to paint them that way. They were as superstitious along previously discussed lines as any other Christians were at that time. They had, however, a unique missionary zeal before Whitby. After that, the Roman church eclipsed the Celtic one. This happened through slightly later, more shorter-sighted men than Pope Gregory.

Gregory the Great is in some ways a mystery to both Protestants and Roman Catholics. This likely comes from our incomplete ability to avoid modern assumptions in our attempts to understand him. On the one hand, he rejected such titles for himself as "Universal Bishop," the substance of which his successors would eagerly embrace. At this time, Byzantium was the center of Christendom. Gregory wrote a letter rebuking the Patriarch of Constantinople for using the title "Universal Bishop." He did this not because he thought it belonged only to Popes of Rome, but because he thought it pretentious for any bishop. [9] This of course did not mean that Gregory did not feel it within his moral prerogatives to rebuke bishops outside of his own normal jurisdiction at times. He still believed himself the successor of Peter and a bearer of Peter's apostolic authority.

On the other hand, Gregory subscribed to many beliefs and practices that Evangelicals would consider Pagan and superstitious. He developed the ***Doctrine of Purgatory*** at length, using dreadfully out-of-context Scripture citations that read the idea into the text. Purgatory was the logical extension of the mentality that had grown from an incomplete view of God's grace surrounding penance. Like many of the Greek styled presuppositions that had infiltrated the faith, it too came largely from the Stoics.

The Stoics taught the necessity of a place of fire after death for enlightenment and the purging of the soul from the corruptions of material life. Without it, they believed no one could enter spiritual peace. They called this state *Empurosis.* [10] Zoroastrians and Babylonians, like many pre-Christian Pagan religions driven by pride in human effort, taught such a place after death. [11] It felt right to a people burdened by guilt over post-baptismal sins for which the sacrifice of Christ now seemed insufficient. Not that anyone at the time thought the church was making less of the death of Christ. Rather, nobody seemed to notice what was happening. At least no record exists of such a controversy.

Neither Rome nor Constantinople had the technology or manpower to erase such a controversy from history. Such power did not even begin to exist until the 20th century. If they had had such power, would they not have used it to erase the Iconoclasts from memory? That Constantinople and Rome saved pro-Icon texts with Iconoclast quotations intact, for argument, shows the Papacy and Patriarchy did not think this way. A controversy against purgatory at this time would have left an enormous paper trail, had people been aware of the implications. It is far more likely that the controversy did not exist because nobody at that time was equipped to see the implications. This meant that the issue was not yet on the Holy Spirit's front burner.

Some might ask how I could write such a thing when Reformation martyrs died to bring us a biblical view of salvation against the corruption the Doctrine of Purgatory created. Others would wrongly see it as an admission that poorly fabricated doctrines like purgatory are not important issues—they are. The operative word is *yet*; as in, "the issue was not *yet* on the Holy Spirit's front burner." Ideally, it would be wonderful to deal with all sin and all human error all at once and get it over with. We simply can't. How well does that work in reality for individuals, let alone nations, and inter-continental spiritual movements like the Christian faith? There's the ideal, and then there's the real. Scripture deals with both.

This brings us back to the mechanics of what was likely fully do-able and see-able at the time. It raises the complex issue of whether it is reasonable for us to expect the center-stage questions of the 6th and 7th centuries to be the same as those of the 16th and 17th centuries or the 21st. One might cry out that salvation by grace alone through faith is always a core issue, and that is true. This is a book on the effect of worldviews on Christian thought in history, however. Did all worldviews during church history provide the same raw material for understanding what Scripture says about grace and faith? Do records show that the Holy Spirit somehow leveled the worldview playing field? Was that even His job? Just how precisely could a teacher in Gregory's day grasp what they read about those concepts?

Certainly, teachers of that day could read a Latin Bible, they had some understanding of grace and faith, and the Holy Spirit was at work. That does not mean they had all of the thought forms available to those who lived in later centuries or to we who live today. We simply cannot say with absolute certainty what men in Gregory's day could take away from Scripture when they read it. In Pope Gregory's mind, God gave grace to man through the gospel and the sacraments of the church. History has long since proved that many of his assumptions were wrong. By today's standards, early medieval concepts of grace were imprecise and skewed by distorting influences. Nevertheless, God would not deal with this problem comprehensively for another thousand years. One might just as well complain about why God tolerated polygamy in the lives of Jacob, King David, and Solomon.

> **"And that servant who knew his master's will, and did not prepare himself or do according to his will, shall be beaten with many stripes. But he who did not know, yet committed things deserving of stripes, shall be beaten with few. For everyone to whom much is given, from him much will be required; and to whom much has been committed, of him they will ask the more."** ***Luke*** **12:47-48 (NKJV)**

We need to consider historical figures like Pope Gregory in the context of their times. To do that fairly, we must compare them with knowledge available during the same period, not with what we can know today. Despite an inadequate view of grace, and all the other fallacies of his day, Gregory the Great managed, by God's grace, to do marvels! He arranged the evangelization of the very people who would make most of later church history happen! Of course, Pope Gregory also furthered spiritual trends that were not at all healthy. He ascribed functionally magical powers to the ritual of the Mass. He was one of the first major teachers to hook these up with being able to help people get out of purgatory. How much of this was simply building on an eroding vision of the past, and how much was something worse, is impossible to say with certainty. God holds us accountable for what we can know and act upon, not for what is half-hidden from our sight and beyond our powers.

While Gregory the Great was one of the brightest lights of his time, clearly his light sometimes shined in spite of what he advocated and taught, rather than because of it. His lifestyle was above reproach and his humility genuine. Still, he held to many bizarre and unbiblical views and practices, some of which would even make many American Roman Catholics today recoil. (I grew up Catholic, so I have a good idea of what might do this.) For example, he avidly encouraged the building of shrines and altars around the dead body parts of martyrs and saints. He wrote that if a person could obtain a piece of a martyr's corpse, and build an altar around it, that they would have life-long good fortune. [12] Only two centuries before, a mainstream catholic bishop named Caecilian had rebuked people for this sort of thing. [13] What had been a fringe element in the church had now moved into the mainstream.

Some say that Gregory followed the documented opinion of a slightly earlier pope, Gelasius. He spoke against a fringe tradition of their day—the legend that Mary was taken up bodily into heaven. In 1740, Pope Benedict XIV called this story insufficiently trustworthy to make into a church dogma. [14] In 1950, however, the ***"Assumption*** (or, taking up) ***of Mary"*** was made an "infallible doctrine of the Roman Catholic Church." This illustrates how foreign traditions over time tend to move from the fringes toward the mainstream, distorting truth as they go.

If Popes Gregory and Gelasius, with Benedict XIV, infallibly rejected the Assumption of Mary as inauthentic; then how can Pope Pius XII infallibly elevate it a doctrine of the church? Catholic sources claim that Gregory, Gelasius, and Benedict XIV had not spoken ***ex cathedra*** or "from the chair" when they discounted the Assumption of Mary. Gregory and Gelasius likely did not know that they were infallible. The idea of papal infallibility had not really been thought of yet, much less been codified as a doctrine. The idea of papal infallibility existed in the time of Benedict XIV, but only as a debatable idea. It, too, took centuries to mainstream.

While Gregory rejected being "Universal Bishop," some of his ideas laid the foundation for a papacy similar to what that title implied. During his papacy, the Roman Popes became custodians of a large tract of Italy called the Patrimony of Peter. Gregory proved an able administrator, doing many charitable works through this temporal trust. While his successors would abuse this worldly power, Gregory did not. He even showed a potential for using such an office for great good. Despite how he personally demonstrated signs of spiritual life, many of his teachings were part of the idea flow that led down to the dead religion of the later Middle Ages. In him, the grassroots superstition of the Germanic barbarian made it fully into the Papal Chair and found a place of acceptance there.

## BIBLIOGRAPHY


1. Shelley, Bruce L. ***Church History in Plain Language*** (2nd Edition), pp.145-147, 1995, Word Publishing, Dallas, Tx.
2. Ibid. p. 142
3. ***Elvira canons***, Catholic University of America on-line library, *"Placuit picturas in ecclesia esse non debere, ne quod colitur et adoratur in parietibus depingatur."*
4. Beckwith, John, ***Early Christian and Byzantine Art***, p. 169, Penguin History of Art (now Yale), 2nd edn. 1979; See also, Mango, Cyril (1977), *Historical Introduction*, p. 1, in Bryer & Herrin, eds., ***Iconoclasm***, Centre for Byzantine Studies, University of Birmingham
5. Warren Treadgold, ***A History of the Byzantine State and Society***, Stanford University Press, 1997
6. Henry Chadwick, ***The Early Church*** (The Penguin History of the Church, 1993), p. 283.
7. Op cit. Shelley. p. 158
8. Bill Cooper, ***After the Flood***, p. 43, 1995, New Wine Press, Chichester, W. Sussex, England; See also, ***Archaeolgica Cambrensis:*** *Journal of the Cambrian Archaeological Association*, Jan. 1876, pp. 291-299
9. Op cit. Shelley, Bruce L., p.167
10. ***Encyclopedia Britannica***, Vol. 22, p. 660, 11th Ed.
11. Hislop, Alexander, ***The Two Babylons***, pp. 167-170, 1st Ed. 1916, 1st American Ed. 1943, 2nd Ed. 1959, Loizeaux Brothers, Neptune, NJ.
12. Op cit. Shelley, Bruce L., p.170
13. Smith, M.A. ***The Church Under Siege***, p. 26, 1976, Inter-Varsity Press, Leicester, England
14. ***Baker's Dictionary of Theology***, p. 69, 1960, Baker Book House, Grand Rapids, Mi.

# 10

# THE MIDDLE AGES, PART 2: THE HOLY ROMAN EMPIRE AND THE EAST-WEST CHURCH SPLIT

## THE HOLY ROMAN EMPIRE: PROTOTYPE FOR EUROPEAN MONARCHY BY DIVINE RIGHT, VERSUS THE RISE OF ISLAM

The Franks became the first Germanic tribe to embrace Orthodox Christianity, starting with the conversion of one of their chieftains, Chlodovocar, in 496 AD. An Arian evangelist, Ulfilas, had already converted the Visigoths and Vandals from Paganism to Arianism, back when the Roman Empire still governed Gaul. By Chlodovocar's time, the Arian Goths had invaded, making the Catholic Gauls in what is now France into a minority. The Pagan Frankish tribes occupied the northlands they had once held as a frontier for the Romans, only now they did so for themselves. History remembers Chlodovocar more commonly as "King Clovis." Clovis' grandfather, Merovech, and his father, Childeric, had served the Romans as mercenaries until the fall of the Western Empire. Historians call Clovis' kingly line the ***Merovingian Dynasty***, after his grandfather's name.

Clovis' wife actually deserves the honor of being the first influential Orthodox believer among the Franks. Queen Clothilde, like many of her sisters today, had difficulty trying to convince her Pagan husband to embrace the faith. It took bringing the war-like Frankish chieftain to the verge of utter defeat at the hands of the Alamanni—yet another Germanic tribe—to break his pride. Clovis, bitter that his own gods had deserted him, promised to follow the Christian God should Christ bring him victory that day. When the fortunes of war rapidly reversed in his favor, the triumphant Clovis agreed to baptism into the Catholic faith. This meant that his entire retinue of warriors, with their families, would also join him in the baptismal waters.

The conversion of the Frankish kings was not a deep one, but it helped restore some semblance of government to part of the ravaged West, though not an efficient one. Many tribes settled in the gutted ruins of the Western Empire during the centuries that followed—Burgundians, Vandals, Sueves, Alans, and Goths, to name a few. Tribal conversions often led to piece-meal loyalty to the Roman Papacy; Catholic versus Arian versus Pagan. The conversion of the Franks and the Angli secured a growing spiritual hegemony in the northwest, but things were not so secure nearer to Rome. The savage Lombards constantly harassed the Patrimony of Peter lands ruled by the Popes. Intrigues and petty wars went on with the Burgundians, and the Arian Visigoths in what is now Spain. The latter half of the 1st Millennium was a time of continual crisis for the church in both the East and West, like a monster with many heads!

To complicate things for all of the Christian West, from Byzantium to Frankland, a new religion started in Arabia during the 7th century. An Arab from Mecca named Mohammed made prophetic claims that he spoke for the same God of the Jews and Christians. He fused half-understood bits of Jewish law and parts of several Christian heresies with the worship of Suenne, an old Sumerian moon god. The result became the militant religious and political movement we know as *Islam*. [1] Living on the edge of a decaying Byzantine Empire, Mohammed's view of Christ came mainly from Nestorians and Gnostics. He took this as mainstream Christianity, just as the Goths and Vandals had taken the Arianism of Ulfilas.

Islam became far more than just a competing religion. It developed into a worldview that undergirded every aspect of life, starting with the political one. A truly biblical Christianity ideally also becomes a worldview that guides how one sees all areas of existence. It, however, does not begin with politics, though it is not apolitical. Nothing that deals with reality can be apolitical because politics is socially necessary to the human condition. It is a good idea to know how these two worldviews differ, especially today.

Many make the naive mistake of assuming that Allah and Yahweh are merely different names for the same God, with the same spiritual agenda. A serious comparative study of the two deities shows that they are not the same, only that Islam used redefined terminology from both Judaism and Christianity. Sometimes the differences between belief systems are more important than their similarities. This is especially so when dealing with where the clashing belief systems take people on a large scale. One would expect to find this sort of thing in the real world, where different ideas have differing consequences.

Seeing the differences between basic teachings in Islam and Christianity is crucial to grasping our history. It is also a key to understanding the many dangers Western Civilization faces today from Jihadists. The Muslim denial of Christ's suffering, death, and deity places Islam's Allah at odds with the God described in the Bible. At least three other conflicting beliefs also make trivial whatever similarities there may be between Christianity and Islam. The first is the difference in how both systems view the nature of divine revelation. The second are the inconsistencies between Allah and Yahweh in makeup and character. The third contrasts how Christians and Muslims see their most basic roles according to their most fundamental teachings.

The Jewish and Christian view of divine revelation is quite different from the Islamic one. The Christian view is that God breathed His word into the lives, thoughts, words, and writing styles of the Bible's human authors. This created a progressive, non-contradictory revelation as His written word. As with any real message, the Bible requires interpretation based on more than just the reader's subjective spiritual experiences. Relying on subjective intuition alone creates a setting where people redefine words too easily. A strong personality skilled at manipulating people can use such a setting to place God into their own personal box. Good Scripture interpretation also needs coherency and logical harmonization. This establishes objective meaning, which enables long-term spiritual stability and growth. It allows Christians to sanity check their individual spiritual experiences, as the Bible commands.

> **Beloved, do not believe every spirit, *but test the spirits, whether they are of God;* because many false prophets have gone out into the world. *1 John* 4:1 (NKJV)**

> **19 And so we have the prophetic word confirmed, which you do well to heed as a light that shines in a dark place, until the day dawns and the morning star rises in your hearts; 20 knowing this first, that *no prophecy of Scripture is of any private interpretation,* 21 for prophecy never came by the will of man, but holy men of God spoke as they were moved by the Holy Spirit. *2 Peter* 1:19-21 (NKJV)**

The Christian view of interpreting Divine revelation also requires that believers have a subjective experience with the Holy Spirit. The "sanity check" happens because the New Testament is an objective truth standard, open to scrutiny with honest and logical interpretive methods. Neither human intellect nor intuition posing as the Spirit can get too far for long. Scripture is the final word until Christ returns. Not even the Apostles could abrogate Old Testament Scripture or the New Testament they were in the process of receiving and recording.

> **8 *But even if we, or an angel from heaven,* preach any other gospel to you than what we have preached to you, let him be accursed. 9 As we have said before, so**

**now I say again, if anyone preaches any other gospel to you than what you have received, let him be accursed. *Galatians* 1:8-9 (NKJV)**

**10 Then the brethren immediately sent Paul and Silas away by night to Berea. When they arrived, they went into the synagogue of the Jews. 11 These were more fair-minded than those in Thessalonica, in that they received the word with all readiness, *and searched the Scriptures daily to find out whether these things were so. Acts* 17:8-10 (NKJV)** (*They did not just believe Paul because he had recently done miraculous stuff involving a demon-possessed slave girl and an earthquake – see Acts Ch. 16 – KGP*)

**Let two or three prophets speak, and *let the others judge. 1Corinthians* 14:29 (NKJV)**

**1 Now the Spirit expressly says that *in latter times some will depart from the faith,* giving heed to deceiving spirits and doctrines of demons, 2 speaking lies in hypocrisy, having their own conscience seared with a hot iron, 3 forbidding to marry, and commanding to abstain from foods which God created to be received with thanksgiving by those who believe and know the truth.**

***1 Timothy* 4:1-3 (NKJV)**

God created an objective reality, and we are His *subjects*. Because the God of the Bible is the God of reality, we should expect His Word to fit reality as far as we can accurately observe it. Here is where problems happen. Fallen human beings too often assume they have a greater ability to observe reality than they really do. False teachers aside, even Spirit-led Christians are not immune to this. We still struggle with our old natures (Gal. 5:16-26) and with both natural and God-imposed limits on our abilities to observe. (1 Cor. 13:8-13)

Without this objective base, any continual attempt to build from subjective spiritual experiences would make chaos of Bible interpretation. This happens today whenever Christians devalue analytical logic as if it were anti-spiritual in itself. Likewise, without a subjective experience of the Holy Spirit, only intellectuals could have access to God's mind. They would categorize Bible truth logically, and endlessly; sometimes to the imposing of artificial limits not intended by the Divine Author. Eventually, their scholastic categories become more real to them than God Himself, until they also end up putting God in a different kind of box. Ironically, people at both extremes of objectivity and subjectivity become certain that the other is "putting God in a box." They too often remain blind to how they do the same thing.

This is not a weakness in the Judeo-Christian understanding of Divine revelation. It is what happens when Christians fail to think clearly about what they believe, why they believe it, and who the Person is that enables them to believe it. This weakness characterizes our own era, but is not unique to it. For that reason, historical context is also important to the Judeo-Christian view of interpreting Divine revelation; again because the God of the Bible is the God of reality. Certain parts of the Old Testament applied only to the nation of Israel. Yet, even these have universal value today as types and metaphors.

By contrast, the Islamic ***Doctrine of Abrogation*** dominates the interpretation of Muslim scripture. To *abrogate* means to over-rule, supersede, or to cancel and replace. Whenever a contradiction arises in the text—and Muslim scholars freely admit to many; verses of the ***Qur'an*** and ***Hadiths*** (the Muslim "Bible") that Mohammed supposedly wrote the latest always supersede those written earlier. This differs sharply from Christianity, where the New Testament ties together and fulfills the spiritual intent of the Old. The New Testament does not abrogate the Old, which God wrote to the nation Israel. It, rather, is a new covenant to a different but related group of people pulled out of all nations (including some from the Jews)—the Church. As such, we can compare the New and Old Testaments to two books by the same author. Though written for different purposes, they share the author's ethical character.

In the Abrogation doctrine, Mohammed could lay out a major moral principle, then a year later, tell his followers the principle had changed. Instead of thinking through the logical contradictions in their holy texts (supposedly penned over 23 years), the Muslim just puts more authority on later commands. Another degree of subjectivism exists in that the author(s) did not lay the sayings of the Qur'an out in chronological order. Sub-schemes of abrogated verses depend on the branch of Islam, though all follow the increasing emphasis on ***jihad*** or "holy war" over time.

In the Christian worldview, believers must harmonize apparent biblical contrasts because God is not erratic in nature. Even when He took drastic action on rare occasions, like the Great Flood and the Exodus judgments, the same bedrock ethic as in the rest of the Bible prevailed. God's revealed character, His fundamental truthfulness, and changelessness expressed in written covenants and promises, gives us a basis for trust. This forced early Christians to think about the nature of truth, and to ask questions of the Bible—something unthinkable to most religions of the day.

The ethics and theology in the Old and New Testament readily agree with each other. People are logically able to take the few passages that seem to conflict as mere contrasts of context. (A remarkable thing, since 40 different authors wrote the Bible over a period of at least 1500 years. One would expect many more hard-to-harmonize passages than there actually are.)

Conversely, in Islamic revelation, all the Muslim must do with apparent contradictions is know which verses of the Qur'an Mohammed wrote latest in his life, then stick more to those. The earlier-written verses are "abrogated" or cancelled out by the later ones. This is extremely important to understand today. The reasons become apparent to anyone who studies the worldview and motives that drive modern Jihadist terrorists.

Mohammed apparently started out as a man of peace, who spoke against the corruption and idolatry of his own tribe at Mecca. The Meccans persecuted him and his followers during the early years of their movement. The verses of the Qur'an supposedly written at this time, teach moral persuasion by example. Mohammed, at this early point, forbade the faithful to match violence with violence. This phase did not last long.

Eventually, circumstances forced Mohammed and his followers to move to Medina or face death. Jews and Christians, called *"people of the Book,"* were not to be molested, but appealed to as potential converts. At this time, "Allah's Prophet" began to permit defensive warfare. Sayings in the revelation from that period reflected this. These verses "abrogated" or superseded the earlier sayings that forbade all violence. Later still, the Medina movement turned to caravan raiding and then conquered Mecca. Teachings from this stage called for offensive warfare against not only Pagans, but also Jews and Christians that refused Islamic law. These began to dominate the developing revelation of the Qur'an.

At this point, early Islamic texts depict a very different Mohammed; a man of growing absolute power who, it would be obvious to Western minds, had become corrupted absolutely by that power. When the daughter of a leading sheik wrote a poem criticizing growing violence in his movement, Mohammed had a volunteer murder her. (Hadith Ishaq 675-676) The same thing happened with a Jewish merchant, whose assassin had been a friendly business acquaintance of the victim before Mohammed ordered the "honor killing." (Hadiths Tabari 7:97, Sahih Muslim 19:4436, and Ishaq 368) People were amazed and terrified by the changes coming over these normally ethical men who had volunteered to perform such killings. (Hadith Tabari 17:187) The Prophet had established conditions that redefined murder into a sacred act.

The later sayings of the Qur'an, from this stage, abrogated or cancelled out earlier restrictions against harassing Christians and Jews. This is how modern terrorists justify their actions based on Islamic revelation. Islamic apologists and Muslims who dislike violence claim that Islam is "a religion of peace," appealing to Mohammed's earlier verses. When Mohammed's earlier, peaceful sayings are convenient or closer to one's personal values, "temporarily abrogating" their abrogation works, too. It is even easier to remember the abrogation of these peaceful verses when Islamic leaders feel the need.

Abrogation, as a way to interpret divine revelation, is capricious. It needs no thought, no searching for truth, no internal logical harmonization—only knowledge of which sayings Mohammed wrote latest in his life. A consistent Christian worldview would find the Doctrine of Abrogation either dishonest or non-rational or both. Muslims and Christians alike have well noted the capriciousness of Allah over the centuries. Abrogation as a guiding principle of interpretation appears to reflect that character. Traditional Judeo-Christian Western logic and ethics cannot help but see through to its fallacy. The Islamic worldview uses Abrogation to formulate its basic definition of truth. [2] Truth is not so subjective or capricious, however. Such ideas have had dreadful consequences.

When Byzantine Christianity had grown stale and corrupt, Islam seemed to promise a restoration of purity. This came through the fiery commitment spawned in its converts. Mohammed seemed originally to admire the morality in what little he grasped of Judaic and Christian writings (he was illiterate most his life). He could not help notice that Christians in the East ignored many of these precepts—particularly those that portrayed God as a hater of idols. He also made no distinction between Nestorian, Gnostic, and Orthodox texts. He concluded that Jesus was just another prophet, and made himself the central revealer of his own theology. One thing Mohammed got right was that his movement would be the scourge of God's chastisement on a self-satisfied and complacent church.

Islam was the worst form of false religion because it appealed to people who really despaired over the spiritual deadness and moral laxity of the church; people who might otherwise have found the central truths of Christianity again. It seemed that what we today call "revival" stood little chance in the Byzantine Church. The chances for a biblical Iconoclasm collapsed against two massive social forces. The first was a popular folk Christianity that lacked discernment, and the second, the imperial church-state's rigid formalism. No help came from the West. Churches there were just as decadent if for somewhat different reasons. The only hope for some on the increasingly fluid borders of the empire seemed to be a spiritual war from outside the Christian system. People seemed too desperate to care just how far outside of it.

After swiftly taking Arabia, Islam swept through Persia and Syria. In time, it conquered right up to the gates of Constantinople itself, but that would take several centuries. Within a single generation, it swarmed west, over Egypt, and across North Africa. It finally cut off the Coptic Church at Alexandria from both Rome and Constantinople. The Copts paid an oppressive tribute to live on as an enclave in Islamic Egypt, where their church has remained much to this day with its own pope and ecclesiastical infrastructure.

The jihad rampaged all the way to Morocco, then north across the Strait of Gibraltar, into Spain. There, Muslim Saracens and Berbers overran the Visigoths, conquering the Spanish peninsula, and northward, halfway into France. The Islamic tide began to turn in 732 AD at the Battle of Tours (also called the Battle of Poitiers). There, forces commanded by Charles Martel, Mayor of the Palace for the Frankish King, pushed back. Martel carefully chose a battlefield designed to hamper the Saracen's huge cavalry advantage.

Martel eventually drove the Islamic Saracens back over the Pyrenees into Spain. This prevented the total rout of Western Christian civilization—such as it was. Fortunately, for us, God does not always look at us the way we are, but rather at what we will become when He is done with us. He sometimes seems to deal with civilizations the same way. Though Martel won a pivotal victory, the Franks were a bunch of yokels compared to the technologically superior Saracens. The Muslims, by now, rode a century-long winning streak. Pride was about due to engineer a fall. Yet there were those in the Frankish kingdom, led by Charles, who knew things had to change or else the Christian West would soon face extinction.

The son of Charles Martel, Pepin the Short, petitioned the Pope for church support of a *coup de'tat*. This would make Pepin not merely Mayor of the Palace, but King of the Franks. By this time, the Mayors had been the real power for many generations, anyway. Since the Pope needed a protector against the hostile Lombard tribes, he agreed to Pepin's request and anointed him King, "By the grace of God." This conferred new standards on how kingship operated among the Franks. Pepin ushered the former puppet king off to a monastery—a new customary fate for those who fell from political favor. This gave evidence that the Christian gospel's effect on at least on some aspects of government proved more than just symbolic. In the old days, people would simply find a defeated rival with a battle-ax buried in his skull.

Pepin's son, Charles the Great, commonly known as Charlemagne, succeeded his father as King of the Franks. He took back part of Spain from the Saracens, and pushed the Slavic Avars out of what is now Austria. Pope Adrian I soon called on him to protect the Papal States from yet another Lombard incursion. Charlemagne responded by marching over the Alps like Hannibal, and attacking the Lombard flank from the north. When he defeated the Lombards, he declared himself their king *"by the grace of God."* Adrian gave Charlemagne a hero's welcome at Rome. The Frankish King, however, while a respecter of the Papacy, was not as swayed by Roman splendor, as Pope Adrian had hoped. He tended to treat the Papal States as part of his own kingdom, much to the Papacy's consternation. Charlemagne even meddled in church affairs, though never without counsel from clerical advisors in his court.

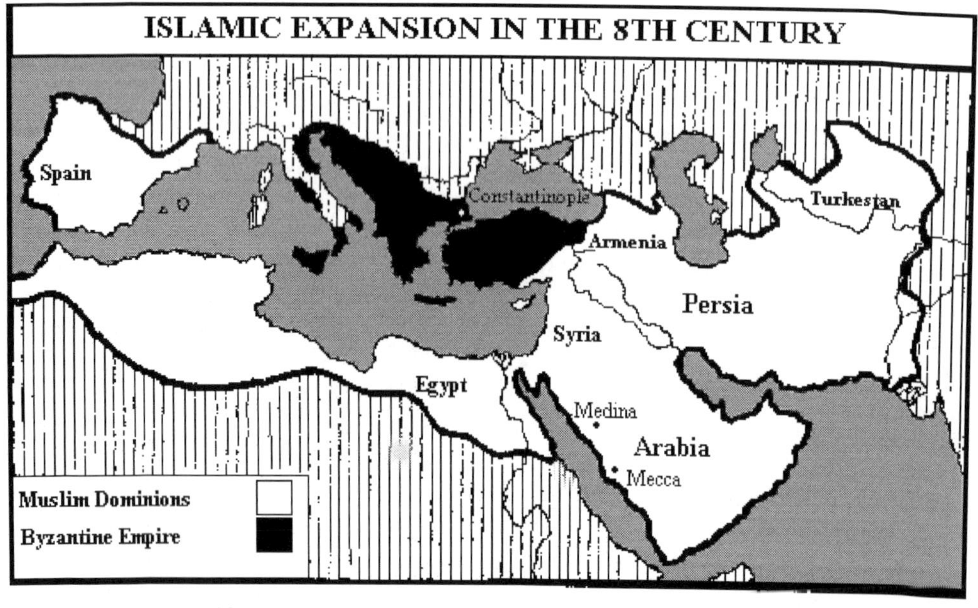


*This map shows the rapid spread of Islam. Though the spread west was rapid, it took a long time for Islam to penetrate Asia Minor all the way to Constantinople.*

Historians call the model of church development from this era ***Christendom***—a combination of the words *Christianity* with *kingdom*. Most people today use that word to mean the sum of all Christian denominations, but that is not the precise definition, nor is it the definition used in this book. Christendom was the Western version of the Byzantine church-state fusion. Charlemagne, effectively, was a political and sociological clone of Constantine. Unlike what had happened in the East, the Popes of Rome were trying to engineer a situation where Charlemagne would be more a tool of the Papacy than the other way around. The Popes had watched from a distance the Patriarchy of Constantinople become a mere creature of Byzantine politics.

They had a major problem here. Charlemagne really saw himself as "the new Constantine." It took considerable intrigue on the Papacy's part to keep him from pulling the strings of church leadership like some Western version of Justinian. These Popes had a real conflict of interest on their hands. They needed this king's goodwill in order to survive, militarily speaking. In the 300 years since Clovis, the Franks had begun to reassemble what appeared to be a revival of the Western Roman Empire to many churchmen. During those same centuries, the Patriarchy of Constantinople had been the center of Christianity, Rome being an outpost. All that appeared to be changing now. The West saw the Iconoclast Movements in the East as heretical attempts to usurp the "true leadership" of the church.

By 800 AD, Charlemagne had defeated a second Lombard uprising. He also rescued Pope Leo III from an attack orchestrated by a large faction of church leaders in Rome that accused him of tyranny and misconduct. After Charlemagne confirmed the Pope's right to rule the Papal States, the exceedingly grateful Pontiff did a surprising thing. Some say without the King's prior knowledge. Likely, Pope Leo and Charlemagne had orchestrated the event with great care. The Pope anointed the Frankish King Emperor of the "Holy Roman Empire." The glory the barbarian chieftains had lusted after for over three centuries now became the sole property of Charles the Great. For him it would be a short-lived glory.

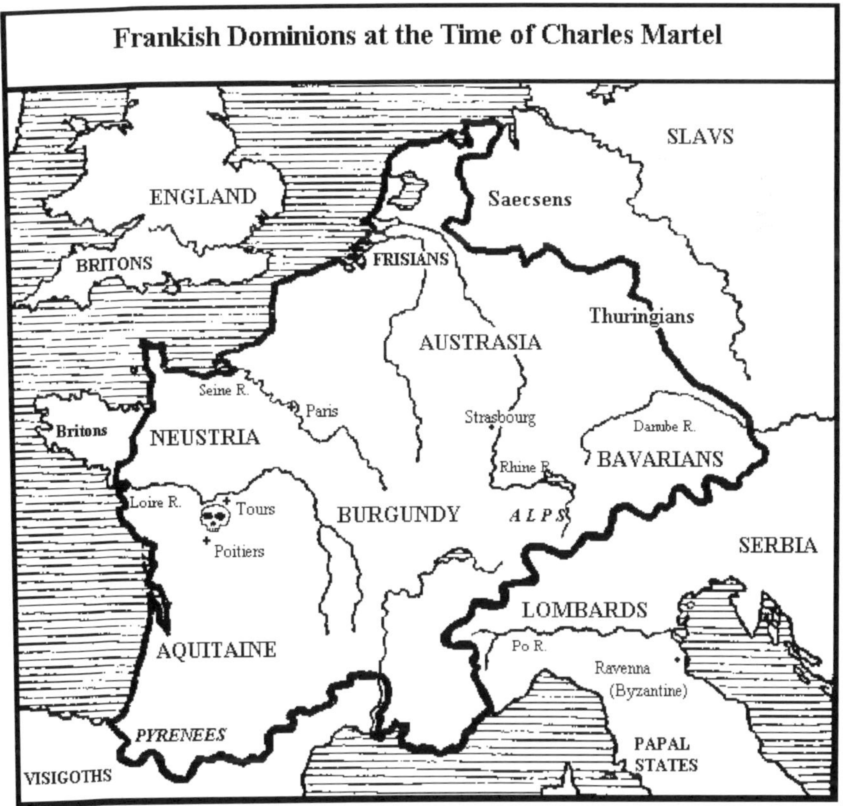


*The Frankish Kingdom of Pepin through a papal supported coup de 'tat*

A brief renaissance of Christian culture blossomed under Charlemagne. Historians have called his line the "Carolingian dynasty" because Charles, Carol, Carl, and Karl are all just different forms of the same name. Entrenched pagan ideas had emerged in Christian terms by now, particularly reflecting Roman and Germanic concepts of a state cult. The Emperor's court scholar, Alcuin, declared that the new Frankish empire had become the fulfillment of Saint Augustine of Hippo's *City of God;* a view that was to set the mold for Medieval Christianity. In this mold, the state existed to help the church establish God's perfect society on earth. In Charlemagne, the virtual clone of Constantine, European monarchies found their prototype—a ruler from a royal family by divine right.

Unfortunately for the Holy Roman Empire, Charlemagne's son, Louis the Pious, turned out a sentimental incompetent; too religiously compliant to Rome for his own good. He remained so, even when the Pope favored the rebellion of his sons against him! Louis was so weak a ruler that he was forced to abdicate. Eventually, Louis' sons divided the Holy Roman Empire among themselves, regressing to an old pre-Carolingian Frankish custom that had fostered much instability. The eastern lands, which continued to bear the name "Holy Roman," eventually became the "1st Reich" of the German Empire, under Otto. The western region eventually reasserted itself as Frankland, otherwise known as *France*.

Soon, these kingdoms buckled under the relentless invasions of the Norsemen, and the southern depredations of Islam. The whole system quickly broke down further into feudalism. Loss of effective government and trade became so acute by the end of the 1st Millennium that some felt that the Second Coming of Christ must be imminent. (***Feudalism*** meant that the only government came through a loose network of semi-independent land barons that effectively owned the serfs who worked their lands.) Ironically, when the Roman Popes finally got their compliant Holy Roman Emperor in Louis, they did not like what they saw, and helped sack him.

The Popes during Charlemagne's reign had indulged in a good deal of intrigue to try to limit the Emperor's power in church affairs. Actually, this had started during Pepin's time. The Mayor-turned-King, like Martel before him, had proven respectful of the Papacy, but not intimidated by it. The intrigue came with a stronger papal form of "universal church authority" to counterweight that of the Patriarch of Constantinople. Pope Leo the Great had laid the groundwork for solidifying the Western church under the Roman Papacy in practice. Gregory the Great had opposed a "universal bishop" even at Rome, protesting a Byzantine claim to universal church authority. For three centuries, the Patriarchs became the highest church authority. Only the fact that they were creatures of the Byzantine Emperor, some of whom had been Iconoclasts, called them into question.

The Popes mainly used two documents to confirm before Pepin and Charlemagne their authority over all the churches. The first, *The Donation of Constantine*, was a complete forgery made by the secretary of either Pope Gregory III or Pope Stephen. [2] Even Roman Catholic scholars admit this document was forged. It wove the tale of how Pope Sylvester of Rome had supposedly healed Constantine of leprosy. A grateful Emperor rewarded him by donating all Christian churches in the empire to the authority of the Bishop of Rome. Such a phony yarn was an insult to Pepin and Charles' intelligence.

The second document, the *pseudo-Isidorian Decretals,* was a partial forgery. It reflected the same political perception as the *Donation of Constantine*. [3] A question we need to ask here is; *why was this necessary if Christians everywhere had known of Peter's inherited primacy through Rome from the start?* This may have revolved more around the Pope's right to govern the Papal States; but what does that have to do with the primacy over all Christian churches that these forged documents proclaimed? **"No lie is of the truth."** (1 John) The

Popes were not content to be the successors of Peter. They also wanted to be the successors of the Roman Emperors who had persecuted and murdered Peter.

Nobody saw how these were opposite, mutually exclusive, bases for spiritual authority.

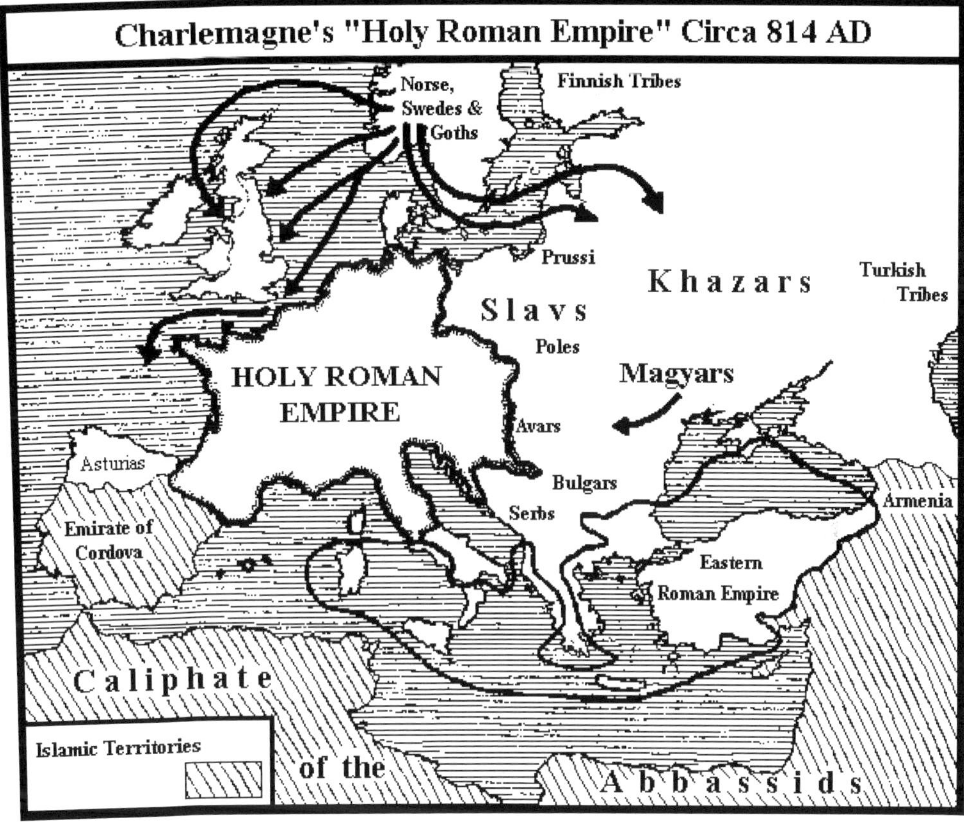


*The Holy Roman Empire was beset by the Norsemen to the North, the Slavs and Magyars to the East, and by Islam to the South*

## Celebration to Sacrament: The Politics of Transubstantiation

Everything is interconnected. If the church is to be the state cult in this world, then its rites potentially become tools of political manipulation—whether anyone intends for them to be that or not. It is mechanically unavoidable by a social form of cause-and-effect. In turn, this has consequences on the spiritual life of the church, which Christ designed to advance God's kingdom, not to become an instrument of the world's.

One consequence is the loss of an experiential reliance on the Holy Spirit at both the grassroots level, and in the leadership systems of the church. If Caesar is lord of the church, even indirectly, then Jesus is not. The blood of several million martyrs punctuates this point. Another consequence is loss of education quality. Whether this came by illiterate warlords or by imperial "bread and circuses" for compliant subjects, made little difference. General grassroots literacy to understand the word of God, even in times before the printing press, aided the spread and deepening of the Faith.

While Charlemagne encouraged literacy, he did not last long enough to bring it to the same grassroots level as during the Roman period. He also had an interest in developing the church further into an effective state cult. The Papacy itself now had a set of small states to govern, so it, too, had a natural interest in controlling education. Not that kings and bishops deliberately plotted at this time to keep the masses ignorant on a vast scale. Satan worked inside their worldview blind spots, as he does against us today. This time, however, history's verdict shows a dishonesty that was clearly visible to church leaders even as they engaged in it.

Before addressing that, we need to realize another factor, which church leaders were not yet equipped to see clearly, because nobody at that time could. Christians would not develop adequate intellectual tools to discern biblical forms of supernaturalism from that of old wives' tales for another thousand years. They did not even know they needed to, beyond avoiding the "black arts." Belief in the supernatural was like belief in air. People were certain they felt it everywhere, but had difficulty telling it from nothingness—unless they were in a hurricane. It would be almost four centuries before Christians in the West returned to addressing a fundamental question; *did God intend for us to understand His word rationally, mystically, spiritually, or by some admixture?* No clear dividing line between the natural and supernatural existed yet in people's minds.

In the 7th century, scholars who taught from Paul's epistles also imagined that what amounted to magical powers would radiate from bones in a martyr's corpse. This lack of clarity on the supernatural had always been around, even before Rome fell. Yet, the power of the Holy Spirit had used literacy to keep Pagan ideas about the supernatural at bay in the church. The most pagan of all ideas to penetrate the church by this time was that religion existed to prop up the state magically, through ritual and priest-craft.

The Holy Spirit of Scripture, and apparently in history, did not seem as eager to endorse a church that functioned as a state cult. I am not merely projecting my own worldview back into another age here. Literacy tempered by Christian faith made a real difference, even in a pre-Modern Greco-Roman age. The 2nd century church viewed ordinances like communion and baptism more mystically than we do today. Yet, limits imposed by literacy helped keep spiritual thinking from decaying to "magical thinking." Literacy builds attention to detail and some ability to keep things in perspective. Such limits later eroded with literacy's decline. The effects of semi-pagan folk religion and state cultism showed, and historians of all faiths recognize this. People now effectively viewed the sacraments more in magical, rather than spiritual, ways.

We saw how ideas had consequences in the way the understanding of baptism degenerated. The Lord's Supper also suffered erosion of meaning in the minds of churchmen during the late 1st millennium. Early Christians allowed for a mystical presence of Christ in the Eucharist, without defining the nature of unknowable things. The definition of "a mystical presence" shifted across time and worldview transitions, though the sacramental words stayed the same. Even 7th century scholars did not always understand the writings of those who went before them with adequate conceptual safeguards. A "conceptual safeguard" is a set of reasonable limits in how people teach ideas, which discourages the learner from taking them to bizarre extremes. Such safeguards may be an implicit product of higher vocabulary that enables things to "go without saying" or an explicit set of control limits. Here, the loss was more implicit.

I mentioned earlier that, before the Council of Nicea, many Eastern churchmen had not used such safeguards in the way they had spoken about the Trinity. Consequently, people in the West sometimes mistakenly thought Easterners worshipped three gods. Eventually, this led to fuzzy thinking, which Satan exploited during the rise of Arianism. Now the same kind of thing was happening with the idea of Christ's presence in the Eucharist. People no longer spoke of the spiritual presence of Christ at communion with the built-in safeguards implicitly understood in earlier times.

In the 9th Century, the abbot Paschasius Radbertus began to preach an excessively physical view of communion. In it, the bread and wine literally transformed into the reconstituted flesh and blood of Christ when a priest prayed over it. [4] Before, and still in the East, priests taught the presence of Christ in the elements as a mystical and spiritual reality. As early as Tertullian, records show that Christians often had a ritual respect for the communion elements. This was perhaps more than mere symbolism, in their minds, yet less than a literal transformation of earthly substances into divinity.

Some of this, perhaps unconsciously, imitated the cakes and *haoma* drink ritual of the Mithras Cult in a popular Roman religion. [5] For most believers of Tertullian's era (early 3rd century), the physical reality of the Eucharist coincided with the spiritual reality. There were no disputes such as what characterized the 2nd millennium. By the 9th century, Radbertus and other churchmen in the West, ceased to make an important distinction. It was one thing to believe that inanimate material elements like bread and wine *somehow coincided with* a spiritual communal reality. It was quite another to think that the material elements *became the same thing as* the spiritual reality. The latter statement describes the Doctrine of ***Transubstantiation*** very well.

Some churchmen now expressed in Medieval "Christianese" the same Pagan idea that led to the practice of ***alchemy***, and the magical theory of ***transmutation of matter***. [6] Whether the product of an age unable to clearly distinguish between substances *"coinciding with each other,"* and *"being transformed;"* or of a deliberate tweak by popes and kings, the state cult mentality of the Holy Roman Empire liked the idea of Transubstantiation. A few centuries later, Pope Innocent III would make it dogma for Roman Catholic communion. [7] Nevertheless, two scholars of Radbertus' day still made this important distinction. Rabanus and Ratramnus refuted Transubstantiation by reasoning from the Scriptures. [8]

Why is this important from a biblical perspective?

Transubstantiation contradicts what Christ said in the context of John Chapter 6, just after he spoke of the need for people to eat his flesh and drink his blood to have life. (Verses 28-63) Romanist theology uses this text to support their doctrine, but that does not stand up to scrutiny. The passage shows the disciples troubled by what the Jews had taken as Jesus teaching cannibalism. After they came to the Lord for further explanation, Jesus assured them in verse 63 that, **"It is the Spirit who gives life; the flesh profits nothing; the words** (in context, the words about eating and drinking his body and blood) **I have spoken to you *are spirit and are life."***

This is a clear statement in the text that Jesus intended a spiritual, not a literal, meaning when he spoke of eating his flesh and drinking his blood. At the Last Supper, Jesus' literal flesh was still on his bones and his literal blood still pumped through his body. Within hours, Roman soldiers would rip that flesh open and shed his blood. The idea of transforming the elements diverts at least some attention from the historical death of Jesus. It inordinately focuses it onto the elements. While many Christians have experienced a mystical union with Christ at Communion without error, the main purpose was to remember the historical act.

As time went on, Transubstantiation became a useful tool in the hands of a Medieval Papacy bent on domination over not only the faith, but also the world. It created artificial dependency, in which people became unduly reliant on the Roman priesthood. Only a Roman Catholic priest could "transform" common wafers and wine into the literal body and blood of Christ. Pope Innocent III made it the official dogma of the church in 1215 AD. The late Medieval Papacy used it, along with the Inquisition and the Mendicant Orders, to maintain control over not only the church, but also all Europe.

## THE LAY INVESTITURE CONTROVERSY AND THE FINAL BREAK BETWEEN EAST AND WEST

With the decline of government after Charlemagne into feudalism, came decline of leadership in the churches along the same lines. Even so, Roman Catholicism, with all its political and spiritual problems, remained the only stabilizing force in Europe. Christianity suffered one of its worst leadership crises because feudal kings and barons appointed bishops for their districts. This meant that, most often, only favor-currying toadies ruled in the churches, with little or no regard to teaching or moral character. History called this practice of secular kings appointing bishops ***Lay Investiture***. The kings were laymen or ***laity***, not being clergy, and *investiture* was the power of choosing whom to ordain.

Lay investiture led to the practice of ***simony***, which was the sale or trade of church offices. Christians named this sin after Simon the Sorcerer, who in the Book of Acts, tried to buy the Holy Spirit from Peter. Even the Papacy of Rome became the plaything of Roman nobles, those of Spoleto, and the Lombard dukes of Benevento. What the popes had hoped to manufacture through the Holy Roman Empire and forged letters had backfired dreadfully. After a century and a half of political breakup in the West since Louis the Pious, Pope John XII tried the experiment again. This involved no political shrewdness or godly wisdom on his part. History remembers Pope John XII best for his sexual degeneracy.

The Italian King, Berengar of Ivrea had invaded the Papal States, and Pope John needed a strong protector. Mimicking smarter pontiffs of an earlier century, he named the fierce Germanic King, Otto the Great, Holy Roman Emperor in 962 AD. This, too, backfired in a big way.

The church soon found that emperors could also appoint bishops, chiefly Bishops of Rome. Church leadership in both East and West were now equally creatures of secular politics. Whenever politicians control church leadership, it is a recipe for corruption. Pope John XII was a perfect example of this. He only made more visible another common problem with the politically appointed bishops and popes of this period. They routinely kept harems full of concubines, and local priests followed their example. He also helped trigger another round of a pattern at work since the 2nd century. Paul had warned against asceticism, that it had no value against battling corruptions of the flesh. (Col. 2:20-23)

No canon law absolutely forbade marriage for priests yet, but the lechery of these church leaders was such that they had wives *with* concubines. Reformers of the period associated marriage for the priesthood with bishops who kept these personal collections of sex slaves. Semi-Docetic Greek assumptions on the nature of sex and marriage had marched to their logical conclusion in church culture. This erroneous association of marriage with sexual sin seemed almost natural to the thinking of the day.

Churchmen from both ends of the moral spectrum routinely demonized women in ways we rightfully call sick. Despite their confusion of asceticism with spirituality, monastic reformers still had access to the New Testament. This had teachings on married pastors impossible to misread completely, despite worldview blind spots. What often tipped the scales was a fear of churches and abbeys losing property to the sons of priests through inheritance. That helped set the coming solution in stone.

Toady-popes and bishops practicing ***priestly concubinage*** heaped abuse on women by licentiousness. Churchmen who wanted reform heaped abuse on them for being "instruments of Satan" to destroy Christian leaders. In the twisted logic of the day, monastics often reinforced a culture that saw women as satanic tools simply because they were women, and men were by nature attracted to them. To address the immodest behavior of some women has always been necessary, just as for some men. To demonize women because men find them attractive was, and has always been, perverse—no matter what kind of religious form one wraps it in.

Bizarre allegoric interpretations of Genesis turned Eden's forbidden fruit into a symbol for sexual intercourse, redefining the meaning of the text. No literal fruit existed in this view. Eve had simply seduced her husband into having sex with her, making married sex the root of evil. This thought was foreign to a Hebrew worldview, and to common sense. It gained enough traction that even some fringe cults today hold to it. Fortunately, this never became dogma even in the Roman Catholic Church. It became popular with Catholic mystics—a growing force in the monastic orders of the day, however.

Regrettably, some truth exists in the modern accusation that monasticism sometimes had unhealthy views of sex and the treatment of women. This did not stem from the Bible's sexual ethics or gender roles, but from the influence of Greek assumptions on the nature of physical relationships. One might complain that the Greeks had no hang-ups about sexuality; that some of our earliest knowledge about the most bizarre forms of sexual deviancy stems from Ancient Greece. While this is true, one must not forget why.

Epicurean, and other self-indulgent schools of Greek thought, believed that giving in to lust was inevitable. They figured there was no point in fighting it. They did not start from an idyllic unshackled sexuality, as some scholars vicariously imagine. They had painful, self-destructive compulsions, whether the Epicureans who gave in to the flesh or the ascetic Stoics who fought it to grotesque extremes. The lie that bodily things are evil just because they are material is an endless labyrinth, no matter which way you turn once you are inside it. The only real answer is to break down its walls and get out. The reformers of the 10th century, for whatever reason, did not do this, though they fixed important problems facing the church of their day.

As the church built from this unfortunate layer of semi-Docetic assumptions, it warped itself to the extent that the Greek worldview expressed in this way. Fortunately, it did not express itself to the degree that the saving truths of Christ's humanity and bodily resurrection were lost, as in Gnosticism. Instead, the worldview came out in ways the early church fathers thought less serious, and hardly worth fighting; hardly worth it until, like a cancer left too long untreated, it choked life from the Faith through perverse extremes at both ends of the moral spectrum. The idea that a pastor could have a healthy marriage and still be spiritual became unthinkable. The gap between biblical marriage and corrupt harem keeping may not have even occurred to most reformers of the era. As bizarre as that sounds, God would wait another 500 years to give this epiphany to another generation of reformers.

Ironically, in the Greek-speaking East, the church was better able to ride out such extremes about marriage, though not entirely. Greek Orthodox priests marry and have families to this day, though high bishops and Patriarchs had to remain celibate. There are many reasons why Eastern Orthodoxy remained less affected by this aspect of the Greek worldview than Roman Catholicism. One might have expected the Greek mindset on sex to be stronger where theology continued to develop in that language.

Two factors may account for the difference. The first is that Greek was the language of the original texts of the New Testament—less communication barriers to the apostolic worldview if expressed in a language you know. The second is that the Byzantine Empire did not have as severe a disruption of culture and education as in the West. Although the Byzantine church experienced the same level of corruption, more conceptual safeguards may have kept reactions to priestly immorality from such extremes.

The movement to reform church leadership in the West centered on the Monastery at Cluny, in Burgundy France. After many struggles between the German Empire and the Italian dukes with their toad-popes, German Emperor Henry III named a Cluny-based reformer Pope in 1049 AD. When Bruno of Toul became Pope Leo IX, he established papal authority of ordination, taking it from the feudal kings—even from the Germanic Emperors. For this, he had help from the Cluny Monastery network, which educated reform-minded priests and monks that evangelized the West. It had become apparent that the major roadblock to purifying the church was that godly men with spiritual motives did not choose its leaders. This was the first of many steps toward protecting the church from the tyranny of a secular government. The sequence of protections matured in the United States Constitution's 1st Amendment, as courts understood it before the 1950s.

Pope Leo IX correctly held that an inability to appoint its own God-ordained leaders was counter-productive to a healthy church. History has called the conflict that followed the *Lay Investiture Controversy*. Leo IX began to sweep house in the West—something that needed drastically to happen. The early death of Holy Roman (German) Emperor Henry III aided this process by leaving six-year-old Henry IV as the new emperor in 1056. A cartel of reformers that had close access to the child emperor took advantage of his youth to make the election of the pope an in-house matter of the church in 1059.

The local Roman church had called its deacons, and other papal assistants, *cardinals* before, but now archbishops from prominent churches throughout Western Europe joined their number. By the beginning of the 12th century, cardinal deacons, cardinal priests, and cardinal bishops merged into a single group; known as the College of Cardinals the Roman Catholic Church has today. It would be the College of Cardinals that would elect the pope from here on out.

Many other aspects of the Roman Catholic Church also began to take their present shape at this time. Unfortunately, connecting concubinage to marriage, and fears of church property loss to sons of priests, also led to enforced celibacy of the priesthood. The Cluniac Reform Movement abolished many evils, like simony, as better accountability revitalized oversight of distant abbeys and diocese. Nevertheless, as we shall often see in history, other blind spots besides a low view of marriage hid in the shadows of the movement's greatest strengths. Pope Leo IX wanted to reach out to the Eastern Church, and tighten bonds that had loosened to where the two branches of orthodoxy remained united in name only. Here his emissaries went too far when they tried to exercise authority in Leo's name over the Eastern Patriarch.

The Patriarch of Constantinople, Michael Ceruliaris, was not party to recent advances of papal power in the West, and viewed them with suspicion. Being a bit of a religious imperialist himself, he wanted nothing to do with Rome's one-sided form of ecclesiastic authority. Of course, Ceruliaris made similar claims for himself. Pope Leo's ***nuncio***, Cardinal Humbert, demanded the Patriarch accept Rome's claim as universal bishop. When Ceruliaris would not, Humbert excommunicated him, and the entire Eastern Orthodox Church. The Patriarch, in turn, anathematized the Western Papacy. So went the final split between the Eastern and Western churches. It did not even happen over any real doctrinal or spiritual issue, beyond arguments about what kind of bread to use for Communion. It came down to just plain power politics.

The Eastern Church became the Greek, Serbian, Bulgarian, Armenian, Assyrian, Russian, and Ukrainian Orthodox Churches. The West evolved into the Roman Catholic Church, and later, the Reformed, denominational, and independent churches of today.

## The Rise of Absolute Papal Power

Not long after Pope Leo IX's time, a protégé of his, Hildebrand of Sovana, became Pope Gregory VII, in 1073. Gregory became one of the main architects of a papacy that would soon reach the pinnacle of its power. Like his predecessor, he continued working to reform the Western Church of simony, and sexual sin within the priesthood. Yet Gregory had a fanaticism that drove his colleagues—even within reformist circles—to call him "the holy Satan" and a "consumingly ambitious person." [9]

Popes had encouraged priestly celibacy before this, but Pope Gregory VII made it mandatory, sealed by vows. He excommunicated any bishops that permitted priests to marry. His enforcement of priestly celibacy required further centralization of church authority under the Papacy. Bishops found their local authority greatly restricted. The Pope could not accomplish one without the other. Pope Gregory VII was also the first Pope to state decisively of the papal office that, *"He himself (the Pope) may be judged of no one."* [10] He also declared that popes had the divine right to depose monarchs and emperors; a bit of a reversal from the Constantine Model of church-state authority (which is not to say that model was any better).

What had begun under Leo IX, as a move to reform the church, through Hildebrand's fanaticism, became one of the greatest corruptions ever to afflict the Christian Church. Christianity now had an absolute human ecclesiastical power that would corrupt its own office absolutely.

## Bibliography


1. ***Encyclopedia of Islam***, eds. Houtsma, Arnold, Basset, Hartman; Leiden: E.J.Brill, 1913, I:302; See also, Ibid. 1971, III:1093, and ***Encyclopedia of World Mythology and Legend***, "The Facts on File," ed. Anthony Mercatante, New York, 1983, I:41; and ***Three Early Christian-Muslim Debates***, ed. by N.A.Newman, Hatfield, PA, IBRI, 1994, pp.357, 413, 426
2. Richard P. Bailey, ***Jihad: The Teaching of Islam from its Primary Sources - The Quran and Hadith***, from the web site ***Answering Islam - A Christian-Muslim Dialog*** (June 2002). **http://answering-islam.org** - Author's note: *This web site is an excellent resource for both Christians and Muslims to gain a better understanding of their fundamental differences and similarities. Bailey's paper explains this issue more deeply than I do and quotes the actual source texts of fundamental Islamic faith in extensive systematic detail.*
3. Walker, Williston. ***A History of the Christian Church*** (4th Edition), pp. 235-239, 1st Edition 1918, 4th Edition 1946, Charles Scribner's Sons, New York, NY.
4. Von Dollinger, J.H. Ignaz (a Roman Catholic source), ***The Pope and the Council***, p.62 and pp. 76-77, 1869, London
5. Op cit. Walker, Williston, p. 248; See also, Smith, M.A. ***The Church Under Siege***, pp. 246-247, 1976, Inter-Varsity Press, Leicester, England
6. Hislop, Alexander, ***The Two Babylons***, p. 259, 1st Ed. 1916, 1st American Ed. 1943, 2nd Ed. 1959, Loizeaux Brothers, Neptune, NJ.
7. Op cit. Walker, Williston, p. 369
8. Ibid. p. 248; See also, Smith, M.A. ***The Church Under Siege***, pp. 246-247, 1976, Inter-Varsity Press, Leicester, England
9. Op cit. Walker, Williston, p. 275
10. Ibid. p. 275-276

# 11

# THE MIDDLE AGES, PART 3: THE ROMAN PAPACY AT THE HEIGHT OF ITS POWER

## THE VICAR OF CHRIST ON EARTH

If the Lay Investiture Controversy lit the fuse, then Pope Gregory VII (a.k.a. Hildebrand) was the bomb. For generations, emperors, feudal kings, and dukes in the fragmented Holy Roman Empire had appointed whomever they wished for church government. This left the church in the grip of royal toadies with little or no regard to teaching, morality, or evangelism. The rise of the Cluniac Reforming Popes—led by Leo IX and culminating with Gregory—brought two other developments. First, a backlash came from secular government. Second, the "idea pendulum" swung to an opposite unhealthy extreme in the wake of the reforming pope's victory.

Pope Gregory VII's ban on layman princes appointing church leaders on pain of excommunication, tossed down the gauntlet. Every feudal lord from the Holy Roman Emperor to the hayseed burger-baron of Yokelburg chose his own bishops. The young German Emperor, Henry IV, reacted by calling a synod of crony-bishops. No one showed surprise when they declared Gregory unfit for the Papacy.

Age and treachery beats youth and enthusiasm, however. Pope Gregory escalated by excommunicating Henry. He then absolved all the emperor's subjects from their fealty oaths. Rebellion already brewed in the Kingdom of Saxony. Henry suddenly faced an insurrection of all his nobles that had the full faith and backing of the Pope, and the entire Roman Catholic Church. To crack down on the church would only make a potential rebellion real.

Most in the West believed in the fires of hell and in a great reservoir of merit from the Saints and the grace of God, which Christ had entrusted the Pope to manage on earth. If some were not so sure about the whole "reservoir of merit" thing, Gregory VII began a tradition of ramrodding the details into what Roman Catholicism has since called "canon law." The momentum of both politics and public opinion shifted now in Rome's favor. The fourth Holy Roman Emperor named Henry stood barefoot in the snow for three days, begging forgiveness, before Pope Gregory would even look at him. While this pathetic display did not settle the issue of lay investiture, it was a decisive victory for the Papacy. Lay monarch-appointed popes still popped up from time to time over the next sixty years or so—the Roman Catholic Church calls these men (among others) "***anti-popes***."

Despite his fanatical heavy-handedness, Hildebrand/Gregory was right about one thing. The church, not the state, needed to appoint church officers of godly calling. To this end, he reinforced the establishment of the College of Cardinals, which from that time on had the duty to elect the Pope. Since the 11th century, the College of Cardinals has usually chosen papal candidates from among their own number.

By now, Western church leadership had evolved into a complex hierarchical system. At the top sat the Pope, followed by cardinals, archbishops, bishops, monsignors (masters), priests (Presbyters), and abbots (monks). Bruce Shelley points out in his book *Church History in Plain Language* that religious authority of this era often overreached itself. Like the ***Gothic*** cathedrals of that time, it soared too high for its support structures, and thus periodically caved in on itself. [1] The Papacy could not create God's kingdom on earth by using religion for political manipulation, any more than Byzantine emperors could by imperial decree.

The Lay Investiture Controversy ended when the church reached a compromise with the lay nobles, several decades after Pope Gregory's death. In 1122, the Concordat of Worms declared that the church had the right to elect its own leaders, but only in the presence of the Imperial Crown or its representative. Everybody eventually seemed able to live with this solution. It gave the church the potential to reform itself, while also keeping secular society intact by recognizing the emperor's place.

Evangelical Christians would also agree with Pope Gregory VII, in principle, that spiritual matters outweigh worldly ones. Where we would have to slam on the brakes was in how he thought the church should apply this principle. The Concordat of Worms only enabled the *potential* for church reform. It could not guarantee that it would. The biggest, most unforeseen source of corruption now festered in the expanding power of the very leaders spawned by the Cluny Reform Movement. In Hildebrand's mind, spiritual leadership over worldly matters meant that the Pope should effectively be a spiritual Caesar over the kings of Europe!

Pope Gregory VII and his successors devised an arsenal of religious weapons for the manipulation of kings and emperors. The conflict between Gregory/Hildebrand and Henry IV became a model. Threats of ***excommunication*** and absolving fealty oaths placed monarchs under the Pope's thumb, in a society based on this form of the Christendom model. People had to be in communion with the church to engage in most anything of social weight. In 1 Corinthians 5 and 6, Paul commanded *local* church leaders to excommunicate people engaged in unrepentant, lifestyle dominating sin. The Papacy had twisted it into a political power tool used against virtually anyone in their way.

In cases where the people stood behind a troublesome ruler, the Pope could take the drastic measure of issuing an ***interdict*** against that nation. An interdict excommunicated the whole country, except for the sacraments of baptism and ***extreme unction*** or "last rites." Churches all over the interdicted kingdom would close up shop, as it were. People were terrified of this. Without the literal grace-sustaining "body of Christ," which only Roman priests had the power to transform from common bread, they believed their souls would slip away from God's favor.

What had started, a thousand years before, as a simple belief in Christ's presence at the taking of Communion; now contorted into an idolatrous mechanism for worldly political and social domination. The machinery was now fully in place. The century after Pope Gregory VII would see these and other methods of religious and political manipulation sharpened to a fine point.

About a hundred years after Gregory/Hildebrand, another pope would rev this machine up to unprecedented levels of power. Pope Innocent III did far more than just formalize the Doctrine of Transubstantiation into a church dogma. The record of his conquests by manipulation and fear makes it hard to imagine much in his character beyond this motivation. Nor was his outlook unique for popes of that period or beyond. Yet more than mere spiritual megalomania drove him (that was just a big part of it). The fanatical vision of Hildebrand/Gregory VII was to build God's perfect society on earth. Innocent III really thought he could bring this to pass. He whole-heartedly did anything it took to advance this political "Kingdom of God," no matter how despicable. In his mind, the end really justified the means.

This kind of kingdom building was another outgrowth of Eusebius' spiritualized view of the Millennial Kingdom. Revelation 20:1-10 teaches that Christ will return to set up his own earthly kingdom for a thousand years. The popes of that era often felt duty-bound to conquer the world in a political and military way, literally, for Christ. Today we might think that only a megalomaniac could believe such a thing—and we would be right.

Concerned Christians began to ask serious questions around this time, as we will soon see.

By now, the idea of papal infallibility had begun to take hold in some parts of church leadership. It was a logical outgrowth of Hildebrand's vision even if it would remain a debatable point for the next six and a half centuries. It only became a dogma of desperation in 1870. Whether Innocent III believed himself infallible or not, he behaved as if he did. At one point he proclaimed, *"The successor of Peter is the* ***Vicar of Christ****: he has been established as* ***a mediator between God and man****, below God but beyond man; less than God but more than man; who shall judge all and be judged by no one."* [2] The word *vicar* means *one who fulfills the duties of another; a substitute; deputy.* [3] The Papacy conveniently forgot 1 Timothy 2:5, **"For there is one God, and one mediator between God and men, the man Christ Jesus."**

The days of such "forgetfulness" reached their peak in Pope Innocent's day, but they were still numbered. By today's standards, very few people had direct access to the Scriptures in their own language. Yet education was on the rise. Many more had access to it than just a century before. Scholars were educated by the church. Even schoolboys had to learn Latin to study the Bible (or anything else). Although the Roman Church's control over learning was powerful, increasing education among the laity began to slowly pry open the stranglehold. Educated people began to ask serious moral, intellectual, and spiritual questions. Getting answers sometimes proved a dangerous up-hill battle. Empire has the same power seduction in religion as in the politics of military conquest; made all the more repugnant by smarmy Christianese terminology and euphemisms.

To give some idea of how Innocent III saw the authority of his office over the secular rulers of his day; consider that he threatened or used the interdict against various kings and princes 85 times during his 18-year stint as pope. He essentially played chess with living game pieces in a German civil war of rival claimants for the throne. At first, he supported one party, then the other, until he garnered the election of his own ward, Frederick II. The youngster had promised to obey papal authority and to go on a crusade. Innocent III also not so innocently expanded the infamous Inquisitions. We will look at more on the Inquisitions in the next chapter. Both secular and church authorities saw heresy as a growing "problem" in a Europe that had begun to question the morality of how the church did business.

Contrast Pope Innocent's hyper-control oriented approach to spiritual leadership with the apostolic model given by Peter:

> **To the elders among you, I appeal as a fellow elder, a witness of Christ's sufferings and one who also will share in the glory to be revealed: Be shepherds of God's flock that is under your care, serving as overseers - not because you must, but because you are willing, as God wants you to be; not greedy for money, but eager to serve; not lording it over those entrusted to you, but being examples to the flock. *1 Peter* 5:1-3 (NIV)**

I do not intend this chapter to be a diatribe against all Catholic popes of every era. Yet we cannot ignore the impact that the popes of this era, and many of their successors, had on the development of church history, doctrine, and practice. I am not citing the exceptions, but a small sampling of the rule. With the rise of men like Gregory VII and Innocent III to the Papacy, one thing had started to happen; just a little here and there at first, but more and more consistently as time went on. After centuries of truth-warping influences on spiritual leadership, people had finally begun to ask a vital question; *what made a church authority truly "apostolic" in character?*

## THE CRUSADES

Control oriented church leadership shown by Popes Gregory VII to Innocent III, and later popes, helped inflame a series of wars between Christian and Muslim states. History calls these "the Crusades." There is a difference between enflaming a conflict and starting one, however. By the 11th century, Islam had taken about two thirds of the Christian world by force. Much of was territory won to Christianity since apostolic times by peaceful preaching of the gospel. Christians did not become warriors without provocation.

Despite this, Islamic rulers often allowed pilgrimages by Christians in small groups from both Eastern and Western churches into the Holy Lands. These went mostly unmolested because Islam, at the time, saw Christian states as the threat; not so much individual Christians, many of whom still lived in currently Islamic cities like Alexandria, Jerusalem, Edessa, and Damascus. Pilgrimages boosted trade, and became an excellent source of income for what we today might call "tourism." Muslims of that era still enjoyed many comforts of high civilization by the standards of the day. They still had far more advanced technology than their European Christian counterparts did.

The Byzantine Empire had long blocked Muslims from penetrating Central Europe. Byzantine Christians had geographic security barriers, like the Mediterranean Sea and the mountains of the Anatolian Plateau of central Turkey. All that changed, when Islamic Seljuk Turks overran Asia Minor. By 1095 AD, the Byzantine Emperor found himself stripped of his southern defenses. Constantinople's near naked underbelly now lay exposed behind the thin veneer of an easily crossed Bosporus Strait. The Emperor sent urgent pleas west, to the Pope. The next Pope after Gregory VII, Urban II, called for the 1st Crusade in response, to help the residual Byzantine Empire defend itself.

The idea of liberating the Holy Lands from Muslim domination to ensure the safety of pilgrims was almost an afterthought. Even most Christian historians suspect that many of the stories of "infidel atrocities" against Christian pilgrims at this time were propaganda spread by zealots like Peter the Hermit; conveniently endorsed by Pope Urban II. The events since 9-11 might tempt us to think otherwise. The available evidence does not support a change of view on this particular point, however. Atrocities came from both sides. Urban had expansionist motives, but he also saw the Crusade as a chance to restore relations with the Eastern Orthodox Church.

The fanatical Hermit led large numbers of paupers from France to useless deaths. He urged them to throw themselves into well-organized Turkish battle lines, shrieking promises of divine protection. Meanwhile, he slinked off to Constantinople to beg military aid from a Byzantine Emperor already short on armies. When Peter returned to the front, he found his "Pauper's Brigade" slaughtered almost to the last man.

Undeterred by any sense of responsibility, and more certain than ever of "the Lord's will," the Hermit ranted on for Christians to join the Crusade. He claimed Christ had appeared to him with promises of victory for those who heeded the call. Few of his raggedy "Pauper's Brigade" remained to contradict him, and they lacked Peter's charisma, anyway. Whether by Pope Urban's worldly lures or those of Peter the Hermit's false spirituality, one thing was certain. The Faith had entered one of its lowest points, in terms of its mainstream view of spiritual authority and sense of Christian identity. Between Pope and Hermit, nothing farther from the words of Christ and the Apostles was possible. Jesus never told Christians to wage war on "flesh and blood" kingdoms.

Contrast this with Islam, where the most literal reading of Mohammed defines "peace" as the forcible conquest of non-believers to Islam. The most natural interpretation of the Qur'an and Hadiths calls for literal warfare against Pagans, Jews, and Christians. For Western Civilization to deny this reality is naïve at best and culturally suicidal at worst. That does not mean Muslim societies have always carried this idea out to its logical conclusion in a bloodbath every chance they had. I am certainly not saying that Christians are better people than Muslims are, by comparing the two worldviews. The Bible teaches that all men are sinners, equally in need of God's grace. History shows that both

Christians and Muslims have behaved thuggishly at times, and at other times with remarkable civility.

Ideas still have consequences in the real world. Similarities are not always more significant than differences, when comparing them. Sometimes it is the other way around. Mohammed personally called for "honor killings," and condoned the rape of female war prisoners, as shown below. Where then will social pressure push an Islamic culture when convinced Qur'anic literalists gain power? Would a society influenced by consistent Biblical literalism really gravitate to that same place? Would not opposition from among those who take the Bible literally be more likely, *given what the New Testament writers actually wrote?*

Here, differences clearly can be more important than similarities in the comparison. Why should comparisons of religious ideas be magically immune to that principle? No other comparison is. Valuing the avoidance of such disputes *at any cost* only creates another belief system that demands acceptance by faith, and a mindless faith at that.

> *Also (prohibited are) women already married,* ***except those whom your right hands possess...*** **Qur'an Sura 4:24** (Context is about liberties that Mohammed permitted his warriors to take with war captives. The term "***whom your right hands possess***" is an undisputed Islamic term for people captured in war, as in *plunder*. By this verse, having sex with married women is adultery, unless she is a prisoner of war! This will become apparent in the way the Hadiths below apply this verse—KGP.)

> *The Believers must (eventually) win through—those who humble themselves in their prayers; who avoid vain talk; who are active in deeds of charity; who abstain from sex, except with those joined to them in the marriage bond, or* ***(the captives) whom their right hands possess—for (in their case) they are free from blame.*** **Qur'an Sura 23:1-6**

> *Not so those devoted to Prayer—those who remain steadfast to their prayer; and those in whose wealth is a recognized right for the (needy) who asks and him who is prevented (for some reason from asking); and those who hold to the truth of the Day Of Judgment; and those who fear the displeasure of their Lord—for their Lord's displeasure is the opposite of Peace and Tranquility—and those who guard their chastity, except with their wives* ***and the (captives) whom their right hands possess—for (then) they are not to be blamed.*** **Sura 70:22-30**

> *We went out with Allah's Messenger on the expedition to the Bi'l-Mustaliq and took captive some excellent Arab women; and we desired them, for we were suffering from the absence of our wives, (but at the same time) we also desired ransom for them.* ***So we decided to have sexual intercourse with them but by observing azl*** (withdrawing the male sexual organ before emission of semen to avoid conception). *But we said: We are doing an act whereas Allah's Messenger is amongst us; why not ask him?* ***So we asked Allah's Messenger, and he said: It does not matter if you do not do it,*** (azl) *for every soul that is to be born up to the Day of Resurrection will be born.* **Hadith, Sahih Muslim 3371**

> ***The Apostle of Allah sent a military expedition to Awtas on the occasion of the battle of Hunain.*** *They met their enemy and fought with them. They defeated them and took them captives.* ***Some of the Companions of the Apostle of Allah were reluctant to have intercourse with the female captives in the presence of their husbands who were unbelievers.*** *So Allah, the Exalted, sent down the Qur'anic verse: "And all married women (are forbidden) unto you* ***save those (captives) whom your right hands possess.****" That is to say, they are lawful for them when they complete their waiting period.* **Hadith, Sunan Abu Dawud 2150** (This is an early "inspired" Hadith commentary explaining the intended meaning of the first verse I cited, from the Qur'an, Sura 4:24—KGP)

> *Narrated Abu Huraira and Zaid bin Khalid Al-Juhani: A bedouin came and said, "O Allah's Apostle! Judge between us according to Allah's Laws." His opponent got up and said, "He is*

> *right. Judge between us according to Allah's Laws." The bedouin said, "My son was a laborer working for this man, and he committed illegal sexual intercourse with his wife. The people told me that my son should be stoned to death; so, in lieu of that, I paid a ransom of one hundred sheep and a slave girl to save my son. Then I asked the learned scholars who said, "Your son has to be lashed one-hundred lashes and has to be exiled for one year."* ***The Prophet said, "No doubt I will judge between you according to Allah's Laws.*** *The slave-girl and the sheep are to go back to you, and your son will get a hundred lashes and one year exile."* ***He then addressed somebody, "O Unais! Go to the wife of this (man) and stone her to death" So, Unais went and stoned her to death.*** **Hadith, Sahih Bukhari 3:49:860**

There is simply too much material like this in the Qur'an, Hadiths, and the earliest biographies of Mohammed. Above, multiple Islamic texts show Allah's Prophet excusing the rape of married female war prisoners (not that rape is any less evil with unmarried captives). Appealing to the principle of comparing past customs to the norm of the times offers no sound argument against my citing these verses this way. Christianity had already produced a higher code of war conduct in Augustine's "***Just War Theory***." Military men had often applied this code from Rome to Byzantium, even among Germanic barbarians!

The fact that men in the Christian West did not always follow Augustine's code is irrelevant. *We are comparing the codes, not Christians and Muslims as people.* The above citations are the Islamic equivalent that quoting Christ or the Apostles would be for Christians.

Complaining that, "I took the verses out of context" will not wash, either. Any citation of any verse in any piece of literature lifts a segment from its context to some degree. Is the degree reasonable or unreasonable; representative or contrary to what the context says? Claiming that citing such passages is invalid just because of the unavoidable mechanics of using quotations ignores their sheer weight and number. It also ignores the literal warfare context of these verses in the texts they come from. Add enough similar citations together from a related body of texts, and one gets a "context."

Nevertheless, in viewing the Age of the Crusades, it is dishonest to present Christians consistently as the "good guys" and Muslims as the "villains." Christian atrocities were equally vile—more so! Christians had a New Testament that forbade such things, while Muslims had a Qur'an and Hadith that encouraged them. Christian soldiers tossed babies into the air and caught them on swords, and raped captive women, too. In what way could they appeal to the Bible to justify such behavior, when Jesus commanded them to, "love your enemies?"

Complaining that the Old Testament also had laws allowing the taking of female war prisoners as chattel engages in a half-truth. The Mosaic Law demanded such women be given the status of wives, and forbade the taking of married women with living husbands. It certainly did not permit the casual rape of prisoners of war. The Mosaic Law, though harsh by today's Christian and Western norms, gave to female captives a level of protection virtually unknown in the ancient world before then. It would remain unique for centuries to come. The earlier Code of Hammurabi does not approach Moses in this regard. Moses was ethically far ahead of a Qur'anic Law that came over 2000 years later.

> **"When you go out to war against your enemies, and the LORD your God delivers them into your hand, and you take them captive, and you see among the captives a beautiful woman, and desire her and would take her for your wife, then you shall bring her home to your house, and she shall shave her head and trim her nails. She shall put off the clothes of her captivity, remain in your house, and mourn her father and her mother a full month;** ***after that you may go in to her and be her***

***husband, and she shall be your wife.*** **And it shall be, if you have no delight in her, then you shall set her free, but** ***you certainly shall not sell her for money; you shall not treat her brutally, because you have humbled her.*"**

**Deuteronomy 21:10-14 NKJV**

Christian historians also know the folly of making the Christians into "the heroes" in the Crusades by some of the testimonies of Christians who fought in them. At least we cannot do this honestly, in the same way that we could morally categorize the Allies versus the Nazis in World War II or the West versus ISIS and Al Qaeda. Christians, in theory, had Augustine of Hippo's "Just War" guidelines, but did not follow them consistently, as we shall see. Islam had nothing comparable to Augustine. Which brings us to another important observation we would do well not to forget; the idea of conversion at sword point is utterly consistent with a straightforward reading of the Qur'an and Hadiths.

> *Fighting is prescribed for you, and ye dislike it. But it is possible that ye dislike a thing which is good for you, and that ye love a thing which is bad for you. But Allah knoweth, and ye know not.* **Qur'an, Sura 2:216**
>
> *Say to the Unbelievers, if (now) they desist (from Unbelief), their past would be forgiven them; but if they persist, the punishment of those before them is already (a matter of warning for them). And fight them on until there is no more tumult or oppression, and there prevail justice and faith in Allah altogether and everywhere; but if they cease, verily Allah doth see all that they do.* **Qur'an, Sura 8:38-39**
>
> *O Prophet! rouse the Believers to the fight. If there are twenty amongst you, patient and persevering, they will vanquish two hundred: if a hundred, they will vanquish a thousand of the Unbelievers: for these are a people without understanding. For the present, Allah hath lightened your (task), for He knoweth that there is a weak spot in you: But (even so), if there are a hundred of you, patient and persevering, they will vanquish two hundred, and if a thousand, they will vanquish two thousand, with the leave of Allah: for Allah is with those who patiently persevere. It is not fitting for a prophet that he should have prisoners of war until he hath thoroughly subdued the land* [Pickthal translates: ***"until he hath made slaughter in the land"***]. *Ye look for the temporal goods of this world; but Allah looketh to the Hereafter: And Allah is Exalted in might, Wise.* **Qur'an, Sura 8:65-67**
>
> *But when the forbidden months are past,* ***then fight and slay the Pagans wherever ye find them, and seize them, beleaguer them, and lie in wait for them in every stratagem (of war); but if they repent, and establish regular prayers and practice regular charity, then open the way for them:*** *for Allah is Oft-forgiving, Most Merciful.* **Qur'an, Sura 9:5** (Often called the "sword verse.")
>
> ***Fight those who believe not in Allah nor the Last Day, nor hold that forbidden which hath been forbidden by Allah and His Messenger, nor acknowledge the religion of Truth, (even if they are) of the People of the Book****, until they pay the Jizya [poll tax levied on non-Islamic people] with willing submission, and feel themselves subdued.* **Qur'an, Sura 9:29** ("People of the book" is an Islamic term for Jews and Christians." KGP)
>
> *Therefore, when ye meet the Unbelievers (in fight), smite at their necks; At length, when ye have thoroughly subdued them, bind a bond firmly (on them): thereafter (is the time for) either generosity or ransom: Until the war lays down its burdens. Thus (are ye commanded): but if it had been Allah's Will, He could certainly have exacted retribution from them (Himself); but (He lets you fight) in order to test you, some with others. But those who are slain in the Way of Allah, - He will never let their deeds be lost.* **Qur'an, Sura 47:4**—all citations, unless otherwise noted, from the *Yusuf Ali Translation of the Qur'an)*

*Allah's Apostle said: "I have been ordered (by Allah) to fight against the people until they testify that none has the right to be worshipped but Allah and that Mohammed is Allah's Apostle, and offer the prayers perfectly and give the obligatory charity, so if they perform that, then they save their lives and property from me except for Islamic laws and then their reckoning (accounts) will be done by Allah."* **Hadith, Sahih Bukhari, 1:2:24** (see also 4:52:196)

*It is reported on the authority of Abu Huraira that he heard the Messenger of Allah say: I have been commanded to fight against people, till they testify to the fact that there is no god but Allah, and believe in me (that) I am the messenger (from the Lord) and in all that I have brought. And when they do it, their blood and riches are guaranteed protection on my behalf except where it is justified by law, and their affairs rest with Allah.* **Hadith, Sahih Muslim, 1:31** (see also 1:130, 1:32, 1:33)

*The Prophet (peace be upon him) said:* ***I am commanded to fight with men till they testify that there is no god but Allah, and that Mohammed is His servant and His Apostle, face our qiblah (direction of prayer), eat what we slaughter, and pray like us.*** *When they do that, their life and property are unlawful for us except what is due to them. They will have the same rights as the Muslims have, and have the same responsibilities as the Muslims have.* **Hadith, Sunan Abu Dawud, 14:2635**

*A man came to the Prophet and asked, "A man fights for war booty; another fights for fame and a third fights for showing off; which of them fights in Allah's Cause?" The Prophet said, "He who fights that Allah's Word* (i.e. Islam) *should be superior, fights in Allah's Cause."* **Hadith, Sahih Bukhari, 4:52:65** (see also 9:93:550 and Sahih Muslim, 20:4684, 20:4685, 20:4686, 20:4687)

*Allah's Apostle said, "Allah guarantees him who strives in His Cause and whose motivation for going out is nothing but Jihad in His Cause and belief in His Word, that He will admit him into Paradise (if martyred) or bring him back to his dwelling place, whence he has come out, with what he gains of reward and booty."* **Hadith, Sahih Bukhari, 4:53:352** (see also 9:93:549, 9:93:555, and 1:2:35) which adds, ***"...and I would have loved to be martyred in Allah's cause and then made alive, and then martyred and then made alive, and then again martyred in His cause."***

*It has been narrated on the authority of Abu Huraira who said: Allah has undertaken to provide for one who leaves his home (only) to fight for His cause and to affirm the truth of His word;* ***Allah will either admit him to Paradise or will bring him back home from where he had come out, with his reward and booty.*** **Hadith, Sahih Muslim, 20:4628**

*Narrated Abu Huraira: While we were in the mosque,* ***Allah's Apostle came out and said, "Let us proceed to the Jews."*** *So we went out with him till we came to Bait-al-Midras. The Prophet stood up there and called them, saying, "O assembly of Jews! Surrender to Allah (embrace Islam) and you will be safe!" They said, "You have conveyed Allah's message, O Aba-al-Qasim" Allah's Apostle then said to them, "That is what I want; embrace Islam and you will be safe." They said, "You have conveyed the message, O Aba-al-Qasim." Allah's Apostle then said to them, "That is what I want," and repeated his words for the third time and added,* ***"Know that the earth is for Allah and I want to exile you from this land, so whoever among you has property he should sell it, otherwise, know that the land is for Allah and His Apostle."*** **Hadith, Sahih Bukhari, 9:92:447**

*Abu Huraira reported Allah's Messenger (may peace be upon him) as saying:* ***The last hour would not come unless the Muslims will fight against the Jews and the Muslims would kill them until the Jews would hide themselves*** *behind a stone or a tree and a stone or a tree would say: Muslim, or the servant of Allah, there is a Jew behind me; come* *and kill him; but the tree Gharqad would not say, for it is the tree of the Jews.* **Hadith, Sahih Muslim, 41:6985 (see also 41:6981-84 and Sahih Bukhari, 4:52:176,177, and 4:56:791)**

Clearly, the fundamental writings of Islam teach that Muslims are warriors by identity—instruments of Allah's judgment to impose his law on earth *in the here and now*, by force. Outward submission to Islamic authority is all that is required. Religion is therefore a political and military tool within Islam, by Mohammed's design.

In contrast, conversion by force is foreign to a natural reading of the New Testament and even the Old Testament. The Old Testament never depicted God telling the Jews to use the threat of war to coerce a people group to convert. In the cases where God commanded Israel to wage war on a tribe, it was as a unique Divine judgment against that tribe. When the Canaanite prostitute, Rahab, of her own free choice helped Israel, God spared both her and her family. Even the lying Gibeonites, who tricked Joshua into protecting them from the other Canaanite kings, had their lives saved through Joshua's oath in Yahweh's Name.

More radically, conversion in the New Testament requires the voluntary change of a person's heart in response to the gospel. Christians are to "preach the gospel" and "make disciples," leaving punitive judgment to Christ, when He visibly returns *in the future*. Christ and the Apostles only commanded Christians to be soldiers in a spiritual warfare sense.

> **11 Take up God's instruments of war, so that you may be able to keep your position against all the deceits of the Evil One. 12 *For our fight is not against flesh and blood, but against authorities and powers, against the world-rulers of this dark night, against the spirits of evil in the heavens. Ephesians* 6:11-12 (BBE)**

This does not mean the New Testament teaches pacifism, only that we cannot convert others by force of arms or political coercion. In general, a Christian's role toward fellow human beings is that of *ambassador*. (2 Cor. 5:20) Christian religion often became a slave to politics in the West, but only as an aberration, not by biblical design. Jesus said, **"Render to Caesar the things that are Caesar's, and to God the things that are God's."** (Mk. 12:17)

This cuts to the main theme learned by most Christians from this period of history. The Lay Investiture Controversy showed the sort of corruption that came when the state controlled the church. The Crusades showed one of many corruptions coming when church controlled state. One reason Christians should oppose utopian ideas is that we were likely first to indulge a fantasy of ***utopia***—that we could build a perfect society on earth.

The only theocracy that will ever escape being a ***dystopia*** is the one Jesus Christ sets up after His Second Coming. Biblical faith cannot produce utopia, but it can have great positive influence on any society. This is so even if the mainstream only sees its virtue for this life—in the same sense non-Jews of the early 1st century saw the virtue of the God of Moses, without converting to Judaism. Of course, it is always best to have spiritual conversions. *The point is that real conversions are always voluntary.* Christ never intended the church in this age to rule the world by force. Only Jesus has the wisdom to do that at his bodily return.

Christians did not learn this principle because they were smarter, morally superior, or more devoted than Muslims were. Often we weren't. It took the mainstream of Christianity centuries to get past this stuff, unevenly, and some in the fringes still have not done so. Nevertheless, the ideas needed to get past such things were already in the fundamental teachings of Christ and the Apostles. They never nonsensically tried to force people to convert. The redemptive raw material to correct the errors of the church came from the word of God. Christianity coddled conversion by conquest only in the most corrupt periods of its history, when it strayed farthest from New Testament thought.

> **16 Be of the same mind toward one another. Do not set your mind on high things, but associate with the humble. Do not be wise in your own opinion. 17 Repay no one evil for evil. Have regard for good things in the sight of all men. 18 If it is**

**possible, as much as depends on you, live peaceably with all men. 19 Beloved, do not avenge yourselves, but rather give place to wrath; for it is written, "Vengeance is Mine, I will repay," says the Lord. *Romans* 12:16-19 NKJV**

**1 Therefore I exhort first of all that supplications, prayers, intercessions, and giving of thanks be made for all men, 2 for kings and all who are in authority, that we may lead a quiet and peaceable life in all godliness and reverence. 3 For this is good and acceptable in the sight of God our Savior, 4 who desires all men to be saved and to come to the knowledge of the truth. *1 Timothy* 2:1-4 NKJV**

The most literal application of the Qur'an and Hadith often drives violence in Islamic cultures, both ancient and modern. This is not because Muslims, as people, are naturally more prone to violence, but because ideas have had their consequences. If the same ideas had flourished in the West to that same degree, we would have fared no better. The assumption that all "Fundamentalist" forms of religion lead to violent extremes, itself, stems from a bigoted dogma. It comes from the presumptuous Secularist bromide that "all religions are alike." This view ignores the fact that different beliefs lead to different lifestyles, and that different conclusions arise from differing worldview assumptions. Since all ideas have consequences, why would religious ideas be any different?

The West today largely accepts without scrutiny the politically correct dogma that "all religions are alike." The motive seems to be a desire to avoid awkward social and historical realities. A serious comparative study of how religions and worldviews sway history should put such nonsense to rest. ***Radical Secularism***, however, has become fanatically committed to this view against all reason.

The 12th and 13th century Christian "hate-mongers" that called for crusade expeditions against the Muslim world were anything but "Fundamentalist" in their approach to the Bible; quite the opposite! In fact, it would be unfair to call many of them "hate-mongers," since they were responding to a real geo-political threat. Even if parts of that threat later proved overblown, how were they to know? Many parts of it were not. Two thirds of a world where Christians had once spoken freely now lay under Islamic domination.

*Conversion in the Christian world had made most of its gains before Constantine, without help from any military expeditions.* After Rome fell in the West, odds had been against isolated missionary monks, who had often contended with hostile warlords using prayer and negotiating skills—as ambassadors. While many stories of Muslim brutality against Christian pilgrims proved false, European kings had no advanced intelligence networks to consult. They had only word of mouth, and the history of the last five centuries.

The power of suggestion by repetition is nothing new, and it worked on Christian and Muslim alike. Pro-Crusade rabble-rouser, Peter the Hermit, was also the first known promoter of praying the ***Rosary***. Babylonian, Egyptian, Hindu, and Greco-Roman cults had used bead chains to count mechanically recited prayers to pagan deities for thousands of years. [4] The Hermit may have borrowed the practice from superficially "Christianized" peoples in Europe or from refugees from the East. Regardless of how it came to him, the resemblance of the Rosary to ancient pagan prayer forms shows its non-Christian origins. It quickly became a popular form of piety in the Roman church.

The Rosary's non-Christian origin by itself would not necessarily have made it a problem. God used many things redemptively that did not originate in the Bible. He still does. The problem is that this form violated the way Jesus told us to pray in the Gospels.

**And when you are praying, do not use meaningless repetition, as the *Gentiles* (*Pagans* - NIV) do, for they suppose that they will be heard for their many words. Matthew 6:7 (NASB)**

Jesus wanted meaningful communication in our prayers.

The Hermit encouraged mantra-like repetitions of rote prayers that drained even biblical verses of their meaning, such as the Lord's Prayer. Emotionally fervent repetitions can generate an altered state of consciousness, when chanted or with music, which makes the mind open to suggestion. Peter filled uncomprehending peasant minds with his militant propaganda. This is not a claim that those who pray the Rosary today are fanatically intolerant or that praying that way automatically leads to semi-hypnotic altered states. I only mean that the practice first arose in that kind of environment. (I have many memories of praying the Rosary as a child at family funerals, and as an altar boy. None involved "altered states." Usually, the priest, and everyone else, seemed most interested in reciting it as fast as humanly possible just to get the thing over with.)

To whatever degree the Rosary played a role in the Hermit's rabble-rousing, the man knew how to generate volatile religious energy. The Christian church has tried for seven hundred years to forget the bloody nonsense that followed, but descendants of Jewish and Muslim war atrocity victims will not let it. The "ethnic cleansing" of Kosovo by Christian Serbia, in the 1990s, showed a leftover sample of this Crusade mentality in the fringes. Most Christians of all major branches of Christianity vocally abhorred what happened there. Many even fought against the regime of Slobodan Milosevic. Of course, during the Crusades, atrocities were not anywhere near a one-sided affair.

While the Hermit stirred up religious fanaticism, Pope Urban II appealed in his speech at Clermont to more worldly considerations. He enticed the nobles of France by telling them that the land could no longer hold them, and that they needed to expand into new territories; the same theme conquerors have used from time out of memory. [5] He also did a new thing destined to create disturbing consequences. Pope Urban II took the reasoning behind penance to its logical conclusion when he introduced the ***indulgence***.

For about nine hundred years, clerics had claimed the power to remit sins to some degree, but always in connection with confession and penitential temporal punishment. Catholics who died before they finished penance on earth supposedly did so in purgatory, after which they entered heaven. Urban II announced a total (plenary) remission of all confessed sins with no temporal punishment here or in the hereafter. This went out to those who went on his crusade *"out of pure devotion."* [6] He then took it a step further by offering the same indulgence to those who could not actually go on the expedition, but who stayed behind to finance it.

Before long, popes offered indulgences for money, to finance anything from local cathedrals to Saint Peter's Basilica, which came a few centuries later. Eventually, the church sold indulgences not only for one's own sins, but also for those of dead loved ones already in purgatory. Soon, purgatory stints conveniently stretched to unknown and unknowable lengths, while moneymaking schemes grew more mercenary. [7] The most shameless hawkers of indulgences even offered them for sins yet to be committed, though this was rare. Today, a watered-down version of this practice continues in the donations given for Masses said for the dead. If the Pope really had the authority to manage God's grace on earth as some form of "treasury of merit," then this sort of thing was the logical outcome.

This begs the nagging question; *what kind of God could entrust such a vital quality of His nature to the hands of men like this?* And why would He even need to? There is a sense in which every believer "manages the grace of God" within their sphere of influence. Christians do not need another human agency to do this for us, and any attempt to set one up is doomed to create silliness or worse. My position does not reject the need for teachers or the need for human authority figures in the church. It does reject the need for mediators between God and the individual, except for the person of Jesus Christ.

In the Gospel of Matthew, the **"keys to the kingdom"** given to Peter, clearly refer to the power of preaching the gospel that saves men, and puts them into Christ's kingdom. Paul, in

Romans Chapter 1, said that the gospel is, **"the power of God that leads to salvation for those who believe."** History has played out to absurdity the idea that Peter, and his supposed successors, had the unique call to manage the sum of God's grace expressed on earth. Is it any wonder that a biblical concept of grace all but vanished during this period?

Not only were the Crusades—and their financing—a spiritual nightmare of demonic comic-opera scale, they were a military and logistical nightmare as well. Thousands of knights marched across Europe, funneling through the Balkans, into the bottleneck that was Constantinople on the Bosporus. These ill provisioned hordes often looted their way to the strait, targeting Jewish communities along the way, robbing, raping, and destroying as they went. If the crusaders found no Jewish quarter, or if what they found was insufficient to satiate the needs of the mob, they would even prey on their fellow Christians. [8]

The Byzantine Emperor, Alexius Comnenus, had called on Pope Urban II to spark the 1st Crusade to bail out his own war-weary troops. The Emperor practically freaked out when he saw the unruly mobs rushing down on Constantinople. While Urban had envisioned this as a possible way to reunite the Eastern and Western churches, Alexius simply put the mobs as fast as he could onto all the boats he could find. Both he and Peter the Hermit, for different reasons, wanted to get them out of the city and to the beaches of Asia Minor—whether they were militarily ready or not. The Hermit wanted to keep his Pauper's Brigade from worldly city temptations, while the Emperor didn't want them dirtying the streets.

After many deaths from inadequate training, the few surviving forces met with trained knights and foot soldiers coming in from the West. In time, these managed to break through the Muslim lines, and drive for Jerusalem. The Hermit took a back seat to the newly arrived noblemen, though he continued to preach the glories of the crusade to the troops. The 1st Crusade eventually succeeded in securing a strip of land along the Mediterranean coast of what is now Israel. The crusaders called this the *Latin Kingdom of Jerusalem.* It lasted only until 1291, when the Muslims inevitably took it back.

To read accounts of this period is to sense that church history had taken a disturbing detour into a Monty Python parody. Christian eyewitness records of the journeys and battlefields painted hellishly surreal landscapes of both faith and madness. Crusaders often cut open enemy dead in search of treasures they might have swallowed in their last desperate moments. Supply lines were so bad that some knights even cooked and ate their fallen Muslim enemies, chatting congenially as they sat around the campfire about the interesting flavor. Shelley cites one crusader's diary that reads like a demented chef review on how the meat had a pleasant taste like "spiced peacock." [9]

As everything else in church history done in accordance with man's flesh masquerading as the zeal of the Holy Spirit, the later Crusades did not even accomplish as much as the first. When the Kingdom of Jerusalem faced imminent destruction in 1147, another mystic, Bernard of Clairveaux, called for the 2nd Crusade. This effort practically fizzled out in its inception, and accomplished nothing. Bernard shows up a bit later, persecuting scholars, when we look at the Scholastic Movements. In a disturbing and dissonant irony, he also wrote profoundly, and often even correctly, on the nature of Christian love. Perhaps Bernard illustrates another example of how blind spots hide in the shadow of strengths. Maybe he was just a hypocrite. I don't know. I wasn't there. I can only report the disparity, not the reasons for it that only Bernard and God know.

The 3rd Crusade became the most famous. Three legendary figures of that period led its armies—Philip Augustus of France, Fredrick Barbarossa of the Holy Roman Empire, and England's Richard the Lion Hearted. Philip turned back, however, and Barbarossa accidentally drowned on the way. Only King Richard followed through to engage the

Syrio-Egyptian Sultan, Saladin, for the prize of the Holy Lands. We remember Richard the Lion Hearted as the king; whose interests Sir Robin of Locksley defended upon his return from the crusade as the legendary Robin Hood. To whatever degree a historical Robin Hood existed, this English king left an indelible mark on European history.

Both Richard and his Muslim counterpart were chivalrous in every sense of the word. They got together and negotiated an end to the fighting, which resulted in roughly another century of borrowed time for the Latin Kingdom of Jerusalem.

The 4th Crusade revealed the nature of the whole series of political, military, and religious games. When Innocent III became Pope in 1198, he started a propaganda campaign to revive a crusading spirit in Europe. Not content to be universal Pontiff, he also aspired to complete his empire building with an army of fanatics to go charging off at his whim. The explosive mess backfired in the young Pope's face when the paltry few knights who showed up could not pay the outrageous transport fees of Venetian shipping magnates. To keep the crusade from sputtering out in its embryonic stages, the knights cut a deal with the Venetians. They agreed to sack the troublesome coastal city of Zara—in Christian territory—in return for transport. Innocent III blew a gasket when he heard of it, and excommunicated the participants left and right. The Venetians had the advantage, however, and took it to help secure themselves yet another strategic port, in addition to Zara.

Internal strife and Islam's advance into Asia Minor had stripped Constantinople and its empire to a dying stump. Venice convinced the crusaders to capture the superbly placed Bosporus port from their Byzantine Christian allies! When news of this reached the Pope, he flew into a rage of crocodile tears and wrote back to the crusaders, calling them all a bunch of sacrilegious whores. Then, being the administrative scavenger that he was, Innocent III named an archbishop for the new "Latin Empire of Constantinople." If he hoped he might salvage a military "reunification" with the Eastern Church in the tattered remnants of the Byzantine Empire, he was hideously mistaken.

The Bulgarians and Muscovites had long ago converted to Eastern Orthodoxy, giving Constantine's church-state machine fresh hosts and new blood. The tawdry affair of "Latin Constantinople" only lasted a bit over fifty years, until 1261. Then, the Roman Catholic Church again lost the city, along with any hopes of reuniting with the Eastern Church for the next seven hundred years. The dying vestige of the Byzantine Empire barely survived this debacle for almost two hundred years more on the collective equivalent of "national life support." This continued to protect the rest of Christian civilization, during its crucial growing pains, from a premature clash with Islam in the European heartland.

Only when the Ottoman Turks took Constantinople, on 29 May 1453, did the Byzantine Empire finally fall. It had lasted over a thousand years as the prototype Christian State. Constantinople afterward became the capital of the Caliphate of Islam. Justinian's Hagia Sophia Basilica became a mosque.

Are we beginning to see a pattern?

The Fall of Constantinople ended the Roman Empire, which had lasted, first in Pagan, then in Christian form, for over 1500 years, and before that, as a republic, for about 550 years, totaling over two millennia; the longest continuous state in human history. The Fall of Constantinople also left Central Europe open to Islamic invasion for the next two hundred years. The Ottomans besieged Vienna several times in that period, but were defeated each time. The last defeat began on September 11, 1683; one of several dates that Muslims refer to as *Al Naqba*, "The Catastrophe." Hatred has a long memory, and those who would stand against it effectively must learn to take the long view.

Historical ignorance is not bliss.

As for the remaining Crusades, they each grew increasingly pathetic in motive, execution, or both. The Holy Lands fell again to Muslim forces in 1291. They would remain in Islamic hands until after World War I. The Crusades were as much a military and political disaster as they had been a spiritual one. The Popes, from Urban II to Innocent III and beyond, had tried to retake the Holy Lands and reunify the Church by political intrigue and military force—the tools of Caesar. They failed on both accounts miserably and made matters a million times worse through their unbridled arrogance. The dreams of Medieval Christendom, with its integrity, had irreparably cracked at the seams.

Soon, they would shatter.

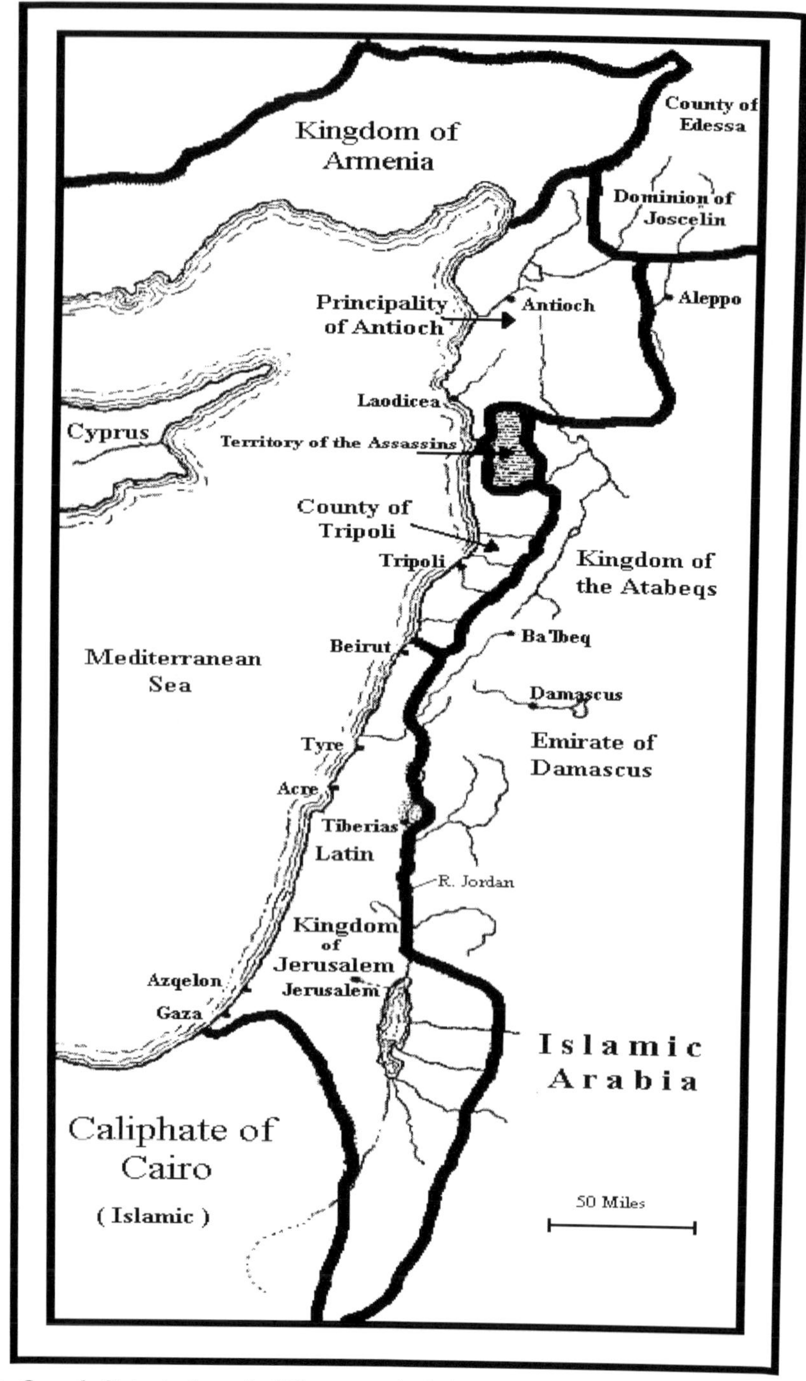


*The Crusade States in the early 12th century, including the Latin Kingdom of Jerusalem.*

## Bibliography


1. Shelley, Bruce L. ***Church History in Plain Language*** (2nd Edition), p.184, 1995, Word Publishing, Dallas, Tx.
2. ibid. p. 185
3. ***The American Heritage Dictionary of the English Language*, vicar**, definition # 5
4. Op cit. Shelley, Bruce L., p. 189
5. Hislop, Alexander; ***The Two Babylons***, pp. 187-191, Loizeaux Bros. 1916
6. Op cit. Shelley, Bruce L., p.189
7. Op cit. Hislop, p. 189
8. Will Durant, ***The Story of Civilization - Volume VI***, p.24; Simon and Schuster, 1950
9. Op cit. Shelley, Bruce L., p.
10. ibid. p. 188

# 12

# THE MIDDLE AGES PART 4: SCHOLASTICISM AND THE BEGINNING OF QUESTIONS

## INQUIRING MINDS AND INFLATED IDEAS

By the Late Middle Ages, many signs showed the sun rising again over Europe's piecemeal "Dark Ages." Mercantile trade exploration flexed the growing muscles of commerce with the establishment of new trade routes, like Marco Polo's overland silk highway to China. Expanding education brought with it new technologies. Monastic inventors rediscovered water wheels and windmills; the fruit of Christian scholars' technological application of ancient classical texts, protected from barbarian raids by generations of monks. Christendom, despite its many failings, had civilized a continent of looting savages that picked at the carcass of Roman civilization. It did so largely by transforming those savages. No other system in history had exerted so vast a civilizing force in so short a time.

This even happened while the church, as an institution, had fallen much from the spiritual and ethical purity of its first few centuries. That loss of purity would have long-term effects, which extended to, and even largely created, our present day circumstances. New questions needed answers, while few church leaders saw that need for what it was. They saw the dangers of a state controlled church from what had happened in the Christian Roman Empire, and the early Medieval Era. Now, at the height of the Middle Ages, church leaders did not realize that they faced the opposite threat.

They sat, secure in their simplistic belief that the Holy Spirit guided their leaders on an institutional scale. The growing potential for institutional atrocities seemed unthinkable because of this, and for one other factor. They also miscalculated the power and penetration of sin in a religious setting. It never occurred to them that there might be horrors spawned by church controlled states.

The previous chapter illustrated one such horror, the Crusades. Here, the church tried to use statecraft and military force to impose Christianity back onto the Holy Lands, and to bring Greek Orthodoxy under Rome's control. By contrast, New Testament Era Christians had spread the gospel through the Holy Spirit's power, using intellectual and moral reasoning. Many other dangers exist when church sects gain control over civil governments, even now. Nevertheless, those snares usually do not lie where today's church-state phobics seem to imagine, if popular culture tells us anything useful. Still, it would delude us to assume that our teaching Scripture verse-by-verse makes our style of Christianity immune to this brand of temptation. (I speak to those who believe, as I do, that expository teaching, book by book, verse by verse, is usually the best way to teach the Bible.)

That temptation can come in ways social conditioning blinds us to, especially whenever a state has recently tried to control the church in some way. We saw this demonstrated in the Byzantine and Western churches, and will see it again in new forms as we approach modern times. The problem is never Christian input, or even leadership (if gained ethically), in the forming of social policy. Nor is it a lack of power in God's word. *It is in sin's potential to work inside even well intended believers who do not use adequate safeguards against the process.*

Behaving as if good doctrine alone protects us from such things is as dangerous on the institutional level as on an individual one. It is relatively simple to admonish individuals to be "doers of the word." Doing so with trans-national church institutions is a bit more complex. In either case, Bible teaching is certainly essential, but the assumption that it alone prevents the sort of thing that happened to the medieval church has a glaring blind spot; *even the most correctly interpreted Bible doctrine can still be misapplied.* It also ignores the historical fact that doctrinal corruption is not the only kind of corruption churches can suffer. Sometimes, corrupt doctrine arrives only after other forms of corruption have cleared the way for it—as we saw during the Christian Roman Empire.

Nor will "being Spirit led" make us immune to the dangers of church controlled states; if by that we mean a contemplative *method* contrived to "develop sensitivity to hearing God's inner voice." Peter the Hermit, and his spiritual successors among the monastics and beyond, thought they had that. The Holy Spirit's guidance is also essential; but imagining that the virtue of a church office or methods of prayer and meditation can conjure up God's presence also has horrendous blind spots. The Holy Spirit is not a power we can inherit or learn to tap into intuitively in five simple steps. Nor can we activate Him by climbing through levels of ascetic discipline toward altered states of consciousness. (Col. 2:20-23)

The Medieval Catholic Church implicitly believed that the Holy Spirit led its leaders, and applied that belief by one or more of the above means. It came to behave as if the Pope and church councils had some sort of magical shield against straying from truth, and thus needed no earthly accountability. In Roman Catholicism, this eventually ended with the reasoning that the Pope was infallible. As with the assumption made about doctrine, the problem here is not the biblical belief that the Holy Spirit guides church leaders; *but in the idea that His guidance automatically removes human limits to what, generally, is knowable.* The Spirit may do so, at times, but the same Holy Spirit designed Scripture Paul the Apostle knew such human limits remained in place even in the 1st century.

> **9 For we know in part, and we prophesy in part; 10 but when that which is perfect is come, that which is in part shall be done away. *1 Corinthians* 13:9-10 NKJV**

Whether an Apostle, a pastor, a teacher, or a disciple; we only know in part. That means we must fold humility into any gift—especially those of miraculous power, knowing, speaking, or seeing. That also applies to gifts of administration and leadership. The passage above is part of an extended exposition on the subject of gifts in the church. God designed our gifts, whether natural or spiritual, to work within a limited situation—we prophesy *in part.* He also made our gifts to operate within the integrated framework of a community body. We need each other at an *organic* level—the root word for *organism.*

Organisms normally grow in both size and complexity over time.

The Holy Spirit's insight into Scripture, likewise, works over time in the Body of Christ to help believers grow honest interpretive methods, *sufficient for their day.* Early on, Christians had faith that Scripture spoke truly about whatever subject it touched on. It is foundational knowledge, on which we may safely build to obey the Great Commission, and to discover and manage the lives and world that God has given us. We grow, both individually and corporately from the "DNA" of God's word. (1 Pet. 1:22-23)

Unfortunately, this does not guarantee that Christian leaders (or any Christian) will never go astray in how they build on this foundation (1 Cor. 3:9-18). Nor is it safe just to sit on the foundation, basking in its perfection, and build nothing on it in the realm of ideas (Matt. 25:24-29). The issues the world throws at us change by generation. Finding timely, biblical answers takes reflection. The war is spiritual, but the battlefield is intellectual, emotional, and relational.

History has rendered its verdict, often justly, that the medieval church went astray in trying to control more than it had any business trying to control. Nevertheless, at least they tried to build something. Everything we enjoy in our Christian faith today rests on things they managed to build rightly from Scripture. Just because there is a stage in any building process, where things are more apt to go wrong than at any other step, does not mean we can skip that step. Things can go wrong at any stage in the superstructure. A "sure foundation" ensures potential for success at all subsequent stages; it does not guarantee that the builders will always live up to that potential.

Most Evangelicals, and even many Catholics and Orthodox, agree that several things went wrong at the "step" we call the Late Medieval Age. That does not mean Christians should skip over this era or write it off completely as wasted centuries. Much more went on than just a massive church system that tried to control things too much.

Of course, we speak loosely when using the word *control* to describe the governmental maneuverings of medieval institutions. Church and state alike had little real ability to control people too closely. The technology to monitor and suggest ideas to large populations did not yet exist. Medieval church and state still made nasty examples of whatever dissenters they caught, whether "heretics," wayward scholars, or, occasionally, Jews. Of course, the more vocal and dedicated the person behaved in a dissenting issue; the more likely they would eventually clash with the system, and gain renown as either a criminal or a martyr.

While Hollywood finds "medieval barbarism" fun to mock, serious historians expose amazing social advances in the Late Middle Ages, even with the true low points. [1] The idea of a simple "medieval worldview" is a myth. Europe, by the early 2nd millennium, reflected a complex hodge-podge of Classical and Byzantine Greek, Roman, Judeo-Christian, Celtic, Slavic, Moorish, and Germanic influences. Literacy had started again to bloom. Scholars began to reason at higher and more original levels, as theories about the nature of knowledge and reality began to take shape. Monasteries gave birth to the university.

One question that engaged thinkers of the period involved the role human reason played in the exploration of Divine revelation. Mystics and contemplatives like Bernard of Clairveaux, the Victorines, and Francis of Assisi often valued subjective spiritual experiences over logic, yet rarely to a complete denial of reason. The Franciscans, for example, included William of Occam and Roger Bacon—key names in the advancement of philosophy toward science. At this point, there were no clear lines between the mystical and what we would call "the scientific," other than, perhaps, Greek logic. Even in their occasional madness, Christian mystics usually had some method. The problem with an exclusively mystical approach was the same then as it is now. Calling reason "unspiritual" robs people of a working biblical "firewall" against extremism.

Nobody really knew that, then, or perceived its importance.

By contrast, the Scholastics honed the tools of logic, later used to study the Bible more clearly. They understood that Christ, as the Divine Logos (the Word), had created an objective reality. This spiritual advance unfolded in the meaning of word *logic* itself, an offshoot of the word *logos*. Scholastics such as Peter Abelard, Albertus Magnus, Thomas Aquinas, William of Occam, Anselm of Canterbury, and Roger Bacon never denied the power of spiritual experiences. They simply improved sanity checks for them. Some straddled both traditions, mystic and scholastic, and saw no conflict.

Since God is a rational Being, who created a reality reflecting cause and effect, then the Holy Spirit also worked rationally. Men could not safely idolize either reason or intuition, any more than they could safely discard either of them. The thinking of such men—usually without their intending it—paved the way for both the Reformation and Catholic Counter-Reformation. It also laid the intellectual foundations of the scientific method.

The scales tipped toward the rational with the rediscovery of Aristotle's works. This sharpened the thinking skills of the educated, even if they tended to rely too heavily on his opinions at first. The faith-assumption that God was a rational Being also expressed itself more consistently as new generations built on the works of the last. English monk, Roger Bacon, predicted that God's creation worked according to laws discoverable by experiment and observation; that men through technology might relieve suffering and improve life by harnessing these "laws of nature." Bacon also favored familiarizing Christian missionaries with the rediscovered learning; to aid them in showing non-Christian peoples what knowledge harnessed by God's word could create. He also called for a reform of theology that went back to the Bible, as he discovered more about the languages of the inspired writers.

Even the bad things of the Late Medieval Period often arose from sincere desires to bring society into conformity with the law of God. The trouble was not always due to power hunger, and rejection of plainly revealed Bible truths. As in all periods of church history, Satan masterfully exploited the blind spots of genuine believers to create ugliness in the name of Christ. Given our spiritual past, we should guard against constantly overlooking biblical truths we think of as secondary. In the enticement to reach lofty spiritual goals that seem primary; "secondary truths" can appear expendable. Too many ignored "secondary truths" have a way of stacking up over time, however. Eventually, they create big problems that make the earlier "lofty goals" seem ugly, out of touch, or unrealistic to later generations.

This describes what happened to the medieval church quite well.

Even at the peak of the corruption penetrating the Christianity of the Late Middle Ages, seeds of change had already begun to sprout. By the 11th to 13th centuries, society based on the Christendom model had made higher levels of education available to more people. Though some Dark Age distortions stayed embedded in the growth of theological ideas, thinkers in the Western Church began to build on their checkered lower floors in ways that were more systematic. Because they built from partly unbiblical ideas, this had both good and bad effects on the church and on society. A fair analysis would conclude that the long-term effects were mostly good.

## Delayed Implications of Scholasticism for Bible Interpretation

On the positive side, men like Peter Abelard began to develop what I like to call, "the philosophical science of asking the right questions." Thomas Aquinas established a biblical and common sense-based philosophy on the value of reason as central to the Image of God in the human person. While showing some evidence of an incomplete view of the Genesis Fall (which we will cover shortly), Aquinas displayed the value of inquiry into the nature of God's creation. This indirectly boosted the arts beyond being mere shorthand for expressing theological truths. It elevated them into something connected to creation and illuminating to the common person. Aquinas' apologetic defense for belief in the existence of God is still among the best arguments in use today.

William of Occam (also spelled Ockham) developed what was later called ***Occam's Razor***; the principle that, *"the simplest explanation for something, needing the fewest assumptions, is usually correct."* Occam's Razor had new implications for the developing science of ***hermeneutics*** or text interpretation. Bible interpreters, at least in theory, could now say that; *"the simplest interpretation of a given passage of Scripture, in its grammatical, thematic, and historical context, is usually correct."* It would be a while before any interpreters actually said that, but it was now possible to express the idea coherently.

Occam himself, as a Franciscan friar, did not carry his own idea out to its logical conclusion in studying the Bible. Yet "Occam's Razor" still held unrealized potential for those who someday would. It would help to shape Luther's, Calvin's, and all Post-Reformation book-by-book Bible interpretation based on ***exegesis***. We mentioned Theodore of Mopsuestia's exegetic Bible interpretation, 900 years before William of Occam; about 1100 years before the Reformation got hold of Occam's Razor. Sadly, Orthodox zealots had slandered Theodore after his death, when a couple of his students went on to back the heresies of Nestorianism and Pelagianism. God gave William better fortune, which gave future Christians better intellectual tools.

We also previewed what *exegesis* is. By doing this in the chapter that covered Theodore, and developing on it here, I am not saying that nobody ever used exegesis before; only that it was not systematically valued for what it is. Constant allegorization trains the mind to read new things into a text. God's word has allegory. Nor is it so time-locked in its application that seeing new allegories in it is always bad. Forcing allegorization as the backbone of Bible interpretation has many dangers, nonetheless. It causes definitions to drift with the changing currents of the times. Scripture loses its timelessness in an unwise attempt to "keep it relevant." The word of God is always relevant in its truths. Such "new allegories," at best, can only illustrate new applications for established truths, not guide Bible interpretation.

Exegesis is the practice of interpreting a text according to its grammatical, historical, and thematic context. *Ex* means *to guide out of,* stressing the value of what is objectively in the text. It is the honest attempt to interpret what a text says, rather than reading one's own ideas into it. Exegesis was a discipline refined over centuries, as the Holy Spirit helped Christians hone their intellectual tools. Such advances enriched our grasp of God's unchanging word in ways applicable to changing historical conditions. Exegesis is the opposite of ***eisogesis,*** where the reader reads things into a text, either from their own presuppositions or from ideas suggested by others.

Many people today think that all interpretation is eisogesis—that everyone just reads into the Bible what they want it to say. No doubt, many do that. In the real world, however, some interpretations are more informed and honest than others. It is possible to tell them apart with good analytical tools. The view that all forms of interpretation merely read our own ideas back into the text ignores more evidence than it explains. It "suppresses truth" by calling "dishonest" any reason for studying ancient texts and ***historiography*** (the mechanics of knowing history), except political power. (Rom. 1:18) The academic term for this view is ***Minimalism,*** a stepchild of Postmodernism and ***Empiricism***; the idea we can know reality only by our senses. [2] Later chapters will explore these views.

While perfect objectivity is humanly impossible, Christians should value the objective and strive for it in Bible interpretation. It is worship to God when we submit to Him by trusting that He has revealed His mind to us in His word. This comes to us in the *object* of a Bible, which has books about real people, places, and times. The science of hermeneutics, or text interpretation, uses the exegetic method to come as close as possible to the inspired authors' intended meaning; and that means substantially and significantly close! While our understanding of language and history are not perfect, they are substantial enough for God to use as a communication medium for His perfect word.

A shared faith rooted in history needs the tools of the historian and philosopher to build on our foundation in Christ. Abelard's art of asking critical questions, and Occam's Razor, honed the methods of exegesis. They began to reverse the effects of Philo's worldview-mismatched, "find the hidden allegory" style Bible interpretation. They cut away, though imperfectly, extraneous layers of cultural assumption that read baseless things into the text. This did not happen all at once nor even in William's lifetime or that of Luther, for that matter—but it happened. Origen, except for *Sola Scriptura,* was largely undone. Papias could now vindicate his early straightforward approach to prophecy from the grave (so to speak).

The Scholastics themselves, in their day, had no idea what they had begun to unleash. Many of them would have been horrified at it—especially William of Occam and Thomas Aquinas. The Razor cut out a clearer view of what the text ***objectively*** said, shedding centuries of what readers had carried in ***subjectively*** by mystical fancy or folk bias. From here on out, the distinction between biblical truth and accreted distortion would become increasingly visible. The Holy Spirit had begun to release the human and spiritual equal of an anti-virus program into the thinking of Catholic Europe. This "anti-virus program" would scan and compile for the next few centuries before executing a repair sequence.

Scholasticism, as a movement, showed that Christianity in the West once again advanced. It boded a blossom of both Renaissance and Reformation at a time when Eastern Christianity stagnated in the false security of dying Byzantium. Eastern Orthodoxy endured through its many shake-ups after the fall of Constantinople. Yet, it seemed it had proved itself too inflexible to reform, too often—at least for the moment. Its center shifted to places like Russia, the Ukraine, Armenia, Greece, and Serbia; where it thrived mostly as state churches under autocracies akin to Rome and Byzantium. The Russian Orthodox Church showed this, as it both fostered and fed off the Czarist Empire, until the Bolshevik Revolution of 1917.

Of course, I'm using a simplification for contrast. Today, there is evidence that parts of Eastern Orthodoxy may be experiencing something akin to revival—in a good sense. Much of it no longer exists in thralldom to autocracy. Orthodoxy may even have preserved in itself something that seems resistant to the Post-modern trend toward trivialization and ***Reductionism***, especially in its view of worship. If so, we all need some of that.

Back in the medieval West, Scholasticism bred seeds of change in both church and state. It was not always so much a spiritual movement as a method of learning harnessed by Christians to build something new.

Christians have tended to react in two ways toward the classical learning of the ancient Greeks. Tertullian and Cyprian shunned all things from Pagan antiquity. Justin Martyr and Augustine followed the Apostle Paul's example in Acts 17, and familiarized themselves with non-Christian thought. Dangers exist in the extremes of both approaches. Scholastics like Peter Abelard and Thomas Aquinas tried to follow Paul's example with varying degrees of success. They redemptively used ***Socratic Dialogue***, and other tools from Greek philosophy, to teach the doctrines of the church more clearly. Though they often genuinely tried to steer away from the Greeks' Pagan fallacies, they did not realize just how much their own setting had already fallen to them. They ran away from such things on a moving platform that slid toward the fallacies faster than any man could run.

As with most great Christian spiritual and intellectual movements, Scholasticism also had some serious blind spots. An application of biblical truth that healed in one century sometimes created problems for the next few. Unchanging biblical principles were never the trouble. Failures to apply them in the wisest ways sometimes were. Without this kind of flexibility, Christianity would have died in Judea in the 1st century. As Pastor Chuck Smith famously put it in the late 20th century, "Blessed are the flexible, for they shall not be broken." He did not mean that truth is flexible, only that what worked in the 10th century will likely not work efficiently, in the same way, in the 21st. There is a difference between *the truth* and *the best way to apply* the truth under a given set of circumstances.

Truth is not about "what works" anyway. Some lifestyles, methods, and worldviews work well in the short run exactly because they avoid inconvenient truths. Yet, nothing that avoids truth can really work over the long haul. Such systems have eventual disaster built into them because they do not fit reality.

However well these systems work for a time, reality always catches up.

## THOMAS AQUINAS, ARISTOTLE, AND THE QUESTION OF PAGAN THOUGHT

Irony flows through the lives of the Scholastics like a variable wind. The very men who triggered the raw ideas, which others, later, put together into the Reformation; also fixed into Catholic theology the doctrines most needing reform. I speak of the accretion of humanistic elements that had slowly crept into the church over centuries. Scholastic monks often revered the Greek philosophers like naturalistic prophets about nature and logic. They gave them authority similar to scholar-saints like Jerome and Augustine on those subjects.

On those topics, the Pagan thinkers seemed to have parity, even excellence, over most comparable Christians to date, in terms of natural ability. It was not that God needed Pagan philosophers to prop up thinking in His church—for that matter, it isn't that God needs Christians to prop anything up either. It seemed so, because God really does use elements of a fallen world system redemptively, without endorsing the sin and error. God brings good out of evil. Christianity had (and still has) a rich history of God doing this. The problems came by the slow buildup of distorting worldly influences on the church. Thinkers locked in the rigid canon of Medieval Roman Catholicism often seemed awkward with the idea of learning from Pagan philosophers. They tended to make them into supreme authorities on the natural world. Perhaps this also reflected the split between the spiritual and material.

Thomas Aquinas did this with Aristotle. Since Aquinas, a Dominican, became the "intellectual champion" of the popes; this fostered a mood where too much dependence on the philosopher's opinions influenced church teaching on everything from nature to ethics. Later papal authorities persecuted Copernicus and Galileo for theorizing that the Earth orbited the sun. This happened in large part because Aristotle had placed the Earth at the center of the universe. [3] Copernicus believed in a sun-centered universe not because he had hard data—he had no telescope to see the sunlit phases of the planets. Rather, as a Christian Neo-Platonist, he saw the sun as a symbol of divine light, which, to him made a better center.

Plato was an odd man out among Greek thinkers, following the mystical math cult of Pythagoras' belief in a sun-centered universe. In Copernicus' day, the issue was mainly philosophical and religious. No adequate telescopes existed yet to provide empirical data. It was also an issue of mathematical ease; Copernicus' sun-centered cosmos, as that of Pythagoras, more elegantly explained planetary motions. While simplicity is usually desirable, and often correct, it does not always turn out that way—Occam's Razor notwithstanding. Exceptions exist today. At the time, based on the little that people could see, Copernicus' system seemed to violate common sense. In the wake of how this debate turned out, many early scientists soon saw mathematics, in the words of Galileo, as *"the language in which the book of Nature was written by the hand of God."*

Some Neo-Platonists eventually began to think they had another line into the mind of God that superseded His Word. If so, it would prove only to be a line into God's most rudimentary thoughts on engineering, with nothing substantial of His character and grace. Mathematically reverse engineering the basic shapes used in a machine gives no insight into the personal heart of its inventor. It tells little or nothing of the Inventor's character, whether the Inventor loves their spouse, or whom the Inventor considers family, friend, or foe. Mathematics is immensely useful, but it cannot tell us the sort of things Scripture can. Copernicus and Galileo understood this in their day, as we shall see later. As the centuries pass from here on out, this will become more important to understanding our own era.

Jumping 200 years back from Copernicus again, to Aquinas and the other Scholastics; they usually did not intend to make Pagan philosophers saints. They sometimes made conscious efforts not to. It happened, again, through the exploitation of their worldview blind spots by the Enemy, using slightly later artists and thinkers. It did not help that the pattern of ***syncretism*** or mixing Christian with Pagan views was already old tradition. The Scholastic Era approach to the Greek philosophers began as a matter of common sense versus extremes. Aquinas admired Aristotle, but the most available versions of Aristotle came through Arab Muslims, who had added their commentary. Excited students at the University of Paris idolized bastardized versions of Aristotle's works; cut with Islamic spin posing as the Philosopher's words. The Bishop of Paris responded by placing most of Aristotle's books on the "forbidden" list.

This raised an important question; *just how far can unbelieving thinkers really "get things right" even on earthly things?* Some Biblicists of the time, thinking to elevate God's word, argued that Christian knowledge was in all things superior. This sounds silly to us, but in the 1100s and 1200s, such issues were not quite so tested. Aquinas argued that natural man, using human reason, could know many things rightly about the natural world without Divine revelation. Hence, Greek logic had value. This would seem to us like a "no-brainer." Whom do you want opening your chest if you need heart surgery, the experienced Pagan heart surgeon, or the Christian first-year medical student? I'll gladly ask the Christian student for prayer, but the Pagan heart specialist is the guy who gets to crack my chest open like a lobster, thanks!

The Pope called Thomas Aquinas in to mediate between the Bishop and the university students. Aquinas agreed with the Bishop that the translations of Aristotle were corrupt, but also with the students, that Aristotle was a worthy study. Unfortunately, the long-term issues were not quite so simple. Either Aquinas himself, or possibly those who later interpreted and applied his writings, came to have an incomplete picture of the Genesis Fall. In this view, only man's will and conscience were fallen, but human intellect potentially remained intact if a person reasoned properly. [4] Yet, *being fallen* and *having poor reasoning skills* are two entirely different things. This would have far-reaching implications for all that would follow in church history and Western Civilization.

It created the beginnings of a rift, where thinkers saw human intellect as increasingly self-sufficient from God's word, as time moved on. Things did not go that direction because logic demanded it. Only perceptions did. One reason it went that way resulted from the existing split in the church's view of authority. If ultimate authority rested in both Tradition and Scripture, and the church by its Tradition had decided what books were *Scripture;* then Tradition was the ultimate authority, mechanically speaking. Since Tradition supposedly included the reasoning that church councils had used to choose which books were Scripture, then much rested on the capacity to reason indeed. The fallacy here rested in the authoritarian assumption that the church had *authorized* Scripture; instead of merely discovering it through research, and agreeing on the nature of what they had discovered.

Another fallacy also embedded itself into this rift about human reason, soon afterward. *It did not logically follow that if Pagan intellects, unaided by Divine revelation, could reason correctly about earthly things; that it meant human intellect was potentially unaffected by the Genesis Fall and its Curse.* Human intellect intertwines with both conscience and will, none of which really exist independently of each other. Distortion in one of these features automatically leads to consequences in the others. Moral depravity adversely affects motives and mental efficiency, even if not all at once. How then could we consider the intellect and will separately in terms of the negative effects of the Genesis Curse? Natural intellect may know natural things truly; but that does not make the foundational assumptions of the Pagan (or the modern secularist) resistant to the self-serving ideas people quietly insert into their reasoning to support their sin. Christian thinkers have no magic immunity here, either.

This had consequences on how Scholasticism came to view the Doctrine of Salvation. If people were not completely fallen, then there was a hypothetical place for them to contribute partly to their own salvation by their own merit. Ideas from the Pagan philosophers; at times used redemptively, at others becoming a distorting influence on Christian thought, now crystallized several man-centered corruptions into theology. [5]

A Christianese form of the Stoic ascetic ideal had long distorted concepts about holiness and marriage. Now, ***Scholastic Theology*** magnified human intellect and merit, burying a biblical view of salvation by grace in a new form of Pelagianism. In fact, opponents of William of Occam even called his view of salvation "the New Pelagianism." Reformation Christians later called the salvation teaching of post-Trent Roman Catholicism "Semi-Pelagian" for even better reasons; it carried the idea that God conveyed His grace through sacramental ritual to new extremes. [6]

The Roman Church at this time often approached the subject of learning not so much as a system of inquiry but as a matter of doctrinaire authority. This spirit showed even when cathedral schools and universities diligently used the outward forms of Socratic inquiry. It wove throughout the culture the way cancerously self-centered forms of individualism weave through ours. The latter is, in fact, a large-scale historical reaction against the former. Today, it has often reached the point of historical over-reaction—but before we treat it as *merely* that, we should consider something. The sense of continued betrayal that stems from systemic abuse of authority is an effect, not a cause. It will not just be the Roman Church guilty of perpetuating this problem, in upcoming centuries.

Aquinas, ironically, the scholar most submitted to papal authority, inadvertently lit the fuse for a string of ideological explosions. Their fallout would leave even most church people seeing the human intellect as detached from any practical need for God's revelation. All real and imagined abuses aside, this was certainly not Aquinas' intent. It became the outcome, however, once people took a broken view of the Genesis Curse to its logical conclusion in the Renaissance, and then in the so-called ***Enlightenment***.

If people could arrive at a truth that was unaffected by sin and the Fall, starting only from themselves by their intellect; then why could they not ultimately arrive at *absolute* truth that way? Aquinas would never have asked this question—nor would have Abelard! The door to it swung open through an incomplete view of the Curse, nonetheless. Other came, later, who not only asked this question, but also insisted that they had the answers in themselves.

Scholastic Era blind spots sometimes hid in the shadow of necessary responses to even worse extremes, more urgent at the time. These came in many forms, from zeal to escape Dark Age illiteracy to the evil side effects of drumming up support for the Crusades, like anti-Semitism. During the Medieval Age, the "idea pendulum" swung from a church culture too swayed by peasant superstition to one driven by nitpicking scholars. That assessment is, of course, a vast caricature, which is likely unfair to many individuals of the period. Still, it captures the mood of the times truly enough in a broad brushstroke sort of way. The worst blind spots came from unbiblical views of authority, and from ones that maybe had a biblical base, but which church leaders applied too carelessly or simplistically.

At times, this made Scholasticism slave to a control oriented papacy, especially in the stream from Aquinas to the Jesuits, some 300 years later. [7] Even the best logic is only as good as the premises at its foundation. If those premises forsake intellectual honesty, and exist only to service the needs and wants of the Roman Papacy (or any establishment); then outcomes stop fitting reality in direct proportion to that lack of integrity. Popes of this period cynically exploited superstition to retain short-term social control, something the more astute of them saw slipping slowly from their grasp. In short, propaganda, rather than a search for truth, sometimes guided scholastic inquiry. *Yet this was much rarer back then than it is today. Back then, a firm belief in absolutes provided some measure of restraint, even if an imperfect one.*

We have nothing as able as Judeo-Christian moral absolutes restraining the prostitution of academics today. Moral relativism offers no such potential. We can so easily poke fun at Late Medieval academics only because of 20/20 hindsight. Bad as they were, power-propaganda incidents were exceptions in Scholastic inquiry, not the rule. What sort of "science" and "history" can we expect today's academies to shape in the long term, based on the logical fallacy of absolute relativism? What forms of fanaticism will such a culture spawn as the 21st century moves on? It is doubtful our civilization will create the civility eventually produced by Medieval Europe. We already see civility dying in our own day.

In addition to the relatively few lapses in medieval academics, an adequate distinction between *what the Bible said*, and *scholastic theories on what the Bible said*, did not always exist. That, too, is a blind spot we have more of today, if for different reasons.

Aquinas may have tried to warn us about that. He pointed out a similar difference between *our conception of something* and the *thing itself* in his writings on metaphysics; part of his thesis that a difference exists between a thing's essence and its existence. [8] Whatever Aquinas intended, this is an important distinction. Christians in the 21st century can miss the needed border between *reality* and *our ideas about* reality as easily as others can. Only God can *completely* align His thoughts with the reality, because only He is all-knowing, and only He created it all. We could spare ourselves useless disputes, both in the church and with the world, by thinking more about this. For it is certain that there are enough necessary disputes to deal with in both places that we cannot and should not avoid.

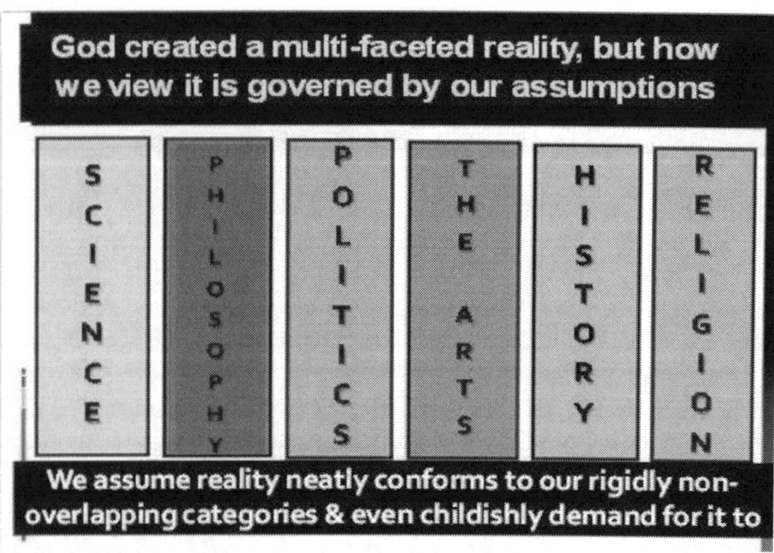


*Theories of knowledge and being – subjects we often take for granted – were cutting-edge during the Scholastic Era. We have forgotten some important categories of thought pioneered by the Medieval Scholastics. Aquinas' distinction between* ***a reality*** *versus* ***ideas about that reality*** *would otherwise clear up many foolish conflicts about "mixing science with religion" or "keeping religion out of politics." In reality, causes in one realm have inevitable effects in the others. This is because God created a reality intertwined by cause and effect relationships not always apparent – such that we can speak of "the Law of Unintended Consequences." 21st century thought arrogantly declares, "Nothing can be certain," as if it had the certainty of omniscience to make such an absolute.*

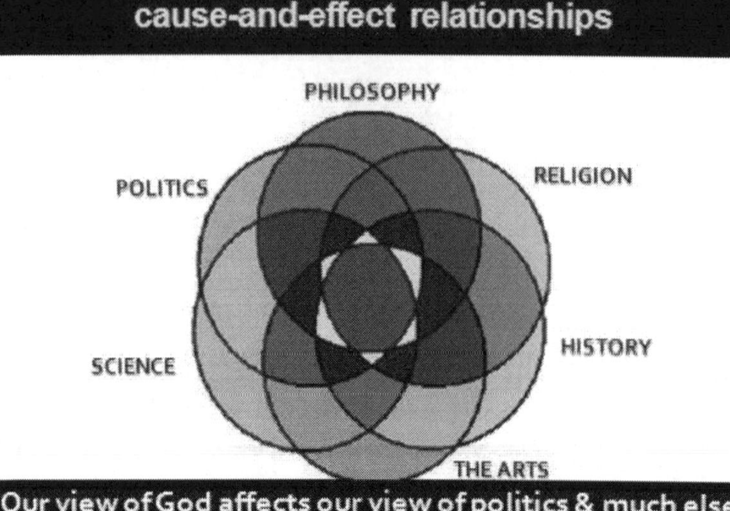

## THE STOIC CORRUPTION OF HOLINESS: A SCHOLASTIC LOVE TRAGEDY

People use the term *Christian* properly in two major senses. The first reflects *a born-again believer,* and that which pertains to a biblical belief system. The second way, also legitimate, is in the sense of *culturally Christian,* as in *that which arose from a culture informed by a Christian Worldview.* A Christian Worldview never saved anyone. That does not mean developing a Christian worldview is unimportant. I have often heard believers try to insist that something culturally Christian is "not really Christian," as if the second sense has no meaning. That is just a trite word game that only confuses and annoys people. Anyone can easily shoot it down with a dictionary. It is easier to specify what one means with more precise terms than to arbitrarily overthrow an established definition.

Likewise, the Scholastic's viewpoints were Christian in the cultural sense, even if the view of salvation that followed grew less biblical. Roman law, Greek philosophy, and Germanic chivalry had entered the church, with a control-oriented idea of authority. Secular thinkers today often like to attribute the latter to a slavish dependence on the Bible. A close examination of medieval thought causes this assumption to break down, however. As the dispute between the Bishop of Paris and the university students illustrate; church intellectuals of the day were often far more on fire for Greek philosophy than for the Bible. These men were charismatic and popular. Some of them could also be dreadfully arrogant.

Having a scriptural set of faith-held presuppositions was not the problem. One cannot think without faith-assumptions of some form, be they theistic, atheistic, or otherwise. Problems come whenever religious or secular authorities seek to control ideas merely to serve their own power agendas. In the 12th century, this required layers of needless speculation to explain away troublesome facts to satisfy papal or kingly powers; details more clearly explained by concluding that the Roman Church or monarch in question had simply erred on some point. (The problem was not unique to the church.)

Though embellished by our pop-culture parodies of history, some medieval corruptions of Christianity really damaged not only doctrine; but also the institution of family itself. The life of Peter Abelard illustrates how far from biblical truth and human reality church culture had fallen in the name of an increasingly bent view of holiness. Abelard lived about a hundred years before Aquinas. He championed the idea that honest doubt leads to honest questions. In Abelard's view, critical analysis led to genuine understanding, which nurtured an educated faith rather than a blind one.

For this reason, he began to subject even the doctrines of the church to questioning; not to discredit them, but so that in comprehending them the Faith would grow. For this, the crusade-mongering Bernard of Clairveaux bitterly opposed Abelard. Bernard was a mystic who over-simplistically saw doubt in any form as the total opposite of Christian faith. He did not believe the tools of reason had much value for understanding God's word. Bernard forgot that the capacity of human reason was a reflection of the *Imago Dei*—the Image of God in man. It did not of itself corrupt whatever it touched simply because it was human. Reason only corrupted truth when it began from dishonest or inaccurate faith-assumptions.

Even so, human reason in a fallen world had no built-in safeguards against people using it as an idol, either. In fact, apart from using it in submission to the word of God, one would tactically expect it to become just that. The assumption that human reason should be independent from the word of God was destined to become the largest, most voracious idol of all. This danger did not mean we must avoid human reason at any cost. Our ability to reason is part of the image of God in us. It is intrinsic to our capacity for understanding and obeying His word. Isaiah the Prophet said, **"Come now, and let us reason together," Says the LORD, "Though your sins are like scarlet, They shall be as white as snow; Though they are red like crimson, They shall be as wool."** (Isaiah 1:18 NKJV)

Peter Abelard was part of the rise of the university as an institution, founder of the University of Paris. He was also a church canon at Notre Dame Cathedral. At first, the universities of Europe were not *places* of learning as much as *a body of teachers* who carried the art of learning wherever they went to speak. In this respect, the university had a similar history to its own image as the church. Both originally saw themselves as a collective of people, rather than of buildings. Abelard was the most popular and effective of the university-style teachers of his day. This presented for him a huge personal problem; one that well illustrates the extreme degree to which Pagan Stoic asceticism had entered the church, and redefined the idea of holiness using the Christianese of the day.

Abelard's life answered the question no one asked: *What happens when Christian culture demands an idealized holiness that fits neither a biblical nor a realistic view of redeemed humanity?*

The terrible answer unravels in serpentine coils throughout the rest of church history and that of Western Civilization, to our own day. Lest one imagine that this was just a "Medieval Roman Catholic thing," history repeats itself whenever enough people fail to learn from it. The false holiness of asceticism always rears its head whenever the world gets ugliest, and the immediate crisis facing Christians involves lack of genuine holiness. It baits the hook. The hook exists to catch Christians *who want holiness,* not those who could care less—Satan already has them!

Peter Abelard was a cathedral canon—a scholar of church law. He was not a priest under permanent vows of celibacy, but in order to continue as a teacher, he had to maintain the potential to become one. The Cathedral of Notre Dame and the later University of Paris were both church institutions. Thus, practically speaking, Abelard's calling still hinged on a vow of celibacy. A few priests were still married at this time, but the powerful Cluniac Reformers were quickly changing that.

A married priest could not advance, regardless of his gifts, or honor as a husband by a biblical definition— neither could a married canon scholar. The tale of Abelard's life reads like one of history's great romantic tragedies. His autobiography is part of a larger volume he wrote called the *History of Calamities*. For at the height of his career, he fell in love with the niece of one of his fellow canons, and desired to marry her.

There is every reason to believe Abelard's love for Heloise was honorable. Although he was almost twenty years her senior, this was common in that day out of economic necessity, and Heloise was in her late teens. Infant mortality rates were high. It took men that long to establish themselves in a society emerging from a feudal economy toward a mercantile one. Girls had to marry in their early to middle teens because they could expect to lose roughly a third of their children, before they reached adulthood, to disease. Aside from that, basic biblical truth about the human condition should have been self-evident. The model of marriage and human sexuality revealed in Genesis 2 is social and relational, not just reproductive. Reducing it to that amounts to a form of ***Reductionism***.

That is what happens whenever we try to fit the Bible into some human ideological mold. We reduce either God, humanity, or both into something less than what they are.

If it does not seem odd that God should use the naming of the animals as the instrument for revealing Adam's need for female companionship, it should. The earliest detailed biblical text on marriage does not even mention procreation, though it is implicit. Genesis 1:28 mentioned it, but only in the same sense as with other animal life. Nothing social, humanly unique, or personal appears until Chapter 2. The concern of God in humanity's case, regarding married sex, is not mere utility in reproduction—it is more!

> **18 And the LORD God said, "It is not good that man should be alone; I will make him a helper comparable to him." 19 Out of the ground the LORD God formed every beast of the field and every bird of the air, and brought them to Adam to see**

**what he would call them. And whatever Adam called each living creature, that was its name. 20 So Adam gave names to all cattle, to the birds of the air, and to every beast of the field. But for Adam there was not found a helper comparable to him. 21 And the LORD God caused a deep sleep to fall on Adam, and he slept; and He took one of his ribs, and closed up the flesh in its place. 22 Then the rib which the LORD God had taken from man He made into a woman, and He brought her to the man. 23 And Adam said: "This is now bone of my bones And flesh of my flesh; She shall be called Woman, Because she was taken out of Man." 24 Therefore a man shall leave his father and mother and be joined to his wife, and they shall become one flesh. 25 And they were both naked, the man and his wife, and were not ashamed.** ***Genesis*** **2:18-25 NKJV**

As a man delivered from bondage to sexual sin, Augustine of Hippo once speculated that pre-Curse sexuality involved no physical desire. In this speculation (and he called it that), the Fall had warped human sexuality by adding strong desire to it. He observed, as we do, that people fed impure desires by fantasy and experimentation; or else had those patterns imposed on them by others through abusive conditioning during youth. Often it was a mix of both. Nevertheless, Augustine's speculation had a faulty view of creation, human nature, and the Curse. It is ludicrous to imagine that Adam's exclamation upon seeing Eve, **"This is now bone of my bone and flesh of my flesh,"** had no desire in it. The words drip with it, and properly so. What happens on the marriage bed is clean. (Heb. 13:4)

One can sympathize with Augustine's wrestling to maintain his personal victory, especially since he was likely first to see problems with Christianized Stoicism. That does not lessen the damage caused by a view of sexual purity warped by practical Stoicism, expressed in Christianese. The ascetic idea that healthy sexual desire in marriage was "a necessary evil" is still a perversion.

Peter Abelard was smart enough to know that no biblical reason existed why he should have to be celibate. Even so, he was not what we might call an anti-celibacy activist. The unruly monks at an abbey he later pastored would soon discover this, to their dismay. In a church system that frowned on theology teachers without the potential for later priestly orders, and which forbade priestly orders without vows of celibacy; Abelard and Heloise were stuck in a difficult situation. Peter insisted on secretly marrying, but Heloise refused at first, not wanting to destroy his ministry. Without a church system that supported common sense, biblical views of pastoral leadership and marriage, hope died for them at some point. They caved to temptation. Heloise became pregnant. (1 Cor. 7:2-5, 1 Tim. 4:1-3, Mark 9:42)

Abelard owned up to being the father, but even after their secret wedding Heloise still refused to publically admit they were married. She feared forever trashing Peter's ministry. Here we see the sheer ugliness of enforcing Stoic asceticism as a counterfeit holiness, "Christian" in name only. Peter impregnating a young woman out of wedlock represented a bump in his ministry, correctable by confession and penance. Biblical marriage, on the other hand, was permanent ruin to a man's calling! A warped church culture cared only for how things looked, not for how they really were. We see this in some form whenever a false holiness takes hold that fits neither Scripture nor a redeemed human condition.

Heloise's uncle Fulbert, Peter's fellow canon at Notre Dame, beat her, and later had Peter castrated by a gang of thugs. Abelard spirited Heloise away to his family for her own safety, and then, to a convent. Both church and civil law, at the time, looked upon Fulbert's actions as justified protection of his family honor. The church allowed Peter to continue teaching. It made him abbot of those aforementioned unruly monks, who, based on all the rumors, expected Abelard would prove as morally compromised and radical as themselves. Peter stunned the monks when he established a series of strict, but fair, reforms that demanded moral integrity and obedience of them.

As for Peter and Heloise, the ill-fated couple continued a life-long correspondence by letters, most of which can still be read today. True to character, they named their son *Astrolabe*, after a compact Greek device used to measure height and azimuth of heavenly bodies before the invention of the sextant. A close relative adopted Astrolabe. Peter and Heloise's positions as abbot and abbess, at different locations, did not permit them to live as man and wife, despite their being married. Marriage was only for procreation, according to the Stoicism-warped church teaching of the day, but that reduced marriage to less than it really was. Marriage is also for Astrolabe to have his mother and father cleaving together at the family core, to provide him both male and female role models.

Gay activists today often portray Christians in court as believing the sub-biblical concept that *marriage is just for procreation*. They often argue that if sterile heterosexual couples and women past childbearing years can marry, then homosexuals, also, should be able. If marriage, and by extension sex, is only about procreation, then the legal sword cuts both ways. The "procreation only" view ignores the broader fact that older couples provide male and female social models for grown children and grandchildren. Infertile couples also serve as wholesome models for both sexes. Male and female have value.

God created humanity in His image not just as individuals, but socially; **"So God created man in His own image; in the image of God He created him; male and female He created them."** (Gen. 1:27 NKJV) Although God is not a sexual being in any physical sense, marriage, and by extension, human sexuality, reflects an intended Divine pattern. Sexual intercourse has always been, in every corner of the earth, the way men and women *consummate* marriages. This pattern is not a religious doctrine, but a human reality.

Church authorities often made life difficult for Peter Abelard in ways that went beyond his tragic personal life. The influential Bernard of Clairveaux secured his condemnation several times at various church councils. Abelard also found himself exiled from Paris after his historical research discovered that Saint Denis (of cathedral fame) was not the Dionysus the Aeropagite mentioned in Acts 17; as church authorities had claimed for a long time. It infuriated churchmen even more when droves of students afterward left the city to sit under Abelard's teaching in the open countryside despite his pariah status. Generations of carelessly vetted Germanic folktales now gave way to scholars who wanted truth.

Abelard saw a need long overdue—a renewed logical harmonization of the major teachings in the church. He had noticed contradictions in the Christianity of his day, both real and superficial. These went far beyond the hasty contrasts people often put forth today as "contradictions in the Bible," though some of those were part of it, too. Because "God is not a man that he should lie," Peter began a rigorous level of logical scrutiny not seen since Augustine. The result was his book, *Sic et Non* (Yes or No), which held a list of doctrinal claims up to examination, and established the Scholastic Method for centuries to come. One late 20th century scholar recapped Abelard's work well:

> *Peter Abelard was the teacher of his generation: preeminent as a philosopher, theologian, poet, and musician, he captured the imagination of almost all with whom he came into contact. His fame as a teacher was unequalled; students travelled from all over Europe to hear him speak, crowds of ordinary people attended his public lectures wherever he went, and it has been said that he was indirectly responsible for the founding of the University of Paris by creating a permanent 'deposit' of students in the city. As a philosopher, he brought the investigation of the "old logic"* (logica vetus) *to its heights; as a theologian, he championed the use of reason and intellect in matters of faith, putting the word theology into use with the meaning it still has today. In philosophy and theology, Abelard's constant and unremitting use of the tools of logic or 'dialectic' – argument, objection, example, counterexample, and the like – helped define the Scholastic method, of which an early example is his* Sic et non *("Pro*

and Con," *circa 1117–1128*). **Peter King, *The Dictionary of Literary Biography*, Vol. 115 (1992): 3–14.**

Of course, Abelard and the Scholastics who followed him only began a process that would take many centuries. They each still held to many dogmas that were, at best, only biblically half-baked. All held to the idea of Baptismal Regeneration. This sent even Abelard after the red herring of trying to find an ethically palatable answer to what happened to unbaptized babies that died. He invented what later became the Roman Catholic Doctrine of Limbo—a place of zero consciousness and no pain. For most of the Middle Ages, until Abelard, the consensus in a Western Church too influenced by the worldview of Germanic barbarians with some Roman law; was that the babies just went to hell. Like Germanic fairy-tales, this came off as a bit dark. Such *ad hoc* inventions are not necessary for doctrines that reason from where Scripture actually speaks, rather than from where Scripture is silent.

*Ad hoc* is a Latin term for adding untestable speculation to an idea to insulate it from the risk that someone might prove it wrong. In this case, *the idea* was Baptismal Regeneration; the doctrine that water baptism conveys God's grace to infants despite their inability to believe or not believe the gospel. This doctrine raised a question, *if the ritual of water baptism conveys grace, rather than the connection of our faith in God's character; what happens to those whom death takes before water baptism?* To keep the idea of Baptismal Regeneration afloat in a way that preserved God's character, Abelard had to speculate. He invented Limbo, despite there being no shred of evidence in Scripture for such a place, or even the need for it. At least Abelard had a more merciful speculation than the one before it.

## THE DISCONNECTS OF MAGICAL THINKING: THE FRACTURE BEGINS

Church elites could not so easily control Abelard's often more objective methods of inquiry as they could those of Thomas Aquinas, a century later. Of course, it helped that Aquinas was a willing participant in such ecclesiastical control. As a Dominican, he made it an intrinsic part of a reasoning system that presupposed "the Church" could not go wrong. This is not to say that he took the indefensible position that individual leaders in the church could never go wrong, only that "the Church" collectively could not do so.

Unfortunately, the logic of this breaks down when one considers that church systems are collectively impacted for good or evil by the worldviews, ideas, interpretations, and actions of individual religious leaders. There is no magic disconnect between individuals and the ideologies, dogmas, doctrines, and events they spawn or influence. It seemed a similar magical disconnect as affected Aquinas' view of the Fall also affected his view of the church.

When Jesus said that "the gates of hell" would not prevail against the church, he was not promising that its religious leadership organs were immune to perversion of purpose or doctrine. Rather, it meant that Satan could not thwart God's purposes for the church in the end. Even if the major part of church leadership corrupted itself, God would still maintain a witness of Himself among His people that would ultimately defeat the counsels of hell. (Counselors in biblical times sat at the *gates* of a city, which were defensive structures.) Aquinas seemingly could not see the idea of *the church* beyond the papal religious system. Yet large portions of the church existed beyond that system in his day, in the East.

Aquinas' work greatly affected the development of what Roman Catholicism calls ***Church Canon*** or church law. For every minuscule aspect of human existence, the church now had some kind of regulation. One remains with the question of; *how is this any different in character from the extra-biblical **Talmudic** religious regulation that Jesus renounced as "the doctrines of men?"* Why would God go to so much trouble to free his people from the bondage of one religious law only to create an even more oppressive version of the same kind of thing? Nobody, of course, intended for the church to turn into that, but it did. Where grace and truth have deteriorated, men inadequately use law of some sort to try to fill the void.

Despite all this, it would still be a mistake to conclude that Thomas Aquinas was merely a tool of the Papacy. He sometimes was, but he was also much more. His contributions to Western thought and culture are too diverse to discuss proportionally in this short a work. His masterwork, *Summa Theologica*, blended Aristotelian and Neo-Platonic thought into an academic tool kit for defending Catholic theology and Christian ethics. His stress on the importance and validity of studying the created world also led to a more biblical view of nature than before. This helped lay foundations for the modern scientific method.

Aquinas laid important groundwork for Western and Christian thought and culture. His simplistic equation of "the Church" to "the Roman Papacy" would also define conflict in Christianity for centuries to come. Likewise, whether from Aquinas or those who co-opted his ideas; the trend toward seeing human reason as self-sufficient from the need of God's word also defined the future ideological conflicts in Western Civilization.

Both chains of conflict would bear the scars of unrealistic "magical disconnects" in thought or response. These would grow more reactionary and violent, as the centuries passed.

## BIBLIOGRAPHY


1. Kirk Lowery, ***Writing History—Then and Now***, *Apologetics Study Bible*, p. xxxi, Holman (2007)
2. Francis A Schaeffer, ***How Should We Then Live? The Rise and Decline of Western Thought and Culture***, Ch. 2, pp. 51-52 (in the 50th Anniversary Ed. Crossway 2005), Revell 1976; See also, Vincent Carroll and David Shiflett, ***Christianity on Trial: Arguments Against Anti-Religious Bigotry***
3. Pearcy, Nancy R. & Thaxton, Charles B. ***The Soul of Science***, p. 39, Crossway Books (1994), Wheaton, Ill.
4. Op. Cit. Francis A Schaeffer, pp.81-82, (in the 50th Anniversary Ed. Crossway 2005), Revell, 1976
5. Ibid. Schaeffer, pp. 82-84
6. Irena Backus & Aza Goudriaan, ***'Semipelagianism': The Origins of the Term and its Passage into the History of Heresy***, *Journal of Ecclesiastical History*, Vol. 65, No. 1, Jan. 2014, pp. 29-31, Cambridge University Press
7. J.H. Ignaz von Dollinger, ***The Pope and the Council***, pp. 214-218; London 1869
8. Gavin Kerr, *Aquinas: Metaphysics*, **Internet Encyclopedia of Philosophy**: *A Peer Reviewed Academic Resource*, http://www.iep.utm.edu/aq-meta/#H4, Queen's University, Belfast, Northern Ireland

# 13

# Prelude to Reformation

## The Inquisition versus Those Who Began to See a Problem

The Scholastics were not the only ones who began to ask questions during this period. An ostentatious view of papal authority had produced a culture of royal pomp in church leadership. Popes and high bishops often led opulent lives, and called themselves "Princes of the Church." A Reformation tradition told of an exchange between Innocent III and his advisor, while they audited the papal treasury. The Pope was said to have remarked, "We need no longer say as the Apostles did that 'silver and gold have we none!'" To which the canny advisor replied, "True, Your Holiness, but neither can we say, 'In Christ's name rise.'" Whether this conversation really took place, it captures the tension, of a rubber band ready to snap, that held the Roman Church in the late Middle Ages.

Scholasticism had allowed the biggest chance for people to read Scripture, until Gutenberg built the first European printing press, around 1450. The Roman Church tightly controlled translation of the Bible into commonly spoken languages of the day, however. This regulation, at first, really hoped to avoid the twisting of Bible texts by deliberate mistranslation. Muslim translators had done this to Aristotle, so church leaders had recent experience in the 1200s to legitimize such a concern. Controls on translating the Bible into commonly spoken languages got out of hand over time, as motives became more convenient, and less honest.

While the Scholastics taught under papal authority, the questions of their students percolated throughout the medieval world. Education no longer confined itself to the cloister, king's courts, and the halls of the super-rich. Urban cathedral schools were open to almost anybody with a strong desire to learn. As public contact with Scripture grew, more people began to see a gulf between the leadership style of the Apostles and papal imperial excesses. The question of what made church leadership apostolic *in character* began to grow more important than what made it so in terms of a bishop see's lineage.

One of the first genuine pre-Reformation reformers was a wealthy merchant in eastern France, named Peter Waldo. Waldo's conversion experience came through hearing a troubadour sing the virtues of Christian monastic poverty. As Jesus had counseled the rich young ruler, Waldo sold all of his goods and hired a couple of priests to translate part of the Gospels into common French. He then memorized huge portions of it, and went out to preach in the streets. When the local archbishop got wind of this, and discovered that Waldo was only a layman, he ordered the preaching stopped. Waldo countered with the question the Apostles had asked of the Temple authorities that ordered them to stop teaching in Jesus' name, "Should we obey God or man?"

Waldo appealed to Pope Alexander III. (This was several decades before Innocent III, who drove the 4th Lateran Council to make Transubstantiation into a dogma of the church, in 1215). Alexander's scholars found nothing outright heretical in the content of Waldo's teaching, but because Waldo was a layman, the clerics did not take him seriously. The Pope ordered him not to preach unless invited to do so by a bishop—something unlikely to happen. Waldo tossed down the gauntlet by answering him the same way he had the local archbishop. The preaching continued, and Pope Alexander III declared Waldo a heretic.

The followers of Peter Waldo called themselves "The Poor in Spirit," but we know them today as the Waldenses. I called Waldo a pre-Reformation reformer, but that does not mean he came out with a clear salvation doctrine of *justification by grace alone through faith alone.*

Scholastic Theology was still in its formative stages. The dominant issue of that day was not so much concerned with how Christ's death and resurrection saved people, as with the quality of life a Christian person should lead. It is not that the first issue was unimportant; it was that few realized yet that a problem had developed there.

The Waldenses were very much a "back to the Bible" sort of group. The keynote Scriptures of the Reformation would be Romans and Galatians. Those of the Waldenses were the Beatitudes—particularly, **"Blessed are the poor in spirit, for theirs is the kingdom of God."** They preferred Catholic priests give the sacraments on pastoral authority grounds, until papal excommunication took away that option. They rejected Transubstantiation, which was not quite yet a universal dogma.

As in later reform efforts, the Waldenses did not wish to start another church, only to bring the old system back into line with the Bible. The problem was that the Roman Papacy *and most people* were high on recent successful reforms—along with ones they only thought were successful. At the time, most Christians in Europe truly believed the Papacy was God's ordained instrument to bring the world into submission to Christ. Many felt safe when popes explicitly placed their system beyond earthly accountability, where kings could not tread.

Most secular authorities and common people saw a person who so much as questioned the *status quo* as heretical. By now, however, the word *heretic* no longer carried a fully biblical meaning. Instead, it could mean almost anything a secular ruler, bishop, or pope wanted it to mean. The content of an allegedly heretical teaching seemed far less important than whether the teacher conformed to the Roman system. Christendom, as a social model that included both the Roman church and the secular states of Europe, had a serious blind spot here. To think that the very answer to the prayers of so many reformers, for strong church authority, could mushroom into new forms of corruption seemed faithless. It appeared, at first, to deny the power of Jesus' own prayer for the church in John 17:6-26.

From the point of view of most people in the 1100s to mid-1200s, a Christian Europe now fully replaced a Pagan one, and better days seemed but an arm's length away! That was not the case, but I am describing what most people tended to see, based on the bulk of writings from that time. The harshness of penalties like burning at the stake and castration were the norm of *secular* government in that day. For a few "disgruntled misfits" to deny the gains of Christendom seemed petty, especially since the Catholic Church really had pioneered so much good. Hospitals in major cities, vast advances in education, and the creation of fair banking laws were a sampling of benefits the church produced. People had little reason that was *easily visible to them at the time* to think otherwise. It is hard for us today to imagine such optimism.

Nevertheless, despite many good works, Christendom had not built an entirely healthy society. A spiritually cancerous growth still metastasized in both the Catholic Church and in Europe's secular states. The church had gone beyond making redemptive use of the world long ago. It, now, not only embraced the world, but also modeled itself after it. Not even religious leaders with full access to Scripture had all the intellectual tools yet to see the problem clearly. The fires of challenge had yet to test and fully reveal the character of Medieval Christendom. While Scripture plainly states that only one mediator exists between God and men, Christ; the Papacy really thought that Christ had deputized that authority to the Roman system, through the Apostle Peter. This proved wrong, but nothing serious had yet happened to challenge anyone's assumptions on that.

The Waldenses were a start to such a challenge, but other groups, like the Cathars, which superficially seemed identical, really were heretical in a biblical sense. This camouflaged the character of the Waldensian Movement to most other European

Christians. Remember, before the printing press, the technology for mass media did not yet exist. People had little independent means to research current events in the light of Scripture. The strong new Papacy had cleaned up a lot of obvious corruption in just a hundred years, even if it failed to see new problems brewing. The Holy Spirit used events in this period, and in those following, to yield better intellectual tools. They came by spiritual discernment only as dark situations unfolded. The same is true today. To what extent, only history will tell.

It is useless to complain that the Holy Spirit would have been sufficient to reveal the errors of this period, at the time, if people had only been open to Him. His sufficiency is not in question. The point is that, except for giving hints in the Letters to the Seven Churches in Revelation Chapters 2 and 3, and maybe a few other passages; the Holy Spirit clearly elected to use the forces of history redemptively and providentially, rather than act directly. One cannot accuse Christians in this era of lack of prayer, either—many other things, but not that. This was the heyday of not only the Scholastics, but of the forerunners of the Contemplative Monastic Movements. The Holy Spirit moved on multiple fronts, through many people, most in the system, and some not. He did not magically erase human limits, however.

Most Christians of the day were simply not aware that a difference between "the Church" and "a church system" even existed. Those coming to such awareness took time to do so.

The powerful mystic Bernard of Clairveaux, referred to heretics as "malicious foxes, who would rather injure than conquer," and who "slink in the shadows" rather than reveal themselves. [1] Consistent with some New Testament reports of heretics, Bernard's description still aroused an emotionalism that demonized. Groups like the Waldenses could not get a fair examination in such a climate. In fairness to Bernard, he opposed using force against heretical groups in favor of argument and persuasion. He also spoke early in the 12th through 15th century "heresy crisis." A range of secular and religious forces that history has collectively called "the Inquisition" answered this "crisis," often poorly. Local bishops formed the earliest inquisitions scatter-shot, in response to heresy charges made by civil authorities against persons and groups.

A few decades later, a new promoter of "apostolic poverty" appeared in Italy. Like-minded to Peter Waldo, he would have also come to Waldo's fate if not for the cunning of Pope Innocent III. Giovanni Bernardone was a cloth merchant, and a burnt out veteran of petty local inter-kingdom wars. He experienced a radical conversion to Christ after being a prisoner of war. We know him better as Francis of Assisi.

As Waldo before him, Francis appealed his right to preach before the Pope. Innocent III proved more calculating than Pope Alexander was. He had also learned from Alexander's mistakes. Instead of laughing Francis out of the court, Innocent made a great show of repentance before him. He then commissioned Francis to preach as the founder of a new monastic order; called a ***mendicant*** order because it used begging as the means to support itself. This approach appealed to dissidents like the Waldenses, Bogomils, and Cathars.

Pope Innocent never really gave up his power lust, nor the political intrigue and luxury that now embodied the Roman church. Francis soon found that, while a great role model, he was hardly fit to administer the new powers the Pope had conferred on him. He asked Pope Innocent's successor to take this administrative burden off his hands. Pope Honorius III did so by appointing Ugolino Cardinal di Conti, later to become Pope Gregory IX, as Francis' advisor. Ugolino, as Pope Gregory IX, launched the first Papal Inquisition in 1231 AD, in reaction to growing dissent against Rome. Earlier "episcopal" or local bishop ordered inquisitions had existed since 1184, but these lacked such sweeping powers.

The Franciscan Order often became the Papacy's "good cop," to the Inquisition's "bad cop," in a ruthless attempt to control or destroy dissident groups. Some Franciscans became inquisitors, but that distinction usually went to another new religious order that we shall consider presently. Like much else in the late Medieval Period, it should be remembered that the Franciscan Order became far more than just this. It produced many great charitable works, some of which continue to bring forth good fruit to this day. While the "good cop" characterization is just, it would be unjust to see that as the entire legacy of the Franciscan Order. Francis, lacking guile and the subtleties of more than a moderate education, died with a vague sense that bad things were happening to his vision. [2] By then, however, he could not have changed things even if he had understood what to change or why.

Another group questioning the Roman church's inconsistencies was the Cathari or "Pure Ones." The Cathars did not have the same kind of beliefs as the Waldenses or the Franciscans; though their movements all responded to the same questions that arose from any attempt to compare the lifestyle and leadership philosophies of the Popes with those of the Apostles. This difference is important. The Cathars not only rejected papal corruption, but also the substance of biblical Christianity. The Waldenses, by contrast, embraced a simple and biblical belief system.

The Cathari, also called "Albigenses" because they began at Albi in southern France, believed in a recycled Gnosticism. Their sense of "poverty virtue" came not so much from a Judeo-Christian understanding of, **"Blessed are the poor in spirit;"** but from the old Greek pattern that made all material things evil and all spiritual things pure. They really were heretical in the biblical sense, while the Waldenses, and a growing number of other dissident groups of that time, were not. That, of course, does not justify what the church did to them.

The Scholastic, Robert Grosseteste, Bishop of Lincoln, also defined heresy in a dubious way. He called it "an opinion chosen by human perception, created by human reason, founded on the Scriptures, contrary to the teachings of the Church, publicly avowed, and obstinately defended." [3] Though more reasoned than Bernard's definition, Grosseteste made a far worse error. He assumed the bottom line authority was not Scripture, but the current teachings of the Roman church. One could not reason in normal ways from the Scripture, if it called into question some aspect of the Roman religious system. Likely, his focus was on prideful obstinacy, which is a motive in real heresy.

Still, Grosseteste's definition showed the blind spot in Scholastic Theology. It failed to deal with built up distortions in the Roman religious system as even a possibility, let alone a reality. Education, by itself, did not erase magical thinking.

Grosseteste, like Aquinas, oversimplified how God's Spirit led the Church. They underestimated just how much church canon was as vulnerable to legalism as Jewish tradition was, at the time of Christ. Their oversimplification compared to another one, often made by 21st century Christians. The Scholastics uncritically equated the methods of their religious system to the leading of the Spirit. One could not work against the other. The Pope's authority was effectively that of the Holy Spirit, in their minds.

Today, the "idea pendulum" has swung to its opposite, possibly more deadly extreme. Christians often refuse even biblical church authority today. They equate the mechanics of emotional impulse to the direct leading of the Holy Spirit. Bad as the medieval oversimplification was, at least it maintained a basis for order. Of course, both extremes are ugly. Abused authority not only hastens the breakdown of order, but of love, and a balanced form of individual Christian liberty. No authority at all creates loveless chaos.

That is what the Inquisition represents—authority abused past repair.

The Cathari and Waldenses, though far apart in their beliefs, were together the first to feel the wrath of the Inquisitions full force. What later became the ***archetype*** for evil in a religious society, began simply enough. Pope Gregory IX (as the earlier local bishops) ordered parishioners queried about their personal beliefs. The aim was not to burn more dissenters at the stake. Ironically, the church's original goal was to stop careless executions of the innocent by overzealous *secular* rulers. This was where the Christendom model of society shot itself badly in the foot. In a legal system formed centuries ago, by the Byzantine Emperor Justinian, then passed on to medieval Christendom; heresy was not merely a matter church discipline, but a civil crime. Heresy was as much a crime against the secular government, as it was the church!

This created an acute problem. Civil authorities often had no clue of what the Bible taught, beyond a few basic Christian distinctions. It was nothing for some power hungry minor official to go nuts inventing heresies that sometimes even the church knew nothing about! It is important to understand that secular penalties like burning at the stake were common state imposed sentences. The Inquisitions, bad as they were, did not invent or introduce such things. Yet, Pope Gregory IX was Innocent III's cousin, and believed Papal Supremacy was the best way to limit the excesses of secular rulers. It never occurred to them that the policy of Papal Supremacy might have excesses of its own.

To make such vast investigations required church officials to perform reams of recordkeeping. Technology of the day was ill suited to the complexity of the task. The system sometimes eroded into a crude medieval thought police, curbed only by its inability to police thought. Bishops discovered more people, with each passing generation, who questioned the methods of the Roman Catholic Church. The very system created to extinguish the fires of discontent, ended up hosing gasoline onto the flames. The more the Roman church tried to tighten its control on the flock, the faster things unraveled, and the harsher measures tended to become. Because "the Church collectively could not go wrong," the more wrong the Church went on a wider scale, the more its leaders lived in denial. The more leaders lived in denial, the more comfortable they became with a schizoid existence.

The religious order that drove the Papal Inquisition began as a mendicant group that consciously tried to imitate the Franciscans. The difference was that its founder, Dominic Guzman, always meant his followers to be frontline troops against heresy. Guzman went out to beg and preach in the "apostolic poverty" style popular with the Cathari and Waldenses. He saw that the imperious speeches of bishops had no effect on people convinced that pomp was a sure sign of corruption. Pope Honorius III allowed Guzman to launch his Dominican Order in 1216. This religious order soon grew its own, more twisted, form of high-handedness, once enabled as agents of the Inquisition, after 1231.

To keep events in perspective, Thomas Aquinas joined the Dominicans at age 19 in 1244, only thirteen years after the Papal Inquisition commenced. The Dominican method started by reasoning with dissident groups, which is not to say that overzealous secular leaders did not flame up the stakes. I'm not saying the Catholic Church was innocent by any means; just that the situation was more complex than a generation fed on Monty Python "not expecting the Spanish Inquisition" has been conditioned to think. Pope Gregory IX's unwavering belief in Papal Supremacy did not help. Instead, it hardened blindness to the gap between Grosseteste's "obstinate defense" of heresy, and a martyr's conviction from God's word.

Secular rulers often proceeded from the assumption that the accused was guilty until proved innocent. An accused heretic often had no right to face his or her accusers. A neighbor with a grudge could simply go to an over-zealous official, make an unsubstantiated charge, and have his identity kept secret. Inquisitor monks had rules they had to work by that at least decreased this sort of thing. The Papacy made great claim that church law forbade their inquisitors to shed blood, and that was true. Of course, inquisitor monks used many of the same interrogation methods as secular authorities. They became adept at extricating confessions from their victims without killing them, using some hellishly devised torture instruments. [4]

To keep things in perspective, the tales of "millions upon millions" killed by the Inquisition are overblown. Inquisitors kept meticulous records, and had others keeping records of their proceedings. There was some accountability to the process—usually more than would be had in purely secular trials of the day. Of course, as time went on, abuses increased, as well as cycles of procedural reform under more conscientious inquisitors or popes. Most often, even those procedures favored the church. They were far from fair, despite being generally better than comparable procedures in medieval secular trials. For example, of 5,400 people who faced inquisitors in Toulouse in 1245-1246, 184 recanted and were set free, 23 got life, and none were burnt at the stake. [5]

The Spanish Inquisition was a separate institution from the Medieval Inquisitions. It came much later, and answered not to the church, but to the Spanish monarchy. It belongs more to the era of the Catholic Counter-Reformation, and we will cover it then.

While most Inquisition trials ended with punishments well short of death, inquisitors could "relax" prisoners to the state. That meant the inquisitor found the prisoner guilty, and the local secular authorities could punish him or her as they saw fit. This usually meant burning at the stake. As time passed, death sentences accumulated against those who refused to deny what often amounted to a genuine faith in the plain meaning of Scripture. Many real heretics and innocents burned as well, so I am not excusing the evil of the Inquisitions, simply placing them in the context of their day.

Catholics and Protestants have both, at times, exaggerated Inquisition death tolls down or up. Radical secularist inflations to propagandize "the evils of religion" are even more dishonest. They pretend that 20th century utopian anti-religion slaughters by Stalin, Mao, the Korean Kims, and Pol Pot lacked fanatical panache. Likewise, people who try to minimize the Inquisitions, as if "that whole Reformation thing" was just a big misunderstanding, stretch credulity. As we saw, a systemic corruption had been growing in the Roman church system since before the period of the Inquisition. No single human cause sufficiently explains the whole.

The nature of historical corruption in Christian church systems is similar, regardless of period, and which system we discuss. Differences are usually a matter of degree or form the corruption takes. Men entrusted to feed the body of Christ the word of God, instead, behaved as parasitic organisms feeding off that body. These words are not too strong for what really happened to a church leadership system that refused to reform after centuries of opportunity and growing awareness. This foreshadowed the 17th Chapter of the Book of Revelation without being its ultimate fulfilment. A Babylonian-styled quasi-pagan world religion will persecute those who believe the gospel in the last days; a gospel preached by Jewish evangelists during the global judgments of the Tribulation. (Rev. 7:2-8, 14:1) The enormity of this prophetic picture shocked John the Apostle when he saw it:

> **1 And one of the seven angels who had the seven bowls came and spoke with me, saying, "Come here, I shall show you the judgment of the great harlot who sits on many waters, 2 with whom the kings of the earth committed acts of immorality, and those who dwell on the earth were made drunk with the wine of her immorality." 3 And he carried me away in the Spirit into a wilderness; and I saw a woman sitting on a scarlet beast, full of blasphemous names, having seven heads and ten horns. 4 And the woman was clothed in purple and scarlet, and adorned with gold and precious stones and pearls, having in her hand a gold cup full of abominations and of unclean things of her immorality, 5 and upon her forehead a name was written, a mystery, "BABYLON THE GREAT, THE MOTHER OF HARLOTS AND OF THE ABOMINATIONS OF THE EARTH." 6 And I saw the woman drunk with the blood of the saints, and with the blood of the witnesses of Jesus. And when I saw her I marveled greatly. *Revelation* 17:1-6 NASB**

Even should today's Papacy be no more party to the development of this end-time apostate religious system than any other denomination or world religion; it is easy to see how the Reformers later took the Papacy of their day for it. Given the Inquisition, and the corruption that constantly put the Vatican in bed with "the kings of the earth," and that Rome is "the city on seven hills" (mentioned in verse 17:9); who could blame anyone back then for making the association? It even seems their view had some validity. Bible prophecy often has multiple fulfillments that match the prophetic pattern more fully each time history repeats itself.

While such a statement might offend some Roman Catholic readers, the prophetic and historic evidence is such that I cannot write it off as mere "Catholic bashing." It is also too much to teach, as some Evangelicals, that Roman Catholicism is the complete fulfillment of this end-time "Babylon." Some prophetic components are not yet in place today, and movements exist in Roman Catholicism that do not fit this description. We do not yet have all the facts, and there are other possibilities developing out there. This is not to exonerate Rome in the end. No religious system of any duration is fully innocent (including the one I write within), and there are many historic and prophetic markers pointing Rome's way.

Either way, I leave all that for prophecy books to explore. My point is that an honest examination of history, and related Bible prophecy, sometimes requires uncomfortable things of everyone, not just of Roman Catholics. It demands we ask hard questions of ourselves that may have even harder answers.

Things are not equal, as our pluralistic culture often demands. Doubtless, I will also offend some Protestants with questions raised by aspects of the Reformation, and some Evangelical responses to Post-Modernism and Islam. I do not wish to offend. It is impossible to discuss history, the nature of the Bible, and worldview issues genuinely without asking questions that offend somebody. Compared to not learning from Christian history, and ignoring worldview issues, the possibility of offending some people is by far the lesser of the two evils.

## The Conciliar Movement of Church Reform

By the 14th Century, Europe was well on its way, economically, toward climbing out of the mire of feudalism. The French, German, and English were beginning to think of themselves more and more as French, German, and English; and less and less as part of a "holy" empire, Roman or otherwise. Land became less essential to the measurement of wealth, and hard cash more so.

For about a hundred years after Innocent III, the Popes kept a self-assured attitude about their place above the secular rulers. Yet signs abounded that the policy of Papal Supremacy had outlived whatever usefulness it once might have had. Secular rulers no longer cared so much about directly electing church leaders. They just wanted to keep fickle popes and bishops from unduly meddling in local affairs of state. Church leaders who thought themselves princes often were no more qualified to handle worldly realities, like warfare, than secular rulers had been to choose godly bishops. Exceptions to that generalization came and went, but they tended to prove the rule rather than break it.

The nature of human authority over both church and state marked the issues of the 13-1400s. The Lay Investiture Controversy had brought the reckoning that it was wrong for kings to meddle in the spiritual realm of how the church chose its leaders. So now, after over a century of excessively political popes, the concept of a rightful "secular" realm re-emerged. As events went on, it became out-of-bounds for the Pope to meddle too deeply with a king's affairs of state, which did not directly involve the Faith. Here again is that historical "pendulum effect" with regard to ideas.

At the turn of the 13th to 14th centuries, a new pope came to the chair with all of Innocent III's power lust, but none of his talent for reading the times and manipulating kings. Few church leaders showed the dangers of Papal Supremacy more than Benedetto Cardinal Caetani did. History better remembers him as the infamous Pope Boniface VIII. Those new to the topic of church history might better remember him as "Mussolini the Titanic" – "Mussolini" for his megalomania, and "Titanic" because of his sinking his own ship while still aboard. To give insight into this pontiff's character and goals, consider that during his famous "Jubilee Year" of 1300, he frequently appeared in imperial robes before visiting pilgrims and cried; *"I am Caesar. I am emperor."* [6]

In Boniface VIII, the schizoid vintage of a church office demanding to be both the successor of Saint Peter, and of the Caesar who had murdered Saint Peter, came to its full septic bouquet. By this time, the Roman Catholic Church owned huge tracts of land in every European country. These lands, and the income drawn from them, had been tax exempt from the kings who ruled over their territories and who protected them militarily. This amount of property went far beyond anything churches enjoy today regarding tax-exempt status. Each of these kings paid gigantic church taxes to Rome—something the United States government never did to any religious institution. It was a classic "heads, the Pope wins; tails, the kings lose" scenario—until two kings came to power that the Papacy could not intimidate.

Edward I in England and Philip the Fair in France found it hard to finance their war against each other. Then they both decided to levy taxes against the extensive church properties in each of their kingdoms. Pope Boniface reacted in a document threatening to excommunicate lay rulers who taxed clergy and church officers who paid. Edward answered back that if the clergy did not pay, he would strip them of legal protection. All English church properties would then be open to seizure by his sheriffs. In France, Philip embargoed all gold shipments and effectively cut off a huge source of the Pope's income. Boniface, tail between his legs, started to back-pedal. He explained that he didn't really mean that the churches could not "help out" in times of emergency, and that the kings knew best what constituted an "emergency" in their own lands.

Pope Boniface's Jubilee Year was an attempt to gain sorely lacked popularity. His deeper motive was to establish forever that the Papal Office sat above all lay monarchs and emperors, even in earthly affairs. By *deeper* I do not mean he put much thought into the affair. In a gesture he doubtless thought mighty generous, the Pope dispensed what is now called a "***plenary indulgence***" to all who would make a pilgrimage to Rome in that year. He advertised this as a full pardon for all sins. At the Jubilee celebrations, Boniface made sure nobody mistook his meaning. He forged a second crown to symbolize his earthly authority. The following year, the Pope was able to test the political waters to see how well all of this took. That was when he discovered he was piloting the Titanic.

The incident involved a certain bishop that Philip had imprisoned on a treason charge. When Boniface VIII commanded that the churchman be released, and took back his earlier taxation concession, Philip proclaimed that Christ had not imparted to the church any temporal authority at all; meaning that the Pope should butt out. Boniface reacted by issuing a new document, called the *Unam Sanctum*, which was the most ambitious papal power claim in all church history. In it, he pronounced that, *"It is altogether necessary for every human being to be subject to the Roman Pontiff."* [7]

Philip escalated by engineering an attempt to legally have the Pope deposed for simony, sexual immorality, and because his election had been illegal. This naked political stab at holding the Papacy accountable, itself, suffered a convenient set of ethics. The King used a brazenly shady lawyer to bring these largely trumped-up charges before an assembly of French churchmen and legal experts. They determined that the Pope must come to France to stand trial. Troops went to Italy and seized the aged Boniface, heaping abuse on him as they went. The old wannabe Caesar died, still in a state of shock, weeks later.

Soon after this, Philip's scheming paid even further dividends. In 1305, the College of Cardinals elected a Frenchman Pope. Yet Clement V never went to Rome. Instead, he decided to stay in Avignon, France, nearer to home. There the Papacy remained through five more French Popes, filling the next seventy-two years. The Avignon Papacy greatly angered the Germans and the English. Until now, the West saw the Papal States as a remnant of the Roman Imperium, apart from, and thus impartial to, Europe's kingdom-states. Now, one of those kingdoms had control of the Papacy. Philip was in danger of exposing the Christendom illusion of a "Holy Roman Empire" as a house of cards.

In 1324, the Holy Roman Emperor, Louis the Bavarian, called a church council more or less like the old universal councils of the Christian Roman Empire. Some Bible scholars had presented him with a paper called *Defender of the Peace*. This document showed from Scripture that the church was not just the papal religious system, but also the community of all believers. It argued that there was no intrinsic superiority for the priesthood because the Book of Revelation called all believers "kings and priests." (Rev. 1:6, 5:10, 1 Pet. 2:5-10) As kings were subject to God's law, so too should be the priests. Popes and bishops were to serve as teachers not overlords, according to this paper. (1 Pet. 5:1-3)

*Defender of the Peace* also argued that binding doctrinal decisions should come by universal church councils, as in the old days. Thus began what history has called the Conciliar Movement to reform the Church. Had it succeeded, this movement would have transformed the Pope into the executive officer of a church council. As such, he would preside over council meetings, but ultimately be subject to the decisions of that council. This would have brought things back closer to the way they had been during the days of Nicea and Chalcedon.

Meanwhile, the Avignon Papacy had become infamous for its funding abuses. Sale of indulgences and the threat of excommunication against those who opposed new church taxes grew to obscene degrees. By 1360, this made it prudent to return the Pope to Rome, lest a European "world war" or some other political disaster result. This solution only sparked some of the most ridiculous events in church history.

In less than a year after his return to Rome, the aged sixth pope from Avignon died. The College of Cardinals, still overloaded with Frenchmen, nevertheless gave in to an angry Italian mob. It elected an Italian to be the next Pope. Urban VI soon proved himself both heretical, and a strutting dictator. His rule became so intolerable that, by the end of summer the same year, the Cardinals got together again. They then informed Europe that an Italian mob had forced them to elect an apostate Pope. Urban reacted by creating an almost entirely new College of Cardinals out of his own handpicked toadies. The French Cardinals then escalated by electing a new pope from among their own group, Clement VII.

Clement soon moved his papacy back to Avignon. This began what history calls "The Great Schism." The Western church now had two duly elected rival popes, each chosen by the same cardinals, and each claiming to be Peter's (and Caesar's) successor.

The implications of this for the Christendom model of society were horrible. Only the cardinals could declare who was really the Pope. Their declarations of August contradicted those of April. Kings and even church officials now had no way to know who the real Vicar of Christ was. On top of all that, both "Vicars" added to the fracas by excommunicating each other. This sent a church dependent on the Roman system for its identity into an identity crisis of comic opera scale. Different countries went with different popes, creating not only division among nations, but minorities in each land for the opposing contenders. Riots broke out in many places. Even the later Roman Catholic Church, often arbitrarily and after the fact, had to choose which of these were "true" popes were and which were anti-popes.

By 1395, people finally found the motivation to take the Conciliar Movement seriously. Yet, even this had a mechanical problem. Unlike in the old days, when Roman Emperors called universal church councils, church law now said that only a pope could call one, and ratify its decisions. Neither rival Pope had any interest in calling a council that could result in his own sacking, which rather mucked up the works. Even if one of them called a council, the other would renounce it as invalid; just as both popes now had their own Colleges of Cardinals, each renouncing the decisions of the other. Church canon here proved just as much a tangle of human regulations around the New Testament as Talmudic law had been around the Old.

The Sanhedrin had used extra-biblical rabbinic traditions as a basis for rejecting their own Messiah. Now, competing popes used extra-biblical Church canon to block calling a universal council needed to save the church from itself! Finally, in 1409, a majority from both Colleges of Cardinals met and agreed they could not allow this absurdity to go on, despite church law. They deposed both rival popes, and elected Alexander V. To make the clown convention complete, neither of the two rivals accepted the legality of this decision. Now there were three Popes, each claiming to be the Vicar of Christ! In a Europe where even one pontiff had gotten to be too much, three were a catastrophe!

Meanwhile, the Conciliar Movement had gained steam in Germany. It, too, dispensed with the technicalities of a church canon developed mostly in the last two centuries anyway. In 1414, the Holy Roman (German) Emperor called a universal church council at Constance, citing as precedent Constantine's call for the Council of Nicea. Representatives even came from the Greek Orthodox Church, acknowledging this return to an ancient pattern of what they considered a truly universal church. As popular support for this council grew, one of the rival popes renounced his claim to the chair. In 1417, the Council of Constance deposed the other two, and elected Martin V as the new Roman Pope.

It seemed that after long last, the Conciliar Movement had achieved meaningful reform of the corrupt papal system. However, absolute power still had the power to corrupt absolutely. Pope Martin's bottom had not even warmed the papal chair before he dissolved the council, and reversed all of its decisions except the one that had put him in power. This great betrayal proved that any opportunity for the papal religious system to reform itself from the inside had long passed. As long as it could act with the kind of total power it claimed was right for the Vicar of Christ to have, truth would continue to warp. The Papacy would continue to make merchandise of Western believers.

The inability of later church councils to revive reform in this rigged-game setting enabled popes to discredit Conciliarism. Not all the blame rested on the Papacy, however. We shall see in the next section that the Council of Constance itself lacked the integrity to keep its word, just as Pope Martin V did. Reformers lost confidence in the Conciliar Movement because of this. If the "good guys" can't be trusted, where does one turn?

This latest wave of corrupt popes crested at the turn of the 15th to 16th centuries, when Roderigo Borgia took the chair as Pope Alexander VI. This murderous sexual pervert compulsively used his office to bring wealth and power to the bastard offspring of his mistresses. A profound hopelessness washed over thoughtful people throughout every level of the church. Up until now, most European believers would have had difficulty imagining a church without the Pope. It was fast becoming clear to some that the only hope for a biblical Christianity lay with believers somehow getting used to the idea.

## John Wycliffe and Jan Hus

Perhaps the first of these radical new thinkers was an Englishman teaching at Oxford named John Wycliffe. His preaching came at the same time as the ***Great Schism***, which served him well as a life-long illustration for his argument that the church had to be more than just the papal religious system. At first, he too thought in terms of reforming the Roman religious system into what he called, *"a Bible papacy."* [8] As the silliness between Rome and Avignon progressed, Wycliffe began to see how the real problem lay deeply embedded in the papal system itself. *Increasing corruption in the Roman Papacy forced Christians to ask just how God delegated authority to the church.* The Roman Christendom model, with the Pope as the Vicar of Christ and head of the Universal Church on earth, now failed steadily in the face of history by recurring vices.

Like the Waldenses, Wycliffe was not fully "Reformation" in his thinking. He did not believe a person could have a real assurance of salvation. Nor did he oppose the use of icons *per se* or think that praying to the saints was wrong. The battle before the church of his day raged in a slightly different theater. It revolved around the nature of social and religious authority. The classical view, arising from Theodosius, passed to the medieval world in the West through Augustine, and in the East through Justinian. It was that God conferred authority, or ***dominion***, on man through the Roman or Eastern Orthodox Churches. Everybody agreed that human authority came from God.

The late medieval papal claim to be able to depose monarchs for immorality, when no real method existed for deposing a pope for the same reason; led to a sense of injustice after so many corrupt popes had risen to the chair. What had become more questionable was just how God actually conferred authority on man. Kings were required, at least in theory, to rule in a state of God's grace, with no ongoing mortal sin on their souls. Why would not Popes subject themselves to that same stipulation? What was only true for kings in theory was not even theoretically true for the Roman Pontiff, for the Pope *"shall judge all, and be judged of no one."* [9]

Wycliffe began to see the need for an objective measuring stick of authority in the church that did not depend on the whim of human pontiffs. He was likely the first to rediscover the Bible as that standard, and apply it in a modern Evangelical fashion. The Oxford Reformer found that almost every church leadership model presented in the New Testament had its opposite in the Roman Popes. This discovery slowly changed his vision from that of looking for a way to bring the Papacy back to a biblical pattern into that of being a full-fledged "Protestant." He saw a need to scrap the Papacy as a church leadership system altogether.

The Church of Christ transcends any one church system, but each church system behaves faithfully or unfaithfully within the historical processes around it. "Historical processes" reflect natural cause and effect inside a fallen cosmos. This is so even when the initiating event(s) are supernatural, and transcend that cosmos and its Fall. This is so even when God inserts new information and power from beyond the fallen space-time universe into that system's cause and effect. The processes that follow such insertions still act according to natural law. Resurrected Lazarus died again, leftover miraculous loaves and fishes rotted just like other loaves and fishes, and manna from heaven still got worms.

We see this playing out prophetically in the Seven Letters to the Seven Churches in Revelation, Chapters 2 and 3. We see it operating in the life of King David, after he committed adultery with Bathsheba, and had her husband murdered. Both King David and five of the Seven Churches committed sins worthy of death or at least (in the church of Ephesus' case) some form of penalty. In each case, God's grace averted the ultimate punishments. Even the two churches that Christ said only good things about were still comprised of sinners in need of redemption.

Nevertheless, in no such instance did God's grace completely suspend earthly cause and effect. "The sword never departed from David's household." The churches were not immune to the effects of their policies, whether they came as Christ's judgments or as the natural results of bad ideas. No magical disconnect protected them from earthly consequences. Wycliffe's observations were just.

Where the Apostles had persuaded men through reason, the Papacy dominated men through fear. Where Peter had counseled church leaders to lead by example (1 Peter 5), the

Popes expected kings to submit to standards that they themselves were unwilling to live by. Where the Apostles had not sought worldly position and power, Roman Popes had often shown themselves willing to lie, cheat, steal, and murder to gain and keep such power. The Apostles had taught a gospel that freed men from religious bondage; a communion ordinance that celebrated Christ's "once-for-all" sacrifice naturally followed. The papal system had encased that gospel in priest-craft, which kept men falsely dependent on Rome's political and religious machinations. On every level Wycliffe looked, he saw glaring contradictions between the system and the Scriptures.

By now, the collection of minor fallacies on the idea of *church,* not attributable to any single source, had grown into a juggernaut. The net effect crushed God's people underfoot, instead of feeding them the word. The idea of a person's ability to have a relationship with God through Christ, as a Bible-centered worldview cultivates it, was in peril. Christendom had politicized ***Sacradotalism***—the idea that God used sacramental ritual to impart His grace through priest-craft, instead of His word—to where it masked the gospel. (Rom. 1:6) Sacradotalism required a priestly class. Clergy had become elite, such that mainstream speech reserved the term "Church" only for them. This was as true in Italian as in Spanish and Portuguese, as in French, as in German, Dutch, Polish, Scandinavian, and in English.

Wycliffe amassed a large following in England, so much that not even the Roman Church dared move against him beyond removing him from his Oxford post. He pursued his work from a country church, using the Waldensian and Franciscan pattern of sending out traveling preachers with sections of Scripture and his tracts. John Wycliffe was the most ardent supporter of translating the Scriptures into commonly understood languages, to date. He reasoned that since inspired writers wrote the New Testament in 1st century marketplace Greek, translations should be in the speech used by everyday people, as much as possible. We would call this a "no-brainer," but the idea was novel in the 1300s.

Wycliffe's aim was not to "start another church," but to help the existing body of Christ free itself from a religious system that, by sound evidences, had become parasitic. One can argue that most people back then, (and even today), lacked the reasoning skills to distinguish between the *Christian Church* and *a religious system spawned by Christendom.* Yet, that distinction exists, nonetheless. The Christian Church preceded the Christendom model of society by many centuries. Social models are temporal forms, even if God beneficially uses some of their elements to work out His redemptive plan. God's redemptive plan, however, does not stand or fall on such time-based forms. Social models decay, and can reach points of no return.

Wycliffe saw the church not as his group of followers, nor as the Roman religious system, but as those who had obeyed Christ by placing faith in the gospel. This contrast, though devastating in the short run to what the Christendom social model had made of the church; enabled a more biblical view of the church to *re-form* over the long term. Yet, this view, founded by Wycliffe, and built upon later by the Reformation, for all its necessity and good, also had limits. It could only ensure a potential for restored church integrity at local levels, not in an upper church system that wanted to have things both ways. Nor could a leadership model such as Wycliffe envisioned ever guarantee that churches, once reformed, would always remain biblical.

The church would no longer be able to fall back on the state, which had no power to enforce genuine reform from the top, down, anyway. It would have to rely once again on the power and leading of the Holy Spirit. It also must trust that enough churches at other locations would do the same, and leave that in God's hands. Christianity would need to sink or swim on the integrity and vitality of its connection to God's word; a Bible that soon would be unleashed on Europe, and the world, by mechanical print technology.

Wycliffe saw a Western Church corrupt, and in factions. Nobody could deny that. Late Scholastic and Medieval thought saw Scripture as a product of the church. Scripture and Church Tradition were equal in authority, with Tradition as the tiebreaker. They believed that the Catholic Church had *authorized* which books belonged in Scripture.

John Wycliffe reasoned that since the church had fallen into corruption and division, and church canon (part of Tradition) had only worsened the problem; it must mean that Scripture was be the higher authority, because incremental human errors had self-evidently corrupted Tradition. This was the logic of trouble-shooting in action. The early church had not *authorized* Scripture—it had simply *discovered* which books had that nature, through research and discussion. The implications, this far down the timeline, were indeed difficult for Christendom. No practical way existed to keep Christians who agreed with Wycliffe from becoming a fourth faction in a Western Church already divided by three Popes.

Despite what Wycliffe's detractors claimed, this was different from the old sectarian Donatist Church of a thousand years before. [10] Though Wycliffe's and Donatist doctrines had one likeness—both put moral limits on church authority—the differences dwarfed this similarity. The Donatists had thought in terms of "their own church against the Catholic churches." Wycliffe saw the true church as a living organism united by the Holy Spirit, rather than by human governmental mechanics. Any similarity was superficial.

The situation facing the church in Wycliffe's day was substantially the opposite of what it faced during the Donatist Revolts. The Donatists had refused to recognize church officers ordained by men whose worst sin had been to surrender already tattered Bible texts to burning. Their sect compounded this by attacking Catholic farms and villages. The sin of many church leaders in Wycliffe's day was systemic, profligate, and spiritually cancerous. They were not a few men who had caved under horrendous pressure. They had become a layer of tyrants, comfortable and complacent in their institutionalized abuse of power. Even their last attempt to reform their own system would soon prove this.

Wycliffe's detractors could not fairly claim that he had taken it upon himself to separate the wheat from the tares—a job beyond any man. He simply pointed out the need for a new model for church leadership; and that the papal system was not an essential element to the Christian gospel, defined by Scripture. While his aim was not to uproot the tares (for Jesus had said that the wheat would then be uprooted with them); he saw a need for the church to adapt to what people today call a new ***paradigm***. Consequently, nobody was ever neutral about John Wycliffe—people either loved him or hated him.

Wycliffe was also the first person to stand up in the modern biblical sense against the idea of Transubstantiation. He connected this view of the Eucharist with the control-oriented church leadership model of his day. In Chapter 10, I mentioned that Rabanus and Ratramnus had spoken out against this teaching long before it became church law. Wycliffe began to teach that the presence of Christ in the Eucharist had more to do with His presence in the heart of the participant than with what happened to bread and wine. He did not deny Christ's presence in the Eucharist, but he had a more complete understanding of what the Eucharist was. Transubstantiation focused on a supposed transformation in the bread and wine, while Wycliffe thought in terms of the whole act, which included the people engaged in it. The spiritual realities within the hearts of the partakers took primary place.

Wycliffe's followers became known as Lollards—originally an insult used against them by their hecklers. The word meant "ignorant mumbler," and implied that the Lollard was uncouth and uneducated. These men travelled across Britain, preaching from sections of Wycliffe's English New Testament translation or from his tracts. Often Lollards lacked formal education, and could not speak Latin, as any formally educated person, lay or clergy, did. They were far from ignorant, however. Wycliffe educated his followers keenly in the Scriptures, and to some extent, history. The difference lay in that he did not make them learn

Latin, a dead language, to do so. Rather, he translated the Bible from Latin into Middle English. He would have used Greek and Hebrew texts, but none was accessible to him.

The Lollards started a chain reaction that would accelerate through William Tyndale, and the other Bible Translators of the 1500s. The result would transform England and the English language. The Middle English of Wycliffe's day did not have words to correspond with many Greek and Hebrew terms. Wycliffe, and later, Tyndale, invented new English words or else pulled new terms in from Greek or Latin. This required an aggressive education campaign for pastors that used the new English Bibles, modeled by Wycliffe's training of his Lollards.

Bible Translation expanded the limited vocabulary of Middle English toward Early Modern English; a language flexible enough to express the high art of William Shakespeare, and to serve the approaching Industrial Revolution. Translators later called Shakespeare in as a consultant, during his old age, on how best to render their work elegantly into English. The result was the first version of the King James Bible in 1611.

John Wycliffe had followers far beyond Britain's shores. A royal marriage between the English king and a Bohemian princess opened Oxford University to Czech students. One of these brought some of Wycliffe's writings back to Bohemia, where they fell into the hands of a young Catholic priest named Jan Hus. Hus immediately saw Wycliffe's point, that the Pope could not truly be the head of the Church, from Paul's Letter to the Ephesians 1:22. **"And He** (God the Father) **put all things in subjection under His** (Christ's) **feet, and *gave Him as head over all things to the Church."*** (NASB) This left no room for the Pope to be the "Vicar of Christ" or earthly head of the Church.

The Greek prefix *anti* does not only means *against*, it also means *in place of.* [11] Wycliffe, and a generation later, Hus, came to a logical conclusion about the Roman Papacy based on this concept. Because of all the opposites between how the Papacy worked, and how the Apostles taught church leaders to operate; and the fact that in claiming to be the Vicar of Christ, the Popes placed themselves over the church "in place of" Christ, only one conclusion seemed possible. The Popes must be ***antichrist***.

As extreme as that must sound to most of today's readers; there is a distinction between calling the Papacy "antichrist" in its methodology and claims, and saying that a particular pope or even all popes in general are *the* Antichrist of the last days. John's first epistle made a similar distinction in 2:18; **"Children, it is the last hour; and just as you heard that antichrist is coming, even now *many antichrists* have arisen; from this we know that it is the last hour."** (NASB) While the Apostle was not talking of popes, but Gnostic teachers, the principle holds that antichrist influences worked in the church even in John's day.

If comparable forces infected the papal system, and even came to control it to a large degree, it would not mean God had forsaken His church. Nor would it mean that Christians should just tolerate it on pretense of "obeying church authority." Once church systems decay toward systemic corruption, they can no longer expect whole-hearted obedience from Christians. God may expect us to obey such systems in some cases, but only as far as they demand of us nothing that clearly violates His word. (Mat. 23:1-4) That sounds simple in theory, but the reality of such a scenario is always far more complex.

Of course, there is a huge gap between "systemic corruption" in a church and a fellowship where leaders have simply made mistakes—even serious ones. We live in a day when Christians feel justified breaking fellowship for the most trivial personal reasons, with the most strained "biblical" pretexts. Most of us live at the opposite end of the "Christian experience spectrum" from Jan Hus—who paid the ultimate price for his convictions. Before we imagine we face that kind of scenario, we had best be sure that we are ready to pay the price Hus paid for coloring it that way, and that our judgment comes from honest review. Wycliffe and Hus appealed to objective truth in Scripture, and the reality of their times, all based on logical analysis led by the Holy Spirit.

In the 500 plus years of church history since, the pendulum has swung to the opposite extreme. In Hus' day, the church system was everything, and the individual, nothing. Today, people feel they can live Christian lives apart from the church, without community and accountability. In Hus' time, church authority was near absolute, and often unapproachable. Pastors in Hus' era often thought nothing of being spiritual tyrants. In our day, church leaders often fear applying even the most common sense, minimally invasive levels of church discipline. The present pastoral situation is a direct consequence of what went before, taken on a broad scale. In the end, neither extreme is healthy; but which do you suppose is ultimately more lethal spiritually? In Hus' era, the church system had built itself up into an "indispensable" idol. Today, the idol too often is just the self.

Hus left us a wealth of writings through which we can know him, and the situation he faced. Church authorities unjustly accused him of teaching many heresies that his own writings show that he never taught. In fact, what happened to Jan Hus showed not only the corruption of the Papacy, but also that of those who desired to reform the system from within. The church council Hus hoped would vindicate him betrayed him in the end. It signaled the doom of any further attempts to reform the Roman Papacy and clergy from within the system. This is not to say that no reforms ever came to the Roman Catholic system; only that it required other biblically orthodox church systems in Western Europe to facilitate them by creating motivation through competition.

The future Holy Roman Emperor, Sigismund, convinced Hus to present his teachings at the Council of Constance, promising safe passage. The Conciliar Movement had created an atmosphere where Hus might reasonably expect to receive a fair hearing. Everyone underestimated the power and influence of the Dominicans, and other Papal Supremacy parties. Despite the silliness of the Great Schism, these could still appeal to the superstitious dread that any idea against the Papacy provoked; and the quite practical dread of the Inquisitions. The Council of Constance, while desiring change, was still too much committed to the idea of reforming the system from within. Nor was it immune to corruption. Its members could not wrap their heads around the idea of subjecting the leadership system of the church to a biblical pattern in spite of itself.

Instead of addressing the issue of reform first, the council prioritized electing a new pope. Even reformers on the council turned on Jan Hus. The policy of Papal Supremacy won out over Conciliarism not for of any great display of reason. That policy had created the conditions that led to the Great Schism to begin with. It came down to procedural priority. Choosing a new pope first meant that council members could shelve church reform for "a more convenient time." Papist council members pressured Sigismund into breaking his promise of safe passage to the Bohemian Reformer. The council imprisoned Hus and branded him a heretic. The secular princes then burned him at the stake in 1415.

The descendants of some of Hus' followers managed to hold out until the Reformation dawned, over a century later. It was an empty victory for the Roman Church that only proved beyond reasonable doubt that the papal system would never repair itself, left to its own devices. God judged the council for its own spinelessness, when its papal appointee, Martin V, returned things to a papal autocracy. He refused to ratify every conciliar proposal, except the one putting him in power.

With all attempts at reform from within tried and rejected, nothing remained but for God to raise up for his church a new kind of leadership system. The resulting ecclesiastical divisions—bad as they sometimes became—would prove the lesser of two evils compared to things going on as they were.

## BIBLIOGRAPHY

1. Walter L. Wakefield and Austin P. Evans, ***Heresies of the High Middle Ages*** New York, NY: Columbia University Press, 1991, p. 133.
2. Shelley, Bruce L. ***Church History in Plain Language*** (2nd Edition), p. 213, 1995, Word Publishing, Dallas, Tx.
3. Jennifer Kolpacoff Deanne, ***A History of Medieval Heresy & Inquisition Lawyer Popes,*** Ch. 3, *Mendicant Preachers, and New Inquisitorial Procedures,* University of Minnesota, (2011)
4. Will Durant, ***The Story of Civilization – Volume IV,*** p.211; Simon and Schuster, 1950
5. Pegg, Mark Gregory. ***The Corruption of Angels: The Great Inquisition of 1245-1246,*** p.126, Princeton, NJ: Princeton University Press, 2001.
6. Shelley, Bruce L. ***Church History in Plain Language*** (2nd Edition), p. 215, 1995, Word Publishing, Dallas, Tx.
7. Pope Boniface VIII, ***Unam Sanctum,*** 1302
8. Op cit. Shelley, Bruce L., p. 226
9. Walker, Williston. ***A History of the Christian Church*** (4th Edition), pp. 275-276, 1st Edition 1918, 4th Edition 1946, Charles Scribner's Sons, New York, NY.
10. Herring, George, ***Introduction to the History of Christianity,*** New York: New York University Press, (2006), p. 230.
11. ***The American Heritage Dictionary of the English Language,*** prefix **anti**; definitions # 4 & 5

# 14

# THE REFORMATION ERA: PART 1

## A BIBLICAL PROPHETIC PERSPECTIVE ON THE REFORMATION

In Revelation 2, John recorded a message from Jesus, to the church at Pergamum. This, with the other six letters to the churches in Asia Minor, is a rare passage of Scripture where Divine inspiration worked by way of direct dictation.

> **I have a few things against you, because you have some who hold the teachings of Balaam, who kept teaching Balak to put a stumbling block before the sons of Israel, to eat things sacrificed to idols, and to commit acts of immorality. Thus you also have some who in the same way hold the teaching of the Nicolaitans.** ***Repent therefore; or else I am coming to you quickly, and I will make war against them with the sword of my mouth. Revelation*** **2:12-17 (NASB)**

The sin of Balaam was that he, a prophet, who knew about and sometimes interacted with the true God placed his knowledge up for sale. (Num. 22:1-19) He made merchandise of the things of God. (Num. 22:20-35) Balaam could not actually curse Israel for his client, Balak King of Moab, because he knew that God had forbidden him to. (Num. 23:4-20) Still, he gave Balak enough information about Israel's relationship with God that the king could exploit the situation. Balak sent the priestess-prostitutes of the local fertility cult into Israel's camp, who seduced the men into bringing down God's curse on their own heads.

For Balaam, the things of God were a way to make money. He studiously held to the form of God's revelation in his refusal to curse Israel. Yet, he violated the substance of it. He "shared the truth" with Balak, doubtless in a most pious tone, that Yahweh hates sexual sin and ritual prostitution. He left unspoken, but clear enough for Balak to infer, that God would curse even Israelites who indulged in such things. (Num. 31:8-16)

A major interpretive theory about the "teaching of the Nicolaitans" is that the breakdown of the name's meaning loosely describes the nature of their heresy. This model maintains that the title *Nicolaitan* is a description of what these heretics did; similar to how the name *Anabaptist*, which means *re-baptizer*, is a description of how the people of that sect (from the Catholic and Lutheran perspective) "re-baptized" converts. This makes sense, since the Book of Revelation not only describes a contemporary situation, but foreshadowed things to come. Without using the ***etymology***, or breakdown of word meanings, the term *Nicolaitan* would just be a meaningless name to future generations. Bible prophecy is pattern. It uses names and images to paint a picture. It also has universal truth. Everything in it has purpose.

*Nicolaitan* is a compound of two Greek words, *nicao,* and *laos*. *Nicao* means *to conquer* or *have victory over*. *Laos* is a word that means *the people*—we get the word ***laity*** from it. [1] The *laity* is those in church who are not clergy—those viewed as "common people" in the pews. From this etymology, many prophetic scholars infer that the Nicolaitans favored church leadership by an elite; instead of Peter's model of leadership by example and reasoning with people. Of course, God calls and gives authority to church leaders that He does not give to everyone in the church, so "an elite" refers to more than just that. Additional human constraints, which countermand some aspect of God's word, must come into play. The elite have other agendas beyond the necessities of church leadership. They give leadership an altered quality from that described in the New Testament.

Given the character of Balaam, and the meaning of the word *Nicolaitan*; the problem in the church at Pergamum was a leadership system corrupted by love of money and lust for power. Christ promised Pergamum that he would in some way come and, "make war against them with the sword of his mouth." The sword of Jesus' mouth is a figure of speech for the word of God, or the "sword of the Spirit" of Ephesians 6:17 and Hebrews 4:12. If a Pergamum-styled church system did not repent of its own volition, Christ himself would somehow raise up a voice that would speak the word of God. He would fight against that system from a place outside of it. *The light of the church would not go out, but it would receive a new lampstand.* (Rev. 2:5, 16, 20-23)

One could also fairly argue that the progressive result of a "Pergamum" styled church system is a Thyatira-like one.

> **18 "And to the angel of the church in Thyatira write, 'These things says the Son of God, who has eyes like a flame of fire, and His feet like fine brass: 19 "I know your works, love, service, faith, and your patience; and as for your works, the last are more than the first. 20 "Nevertheless I have a few things against you, because you allow that woman Jezebel, who calls herself a prophetess, to teach and seduce My servants to commit sexual immorality and eat things sacrificed to idols. 21 "And I gave her time to repent of her sexual immorality, and she did not repent...'" *Revelation* 2:18-21 (NKJV)**

The Church of Thyatira, despite its increasing good works, still tolerated forms of adultery and idolatry. It permitted the source of that bad teaching a platform, typified by this prophetess, Jezebel. All the names and imagery in the Book of Revelation finds its meaning in the Old Testament. Jezebel was the foreign idol-worshiping wife of King Ahab, who ruled at the height of the wealth and power of the northern kingdom of Israel. Ahab and Jezebel attempted to syncretize or mix the worship systems of Yahweh with that of the Canaanite Baals. The use of Jezebel's name was emblematic for the introduction of idolatry to God's people.

Bible prophecy usually links adultery with idolatry. God called Israel His wife in the Old Testament. The church is the Bride of Christ in the New. (Ez. 16:1-34, Hos. 2:1-16, Eph. 5:23-33) Mention of sexual sin in the Thyatira Letter includes the idea of spiritual adultery—a recognized term for idolatry. This logically extends to restricting or forbidding marriage, which sets people up to fail at sexual purity by ignoring God's design in human nature. (Gen. 1:26-28, 1 Tim. 4:1-3, Heb. 13:4, 1 Cor. 7:1-3) Pagan temples often considered their priests and priestesses "married" to the god of the temple, which forbade them to marry in the normal sense.

After 1500 years, most of the church had come to this place. Ritual syncretism, Pagan folk religion, selling indulgences and relics, and now Greek philosophy as a major influence in theology, had corrupted church culture. Worse, the system had rejected repeated opportunities to repent. The case for a Pergamum to Thyatira descent is strong.

I want to make clear, as Christian philosopher of history Francis Schaeffer did, that the ***Reformation*** was no golden age either. [2] It involved some seriously unbiblical aspects—things I will cover just as frankly as the failings of the Medieval Roman system. One problem, likely unavoidable at first, was that, by the very necessity of being forced to form new church systems; the Reformation embraced a "lesser of two evils" approach. What I mean is that the reformers had no alternative but to sacrifice one biblical principle to preserve another, more essential one.

The original leaders did not intend this to happen. We will see serious effort among some reformers to prevent it. Of necessity, large-scale church unity took a back seat to a biblical doctrine of individual salvation. Both are biblical. Yet, without a biblical concept of salvation, that form of church unity only preserved a growing illusion.

Later, this pattern made it easier for Reformation-based churches to divide over less than crucial issues. Despite this, the Reformation pointed the way to a comprehensive return to scriptural authority in the church. By contrast, the Roman Catholic Church at this point had rejected reform of any substantive kind. Rejected by Rome, the Reformers shed the Roman system, and later, even some transitional Reformed and Lutheran ones, as dried husks. This sometimes left good individuals flailing in the turbulent wake of historical forces too large for any one person.

As in other eras of church history, we should not assume that because people were responsible for their choices, and had growing access to the Bible; that it meant they all had the same information we have, framed for them as clearly as hindsight frames it for us. That is neither realistic nor fair. We can see it as "biblical" only in a very shallow sense that accepts the existence of the Bible at the time, with the same content, but looks at no other factors. God did not breathe His word, and have men write the Bible into a historic vacuum. Nor did people understand it except by how the Holy Spirit used events and the tools of the time to illuminate it. This was not a limit on the Spirit, but upon the people He chose to work through. While God is free to lift human limits, and sometimes does, He is not obligated to do things that way.

## The Timing was Ripe

The stage had been setting itself up toward that series of ideas and events history calls the Reformation for many centuries. For pastors, ministers, and other Christians, who like I do, approach church history with a doctrinal mindset of great concern for salvation, and evangelism; a disturbing question must rise to the forefront: *Why now?*

Why did the Reformation happen so late, when hindsight suggests that biblical views of grace had eroded in Christian thought and culture centuries before? Why did God allow earlier efforts at reformation to fail for so long, if nothing less than teaching about eternal salvation was on the line? We can fall back and say, "God is sovereign," because He is. Yet *only* saying that *here* dodges the question, instead of shedding light. It would make the majesty of God's sovereignty seem less than what it is. God is also many other marvelous things, all of which work together with His sovereignty. One thing we cannot say is that the issues were not really so crucial. God's word implies otherwise.

I have even seen some pastors avoid the entire subject of church history to avoid this question (they even told me they were doing this). To find a biblically reasonable answer does not require that we avoid our own history. Nor does it require us to compromise doctrine or to doubt God's love and sovereignty. We already explored certain aspects of the matter by recognizing the economic realities; that owning a personal Bible did not begin to become possible until around this very time. The question of why God only allowed the Reformation to come when it did is in some ways unanswerable. The best historical models explore the patience and mercy of God. I anchor my views on the implications raised by the Reformation's timing to something Jesus said about how God judges.

> **47 "And that servant who knew his master's will, and did not prepare himself or do according to his will, shall be beaten with many stripes. 48 "But he who did not know, yet committed things deserving of stripes, shall be beaten with few. For everyone to whom much is given, from him much will be required; and to whom much has been committed, of him they will ask the more."** ***Luke*** **12:47-48 (NKJV)**

God does not expect His children to do things He has not equipped them to do. Having the word of God is not the same as being able to study, mass-produce, and spread it efficiently. An ability to know and obey God's word imprecisely is not the same as being able to do so precisely. Many earlier believers expended far more of themselves in God's service to do imprecisely what we today can do with much greater precision, much less effort; but often don't bother doing. I include myself in that scathing indictment.

Nor is this recognition a denial of the power that the Holy Spirit gives to believers. I speak of normal potentials confined by historical limits. A more obvious example would be like realizing that Paul could not have traveled 60 miles per hour along Roman Roads in the 1st century to spread the gospel. It is useless to object that he could if God had wanted him to. That is not in question. God evidently chose to operate within certain natural limits, voluntarily, for His own glory.

As crazy as it sounds, I have heard such objections coming from otherwise well-rounded believers often enough that I began to suspect that I might be dealing with a worldview blind spot here. I also might be wrong about that. Either way, I ask forgiveness of the reader if the way I am writing right now seems condescending. I do not intend it that way.

The next best speculations on God's timing of the Reformation look to the need for social stability during the earlier Middle Ages. Roman Catholicism was the foundation of medieval culture—the cement that unified the new Western civilization. Without some unity in the West, Islam would have swept unhindered into France, Britain, and Germany. When Constantinople fell, it would have meant the end of Christian influenced civilization. All of this deals with the social mechanics of cultures in conflict; a part of the reality God allowed after the Curse. None of it is a statement on what God could or could not have done had He chosen.

Disturbing undercurrents lurked under the oily calm surface of late medieval society. In terms of external Roman Catholic-styled piety, everything seemed great—if one did not look too closely. Germany in particular had a thick layer of traditional religious zeal floating like a slick of heavy crude on troubled waters. The perverse splendor of the church system at that time captivated even those who knew and lamented its moral and spiritual bankruptcy. Its claim to be the heart of Christ's authority on earth intoxicated.

By now, better lay schooling, with the spread of Scripture via the printing press, opened more eyes to conflicts between biblical teaching and church practice. Yet denial reigned in many quarters, similar to the thinking a drunk uses, today, to ignore his own impairment to drive. A sense of helplessness also gripped Europe with the feeling that, in the failure of Conciliarism, the only valid method of church reform had died. After the Great Schism, nobody wanted to risk anything that might again divide the church. The stability of society itself seemed to be at stake.

Nevertheless, a growing number of thinkers began to drink some proverbial black coffee, and grope their way out of the haze. We know them as the Christian Humanists, not to be confused with today's anti-Christian Secular Humanists. They drove much of the new popular thirst for education among the laity, as the Scholastics had a few centuries before. Christian Humanists like Desiderius Erasmus and Johannes Reuchlin made studies of Greek and Hebrew Scripture manuscripts more accessible to European scholars. Before, as in Wycliffe's day, scholars had been limited to Latin texts.

Biblical perspectives that we now take for granted, which lay forgotten, or mislaid for many centuries, re-emerged through the translation work of Erasmus and Reuchlin. One was how Jewish writings revealed the original Hebrew context of New Testament theology. While Dominicans suppressed Jewish literature, men like Reuchlin stood up and shouted against this tragic triumph of ignorance and fear. The Christian Humanists helped shape the idea development of a young law student-turned-monk named Martin Luther.

As an Augustinian monk, Luther read the anti-Pelagian works of Augustine of Hippo. Augustine's views on salvation by God's grace alone also greatly influenced the young friar. Chapters 8 and 12 discussed how Pelagianism denied that men were sinful by a nature passed on through the Fall, and could thus merit God's favor through their own good works. Semi-Pelagianism, which Luther also later opposed, taught that a combination of God's grace and human merit saved men; a concept that by this time dominated the Scholastic Theology of the Roman Catholic Church. Luther was far from alone in referring to the major Scholastic view of salvation as *"the new Pelagianism."* [3]

The logic of William of Occam also influenced Luther. He rejected William's Scholastic Theology because he saw real conflicts between Occam's Bible doctrine and Occam's logic. Remember that a major tension during the time of the Scholastics had touched on whether reason and logic applied to interpreting Scripture. Luther applied "Occam's Razor" to Bible interpretation—something William had failed to do. In William's time, disagreements between biblical teaching and that of the church always defaulted to the church's established view. By Luther's day, trouble proved increasingly rooted in such blind authoritarianism.

Origen's idea of *Sola Scriptura*—only Scripture—as the church's highest authority offered the only workable answer. Luther usually held the view of a Bible passage that made the fewest assumptions, given historical, grammatical, and thematic contexts. He made a few exceptions to this rule, as we will see, but he started the trend.

Something personal also tied Luther's convictions into a coherent Bible-based theology. Martin found that the more he tried to satisfy the demands of church law through the Sacrament of Penance, the more burdened and miserable he became. He believed in the power of the sacraments to convey God's grace to him. He just did not actually experience forgiveness or peace with God by doing them, or the other religious works the Roman Catholic Church imposed. Nor was it for lack of effort or desire. Luther, if anything, was a compulsive penitent as a young man. Nor was he alone.

The problem was as theological as it was relational. Accumulated traditions that focused on human merit had muddied the biblical doctrine of salvation. The church's concept of grace no longer resembled in character what the New Testament actually taught in its plainest sense. We saw how biblical assurance of salvation (1 John 5) became the logical, if unintentional casualty of the Christian Roman Empire fusion. We then followed how the medieval church inherited and built on this, partly refuting yet partly absorbing Celtic distortions of the nature of sin and grace. Yes, the Holy Spirit also redemptively used parts of these worldviews positively, but that did not magically keep bad ideas from also having their consequences.

Now, Germany and the rest of Europe had all a religion could offer—rich traditions, social structure, a tough moral code (even if folks only followed it outwardly), and a parade of festivals. They had everything except the personal peace with the Living God promised by the gospel. It was possible to know all *about* God, but the church largely had forgotten how to know him. The main thing that had set biblical Christianity apart from all other world religions, like the Emperor's Clothes, was now conspicuous by its absence.

Not that many people at the time could have put this lack into words as I have just done. It took Luther many years to put his finger on it. It involved questioning the foundational faith-assumptions of medieval Roman Catholicism—not its Bible-based ones; but those pureed into the mix from the other worldviews that had become the lens through which people now viewed even many biblical practices. Once again, the pattern emerges. People often accept conclusions about what to believe from others. They do not usually think about the assumptions that under-gird their own belief systems. Only after their life and culture has gone wrong for a long time does this even become thinkable to most people. Even that does not mean they actually follow through by examining their assumptions.

Most people never question their faith-assumptions no matter how bad things get. Many choose to live in various forms of denial, rather than ask God how bad things really are. In late medieval Europe, a hovering sense of dread in people's lives told them something was missing. They lived under fear of punishment that lavish layers of religious zeal could not ease. The passion of penitential works only increased this dread as salt water does thirst.

The problem had not developed overnight. Neither would the solution.

## THE SPARK THAT IGNITED EUROPE'S VOLATILE VAPORS

The event that set the whole thing off involved the sale of indulgences. The fabulous St. Peter's Basilica was under construction, and like most papal projects of that time, way over budget. The Pope sent a rather slimy Dominican monk, Johann Tetzel, to hawk indulgences in Germany, where piety and pageantry both ran high.

Tetzel was the 16th century version of the poofy-haired televangelist who plies "prayer cloths," cut out paper hands for laying on the sick, and drives into town in a stretched limo. Like the heretic, Arius, he came armed with a jingle for every occasion. *"When into the coffer a coin does ring, out of purgatory a soul does spring!"* was one of his favorite ditties. [4] The German of that period and English are similar enough that the words for *spring* and *ring* rhymed in both tongues. Tetzel brought the crassness of the whole indulgence phenomenon to an all-time low. He was just the stimulus Luther needed to speak out.

The Tetzel-indulgence affair prompted Luther to nail his famous *95 Theses* to the door of Wittenberg Castle. A ***thesis*** (singular of *theses*) is a point of argument expressed as a proposition. Luther amassed 95 of them and posted them, after the tradition for scholarly debate in those days, on the door of the place where the university met. To read them today is to be surprised that so mild a collection of statements could have created such a fuss. Luther did not attack the Doctrine of Purgatory or the concept of penance. He did not even question the Pope's authority to grant indulgences, just their effectiveness after death, into purgatory. Most Protestants would be shocked at how Roman Catholic the theses sounded.

In fact, like the reformers before him, Luther at first had no intention of dismantling the papal religious system or "starting another church" as Roman Catholics might see it. His concern lay in getting rid of the corruption, rather than challenging the assumptions from which the Roman system of Christendom built. Only as the Papacy reacted to the questions he posed did it become clear to Luther that the real problem laid in the Roman system itself. His earlier *97 Theses* had questioned the supports of Aquinas and William of Occam's Scholastic Theology more boldly than the *95 Theses* challenged indulgences. The *95 Theses* hit Rome in the pocketbook, and therefore got a sterner response.

Luther had hoped to reason with the Pope by demonstrating how men like Tetzel abused the Papal power of granting indulgences. In June of 1518, Pope Leo X ordered his Dominican book censor to write in reply; *"the Roman Church is representatively the College of Cardinals, and moreover is virtually the Supreme Pontiff,"* and; *"he who says that the Roman Church cannot do what it actually does regarding indulgences is a heretic."* [5] In other words, the Papacy equals *the church* and heresy is whatever the Pope wants it to be—right or wrong. As Wycliffe and Hus a century before, Luther had his face rubbed in how the problem lay at the heart of the Roman system itself, not just corrupt appendages like Tetzel.

Luther's fate would have been much like that of Jan Hus had it not been for the protection of a powerful German prince, the elector Frederick the Wise. Inevitably, however, this embroiled Luther in the politics of his era far more than he would have liked. With the church and state so intertwined, such embroilment would have been unavoidable eventually anyway. If not for Frederick, the ethically decaying political and religious arms of Christendom would have smothered the Reformation in its infancy. These appendages had done so to Hus and his followers, at the Council of Constance, the century before. The spiritual gangrene had only advanced in that time.

It is not that Luther would have agreed with the idea of the separation of church and state in the original American sense. He just did not believe in the use of military force in spiritual matters. Nor could anyone see clearly at the time the inherent problems of state churches. That began as a lesson of history, in hindsight of what happened to Luther. The more the politics of his times swept him up, the more military power became an inevitable tool of the princes protecting him. God did not seem to offer any visible alternatives to princely protection. While Christianity is not primarily political in motive, it cannot be apolitical, either. The war is spiritual, but since the battlefield is intellectual, and ideas have consequences—some of which are political—it is impossible to avoid all politics.

Other forces drove the politics, too, besides princes. For example, some German Humanists called for a military campaign against Italy to free the empire from papal religious tyranny. Another incident flared when peasants took Reformation ideas to their logical conclusion in the political realm. They declared serfdom an unjust abuse of power. Soon peasants were in open and violent revolt.

Though at first sympathetic to many of the peasant's complaints, Luther was eventually obliged to stand with Frederick and the other princes. In the end, he urged them to crush *"the robbing and murdering hordes of peasants"* with the very military force he had opposed in more religion-based controversies. [6] Of course, once things come to bloodshed, it is no longer just a spiritual issue confinable to gentle persuasion.

As time went on, worse compromises came. Many were unavoidable, but some could and should have been. Despite his reforming doctrine of grace, and growing suspicion that the Papacy was antichrist, Luther had yet to move beyond the "Constantine Model" of church-state relations. He merely proposed that, instead of a Roman controlled church, there be national churches united in spirit. This was a small step in the right direction. It took ultimate control of the "Universal Church" from human hands, and left it, in theory, with the Holy Spirit, working through councils made of national and local churches.

It did not occur to early reformers that "national churches" would only behave as smaller clones of the Roman Empire-Church fusion. This kept the church in bed with the state, with only a quick change of the sheets, and doomed Luther to further political entanglements whether he liked them or not. Constructive change never comes easily and rarely overnight.

The Peasant Revolt marked the end of the brushfire-like expansion of the Protestant cause. The common people felt betrayed by Luther's stand with the princes. However, that did not mean that Lutheran ideology and theology did not continue to spread. Increasingly radical reformers, and some less so, emerged, whom we will cover in the next chapters.

The significance of the Lutheran breakthrough rests in more than just restoring a biblical doctrine of salvation. It began a centuries-long repair sequence of the amassed deviations from Scripture that had taken the church from the purity of its roots. Doctrines and applications that came from blending Greek assumptions and Pagan superstition with Christian tradition now began to stand out, as exposure to God's word increased. This enabled the correction or removal of contaminated teachings from those that could claim a genuine Hebraic and biblical base.

A couple chapters ago, I compared this to an anti-viral repair sequence for Christian thought and culture. This was an overly simplistic analogy, perhaps—and certainly not a complete picture. It is a good picture nonetheless. God's word was now able to reach more people in their own languages at a time marked by the availability of better interpretive tools. This happened slowly, unevenly, as small groups applied Scripture more consistently as the highest church authority. Even ideas Luther thought central, like Transubstantiation, ultimately failed his test of *Sola Scriptura*. The Holy Spirit filled men who passionately desired God's word. He used them to develop a growing array of exegetical tools that slowly gave better interpretation skills to more of God's people.

This sifting also began to cut away the semi-Docetic stigma on marriage that viewed married sex as "a necessary evil." Luther took former nun, Katerina von Bora, as his wife, writing boldly, but tastefully, of their conjugal passion for each other. After many centuries, churches could now fully apply Paul's Pastoral Epistles again in the real world. Christians once more had the straightforward test of Scripture to tell if men were capable of handling pastoral responsibility. They could see if such men lovingly handled their own wives and families (among other things) decently and in order. (1 Tim. 3:1-5)

This did not mean Protestant forms of asceticism's false holiness never happened under similar conditions to those shown earlier. It meant we now had a coherent way to use Scripture to expose it when it did. Christians now had an increasingly effective interpretive method that let the Bible say what it plainly said in normal language to everyday people.

Pope Leo X died in December of 1521. The College of Cardinals replaced him with a man of traditional medieval views on orthodoxy, yet one who despaired over the same moral corruption as Luther. However, Pope Adrian VI did not last long enough to make any effective contribution to change. He understood one thing that neither his immediate predecessor nor most of his successors seemed to, though. Pope Adrian declared that the Lutheran Movement was a judgment from God against the Roman Church because of its failure to reform itself. [7] He aimed, as Pope, to make the moral and administrative changes necessary for the Papacy to regain its ethical vigor.

Unfortunately, Pope Adrian VI still had a blind spot, which continued in those who followed him. He strongly opposed the idea that philosophical, moral, and administrative corruption over the centuries could affect the development and application of church doctrine. He reasoned that the Spirit would never allow "the Church" to become apostate, and saw no distinction between "the Church Universal" and a church system. Thomas Aquinas' magical disconnect of cause from effect in this isolated realm continues within Roman Catholicism to this day.

Although the Roman Catholic Church regained and retains many positive qualities and influences, the failure to recognize a cumulative impact of non-biblical worldviews on doctrine and practice reflects a certain unreality in the mix. God's love for His people is not contingent, however. Pope Adrian VI understood his times remarkably well, even if he did not recognize the root of the problem. Reformation of the church from outside the Roman system was indeed God's judgment against that system. Yet I wonder how well sometimes both Protestant and Catholic polemics understand the implications of that.

When God disciplines a church, He does so in love, as with erring children. Yes, there is a difference between an individual and a religious system. Any religious system involves many people, some truly redeemed, others not. There is not only human sin and stubbornness involved, however; there are also individual human limits to what is knowable at the time. Long-term tumults of history separate people, and groups of people, from each other in a kind of fog of war. Individuals in the 16th century began to have both greater access to God's word, and responsibility to its light. Nevertheless, the Holy Spirit has never given equal levels of every spiritual gift to every believer in any age. Otherwise, what need would we have for one another? (1 Cor. 12)

It took the "outside" influence of the Reformation; competing religious systems of a *biblically* orthodox Christianity, to force the Roman system to deal with problems it had repeatedly proven it would never have dealt with on its own. Nor did that system deal with all of them. Serious blind spots remained. Some distorting worldview mixtures, long entrenched in Christianese language, continued to combine with the effects of past ethical lapses; for example, the confusion of asceticism with holiness, and its bitter fruit. The impact of this on some Roman Catholic doctrines, and their applications, continued almost without challenge from inside the system. Ethics and motives often improved, but doctrinal reactions to the Reformation reinforced key distortions.

Mismatched worldview presuppositions have consequences in the realm of ideas and teaching, as they do in any realm. Ideas govern behaviors, which influence the formation of new ideas, and affect the development of older teachings in how people see, interpret, and apply them. It is necessary to discuss both the positives and the negatives of this to have an honest grasp of worldviews and church history. The word of God gives us an anchoring point for such discussions, for the gospel is **"the power of God to salvation for everyone who believes."** (Rom. 1:16)

Central moral teachings, along with those on the nature of Christ, and how He relates to God the Father and the Holy Spirit, remained intact in Roman Catholicism. So did the historical Incarnation, death, and Resurrection of Jesus. Still, the Roman and Medieval Eras shrouded other central doctrines, which we might call secondary only because they dealt more with human salvation than with God's identity and nature. It is essential to know which god is really God. It is also vital to have as clear a view we can of the gospel that is the power of that God to salvation for those who believe. Salvation by grace alone through faith, and personal assurance of salvation based on God's promises, could no longer be second.

Without accepting even the possibility of bad effects like those described above, the Roman system reached a roadblock of sorts. It could not internally allow an all-embracing biblical pattern of reform, at best only partial ones. This was so no matter how sincerely people lamented the corruption in the system. A distinction had to be made between the Roman system (and any church system) and the Body of Christ Universal. One is a device of organizational social mechanics designed to get a job done. The other is an organism made up of all those who, by faith, have been regenerated through the gospel by the Holy Spirit's power. We need systems, but the Church organism must take precedence over them.

The Reformation forced Christians to choose one over the other at a unique time in history.

## BIBLIOGRAPHY


1. Newell, William R. ***The Book of The Revelation*** commentary, p. 51; Moody Press, Chicago (1935)
2. Schaeffer, Francis A. ***How Should We Then Live? The Rise and Decline of Western Thought and Culture***, p.84, 1976, Fleming H. Revell Co. Old Tappan, NJ. See also Schaeffer, Francis A. ***The Great Evangelical Disaster***, p. 22; Crossway Books (1984)
3. Walker, Williston. ***A History of the Christian Church*** (4th Edition), p. 358, see also pp. 423-425, 1st Edition 1918, 4th Edition 1946, Charles Scribner's Sons, New York, NY.
4. Shelley, Bruce L. ***Church History in Plain Language*** (2nd Edition), p. 240, 1995, Word Publishing, Dallas, Tx.
5. Op cit. Walker, Williston, p. 427
6. Op cit. Shelley, Bruce L., p. 243
7. Op cit. Walker, Williston, p. 434

# 15

# THE REFORMATION ERA: PART 2

## PHILIP MELANCHTHON AND THE DEVELOPMENT OF LUTHERANISM

Well before 1530, the Holy Roman (German) Emperor, Charles V, had already labeled Martin Luther an outlaw. In 1521, Charles had summoned an imperial assembly (called a ***diet***) at Worms to hear Luther present his case. Yet he was unimpressed by the gruff and sometimes reactionary reformer.

History often has its own sense of humor. The Diet of Worms began a string of events that permanently divided the Holy Roman Empire. Germany's so-called "1st Reich" hung on only by political life-support until the Napoleonic Era of the early 19th century. When I first heard of this diet, I saw the bizarre mental image of a group of Monty Pythonesque medieval dignitaries eating worms while their nation died. It is a bad pun, but the polarization of forces into Catholic and Lutheran camps among the princes marked a rift no nation could long survive in a healthy way. Much of this section summarizes events from 1523 to 1545.

With Luther hidden by Frederick the Wise, and then by Frederick's brother, John of Saxony, pastoring the Lutheran Movement fell to Philip Melanchthon, an ally of Luther. Melanchthon was a Greek scholar trained in the tradition of his Humanist granduncle, Johannes Reuchlin. By 1529, Luther took on a secondary role, first for his outlaw status, and later, as people's awareness of certain political compromises grew.

The worst concession involved Luther's reluctant consent to a secret bigamous marriage for the lecherous Prince Philip of Hesse. Philip took a key role in the Reformation's military survival, despite his lust for a teen-aged girl. This smeared Luther's reputation badly at the hand of Catholic polemics. Sexual sin is often biblically associated with heresy—the last thing the reformers needed at the time!

Luther warned Philip gently, but repeatedly, against this "marriage." The reason for Luther's unusual gentleness was that Philip protected Lutheran congregations more and more as the years went on. The Prince kept bringing the matter up, apparently because his conscience bothered him quite a bit. This was unusual for a period when royalty routinely swept their infidelities under the rug. Philip had already made up his mind to go through with the bigamy, however. Only then did Luther and Melanchthon reluctantly urge him to keep it secret, which clearly did not work so well. "Fear of man" results whenever the church becomes dependent on the state. [1] Although less in the forefront, Luther continued to be a primary writer and ideologue of the movement, despite the compromises.

A long and grueling war against King Francis I of France prevented Emperor Charles V from enforcing the Edict of Worms against the Lutherans. Ironically, the Pope himself ensured the survival of the Lutherans in Germany. After Adrian VI died, the College of Cardinals elected the Italian statesman, Giulio de Medici, Pope. He took the name Clement VII—Roman politics had declared the earlier French Clement VII an ***anti-pope***, so his number no longer counted. The Medici family often seemed more concerned with political and economic power than with church doctrine. Hence, the emphasis of the Papacy briefly shifted—not so much in action as in motivation.

The power of the German emperor in Italy alarmed the new Pope, which caused him to side with Francis I in the war. This gave the Lutheran princes almost a decade to consolidate their military and political positions; enough so that when the war finally ended, and Charles V returned, it forced him to give only lip service to carrying out the Worms Edict. He pushed for reconciliation instead. Clement also seemed interested in some measure of reconciliation. War could not have been good for de Medici family businesses. Resolving things with Charles V, the Pope sent his legate, Lorenzo Cardinal Campeggio, to manage Roman interests in the new Reichstag. The main point of discussion was the Lutheran party's place in the empire. The Reichstag was the German equivalent of the British Parliament.

Melanchthon, in many ways, had a personality the polar opposite of Luther. Where Luther could be earthy and blustery; Melanchthon was soft-spoken, and willing to look for ways to heal the breaches with both Rome and other reforming parties Luther did not trust. Melanchthon wrote the *Augsburg Confession*, a statement of common ground to unite the Evangelical Lutheran churches in Germany.

Unfortunately, earlier attempts to unite with the other major reform movement, in Switzerland, had failed. This was largely due to Luther's insistence that a form of Transubstantiation must remain core to teaching on the Eucharist. Other reformers saw Transubstantiation as the manipulation tool Romanism had used to keep Europe in superstitious bondage to an idolatrous perversion of the Eucharist. They also understood a difference between ritual and spiritual reality.

While the *Augsburg Confession* spoke in mild, non-threatening terms in its approach to the Roman Church, its central theme was salvation by grace alone through faith. It explained how everything in Christian living sprang from understanding how Christ's work alone brings salvation to the individual.

> **8 For by grace you have been saved through faith, and that not of yourselves; it is the gift of God, 9 not of works, lest anyone should boast. 10 For we are His workmanship, created in Christ Jesus for good works, which God prepared beforehand that we should walk in them. *Ephesians* 2:8-10 (NKJV)**

Grace and a faith-held assurance of salvation resulted in good works for the genuine believer. Works and sacraments did not generate or convey grace; they reflected its presence after the fact. God's unmerited favor came through faith in the gospel, which is **"the power of God for the salvation of everyone who believes."** (Rom. 1:16b NIV) Melanchthon showed in his document that the Lutheran Movement securely grounded itself in things widely accepted by earlier Catholic thinkers. It was not a **"new wind of doctrine."** (Eph. 4:14)

Cardinal Campeggio ordered the *Augsburg Confession* subjected to the scrutiny of local Roman Catholic scholars. Chief of these was one of Luther's most bitter critics, Johann Eck. Eck and the other ***Romanist*** scholars gave a reply so harsh that even the pro-Roman Emperor and the Catholic princes rejected it. [2] It was as if Melanchthon had said to the assembly, "Hey, work with me here. The fate of both the church and the empire hangs in the balance."

Yet the Emperor found, to his short-lived dismay, that radicals of his own camp would send Europe through a meat-grinder rather than risk even a speck of power lost to Rome. During the years of Emperor Charles' absence, the princes had effectively partitioned Germany into zones. If a prince was Catholic, everybody who lived in his region was Catholic, with no choice but to comply or move (and few allowed peasants to move). If a Prince was Lutheran, then everybody under him was Lutheran.

The other reform groups had no representation. Often the Lutherans persecuted them as harshly as the Roman Catholics did. This made Lutheranism the state religion in parts of the empire, with claim to all church properties in those zones, and Catholicism in other parts; all spread out like a glommy pan of oil and water that would never truly mix. Essentially, these were just more Christendom church-state clones popping up out of the woodwork, even if they were getting smaller and smaller. Negotiations between reforming groups went on, but often badly.

Reconciliation attempts soon fell apart due to the words of a talebearer. The Lutherans began to mobilize for their defense under a military coalition headed by Philip of Hesse. A forged letter convinced Philip, with John of Saxony, brother of Frederick the Wise, that the Catholic forces were mounting for a surprise attack. With hostilities aroused, a new imperial diet at Speyer in Germany did not look promising.

An earlier Diet at Speyer, in 1526, had suspended enforcement of the Diet of Worms edict. In 1529, another Reichstag Diet at Speyer ordered Roman worship forms restored, and all former rights of the Roman Church returned. Momentum in favor of this new edict grew under a Catholic plurality and emperor. This meant dismantling all the Lutheran churches that had virtually replaced the Roman ones during the war years.

Unable to counteract this legislation any longer, the Lutheran princes issued a formal protest, called the *Protestatio*. This document placed the name ***Protestant*** upon Reformation-based churches. It now seemed that Philip of Hesse's defensive league would be essential to prevent the marginalization of Luther's Reform Movement. Not only did the wake of the Diet of Speyer's political reaction threaten the Reformation; the movement itself had become rife with divisions and hostile competition from other reform-minded groups.

It seemed the worst Roman Catholic prediction against Luther's theology—that of fragmentation—was in danger of proving true.

## Ulrich Zwingli and the Swiss Reformation

The other reform movement, alluded to above, grew in Switzerland. It centered on the teaching of a Catholic priest by the name of Ulrich Zwingli. Like Luther, the Christian Humanists Erasmus and Reuchlin also heavily influenced Zwingli. Many of his biblical insights came through his being a Greek and Hebrew scholar. By now, such studies had uncovered vital literary and historical data. It enabled clearer discernment between living Bible teaching, and the dead superstition or philosophy the church had picked up from non-biblical worldviews. This filtration, too, is a redemptive need when things go bad. Scripture warns the church against imitating the world.

Zwingli often saw more clearly into this realm than did Luther. As Wycliffe before him, he noticed something about the natural language use in the Last Supper accounts of the Gospels, and of John, Chapter 6. Literal interpretation does not require that we ignore clear signs of figurative speech; only that we do not wrongly consider something "figurative speech" when usage, context, and grammar show otherwise. Zwingli saw that common sense demanded a differing interpretation of communion than that of Transubstantiation.

If Christ meant that He literally transformed the bread He held in His hand into His body, then it would mean that His physical body was in two places at once. The word construction of these passages resembled metonymies often used in other parts of Jesus' teaching, like when He said, **"I *am* the *door* of the sheep."** (John 10:1-9) A ***metonymy*** is a figure of speech where one object symbolically describes another; for example, "the throne" refers to a *monarch or a monarchy*, or "counting heads" for *counting people*.

The language of Jesus' day was full of such figures of speech, and they richly inhabit the Gospels. Nobody would have ever argued that the Gospel of John taught that Christ had literally transformed himself into a door, but in a way people could not see or feel. Nor would the blessing of doors by a priest literally make them into "Christ," so that people who walked through them regularly literally became His sheep.

The core idea of communion was the celebration of a spiritual reality provided through Christ's physical death in space-time history; not a focus on what happens to bread and wine metaphysically, when a priest prays over them. This bit of cold water to the face was simply too much for Luther, who bitterly opposed the Swiss Reformers. He even told one of Zwingli's associates that, *"You have a different spirit than we!"* [3]

Another argument between Luther and Zwingli centered on the place of music in worship. While this may not have been as big an issue as the nature of communion, it resembled an argument in churches of America today. Zwingli believed in the exclusive use of the old sacred music of his day. Luther, an accomplished musician, often took popular bar room tunes and gave them sacred lyrics. Ironically, many old time hymns we treasure today, like, *A Mighty Fortress is Our God*, originated as "worldly bar room tunes" from Luther's day. [4]

Music is a part of the world of ideas, with a natural progression in its development. Our music should reflect our Christianity in some sense. Yet, it is usually not a good idea to put artificial or provincial restrictions on what styles of music can be useful to God or not. History has vindicated Luther in this, by how well his hymns have survived the test of time. While not all our contemporary Christian music styles will survive that same test, some no doubt will—if the Lord waits another generation or more to return. Even what does not survive is still a part of history's picture of musical development. It interacts with and sometime provides some part to that which endures. Art is not simple. We cannot restrict it based on some traditional or personal taste without reducing it to something less than what it is.

While music is not isolated from correction using biblical principles, no living art exists without the risk of getting things wrong. Nor should the sense of "a biblical place for art" be so restrictive that only a non-artist could feel comfortable under it. When artists with a Christian worldview do not feel free to try new things in their church communities, culture fossilizes. If Zwingli had had his way, we would be stripped today of many of the greatest hymns and spiritual songs of the last 500 years.

We need to avoid taking a simplistic "good guy-bad guy" mindset when it comes to the bitterness between Luther and Zwingli, with Luther as the contentious guy. The reformers were as fraught with worldview blind spots as anyone was at the time. Another reform movement in Switzerland began by breaking from Zwingli's teaching. This group believed in following Scripture as the model for how to practice all of life, particularly in ordinances like baptism. They pointed out that infant baptism was not valid because, in Scripture, the church only baptized with water those who converted. Conversion required a positive response to the gospel. This new reform group stressed the need for genuine spiritual regeneration, as most modern Evangelical churches later came to do.

Just as Luther could not deal with Zwingli's denial of Transubstantiation, Zwingli disowned any Bible-based rejection of Baptismal Regeneration. He derisively named this group, which Chapter 17 will cover in more detail, the ***Anabaptists***. Zwingli, and the Swiss Reformers, saw this sect as advocating the total dismantling of the Christian social order, as everyone understood it. Like the Lutherans, the Swiss had yet to get beyond the old church-state fusion model of Christendom. Thus, the Anabaptists seemed a looming threat. People saw Baptism as the gateway to participate in Christian society.

The early reformers reacted to this abstract menace as the Roman Papacy had to Zwingli and the Lutherans. They put Anabaptists to death by drowning, in a cruel mockery of their emphasis on educated believer's baptism.

We Evangelicals often think of the Reformation in such glowing terms that it sometimes shocks us to learn of such things. Keep in mind that at this moment in history, Islam, in the form of the Ottoman Empire, was poised to besiege Vienna—deep in the heart of Christian Europe! Muslims thought in terms of "Muslim states versus Christian states." Luther called for Christians to take up arms against the invaders, based on Augustine's ***Just War Theory***. Christians had also thought in terms of *Christendom* since the Roman Emperors Theodosius I, and Justinian. This was, by definition, *a state protecting the church, which spiritually nourished that state*. It fit the "kingdom model" of the last 1000 years, during which the Holy Spirit seemed content to protect the church from outside attack in just that way.

Only now, did some Christians begin to discover that another way was possible, and even desirable. The biblical justification for this new way was not yet clearly visible to many—given the big picture at the time—even to the reformers who knew Christendom's flaws. Focusing on a single issue, without regard to anything else, rarely leads to a balanced biblical outlook, even when that "single issue" has a biblical basis. Disrupting the social order during wartime, with Muslim armies deep in Christian territory, did not seem wise even to most who agreed that Scripture did not teach infant baptism. More than a doctrinal dispute about baptism seemed to be at stake, even though history later proved fear of the Anabaptists grossly overblown. It comes back to what was knowable at the time, given the full scope.

Chapter 17 will show that the Anabaptist Movement, as any movement, took time to mature. There were even a few fanatical and seditious fringe elements, though not nearly as many as some Roman Catholic polemics claimed. The fanatical fringe did not characterize the Anabaptists or their theology as a whole.

History finds in the Anabaptists an early transition toward a modern Evangelical Christianity; freed from the imprint of Constantine's spiritual DNA.

## John Calvin and the Export of Reformed Theology

Perhaps the greatest theologian produced by the Reformation was a French man by the name of Jean Cauvin. We know him today as John Calvin. Unlike the older reformers, Luther and Zwingli, Calvin grew up in an environment of wealth and means. His father had set him up to be a member of the upper-class priesthood. These flittered about the aristocratic families of Paris like hummingbirds drinking nectar from flower to flower.

By the time of Calvin's secondary schooling, the works of Luther had penetrated France, and stirred up great philosophical debate. John remained a Christian Humanist during those years, his mind stimulated by the questions Luther raised, but his life essentially unchanged. In this, he looked like many American Christians today, softened by a wealthy culture, and removed from the logical results of his own Bible-based ideas. For up until now, the Reformation in France had largely taken the form of an intellectual diversion for educated nobles. That was about to change.

Nicholas Cop, a Humanist friend of Calvin, gave an inaugural speech at his election as rector for the University of Paris, in 1533. Cop made a passionate cry for church reform using language easily identified with that of Luther and Erasmus. The effect was like setting off a bomb in the royal palace. King Francis I, disturbed by the healing of the breach between the Pope and his rival, Emperor Charles V, decided to ingratiate himself again with his old ally, Clement VII. Francis ordered the arrest of reformers and their sympathizers.

For the first time, Calvin began to see what his developing ideas might cost him. Until now, he had not expressed any desire to actually separate from the Church of Rome. Not long before this incident, Calvin experienced what he later called his "unexpected conversion." [5] This involved a new realization that God, in His Divine providence, had radically changed Calvin's heart from one of stone into a teachable heart of flesh. To put it in the language of our day, Calvin's heart finally caught up to where his head had been going for a long while. Now, he had to flee for his life, which added a new dimension to his already vivid conversion.

King Francis I had a bit of a conflict of interest, politically. On the one hand, he wanted to maintain his ties with the Papacy by persecuting reformers in his kingdom. On the other, he was trying to stir up the Protestants in Germany to revolt against Charles V by offering them an alliance. To do this, he explained that his persecution of the French reformers had nothing to do with their beliefs, but an insurrection they had stirred up against him. This bold-faced lie got the pen of Calvin moving on a point-by-point response that explained the position of the French Reform Movement. Published in 1536, under the title *Institutes of the Christian Religion*, it began with a personal letter of polite rebuke to the King.

Calvin's followers later expanded *Institutes* into a watershed theological work that believers today still read and quote. In it, Calvin stressed God's electing grace, which predestines the believer, apart from anything in the person's make up that stirs Divine favor. God created man originally in an innocent state in the Garden of Eden. Adam was capable of obeying God, and doing works that pleased Him. Humanity lost both its goodness, and its power to please God, when Adam fell. This tendency toward sin passed to Adam and Eve's children from their parents—indeed, all creation reflected its futility. (Rom. 8:18-24) No human work today can earn divine merit because of this. Man is born helpless and hopeless in his natural condition, alienated from God. This was the bad news, which made the good news of the gospel so necessary.

Because Christ paid the penalty for sin on the cross, some people are undeservedly saved from this condition, and its damning consequences. Even a person's ability to repent and choose Christ is a work of elect grace caused only by God's love. Calvin refined many of Augustine's ideas, though it seems he often did so without falling into some of Augustine's extremes. It will become apparent, later, that not all of his followers would be quite so careful, however.

After fleeing France, Calvin ended up in Geneva, Switzerland. There, he met city leaders who wanted reform. Geneva became a haven for refugee reformers from Germany, France, Italy, the Netherlands, England, and Scotland. The French Reformer and the city elders seemed to imagine at first with wild hope that they could create an almost ***utopian*** "model Christian society." Calvin also taught from Scripture that the Holy Spirit ***regenerated*** and ***sanctified*** believers. While this is gospel truth, it did not guarantee that believers always drew realistic inferences from it. Sometimes it took time to learn the best way to apply these truths practically.

What historians later called "Calvin's Geneva Experiment" seemed to assume that reformers could create ideal Christian societies, starting only from the Bible. This seemed possible by virtue of the Holy Spirit's regenerative and sanctifying work in individuals; who would then vote their consciences under the Spirit's leading.

Yet how was this much different in principle from what the Medieval Catholic Church had tried? The assumption that gifts of the Holy Spirit shielded church leaders from error had helped embolden undue trust in the policy of Papal Supremacy. Was there any greater basis for assuming that gifts of the Holy Spirit magically shielded voting lay believers from error in the same way? History would likewise show not. Calvin's careful exegetical approach to Scripture ultimately exposed the fallacy in both his own "idealized society," and that of the Papacy's "Christendom." The Bible not only showed human beings as sinful in their natural state, but that Christians continued to struggle with their old nature after conversion. This meant that no human being could be trusted with too much power without some form of checks and balances.

Such a realization, later, had deep implications for both secular politics and church leadership. It would take generations for those to mature, however. Calvin made great progress here, but did not work it all out in his own lifetime. When I wrote that Calvin's "Geneva Experiment" tried to create a "utopian society" based on Reformed Christian principles, I did not mean that he called it a "utopia." Nor was it utopian in the modern sense; no man-centered ideology pretended to have a cure-all for the evils of the human condition in this life, apart from the cross. It was only utopian in some of its naïve early expectations, which it soon had the substance to outgrow.

Thomas More, author of the book *Utopia*, a satirical novel about an ideal island society, lived at the same time as both Luther and Calvin. More published *Utopia* a year before Luther nailed his *95 Theses* to Wittenberg Door. A staunch Roman Catholic, and later, a vehement opponent of the Reformation, More wrote mostly before Luther and Calvin. Marxists later seized upon *Utopia's* communistic approach to the ownership of property. Most scholars today realize that More's satire exposed the futility of trying to build ideal societies. As we shall see, all utopias have a nasty habit of becoming *dystopias*. Like *Christendom*, ***dystopia*** is a mix of two words—*dysfunctional* and *utopia*. The word *utopia* itself is Greek for *no place*, as in, *no such place can exist*. Calvin, and all biblically literate Christians after him, would likely attribute this to the reality of sin.

It is doubtful that Thomas More could have influenced Calvin much, given More's views. The Geneva Experiment was "utopian" only in one sense. At this early stage, it had not yet reached the maturity to see its own limitations. It rapidly failed in its earliest form. The city's political opposition won the next elections. This forced Calvin to move to Strasbourg for almost a decade, where he met with Philip Melanchthon. However, shady political dealings caused the opposition clique in Geneva to lose favor in the eyes of the people. Eventually the pro-Calvin faction came to power again. They sent a messenger to Strasbourg to fetch back the now reluctant social reformer.

Calvin had married, and settled down in the ministry at Strasbourg. After much prayer, he concluded that the Lord was leading him back to Geneva to try for that model Christian society again. This time he met with more success, but not without some low points.

As things developed in Geneva, a "Christian dictatorship" mentality still reared its head. A thousand years of the Christendom model for church-state relationships did not die easy. The enforcement of church doctrine as civil legal code outside the church created an inevitable "thought police" type environment. Not everyone in Geneva followed Calvin. The naturally freethinking Swiss began to find this distasteful, even though most of them still agreed with the dominant doctrines. Calvin banished dissenters most of the time. At one point, however, Reformed magistrates had a refugee doctor from Spain burned at the stake for persistently teaching against the Trinity. Old ways, no matter how ineffective, are even more difficult to shake at the cultural level than on the individual one.

Despite the "Constantine Clone" still showing in the Geneva Experiment, Calvin became more convinced, as time passed, that civil government should be separate from the church. Though he still thought in terms of a Christian state, he kept the zones between civil and religious authority more sharply divided than most Europeans did at the time. It was one thing to reach a conviction in principle. It was quite another to figure out how best to put it into practice after so much entrenched history. Some things maybe had to wait for another day. Another work took center focus, and likely had to, at Geneva.

John Calvin founded the Geneva Academy in the safety of his "Reformed safe house" city. This institution trained Calvin's fellow refugees, who then returned home to export Reformed Theology all over Europe. In this way, the Reformation came to Scotland, the Netherlands, and back into France. It also penetrated the already separated-from-Rome Church of England, where strong parties had come to sympathize with Luther and Calvin's teachings.

Strangely, the splitting of the Church of England from the Papacy had nothing to do with the Reformation—not at first. That was about to rapidly change.

## BIBLIOGRAPHY

1. ***Time Magazine***, March 24, 1967, pp. 70-74, see also John Alfred Faulkner, ***Luther and the Bigamous Marriage of Philip of Hesse***, *The American Journal of Theology*, Vol. 17, No. 2 (Apr., 1913), pp. 206-231, Published by: The University of Chicago Press Stable URL: http://www.jstor.org/stable/3154607
2. Walker, Williston. ***A History of the Christian Church*** (4th Edition), p. 457, 1st Edition 1918, 4th Edition 1946, Charles Scribner's Sons, New York, NY.
3. Ibid. p. 456
4. Grout, Donald J., ***The History of Western Music*** (4th Edition), Ch. 8, p. 310, (1988), W.W. Norton & Co.
5. Shelley, Bruce L. ***Church History in Plain Language*** (2nd Edition), p. 258, 1995, Word Publishing, Dallas, Tx.

# 16

# The Reformation Era: Part 3

## The English Reformation

The transition of the Church of England from Roman Catholicism to the Reformation is an odd tale that this compact a work of can hardly do justice to. It has enough intrigue, sordid marriages, irony, and betrayal to busy novel and film writers for hundreds of years. As most history, it is also weirder than fiction. A contemporary of Luther, King Henry VIII was a political intellectual of traditional Roman Catholic views. Though he respected several Christian Humanists, he had no sympathy for Luther, or for Zwingli and Calvin, later on. Pope Leo X named Henry a *"Defender of the Faith"* for his writings against Luther. King Henry VIII also burned the first English Protestant martyrs at the stake.

Despite Henry's theology, his Tudor heritage sprang out of Wales, and had a Celtic Briton flavor. [1] The office of the Pope of Rome did not overly intimidate him, when push came to shove. Moreover, push did come to shove, because Henry had a serious political problem. He had no male heirs. Rival factions already vied for position in a looming power vacuum-driven feeding frenzy, even while the King was still in his prime. The infamous War of the Roses (which started from such a power vacuum) still lived in the memory of older generations in Britain; much the same way Vietnam is still alive in the memory of older Americans today. Nobody wanted another War of the Roses.

The story of Henry's bed hopping through six wives, and many mistresses, is a long and complicated one; full of intrigues that had much to do with Catholic and Protestant factions trying to gain favor in his court. Henry's ruthlessness is the stuff of popular song and legend. However, our purpose is to trace the development of major ideas in church history, so we do not have much space for this historical bunny trail. Suffice it to say, that Pope Clement VII refused to grant Henry a divorce from his first wife, Catherine of Aragon. The Pope's recent reconciliation with Emperor Charles V forced him to favor German wishes, if they did not violate church doctrine. [2] Catherine was Charles' aunt. Clement could also truthfully claim that Roman Catholicism taught against divorce and remarriage.

Why can we not give Clement the benefit of the doubt here? We can, and even should, if we isolate the issue only to the marriage, and leave political motives out of it. Certainly, the Catholic Church takes a hard line on divorce; even if it legalistically ignores New Testament exceptions that allow remarriage—which did not apply to Henry's case. Nevertheless, the Papacy often gave "annulments" to royal marriages for lesser reasons than potential civil war. One could argue Henry's case only as a "lesser of two evils" that considered saving lives in the national "big picture." There is another reason we can give Pope Clement the benefit of the doubt on his denying Henry a divorce.

Henry used bizarre interpretations of Leviticus 18:16 and 20:21 as his biblical reason for allowing the divorce. His lack of an heir would not have flown because he had a daughter, Mary. He wanted a male heir, or at least more than one sickly girl. Any scholar should have seen through his bad reasoning. Henry claimed that his conscience troubled him deeply over his union with his brother's wife. Catherine of Aragon had been the widow of Henry's deceased brother, Arthur, before Henry married her. Leviticus forbade committing adultery with the wife of a still-living brother, not marrying a brother's widow. We know this because Deuteronomy 25:5 commanded marrying a brother's widow if she had no sons—a practice called *levirate marriage*. Marriage only lasts until death parts a couple, anyway. (Rom. 7:1-3)

Henry carefully engineered the rise of Thomas Cranmer as Archbishop of Canterbury, in March of 1533. Pope Clement confirmed the decision. Both Pope and King later found that Cranmer's creampuff-like personality hid alarming political and theological beliefs. Cranmer had secret Protestant views, despite his outward political bendiness in Henry's hands. A month after his appointment, the new Archbishop voided Henry's marriage to Catherine of Aragon, and sanctioned the King's new wife, Anne Boleyn. Soon, Anne gave birth to a daughter, who would one day rule as the formidable Queen Elizabeth I.

The Pope threatened a ***bull*** of excommunication against Henry VIII. King Henry escalated by ramrodding several legislations through Parliament that nullified the Pope's authority over the Church of England. Henry had himself declared head over the English church, replacing the Papacy with the Crown, except in powers of ordination. (Nobody was stupid enough to want another lay investiture controversy.) Thus, the first stage of the English Reformation had nothing to do with Reformed theology. Archbishop Cranmer kept his secret sympathies hidden for much of Henry's reign.

The English situation nevertheless threw the ecclesiastical situation into a state of flux, which made it more open to Reformation influences. God redemptively used Henry's lustful verse splitting and Cranmer's spinelessness, just as He had once used the evil motives of Caiaphas and Pilate. Even so, Archbishop Cranmer worked toward Protestantism as far as his loyalties to Henry allowed; which was not much, at first. Henry insisted the Church of England stay doctrinally Roman Catholic, except for its non-submission to the Pope. Cranmer sometimes got the King to vacillate a little, yielding to Protestants on limited points. Sadly, near the end of his life, Henry VIII reverted to hardline Romanism (though still minus the Papacy). This cost the lives of several Protestant martyrs.

The real English Reformation went on mostly behind the scenes, at the grassroots level. This made it all the more effective. As early as 1520, a secret alliance of pastors and lay scholars regularly studied Luther's writings at a pub called "The White Horse Inn." Included in this "league of extraordinary gentlemen" were Thomas Bilney, Robert Barnes, William Tyndale, Miles Coverdale, Archbishop Cranmer, Nicholas Ridley, Hugh Latimer, and Matthew Parker; names that show up in church history books as great reformers and teachers. Bilney, who shepherded the Whitehorse Pub group, led both Cranmer and Latimer to the Faith. All but Parker and Coverdale would die as martyrs.

Miles Coverdale, while in exile, produced, with Cranmer's assistance, the first complete English Bible in 1535; and had it printed, most likely at either Zurich or Antwerp. They then exported finished editions back to Britain with help from another closet reformer of Cranmer's circle—Thomas Cromwell (~1485-1540), not to be mistaken for the later Puritan "Lord Protector," Oliver Cromwell. (Oliver descended from Thomas' sister. Her offspring later took Thomas' surname, long after Cromwell's execution, perhaps once it became clear that Protestantism had won the heart of England.)

A legal and political genius, Thomas Cromwell had drafted Henry VIII's anti-papal laws. He had the reputation of a ruthless manipulator; a survival skill learned, first as the assistant to the infamous Cardinal Woolsey, and then as King Henry's advisor. This "survival skill" eventually failed him during that last career opportunity. Few who got so close to the King could survive Henry VIII's whimsical and volatile temper. Having hitched his chain to Henry's second wife, Anne Boleyn, during her rise, Cromwell spiraled into disfavor in the years after her execution. The continual slander of him to Henry by old-line nobles and Catholic sympathizers greased the skids. The nobles resented Cromwell's common origins; and the Catholic partisans, his Protestant leanings.

While, at times, a backstabbing "lawyer's lawyer," there is some evidence that Cromwell sincerely cared about church reform, and his country. His motives seemed, and likely were, however, sometimes murky. He did much to advance Reformation teaching within the Church of England, a good deal of it behind the scenes. Not three years after the first release of Coverdale's Bible, the first of three new editions (each authorized by King Henry VIII) came out in England. It is difficult to imagine how this could have happened without the knowledge and support of Thomas Cromwell.

This emboldened other Bible translators in their work. These added pro-Reformation study notes, many of which simply exegeted the text. This often looked bad to traditional ***episcopal*** oriented church leaders and royalists. John Rogers finished William Tyndale's work, releasing it as the *Matthew Bible* under the pseudonym "Thomas Matthew." This shielded his covert translation work during times of sporadic persecution. Tyndale's Bible became the basis for the *Great Bible, Bishop's Bible*, and the *Geneva Bible* from 1560 to 1599. These translations released so many new editions because the English language expanded so rapidly during that century. This greatly increased the availability of Scripture to all who could read. It also ensured that English-speaking peoples could compare church practice to a New Testament model with growing consistency and precision.

The Bible translation explosion of the 1500s enriched the English language in ways people rarely value today. It expanded vocabulary from the flat Middle English of a century before; to the rich Early Modern English used by William Shakespeare. [3] When Shakespeare wrote his plays, three generations after Tyndale, Early Modern English proved itself a vehicle for high art. None of Shakespeare's plays would make much sense to an audience without a working knowledge of Tyndale's English Bible, a main source of "the Bard's" poetic allusions. The Renaissance, Humanist translation work, the printing press, and better lay education under the Tudor Dynasty all helped; but Bible translations and the Reformation-driven thirst for God's word provided the passion.

Translators often had to invent new English words for Hebrew and Greek terms and ideas for which the English of the time had no equivalent. Then they aggressively educated pastors and lay leaders who used the new translations. Literacy and expanding ones vocabulary became spiritual priorities for those given the gift of God's word in their own language, often for the first time. Our language was the outcome—or at least it once was.

As the English language collapses in our own day, idea categories blur, erase, and become trivialized by a culture that dumbs people down. What attitude should our church cultures have toward language skills? What attitudes about language use should we reward, and which should we stigmatize? Are all "big words" really that scary, too confusing, and bad for people? What about today's prideful, popular demand for a "McTheology" that reduces words, and the ideas they carry, to less than what they are? The Bible is self-evidently a complex set of many literary forms translated for us from other languages. Should we not treat vocabulary as a tool that helps us express its ideas more precisely and truthfully?

Although people can abuse any tool through pride, that does not make the tool itself useless or counterproductive. The common or Koinae Greek of the New Testament is rich and multi-layered compared to today's video and text messaging reduced English. Do American church cultures encourage or discourage people from increasing their literacy and language skills today? What should we reinforce at a time when powerful forces seek to erase or make simplistic mockeries out of important biblical ideas on so huge a scale?

The Protestant Reformation drove the idea of universal literacy; that all children should attend school and learn to read—something we take for granted. Luther, Calvin, and Zwingli each strongly advanced universal education; the principle of *Sola Scriptura* made this a logical necessity. [4] This, at that time, novel idea left an enduring footprint on Western Civilization. Certainly, one does not need to be a Christian to appreciate the boon of universal literacy. It is, however, important to recognize the origin of ideas, and the forces that gave them traction on the road to becoming widespread practices.

We live in a day when utopian thinking in American education tries to hide the impact of biblical faith on our history from new generations. [5] There is a reason our society looks more and more like a dystopia each year. I remember a time when this was not so. A Polish college student recently captured in her thesis a balanced historical view on the effect of the Reformation on Early Modern English.

> *In the Modern English period, the beginning of which is conveniently placed at 1500, numerous new conditions began to play an important role, conditions that previously either had not existed at all or were present in only a limited way, and they caused English to develop along somewhat different lines from those that had characterized its history in the Middle Ages. The new factors were the printing press, the rapid spread of popular education, the increased communication and means of communication, the growth of specialized knowledge, and the emergence of various forms of self-consciousness about language.*
>
> *The role of English was given impetus by the Protestant Reformation, which placed a religious duty of literacy on all, and provided national texts for the purpose: the vernacular Bible and Prayer Book.* **Marta Zapala-Kraj, *The Development of Early Modern English: The Influence of Shakespeare on Early Modern English***

Henry VIII's third wife, Jane Seymour, died after giving birth to his long desired son, who came to the throne at age nine as Edward VI. Edward became England's first real Protestant monarch in faith and conscience, rather than political pragmatism. Archbishop Cranmer now worked more openly to advance the Protestant cause, though he was still one of the less radical of England's reformers.

With the general liberty brought on by Edward's rise to power came increased confusion in church affairs. One might argue against the young King's Reformation-based convictions (as many did) by superficially citing that "God is not the author of confusion." (1 Cor. 14:33) Yet that would not be a sound analysis of the full picture. It would misapply the passage to history. By the mid-1500s, Calvinism penetrated both England and Scotland. The English reformers were themselves divided into several camps. This was only the kind of "confusion" that Jesus warned would sometimes result when people put Him first.

> **"Do you suppose that I came to give peace on earth? I tell you, not at all, but rather division. For from now on five in one house will be divided: three against two, and two against three. Father will be divided against son and son against father, mother against daughter and daughter against mother, mother-in-law against her daughter-in-law and daughter-in-law against her mother-in-law."**
>
> ***Luke* 12:51-53 (NKJV)**

The above passage describes the situation among Henry VIII's children quite well.

Each of the three following monarchs, whom Henry directly sired, represented three major factions in the nation. Young Edward favored the newer radical Calvinistic element. These would settle for nothing less than a biblical church, purified of what they called "popery." They later became the Puritan, Nonconformist, and Separatist movements. At the opposite end of the spectrum, Mary was the reactionary. She demanded unconditional return to Roman Catholicism by any means necessary. Elizabeth understood the need for change, but favored a more gradual approach. She embraced a range of conservatives, some with doctrinal and liturgical positions but slightly changed from Catholicism; others, wanting a Lutheran-style state church, with Transubstantiation left open to civil debate.

Archbishop Cranmer prepared some "articles of religion" designed to help smooth out the bumps. He submitted these to a council of six theologians, among them the famous Scottish Calvinist reformer, John Knox. Knox later pioneered the ***Presbyterian*** movement for church government in Scotland. This method of church leadership replaced archbishops with a board of elders or presbyters; just a step farther along from what Cranmer was doing in submitting the articles to the six. We will cover changes in church government in the next chapter.

By 1553, it became clear that the frail young King Edward was dying of tuberculosis. That meant trouble. Mary Tudor came next in line to the throne, the Roman Catholic reactionary daughter of Catherine of Aragon. By the time of Edward's death, the majority of England had become Protestant. Nevertheless, in the battle for succession, Parliament reversed Cranmer's ruling on Henry VIII's marriage to Anne Boleyn. It declared his marriage to Catherine of Aragon legal. This removed any potential to challenge Mary's rise to power based on her legitimacy. History remembers Mary Tudor as "Bloody Queen Mary." People named an alcoholic drink after her in the 20th century, consisting of vodka and tomato juice, called a "Bloody Mary." Odd, the historical footprints one leaves.

Not just reactionary in personality, Mary reflected the Roman Catholic paradigm of her times. She tried to impose her religion from the top down upon a people whose grassroots sentiments the Reformation had already won over. Queen Mary launched the most intense persecution against Protestants England would ever see. Her first victim burned at the stake was the Bible translator, John Rogers, who died in February of 1555. Crowds of well-wishers cheered for him as he was marched to the flames, showing how odious the dictates of Mary were to the average person. She had Hugh Latimer killed also, that same year.

Not satisfied, the Queen had bigger fish to fry, if the reader will excuse the expression. If Mary could strike at the highest bishop in the Reformed camp, she could not only rid herself of a big political foe, but also score a major propaganda victory. This seemed a great strategy to her. Unfortunately, Archbishop Cranmer simply did not seem cut out for heroic displays like burning alive on principle. (It was that whole, "him being a notorious creampuff," thing.) Cranmer denied his faith while imprisoned by Mary, and signed a document to that effect. The Queen hoped to discredit the English Reform Movement by this, and never intended to stay Cranmer's execution. She only delayed it to milk the recantation for all it was worth. This was not her only miscalculation.

People are often more than what they seem on the surface, especially when the Holy Spirit gets hold of them. At the hour of his public execution, Cranmer received a fresh infusion of courage from the Spirit. He loudly took back the denial of his faith, and somehow held the hand he had used to sign the document to the flames, burning it before the fire reached his body. [6] Crowds watched and heard, as he screamed out his last sermon in the blaze—one of personal repentance.

A contemporary of these martyrs, John Foxe, collected accounts of the heroic deaths under Mary's bloodbath. He published them in a paper that set England even more strongly into Reformation convictions. He later combined that paper with other records of martyrs from throughout church history, and across Reformation Europe. English reformers soon re-published it as *Foxe's Book of Christian Martyrs*—a work still well known in Evangelical churches today.

Insecurity and poorly thought-out ideas often drive reactionary personalities, no matter what belief system they hold. (The Protestants had them, too.) Mary had been married to the son of Emperor Charles V, Philip, who would soon become King Philip II of Spain. She felt cursed by her own inability to give her husband a child. Her neurotic phobias seized on the idea that she went childless because God was punishing her for not doing enough to execute "His judgment" against Protestant "heretics." This sallow wretch of a woman kept the persecution on until her death in 1558. While the carnage did not equal that seen by the Dutch Reformers under the Spanish rule of her husband, nearly 300 persons died at the stake. Over 50 of them were woman and children. [7]

By the time of her demise, Mary's reign had become so repulsive to the English people, that many welcomed the moderate Protestant Elizabeth I to replace her. Elizabeth, though more a politico than a reformer herself, would go on to become one of the greatest monarchs England had ever known. She restored many of the reforms of her half-brother Edward, but insisted that change move more slowly, to the frustration of the emerging Puritan Movement. While she may not have been the best thing for those wanting to fast track a fully purified church, she appeared to be the best thing for England as a whole.

That likely was God's best. England now carried in its national womb the embryos of a series of "great awakenings." Each would unfold in its turn, from then on until the 20th century.

## THE ROMAN COUNTER-REFORMATION AND THE COUNCIL OF TRENT

By the mid-16th Century, the Papacy had begun to get its act together into an effective response against the Reformation. The more theology-minded Pope Paul III replaced Clement VII in 1534. He was the first of several popes who not only sought to crush the Protestant movements, but to pick up Pope Adrian VI's desired reforms against clerical and moral abuses. Church historians have called this the ***Counter-Reformation***.

The Reformation was a huge shock to the Roman church system. Imagine this system was an individual. The shock would compare to that of a person having his arms or legs cut off, and being unable to do normal things people find second nature. Accustomed to absolute church authority, and to considerable amounts of political influence over far-off places like Britain; the forces of reform and the secession of the Church of England frustrated Rome in a way akin to what a fresh amputee might feel. If the Roman Papacy really equaled *the Church*, then it meant "the Church" was now a cripple. On the other hand, if the church was the "called-out ones" of Jesus Christ, then it had taken on new forms better able reach the peoples of the late 2nd Millennium.

Either way, the Reformation forced the Papacy to respond. Part of that response had to deal with the most glaring of the institutionalized abuses that had brought on all the trouble to begin with. The Papacy now welcomed Conciliar Movement ideas, which it had rejected bitterly only a hundred and fifty years before. They fit them to a Romanist agenda, but it still brought administrative reforms that cleansed abuses from the religious orders and local parishes. [8] This overhauled the systems for getting indulgences, removing the "Tetzel-like" elements. Still, it left the assumptions underneath the idea of indulgences unaddressed. Pope Paul III also embraced the Christian Humanists. These had usually stayed neutral, except the few that had wanted a revolt in Luther's day.

Inquisitions continued, notably in Spain, where an important change of structure occurred. Queen Isabella and Francisco Cardinal Jimenez made a lively go at pro-papal reform, which history recalls with both horror and satire. The Spanish Inquisition however, despite its focus on heresy, answered to the Spanish Monarchy, not the Pope. Catholic monks still peopled its investigative arm, however. In Christendom-styled social systems, which continued in Catholic countries, heresy was still a civil crime. The Spanish Inquisition zealously cleaned up personal sins in the priesthood. Yet that most odious and lampoon-inviting deviance remained, precisely because nobody saw it as a perversion.

The last stab of a long-buried Greek-Semitic mingling of worldviews had people trying to "save the soul," even if it meant putting the body to a cruel death. This produced bizarre delusions in the perpetrators, and much worse in the victims. Inquisitors really believed they were helping their victims to eternal salvation. The religious drive in man's fallen nature cannot create healthy spirituality. That takes a genuine regenerative work of the Holy Spirit that no ritual or religious system can generate. Unwillingness to deal with doctrinal corruption the same way as moral and administrative kinds, led to schizoid forms of church reform more in Roman Catholicism than in the Reformation.

Some of the Reformed systems also suffered such incidents of schizoid inconsistency. The freer Reformation-based approach to Bible truth, however, in time, led Protestant countries to the tools to reject such things within their own systems. By "freer" I mean not only more freedom of human choice, but freedom for the Holy Spirit to move in people whose hearts were touched by Scripture and worship forms in their own tongues. In contrast, force of arms from outside of Rome, through the Italian Revolution of the mid-19th century, abolished the last inquisitions. [9]

As the Dominicans drove the medieval inquisitions, Jesuits became the heart of a more broad-based Counter-Reformation. This movement did not make the mistake of relying too much on inquisitions that could no longer penetrate all of Europe with impunity. Unlike the Dominicans, the original Society of Jesus did not grow from the desire to be a front line force against Protestantism. The vision of its founder, Don Inigo de Onez y Loyola, was that of evangelizing the Muslim world. Yet, Ignatius Loyola, as people came to call him, had also placed obedience to the Pope in the central place of his mission statement.

Some of Loyola's followers, like Francis Xavier, went on to do missionary work in the Far East. These began to see the inadequacy of that Roman Catholic mission model of religion by imperial force from the top down. Of course, not all Catholic missions had operated that way, even during the worst of times prior to the Reformation. The feel of this method's "normality" at the time was yet another side effect of the fusion of *Christianity* with *Kingdom* intrinsic to the Christendom model.

The Popes of the Counter-Reformation knew one thing fairly well. They needed soldiers with cleaner hands than the stereotyped "Dominican henchmen" to lead an effective charge against Protestantism. Jesuits combined Christian Humanist and Renaissance individualized education with submission to the Pope. They became perfect front-line troopers for the ideological battle. Few groups have so successfully preserved both intellectual versatility and singleness of purpose. Usually an institution ends up sacrificing one for the other.

The changes of the Counter-Reformation created much of the Roman Catholicism people know today. These came primarily out of the Council of Trent. Pope Paul III called this synod at the prodding of Emperor Charles V in 1545. It lasted, off and on, through a checkered history of twenty-five sessions, until 1563. Scheduling has always been a powerful political tool for quietly controlling outcomes. This council habitually voted on its most vital doctrinal issues when the fewest delegates were present (72 out of about 2000). [10]

Unlike the Council of Constance, with its proportional body of churchmen from all affected nations, Italian bishops with a smaller bloc of Spaniards controlled Trent. These dominant parties were directed by Jesuits, notably Diego Lainez and Alfonso Salmerone, who were tied by special oaths to the Pope. They saw to it that a most rancorous anti-Protestant mood prevailed. Trent was a "universal council" in name only. This was so even if one equates the Roman Catholic subset to the "universal church whole," as Roman Catholicism tends to do. In other words, not even a truly representative ratio of Roman Catholic bishops was present.

In these ways, the Papacy engineered the doctrinal decisions at Trent. The wording in some of their statements shows that their perceptions were somewhat distorted; especially about what they thought most Protestants believed about the ***Doctrine of Justification by Faith***. Even some of the bishops present could not shake the idea that Jesuits now defined doctrine largely around whatever they thought Luther would hate. [11]

A long list of ***anathemas*** damned anyone who believed in justification by grace alone through faith. This happened even over the objections of several astute Romanist theologians. They pointed out that this particular part of Luther's theology had a firm basis in both Scripture, and the teachings of Saint Augustine of Hippo. [12] One of them, English prelate, Reginald Cardinal Pole, could hardly be accused of being a Luther sympathizer. He had worked with "Bloody Queen Mary" to try to re-Romanize England!

Listed below is a small sampling of pertinent canons from Trent about the doctrine of Justification by Faith. The Jesuit bloc tried to word many of them to skirt the accusation of Pelagianism. Yet, in substance, these canons reveal that Trent had the doctrinal effect of reinforcing many of the accumulated distortions examined earlier. They also removed plainer, more Bible-centered views from further attention.

> *CANON XI.-If any one saith, that men are justified, either by the sole imputation of the justice of Christ, or by the sole remission of sins, to the exclusion of the grace and the charity which is poured forth in their hearts by the Holy Ghost, and is inherent in them; or even that the grace, whereby we are justified, is only the favour of God; let him be anathema.*
>
> *CANON XII.-If any one saith, that justifying faith is nothing else but confidence in the divine mercy which remits sins for Christ's sake; or, that this confidence alone is that whereby we are justified; let him be anathema.*
>
> *CANON XV.-If any one saith, that a man, who is born again and justified, is bound of faith to believe that he is assuredly in the number of the predestinate; let him be anathema.*
>
> *CANON XXIV.-If any one saith, that the justice received is not preserved and also increased before God through good works; but that the said works are merely the fruits and signs of Justification obtained, but not a cause of the increase thereof; let him be anathema.*
>
> *CANON XXV.-If any one saith, that, in every good work, the just sins venially at least, or-which is more intolerable still—mortally, and consequently deserves eternal punishments; and that for this cause only he is not damned, that God does not impute those works unto damnation; let him be anathema.*
>
> *CANON XXX.-If any one saith, that, after the grace of Justification has been received, to every penitent sinner the guilt is remitted, and the debt of eternal punishment is blotted out in such wise, that there remains not any debt of temporal punishment to be discharged either in this world, or in the next in Purgatory, before the entrance to the kingdom of heaven can be opened (to him); let him be anathema.*

Until Trent, biblical assurance of salvation was maybe an unintentional casualty of the Roman church-state fusion. Now it received condemnation as if it were heresy. In contrast, what does the Apostle John say about why he wrote his first general epistle?

> **10 He who believes in the Son of God has the testimony in himself. He who does not believe God has made him a liar, because he has not believed in the testimony that God has borne to his Son. 11 And this is the testimony, that God *gave* us eternal life, and this life is in his Son. 12 *He who has the Son has life*; he who has not the Son of God has not life. 13 I write this to *you who believe* in the name of the Son of God, that you may *know* that you *have* eternal life. *1 John* 5:10-13 RSV**

Verses 10-13 clearly states the plain biblical argument against this portion of Trent's dictates; "**He who believes in the Son of God has the testimony in himself.**" John wrote to those who believed on the Son of God that we might *know*—present tense—that we *have*—not *might have*, not *could potentially have*—eternal life. Post-Trent Roman Catholicism says we cannot know any such thing, except by a direct revelation from God. Nevertheless, God has spelled it out in His revelation to all believers, right here, in I John.

Other beliefs also received *anathemas* at Trent. The Council tried formally to make *the Church* Universal synonymous to the Roman Papacy. It finally made the huge leap of declaring church tradition equal in authority to the Scriptures. The argument went that the church decided which books became Scripture. This was not even a half-truth in the sense that they stated it. The church only *discovered over time through research* that certain writings, directly connected to apostles or their associates, had divinely inspired properties; like fulfilled prophecy.

The Council made the ***Apocrypha***, rejected as Scripture long before by earlier church councils, fully canonical. They did this to support unbiblical practices in the church. Some read a prayer-for-the-dead teaching, after the fact, into an incident recorded in one of the *Maccabees* accounts. [13] This was a logical fallacy, at best.

In fairness, we should recognize that Trent granted safe passage to the German Reformers so that they could present their views. In that, they did better than the Council of Constance. The Council also revamped the entire Catholic clergy. Seminaries went up in every bishop's see, with accountability systems that, even a few decades earlier, would have been unthinkable. A moral and administrative reformation was definitely underway, despite the problems already discussed.

While Trent allowed some leeway for future dialogue with the Reformers, the direction of such discussions had to go only one way. This is one reason why talk of Protestant reunification with Rome today is ultimately a superficial, feel-good solution. It trivializes a complex issue. Vatican II, the most recent and ecumenical of Roman Catholic councils, affirms all the rulings of Trent and Vatican I (1870). [14] Vatican I made Papal Infallibility a dogma. It became more than just awkward for Rome to place Scripture above Tradition without admitting to being in the wrong. This dynamic reduces even recent, emotionally genuine concessions to the Reformation to a form of doublespeak.

It is not that I think modern Roman Catholic Ecumenicals are not sincere—quite the opposite. It is common sense idea mechanics. The Vatican's past reactionary stances (Trent and Vatican 1), have painted the Papacy into a corner. The system cannot admit to ever making substantial erroneous doctrinal decisions in the past, even if it wants to. One cannot have meaningful negotiations with someone who cannot admit to being partly wrong in a significant way. Recent apologies from Popes John Paul II, Benedict XVI, and now Francis I, over past persecutions, while emotionally genuine, do not address the core issues. They admit that Rome might have been wrong to persecute, but not in their reasons for doing so.

Reformation-based churches, and their descendants, have no such intrinsic roadblock to prevent them from being able to admit wrongness in their more reactionary teachings. This does not mean Catholics and Protestants cannot work together effectively to be salt in the world. We can work well together for social reform, traditional marriage, and against abortion, for example. Nor does it mean that we, as individual members of Christ's body, cannot recognize spiritual integrity in other individual Christians across denominational lines. We should treat each other with love, dignity, and respect.

One way doing this is by thinking past the stereotypes. Love also demands the door be open to share a biblical gospel, should we become reasonably convinced we are not dealing with Spirit-led influences in the other group. Even stereotypes sometimes reflect actual patterns. People need the opportunity to define themselves as individuals, however. People are usually more complex and diverse than the groups they grew up in. Yet, the influence of that group exists to varying degrees, and in varying mixtures. That is true of us, too, in ways we are often least aware of. People who complain that this is too complex need to grow up! We are not dealing with one-size-fits-all Catholic (or Protestant) units, but individuals.

The market place of ideas must stay open between individuals, even if the exchange can work both ways, and even at the risk of being misunderstood. Jesus, toward the beginning of his last Passover evening talk, in John 13-18, said in 13:35 that the world would recognize His disciples not by creeds or confessions; but **"by the love you have one for another."** Love sometimes must say things that others do not want to hear. At others, love must agree to disagree, knowing our inability to see another person's heart and motives.

Unity of the Faith in ***agape*** love is not the same as clerical uniformity encased by a hierarchical religious system. The existence of such systemic uniformity does not create true church unity even where it goes unchallenged. Medieval and Reformation history shows that clerical and ritual uniformity can even hide a severe lack of love-based unity. It also can mask a widespread deficit of genuine conversion among the members of the visible church. Like real spiritual regeneration, leaders cannot mandate reform from the top down. It must grow, painfully, and often in ways that to earthly eyes appear disorganized and non-uniform, from the grassroots up.

## BIBLIOGRAPHY


1. Cooper, Bill; ***After the Flood***, p. 43; New Wine Press, W. Sussex, England (1995)
2. Shelley, Bruce L. ***Church History in Plain Language*** (2nd Edition), p. 266, 1995, Word Publishing, Dallas, Tx.
3. Shaheen, Naseeb (1999), ***Biblical references in Shakespeare's plays***, University of Delaware Press, p. 18.
4. Dr. Riemer Faber, ***Martin Luther on Reformed Education***, *Clarion* Vol. 47, No. 16 (1998), (Online at http://www.spindleworks.com/library/rfaber/luther_edu.htm) Dr. Riemer Faber is professor of Classics at the University of Waterloo in Ontario, Canada
5. David Barton, ***Revisionism: How to Identify it in Your Children's Textbooks***, Wall Builders (http://www.wallbuilders.com/libissuesarticles.asp?id=112) (Note: *While Barton is often accused by leftist sources of being a revisionist, I have found him far more quick and willing to self-correct his own material, when he finds he has made an error, than any of his detractors have been. He writes articles revealing his own past mistakes, or the discovery of evidence that calls into question a source he once used. Barton's position is not the straw man that many Wiki sites portray.* ***He does not believe that all the Founding Fathers were Christians, but that Colonial America thought within a Christian worldview that generally honored and built on, rather than disparaged or ignored, the Bible***. *This would be self-evident to anyone who bothered to read the source documents of that era, even those by American Revolution Era deists. (Who were a small, but significant, minority.) Nor is Barton a proponent of "morality myth American history," like the fabricated story of Washington chopping down the cherry tree. He is concerned, rather, with powerful ideologues in education, who effectively edit out what is objectively present in the documents of the time. A good example of this would be history textbooks that fail to mention the main reasons Pilgrims and Puritans came to America, as if Christianity had little to do with their motives. I would challenge people to check his books out for themselves.*)
6. Foxe, John; ***Foxe's Christian Matyrs of the World***, p.503; (1571) revised by Moody Press
7. Ibid. pp. 510 - 584
8. Op cit. Shelley, Bruce L., pp. 273-274
9. Hunt, Dave; ***A Woman Rides the Beast***, pp. 128-131; Harvest House (1994), Eugene, Or.
10. Walker, Williston. ***A History of the Christian Church*** (4th Edition), pp. 509-510; 1st Edition 1918, 4th Edition 1946, Charles Scribner's Sons, New York, NY.
11. ***Storia del Conc. Di Trento***, v. 453; edited in Milan in 1844; see also Von Dollinger, J.H. Ignaz; ***The Pope and the Council***, pp. 68-69, 78; London, 1869
12. Op cit. Walker, Williston, pp. 505-506
13. Geisler, Norman L. and MacKenzie, Ralph E.; ***Roman Catholics and Evangelicals***, p. 162 points 4 & 6, also pp. 334-335; Baker Book House (1995)
14. Flannery, Austin O.P., gen. ed., ***Vatican Council II: The Conciliar and Post Conciliar Documents*** (revised edition) vol. 1, p. 412; Costello Publishing (1988)

# 17

# THE REFORMATION ERA: PART 4

## A DARK SIDE TO THE REFORMATION

We touched on the growth of anti-Semitism in the church, starting in the 2nd Century with Marcion, and moving through the Medieval Age. In many ways, this ugliness grew more perverse and virulent as time went on. It is to the eternal shame of the Reformers that they ignored this corruption of Christianity, and even sometimes reinforced it. Luther himself passionately denounced the Jews in terms that sometimes made it sound as if they were knowingly in league with Satan, as a race. [1] Portions of his booklet-sized rant, *The Jews and Their Lies*, even read like a Hitler speech. This went far beyond the needs of a reasoned expose against institutionalized rejection of Jesus as Jewish Messiah. [2]

Luther, at first, seemed sympathetic to Jews, owing to their frequent poor treatment by many Catholics. He saw this as an opportunity to reach out to a number of them. When the Jews he reached out to did not convert to Christ, he seemed very much to turn on all Jews with extraordinary viciousness.

In those days, priests, and preachers—indeed, most everyone—routinely stigmatized whole people groups based on bad experiences with an individual or a small sampling of the given group. Ethnic bigotry was a cultural institution, back then. It was bad, and dumb, but it characterized the times. Our society shows a foolishness poles apart, when it endorses self-destructive ideas and behaviors through undue fear of intolerance. The latter is, in fact, a long-term over-reaction to the former—another example of the Pendulum Effect. The idea that Jews deserved abuse for the role some of their ancestors played in Christ's death was the stupid conventional wisdom of Luther's day. It warped how that culture understood the words of Jesus and Paul, and how they applied them to relationships with Jews in later eras.

Jesus had once said, **"You are of your father the devil"** to the Jewish religious leaders who had plotted to murder him. These men had no excuse for their self-righteous blindness to Scripture, as most Jewish scholars understood it in the century before the birth of Jesus. Daniel 9 gave a timeline that had many of them expecting the Messiah in that generation. Christ was fulfilling detailed prophecies on a huge scale. [3] Even non-Christian Jewish writers of the 1st century, like Josephus, wrote of the miracles of Jesus as if they had happened. [4]

It is also true that, as individuals, we are either **"children of God"** or of the **"serpent's seed."** (Gen. 3:15) It is only possible to be *for* Jesus or *against* him—there is no neutral ground, according to Scripture. This applies to everyone, from all social stations, and cultural backgrounds. It has more to do with a person's teachability and desire (or lack of it) to know God, than with the values of their upbringing, even an anti-Christian one. There were many Jews alive at the time of Christ who had the same background as those religious leaders, and yet responded well to the gospel. God looks at the heart response.

People cannot help where they were born or raised. An honest person, however, reaches a place where they ask, at least on some level, whether the things their family taught them to believe as children are actually true. Any honest thinker must question their fundamental assumptions about reality at some point. Otherwise, they cannot claim to care about truth. In John 4, Jesus told the woman at the well that God insisted on being worshipped **"in spirit and in truth."** A Samaritan upbringing had conditioned the woman to be hostile toward Jewish concepts of worship. Many worldviews, today, condition the people that grew up within them to be hostile to Christian ones. Jesus effectively told her that neither Jewish nor

Samaritan worship forms impressed God. He also said more or less that, in terms of prophetic knowledge and Messiah's descent, **"salvation is of the Jews."** (John 4:22)

Jesus did not attack the woman because she was Samaritan. He simply leveled the playing field in a way that showed Jews were no better than Samaritans were. He also told her the truth, though it touched on something offensive to a Samaritan viewpoint.

God does not give everybody in this life the same amount of information or natural ability to use in searching for truth. Yet, Scripture also says that God considers this; **"But he who did not know, yet committed things deserving of stripes, shall be beaten with few. For everyone to whom much is given, from him much will be required..."** (Luke 12:48a NKJV) The important thing is an honest heart. Anyone with that can follow the evidence, and consider the possibility that they might be wrong about things they have not heard all sides about. The religious leaders Jesus rebuked had more detailed prophetic information available on how to recognize their Messiah than they needed. Daniel 9 even provided a timeline that had many scholars of Jesus' day sure that he would come in their generation.

Luther's words against the Jewish communities of his era went far beyond what Jesus said. They came only after many centuries of Christians persecuting Jews in various ways, and portraying them in degrading images and theater roles. Printed posters of the day, called "broadsides," often had anti-Semitic themes, particularly in Germany. One sample I examined was a popular etching from 1475. It showed several traditionally dressed Jewish scholars on their knees, sucking the udders of an enormous, demonic-looking sow. As if to suggest bestiality, some of the scholars approached the animal's hindquarters. This explicit, disgusting imagery was not rare for that period. People even posted broadsides where children saw them.

Late Medieval culture excluded Jews from most aspects of society because they were not in fellowship with the church. Popular literature often characterized them as sorcerers and loan sharks. Their kosher diet frequently kept them healthier than the average European, and banking was one of the few social institutions open to them. Centuries of habit and rancor make for powerful walls. Luther had unrealistic expectations if he imagined Jewish leaders would flock to Christ just because the Reformation had a new approach to Christianity. To outsiders, like the Jews, the differences were not terribly evident. The warped view of Jesus the churches gave to them, by now, reinforced tremendous barriers.

What does Scripture really say about the current relationship of the Jews, as a people group, to what God is doing in this age? Paul, speaking as a Jew, wrote:

> **I am speaking the truth in Christ, I am not lying; my conscience bears me witness in the Holy Spirit, that I have great sorrow and unceasing anguish in my heart. For I could wish that I myself were accursed and cut off from Christ for the sake of my brethren, my kinsmen by race. They are Israelites, and to them belong the sonship, the glory, the covenants, the giving of the law, the worship, and the promises; to them belong the patriarchs, and of their race, according to the flesh, is the Christ. God who is over all be blessed for ever. Amen.** ***Romans*** **9:1-5 RSV**

> **I ask, then,** ***has God rejected his people? By no means!*** **I myself am an Israelite, a descendant of Abraham, a member of the tribe of Benjamin.** ***God has not rejected his people whom he foreknew.*** **Do you not know what the scripture says of Elijah, how he pleads with God against Israel? "Lord, they have killed thy prophets, they have demolished thy altars, and I alone am left, and they seek my life." But what is God's reply to him? "I have kept for myself seven thousand men who have not bowed the knee to Baal."** ***So too at the present time there is a remnant, chosen by grace. Romans*** **11:1-5 RSV**

Paul addressed something more to the point of having a proper Christian attitude toward the Jews, later, in Romans 11. Comparing Gentiles to "wild olive branches" and Jews to cultivated ones, Paul wrote:

> **17 And if some of the branches were broken off, and you, being a wild olive tree, were grafted in among them, and with them became a partaker of the root and fatness of the olive tree, 18 *do not boast against the branches.* But if you do boast, remember that you do not support the root, but the root supports you. 19 You will say then, "Branches were broken off that I might be grafted in." 20 Well said. Because of unbelief they were broken off, and you stand by faith. Do not be haughty, but fear. 21 *For if God did not spare the natural branches, He may not spare you either.* 22 Therefore consider the goodness and severity of God: on those who fell, severity; but toward you, goodness, if you continue in His goodness. Otherwise you also will be cut off. 23 *And they also, if they do not continue in unbelief, will be grafted in, for God is able to graft them in again.* 24 For if you were cut out of the olive tree which is wild by nature, and were grafted contrary to nature into a cultivated olive tree, *how much more will these, who are natural branches, be grafted into their own olive tree*? 25 For I do not desire, brethren, that you should be ignorant of this mystery, lest you should be wise in your own opinion, that *blindness in part has happened to Israel until the fullness of the Gentiles has come in.* 26 *And so all Israel will be saved,* as it is written: "The Deliverer will come out of Zion, And He will turn away ungodliness from Jacob; 27 For this is My covenant with them, When I take away their sins." 28 Concerning the gospel they are enemies for your sake, *but concerning the election they are beloved for the sake of the fathers.* 29 For the gifts and the calling of God *are irrevocable. Romans* 11:17-29 (NKJV)**

This passage speaks clearly on several points. Christians have no business feeling superior to Jews. God can and will someday restore national Israel to a faithful relationship with Him through Christ. This does not describe the situation today, when individual Jews may receive Christ, but the nation *as a nation* rejects His messianic claim. Christianity rests on the foundation of a Jewish worldview, as it had developed by the early 1st century. God loves the Jews, and His calling of them as His chosen people is irrevocable or non-reversible. Verse 26 does not mean individual salvation happens to every single Jew; any more than every individual baptized and raised in the church experiences automatic salvation. It means that Christ will restore and save all the components that make Israel a nation.

The Book of Revelation speaks of 144,000 Jewish evangelists from the Twelve Tribes of Israel that God seals before the beginning of Great Tribulation. (Rev. 7:1-9) What this means is that the church does not replace Israel. Faithful members of both may lay claim to the broader category of being God's elect. The term *elect* includes all who have believed God throughout history, from before the nation of Israel existed, to believing Israel, to the church, then to those who believe after Christ removes the church. During the Church Age, Jews who believe the claims of Jesus belong also to the church, as seen in the following Scriptures.

> **There is neither Jew nor Greek, there is neither slave nor free, there is neither male nor female; for you are all one in Christ Jesus. *Galatians* 3:28 (NKJV)**

> **Do not lie to one another, since you have put off the old man with his deeds, and have put on the new man who is renewed in knowledge according to the image of Him who created him, where there is neither Greek nor Jew, circumcised nor uncircumcised, barbarian, Scythian, slave nor free, but Christ is all and in all.**
>
> ***Colossians* 3:9-11 (NKJV)**

**For there is no distinction between Jew and Greek, for the same Lord over all is rich to all who call upon Him.** ***Romans*** **10:12 (NKJV)**

**And when there had been much dispute, Peter rose up and said to them: "Men and brethren, you know that a good while ago God chose among us, that by my mouth the Gentiles should hear the word of the gospel and believe. So God, who knows the heart, acknowledged them by giving them the Holy Spirit, just as He did to us, and made no distinction between us and them, purifying their hearts by faith."** ***Acts*** **15:7-9 (NKJV)**

**Therefore remember that you, once Gentiles in the flesh—who are called Uncircumcision by what is called the Circumcision made in the flesh by hands—that at that time you were without Christ, being aliens from the commonwealth of Israel and strangers from the covenants of promise, having no hope and without God in the world. But now in Christ Jesus you who once were far off have been brought near by the blood of Christ. For He Himself is our peace, who has made both one, and has broken down the middle wall of separation, having abolished in His flesh the enmity, that is, the law of commandments contained in ordinances, so as to create in Himself one new man from the two, thus making peace, and that He might reconcile them both to God in one body through the cross, thereby putting to death the enmity. And He came and preached peace to you who were afar off and to those who were near. For through Him we both have access by one Spirit to the Father. Now, therefore, you are no longer strangers and foreigners, but fellow citizens with the saints and members of the household of God, having been built on the foundation of the apostles and prophets, Jesus Christ Himself being the chief cornerstone, in whom the whole building, being joined together, grows into a holy temple in the Lord, in whom you also are being built together for a dwelling place of God in the Spirit.** ***Ephesians*** **2:11-22 (NKJV)**

God setting one nation apart from all other nations is different from God calling an assembly of people out of many nations (including some from the special nation). That is the contrast between Israel and the church. It's an "apples and oranges" thing. Both are fruit, but they are not the same. Both are elect, but in somewhat different senses. The issue here is the reliability of God's promises. God made unconditional promises to Abraham, and his offspring through Isaac. He did not let Israel off the hook if they rebelled as a nation, nor does he allow individuals to get away with sin. Saying the church permanently replaces Israel as the chosen people, however, makes God a liar.

**And the LORD said to Abram, after Lot had separated from him: "Lift your eyes now and look from the place where you are-northward, southward, eastward, and westward; for all the land which you see I give to you and your descendants** ***forever." Genesis*** **13:14-15 (NKJV)**

Forever, in the original Hebrew, means *forever.*

**"And I will establish My covenant between Me and you and your descendants after you in their generations, for an** ***everlasting*** **covenant, to be God to you and your descendants after you. Also I give to you and your descendants after you the land in which you are a stranger, all the land of Canaan,** ***as an everlasting possession;*** **and I will be their God."** ***Genesis*** **17:7-8 (NKJV)**

While individuals and entire generations, through disobedience, may not experience the benefits of the promise, God's promise itself does not become void. God does not disown the Jewish nation permanently, but revisits them in a future generation. For example, He judged the Jews of Jeremiah's generation, but restored those of Zechariah's. The promises to the Jews as a nation remained.

Ideas have consequences. Because the Reformation failed to deal with the heresy that the Church permanently replaced national Israel as God's elect, hatred of the Jew continued. I do not think it random that Nazism later arose in Germany—Luther's main sphere of influence and that of much folk Roman Catholicism. The racism of the Nazis did not originate in an historic and cultural vacuum. Hitler, like anybody, absorbed ideas commonly held true by much of the culture around him. One strong factor in his thinking was the rise of Darwinism—a subject for a later chapter. Still, the anti-Semitism of Luther and many medieval Roman Catholics grew into the popular culture a young Hitler later embrace.

Adolf Hitler built upon this grassroots view of the Jews, adding what he thought was a scientific base by applying Darwinism socially. He brought forth the Holocaust by carrying both out to their logical conclusion.

## THE ANABAPTISTS: ANATOMY OF A SPIRITUAL MOVEMENT

Luther also alienated many commoners by his stand with the princes against the Peasant Revolt, not the Jews only. His work had started a great process that began to elevate Scripture back up to its proper place in the church. Yet Luther himself could not live with some of the implications of what that process eventually brought forth.

A unique pattern emerges whenever new movements of the Holy Spirit happen. Students of history can see it whether the Spirit moves in distinct generations or in specific ethnic or social groups. It also shows in movements that affect whole regions of multi-ethnic peoples or many generations. The pattern is consistent enough that we can build historical models of it. Church history often calls these events "revivals."

A revival model begins with God pouring His Spirit out upon a small number of people. They have a powerful experience, which points them back to the Bible in a meaningful sense involving personal repentance from sin. They also show a conversion from a self-centered existence to a more God-centered one. These people then rapidly win others to the Faith, with signs of the Spirit's love and power following them. The signs are not always identical to what Mark 16 describes, but they do confirm in some way that God is at work.

People often display an exhilarating rush of spiritual power during this stage of the pattern. Spontaneous works of God in their lives mark this, which often contrast sharply to the established religious ways of thinking and doing things. This happens because of an observed tendency for church systems to drift from Holy Spirit to humanly engineered control. This even takes place when the intent of the system is to prevent such drift. The new spiritual work is unrestricted and exciting. Those qualities then begin to attract people with other motives than repentance and regeneration. This is where the first crisis hits.

Growing numbers want to experience the excitement for its own sake. Sometimes this involves manifesting some of the more spectacular gifts of the Spirit in ways that draw attention to the gifted. Others come, as Simon the Sorcerer did in Acts 8, to use the movement's backdrop to get spiritual power over people, and gather a following. These "wolves in sheep's clothing" mix with the genuine converts, often indistinguishable from them for a time, even to the discerning. Fringe elements also appear that are perhaps more immediately visible, but which can become just as dangerous.

The **"mystery of iniquity"** (2 Thes. 2:7) describes a process of spiritual decay that usually does not progress to its deadly final phase overnight. Soon, weird **"winds of doctrine"** (Eph. 4:14) and fanatical altered states of consciousness begin to manifest among the movement's fringe. This often happens at a time when genuine, but immature believers are numerous, and therefore most apt to misapply Scripture in some way on a large scale. As we saw earlier, this can make both fringe practices and outright false teaching seem plausible.

Having experiences for experiences' sake slowly seems to wrestle against an emphasis on knowing God through His word, by the leading of the Spirit.

This can entangle even genuine believers for a time. What I call the "fringe" moves so closely among those truly stirred by God that people who only see things from the outside confuse the two. Even after those inside the movement begin to suspect that something is wrong, outsiders associate the fringe with the mainstream. This danger comes with the first phase of most spiritual movements in Christianity. The fact that it takes time to discover what is really going on complicates the problem. It would be wrong to judge anyone too quickly, based on superficial qualities that could have several explanations. Why would this be so hard to discover? Does not Scripture say that we can tell by their fruit? Yes, but fruit takes time to mature and ripen.

Sometimes new believers, and even zealous young teachers, are so excited with what God is doing, and so inexperienced, that they say and do dumb things—I know I did. I would not want people to judge the validity of my conversion and ministry based on some of the things I said and did during my early years in the Faith. In fact, I did so many weird and dumb things as a new believer that I got disgusted with myself for a long time. Then there are clashing temperaments and styles of using spiritual gifts—differences God intends us to have for good reasons. Some church movements attract people of one God-given personality profile and repel those of another—not for sin issues, just individual natures. Ideally, Christian movements should make room for a variety of temperaments.

Christians should not react against people simply because they are different. God created people with many temperaments and gifts to add flavor to the church, and to offer a rich variety of service. Differences do not always represent a clash between the true and false. Even when people behave in ways that look questionable to us, things may not always be what they seem. Discernment takes time and attention. Satan sometimes uses this scenario to discredit the public perception of a genuine movement of God. At such crisis points, the spiritual movement might go one of several directions. It may move to deepening study and application of biblical lifestyle patterns, or reject such changes, which brings stagnation. The movement could even break apart and die.

To survive in a healthy form, Christian movements must apply leadership models that discourage fringe elements, but encourage the Bible's teachings, and ethics. This time of streamlining is both necessary and dangerous. It is necessary because it keeps the fanatical and self-promoting out of leadership. It can be dangerous because the temptation to rely too heavily on method, instead of the Holy Spirit, quietly asserts itself. History has shown that every leadership system in the church succumbs to at least some of the dangers built in to this phase of the model, given enough time. Some do so faster than others do, but none is immune. Systems that succumb too much become relics. Men end up trying to do what only the Holy Spirit can; regulate God's work in people's lives.

Avoiding method and church organization has near instant risks, however. It is misinformed to view spontaneity itself as a sign of spiritual life, as if logic and structure are at war with passion and intuition. That slant in church culture is itself the product of a worldly philosophy, as we shall see later on. The Holy Spirit is not against developing good methods for doing things. He leads us to think and plan, too. Just because things can go wrong at a given stage of development does not mean we can skip that stage, or that the Spirit wants us to leave that step out of the process. That is true of forming church leadership structures and learning to reason philosophically from a book-by-book interpretation of Scripture.

Most pastors today would agree that biblical order aids healthy church life. Most would also agree that over-rigid, control-oriented micro-management does not. Religious systems can unconsciously encourage one or the other as they grow and take on a life of their own. If that "life" is more humanly inspired than of God, systemic decay becomes only a matter of time and degree. This is true whether the driving force is Jewish legalism, Greek philosophy, and Roman law, or today's ***Materialism, Rationalism***, and ***Postmodernism***.

Often people are not aware of the decay process until it is well advanced. God then must do a new work to get the church back on track. The question we need to ask of ourselves is whether this progression is inevitable or can we delay and possibly even prevent it with God's help? The choices Jesus offers the Seven Churches in Revelation 2 and 3 imply that this progression is not inevitable, which suggests we can delay and prevent it. That is consistent with Jesus' calling his disciples the "salt of the earth." (Matt. 5:13) Salt, among other things, inhibits decay.

Speaking from my own familiar church system, I see many Calvary Chapel pastors giving serious thought to this. It appears that "Calvary," as a movement, has shifted into the "streamlining" phase of this model. Some have lamented this. The older I get, however, the more convinced I am that it is a mistake for believers who want deeper levels of spiritual experience to abandon churches at this stage. They do so because they mistakenly assume that more focus on studying and applying the word means human intellect has deadened the revival. The opposite is usually true. Despite dangers, perceived or real, the greatest promise for lasting spiritual power and ministry matures during this streamlining phase. The Holy Spirit does not grow bored with us as we mature. Nor is there growth without risk.

Jesus addressed this problem when he spoke about wineskins. After the disciples of John the Baptist had compared the way Jesus' disciples did things with the way the Pharisees and their own group practiced religion, the Lord told them a parable.

> **He told them a parable also: "No one tears a piece from a new garment and puts it upon an old garment; if he does, he will tear the new, and the piece from the new will not match the old. And no one puts new wine into old wineskins; if he does, the new wine will burst the skins and it will be spilled, and the skins will be destroyed. But new wine must be put into fresh wineskins. And no one after drinking old wine desires new; for he says, 'The old is good.'"** ***Luke*** **5:36-39 RSV**

New wine is often idiomatic for a new work of the Holy Spirit. The wineskins would be akin to the cultural traditions and religious systems that contain the Spirit's expression through the church in this world. Old wine in old wineskins is the aged relic of a past work of the Spirit, fondly enshrined, but largely stagnant and fermented by the yeast of foreign elements. (Yeast is usually a metaphor for corrupting influences, or at least for foreign ones, in Jewish tradition.) The old skins are well worn and comfortable, but it is in the new where God's most current work tends to happen.

The ***Anabaptists***, also called the "Radical Reformers," were a textbook picture of this model. Some who had worked with Luther came to believe, through their own study of Scripture, that he was, as one put it, just "a half-way reformer." [5] Others, in Switzerland, came to feel this even more strongly about Zwingli. Felix Manz and Conrad Grebel, who began as Zwingli's followers, argued that nobody followed the pattern for baptism described by Scripture. Spiritual regeneration, in the New Testament, came after a person believed the gospel. Conviction of sin led to a convinced change of heart. Since babies lack the capacity to know what they believe, Manz and Grebel declared that it was useless to baptize infants. They held that such baptisms were not valid because of this.

Many Evangelicals and Fundamentalists of today agree with this basic Anabaptist belief. It seems only sensible that the most natural biblical order of things should be the right way. Earlier, I wrote that the name *Anabaptist* was actually a misnomer used by Zwingli and other enemies of the Radical Reform Movement; based on the incorrect feeling that they were re-baptizing people, when Ephesians 4:5 said that there could be only "one baptism." Of course, Anabaptists agreed that there was only one baptism. They simply felt that it was the one performed after the biblical pattern of educated adult immersion. Manz and many of his followers were put to death for this conviction not only by the Roman Catholics; but also by other Reformers, notably Zwingli and the Lutherans.

Another leader, Balthasar Hubmaier, influenced the movement after Grebel died of plague in 1526, and the martyrdom of Manz a year later. Hubmaier fled to Moravia, escaping Zurich after denying his beliefs under torture on the rack. This denial troubled him greatly, and once in Moravia, he began to preach his true convictions again. In his 1526 Short Apology, he wrote, *"I may err – I am a man – but a heretic I cannot be... O God, pardon me my weakness."* [6]

Hubmaier was one of the few Anabaptists to promote the necessity of government, Just War Theory, and Christian service in the military. This brought him into sharp conflict with Hans Hut, father of the Anabaptist sect known as the Hutterites. Hut preached that the world would end in 1528. Despite his missing that one by at least 500 years, Hut continued to gather followers. His sect later simplified his message around the core Anabaptist beliefs, sharing similar roots as the Amish and the Mennonites. Sects of Hutterites eventually migrated to North America, and settled in isolated villages and farms, mostly in the Northwest.

In contrast, Balthasar Hubmaier's views helped moderate the Radical Reform Movement, refining the things they got right, like the rejection of Baptismal Regeneration, into coherent doctrines. This enabled the cross-pollination of such teachings to other reform movements, and worked against the general Anabaptist tendency toward sectarianism. His education and study of Scripture was deeper than what often prevailed during the early Radical Reform Movements. Hubmaier's teachings also survived him, and the test of time. Those teachings helped turn what could easily have become a rabble with a superficial popular theology into a maturing belief system.

Hubmaier's faith also proved strong in the end. Austrian forces martyred him, after the Catholic Prince Ferdinand took over Moravia and captured him. Balthasar died by burning at the stake, while the authorities tied a stone around his wife's neck and tossed her into the Danube. The Moravian Brethren churches grew around his teaching.

I try to show both the strengths and weaknesses of the reforming movements of church history, and their leaders, for several reasons. One is to discourage romanticizing them. Christians have often walked a thin line between healthy admiration and idolizing the heroes of the Faith. This is as true of 21st century American believers, removed from most persecution harsher than losing a few friends; as it was of late 4th-early 5th century Roman Christians idolizing the 1st, 2nd, and 3rd century martyrs. The variables differ, but the damage to realistic spiritual expectations remains. It is possible to respect the role models of the Faith, and to learn from them, without reducing them to idols—of either Catholic or Protestant form. The Bible does this well in how it depicts both the triumphs and failures of figures like Noah, David, and Peter.

The Anabaptists, like most Christian movements, began with many grassroots groups in loose alliance. Some governed themselves by straightforwardly biblical teachings, others by quite bizarre ones. Even the "straightforwardly biblical" groups tolerated some ideas we would find cultic. They were "straightforwardly biblical" only in a selective sense. For example, many held to a view similar to what we call "soul-sleep" today—the idea that dead believers sleep until the Resurrection. Most had a ***sectarian*** approach to the church, though some did not. *Sola Scriptura* was, and possibly still is, a work in process, moving from core teachings to secondary ones.

It did not take long for a "fringe element" to manifest itself among the Anabaptists. If the reader thinks calling such fanatical forces "satanic" is too strong a term, consider the following profile.

*He claimed to be a prophet, then Jesus Christ returned, and the reincarnated King David. He took the wives of his male followers as his own harem, and made the men go celibate. He also advocated the overthrow of the government, until government forces finally surrounded him and his followers, and burned them together in the house that he had fortified against "the coming Armageddon."*

Am I describing David Koresh, and his "Branch Davidian" cult of Waco Texas, in the 1990s? Not this time—it is the story of Jan of Leiden, in Munster Germany of the 1530s, an Anabaptist leader who took himself far too seriously. Satan played a re-run at Waco.

Another Anabaptist fringe preacher, the dreadfully uneducated "street prophet," Melchior Hoffman; spun raving sermons about end-time prophecy. One of his rants made Strasbourg into the "New Jerusalem" of Revelation 21:2-27. Somehow, he did not notice the absence of gold-paved streets, and the fact that God had never lowered Strasbourg to earth.

Clearly, Melchior did not draw his ideas from the text in its literary and historical context, but let impulse, emotion, and, likely, demonic visions sway him. I say "likely demonic" for a simple reason. At this point in church history, the Holy Spirit worked through many forces to build sound interpretive skills for Christians who now had an available Bible. Melchior's reading of his own private, contextually disconnected impulses into Scripture created a shallow illusion; that Bible prophecy can mean anything anyone wants it to mean, if they can just get enough people to follow them. This is a delusion that traps immature believers today, and keeps unbelievers from taking the Bible seriously.

People called Hoffman's followers the Melchiorites. Though I call him a "fringe element," that is not to say that he did not divert a sizable number of Anabaptists from the truth for some time. Melchior is visible as a "fringe" teacher largely through hindsight. His sect is a historical curiosity, today. Other forces grew from the Anabaptist Movement, like Hubmaier's teachings, which shaped modern Protestant theology in healthy ways. When Roman Catholic polemics look at the Anabaptists, they usually take the Melchiorites as their test sample. They infer that his views characterized the whole movement. This is unfair, but it illustrates our model in how people view movements from the outside.

When God brings revival, He raises up a group of people who in some way genuinely turn back to Scripture. Satan (who is a real entity with a real agenda) then tries to cluster a tightly packed wad of freakish elements around and within this group. The bizarre elements, if successful, become confused with the godly ones by those outside. They penetrate and pollute the godly movement if the latter fails to confront them, thus destroying the work. This progression takes the time necessary for the spiritual battle to unfold, and the "fog of war" to dispel. What seems clear to us, after the fact, is not so clear to the immature movement at the time. If I were an enemy to the spread of the gospel, this is exactly the kind of scenario I would try to engineer.

Fanaticism and violent government reaction ravaged much of the early Anabaptist Movement. Some, like Jan of Leiden, and Melchior Hoffman, called for and practiced armed revolt. A young preacher, ironically swayed at first by Melchior Hoffman, went on to become part of the solution. Menno Simons despaired over the havoc wreaked by the lack of discernment shown during the early stages of the Anabaptist Movement. He began to pick up the pieces by teaching simply out of the Bible, book-by-book and verse-by-verse. Although he avoided reasoning much from the text into the issues of his day, even to where it is sometimes hard to know his positions even on basics, like the Trinity; Simon's simplified teachings most often came from what he knew of the Bible's thematic and historic context. God blessed his heart and his work. Others imitated his example.

Soon, small groups were studying the Bible this way all over northern Europe. Both the Roman Catholic Church and the mainstream reformers continued to persecute such people bitterly. Yet, these small groups gave a powerful testimony freed from the earlier fanaticism that had marred the Anabaptist Movement. The followers of Menno Simons eventually called themselves *Mennonites* after his first name. Many eventually immigrated to America, and they are still around to this day.

## CROSS-POLLINATION: DAWN OF THE DENOMINATIONS

Lest we imagine that the more balanced Anabaptist fellowships, like those of Hubmaier and Simons, resembled our own late 20th–early 21st century independent churches too much; we need to remember perspective. Our "balanced Anabaptists" would view today's Evangelicals and Fundamentalists as the first reformers did them—heretical. We would not find their reasons biblically consistent for doing so. The reverse would also be true, were we to encounter groups today with some of the doctrines embraced by many Radical Reformers. Many might find that hard to understand because the Bible is clear.

One cannot accuse the Bible fairly or reasonably of being unclear because of such things. The differences among interpreters with logical and honest exegetical methods are not large enough. The Holy Spirit uniquely opens the comprehension of the Bible to believers who apply themselves. That is not the same as saying Scripture is otherwise unintelligible, just that those without faith do not discern its spiritual magnitude. (1 Cor. 2:12-14) After my conversion in 1978, I had a working grasp of the Bible in less than a year and a half, with only a high school education. It would have taken me many times longer, with full-time teachers, to understand it merely on an intellectual level otherwise. Even then, I would have still been blind to its significance and timeless relevance.

A more realistic explanation exists for why honest people, seeking the Holy Spirit's lead, see varied things from the same Bible. The many worldview assumptions, historical stresses, and intellectual tools used in its interpretation over 2000 years would naturally yield some variation. Yet these forces all have a human root. Different people were better equipped to see certain things in the Scripture at some periods of history than in others.

No writings of similar age do any better in terms of clarity, and most do considerably worse. It is foolish to fault the Bible just because honest people can see somewhat different shades of meaning in parts of it. That is true of any writings, ancient or modern. Not all variances are bad. Many truths have multiple dimensions and applications. Not all variances are contradictions, either. Many involve ranges of related possible meanings that sometimes each need to be tested.

What the Bible reveals about the nature of the church illustrates this. This topic came into focus as Luther, Calvin, and the Radical Reformers all sought better ways to apply what Scripture said about it. For example, even our "balanced Anabaptists" often went terribly wrong in their concept of the church. This often happens when people try to respond to a serious error. They fly to the opposite extreme from the first mistake, and end up making new and different ones. The Radical Reformers mostly formed ***sectarian*** movements, not ***denominational*** ones. That is, they came to see only their own insular groups exclusively as "the true church." Ironically, they made a different form of the same error as that of the Papacy—the extreme they so strongly opposed!

The Reformation was clearly a work in process.

Most people take the words *sect* and *denomination* to mean the same thing. This is not precisely so, in the historical sense. Christians that have a *sectarian* concept of the church believe that only their religious system has the truth, and that all others, no matter how similar in belief, are counterfeits. Believers with a *denominational* view see truth in other like-minded Christian movements. They have no trouble fellowshipping with believers from other groups. Christians who are "denominational" in this sense can embrace a unity of the Holy Spirit with believers from other church systems. They see them as members of the universal body of Christ. For example, though I am not a Baptist, I do not see my Baptist friends as "less Christian." That is not because I think doctrine is unimportant. Rather, the many commonalties outweigh the trivial differences.

The sad fact that people in denominational churches sometimes behaved in sectarian ways blurred the meanings of these two words. Today's independent fellowships (including the one I work in) call themselves ***non-denominational*** for a tragic reason. People have come to connect denominations with sectarian conduct. My bringing out the blurring of categories here is not just word wrangling. Words carry meaning. Nothing stops non-denominational Christians from acting in sectarian ways, too. When this happens, it can become too easy to imagine innocence, while waving the "non-denominational" flag.

The removal of the distinction between *sect* and *denomination*, however, makes such problems harder to address. *Issues that are far more important than this one suffer when meaningful distinctions vanish with the words that describe them.* This is especially true at a time in history when church cultures seem to feel that having a smaller vocabulary aids, rather than hinders, the communication of truth. While the latter may sometimes be true on an individual scale, in the short run, the long run reveals another story. What happens then is that people operate under an illusion that they really understand each other, until a catastrophic event tests the situation, and shows that they do not.

The cultural encouragement of small vocabularies creates lack of precision in conveying ideas. Important thoughts and distinctions are harder to express until eventually people lose knowledge of them. People can even become unaware that they are using the same words in the same way to mean very different things. This is not the same as being "a person of few words" in the sense of being self-controlled in our speech. The worst form of confusion is the kind that people do not know they have. Churches and nations have crumbled over less, though not usually instantly.

Of course, this particular blurred meaning, between *sect* and *denomination*, is a simple one, easily fixed by a little common sense. I bring it out to illustrate a major difference between the Reformation period and our own. The era of the Reformation was a time when languages like German and English gained precision. Western languages had to deal with new ideas introduced by a more available Bible, and an increasing number of books. Our own day is a time when precise language is rapidly collapsing, and important thought categories are becoming blurred and even erased. We often call this being "dumbed down."

We also live in a time when communication technologies artificially shorten attention spans, making it harder for us to think deeply. This has looming implications for our ability to preserve Bible-teaching churches today, which we will cover in later chapters.

The Bible's growing availability, plus new church systems, forced Christians in the Reformation Era to think more carefully on what the church actually is. How was it possible for them to affirm visible unity in the body of Christ universal under what seemed to be, and often were, chaotic conditions? In what ways were they successful, and in what ways, not so much? These are all important questions for us to ask. They affect our view of the church.

We might describe the Roman Catholic approach to "church" as semi-sectarian, at least relative to this topic. We cannot call it fully sectarian, because it still leaves room for the idea of "separated brethren" in Eastern Orthodox and Reformation churches. Yet, we cannot call it truly denominational, either, because it treats such "separated brethren" as second class Christians, cut off from the "true church." Because Trent defined "the church" as synonymous to the Papacy, no other outcome was possible within that framework.

To the traditional Roman Catholic way of thinking, the fact that denominations exist at all is scandalous. Medieval Christendom assumed that one church system equaled one church, as a universal whole. The Roman Empire had left its stamp on the church's self-image, yielding a rigid episcopal hierarchy that mirrored imperial government. It was more than just that, however. A sincere conviction often appealed to Jesus' prayer for unity in John 17, even if the imperial stamp had marked how they thought that unity should work. It is unreasonable to deny that an easily visible form of unity between churches suffered in the Reformation. It also had done so in the East-West split 500 years before. Church authority and structure do not lose all importance simply because people corrupt a form of it on a grand scale. That would not be true even after Christians corrupted many forms of it.

God's precepts are still true even when we screw them up.

History seems to suggest that God was slow to allow reform to come from outside the medieval church system, despite how bad it often was. It seemed that He really wanted to preserve structural singleness for the church in medieval culture, as long as it was possible to do so. Yet, this could not go on forever under the conditions that existed in post-Roman and Medieval Europe. Too much essential truth was in jeopardy, leaving too much at stake. A single church system was desirable as long as it had enough integrity to uphold its purpose. In the end, it was not God's purpose for the church to fuse the Faith with worldly ideas of what a kingdom should be. God would not let the Christendom model go on forever at the expense of righteousness, truth, or scriptural integrity.

The new denominational church ***paradigm*** removed a lot of human political power from the "upper church." It focused on the local church, and ceased to worry about whether people saw the upper church system as a single political unit. This new approach assumed that the Holy Spirit was capable of keeping the regenerate in sufficient harmony with one another locally. Pastors could come together and call representative church councils to handle regional issues as needed. Human imperfection and strife sometimes marked this new paradigm. Yet, the truths preserved and re-emphasized by it were no more expendable than those about Christ's nature were, 1100 years before. It was a needed course correction, but not without counter-currents and unintended side effects.

Despite such side effects, the church regained potential to be a spiritual organism made of God's people, instead of a distant political-religious caste ruling by fear. As with all potentials, this did not guarantee Reformation-based churches, or even individual Christians, would go there. Yet, many did. The dynamic of *Sola Scriptura* also took on a life of its own. God has promised that His word would never return void without accomplishing what He sends it out to do. (Is. 55:11)

The Reformation also preserved and restored the potential for the church, or at least a remnant of it, to regain its biblical character. That was so even if, as a side effect, one familiar application of biblical truth needed to give way for new ones. This was the ability for Christians to apply the Bible's principles on church unity by imposing only one earthly system in the West. Christianity already had a separate religious system in the East. As we saw, however, the cost of enforcing that one system masked even worse departures from unity in the Spirit, based on a biblical definition of love (1 Cor. 13). Jesus' prayer for oneness in John 17 was about something deeper than the shell.

Whether one views this as the lesser of two evils or as a necessary Spirit-guided process to wrest actual control of the universal church back from human imperial manipulations; at least three things are certain. One is that God allowed those manipulations, and even used them for a time to shape His work. He used the evil plots of men to work His plan of redemption in the crucifixion of Christ, so there is no moral trouble with God bringing good out of evil in church history. He never endorsed the evil. Secondly, God holds church systems accountable even in this life, just as he held the many governing systems of Israel accountable. God judged the governments of Israel in the Old Testament many times. He took them from patriarchy to theocracy to monarchy, and even made them conquered vassal states, without destroying the Jews as a people.

Thirdly, we in churches that sprang, either directly or indirectly, from the Reform Movements can never go back to the way it was before without losing more than we have gained. The ability to respond to fast-paced historical changes requires freedom to move, and local authority on the ground. Even with the advent of the Internet, distant authorities are not truly "on the ground," they only think they are. In reality, virtual "on the ground-ness" is like virtual anything else—one only sees filtered versions of the situation, not the situation itself. More importantly, doctrine has not outlived its day. Just as a ship must keep watertight integrity in its compartments, doctrinal integrity is still essential to a healthy church. A transition toward many church systems is good redundant engineering on the Spirit's part, so long as we maintain love for one another.

Consider how some of the modern denominations developed.

New and heartier breeds of flowers come through a process called *cross-pollination*. In the same way, many of today's Christian denominations came through a cross-pollination of ideas from one Reform movement into the others. The English Puritans were a mix of Knox's Scotch Calvinist Presbyterianism and the Anabaptist stress on a conversion experience, and believer's baptism; except with a denominational rather than sectarian view of the church. Out of them flowed the modern Congregational and diverse Baptist fellowships. The many Presbyterian denominations grew from Knox's Calvinism, too, but without Anabaptist views. Most Presbyterian churches still baptize infants because historical Christianity did through most of its history, even if not at the start.

Exporting Calvinism from Switzerland to the Netherlands, England, Scotland, and back to France, cross-pollinated biblical ideas to many groups. It eventually led to the breaking down of some of the walls that had divided the Reform movements so bitterly during Luther and Zwingli's day. It also sometimes helped to erect new ones. Calvin's followers developed on his ideas after his death, and amended them, sometimes in admirable ways, other times less so. One of the best known of those who built upon Calvin's thinking in the Netherlands was a theologian named James Harmenszoon. We know the Latin form of his name better, Jacobus Arminius, because history named his school of theology *Arminianism*.

Arminianism countered some extremes growing in third and fourth generation Calvinism. By this time, elements of speculation had entered parts of the Calvinist system. All have sinned and fallen short of God's standard. The wages of sin is death, such that eternal life is God's gift to the undeserving, paid in Christ's blood. God's grace saves us, when we put our faith in the work and person of Christ, not anything we initiate as a good work designed to earn God's favor. (Rom. 3:21-26, 6:23, Eph. 2:8-10) That is gospel truth promised by the word of God. By the early 1600s, some Calvinists began to speculate that exercising faith itself was a work; that faith came totally from God, and not at all the believer. This is true, in one sense, but not in another.

It is true in the sense that exercising faith involves a person making a real choice. Yet, people cannot come to Christ from their fallen state without the Father drawing them through the Holy Spirit (John 6:44, 65, 1 Cor. 12:3). The blindness Satan puts on all who are naturally born into this fallen cosmos makes it impossible for anyone to perceive God or come to Him, without help from the Holy Spirit. (John 3:3-8, 2 Cor. 4:3-4) The sense that the speculations in Calvinism were not true is in the assumption that *faith is a work*. This would lead to some half-baked ideas in both camps. Arminius stressed that God saved us by grace *through faith*, and that Scripture makes a distinction between *faith* and *works of the law*.

> **9 So then *those who are of faith* are blessed with believing Abraham. 10 For *as many as are of the works of the law are under the curse*; for it is written, "Cursed is everyone who does not continue in all things which are written in the book of the law, to do them." 11 But that no one is justified by the law in the sight of God is evident, for "the just shall live by faith." 12 *Yet the law is not of faith*, but "the man who does them shall live by them." *Galatians* 3:9-12 (NKJV)**

A person can try to perform the works of the law without faith, and possibly get some of it right as far as outward appearances and even intentions go. Both Calvin and Arminius agreed that such a performance, however shiny to onlookers, could not save anyone from their sins. Saving faith is something distinct from a "work" in the "trying to be righteous by keeping the works of the law" sense. Nor is Satan's power over the world so complete that the blindness he imposes on unbelievers makes faith impossible. Everyone has at least some light, which people may trust by faith or ignore. The light shines from Christ.

> **1 In the beginning was the Word, and the Word was with God, and the Word was God. 2 He was in the beginning with God. 3 All things were made through Him, and without Him nothing was made that was made. 4 In Him was life, and the life was the light of men. 5 And *the light shines in the darkness*, and the darkness did not comprehend it... 9 That was *the true Light which gives light to every man coming into the world*. 10 He was in the world, and the world was made through Him, and the world did not know Him. 11 He came to His own, and His own did not receive Him. 12 *But as many as received Him, to them He gave the right to become children of God, to those who believe in His name*: 13 who were born, not of blood, *nor of the will of the flesh, nor of the will of man, but of God*. 14 And the Word became flesh and dwelt among us, and we beheld His glory, the glory as of the only begotten of the Father, full of grace and truth. *John* 1:1-5, 9-14 (NKJV)**

Not only does the image of God in man reflect from even a fallen human conscience, though in a distorted form; faith is foundational to the very human ability to know things—anything. Hebrews 11:1 is just as true for the unbeliever as it is for the Christian. Unbelievers simply hope for a different ultimate reality than Christian do.

> **Now faith is the substance of things hoped for, the evidence of things not seen.**
> ***Hebrews* 11:1 (NKJV)**

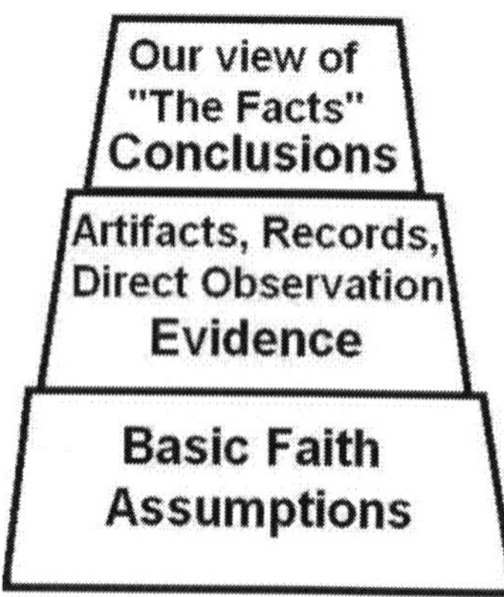


The word *substance* in Greek is *hypostasis*, *hypo* means *under*, and *stasis* speaks of the state of things. *Hypostasis* is that which undergirds, or holds up, the state of things. The "state of things" includes that which we may observe and test, and how we know what we know about those things. If faith is the *hypostasis* of what we hope is true about reality, then faith undergirds how we interpret evidence and information. It colors how we fill in the blanks when we run out of evidence, and life still demands choices of us based on incomplete information. Nobody has complete information, except God. Faith is at the base of every set of worldview assumptions, ancient or modern. We can truly call such presuppositions *faith-assumptions*. Faith holds up all belief systems, not just Christianity. Here I do not mean faith-in-God, but *faith*, as in accepting *unprovable starting assumptions*.

Since everyone has the capacity to exercise faith, it is a matter of whether they do so in accordance with the light God gives them, to lead them toward Christ. This describes faith in its *epistemological* sense, as a foundation for knowing. ***Epistemology*** is the study of how we know things—the mechanics of how we know stuff. Some of Arminius' arguments brought out the common nature of faith to human knowledge, to turn the discussion back toward the *object* of saving faith—Christ. The Calvinists rightly stressed God's sovereignty. Yet, about three generations after Calvin, Calvin*ism* reached a phase that all schools of thought hit, eventually. In trying to distill Calvin down to easily teachable points, influential leaders within the movement began to oversimplify what Calvin actually said; even to the point of misquotation.

Arminius' chief opponent was a third generation Calvinist of the Dutch Reformed church, Franciscus Gomerus, who was born a year before Calvin died. A young man, Hugo Grotius, watched Gomerus debate Arminius first hand. He described Gomerus as a man of "deeply rooted faith," and a "forceful defender of the Calvinistic doctrine." Grotius also described him as a "mediocre scholar." [7] Arminius vastly outmatched Gomerus in both intellect and willingness to try to see things from both sides. This does not mean Arminius was right about everything. It just meant Gomerus lost the debate, and resorted to character assassination. He called Arminius a "Pelagian" without proving it, and tried to associate him with a local Jesuit priest. The observer, Grotius, became an Arminian.

After Arminius' death, the same thing happened to his followers as what had happened to Calvin's. As with Calvin, many of the extremes attributed to Arminius came generations after he died. His supporters also oversimplified his position, sometimes even more dangerously than Calvin's followers had those of Calvin; for at least the Calvinists erred on the side of God's sovereignty. Arminius himself laid a foundation for at least one of the errors attributed to him, however. He taught that Romans 7:14-25 only described Paul's experiences with the law before becoming a Christian. Paul wrote the passage in the present tense, however, which meant that he sometimes still had his little spiritual winters of failure.

Christians may likewise expect, sometimes, to experience spells of personal defeat, where they end up doing things they hate. (Rom. 7:25) This is not because God's promises, or the power of His Spirit failed, nor always even because the Christian is "trying to do things in his own strength," (although that is often the case). Sometimes God allows us to fail even when we do not want to, for reasons of His own. When He does, at least it is only temporary. Victory comes eventually, even if sometimes only in the end, as promised.

People often seem to think that Arminians do not hold to a doctrine of predestination. The real difference between Arminianism, and the ***5-point Calvinism*** that developed after Arminius' death, concerned how each group believed God made His decisions in election. Arminius and his followers stressed Romans 8:29-30 in their view.

> ***For those whom he foreknew he also predestined*** **to be conformed to the image of his Son, in order that he might be the first-born among many brethren. And those whom he predestined he also called; and those whom he called he also justified; and those whom he justified he also glorified.** ***Romans*** **8:29-30 RSV**

Arminius did not see God's predestination of the elect as governed by mere foreknowledge of choices people made for the gospel, as often claimed. He viewed the issue of predestination as relevant only to dealing with man as he became after the Genesis Fall. God did not predestine the majority of humanity to damnation simply because He created us, knowing that Adam would fall. He created knowing that, but that is not the same thing as programming man to fall. God predestined a way of redemption, based on the "Lamb slain from the foundation of the world." (Rev. 13:8)

In Arminius' view, God knew the future choices of every person, left to them, would end in damnation—just as Calvin did. God did not leave people to themselves. Election was still a work that began in eternity. The difference was that Arminius saw a role for human choice in the process—not as what determines God's election, but as a response to God's grace. In other words, God, in His sovereignty, gives people some space to choose, and holds them accountable for their choices. God is sovereign, unrestricted by anything except for His own good nature. He is free in His foreknowledge to consider human choices if He wants to, without making them the final determiner of election.

This conforms to how God treated Cornelius the Centurion. God acknowledged the man's prayers and generosity, but still directed him to Peter and the gospel. Cornelius' good works could never save him, nor were they sufficient to impel God legally to act in his behalf. Yet, God was free to consider them if He found them relevant in some way. Either way, Cornelius still had to hear the gospel and submit to Christ.

> **1 There was a certain man in Caesarea called Cornelius, a centurion of what was**
> **called the Italian Regiment, 2** ***a devout man and one who feared God*** **with all his**
> **household,** ***who gave alms generously to the people, and prayed to God always.*** **3**
> **About the ninth hour of the day he saw clearly in a vision an angel of God coming**
> **in and saying to him, "Cornelius!" 4 And when he observed him, he was afraid,**
> **and said, "What is it, lord?" So he said to him, "*Your prayers and your alms have***
> ***come up for a memorial before God.*** **5 Now send men to Joppa, and send for Simon**
> **whose surname is Peter. 6 He is lodging with Simon, a tanner, whose house is by**
> **the sea. He will tell you what you must do."** ***Acts*** **10:1-6 (NKJV)**

Romans 8:29 seems to allow for this idea about the role of God's foreknowledge in election, and likely even calls for it. Predestination, in this sense, is the outworking of God's predetermined grace; instead of an arbitrary decision that God made without regard to the Fall, where God simply preordained some to salvation and others to damnation. This is the positive side of Arminianism. It showed God predestining the elect without damning people who could not choose differently because God had individually cursed them to the pit before birth. The operative word is *could*. People are damned because they *would* not make any other choice in the matter, no matter how God caused light to shine on them, not because they *could* not. God is not morally obliged to try every means to reach those whom He already knows have made themselves unreachable.

Of course, God knew that most people would choose poorly before He created Adam. That is not the same as Him programming them to do so, or stacking the deck in such a way to force this outcome. People today often tend to assume that these things are the same, but they do so only by erasing real moral distinctions. Programming reduces Adam to the robot in the TV show and movie, *Lost in Space*. At a certain point in elapsed time, God has triggered him to self-destruct. That does not fit the human condition, nor does it fit any reasonable sense of justice.

"Stacking the deck" implies that God is both unjust, and has no valid reason to test His own creation because of His foreknowledge. Only the idea that sin is a devouring evil that humanity's earliest parents brought into the cosmos, (despite God's warning), fits the text, and what we see today. **"On the day you eat of it, *dying*, you shall die."**

Within the Arminian model, even the elect cannot simply choose salvation. It requires God's proactive grace that sets them up to make the right string of choices under providentially arranged circumstances. This ultimately involves how and when they hear and believe the gospel. In this view, the unsaved would not place their faith in Christ no matter what God's providence arranged. Without God's grace, and apart from God's sovereignty, nobody would find salvation. Today, moderate Calvinists recognize that this is not a matter of man's will trumping God's sovereignty. They might express the matter in different terminology, but they would agree that the human will, while not free in the absolute sense, does in fact have a real choice.

Although neither a full Calvinist, nor a full Arminian, I would suggest that the term *real choice* is better than *free will* for this discussion. The human will is self-evidently limited, at least by the range of choices in a given situation, and by its level of willpower. Even those with willpower supplied by the Holy Spirit, only have the level of strength that the Spirit desires them to have. **"I can do all things through Christ who strengthens me,"** assumes that the things one is doing fall within the will of Christ who strengthens. (Phil. 4:13)

What we today call *5-Point Calvinism* came in the wake of the Arminian debates. Calvin's successors reacted to Arminius' views on predestination in ways that Calvin himself likely would not have. This is particularly so on 2 of the 5 Points, *Limited Atonement,* and *Irresistible Grace*. Limited Atonement is the idea that Christ did not really die for all people, but only for the "elect." [8] This view calls for an unnatural interpretation of Scriptures like 1 Timothy 2:1-4 and 2 Peter 3:9. It also makes invalid assumptions and associations regarding God's will.

> **First of all, then, I urge that supplications, prayers, intercessions, and thanksgivings be made for all men, for kings and all who are in high positions, that we may lead a quiet and peaceable life, godly and respectful in every way. This is good, and it is acceptable in the sight of God our Savior, *who desires all men to be saved* and to come to the knowledge of the truth. *1 Timothy* 2:1-4 RSV**

> **The Lord is not slow about his promise as some count slowness, but is forbearing toward you, *not wishing that any should perish,* but that all should reach repentance. *2 Peter* 3:9 RSV**

These scriptures suggest that God has a genuine, though unrealized desire to save everybody. They also suggest a realm of limited, yet real, human choice. How else could any of God's desires go unrealized, unless He had willfully set aside some human domain where our own choices could bring forth their own consequences? The extreme Calvinist assumption is that this is a matter of God's sovereign power versus human will. There is a lot of evidence to suggest that the issue is not really about that, at least not completely. We cannot accurately view God as weak or ineffectual if it is also His sovereign desire for man to have a real choice. It would seem that, at least on some levels, an obstinate sinner could resist God's grace if that is how God designed things to work in His redemptive system. Not all grace is irresistible.

Proof that Calvin would not accept the doctrine of Limited Atonement, in the sense that later 5-Point Calvinists implied, comes from Calvin's own pen.

> *And the first thing to be attended to is, that so long as we are without Christ and separated from him, nothing which* ***he suffered and did for the salvation of the human race is of the least benefit to us.*** **John Calvin, Institutes, 3.1.1**

> *I approve of the ordinary reading, that he (Christ) alone bore the punishment of many,* ***because on him was laid the guilt of the whole world****. It is evident from other passages, and especially from the fifth chapter of the Epistle to the Romans,* ***that "many" sometimes denotes "all."*** **John Calvin, Comments on Isaiah 53:12**

> ***The word* many *does not mean a part of the world only, but the whole human race... It is incontestable that*** *Christ came for the expiation of the sins of the whole world.*
> **John Calvin, Eternal Predestination of God, *IX*.5**

A fuller list of Calvin's own words on the subject comes in Norman Geisler's *Chosen But Free: A Balanced View of God's Sovereignty and Free Will.*

Nevertheless, Calvinist opposition to Arminianism also sometimes had legitimate biblical concerns. Calvinists emphasized the sovereignty of God in the process of election, as it appears in Romans 9. *Sovereignty* is the biblical teaching that God, as Creator, has the right to dispose of His creation as he sees fit.

> **And not only so, but also when Rebecca had conceived children by one man, our forefather Isaac, though they were not yet born and had done nothing either good or bad, in order that God's purpose of election might continue, not because of works but because of his call, she was told, "The elder will serve the younger." As it is written, "Jacob I loved, but Esau I hated." What shall we say then? Is there injustice on God's part? By no means! For he says to Moses, "I will have mercy on whom I have mercy, and I will have compassion on whom I have compassion." So it depends not upon man's will or exertion, but upon God's mercy.**
>
> ***Romans* 9:10-16 RSV**

This part of the passage deals more with national election of Israel as God's chosen nation, than with election of persons for eternal salvation. Paul quotes Malachi 1:2-3, after citing Genesis 25:23, which only says, "the elder (Esau) shall serve the younger (Jacob)." Malachi spoke of the nations spawned by Jacob and Esau representatively. His words may not even mean that God hated Esau the individual, though He despised Esau's cavalier attitude toward his birthright and the blessing. Genesis shows Jacob and Esau at peace with each other, after Jacob returned from Laban, and when they buried their father together. Genesis does not show God singling Esau out for further individual disgrace, beyond losing birthright and blessing. There is a difference between a person and a nation figure-headed by that person.

Even so, Romans 9:15-16 applies to both national and individual election. In either case, the initiative belongs to God's grace, not to man's will. Only God can elect to reach out from eternity to save a nation or an individual, man cannot generate it from inside time and space. The issue appears to be irresolvable in some ways.

Both Arminian and Calvinist camps have since carried their opposing perspectives to logical, if sometimes contrived conclusions. Extreme Calvinists engaged in intellectual contortion to jam Scripture into the grid of Limited Atonement and Irresistible Grace. This erased the reality of human choice from their system, and produced a manufactured view of Divine Sovereignty. Likewise, extreme Arminians drifted from a biblical view of God's Sovereignty and Assurance of Salvation. They opened the door for relational insecurity to drive a "salvation" contrived by human method. (We will see how, later.) Extreme Arminianism fell to something Gomerus had unfairly accused Arminius of; a virtual Semi-Pelagianism where people felt "saved by grace, but kept by works."

Speaking again from within my familiar church system, I have heard Calvary Chapel pastors call themselves "Cal-minian," when asked where they stand on Calvinism and Arminianism. They are not trying to evade the issue. They are simply advancing an approach that places the Bible above systematic theologies, so that Scripture may address the issues naturally, on its own terms. Systematic theologies often have a historical shelf life, while the word of God is eternal. Systematic theologies try to express what Scripture teaches to the worldview of the period in which they developed. They are often necessary. Yet, they should be re-evaluated when new data affects the worldview the theological system serves. We live in such a time.

*When I speak of systematic theologies, I do not mean exegetically interpreted, book-by-book, verse-by-verse Scripture.* I refer to those layers of human reasoning that necessarily connect what Scripture teaches to the worldview of when and where the system formed. **"For by grace are you saved through faith, and that not of yourselves, it is the gift of God, not of works, lest any man should boast;"** is a straightforward statement of Scripture. *Calvinism* is a systematic theology to correlate that statement with other biblical data for European Christians of the last four centuries. Western European Christians of that period all had worldview assumptions, some of which have since proven not to reflect reality as well as once thought.

This book does not pretend to solve the Calvinist–Arminian conflict. It merely comes at a time when one of the worldview assumptions undergirding both sides in that debate needs re-evaluation. I speak of our assumptions about the nature of time and space. At the time of Calvin and Arminius, and until very recently, people viewed time as absolute, and disconnected from space and the objects in space. Just as most Christians thought the sun orbited the earth, until the 1500s, because that was what almost everyone thought; so many Christians, even today, still think of eternity as just endless amounts of time, stretching into the past and future. We did not have the vocabulary or intellectual tools to think of time any differently until the mid-20th century.

We now know with increasing experimental certainty that time is a part of space. It is not a constant. The rate that time passes locally decreases relative to the effects of gravity and velocity. This describes Einstein's Theories of General and Special Relativity in a nutshell. We also know that space has expanded because we can see that the light from distant galaxies shifts into the red end of the spectrum. Light waves from objects moving away from us shift to the red end of the spectrum, while those coming toward us shift to the blue. This implies that time had a beginning, just as the Bible says. It also implies that eternity is a state outside of time, not merely endless amounts of time stretching into the past and future.

*The Bible will always teach the predestination of the elect according to God's sovereign will.* This new knowledge about the nature of time however, opens the door for us to understand this better. *A Divine act, made from eternity, outside of time, to predestine a believer for salvation, is not in logical conflict with that believer also having a real choice inside space and time.* It may be that the sort of biblical language paradox found in the Calvinist–Arminian debate is exactly what we should expect. The Bible, after all, is a communication that ultimately comes to us from a Being who is outside the space-time continuum.

God sees the past, present, and future from a higher dimension, which has the properties of cause-and-effect; but from which all of time appears as a great eternal "now." His works and thoughts reflect that realm, and election is a work of God from the eternal. Science has learned experimentally in physics that time is a physical property, a created thing. Eternity is therefore not just endless amounts of time but something beyond. Scripture speaks of election and predestination from a divine perspective, above our linear time flow. It also speaks of human responsibility to "choose life" within our frame of reference in linear time.

The Calvinist view, with some Anabaptist influences, went on to shape Baptist and Fundamentalist denominations and movements. A moderate Arminian view came, through John Wesley, passed to the Methodist, Holiness, and Pentecostal churches. There is biblical truth in both positions. They are both right about what they uphold, but generally wrong about what they deny.

## BIBLIOGRAPHY

1. ***Time Magazine***, March 24, 1967, pp. 70-74
2. Martin Luther, ***The Jews and Their Lies***, (1543), Michael, Robert, ***Holy Hatred: Christianity, Antisemitism, and the Holocaust***. New York: Palgrave Macmillan, 2006, p. 112.
3. Flavius Josephus, ***Antiquities of the Jews, Book XVIII 3:3***, *circa* 100 CE – (Note: *Though some modern scholars have tried to discredit this section of Josephus for ideological reasons, the Josephus text is stylistically uniform and shows great internal and external evidence of genuine late 1st century authorship. A Syriac version also exists that never resided in the Vatican library, which is virtually the same in all the points that have to do with Jesus. For a better understanding of what the Jewish leaders of Jesus' day had available to them as far as prophetic information on Messiah and how later Jewish and Christian scholars obscured things, see also:* Smith, Chuck, ***The Search for Messiah***, The Word for Today Publishers)
4. Mark Eastman, Chuck Smith, ***The Search for Messiah***, *documents in detail the extensive degree to which Jews of the final century BC held a messianic expectation for the approximate generation in which Jesus was born, based on pre-Christian prophetic interpretation.*
5. Walker, Williston. ***A History of the Christian Church* (4th Edition)**, p. 436; 1st Edition 1918, 4th Edition 1946, Charles Scribner's Sons, New York, NY.
6. Vedder, Henry Clay (2009) [First published 1905].***Balthasar Hubmaier: The Leader of the Anabaptists***. LaVergne, Tennessee: Kessinger.
7. Rabbie, Edwin (1995). ***Hugo Grotius: Ordinum Hollandiae ac Westfrisiae Pietas, 1613***. Brill.
8. Norman L. Geisler, ***Chosen But Free***, *Appendix 2: Was Calvin a Calvinist*, pp. 199-205, Bethany House, (1999, 2001, and 2010)
9. Larry Taylor, ***Calvinism vs. Arminianism – A Discussion of Doctrine, What is Calvinism?*** See also, Smith, Chuck; ***Calvinism, Arminianism & The Word Of God - A Calvary Chapel Perspective***; both are available on line at (http://www.calvarychapel.com/library/smith-chuck/books/caatwog.htm)

# 18

# Reason and Renewal: Part 1

## Stalemate: The 17th Century Religious Wars in the Big Picture

The Roman Catholic Church found, in the Reformation, a religious movement it could not crush by political, military, or ideological means. Conversely, the Reformation found that it could only go so far in its battle to free the church from Romanism, largely due to its own divided nature. The Lutherans were almost as hostile toward the Calvinists as the Catholics. Both Lutherans and Calvinists alike hated the Anabaptists.

The Anglican Church had pro-Presbyterian Puritans resisting the pro-Episcopalian "high church" party, to the annoyance to Queen Elizabeth I; who had replaced Philip II's dead wife, Mary Tudor, on the throne. We saw that *presbyterian* describes a church government model led by a board of presbyters or elders. The word *episcopalian* refers to a church led by a hierarchy of bishops. A single archbishop, like a pope, patriarch, or the Archbishop of Canterbury, sits atop this ranking order. The Queen wanted reform happen in stages, at a pace her nation could absorb with order. Elizabeth desired stability in England, and fought the earliest of the major Religious Wars, with Catholic Spain, mostly at sea. The Royal Navy sank the Spanish Armada when it became clear that Spain intended to invade England.

As the long reign of Elizabeth I progressed, some in the Puritan camp began to see what the Anabaptists had seen on the continent for some time. As long as the Christendom state church social model prevailed, nobody in either secular or religious power would ever restore a truly New Testament styled church. It was not in their interests. Nowhere in the New Testament is there a hint that Christ and the Apostles wanted the church to fuse with a worldly state. Conversion happened to individuals, not states. The unholy injustices required to maintain the politics of a Reformed state church proved no less oppressive than what it took to sustain the Roman system. This group of Puritans began to formally separate from the Anglican Church, and became known as *Separatists* because of it.

Unlike most Anabaptists, the Separatists had a denominational rather than sectarian view of the church. They held that many individual Christians of good faith remained in the Anglican Church, but the religious system itself bore no resemblance to a church in the New Testament sense. They believed that the Anglican religious system had proved itself an anti-Christian institution, just as the Roman system had done. Separatists argued that first Rome, and now England, as kingdoms of *this* world, had subverted Christ's institution of the church. They formed local congregations to live out their right "as the Lord's free people." [1]

The Roman Catholic Church had a propaganda field day with so many conflicted Reformation factions. The regimented Counter-Reformation often made the bickering Protestants look silly to people who might otherwise have joined the reformers. In time, spiritual and ideological stalemates turned into political and military ones. State churches left no other outcome possible, if only because states tend to go to war with each other. The Catholic Church, though far from neutral in the wars of Europe, often at least gave an appearance of rising above the petty squabbles of secular kings. Rome, when the system worked on a political level, even sometimes brokered peace among her secular "children."

Now, the Catholic Church, through Catholic emperors, kings, and princes, wanted to take Protestant kingdoms and cantons by force. People had reduced the idea of church reform to a formula of cartoonish proportions, on both sides. If the political ruler was Catholic, the nation was Catholic—if Protestant, then Protestant. Few thought in terms of individual convictions yet, but that was beginning to change. As with all attempts to oversimplify complex problems, the results were not simplicity, but more complications.

The Religious Wars proved both intricate and far-reaching. I certainly cannot do justice to them here, merely try to show how they fit into the historical big picture. The growing sense of stalemate between Catholic and Protestant interests was not encouraging for either side. A protracted war between Calvinist Huguenots and the Catholic League bled France down from a world power to a mere buffer state of Spain, and then England. Intrigue plagued the English crown, as Philip II of Spain plotted with the Catholic Mary Queen of Scots to murder Elizabeth I. When Elizabeth discovered the plot, she had the Scottish Mary executed. The Catholic hierarchy in England had to go underground.

The English war with Spain that destroyed the Spanish armada in 1588, also made the Netherlands safe for the Reformation. The Spanish had ruled the Lower Countries up until that time, ruthlessly persecuting the large Protestant population. Elizabeth had no children, which opened the door for the Scottish Stuart Dynasty to succeed her on her death, in 1603. Secret negotiations with her Chief Minister, Sir Robert Cecil, helped the nominally Catholic Scottish King, James VI, to become King James I of England—first king of "Great Britain."

James I was the only son of Mary Queen of Scots, but had received some Protestant schooling after the execution of his Catholic mother. While fascinated by theology as an abstraction, he never converted to Protestantism. His commitment to Roman Catholicism seemed lukewarm to many, as well. This might explain, at least in part, why James had no interest in returning his United Kingdom to Roman Catholicism. He knew Protestantism had won England and Scotland over. Instead, he tried to play one Reformed faction against the other. His main concerns in church affairs were political.

With Roman Catholicism still illegal in England, James I aligned himself to the Protestant Episcopalian Party. He believed that church government by an archbishop most closely resembled monarchy. He perhaps felt that if he could not have Roman Catholicism, he should at least have that form of Protestantism most like it. This would eventually prove a failed attempt at more than just political survival. Though he persecuted the Separatists, James accommodated Puritans that remained in the Anglican Church. He promised them an authorized English Bible if it left out anti-Episcopal study notes, like those of the 1599 edition of the Geneva Bible. This resulted in the King James Bible of 1611, still widely read to this day.

Though Catholic, both James, and his son, Charles I, endorsed the "High Church" Anglican party as an application of James' political adage, "No bishop, no king." [2] James foresaw that if Presbyterianism toppled bishops as the highest church authority, the pattern would soon go secular. Back then, secular government tended to imitate church government. To King James, Presbyterianism smacked of Republicanism, which kept the Stuarts on their toes. James proved right about that. Parliament Forces executed Charles I, during the English Civil War, which ended with the Puritan, Oliver Cromwell, as "Lord Protector" for a generation.

Compared to what was happening on the continent, however, the English Revolution was tame. Cromwell's death, in 1658, enabled Charles' son, Charles II, to regain the throne. Charles dissolved Parliament multiple times, and ruled for his last few years as an absolute monarch. His heir and younger brother, James II, was openly Catholic. When James sired a Catholic heir, Parliament called upon his nephew and brother-in-law, the Protestant William of Orange to take the throne. After William landed with an invasion fleet, James Abdicated, and fled the country. James' Protestant elder daughter, Mary II and William III ruled as co-monarchs. They signed a bill of rights that made the United Kingdom a constitutional monarchy. Historians have called this the Glorious Revolution.

In Germany, the bloodbath of the Thirty-Year War stormed for over a generation, climaxing the great Catholic-Protestant stalemate. The Lutherans and the Catholics slugged it out for year after bloody year, wiping out fighting men faster than new ones could come of age. The few Calvinist German cantons finally joined in, for the first time gaining recognition in the form of grudging gratitude from the Lutherans. Catholic forces led by Duke Albrecht von Wallenstein vastly outnumbered the united Protestant armies.

The war turned well for the Protestants only after the Lutheran Swede, King Gustavus Adolphus, intervened. He defeated the Catholic Imperial forces at the Battle of Lutzen. Only after Adolphus died in that battle, did many Protestant princes take courage from his example and unite against Wallenstein. The war continued, until the Holy Roman Empire bled down to an anemic shadow of its former self. The empire would hang on, through the staying power of the Hapsburg Dynasty, until reorganized in 1809 into the dual monarchy of Austria-Hungary.

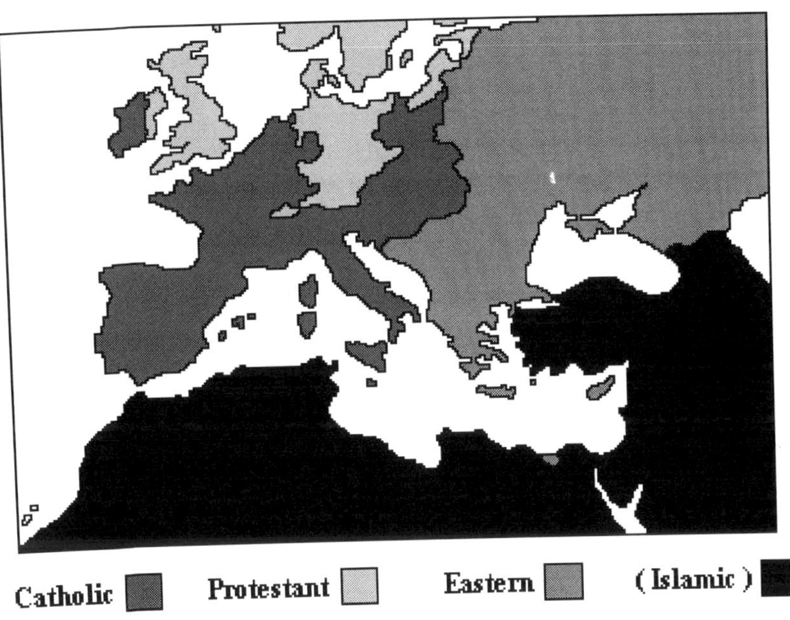


*The division of Catholic and Protestant Europe was not truly as clear-cut as this overly simple map depicts. The Balkans shifted back and forth between Islamic and Eastern Orthodox dominion. In all of the respective countries were sizable cities and enclaves where dissenting belief systems dominated.*

When it became apparent, at last, that the Catholics could no longer retake lands held by Protestant interests, and Protestants could not militarily "liberate" Roman Catholic lands; the war petered out from exhaustion. It settled no real issues, except the grudging agreement of both sides to let each other have whatever lands they had gained at a certain point in the conflict at "The Peace of Westphalia." The war stripped the German Empire of trade, and wasted its population of 16 million down to less than 6 million in one hellish generation. [3] Imagine living in the wake of a generation-long war, where two thirds of America's 300 million people had died. Now imagine this war had been between two groups of Christians, whose main dispute with each other was over the way God saves people.

Of course, there was far more to the Thirty-Year War than a religious dispute. The war happened because churches were married to states in a way that God's word never prescribed. States will always have territorial ambitions and strategic interests. Christian religious systems used warfare no more than any other belief system, *religious or secular*. To get Christian church systems to view violence as a tool for church policy required a departure from the New Testament model of the church. The wars were not really about church policy, but state policies. The churches came in because the states identified themselves with those churches. That, and Christian individuals still have a struggle with their flesh. Fanaticism is a human problem, not a uniquely religious one. It is certainly not one that Christians show any more than others do.

It is easy today to characterize the Religious Wars as an orgy of militaristic Christian hypocrisy, but that would not be completely fair. For much of it, Protestant factions were literally fighting for their lives, and for the right to worship as conscience directed. In England, fear of another staunch Catholic monarch like Mary Tudor, however unlikely; led to irrational laws and persecutions against all Roman Catholics. In France, Catholic forces virtually wiped out the Huguenots without mercy. Circumstances eventually forced even many Christians who despised the idea of religious wars to fight in them out of raw self-defense.

Atrocities happened on both sides. Wars that last more than a generation produce a great deal of social discontent. Many people were, by this time, disgusted with all the bloodshed and hypocrisy in both Roman and Reformed churches alike. It seemed to many at this time that Christianity in all its forms was the cause of all the woes in Europe. The Religious Wars sowed brooding emotional seedbeds for an openly anti-Christian ideology to flower in the next century; a weed fertilized by war's jaded aftermath. It would grip the West by its color and promise, only to slowly rot everything touched by its leaves. In the end, it would become hypocrisy, to fight hypocrisy.

Before any of that became clear, history would call this movement the *Enlightenment.*

## HOBBES AND VOLTAIRE, THE REVIVAL OF EPICURUS IN THE FRENCH ENLIGHTENMENT

Francois-Marie Arouet, better known by his pen name, Voltaire (1694-1778), is often called "Father of the Enlightenment" by historians. He grew up in a Europe reeling in the aftermath of the Thirty-Year War and French Confessional Strife. Roman and Reformed churches, each married to secular states, had habitually used political and military power to deal with spiritual and intellectual problems, a long time. It grew clearer each year that the Christendom church-state had failed as a just social model.

If Voltaire was the "father" of the Enlightenment, a slightly earlier figure, Thomas Hobbes, was the "grandfather." He watched from a distance the Religious Wars play out.

Hobbes (1588-1679) believed that God was unknowable. He wrote that everything in human experience—will, emotion, thought— stemmed from material and mechanical processes in the human body. Thus, in his mind, Christian doctrine was only a systemic pretense to power. Hobbes also became first to revive the worldview of Epicurus as a foundation for understanding the human condition. In doing so, he became the first major modern philosopher of ***Materialism***. He published his philosophical opus, *Leviathan*, in 1651, three years after the Thirty-Year War ended. Hobbes then fled to France because of the book's anti-Christian tone. There, he became a big part of the intellectual compost from which Voltaire and other late 17th and 18th century French intellectuals grew.

Hobbes was not alone on that compost heap.

Huge moral and spiritual blind spots undermined not only Roman Catholicism, but the Reformation as well. Slavery based on race, the unjust use of wealth, and the willingness to wage unjust wars in the name of Christ, were just a few issues running out of control. The Bible addresses such things, at least in principle, if not directly. Such evils festered not because churches obeyed Scripture, but because they systemically failed to do so. Mainstream Christianity had imagined itself able to fix, by its mere inclusion into it, what nothing less than Christ's Second Coming could—Satan's world system. Instead, that world system had built itself right into the churches, giving them its own flavor and disease. (Matt. 5:13, John 12:31, 14:30, 16:11, Rom. 12:1-2, 2 Cor. 4:4, Rev. 2:12-16, 18-25)

Voltaire wrote, "*Every sensible man, every honest man, must hold the Christian sect in horror. But what shall we substitute in its place? You say. What? A ferocious animal has sucked the blood of my relatives. I tell you to rid yourselves of this beast, and you ask me what you shall put in its place?*" [4] Given his time and place in history, one can emotionally understand how Voltaire saw Christianity this way. An appeal to emotion is not a sensible or fair case, however. One should also see his logical fallacy in attributing the church's corruption to the core doctrines of the Faith. It should also be easy for us to see how some people today might feel as Voltaire did, given how academics and cinema often present church history.

We should not ignore the atrocities. This book does not. Neither should we gloss over the vast positives of church history, or church history itself, for fear of facing such things.

Voltaire and his ideological allies believed that Christianity needed to be de-fanged. To do this effectively, in their minds, required not just institutionally parting church from state. It also meant getting grassroots people to question, and reject Christianity's core doctrines. As a means to this end, Voltaire, as Hobbes before him, dusted off the ancient worldview of the Greek philosopher, Epicurus. He then re-tooled it to fit their current situation. Epicurus built his worldview on the premise that the highest human good was to be emotionally detached and undisturbed. He saw, in his day, fear of the Greek gods as the source of what disturbed people most. Voltaire, likewise, saw the Judeo-Christian God as the problem. [5]

Epicurus could not prove that the Greek gods never interacted with people. Voltaire had even less of a basis for demonstrating that the Creator God of the Bible never did so. The Greeks had never viewed their gods as creators of nature, merely as controllers who had seized that mastery from an earlier set of gods, called the Titans. The God of the Bible, as Creator of the universe, stood on firmer philosophical ground in His ability to interact with what He had made. What Being powerful enough to create reasoning creatures such as man would not also be capable of interacting with His own creation? What sensible good purpose would prevent this Creator from doing so? What Genesis answered by Creation, Fall, and Curse; Voltaire and his peers needed a better explanation for. This was no small task.

Voltaire placed great hope in science someday discovering such an explanation. He had his hopes dashed, at first, by the fact that the greatest scientific mind of his day, Sir Isaac Newton, believed in a supernatural God. Nor was Newton an exception. The best that reactionary Enlightenment philosophers could do was to revamp Epicurus. They set up their grid of faith-assumptions to exclude any possibility of Divine interaction with men. Philosophers call this is an *a priori* assumption—something assumed to be true prior to examining any evidence. [6] Direct interactions with God had not happened visibly, on a large scale, since New Testament times. Since these ideologues held churches and the Bible suspect, Enlightenment truth claims felt realistic to them.

Nothing in everyday life seemed to disprove their claims. At this point, materialists did not reject the idea of a Creator God, only that He had interacted with humanity in a meaningful way. Hobbes, Voltaire, and later Enlightenment thinkers, pushed the religious ideology of ***Deism***. Deism is a belief that a god created the world sometime in the remote past, and then left it to run on "automatic pilot." In Deism, there is a creator, but no revelation of that creator. The laws inherent in the creation bind that creator, who is powerless over them. God is silent, distant, and uninvolved with humanity. Man cannot know God even if he wants to.

While Voltaire believed in a god after the deist fashion, he demanded silence of this god. Agnosticism was still, even in the deist mind, logically weak, given the self-evident complexity in nature. That logical weakness became the "squeaky wheel," as time went on. It demanded something plausible to explain apparent complexity apart from God.

In the Scholastic Era, thinkers had, I think inadvertently, launched human reason on a course toward separation from Divine revelation. The Renaissance continued this curve, while Reformation thinkers reversed it to varying extents. Now, the Enlightenment made the autonomy of human reason cry for completion. It transplanted reason onto another set of worldview assumptions, hostile to the Judeo-Christian ones. Quietly, a new set of cultural desires, hopes, and imperatives began to grow within the old institutions so foreign to their worldview DNA. This new "DNA" slowly began to rewrite everything from law to religion to cosmology. Once science turned, it accelerated the shift.

Foundational to this change was a new view of humanity. This involved a new view of morality. Not necessarily a change of moral behavior, at first—that would not come on a large scale until the 20th century—but *a new view of what morality was.* In the Christian view, morality is an echo of God's righteousness, even in our fallen condition. It originates with God, and reflects His holy and loving character. The Enlightenment defined morality as a product of human custom and convention. This viewed made it a mere resource subject to human engineering, through social and political manipulation.

Voltaire's Deism seemed to assume that if the real God had ever revealed Himself; then surely reasonable men would have a clearer understanding of who He was—there would be no religious sects. This assumption had a naïve faith in human honesty that flies in the face of what we see, even in the best of us, on truth telling. It also demanded that God jump through man-made hoops. It was unrealistic. This new view of humanity denied that man was a sinner by appealing to its new morality, which had redefined sin.

Deists also limited their god to using only the laws of nature to create. This made the god of Deism as trapped in the ***machine of the cosmos*** as men and animals are, only more powerful. The deistic god somehow manipulated matter in an eternal universe to make the earth, and life on it. By *machine of the cosmos,* I mean *the universe, as it works by knowable mechanical laws.* For example, gravity holds the earth at the exact distance from the sun to support life. Plant machinery makes oxygen from carbon dioxide, given off by animal machinery. This all works in an intelligently designed system. This "machine view" is accurate as far as we can see it. Deists share it in common with Christians.

Where Christians and deists differed was in the reduced size of the deist god. The Bible's God is eternal, and outside of the temporal "cosmic machine," yet omnipresent throughout it. This is what Christian theology means when it calls God *transcendent.* God can intervene in the cosmic machine from beyond, at will, and man, created in God's image, is not just a mere cog. Humans have real power to choose in a limited domain. Man can operate above the mechanical level to affect things in ways that have eternal consequences beyond the cosmos. For deists, there is no "beyond the cosmos."

The deist view required a new history, theology, and science. As time went on, the Materialism in it also demanded a new cosmology.

Voltaire and likeminded thinkers, *by faith,* rejected any possibility of the supernatural, and of a god who works in that realm. Though they would have hated the term *faith,* they accepted their assumptions that way, of necessity, since they were unprovable. Voltaire spread philosophical Materialism, but dressed it up by calling it ***Rationalism****. This kind of Rationalism is not a commitment to rational thought; rather it is the arbitrary assumption that only materialistic ideas can be rational.* When I say "***materialist,***" I do not necessarily mean "greedy for stuff" as many people who use that term today mean. Philosophical Materialism assumes that only the material world we can see and touch is the real world.

Science popularizer Carl Sagan used to express his faith in philosophical Materialism in a brief litany at the beginning of each episode of his late 20th century PBS show, *Cosmos,* when he said; "*The cosmos is all that is, or ever was, or ever will be.*" Many people do not even realize that this was a religious statement, not a scientific one. Like the Greek idea that "all material things are automatically corrupt," this, too, is a faith-assumption, not a conclusion drawn from evidence. Either the universe is *contingent*, that is, *held together by something greater*, and beyond itself, or the universe is eternal. If the latter, we can reduce creation's apparent complexity to the mere interactions of simple particles. Of course, the "particles" are proving to be anything but simple, as time goes on.

Atomic theory does not demand that the universe, and all matter in it, be eternal, either in its ancient Greek form or in that of today. Epicurus used Democritus' ideas on atoms as materialists try to use atomic theory now. *They try to suggest* that nature only *seems* complex, but really is random and simple at its basic level. If matter is eternal, and nature only seems complex, but is not as complex as it seems, then matter still might be the ultimate reality. No God need apply. Yet, "particles," whether atoms, molecules, or living cells, have proven far more complex in form and behavior than 18th century Epicurean Revivalists bargained for. Even if particles were such simple things, their tendency to exist together in complex forms—like grains in the concrete of a skyscraper—would not make nature self-existent.

Most people today, though not philosophical materialists, do not realize how many of their root ideas stem from Materialism. For example, the near universal assumption that "rational explanations" in nature must appeal to unguided material causes; *despite evidence to the contrary or how improbable many unguided causes are*. This excludes *purpose* as an explanation without proving purposelessness. It turned out that many 17th and 18th century guesses about created purpose, or ***teleology***, in nature were wrong. That did not prove *purpose* itself was an invalid inference. That would be appealing to a ***straw man argument***.

Early scientists and their forerunners had no trouble thinking in terms of Divine purpose in nature. Copernicus routinely described the sun metaphorically in terms of its created purpose as, "*the Lamp, the Mind, the Ruler of the Universe [who] sits upon a royal throne ruling his children the planets which circle around him.*" [7]

Materialistic assumptions can mold the thinking of Christians, too, who are not themselves, materialists. This happens through what philosophers call the "God of the Gaps" trap. This trap rests on at least two false faith-assumptions. The first is that because science will never know everything, *we will always need God to explain those things that science either does not or cannot explain*. The second assumption is that *the discovery of a naturalistic mechanism removes the need for God—as if we need God merely to explain what we do not understand*. Both assumptions covertly assume that Materialism is true. They force the idea of *God* further into the margins, as scientific knowledge grows—if we buy into them.

Many Christian thinkers, even before Hobbes and Voltaire's times, knew better than to appeal to the supernatural just because they ran across something they did not understand. Some mystics and many believers of modest education did not know better. Yet, even Christian apologists could not always rule out the supernatural *a priori*. We saw in Chapter 12 that Medieval Christian thinkers also understood that, at the bottom of all natural law, must be a cause greater than that law—a *super*-natural cause. Faith in an orderly, lawful Creator had caused these Christian intellectuals to think in terms of the "laws of nature" to begin with. Faith in the biblical God also gave them confidence that they could discover those laws by experiment and mathematical reasoning.

The writings of scientists in the 16th through early 19th century abounded with references to God as the Divine Engineer, and praises to His genius. Early scientists borrowed richly from Aristotle or Neo-Platonism, but they filtered the ideas of Pagan philosophers through a biblical view of God. Enlightenment philosophy did not lead to modern science. It eventually infected science, but it did not *and could not* give birth to it. Modern science, as a discipline and method, had already developed before the Enlightenment came along. It grew from a very different philosophic base. [8]

## THE RISE OF MODERN SCIENCE ON CHRISTIAN STARTING ASSUMPTIONS

Unlike ancient Pagans and Pantheists, Christians felt safe studying the natural world because it was no longer viewed as a deity, but a created thing. To Pagan mystery cults that worshipped natural forces, experimenting with those forces risked divine anger for something akin to looking up Mother Nature's skirts. Nobody felt that could end well. This did not mean a Christian worldview disrespected nature. The natural world still had dignity because it was God's creation and property.

We last touched on the history of science, and its relationship to the church, in Chapter 12. To take it up again, we need to jump back in time some four centuries. The development of science, both as a method and institution, stretched from the Scholastic Era, through the Renaissance and Reformation. It only met Enlightenment Materialism late in the game, mostly during the 18th century.

The Reformation renewed the Medieval (and biblical) view that God is a rational Being. The Renaissance, though man-centered, restored Greek philosophy in both its Aristotelian and Neo-Platonic forms. It suffered from an incomplete view of the Genesis Curse. Aquinas had introduced the idea that the human will had fallen, but that the intellect was potentially unaffected, if a person reasoned properly. [9] Pre-Renaissance Scholastics often saw Aristotle as a "naturalistic prophet" on issues of science and nature.

Francis Schaeffer showed how later artists popularized this idea; illustrated by the fresco of Andrea de Firenze in the Spanish Chapel in Santa Maria Novella, at Florence. Aquinas is enthroned in the center of the fresco. Lower down are Aristotle, Cicero, Ptolemy, Euclid, and Pythagoras placed in the same group with Augustine of Hippo. [10]

We saw that Aristotle taught the earth was the center of the cosmos—the sun, in his model, revolved around the earth. A minority of Neo-Platonic thinkers, like Nicolaus Copernicus, saw the sun mystically, as symbolic of the divine principle. He believed in a universe with the sun at the center. Copernicus offered a ***heliocentric*** (sun-centered) universe because it fit his Neo-Platonic philosophy; stated in strong Christian religious language. Faith motivated his search, which only later began to yield mathematical proof, and later still, evidences, based on observation. [11]

A century later, when Galileo also proposed that the earth orbited the sun, the Roman Catholic Church reacted, not because it violated the Bible. Instead, they had accepted the teachings of Aristotle through in Aquinas' Scholasticism. [12] Galileo actually used some biblical arguments to defend his position. He showed how Scripture speaks from an earth-bound point of view when describing the heavens, not in an absolute sense where the sun must move around the earth. For example, the author of the Book of Joshua wrote divine truth accurately from a human point of view. Relative to where the children of Israel observed from, on that long day, the sun indeed stood still.

Linguists call this ***phenomenological language***, a form of word usage that appears in every language. The author of Joshua, by using the historical narrative genre, never intended the text as a cosmological statement that the sun orbits the earth. Even where Psalm 19:6 says that the sun goes forth in a circle **"from the end of heaven,"** it speaks in a way that makes sense even to a modern person. The sun does indeed orbit the center of our galaxy, which is also in motion. An absolute earth-centered universe arose not from the Bible, but Aristotle's starting assumptions. Actually, the Scriptures made equal sense whether reading them through a heliocentric or ***geocentric*** (earth-centered) worldview.

Galileo appeared to have understood Scripture in a natural, rather than a woodenly literal way. People often ridicule a reasonable, literal interpretation of Scripture, today. It is equally silly to pretend the Bible has no figurative language, or that it uses language abnormally. An abnormal use of language would be to take an obscure detail, and make it the central focus of the text. There have been times when Christians used poor judgement in discerning figures of speech made in the Scriptures. The Galileo Incident was such a time. Avoiding a woodenly literal interpretation of the Bible is not the same as shaping Scripture to fit current popular philosophy.

Detecting phenomenological language is not as hard today as it might have been five hundred years ago. We hear it whenever a weatherman says that the sun will rise at 7:00 AM. We all know that the sun does not actually rise. Instead, the local coordinates on earth's rotating surface cycles past the meridian of its dark side into sunlight. We would never think of attacking the accuracy of meteorology based on a woodenly literal interpretation of the weatherman. *The weatherman is still describing a real event set to occur within a real time frame.* The Bible does the same thing when it uses language from an earthbound point of view.

Even so, Galileo's theory of planetary orbits did not *seem* natural at the time; either to the common sense of what people saw in the sky or to an intellectual community steeped in a Christianized version of Aristotle. A more human detail also messed things up. Galileo had an arrogant temper, visible in his letters to Johannes Kepler. This made needless enemies for him in both scientific and church leadership communities. In those days, this often meant the same circle of men. The church sponsored most scientific work, and some scientists were also clergy or at least worked in the church.

Galileo annoyed other scientists because he would not share data. The Pope reacted harshly, in part, because Galileo had published a comic strip-like tract where a buffoon character, Simplicio (meaning *stupid*), stubbornly rejected heliocentric experimental results. Galileo drew Simplicio with the Pope's face. Robert Cardinal Bellarmine, who judged part of the Galileo case, had no problem with the sun-centered model as a theoretical construct. He just cautioned against calling it a proven fact because many Scriptures pictured the sun as circling the earth. He wanted time to study how the Bible used its language on the subject.

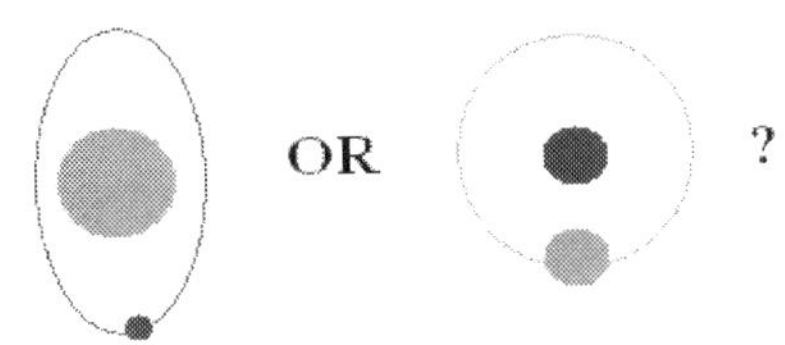


**Scripture makes sense through either lense.**

***Philology*** is the study of literature, and the mechanics of how it uses language. The science of philology had not yet designed words to discuss *phenomenological language use* clearly in Galileo's time. This was how scholarly men could miss seeing that the literary genre of a text affects even its literal interpretation. *Genre* is *form of literature*—for example, historical narrative, poetry, or epistle. The Bible has books of these, and many other genres. Today, we know this kind of language lets weathermen, the Bible, and everyone else picture how the sun *appears to behave* during a literal event, instead of its *actual motions*. This "language of appearance" does not break the rules of literal interpretation. Nor was God using deceptive language, any more than the weatherman is.

None of the Bible texts that describe the motions of heavenly bodies is *about* the motions of heavenly bodies. Such descriptions are incidentals. Both Galileo and Bellarmine intuitively understood this, but lacked terms that could easily address the issue for the public. The problem the church had with the sun being at the center stemmed not from Scripture. It came from over-dependence on the worldview of Aristotle, and from the fact that, until then, nobody had much reason to examine the other possibilities. Many Jesuits agreed with

Galileo's ideas, but could not join him because of the confrontational way in which he often framed them. [13] Brilliant men can sometimes be their own worst enemies.

Nor was this a uniquely Roman Catholic form of arrogance. It may not even have been arrogance at all, at least, not at first. Reformers, like Calvin, took the earth-centered view simply because it seemed most natural at a time when very little seemed to ride on the matter. Yet times were clearly changing. Much would soon ride on it, indeed.

The growing emphasis on reason held many positive implications for Christianity. It often forced Christians to sharpen their thinking skills in ways that affected their ability to defend the faith and to interpret Scripture sensibly. Isaac Newton was born the year Galileo died, in 1642. He wrote many Bible commentaries, devoting most of the latter portion of his life to Bible study more than to science. [14]

Newton pioneered what science philosophers later called the ***Mechanist*** philosophy in physics. This view, as its name suggests, emphasized the machine-like precision often found in nature. It might surprise many people today to learn that Newton created his mechanist system largely to defend against rising anti-God ideology after the Religious Wars. [15] He pointed out what should have been self-evident; that any machine testifies to the existence of an engineer. Romans Chapter 1 puts it this way:

> **For what can be known about God is plain to them, because God has shown it to them. Ever since the creation of the world his invisible nature, namely, his eternal power and deity, has been clearly perceived *in the things that have been made.* So they are without excuse. *Romans* 1:19-20 (RSV)**

**Newton's Original idea on mechanics.**

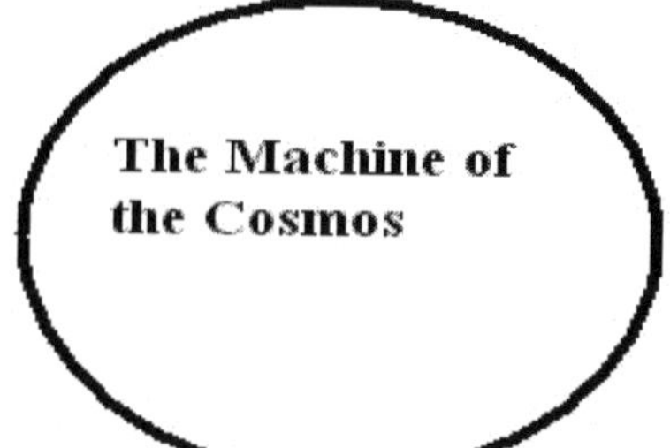


**God is outside the machine and can intervene from outside - we call this a "miracle."**

*Newton missed that if God did anything to the universe from outside the mechanism, it would involve new energy, information, and matter inserted into the system – the very essence of a miracle. He proved to be wrong in his proposals about how God adjusted the creation from time to time, while his own faith in the miraculous wavered. The mechanistic universe, under normal conditions, would be a closed system, open only to its Maker. Today, we can better express biblical supernaturalism as "God's Back Door" to Reality's "program."*

Voltaire hated this situation, because he could not believably discount Newton's science. Worse (for Voltaire), Newton loudly rejected the Enlightenment's Materialism. Nevertheless, Voltaire was a genius of another sort. As a historian writing history from a materialistic worldview, he took Newton's mechanistic model of the universe, and downplayed its main logical implication. Voltaire had no problem with the existence of a creator. Any machine needs an inventor. Enlightenment thinkers had no sensible naturalistic explanation for the universe. Voltaire, and others of his mindset, derided Newton's belief that God must adjust His creation periodically, as man-made machines need adjustment.

It turned out Newton was wrong about that. Although entropy wears creation down, the universe requires no periodic corrections on God's part from outside. He merely holds it all together. Newton's idea that God needed to adjust comet orbits sometimes, fell into the "God of the Gaps" trap through Newton's own diminished faith in miracles. Newton believed nature had a supernatural origin as God's creation, and he believed in Divine providence. Unfortunately, he did not relate biblical miracles with the idea of God inserting new information, matter, and energy into the created system. He viewed nature as a watchmaker, not as a virtual reality computer programmer. This was not surprising, since computer analogies were not yet possible.

The problem at the dawn of the 18th century was that even Christian thinkers often underestimated the size and power of God. Bond University *Journal of the History of Ideas* writer, Peter Harrison, captures the view of Newton and his generation of scientists well.

> *Newton's apparent ambivalence towards miracles highlights what to many commentators is one of the most curious features of seventeenth-century natural philosophy. Leading scientists of this era, almost without exception, had a dual commitment on the one hand to a science premised upon a mechanical universe governed by immutable laws of nature and on the other to an omnipotent God who intervened in the natural order from time to time, breaching these "laws" of nature.* ***This puzzle is heightened by the fact that (in England at least) those figures who were at the forefront of an advancing mechanical science were also the most staunch defenders of miracle. The Christian virtuosi of the Royal Society—Robert Boyle, Thomas Sprat, and John Wilkins, to take the most prominent examples—insisted not only that miracles could take place but that they played a vital role in establishing the truth of Christian religion.***
>
> ***Newtonian Science, Miracles, and the Laws of Nature****, Peter Harrison,*
> ***Journal of the History of Ideas****, Bond University, 1995*

Newton, Boyle, Sprat, and Wilkins were not deists, but their assumption that miracles somehow "broke" natural laws was something deists often seized on. Deists often felt that God could not ethically break laws of nature because they were *laws*. This argument pushed the bounds of silliness. Discussions about "higher laws" or "unknown natural laws" abounded, but these failed to address the essence of a miracle. Today, we know that all good computer programmers leave themselves "back doors" to insert new lines of code into their virtual reality matrices. Why would God be less efficient than today's virtual reality programmers would?

Newton particularly struggled with parts of Biblical theology, even with his great respect for the Bible. He had doubts about the Trinity, and his view of God's sovereignty and power was clearly incomplete. The mechanists had a worldview blind spot, too. For all their focus on laws of motion, and order, they missed the role of *information* as a fundamental reality. There was also the assumption that everything God had made was part of the universe. They suffered the same assumptions about the absolute nature of time found in the Calvinist-Arminian controversy. Like the deists, they had trouble picturing the universe as a box with an outside, even though they insisted God transcended His creation.

This was a time when ideas were in flux for believers, as they tried to translate biblical truth to an intellectual setting that grew more complex each decade. For those looking for a reason to abandon the faith, the time seemed ripe to construct believable models to justify their doing so. Voltaire was young while Newton was old, so he did the bulk of his work after Newton's death. Enlightenment ideology exploited an emotional perception that if humanity knows how things work, then God becomes redundant. People commonly felt that if we knew the mechanical principles on which nature worked, spiritual causes would somehow become obsolete. This feeling also assumed an emerging Materialism.

It even became a great fear in the minds of thoughtful people in that day, and is still so among some today; despite the fact that mechanics in nature still points objectively to an engineer-creator. (The modern attempt to classify this as an "anthropocentric, or man-centered, illusion" is superficial. It depends on models that assume that claim is already true. This attempt effectively shrugs at the evidence for design in nature, and says, "Of course everything *seems* designed, it would have to, given the way things turned out.")

A gulf divided the early scientists from Enlightenment philosophers like Voltaire. Newton, Boyle, and the others, by faith, believed in a uniformity of natural laws in a universe that was an ***open system*** with respect to God's ability to act on it. [16] In all other respects, nature was a ***closed system***, but not to its Creator. The early scientists held that the Creator of natural law must be greater than that law, thus able to intervene from outside and above it, whenever He wished. Some, like Newton, missed this as a mechanical description of miracles. In the Computer Age, Divine interventions into history are how biblically and scientifically literate Christians see miracles.

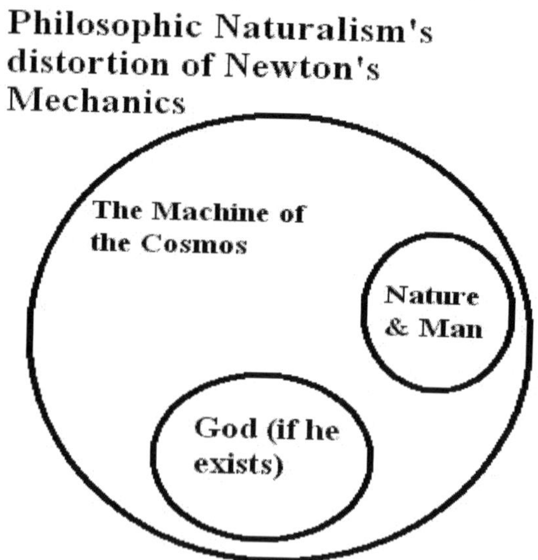


Men like Voltaire, on the other hand, equally by faith, believed in a mechanical uniformity of natural laws in an absolute closed system. God was not outside the machine, but a part of it, trapped, and unable to intercede in any way beyond natural laws. No experiment proved this emasculated mechanist view true. It was merely the popular assumption in the Enlightenment's growing circle of influence. [17]

The Enlightenment carried Renaissance Humanism to its logical end. Man, starting from himself, could perfect himself through reason, in this view, without help from God. Nonetheless, the Enlightenment in the 18th century was still a philosophy driven by emotional reaction; a hypocrisy men like Isaac Newton saw through. It had yet to find much validation in the hard sciences for all of their mechanistic and rationalistic talk. Science itself had to undergo a foundational philosophic shift in its faith-held starting assumptions for that to happen. That would take several generations. For that reason, we will cover much of it as we discuss the 19th, 20th, and 21st centuries, and today's situation.

Because science began as a method for studying the patterns of *nature*, its methodology, by definition, was *naturalistic*. Early scientists accepted this limitation. They knew that other systematic methods-of-knowing existed for things like history, and Divine revelation. This, by itself, involved no denial of the supernatural, God, angels, and demons. It merely recognized the limits of the scientific method as an epistemology or *way of knowing things*. Science can only predict natural phenomena according to how they act without interference from outside of nature. It is useless, as the main method to study history, for example, because we can only reenact history, not experimentally repeat it. Science cannot study theological truth, not because such truth is not real, but because God is beyond our experimental reach. Science philosophers call this principle ***Methodological Naturalism***.

Epicurus taught that the value of knowledge lay mainly in its ability to protect us from disturbance, and to better our quality of life. Whether the knowledge represented moral truth was of secondary concern to him. The worldview shift driven by Enlightenment Materialism caused a slow change in the idea of Naturalism. This happened concurrently with the Industrial Revolution, when new technologies slowly began to improve the quality of life for many in Western Europe. These technologies all built from the improving understanding of physics and chemistry, which began to place science more into the public spotlight. Discoveries of the day often amazed people at public exhibitions.

As the revived Epicureanism slowly penetrated academic and political elites, *science became the focus of hope for a better life*. In the vacuum left by growing rejection of Christianity, chiefly in France and Germany, this hope grew into an effectively religious belief *about* science. Nobody noticed that there was a difference between science and *a belief about* science. *Methodological* Naturalism slowly mutated into *Ideological* Naturalism. The first is *a method for studying nature*; the second is *a faith-based hope in the benefits that method will bring.* In no way am I diminishing the advances science has given us. Science is the most powerful tool for studying nature we know. It is not the bad guy, here.

While science is good, not all beliefs *about* science can make that claim. Consider the differences between Naturalism as a method and as an ideology:

**Hope in a method of studying nature became a faith-based ideology—The 2 Naturalisms: Method vs. Ideology**

| Method | Ideology |
|---|---|
| • Scientific Method is limited in what it can know to the created realm (nature) | • Behaves as if Science is the ultimate way of knowing *all* aspects of reality |
| • Best used on observable & repeatable processes | • Distrusts Legal-Historic way of knowing history & declares Divine Revelation obsolete |
| • Can recognize the need for other ways of knowing for other aspects of reality | • Declares the realms of other ways-of-knowing to be imaginary or "non-real" |
| • Can assist other ways of knowing | • Denies the integrity of other ways of knowing automatically |
| • Has no built-in chip on its shoulder | • Has one huge shoulder chip |

Popular culture has not only blurred the difference between *science* and *a belief system about science*, or ***Scientism***. It suffers an anemic view of science history that only lists discoveries; but fails to describe the religious and philosophical assumptions that generated the methods that brought them about. [18] Worse yet, popular media often feeds people a false view of science as born from a struggle between "rational" Materialism against a "superstitious" Christianity. [19] This describes a view of science history popular from the middle 19th to middle 20th century, called ***Logical Positivism***. Historians now roundly reject this view for its shameless propaganda. It fails to consider what the source documents from early scientists actually said about their own motives and inspiration.

To read the deep and heart-felt praises to God in the letters of Johannes Kepler, Carolus Linnaeus, Blaise Pascal, Robert Boyle, and countless other pioneers of science; is to wonder where this supposedly all-pervasive "battle between faith and knowledge" was really going on. It apparently went on only in the imaginations of men like Voltaire and David Hume, and a century later, in the Darwinist propaganda of Thomas Huxley and Ernst Haeckel. The few scientific discoveries, before the 19th century, that involved church opposition were conflicts between popular *scientific* views that had gained church support through the academics of the day. [20] They did not represent clashes between science and the Bible.

Even during and after Darwin's time, we shall find that the real battle was not between faith and science; but between materialistic or pantheistic faith-assumptions and theistic Judeo-Christian ones. Before Newton and the others, Sir Francis Bacon placed the dignified role of science into perspective. In doing this, Bacon also made one of the clearest, most concise statements on the nature of the Genesis Fall ever made. In his *Novum Organum Scientiarum* (1620), he wrote:

> *Man by the Fall fell at the same time from his state of innocence and from his dominion over creation. Both of these losses, however, can even in this life be in some parts repaired; the former by religion and faith, the latter by the arts and sciences.*

Notice that Bacon did not see the world of knowledge as walled-off compartments, whose separate disciplines never effectively touched each other; the fragmented way that the sciences and theology are often treated in relation to one another today. For Bacon and the original scientists, science was not something totally divided from the consideration of God and his work. The consideration of God's work, and our duty to understand it, motivated the early scientists to seek truth in this way.

Our first command from God in Genesis was to manage the created world—to "have dominion" over it in a positive stewardship sense. Science and faith mesh well in the matrix of the reality humanity observes. Even 17th century thinkers who may not have been biblical Christians, like Rene Descartes, thought primarily in Christian worldview terms. They had confidence that because God was a rational Being, who created orderly systems in nature, man could learn of nature and apply that knowledge technologically.

In contrast, the Chinese had shown vast knowledge of many technologies unknown in the West. Yet, they had no enduring confidence that the universe operated by uniform rules. The Far Eastern religious worldview, where things worked either randomly or in unchanging cycles, disabled the growth of a science based on experimentation. Randomness gives zero confidence that natural laws are even possible. Immutability quashes the hope that things can improve. Therefore, it never occurred to them to devise a cohesive scientific method with which to build on the technology they already had.

Science, as an institution, is not necessary to the invention of many technologies. Happy accidents and genius still happen. Science, however, institutionalizes and harnesses discovery. It takes what once happened by happy accident, and disciplines it into a reliable force for advancement.

Likewise, Islamic Arabia, once far more advanced than Western Christendom, eventually lost interest in science. Allah was too capricious. [21]

I am not saying that Christian presuppositions alone allowed science, as we know it, to develop in the West. Many mystical influences came from Neo-Platonism, and reasoning tools from other Greek philosophies. Also social, military, and political forces worked, the bulk of which are too complex to deal with here in full. Nevertheless, the Christian emphasis on a rational God was an undeniable cornerstone. Alfred North Whitehead and J. Robert Openheimer, scientists of the early to mid-20th century, and not professing Christians, were quick to make this point. Whitehead called Christianity, *"the mother of modern science."* [22]

## Christian Reactions to Deism: Jansenism and the Pietists

The materialistic Deism of Voltaire and other Enlightenment thinkers evoked two proper reactions from the churches. One came from Reformed Christianity, and the other from within a small portion of Roman Catholicism. Ironically, these separate camps reacted by coming to the same basic conclusions on how best to counter the influence of Deism. Both Catholic Jansenists, and Protestant Pietists, stressed the individual believer's need to have a personal relationship with God through the work of Jesus Christ. We find this idea all over the Bible, yet Christianity had seemingly left it for centuries to gather dust.

Blaise Pascal, a Catholic Jansenist, and well-known scientist and mathematician, wrote widely on having a personal faith and relationship with God. He became known for "Pascal's Wager"—the statement that believers lose little now, and gain everything later, by placing their faith in Christ; while the unbeliever gains little, but loses all in the end by betting on God's nonexistence or indifference.

Pietists in both Calvinism and Lutheranism became a major revival influence in the 18th century. They ignored barriers of sect, social class, and denomination if they saw biblical light in other groups. Much of today's Evangelical theology on individual salvation, which terms Christ our "personal Lord and Savior," stems from their renewal of these Bible truths. Until Pietism, Reformation theology had often been mainly scholarly in its nature, and often unevenly applied. The Pietists emphasized small Bible study groups in much the same way we see done today in many independent Bible oriented churches. This brought personally applicable biblical theology to the masses on a large scale.

Many Pietists joined with remnants of Anabaptist fellowships that had, by this time, learned from the English Separatists to drop a sectarian view of the church. A fusion of the followers of Balthasar Hubmaier in Moravia, with Calvinist and Lutheran elements, became the Moravian Brethren church led by Count Zinzendorf. The Brethren grew into one of the most amazing Bible-based missionary movements of that era, likely of all church history. Moravians sometimes sold themselves to Muslim slave traders to bring the gospel to the Islamic world of the Ottoman Empire.

With the Pietists and Jansenists, Christians began to get in touch again with God's tender heart, and His passion for lost souls. Church systems, Eastern, Catholic, and Protestant alike, which had been cold and aloof for far too long, desperately needed this. Yet, this, too, had potential blind spots that, after several generations, began to actualize. By the 19th century, Pietist emphasis on an emotional personal experience with God began to take shortcuts. People often sought it at the expense of maintaining the equally important realm of Spirit-led intellect and reasoning skills. An untrue belief that "true spirituality" and reason were incompatible began to form in some quarters. In time, even a rationally defendable concept of Divine revelation began to suffer, as spirituality and reason seemed in growing tension.

It is often true that people begin to believe a thing, if only they hear it repeated often enough. The Enlightenment's frequent, often clever mockery of Christianity in the 18th century aided this effect. Even many Christians, in a variety of denominations, began to believe that "faith" and "reason" were at war by nature. Because people generally drew hope from their faith, reason began to take on the aura of an enemy to grassroots Christians of many stripes. In a great irony, this artificial outlook not only plagued Pietists, it also demoralized some of the students of Voltaire.

## ROUSSEAU AND ROMANTICISM: FREEDOM WITHOUT RESPONSIBILITY

The mechanist view of man and the cosmos fostered by Enlightenment Rationalism, also resonated with another force in 18th century Europe. The Industrial Revolution had started to change an agrarian civilization into an industrial one. New ideas and inventions began to accelerate on a curve that would soon go exponential.

Ideas, as always, have logical consequences. If people, at the bottom line, were only machines in a purely mechanical universe, with nothing beyond it; why not use men in mechanistic and ***utilitarian*** ways? Why should we not train underprivileged children to do dangerous and repetitive menial jobs in sweatshops and mines? Why should we not work men to death with low paying sixteen to twenty hour workdays, six, and sometimes seven days a week? People were certainly plentiful and easy enough to replace.

Jean Jacques Rousseau (1712-1778), a student of Voltaire's mechanistic views, sensed trouble in the emerging picture. He grew depressed at people dehumanized into mere machines of the Industrial Revolution. He parted with his mentor's deification of reason in favor of his own philosophy of ***Romanticism***. This was a feelings-based view of reality that idealized an absolute freedom for the individual. Rejecting a Christian view of ethics, Rousseau's idea of freedom came without a Bible-based model. His idea of liberty came without enough responsibility, and with no limits based on Divine absolutes.

Rousseau proclaimed that Man was, by nature, good. Only the evils of repressive Christian and industrial civilization had corrupted him. He believed that society could rest on a "social contract," in which individual freedom would coalesce somehow into a mass "general will" of the newly "enlightened" people. Society would educate evil out of people, as a utopian paradise of individual liberty emerged. If an individual opposed the "general will of the people," then that person would theoretically be *"forced to be free"* according to Rousseau. [23] The unreality of his views led to the French Revolution's Reign of Terror. Rousseau's disciple, Maximillian Robespierre, carried out the "people's general will" on tens of thousands using the guillotine.

In the end, Robespierre himself had his own guillotine experience, when the "people's general will" failed to perform as promised. France fell to the dictatorship of Napoleon Bonaparte, who took the title of Emperor.

Rousseau's views also had a great influence on the Bohemian Ideal—a free sex lifestyle that tried to shed the limits of civilization, and return to nature. The hippie movements of the 1960s bore the signature of his influence. So did many late 19th and early 20th century post-Impressionist artists. Francis Schaeffer records how the painter, Paul Gaugin, tried to live the life of Rousseau's idealized "noble savage" and ended in deep depression after a failed suicide attempt. [24]

The Marquis de Sade carried this "return to nature" style ethics to its logical conclusion in the early 19th century. He based his morals on the fact that, in nature, the strong prey on the weak. We get *Sadism* – the brutalization of women or of other weaker men as sex objects—from his name. Yet, jurists irrationally still try to work from concepts of ***Naturalistic Law***, as a basis for law and morals apart from the Bible. [25]

As the oft-quoted line in the 1986 re-make of *The Fly* says, "Be afraid. Be very afraid."

## A COMPARISON OF EFFECTS FROM TWO OPPOSING WORLDVIEWS

Let us briefly compare the directions taken by law and government in the man-centered Renaissance-based south of Europe; versus the more Bible-centered Reformation-based North. The Enlightenment was, of course, more than an emotional reaction to the corrupt spiritual climate of the institutional churches after the Religious Wars. It came as the next logical step of a Humanism that, by now, had drifted far from its Christian roots.

While the Reformation did not produce an ideal society, it did teach the biblical doctrine that all men were sinful in their fallen nature. Because of this condition, no one man or group of people could be trusted with too much power. This view of the human condition supplied the logical base for the constitution of England's relatively bloodless Glorious Revolution. [26] The constitutional monarchy's bill of rights made Parliament and the judiciary equal to the King. Colonial America appealed to this legal foundation in the 1770s, when it protested against taxation without representation. It also modeled its own Constitution after it.

In 1644, Samuel Rutherford published a book titled, *Lex Rex*, or *Law is King*. In this remarkable concept, the King was no longer the law, but rather the first citizen subject to the law. It created the potential for a government where leaders were empowered to do good, but hindered from doing evil. Rutherford was a Scottish Presbyterian Calvinist. One can see two patterns in history. One is that wherever a Reformation-based faith freely emerged, governments that guaranteed liberty without chaos followed. The second is that wherever such faith continued to influence public cultural norms, governments that secured realistic individual liberties endured. Whenever that biblical concept of man and government was lost, tyranny reasserted itself in one form or another. It often re-emerged in a worse form than what had existed before. [27]

Contrast this with the political ideology of Nicollo Machiavelli, who wrote earlier from a Renaissance humanist base. We find in Machiavelli's *The Prince* a manual for how to manipulate henchmen, the masses, the church, and other parts of society with complete indifference to ethics. [28] We get the adjective ***Machiavellian*** from this author's name. Historians use the term *Machiavellian* for the amoral exploitations of men like Adolf Hitler, Benito Mussolini, and Slobodan Milosevic; who each put Machiavelli's theory into practice. Machiavelli is a staple in political science classes today.

An Enlightenment philosophic base produced a near instant public bloodbath. Voltaire had hoped to see a "bloodless revolution" in France like the Glorious Revolution he had witnessed during his youthful exile in England. The French, however, were not operating from a Reformed Christian view of humanity. They followed Rousseau's idea of man being innately good in his present condition. [29] They did not see people as naturally sinful and power-hungry. It, therefore, did not occur to the French revolutionaries to build institutional safeguards against mob power into their system.

A culturally strong grassroots Christian influence in America tempered their revolution. It indirectly helped people see the wisdom of a system of checks and balances to prevent any one group from getting too much power. In contrast, the faith-assumptions of the French Revolution choreographed events to end in a meat grinder for human flesh.

This is also an illustration of what happens when the church loses its salting effect on culture. Jesus had called his disciples the "salt of the earth" during his Sermon on the Mount. Salt, in Jesus' day, was an agent used to prevent the rotting of meat, as well as to add flavor. In this sense, Jesus said that his followers were to inhibit corruption in the world, and add godly flavor to culture through their influence. This, of course, assumed that the churches would function the way Jesus and the Apostles had taught Christians to behave.

The Pietists and Jansenists were tiny minorities, potent in faith, but too small to affect state churches on a scale that could hold back the fall of Christendom to a secularized worldview. Schaeffer described what happens when a society rejects Divine absolutes. An elite person or group must step into the resulting moral chaos and enact arbitrary human absolutes to keep order. [30] These arbitrary absolutes always serve whatever agenda the elite pushes, rarely the good of the nation and never of its people.

The Reformation, which preached *Sola Scriptura* as its basis for authority, also became corrupt in some ways. Yet, where it was corrupt, it was being *inconsistent* with its own beliefs and starting assumptions. When bloodshed and corruption arose out of Renaissance and

Enlightenment based governing principles, it did so utterly *consistent* with the assumptions of those systems. They carried in them the seeds of their own breakdown.

The biblical view of humanity taken more or less by Britain, and passed on to the United States, gave a person rational footing to hold both the state *and the people* answerable. They could lift their Bibles up to say that slavery or child labor sweatshops were evil. Public opinion and government policy had a basis for a realistic hope in the potential for change because their worldview assumed moral absolutes. In Revolution France, no rational basis existed for such things. People there made many passionate emotional stands for justice, but they had no watertight rational base underneath them.

Read *A Tale of Two Cities*. England and America were often hypocritical in their policies on slavery, and the colonial treatment of indigenous peoples. Nevertheless, at least the Reformation-based worldview there raised a reason-based hope that objective truth existed, and should thus be defended and embodied. People working from a Bible base could stand up and hold government, churches, and industry morally accountable. A cultural basis endured for swaying public opinion more consistently for the good. *That can only happen in a society that recognizes the reality of divine absolutes and objective truth.*

It will become evident in following chapters that this was how Britain abolished slavery based on race. Sadly, it will also be evident how the church lost much of its "salt" when this biblical social dynamic, later, eroded even in Britain and America. Only the sporadic revivals of the 18th through 21st centuries have kept churches alive enough to present any witness at all for truth. This usually happened through inspired individual Christians, rather than the church as an institution. For by this time, the church, as it existed within most institutional structures, was essentially dead, salt-less, and **"fit for nothing but to be cast out and trodden under the foot of men."**

The widest latitude of political liberty without social chaos rose in the Judeo-Christian West not by fluke, but by logical cause and effect. Christian spiritual liberty *alone* may not have been enough to bring about such a thing, but it was certainly the main and necessary foundation. The acceptance of a Judeo-Christian worldview on human value into any political situation has always improved things. It may not happen at first or directly, but improvement on some level happens. Likewise, suppression of Judeo-Christian views of human value has always furthered tyranny. This does not mean liberty always blossomed whenever an individual Christian ruled. It only means that law based on a Judeo-Christian view of Creation, Universal Curse, Redemption, and Promised Restoration advance individual liberty without chaos. This is verifiable.

Earlier, less-developed, examples exist of this thesis in action. When Constantine became the first Christian (or at least "Christianesque") Roman emperor, he abolished gladiatorial games, crucifixion, abortion, and infanticide. He also established more humane prison conditions. These reforms produced an elevated sense of human worth within the Roman legal system of the time. Despite the fact that Constantine, and his sons, remained despots, who sometimes did the corrupt and arbitrary things despots frequently do; this modest *yet real* change began to set the Western world on a new course. Sharpening ideas about how law should protect human dignity and property marked the centuries that followed at an accelerated pace.

After Rome fell, the conversion of the barbarian tribes, even when the church itself had become decrepit as an institution, took only one or two generations. Head hunting, sometimes even ritual blood-drinking, animistic savages became Frankish, and then English, villages under the rule of law. This took more than just a Judeo-Christian concept of law, however. It required an increasingly biblical view of reality in the people governed. Most of all, it required the sanctifying power of the Holy Spirit. This set the stage for the Magna Charta, and for all the legal developments to follow, right up to the United States Constitution.

The benefits of individual liberty without chaos became possible because people had a sense that there was a higher universal law from God. Earthly kings were now (at least in theory) accountable to that higher law. Exactly *how* kings were accountable was a matter of dispute for some time. The idea, nevertheless, took hold that kings were in fact accountable. The flipside of that was that nobility, and eventually all people, had natural rights that came to them from their Creator. The invention of the printing press, and the Reformation of Christianity it helped enable, were major breakthroughs that accelerated this process.

A Bible, before, had cost the life savings of a wealthy man. (Consider Peter Waldo, the merchant who, in the 12th century, had sold all he owned to pay monks to translate portions of the New Testament). Now, Bibles were affordable to a growing middle class. Having the Bible in spoken languages drove, first church and then political, reform by mechanical result. People were no longer dependent on church and political leaders to know what truth was. They could read God's word for themselves if they took the time to become educated.

With the Reformation, came a biblical view of spiritual liberty. This gave birth to a political view of individual liberty that did not bring social chaos. The Bible made known God's higher law, to which man could hold church systems and governments accountable, by developing systems of legal redress. This remained possible on a large scale however, only so long as the culture respected the Bible as God's higher law. Once society lost this view of spiritual liberty, all that remained was human government, with its arbitrary edicts, to keep order.

The church's long-time love affair with the State; first through Constantine, then in his European Monarchy clones, and finally in the Reformed state churches, now drew to an exhausted close. The aging bride no longer seemed so attractive to her lovers, and so they began turning her out into the street. For most clergy these were dark and frustrating times. Yet, for the repentant, moved anew by the Holy Spirit, who brought God's word to the grassroots level, an era of new vision and opportunity beckoned.

A Great Awakening stirred on the shores of a New World.

## BIBLIOGRAPHY


1. Compiled by Verna M. Hall, ***The Christian History of the Constitution of the United States of America***, p. 25, citing Leonard Bacon, ***The Genesis of the New England Churches***, NY: Harber & Brothers [1874], (1960, 1966, 1975, 2006)
2. Ed. Elizabeth Knowles, *"James I,"* ***The Oxford Dictionary of Quotations***, *Oxford University Press*, 2004. Oxford Reference Online. Oxford University Press
3. Walker, Williston et al. ***A History of the Christian Church***, The Reformation, Ch. 13, Pg. 534, Copyright 1918 by Charles Scribner's & Sons.
4. Multiple sources cite this quote as Voltaire's, but none specify where and when he wrote it. Even if it should prove a spurious quote, it is consistent in tone and style with a large body of Voltaire's anti-clerical statements for which there is firmer documentation.
5. Benjamin Wiker, ***Moral Darwinism***, pp. 170-177, & pp. 205-206, IVP 2002
6. Ibid. pp. 18-27 –In fact, this is the thesis of Wiker's book.
7. Nancy Pearcey, ***Saving Leonardo***, Pg.188 ©2010 Broadman & Holman
8. Pearcy, Nancy R. & Thaxton, Charles B. ***The Soul of Science***, pp. 17-122, Crossway Books (1994), Wheaton, Ill. See also, Schaeffer, Francis A. ***How Should We Then Live? The Rise and Decline of Western Thought and Culture***, pp. 130-165; 1976, Fleming H. Revell Co. Old Tappan, NJ.
9. Schaeffer, Francis A. ***How Should We Then Live? The Rise and Decline of Western Thought and Culture***, p.52, 1976, Fleming H. Revell Co. Old Tappan, NJ.
10. Ibid. pp. 51-52
11. Pearcy, Nancy R. & Thaxton, Charles B. ***The Soul of Science***, pp. 63-66 & pp. 75-76, Crossway Books (1994), Wheaton, Ill.
12. Ibid. pp. 60-62
13. Ibid. pp. 38-42
14. Op cit. Schaeffer, Francis A., p.135, see also, Pearcy, Nancy R. & Thaxton, Charles B. ***The Soul of Science***, pp. 88-95, Crossway Books (1994), Wheaton, Ill.
15. Davis, Edward B., ***Newton's Rejection of the 'Newtonian Worldview': The Role of Divine Will in Newton's Natural Philosophy***, in ***Science and Christian Belief***, 3, no. 1, (1991), p. 113 – *Davis cites the writings of Samuel Clark, Newton's friend and publicist, who personally consulted Newton on this same matter.*
16. Op cit. Schaeffer, Francis A., p.138-143
17. Ibid. pp. 146-147
18. Op cit. Pearcy, Nancy R. & Thaxton, Charles B., pp. 63-66 & pp. 74-78
19. Ibid. pp. 46-49
20. Ibid. pp. 37-42
21. Needham, Joseph; ***The Grand Titration: Science and Society in East and West***, p. 327; University of Toronto Press (1969). Cited also in Schaeffer, pp. 142-143
22. Whitehead, Alfred North; in the ***Harvard University Lowell Lecture*** entitled, ***Science and the Modern World*** (1925). See also, Oppenheimer, J. Robert; ***On Science and Culture***, ***Encounter*** magazine, Oct. 1962. Cited also in Schaeffer, p.132.
23. Op cit. Schaeffer, Francis A., p. 155. See also Rousseau, Jean-Jacques; ***The Social Contract*** (1762)
24. Op cit. Schaeffer, Francis A., p.159-161
25. Marquis de Sade; ***La Nouvelle Justine***, (1791-1797). Cited also op cit. Schaeffer, p. 159.
26. Op cit. Schaeffer, Francis A., p.120-121
27. Ibid. pp.108-110; see also, Rutherford, Samuel, ***Lex Rex*** (1644)
28. Op. Cit. Schaeffer, Francis A. p. 112
29. Ibid. p. 154
30. Ibid, p. 224

# 19

# Reason and Renewal: Part 2

## The First Great Awakening—George Whitefield, Jonathan Edwards, Isaac Backus, and Colonial Piety

By the 18th century, Christianity as the dominant worldview was far down the road of fragmentation and breakdown in Europe. Christians needed a new model for the church's role in society and individual life. This was not simply to stave off the fall of Christian civilization, but to preserve gospel truth and spiritual life in churches re-formed by the events of the last two centuries. A stereotype, unfortunately with some truth in it, has churches notoriously bad at keeping up with ideas and events around them—even those it must resist. The church being ahead of the curve is almost unheard of. Many were only now beginning to realize that the "Emperor" of Christendom's church-state fusion had no clothes.

Before accusing me of cynicism or being condescending, I hope the reader will remember that the Lord once made a similar lamentation.

> **And his lord was pleased with the false servant, because he had been wise; for the sons of this world are wiser in relation to their generation than the sons of light.**
>
> ***Luke* 16:8 (BBE)**

By the early to mid-1600s, Puritan Separatists from Britain had begun to colonize the Massachusetts Bay area. The English crown, and its high church, saw this as a humane way to rid themselves of a constant irritant. The Pilgrims and Puritans relished the opportunity to test their ideals in a new world, where they could self-govern and set policy. Both groups were committed to the idea that the church must be a community of the experientially converted. Only such church members could be trusted to make laws, in this view. The Puritan experiment in New England was convinced that it could create the Calvinist dream of a spiritually pure Christian society on earth.

The Pilgrims had colonized American shores for more practical anxieties, to which a growing number of Christian parents, today, might relate. Pilgrim pastor John Robinson had concerns for the upcoming generation of his Separatist exiles, from Scrooby, England, living in Holland. Parents agonized over the spiritual welfare of their children—how to foster a biblical culture in the cosmopolitan merchant cities of Holland. On top of that, the war between the Dutch and Spain had shown how easily a Spanish invasion in mainland Europe might put Roman Catholic monarchs in control. Their safe-haven, uncertain at best, could again become subject to the Spanish Inquisition.

This had happened in Holland, not long before. Robinson's flock faced the very real menace of falling out of the Anglican Church's frying pan, into the Spanish Inquisition's fire. *Monty Python's Flying Circus* has assured us all, since 1970, that, "Nobody expects the Spanish Inquisition." In Holland, at the time of the Pilgrims, however, almost everybody expected it, with good reason. This motivated the Pilgrims from Scrooby to depart once again, this time for the New World. They left aboard the merchant vessels *Speedwell* and *Mayflower* in 1620. Only the *Mayflower* made it, after they had to abandon *Speedwell* 200 miles west of land's end, with over half of the Pilgrims' supplies. *Mayflower* reached what is now Provincetown, Cape Cod, just before winter. They crossed Cape Cod Bay to "New Plymouth," where they wintered aboard ship.

In some ways, the Pilgrim Colony, and the slightly later Puritan one at Boston, signaled another dying gasp of Christendom's church-state paradigm. Yet these colonies formed many important steps in the transition to modern Evangelical Christianity. The Puritans applied some of their views on experiential conversion by the Holy Spirit naïvely, yet it would be wrong to view them only through that lens. They tried to require it as a prerequisite to participate in civil government. Even so, the idea of a genuine conversion to Christ needed reviving. People really did need to experience the grace of God on a personal level, and demonstrate its sanctifying results. In this sense, what happened in the colonies was parallel to, and heavily influenced by, the Pietism going on in Europe.

The Puritans were not wrong for wanting to encourage people who really experienced the work of God in their lives to fill their churches. All believers want this in one way or another. Where they made their mistake was to believe that they could make political rules that would guarantee the situation. In 1648, the Massachusetts Bay Colonies adopted the *Cambridge Platform*; an attempt to codify the burning desire of the first generation colonials. They hoped to prevent their churches from slipping away from a living experience with the Holy Spirit, into formalism, and then apostasy, as they had seen churches do in Europe. Any spiritually living movement would have similar concerns. They were painfully aware of church history and did not want to repeat it.

That the Massachusetts colonies soon repeated history by the very policies they passed to keep from doing so shows the cycle we found in Christian spiritual movements. (Likely, it is true of any movement.) The platform declared; *"The doors of the churches of Christ on earth do not by God's appointment stand so wide open, that all sorts of people good or bad, may freely enter therein at their pleasure."* [1] It was necessary for people who wanted to join the church to be *"examined and tried first."* Generally, that meant they had to testify of their conversion experience. This included being able to demonstrate repentance from sin, faith in Christ by their lifestyle, and explaining what God was currently doing in their life.

That may not be an unreasonable expectation for church membership. Christians need to talk of their faith, examine themselves, and be certain of God's promises, as they live them out. The fact that church membership was required before a person could vote or hold political office in the colonies made things problematic. As time went on, fewer people felt sure that they could tell if they had undergone "conversion" or if they had showed an adequate level of repentance from inward sin. Their parents were Christian, and their own upbringing in Christian homes meant that they were also Christians. Yet, as Chuck Smith often said, *"There are no spiritual grandchildren in the family of God."*

The children and grandchildren of the first generation colonists heard of the vivid conversions of their forebears, and stood in self-doubt. In addition, every generation must have a living relationship with Christ through the Holy Spirit and by the word of God. No legislation of a Christian society can artificially manufacture this, however well meaning. Believers can only cultivate an environment that encourages conversion and discipleship through the un-coerced participation in the ministry of the church. This means a rich teaching and learning ministry, peppered with evangelistic messages, and outreaches to the poor and those with special needs.

Postmodern people often look back with scorn on the Puritans because they tried to "legislate morality" in this way. That is a myopic point of view. Except for some zoning and tax type codes, law by definition is legislated morality. The real question is, *whose morality is being legislated in any given time or place*? Even those third and fourth generation Puritans, who grew tired of mechanically required spirituality, still felt the God of the Bible guided their destiny. They, too, believed that obedience to a Christian code of conduct was the only sensible basis for law. They merely replaced the more spiritually oriented goal of their fathers with the political goal of liberty. Yet, even their definition of liberty stemmed from the Bible. It linked freedom with moral responsibility to God.

It was not so much morality that the Puritans tried to legislate here, as spiritual regeneration. Just as sacramental ritual could not bring regeneration, so making regeneration a condition for public office did not guarantee enough such people to run the system. As is often true, the idea of "regeneration" became more exclusive, and hard to live up to, with the "refinements" of each new generation.

The legalism this policy spawned became as burdensome as it was impractical. Only God knows the number of the truly regenerate. A healthy believer should have an assurance of salvation, and "bring forth fruit worthy of repentance." Yet, there is no realistic way to fully mandate this even in the church, let alone in society. By 1662, membership in the New England colonial churches had dwindled. To keep the system from falling apart, the colonies enacted the "*Half-Way Covenant*." This allowed those who were unsure of their spiritual regeneration to participate in church without being in full communion. "Unsure people" met the minimum requirement of church membership to vote or hold public office, which kept the system manned and afloat.

The Halfway Covenant drove an unhealthy rift through Puritan society by promoting religious snobbery. This, in turn, generated a great deal of frustration and hypocrisy among young and old alike. By the 1690s, all the fuss over who was spiritually "awakened" or not seemed like a politico-religious game to a new generation. This disheveled spiritual mood formed the backdrop for the scandalous Salem Witch Trials of 1692. A late 17th century version of the lurid curiosity and paranoia that drives tabloid sales and conspiracy theorists today fueled the witch-hunts. [2] Prominent pastors, led by Increase Mather, interceded to end the trials, which, many agreed at the time, had gotten out of control.

> *In* Cases of Conscience *Increase Mather forcefully related his distrust of spectral evidence to convict witches. He argued that it would be better that ten witches go free than the blood of a single innocent be shed. One Mather biographer wrote that, "No zeal to stamp out crimes ever drove him from his belief that, whatever the fate of the guilty, the innocent must never be in peril."* Matthew Madden, ***Increase Mather: Salem Witch Trials in History and Literature****, an undergraduate course, University of Virginia, Spring 2001*

In 1691, Massachusetts Bay formed a new charter that based the right to vote and hold office on the ownership of property, and not church membership. Another anemic clone of the Christendom Church-State bit the dust with a whimper.

By the early 18th century, colonial piety settled into a spiritual stagnation as dead as the "popish" Church of England their great grandparents had escaped. Although their attempts to ensure spiritual regeneration by statute had led to widespread silliness (as they always do); the genuine concern of the first generation settlers for spiritual renewal and holiness was not at all silly. We might fault the Puritans for some of their dubious social solutions—as if we, today, are doing better. Yet their diagnosis of the central need in the church for this basic biblical dynamic was not off target.

The dawn of the 1700s saw rising public drunkenness and bar fights in New England, and many new brides who "miraculously" gave birth after pregnancies of only four or five months. One thing had become apparent. Mechanical church attendance in a culture defined by rules based on biblical morality was unable to produce the kind of society Puritans of either stripe had hoped. God had mightily moved in the lives of their forefathers, but this did not make the Puritan colonists immune to an unintended blind spot. They had unrealistically raised their expectations of the kind of social order within grasp of human government. Man neurotically tried to take control to make sure spiritual vitality would never again fade away. He didn't necessarily mean to. He just did.

The classic Galatians 3:3 rhetorical question sums it up nicely, **"Having begun with the Spirit, are you now ending with the flesh?"** It was also the classic story of church history in microcosm. If we are not careful, it will be the classic story of our present-day churches, as well as each of our individual lives—if it isn't already. It seemed as if the dominant church social model of the last 1400 years had to die to itself completely in the New World. Only then, could biblical faith experience any kind of full germination in new soil.

The Great Awakening began like a major river, from several independent springs and tributaries that joined downstream to make a unified rush for the sea. This river, and its branches, swept over the drought parched spiritual ground of the colonial churches, beginning in 1720. That it began in widely scattered places, with people who were not in contact with one another, at first, is evidence of the Holy Spirit's orchestration. It started in the Raritan Valley of New Jersey, where a newly arrived Dutch Reformed pastor of Pietistic conviction named Theodore Frelinghuysen began to reach the hearts of the local farmers. Evangelist, George Whitefield later described it, using classical English understatement, as *"an ingathering of new members"* into the church. [3]

Soon the spiritual eddies flowed together with those from the Pennsylvania "Log College" of Scotch-Irish Presbyterian, William Tennant. The growing river meandered south, where it met with the ministry of Samuel Davies. Davies was busy planting revivalist Presbyterian churches all across Virginia. Another southerner, Shubael Stearns, did the same thing among the Baptists. Meanwhile, in New England, a spring had broken through the dehydrated soil to begin a new stream that would encompass all of Massachusetts Bay, and beyond.

In the western Massachusetts hamlet of Northampton, a young pastor took over a church of some 200 families steeped in what he called an *"extraordinary dullness in religion."* He complained of the frequency of public drunkenness at the taverns, and of what he called the *"lewd practices"* among the young men and women of the community. [4] His name was Jonathan Edwards, and everything he lamented in the spiritual condition of New England was about to change.

Edwards wrote that in December of 1734, *"The Spirit of God began extraordinarily to set in;"* and that a *"great and earnest concern about the great things of… the eternal world"* washed through Northampton. [5] People remember Edwards for his most famous sermon, *Sinners in the Hands of an Angry God*. From this, they develop a stereotype of him as the original shrieking hellfire and brimstone preacher. Actually, Edwards was so nearsighted that he had to hunch over his pulpit and practically read his messages in a kind of monotone. He was an intellectual and a scholar, the third president of Princeton University. Today's glitzy world of flamboyant televangelism would dismiss him casually and stupidly as "un-anointed" for his lack of charisma.

The Holy Spirit, on the other hand, worked powerfully through his preaching. Edwards' sermons drew listeners into such a real and potent awareness of God's presence and holiness that many would cry out in terror and wonder at the tangible sense of impending eternal damnation apart from God; and the nearness of God's mercy and forgiveness. Emotional enthusiasm grew so intense in the congregations that Edwards had to pause in his teaching to allow the people to calm down. At first, he was tolerant of these "enthusiasms" as he called them, not wanting to dilute the powerful work of the Holy Spirit or risk quenching it in any way.

As time went on, however, it grew more and more clear that many people came to the revivals just to experience the "enthusiasms" like some new kind of stimulant. Soon, it became the worst kind of distraction from the real work of the Spirit, the teaching of God's word. Edwards gave us several eyewitness impressions, as a pastor, of what he saw going on around him as the Great Awakening went on. His observations about the waning days of the revivals are telling.

*Lukewarmness in religion is abominable and zeal an excellent grace; yet above all other Christian virtues, this needs to be strictly watched and searched; for it is that with which corruption, and particularly pride and human passion is exceedingly apt to mix unobserved.*

*Many godly persons have undoubtedly in this and other ages, exposed themselves to woeful delusions, by an aptness to lay too much weight on impulses and impressions, as if they were immediate revelations from God, to signify something future, or to direct them where to go, and what to do… And it is particularly observable, that in times of great pouring out of the Spirit to revive religion in the world, a number of those who for a while seem to partake in it, have fallen off into whimsical and extravagant errors, and gross enthusiasm, boasting of high degrees of spirituality and perfection, censuring and condemning others as carnal.*

***Works of Jonathan Edwards, Vol.** 2, excerpts from pp. 264 & 265*

It would seem Edwards' remarks track with the spiritual movement model described in Chapter 17. Even as the Awakening reached its peak, the seeds of its own demise were already planted and firmly taking root. Let us first consider the climax, and some of the Awakening's lasting legacy, not focus only on negative side effects.

George Whitefield, the great English revivalist, and friend of the Wesley brothers, came to the colonies in 1739. He made a grand sweep north from Georgia, as if to channel the various tributaries of the revival together into a single roaring flood. This not only united the Awakening into a cohesive movement, it tied it to the Wesleyan Revival in Britain. The two revivals supported each other across the Atlantic through prayer, funding, and sometimes an exchange of speakers. Whitefield made it to New England in 1740, where he preached at Edwards' church. Soon after that, Edwards and other revivalist pastors did a regular traveling circuit. They guest spoke at one another's congregations in what became a traditional pattern that has hung on to this day.

At one of these mobile evangelistic meetings in Connecticut, a 17-year-old young man found repentance and the "inward witness" of the Holy Spirit. Isaac Backus would have a compelling impact on how future America came to understand the relationship between church and government. Unlike the Puritan settlers, the converts of the Great Awakening shook off Christendom's church-state fusion. Backus spearheaded a conviction on the church's role in society that historians call ***voluntaryism***. (One should not confuse this with an unrelated term—*voluntarism*, minus the *y*). Voluntaryism held that no government could force real conversion and spiritual regeneration on people, from the top down. Any attempt to force this has always, and will always, backfire in nasty ways.

The Puritans, with their watered-down church-state ***Congregational*** charters, were aghast at this new idea. *Congregational* refers to that uniquely American form of church government where the congregation of members all had voting rights. Episcopalian leadership looked like monarchy, and the presbyterian model, a republic. The congregational form of church government resembled pure democracy. Pure democracy always sounds good until you actually have one. Soon, an unmanageable bureaucracy of committees sucks time and energy from the ability to make capable and timely decisions. A charismatic demagogue often churns to the surface, who dominates by working the system. The situation then becomes more autocratic than any monarchy.

Colony-backed congregationally led churches still had the form of state churches. Roger Williams fled Massachusetts to found Rhode Island because he had a different view on certain doctrines from the Puritan party line. By the early 1700s, many little unofficial autocracies gripped Congregational systems, wedded to local civil governments. Church membership was down. Then, along came the Great Awakening to challenge the *status quo*. *Status quos* being what they are, we can thank God the Puritan charters, by this time, mostly just empowered church and civil leaders only to be aghast.

Isaac Backus and his peers had stumbled for the first time upon something we take for granted in American Christianity today. He held that it was useless to constrain people legally to believe, and that any effort to do so does more harm to the cause of Christ than good. The Great Awakening thus marked itself as one of the first modern expressions of Evangelical faith. In it, intellectual and moral persuasion became the only legitimate tools for spreading the gospel. It was the job of the church, not the state, to sponsor and support evangelism. This fell out quite logically from the Calvinist idea that election, and then sanctification, were works of God and not men.

Therefore, adherence to the principles of Scripture must be voluntary, and not coerced by government. In that way, only the truly converted will want to do the work of the church. Those who do not really wish to be there, will be free to go their own way in this life, and responsible to deal with the eternal consequences.

This was not to say that secular leaders could not apply Bible principles generically in politics to make sensible laws; or in any application of ethics, as claimed today. While voluntaryism also had problems, it proved a far better approach than the political coercion that had marked so much of church history. It left the door open for general biblical ideas to impact politics for good, without making the government sponsor any one denomination. The real concern, however, was the harsher scenario of making the church a slave to the government's political agendas. This idea set the stage for what later appeared in the *Constitution of the United States* Bill of Rights, regarding what Jefferson, later still, called the "separation of church and state." It also opened the door for one of the strangest, most remarkable political and social alliances in history.

Unlike their French counterparts, American deists accepted a Christian philosophy that rejected the idea of state churches as they did, if for other reasons. Today, a secular academic world seeks to recast the American Founding Fathers as deist skeptics. This is historic revisionism—to the extent that we often see it done. The most effective revisionism bases itself on a kernel of truth, however. A small, but significant, minority of the Founders were deists, like Thomas Jefferson. Jefferson published a version of the New Testament with all accounts of the supernatural removed from it. Nevertheless, he came at least, to believe in a God that will judge human hearts and actions in the end.

> *God who gave us life gave us liberty. And can the liberties of a nation be thought secure when we have removed their only firm basis, a conviction in the minds of the people that these liberties are a gift from God? …That they are not to be violated but with His wrath? Indeed, I tremble for my country when I reflect that God is just, and that His justice cannot sleep forever.* –Thomas Jefferson, ***excerpts of his writings inscribed on the walls of the Jefferson Memorial in Washington DC***

Of the American deists, only Thomas Paine, and Ethan Allen showed anything like the rancorous anti-church attitude found in France. Other Founders, though not deists, and possibly even Christian, or at least nominally so, had beliefs somewhat influenced by Deism. Some of this minority among the Founders became Universalists and Unitarians during the 1790s through 1820s. Many deists felt more at home in these theologically non-Christian, monotheistic bordering on pantheist religions. Together, these groups made up a small, vocal bloc; but one which still thought in culturally Christian terms, with moral absolutes consistent with Judeo-Christian ones.

We who are Conservative Evangelical Christians, today, often say that the Founding Fathers established the United States as a Christian nation. When we say this, we should be very clear about what we mean by "Christian Nation;" especially since President Barrack Obama announced to the world that America is no longer Christian. We Christians cannot indulge in counter-revisionism. We do not mean that the Founders established a ***theocracy***—I actually heard a preacher, fishing for words at an intense moment, blurt that out on the radio. He misspoke, rather than expressed his actual view. I had the chance to meet him, and speak to him about it. He agreed it was the wrong idea.

The Founders established a secular constitutional republic. It was *secular* in the sense that it had no ties to a formal state church denomination. It was not an *ideologically* secular republic, which banned Judeo-Christian social ideas from public policy. It did not govern only from ideas with no cultural and spiritual connection to the Bible. Any casual read of source documents written by the Founders would easily disprove this present-day myth.

A modern ideological *Secularism* marked the French Revolution, not the American one. Ideology functions the same way as religious dogma at the epistemological level; that is, in the mechanics of how we process ideas. The French Revolution, and every revolution since marked by an ideological Secularism, showed fanaticism at least as great as in any Christian religious war. What such revolutions lacked was as many potential influences toward moral restraint. Those who think themselves unaccountable to God are less likely to behave as if they are. Robespierre, Lenin, Stalin, Mao, and Pol Pot prove that much. Hitler and Mussolini had some nominal connection to the church, but did not have biblical belief systems.

Nor do historically literate Conservative Christians mean by a "Christian nation" that the Founders were all "born-again Christians." Many were, based on their writings, but many were also "high church" Episcopalians, who did not think in terms of having a conversion experience. Others had formal church affiliations because of social expectations. These thought in secular political terms, similar to John Locke. Locke took the theological concepts in Samuel Rutherford's *Lex Rex* and secularized them for political use. By *secular* and *secularized*, I do not necessarily imply anything bad, here. Until recently, the term *secular* had simply meant *that realm of life that applied civically to everyone, not just the church*.

What we mean by "Christian nation" is that the Founders thought and wrote within a generally Judeo-Christian worldview framework. They had a view of law based on moral absolutes consistent with those in the Bible. Although they recognized no allegiance to a particular denomination or sect in their political writings, most evidenced genuine respect for the Bible. They spoke freely of the Creator, and built from biblical concepts, as in the *Declaration of Independence*, and in the U.S. Constitution's Bill of Rights.

> *We hold these truths to be self-evident: That all men are created equal; that they are endowed* ***by their Creator*** *with certain unalienable rights; that among these are life, liberty, and the pursuit of happiness; that, to secure these rights, governments are instituted among men…*
> **The Declaration of Independence**

> *As Constitution signer John Dickinson explained,* ***an inalienable right was a right "which God gave to you and which no inferior power has a right to take away."*** [148] *John Adams similarly attested that the* ***inalienable rights of man were rights "antecedent to all earthly government; rights that cannot be repealed or restrained by human laws; rights derived from the great Legislator of the universe."*** [149] *It was from among such inalienable – or natural – rights that the framers specifically identified the right to life, liberty, property, self-protection, pursuit of happiness, etc.*
> *David Barton,* ***Evolution and the Law: A Death Struggle Between Two Civilizations,***
> *(Barton cites Bill of Rights framer, John Dickinson, and 2nd President, John Adams)*

What we mean by "Christian nation" is that the Founders (whether Christian, Universalist, or deistic) wrote in ways that honored God's place in society. They were not inherently hostile to Christian faith, and established a nation that reflected that kind of morality. They were not in the business of coercing changes in peoples' belief systems. They did not create government schools designed to subvert the family ethics of a mostly Judeo-Christian people. Nor did they introduce morally and medically self-destructive lifestyles to the young under a pretext of "sex education" or "sensitivity training."

We mean by "Christian nation" only what historical source documents confirm; that the Founders worked from a culturally Judeo-Christian worldview, even if some of them did not hold biblically orthodox views of God.

Exactly which Founder fits in what category is sometimes open to debate, as we shall see with Benjamin Franklin. Franklin rebelled against his Puritan upbringing, entered adulthood in Philadelphia under deist influences; but, through long friendship with George Whitefield, likely died as a prodigal Christian. [6] Franklin's writings fit that progression. Of course, no one can say absolutely. We can only go by the source writings.

In the late 18th century, Enlightenment-influenced deists like Thomas Jefferson, Ethan Allen, and Thomas Paine formed an odd, but often friendly alliance with the children of the Great Awakening; represented by such figures as Patrick Henry, Benjamin Rush, John Witherspoon, Samuel Hopkins, Samuel and John Adams, James Madison, and Roger Sherman. Both ideological forces in the Continental Congress recognized something important. Any attempt of one to suppress the other would only lead to either a Christian or a secular tyranny. The only valid constitutional concern was about the negatives of a state church denomination. Nobody foolishly imagined a "right" not to experience any social presence from a majority opinion.

Most everybody understood a need for genuine tolerance.

This is not the distorted view of "tolerance" bandied about today in the name of separation of church and state, where "freedom of religion" has become "freedom from religion." People do not have the right to have their worldviews artificially shielded from all challenge from civil intellectual or moral reasoning. Many of the Founders saw how biblical ethics provided an important moral foundation in society; that without such a base, the guarantees of liberty in the Bill of Rights could not work.

> *It is religion and morality alone which can establish the principles upon which freedom can securely stand. The only foundation of a free constitution is pure virtue.* John Adams [7]

> *Our liberty depends on our education, our laws, and habits… it is founded on morals and religion, whose authority reigns in the heart, and on the influence all these produce on public opinion before that opinion governs rulers.* Fisher Ames, framer of the First Amendment "Establishment Clause" [8]

> *We have no government armed with power capable of contending with human passions unbridled by morality and religion. Avarice, ambition, revenge, or gallantry, would break the strongest cords of our Constitution as a whale goes through a net.* ***Our Constitution was made only for a moral and religious people. It is wholly inadequate to the government of any other***. John Adams, October 11, 1798, Letter to the officers of the First Brigade of the Third Division of the Militia of Massachusetts [9]

> *The highest glory of the American Revolution was this: it connected in one indissoluble bond, the principles of civil government with the principles of Christianity.* John Quincy Adams, in a speech addressed to the House of Representatives, July 4th, 1821 [10]

Consider what even the supposedly dyed-in-the-wool deist, Benjamin Franklin had to say at the Constitutional Convention of June 28, 1787:

> *I have lived, Sir, a long time, and the longer I live, the more convincing proof I see of the truth - that God governs in the affairs of men. And if a sparrow cannot fall to the ground without His notice, is it probable that an empire can rise without his aid? We have been assured, Sir, in the sacred writings, that 'except the Lord build the House, they labor in vain that build it.' I firmly believe this; and I also believe that without this concurring aid we shall succeed in this political building no better, than the Builders of Babel: We shall be divided by our partial local interests; our projects will be confounded, and we ourselves shall become a*

> *reproach and bye word down to future ages. And what is worse, mankind may hereafter from this unfortunate instance, despair of establishing government by human wisdom and leave it to chance, war and conquest. I therefore beg leave to move - that henceforth prayers imploring the audience of Heaven, and its blessings on our deliberations, be held in this assembly every morning before we proceed to business, and that one or more of the clergy of this city be requested to officiate in that service.* Benjamin Franklin, 1787 [11]

The point that all these, and many other, source documents make is clear. The U.S. Constitution can only successfully govern a people with a voluntary consensus, based on worldviews that have the same moral absolutes. They need not all belong to the same religious denomination, and they need not all have the same theology. However, they do require an ethical consensus centered on the respect of moral absolutes based on a law higher than human law. A people without such a consensus would soon make chaos of the freedoms our Constitution offers. It is mechanically impossible to have things both ways.

It would seem that Benjamin Franklin, who had been close friends with George Whitefield, might have relented in the end, possibly at fond memories of Whitfield's many attempts to win him to the Faith. Whitefield had died seventeen years before, in 1770. In any event, age now wore on Franklin. Within three years, he, too, would be dead.

By the time of the American Revolution, the Great Awakening had already died out. Yet its legacy in the American concept of religious liberty, as people and the courts commonly understood before the 1960s, lived on. In all, the colonial Awakening lasted only a little more than twenty-five years. Jonathan Edwards' biographer, Ian Murray, recounts Edwards' personal assessment of why the revivals died out.

> *He came to believe that there was one principle cause of the reversal, namely, the unwatchfulness of the friends of the Awakening who allowed genuine and pure religion to become so mixed with "wildfire," and carnal "enthusiasm," that the Spirit of God was grieved and advantage given to Satan.*
>
> *Ian H. Murray, **Jonathan Edwards: A New Biography**, p. 126*

As with other revivals, the Awakening not only generated light, but also heat. As time went on, the heat began to burn out the light. Church splits and infighting began to gnaw at the foundations. Between that and the unfettered popular "enthusiasms," the whole thing just flew off in different directions. Edwards lived to see the Awakening dwindle, and commented on it. His words are an instructive bit of providence for us today. We can learn from past mistakes—especially ones spelled out so clearly for us in the writings of men like Edwards. Believers do not have to sabotage the work that God is trying to do in our own generation, the way it happened in the 18th century.

One thing is certain, when we factor in human nature. We are bound to be making enough original mistakes of our own.

## JOHN WESLEY AND REVIVAL IN THE INDUSTRIAL REVOLUTION

The Great Awakening was part of a broader revitalization of Western Christianity during the middle of the 18th century. The Pietists and Moravian Brethren had revivals in Germany and Central Europe. Meanwhile, a skinny little Anglican preacher discovered the meaning of God's power through the gospel in his own life. He would become the unlikely father of the Methodists, as well as the later Holiness and Pentecostal movements. Unlike his American counterparts, he would see Scripture with an Arminian view, despite respectful and brotherly friendship to Calvinists, like George Whitefield.

The story of John Wesley (1703-1791) reads a little like the old Don Knotts film *The Reluctant Astronaut* in colonial garb. While he crossed the Atlantic to take up a pastorate in the Colonies, Wesley's ship encountered a terrible storm, and seemed in danger of sinking.

The young minister surprised himself at how terrified he was of dying. All the while, gathered in the hold, a band of Moravian Pietists with their wives and children sang and worshipped in the midst of the sea's fury. When the storm abated, Wesley marveled at them and asked whether even one of their children had feared death. The Pietist settlers explained the implications of the gospel to this gospel preacher. Wesley came away with the profound awareness that these people had something he lacked. When his pastorate in the Georgia Colony bore no fruit, except a broken romance, Wesley returned to England depressed over his sense of failure.

It was not that Wesley had been exactly out of touch spiritually up until that time. He had led a Bible study fellowship at Oxford, along with his brother Charles, and George Whitefield. They had dedicated themselves to the renewal of a first century style Christianity in the Anglican Church. Their group had also been concerned over the growing popularity of Deism at the university. John had been their natural leader, despite his freely admitting that he lacked the spiritual peace that normally came with that territory. The popular deist clique had labeled them with all sorts of mocking names. One of them, *Methodist*, took hold—just as the first century believers had been derisively called "Christians" first at Antioch. (Acts 11:26) Believers can proudly wear the name of "Jesus Freak" in the same way today.

Wesley had left this group for the colonies, full of missionary zeal. His Bible-centeredness all along made his return more difficult to take. It was not as if he had started out as a "high church formalist" with no heart for God's word. This very pride in his own background only contributed to his spiritual emptiness. He had made the mistake of trying to emulate Christian virtue in his own strength and that strength had inevitably failed him.

John Wesley discovered the real meaning of spiritual empowerment when he looked up one of his old Moravian friends, who had come to live in London. The Moravian explained that regeneration was more than just a doctrine, but a gift from God John had to receive experientially. It happened quietly one night, while John read Luther's introduction to the Book of Romans. The inner witness of the Holy Spirit filled him with assurance of the forgiveness of sins.

Brief Sunday homilies were not sufficient for John to communicate the depth of what he had experienced or what God wanted him to do in the church. The senior rectors were displeased with so much Bible teaching to a laity who was not supposed to understand it so well. Wesley began reluctantly to preach outdoors, at George Whitefield's urging. John felt uncomfortable with the idea of souls being saved, and nourished, outside of a church building. He soon lost this cultural inhibition with unparalleled abandon, when he saw the thousands come to Christ in response.

The Methodist Revival swept first through Bristol, melting the hearts of the hardened coal miners there. I think that the work among the coal miners represents one of the most significant aspects of Wesley's ministry. The Industrial Revolution had increased the demand for coal and the demands made on the miners. Human exploitation bred by the Enlightenment Materialism of wealthy manufacturing moguls made harsher conditions for workers. Too often, at first, the high church ignored this, its emphasis on form and intellectualism tuned to the trends of the educated upper class instead. Wesley came like a breath of summer air into a culture where **"the love of many waxed cold."** (Mat. 24:12)

The Methodist impact on the Anglican Church, and their eventual separation from it after Wesley's death, is well known. Less likely to be acknowledged nowadays are the positive effects the revivals had on culture in general; and on the twin scandals of industrial child abuse and slavery based on race in particular.

## John Newton, William Wilberforce and the Abolition of Slavery in Britain

The social ills of the 18th and 19th centuries read like a scarlet letter *H* on Anglo-American civilization—for *hypocrisy*. Christian churches, as institutions, often seemed strangely double-minded. Their responses to abuses of humanity brought by the new industrial society, at first, seemed to mirror whatever social class the church served. On the one hand, traditional church institutions religiously supported charity; while on the other, they did not speak out consistently against social abuses perpetrated by wealthy patrons.

People saw the slave trade in the latter decades of the 1700s as vital to British commerce and national security. The Methodist revivals shook the institutional churches. It forced complacent believers to face the logical inconsistency of tolerating slavery based on race, and brutal child labor, in a Christian culture.

Nobody illustrated the moral strain this put on the soul of the thoughtful, or even the not-so-thoughtful individual, as did John Newton. A rowdy slave trader, and Royal Navy deserter, who bordered on the buccaneer, Newton worked a ship running between the Ivory Coast and the West Indies. Shipmasters packed Black Africans aboard like sardines, chained to the deck in abominable stench and filth. The Holy Spirit used Newton's exposure to the revivals in England and the colonies, plus Thomas A` Kempis' *My Imitation of Christ*, to bring gradual, yet in time, deep conversion in this crusty reprobate. Newton entered the ministry, and became one of the outstanding opponents of the slave trade as his Bible-based convictions grew.

People know John Newton more commonly for the great hymns he composed, the most popular and enduring of which is *Amazing Grace*. Understanding the man's background, it becomes plain that the words; *"Amazing grace how sweet the sound that saved a wretch like me,"* were no mere religious hyperbole.

If the moral tug of the revivals reached the common sailor, they exerted a force just as profound ashore, even to the highest levels of government. Parliament statesman, William Wilberforce, joined a small group of politically connected Bible students known as the Clapham Sect (for their meeting in that suburb of London, not because they were sectarian). They worked tirelessly toward the legal abolition of the slave trade. In the late 1780s, this goal seemed about as likely to succeed as the overturning of *Roe versus Wade* does to pro-life advocates today. When Wilberforce gave his first Abolitionist speech before Parliament, in 1789, few people took him seriously.

The Clapham fellowship blitzed public opinion with tracts that revealed the sheer brutality of slavery. It gradually won over an increasing number of prominent people. Wilberforce harnessed the moral outrage of public opinion, and brought it to bear like a naval broadside against the government. He had at his command a moral and spiritual consensus still well fired with the flames of the Methodist Revival, the most enduring of all the 18th century awakenings. By 1807, Britain not only outlawed the slave trade, it did so cheerfully, with a great applause never before or since seen in Parliament.

One wonders if the Americans might have also abolished slavery this early, if only the Great Awakening had gone on a bit longer. The politico-economic rationalizations for keeping slavery alive in the new United States were no more powerful than those the opponents of Wilberforce raised. However, by the late 1700s, the churches in America were again in steady decline. The issue of slavery there would have to wait for another generation.

## BIBLIOGRAPHY

1. ***Cambridge Platform*** (1648) – cited in Bruce L. Shelly's ***Church History in Plain Language***, p. 343
2. Starkey, Marion L.; ***The Devil in Massachusetts***, Editor's Preface & pp.1-4; (1949) Time Inc.
3. Shelley, Bruce L. ***Church History in Plain Language*** (2nd Edition), p. 345, 1995, Word Publishing, Dallas, Tx.
4. Ibid. pp. 345-346
5. Ibid. pp. 345-346
6. Eidsmoe, John, ***Christianity and the Constitution***, Baker Book House, Grand Rapids, Michigan, 1987, pp. 192-195, & p. 206, see also, Frank Lambert, ***The Religious Odd Couple***, Christian History, Vol 12 No 2 Issue 38, pp. 30-32
7. Charles Francis Adams, ***The Works of John Adams, Second President of the United States***, editor (Boston: Little, Brown, 1854), Vol. IX, p. 401, Letter to Zabdiel Adams dated June 21, 1776.)
8. Fisher Ames, ***An Oration on the Sublime Virtues of General George Washington***, (Boston: Young & Minns, 1800), p. 23.
9. Op cit. Charles Francis Adams, pp. 228-229.
10. Cited by John Wingate Thornton, in ***The Pulpit of The American Revolution***, 1860
11. John Bigelow, ***The Life of Benjamin Franklin***, J.B. Lippencott Co., 1893, footnote, pg. 378, "The following note is appended in the handwriting of Dr. Franklin to the original draft of this speech: 'The convention, except three or four persons, thought prayer unnecessary.'" A secondary source gives the same notation as a footnote on pg. 452 of Max Farrand's ***Records of the Federal Convention***, Yale University Press, 1911. ***The situation described in this note compelled Franklin to act by calling for prayer***.]

# 20

# The Time of Shifting Foundations

## Materialistic Faith-Assumptions in Philosophy and Theology: the Rise of Liberalism

In the 2nd through 5th centuries, Greco-Roman believers viewed their Christian faith through different basic assumptions about reality than did the earliest Hebrew disciples. Christians could accommodate the Greek worldview sometimes. Its presuppositions did not deny the existence of a spiritual or supernatural reality. The church adapted, but also had identity and ideology distortions in proportion to its acceptance of some Greek notions contrary to Bible content. This created a pattern of problems, which eventually made the Reformation necessary.

At the dawn of the 19th century, a new and far more dangerous shift in foundational faith-assumptions about reality undermined the walls of Western thought and culture. Not only was the emerging worldview more antagonistic to biblical faith concepts than the older Greco-Roman one; it came at a time when churches were far less ready, and far less unified in their spiritual and intellectual response. The fact that Christianity was still culturally dominant, in the political and the moral worldview senses, did not protect the Faith. In some ways, it only made matters worse. Christians of the 19th century hugely misjudged how fragile a hold Christian thought and culture really had on Western Civilization.

If a growing consensus saw only the material world as the "real world," and the Bible did not fit that view; then the idea that the God of the Bible was the God of reality must ultimately lose its cultural power. That is what most people today believe has happened. Some want to believe that. Others do so merely because they have never seriously questioned the idea to see if it really holds up. The second group may believe it because they think science has already proved that materialism is true. Either way, if the God of the Bible is not the God of reality, then the Christian gospel, and everything it offers, is just a fantasy. Enlightenment rationalists saw this more clearly than most Christians did. This was their goal in reviving Epicureanism, and re-tooling it to de-bunk the Christian worldview.

Nor did it take a massive academic conspiracy to send things along this trajectory. All it took was a similar mindset in several influential academic schools, which exploited the worldview blind spots of their society. It only took that, and a spiritual enemy who used that dynamic in a far more conscious and coordinated way. While a few academics, like Thomas Hobbes, Spinoza, and Rousseau, actively conspired to revive Epicurus, most were simply gamed by their own blind spots. [1]

On the bright side, the Reformation dynamic was still alive in many quarters, bringing Scripture to bear as a measuring stick and filter for what was coming. The 19th century revivals also blossomed; a series of highly effective soul-winning ventures built on the Reformation, Pietism, and the two Great Awakenings, but mostly on God's word. God used these, and similar works, to restore and revitalize the preaching of the gospel's saving truth. This ensured that reasonably biblical teaching and worship forms survived and grew, where allowed to do so. On the other hand, that cycle could not work uniformly in all churches. Breakdown went on in churches mostly unprepared for the ideological attacks soon coming, not only from outside, but from trusted education institutions within.

I call this the *Time of Shifting Foundations* because the superstructure of Western culture began to detach from its Judeo-Christian base. It shifted, and then reattached onto a new foundation of starting assumptions about truth and reality. This new base was hostile to the content of the old foundation. I do not mean that persecutions broke out, although that did happen in France, and later, under Marxist regimes. I mean that the assumptions of the new foundation radically opposed those of the old one. They could not reasonably lead to the same social outcomes, given the same evidence.

Picture this like a bottled water plant built over a natural spring of clear crystal purity. People depend on the water because most of the local wells are bad. Then, one day, a fleet of helicopters come, and lifts the factory from its foundation. The helicopters fly it away, and lower it onto a new well system polluted by industrial waste. The people who buy the bottled water suspect something has changed, but can't tell what, without testing the water or knowing about the factory relocation. In the same way, the new worldview scooped up and transplanted the culture of many churches onto a new intellectual foundation; one that assumed that what these churches had historically believed and taught was fraudulent.

What was this emerging worldview, and how has it affected the teachings of the church in the most recent two centuries?

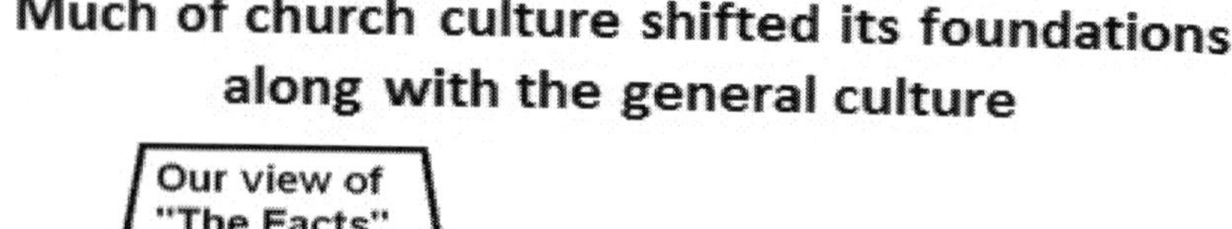


I began to cover the academic revival of Epicureanism after the Religious Wars, how it drove the rise of a rigorously materialistic worldview, in Chapter 18. To understand this worldview's effect on religion, we must understand how it affected the way people viewed science. I do not mean how it affected science itself. The next section of this chapter will cover that. We saw in Chapter 18 that *science*, and *how people view science*, is two different things. For clarity, historians of Western thought and culture call the latter ***scientism***. We also saw how Methodological Naturalism; the *idea that scientific methods can only deal with natural phenomena*, drifted toward Ideological Naturalism. This, too, describes the hope that science would prove the ultimate way to know all things, and thus solve man's problems.

Men like Voltaire, in France, emphasized a form of Isaac Newton's Mechanist science philosophy stripped of some of its logical implications. Newton had stressed the mechanical nature of the laws of physics as a way of defending the idea of an intelligent engineer God. Voltaire and others like him, responded by playing on a popular fear-based fallacy; that a universe that operates by mechanically explainable laws has no need for a supernatural God. Voltaire's Deism admitted an intelligent creator, but only one as trapped in the machine of the universe as men were, even if more powerful than us. This god was limited to using only nature's laws, however. We had no more hope of knowing it than an ant has of knowing us.

While such a view might superficially sound plausible, it has no real basis in cause-and-effect reason. One might develop an emotional fear that natural law would make a supernatural God unnecessary, as even many Christian thinkers did at this time. It was still a fear based on a lack of understanding. I do not mean a "lack of understanding" of the laws of nature, as in a "God of the Gaps" argument, but a lack of knowing what logically follows what. No one on either side of the gulf between the Enlightenment and Reformation understood the effects of man being able to explain how the universe worked.

Certainly, there was an over-estimation of man's abilities here, typified by arrogance on the Enlightenment side, and by fear on the more-or-less Christian one. Even so, it does not logically follow that if the cosmos works by understandable natural laws, then a supernatural God becomes pointless. This is because mechanics in nature, as in human industry, still demands an engineer outside the machinery to have designed and built it. The fact that miracles are not common, that God has structured creation to function by predictable principles, and that He is usually happy to let it do so; does not mean that God cannot and does not sometimes interact with the flow. Nor would it make a record of such interactions in history innately impossible.

Nature is a system of effects, some of which are secondary causes. Science shows that all effects have less usable energy and order than their causes. Therefore, nature demands a *super*-natural cause. Philosophical materialism is not a logical necessity for science. Science began, and functioned for some time, without it.

Though deists admitted the creation work of a "divine engineer" in nature, they rejected that this engineer had revealed Himself as the God of the Bible. Yet, their distaste for the Christian revelation of God was an emotional response, not a truly rational one. This revulsion predated Darwin by almost two hundred years. All during that time, many materialistic rationalists searched. In quiet desperation, they hoped someday to find a scientifically plausible origins model with no need of a supernatural creator. If the discipline of science proved, at first, a hard nut to crack for Enlightenment "Neo-Epicureans," philosophy was often as pliable as silly putty. It quickly shifted to the new view because, too often, ideology can pose as philosophy.

Ultimately, philosophy and ideology, not science, shapes the popular mind, which includes the way people view science, and interpret evidence. Here is a subtle line between *philosophy* and *mere ideologies that use philosophy*, such as Epicureanism, Marxism, and Postmodernism. *Philosophy* is a tool set applicable for understanding the nuts-and-bolts of any belief system. An *ideology* is itself a belief system. Even academics sometimes carelessly use these two words interchangeably, however. I probably have, also. Language is not always as precise as the ideas it must express. Philosophical reasoning skills are important tools for anyone. Ideologies, on the other hand, each have their own premises, which often involve making faith-assumptions as dogmatic as those of any religion.

Ideology also expresses itself in the language of reason, even when it violates reason. This lends it to easy propagation in arts and entertainment media. Perception can be powerful, even when based on a logical fallacy. The mechanics of Newton were a wonderful thing when viewed as the handiwork of a loving Creator. Yet, when Deism downplayed the logical implications of having a Divine engineer, and then ***Agnosticism*** seemed to remove them, the same mechanics became a trap for the human soul. Without the assumption of a designer in nature, its mechanics becomes meaningless, and even harmful.

Agnosticism was the next logical step for philosophical speculation, a generation after Deism. While a deist assumes God exists, but claims He is unknowable, an agnostic assumes that there is no way to know if there is an unknowable god or not. He wraps the whole idea of *God* in a suggestion of irrelevance, even when talking about origins. An up-and-coming generation of materialist academics had popularized this suggestion, over fifty years *before*

Darwin. By then, Epicurean assumptions had shaped an academic thought culture starving for an origins account without a supernatural God. The reason for this hunger was simple. A materialistic worldview could not long hold the ground it had recently taken without one.

Yet this was an entirely artificial "need." Science and reason did not truly demand it; only an ideology making religious pretensions, using the subtly redefined terminology of science and reason did. Every worldview needs its own creation myth as every car needs a chassis.

Under Newton's assumption of an open-system universe (with respect to God's ability to act into it from beyond), understanding the mechanics of natural laws enhanced our concept of what the psalmist taught when he said; **"I am fearfully and wonderfully made."** (Ps. 139:14) In the Enlightenment's faith-assumption of an absolute closed-system universe, God appeared to grow less and less relevant to modern life. This presumption suggested that the laws of nature implied people were ultimately meaningless biochemical machines, with no real free will, and nothing more than that. It did this not because any evidence objectively proved such a thing. Rather, this assumption force-marched the interpretation of the evidence. That same grid also prevented asking any questions of the evidence that might lead to alternate conclusions; applied Epicureanism in action.

Ideological Naturalism ruled out questions of purpose and design.

This artificially divided the logically related idea couplets of *form and function* from *design and purpose* in the study of living things. Many 19th century biologists did this with starry-eyed faith in the simplicity of the "simple cell" and of atoms. Epicurean Naturalism relied on this hope; that universal simplicity in the micro world, where particles would prove to work randomly, or through a few simple principles, could explain away all the apparent design complexity in the visible macro world. The problem for trying to sustain this outmoded view of science is that the evidence has not cooperated over the long haul.

Modern molecular biologists now know the cell is extremely complex. Early training still attempts to condition them not to see this logical disconnect. Reality, however, forces them to use design-engineering models to study the increasingly complex cell. Early conditioning to ignore the implications of why this is necessary can only go so far. Using design-engineering models is unavoidable. Early conditioning only makes it seem "outside of their field" for researchers to consider the implications of why. Still, an environment of hyper-specialization often detaches scientific questions from philosophical ones to save time.

Modern cosmology plays a similar game in looking for a unified field theory—a "theory of everything." Even if they find such a sublime simplicity in the basic building blocks of the cosmos, it still would not prove that matter is the ultimate reality. Not in a universe where we know that space is expanding, carrying along the matter in it. This implies an origin point when everything was together. Though wrong about much else, the Big Bang model at least got that right. Yet, this only happened after a wasted century; while materialists tried desperately to make "eternal universe" Steady State cosmologies work. Simple structures at the subatomic level would only prove that a vast intelligence made some basic building blocks, and used them to build a breathtakingly complex creation. Think of a Lego Boston.

This non-compliance of the evidence to late 19th century expectations prompted world-renowned astrophysicist, Dr. Robert Jastrow, to write the following, in the 1970s.

> *For the scientist who has lived by his faith in the power of reason, the story ends like a bad dream. He has scaled the mountains of ignorance, he is about to conquer the highest peak; as he pulls himself over the final rock, he is greeted by a band of theologians who have been sitting there for centuries.*
>
> *Robert Jastrow,* ***God and the Astronomers****, 1978, W.W. Norton & Company (NY/London)*

Things seemed far more optimistic for the ideological naturalist, in the 1770s. The successful technological application of findings made by hard sciences like physics and chemistry gripped the imagination of philosophers in the 18th through 20th centuries. These men drove Naturalism faster into ideological territory, as they imagined that they could and should study all other subjects this way, too. They were not always wrong in trying to apply the scientific method to certain aspects of disciplines like anthropology. They just had a serious blind spot in doing so from an ideologically naturalistic grid.

Human beings also have a spiritual dimension to them. Biochemistry has not disproved this, as so many lay people popularly suppose when they confuse *science* with *scientism*.

Atomic physics and chemistry often had to reduce large numbers to practical size. The hard sciences thus employed a tool set for this that we might call *methodological reductionism*. The mathematics of scientific notation illustrates one legitimate example of this in action. Materialist scholars pushed more and more to study humanity only on naturalistic lines. As a side effect, ***Reductionism*** quietly turned into its own covert ideology. Most people were barely aware of its growing presence. Popular thought soon insisted that we must explain all of reality *only* in terms of some materialistically determined lowest denominator. This "lowest denominator" determined the course of all things; human beings were *just* the helpless product of whatever process came into vogue as that lowest denominator, be it chemical, environmental, or genetic.

Thus began the debate over whether nature or nurture determined behavior.

The debate itself started from the assumption that something other than a person's choices *determines* or causes their behavior. Philosophers call this ***determinism***. Man's mind is *only* a mass of biochemically charged electric impulses. Human sexuality is *just* a mix of genetic programming and environmental stimulus. While these examples each include some truth, electrochemical reactions occur in the process of thinking, and sexuality includes genetic and environmental inputs; determinism uses reductionism to express the assumption that such things were the sum total. This assumed more facts than were actually in evidence.

Satan has used determinism and reductionism to destroy more Christian lives in the last two centuries than Satanism, the cults, legalism, and New Age thought combined. It should disturb us that most Christians cannot even use these words in a sentence coherently.

The facts do not demand deterministic and reductionist results—faith-held starting assumptions do. Yet, Francis Schaeffer has pointed out that, "*people cannot live like that.*" [2] Even those who want deterministic ideas to be true, to avoid responsibility for their own desires and behaviors, cannot live like that consistently. In the frame of reference demanded by any form of reductionist determinism, all love and freedom must also logically perish. If some form of mindless mechanical process determines everything in our nature, then freedom of choice, and thus, love, is an illusion. That is what determinism is—the idea that mechanical forces *determine* our behavior, and that human choice and spirit are *just* illusions.

Materialism force-marches evidence to the conclusion that biochemistry determines behavior. Yet, this fails to pass scrutiny each time people make choices against a biochemically stacked deck. Every time a battered woman chooses to end an abusive relationship, she chooses to override the oxytocin hormone bonding her emotionally to her abuser. Oxytocin is one big reason why such women have a hard time breaking free. This hormone floods the female system when they become sexually active, and when they have children. [3] Sinful humanity has used for evil something that God created for good, oxytocin —the hormone that helps bind mothers to children and wives to loving husbands. The human condition really has objective properties.

The Christian worldview does not deny that biochemistry plays a role in human behavior. It only rejects the idea that it *determines* behavior. A more realistic statement is that *biochemistry affects the ease or difficulty with which people can make certain kinds of choices.* Biochemistry acts as an emotional retardant or accelerant—not the ignition. It does not make choices against immoral sexual desires or orientations impossible; but it certainly can make them harder for some people, under some conditions—especially if bad choices or abuse in the past has reinforced the destructive desire. Seeing nature or nurture, or even a mix of the two, as behavior determinants ignores the very existence of people who overcome unwanted behaviors and desires. This population is large enough that most people know at least one.

The Christian worldview fits reality better than its materialistic alternatives. It recognizes difficulties that come from biochemistry, a product of glands, which are part of our flesh. It explains, while giving hope, that people can overcome a biochemically stacked deck. A Bible-informed worldview, when taken seriously, can potentially make sense of more facts than one governed by Ideological Naturalism. *It does not guarantee all or even most believers will make sense of those facts – Christians must still see the need, and apply themselves, but it provides the potential.*

As in earlier transitions the Faith made in church history, we need to remember what was knowable to people two hundred years ago. Most people, even most intellectuals, at the turn of the 19th century did not consciously think about all this stuff. A few considered some of it, but most often, those few were not the Christians, but enemies of the Faith. Case in point, Jeremy Bentham, the Father of ***Utilitarianism*** – the idea that people should be valued only by their usefulness to society. Bentham rejected the idea of natural and inalienable rights because they implied a Divine legislator, which revealed a relationship between theology and law. This set him at odds with the prominent Christian legal scholar, Sir William Blackstone. Bentham claimed that Utilitarianism made a better basis for law and government than Judeo-Christian ethics did. He carried Materialism to its logical, absurd, conclusion.

Bentham at one point favored the abolition of graveyards so that soap factories could render fat from dead bodies. Waste not; want not! He willed his own body to be stuffed and put on display at the University College Museum, in London. Bentham wanted to be a monument to his brave new Utilitarian world. The university followed his wishes for a number of years, until the "monument" became a regular target for student pranks. This, too, proved a certain objective property in the human condition. People tend to make fun of truly stupid ideas, especially when potentially smart people float them. To put it another way, **"Professing to be wise, they became fools..."** (Rom. 1:22)

No wonder some of Voltaire's own students could not live with such implications!

Chapter 18 showed that Rousseau turned from pure Rationalism to what philosophers call *Romanticism*; a feelings-based view of reality that assumed the basic goodness of people, as long as they remained uncorrupted by "civilization." David Hume pushed the same ideas in England, even going so far as to deny the validity of the concept of ***cause and effect***. [4] These men laid the intellectual groundwork for the array of lifestyles today, which stem from the Sexual Revolution, including the Gay Liberation Movement. All deny any role of choice in sexual orientation by assuming a deterministic model of human psychology. These are no longer just lifestyles, but social ideologies based on worldviews that demand the divorce of sexual desire and behavior from moral choice.

Rationalism, and Romanticism, the two main idea flows from the Enlightenment, though superficially antagonistic toward each other; actually kept a deeper cooperative relationship with each other in modern thought. Romantics drifted toward a fuzzy Pantheism in their thinking on humanity, God, and nature, while the rationalists kept their materialist frame. Yet, each flow of ideas drew from the other for mutual support as needed.

***Pantheism***, for those not familiar with the term, is the idea that everything in the universe added up together equals "god." *Pan* means *everything* and *theos* is Greek for *God*. This view of god is that of an impersonal quasi-spiritual energy that inhabits nature; not of a personal being like the God of Scripture, who communicates ideas through words that have definite intellectual content. Several forms of Pantheism exist, but this definition will do for now. George Lucas illustrates a contemporary example of western-styled Pantheism. He used his theology extensively in making "the Force" of his *Star Wars* movie series. Lucas depicted the

Force as an impersonal energy in the universe with a positive and negative pole, like electromagnetism. He added enough inconsistent moral overtones to make the movies fun.

The people in the *Star Wars* movies tapped into the force and used it. If they practiced "Jedi mind tricks" well enough, the Force even overwhelmed them, as if by a kind of energizing radiation. Thought and volition only got in the way whenever one tried to use the Force, however. Nowhere did the concept of loving and obeying the Force come into play because people can only love and obey a personal being. The god of Pantheism is impersonal and natural-force-like enough not to bother materialists. It also gives enough of an illusion of spirituality to satisfy romantics. It also fits well with today's moral and cultural relativism.

By the end of the 18th century; Enlightenment Rationalism or to the growing pantheistic Romanticism of Rousseau's school won over the philosophy departments in most European universities, and some American ones. Yes, it really happened that early. The same universities that taught philosophy and the humanities also offered theology, science, and law. It was inevitable that Enlightenment assumptions infect these disciplines.

Evidence of the overall weakness in much of mainstream Protestantism came in the early 19th century. Theology was the first major discipline to cave in to the new worldview. One would expect theology to be the last holdout for a Judeo-Christian view of truth and reality, only succumbing after science and then law. The very opposite was true, except for a few loud, dissenting voices, like the revivalists. They continued to build their thinking from a Reformation and Pietist foundation.

We can describe ***Liberal Theology*** as the Enlightenment's materialistic Rationalism and Romanticism voiced in religious words. By the 19th century, the experiment of studying culture and religion using laboratory-like methods of hard sciences (like physics and chemistry) had become a trend. Nevertheless, these subjects do not lend themselves so consistently to that form of analysis. Therefore, it was impossible to apply the methods of the hard sciences to them accurately, across the board. Sometimes they could, but not with the confidence that one could reasonably expect from the hard sciences.

This opened the door for romantic theories to exact their pound of flesh in these subjects also. Social "soft sciences" like psychology, sociology, and anthropology were born out of the attempt to study humanity this way. [5] Along with this trend, came a growing number of men indoctrinated into the closed-system mechanistic view of nature at the universities. The same schools not only trained men for the sciences, but in theology. Most universities started as church institutions, in fact. Men in the hard sciences sometimes held out a little longer against the worldview shift. A number of scientists resisted absolute philosophic Materialism, for example, Michael Faraday, Louis Agassiz, Gregor Mendel, Matthew Maury, Lord Kelvin, and Louis Pasteur.

The fall of theology, by contrast, was often near instant in the major schools.

Georg W.F. Hegel, a theologian of the German Evangelical Lutheran seminary at Tubingen, redefined truth in a seriously corrosive way. In classical logic, if something were true, then its opposite would be false. In Hegel's system, truth came by taking two opposing ideas, a ***thesis*** and its ***antithesis***, and combining them to form a ***synthesis***. [6] We get the word *synthetic*, meaning *artificial*, from this word. The implications of this in theology were often devastating, especially when combined with materialistic assumptions on the nature of Scripture, and the growing pessimism over the value of reason that had affected even the later Pietists by this time.

Jesus stated his teachings as propositions of truth, the opposite of which were false. Hebrew and Greco-Roman alike would have understood them that way, and there is no reason not to understand them that way today. For example, Jesus said, "I am the way the truth and the life, no man comes to the Father but by Me." This means anyone who seeks God another way, will not find Him.

Hegel's definition of truth would arbitrarily change all that.

Someone might answer Jesus' truth claim about how to get to God with its antithesis, perhaps, *"All roads lead to God."* Then, through dialogue, the "truth" could be fabricated that, *"Many, but not all, roads lead to God."* The real-world problem is that Jesus did not say that, and He is the only one truly in a position to know.

Hegel's system of defining truth has, in our own day, penetrated all the way to the grassroots. People no longer think in terms of morality as absolutely right or wrong, or a statement as being true or false, but as being relative. That is, *truth* as seen today, is not a position that stands against that which is false; but is the moderate halfway mark between two opposing extremes *no matter what those extremes may be*. This is especially evident in today's politics and religion. If someone believes strongly in anything, like the sanctity of human life, people label them "extremist."

The only thing extreme about this is that the claim that "there are no moral absolutes" is a logical fallacy. To insist on it, arbitrarily establishes a moral absolute! It is also a tyrannical absolute. People who say this expect the rest of us to go along with their absolutist claim that there are no absolutes, as if it were the only exception to their own rule! I like to call this the "Gee, Obi Wan, Scenario," after a little incident that happened to my daughter and I at the theater. Gotta love those *Star Wars* movies!

My daughter graduated from high school in 2005, the year the last *Star Wars* prequel came out. She and her friends invited me to come along to the midnight premier of *Star Wars, Episode III: Revenge of the Sith*. The climax of this special effects extravaganza had Obi Wan Kenobi, and a griping young Darth Vader (before all his cyborg accessories), fencing their final showdown with light sabers, on a volcano planet. (Why is there always a handy volcano planet around for such things, anyway?) George Lucas decided that this was the time to hammer his "gospel" home to moviegoers everywhere. He did this by having young Darth bleat out his own whiney quotation of Jesus Christ, by saying, "If you're not with me, you're against me, Obi Wan!"

To which Obi Wan answered, with all the self-righteous fury Lucas could write into him, "Only a Sith deals in absolutes!"

That was when I broke into shrieking laughter. Some of my daughter's friends looked at me oddly. A middle schooler dressed as Yoda glared at me, as if to say, "Laughing, why is he?" My daughter and a couple of her friends got it, and started to chuckle, but at a more subdued volume.

All this happening in a few seconds, I said, loud enough for many rows to hear, "Gee, Obi Wan, are you *absolutely* sure?"

This demonstrates two things. One is the logical fallacy of moral relativism. The other is that you just can't take me anywhere.

It will always be true that some lesser issues occasionally need moderation. Yet, it is anesthesia to all ethical and intellectual sense to make moral relativism the foundational concept of truth.

The thinking of men like Hegel was able to affect theology so dramatically for several reasons. For one, except for the revivalists, Christians in a variety of settings experienced confusion about the nature of their faith, beginning around this time. In Germany, the School of Higher Criticism re-examined Bible texts starting from materialistic faith-assumptions. The "Higher Critics" discounted accounts of the miraculous as written generations after the fact, based on oral stories that had attained exaggerated mythical status. They did this even in cases where text evidence, and external sources, overwhelmingly favored early authorship.

The "Higher Critics" assumed that because nothing supernatural could really happen; historically fulfilled Bible prophecy had to come from later than traditionally claimed, after the prophesied events had taken place. Late 18th-early 19th century text scholar, Julius Wellhausen, saw that different writing styles sometimes showed up in the books of the Pentateuch, credited to Moses. The worldview prejudices of the Higher Critics caused them to miss the simplest, most reasonable explanation for this. They also drove the exaggeration of every minor contrast into "evidence" for usually four sets of later, non-Mosaic authors.

The simplest explanation for what Wellhausen saw, which fit the evidence best, was far less elaborate. Christians had always understood the Bible as God's word composed through human authors. The inspired writers and editors, during the ~1000-year formative era of the Old Testament, merely updated the language, as needed. They inserted God-breathed editorial clarifications for later generations.

It did not occur to materialist German scholars to think realistically about the language challenges Ezra faced upon returning from Babylon. In "giving the sense" of the Law to the people, Ezra, and his scribes, did not merely do as pastors did when teaching from the Bible. Hebrew had changed radically as a language during the 70 years in Babylon. To get a feel for this, try reading the Middle English of Chaucer. Better yet, consider that the Paleo-Semitic of Moses compares to the Hebrew of Ezra's day; much like us rendering a legal code written in the Old English of *Beowulf* would for 21st century English speakers.

Þær æt hȳðe stōd hringedstefna
īsig ond ūtfūs æþelinges fær.
ālēdon þā lēofne þēoden,
bēaga bryttan on bearm scipes
mǣrne be mæste.

*A verse of* Beowulf *in Old English*

Major authors, like Moses, Ezra, and Solomon, likely also had teams of scribes available. God also breathed through these, who helped, under supervision, to render parts of the text, very little of which God dictated directly, as He had the 10 Commandments. Nothing prevents God from providentially using what would otherwise be normal human means in the inspiration of His Law. These methods would leave the same kinds of artifacts as any other written record authored by men. Differing writing styles between an original author and a later, inspired editor making explanatory expansions do not threaten inspiration.

As with most others who reject the idea of the Bible's Divine Inspiration, the Higher Critics indulged in a form of "straw-man" argument. They did not debate the actual position, but an absurdly simplistic caricature of it. They then knocked down that dummy version before a less-informed public, as if their parody of Inspiration and Inerrancy were what informed people who held those views really believed.

God using real human personalities and methods to shape Scripture detracts nothing from His word. As Jesus is the Living Word of God made flesh, so the Bible is the written word of God, authored through gifted men who used their own human thoughts, methods, and writing styles. It is not an *either / or* issue, but a *both / and* one.

Higher Critics, building on Wellhausen, re-classified Old Testament texts to fit what scholars call the ***Documentary Hypothesis***. Suddenly, the Old Testament no longer seemed to be what it claimed. The Documentary Hypothesis, also called the J.E.P.D. Theory, is the idea that Moses and the Prophets did not write the Old Testament; but various groups of text redactors did, late, after the Babylonian Captivity. In this view, the parts of Scripture that call God *Jehovah* or *Yahweh* (J) came from different sources and periods than those sections that call Him *Elohim* (E). A third text source, the Priests (P), supposedly finalized the documentary (D) process, after the time of Ezra.

The Documentary Hypothesis comes in several forms, each highly speculative. None has convincing support evidence, except the above-mentioned style differences. Writing styles change with subject and literary genre, just as easily as by author, however. I do not use the same literary form when I write poetry, as when I write history or my novels. We can better explain the style changes as a signature of God providentially arranging the Old Testament, using men. They result from the linguistic mechanics of one or two language update revisions by later, equally inspired authors, during the ~1000 years between Moses and Malachi. Did God *need* to do things that way? Of course not! The available evidence simply seems to suggest that, for whatever reason, He chose that method.

The Documentary Hypothesis appears to have one main purpose. It gives an ideologically naturalistic just-so story for the origin of the Mosaic Law, and the Old Testament. As its ideological bias is exposed, today, trendy books on Old Testament origins grow more shrill about one thing; the repetitive, yet unconvincing suggestion that Jewish Scripture is fiction. Too many folks are catching on that the foundation of the Documentary Hypothesis sits on patches of eroding sand. People at the dawn of the 19th century still trusted that academics, as an institution, always worked from evidence in good faith. Even many scholars, at the time, underestimated how much faith-assumptions set the grid for interpreting evidence, and for which questions seemed pertinent or not.

The idea that academics, as an institution, could so prostitute itself to one ideological assumption was unthinkable at the time. That was largely what enabled it to happen. All so-called "modern theology" rests on Documentary Hypothesis views of the Bible. [7] The result, as the 19th century went on, was that many in church leadership no longer viewed Scripture as a history of events in the real world. Many Liberal theologians took the logical next step of admitting that if they could not rely on Scripture historically; then they had no good reason to rely on it ethically or theologically either.

Many have built much on Liberal Theology, so much that most do not wish to desert the structure, no matter what evidence comes in. This is so even if its foundation is not really the commitment to reason advertised. The rise of Postmodernism, and its denial of objective truth, has also since created an atmosphere where few see the need to re-evaluate. If truth is whatever the consensus says it is, then "does it work?" seems like a more important question than "is it true?" does. The problem is that lies often work very well in the short run, but in the end, will cause the entire system to collapse. This is because important decisions based on faulty information eventually lead to disaster in the real world.

Perception is not the same as reality. Returning to Scripture is not the same as going backwards, regardless of how the popular culture misrepresents the idea.

Most believers in the 19th century had soured themselves on reason. Even educated Christians often failed to notice how the assumptions of Enlightenment-style Rationalism drove conclusions of the higher critical schools; not concrete evidential discoveries. The foundation of Higher Criticism stood, at the bottom line, on little more than ideological peer-pressure. Other scholars accepted it virtually without criticism by the late 19th century, as no view before or since. [8] Why?

Higher critical schools shaped more theologians in their own image, throughout the 19th and into the 20th centuries. This caused what seemed like the logical self-destruct of the intellectual foundations of a biblical Christianity before the eyes of the world. The church leaders entrusted to teach the word of God, instead subverted trust in the word's reliability! This caused those who had always depended on the universities to educate men for Christian service to doubt the validity of their own faith. It made it easy for philosophies, like that of Hegel, to influence church doctrine. People will follow the ideas of men who seem confident in what they say. Scholars like Hegel seemed to know what they were talking about at a time when many believing people were not sure that they did anymore.

Few people illustrated the believer's dilemma, at this time, better than Soren Kierkegaard did. Like Hegel, both secular and religious thinkers have built on Kierkegaard's writings.

Biblically informed people have drawn a variety of conclusions about him, both good and bad. His devotional writing is rich, influenced much by late Pietism with its emphasis on an experiential relationship with God. His stress on Christian "neighbor love" places him in the edifying category, on that topic. [9] Yet, we see in him an increasing tension between the devotional and the intellectual. This tension soon fractured, leaving a lasting chasm between how today's Christians often view faith versus the intellect.

Many refer to Kierkegaard as the "Father of ***Existentialism***." [10] Whether this is completely fair, I do not know. Existential philosophy certainly came through those who built on at least some of his work. One wonders, however, if those who carried his ideas that direction might not deserve the title more than Kierkegaard does. Existentialism is the idea that reasoning over objective external issues leads nowhere. People must each authenticate themselves on their own terms, through a defining act that gives meaning to the individual's life. Kierkegaard died young, at age 43, possibly before he had time to let his fracture between "faith" and reason work all the way through his own life. If so, this was fortunate for him—horrible as that sounds.

Kierkegaard correctly insisted that real faith leads to authentic acts of love. It is hard to imagine how this focus could have any significant worldview blind spots, much less ones capable of the damage soon to come in their wake. It was not what he insisted on that was the problem, rather what he failed to insist on. The reason Kierkegaard's followers took his ideas in a harmful direction was his pessimism about reason. One sees it displayed in some of the titles of his works, like *The Concluding Unscientific Postscript* and *Philosophical Fragments*. I prefer to think of Kierkegaard as one of the earliest modern Christian victims of the artificial, but popular, view that faith and reason are natural enemies.

Even if he did not think this consciously, Kierkegaard's view of faith seems to have reflected it as an underlying fear. It was he who coined the term, *"leap of faith"* to mean a jump outside of reason to a place of optimism about Christian meaning and ethics in spite of, *and without dealing with*, what the skeptics said. [11] While this may not have been his intention, the idea of a faith divorced from reason resulted in those who took his thinking further.

Many believers at the time, thinking more or less from a Pietist base, seemed to almost unconsciously associated reason with faithlessness. This likely stemmed from the Enlightenment's lampooning the Christian faith. Instead of using reason to develop a more effective system of apologetics to answer the issues raised by the critics; many who came after Kierkegaard, in effect, threw up their hands in exasperation and retreated from the intellectual scene. I do not think that this was necessarily his intention, simply an unanticipated side effect. Eventually, apologetics caught up with the issues, but too late to stop the rise of Liberalism and Evolutionism as dominant forces in mainstream churches.

Much of late 19th century mainline Protestantism seemed to think it could motivate people to believe in God, and embrace Christian virtues anyway; that it did not matter if secular and Liberal skeptics turned out right about the Bible being full of errors. It did not occur to many people to question the assumptions undergirding the claims spouting from the German schools. Academics, some non-Christian, have disproved many of those claims long ago. Much thinking continues to build on them, anyway. [12] Kierkegaard was probably not fully a Liberal in the sense people understand today. He illustrates well the eroding effect Liberal Theology had even on believers with a deep and abiding love for Christ.

Those who fully followed Liberal conclusions about the Bible seemed to fall into two basic groups. One logically rejected historic Christianity lock, stock, and barrel. This group turned to various forms of Pantheism and ***Universalism***, the latter being the basic idea that "all roads lead to God." Some of these left for already separate church systems, like the Unitarian Church, for example. Most stayed in mainline Protestant denominations, and heavily influenced their development away from a biblical worldview.

The other broad Liberal clique tried to salvage something useful from the wreckage they felt had been made of historic Christianity. Included in this category were those involved in the so-called "Search for the Historic Jesus" movement. This school combed the New Testament, and tried to remove the supernatural. They hoped to sift from the minimalized text a non-miracle-working "historic" Jesus to fit their materialistic bias. [13] The effort was a dismal failure, despite attempts made by today's *Jesus Seminar* to revamp its tried-and-found-wanting approach to historic truth.

It failed intellectually for two reasons. The first was that taking the supernatural from Jesus left little behind. An ethic so focused on internal motive demands supernatural power beyond human moral strength to live by. It defeats the Seminar's ideology as much as any overt miracle does. The second reason was that it violated the main premise of historic analysis to assume what "historic Jesus" thinkers did about the reliability of the New Testament. *Aristotle's Dictum* states that *the benefit of the doubt must go to a text that claims to tell a history, not to the ideology of the critic.* [14] Without this premise, it is impossible to have any historic knowledge. A writer from or closer to the times has a better view than we do.

Many of the assumptions made in Liberalism were entirely arbitrary. The philosophic prejudices of the critics often guided their research instead of an objective search for truth about the claims made by the manuscripts. The spiritual and moral vacuum left by the dominance of Liberal Theology in German culture, during the 19th and into the 20th century, contributed to the backlash of Nazism; and the social ills in Germany and Austria-Hungary that long preceded it. Divorce and illegitimate births hit record levels. Homosexuality grew rampant in both German and Habsburg armies and governments. Freud proclaimed cocaine the "wonder drug" for depression. Intellectuals deluded themselves in a romantic return to Norse Paganism, visible in the operas of Wagner, and the books of Nietzsche.

Theological Liberals, like Albert Schweitzer, hoped to preserve the morality of Christ with a "historic" Jesus. Yet, his own study in this area revealed the intellectual futility of trying to separate the supernatural from the life of Christ. This humanitarian doctor did much to help the suffering in Africa, and hoped that his example might shine a light of ethical Christianity. Yet, without a biblical understanding of who Jesus is, and working from faith-assumptions hostile to what the Bible tells us about truth and reality; it was unrealistic for men like Schweitzer to expect this. [15] Such human righteousness withered and died at the onslaught of a truly demonic evil like the Nazism that came a few short decades later.

Because the philosophic shift came first in the universities, most of which had religious ties, it rapidly spread to the seminaries. This happened first in Germany and France, then in Britain, and America. It effectively hijacked the leadership of most every major Protestant church system in less than three generations. It happened in German Lutheranism first, then the Reformed denominations. By the early middle part of the 20th century, Anglicanism, and then Methodism, and much of Presbyterianism and Congregationalism fell.

This apostasy was much worse than that of Roman Catholicism, in terms fidelity to God. At least Catholicism held on to theological orthodoxy about the nature of God. Protestant apostasy also resulted, indirectly, in many times more deaths. It enabled 20th century genocides, especially those by the Nazis, through cultural decay from the loss of spiritual salt at the institutional level. Of course, collaborators and martyrs came from both camps, too—I'm talking about large-scale effects on a larger population.

Remarkable Christian individuals also still stood firm, as we shall see. These men and women were, mostly, voices crying in the wilderness. By God's grace, their voices carried farther and wider than anyone expected them to. I pray our voices will do the same.

The social and spiritual effects of Liberalism in Britain were about a generation behind those in Germany. Its effect in America is about a generation behind that in Britain. I am convinced that the continuance of some indirect biblical influence in Britain, and more of it in America; is one of the few things that have kept social conditions remotely sane in the West since the end of World War II. Will biblical churches influence the 21st century effectively, go isolationist, or dilute the truth in the bankrupt worldview of Postmodernism?

The fourteen years since the first edition of this book have mostly seen the scales tipping disastrously toward Postmodernism. Yet hope remains.

## Materialist Faith-Assumptions in Science: The Rise of Evolutionary Thought

After the Galileo Incident, scientists began to be more careful how they built from biblical assumptions a scientifically informed view of the cosmos. Few doubted that Scripture had a foundational place in that process. Nor did they doubt its accuracy on points of history and nature, when read with care to language conventions. Early scientists understood the limits of science to the study of observable and experimentally repeatable natural phenomena. ***Methodological Naturalism***, at first, focused on *experimental method*, not *ideological assumptions* trying to sway outcomes. It fit a worldview consistent with Scripture, being its intellectual child.

Enlightenment faith-assumptions then began to shift the idea of science onto a base of hard Materialism. Methodological Naturalism became *Ideological Naturalism*; a belief system based on the hope that science would answer all of humanity's questions, and religion would become obsolete. This shift broke the connection in science philosophy with the worldview that had enabled science, as we know it, to happen in the first place.

Here's the rub—what many academics today call "Methodological Naturalism" is mostly Ideological Naturalism. Whoever wins the culture war often writes the history, and defines the terms. This does not mean everyone who uses the term that way is intentionally dishonest, only that the change in meaning came mechanically in the worldview shift. Methodological Naturalism *in practice* became more ideological. The method became less and less honest, even if individual scientists were not intentionally so. Consider how contemporary chemical evolutionist, Richard Dickerson describes science:

> *Science, fundamentally, is a game. It is a game with one overriding and defining rule: Rule No. 1: Let us* see *how far and to what extent we can explain the behavior of the physical and material universe in terms of purely physical and material causes, without invoking the supernatural.*
>
> *Richard Dickerson, chemical evolutionist,*
> ***The Game of Science, Perspectives on Science and Faith****, Vol. 44, p. 137, June, 1992*

To the early scientists, science was a search for knowledge about how the universe operated. It was not a game. It had dignity as a serious search for truth, even if the scientist had to hold that information only tentatively because further data could prove it wrong. Early scientists rarely pontificated on realms more properly addressed by the legal-historic method or by Divine revelation. They did not treat those realms as imaginary and explainable only by using the scientific method. Knowing the difference between science and ***scientism*** helps the Christian understand how this particular worldview transition happened, and gives us terms to discuss it.

In Voltaire's day, James Hutton began to change the interpretation of the fossil record from a partly biblical ***Catastrophism*** to the ***Uniformitarian*** view. British geologists did not greet Hutton's hypothesis so well in the mid-to-late 18th century. The worldview shift had not yet gotten that far. By the 1830s, Sir Charles Lyell circulated Hutton's Uniformitarian Hypothesis with more success. Scholars had become more open to the rising tide of materialistic Rationalism. Lyell was also a lawyer by profession. He encouraged his supporters to use political tactics, like ignoring competent opponents and debating only less competent ones, to undermine the reputations of scriptural geologists. [16] Several competent geologists raised scientific problems with ***Uniformitarianism***.

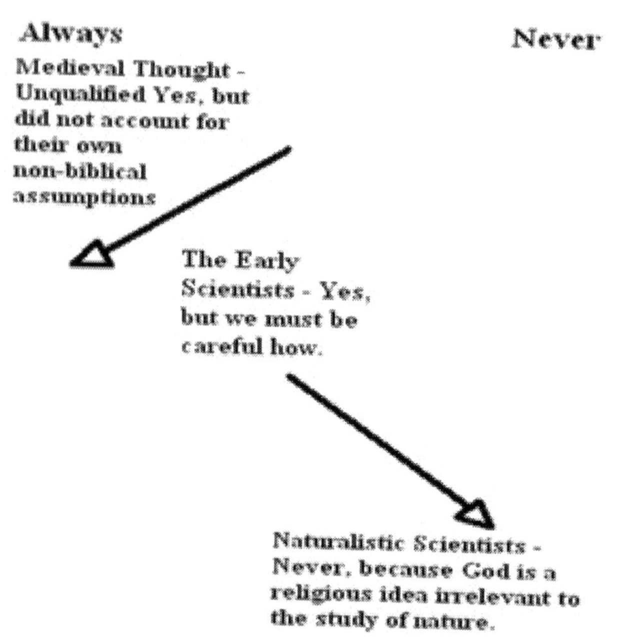


*"Always," "Yes," or "Never" answer the question;* ***can science start from biblical assumptions about reality****? Medieval thinkers lived before the discovery or invention of many of the thought tools needed to detect the assumptions they brought to the text, without knowing it. Early scientists generally held a biblical view of reality. They were only just finding how they might bring unconscious assumptions to the texts that were not always valid. Thus, their uncertainty was usually reasonable. If allowed to question in an intellectual environment that continued to take the effects of the Curse seriously, scientists might have advanced faster in several ways. This will become apparent in later chapters of this book. After Naturalism became materialistically ideological, rather than just methodological, the worldview environment that science was born in, as a discipline, shattered.*

*People increasingly viewed only the material world as "real," and, in direct proportion, saw spiritual realities as "imaginary." By the mid-19th century, matter, energy, space, and time became "the fundamental entities of reality" in the shifted Western worldview. People saw* ***information****, being a construct of the human mind, as merely imaginary. This is why 20th century scientists found the DNA code and Quantum Physics so profoundly disturbing. Such discoveries implied that matter was not the ultimate reality, and that even space-time had a beginning. The fact that we have built a complex technology on the science of Information Theory shows that the list needs a new fundamental entity on it –* ***information****. Materialism just does not describe what we now know about reality at the bottom line. This was not what most 19th and 20th century scientists had expected to find, and many are still trying to hang on to the old view. The danger is that political correctness is shutting down the marketplace of ideas.*

*An academic system committed to materialism diverts much time and intellectual energy into keeping students from seeing this. It must create unprovable "just-so stories" either to keep outmoded models afloat or to breed views of the new discoveries consistent with traditional late-19th century "science orthodoxy."*

**The Worldview Shift broke connection with the assumptions that had fostered the idea of the scientific method to begin with**

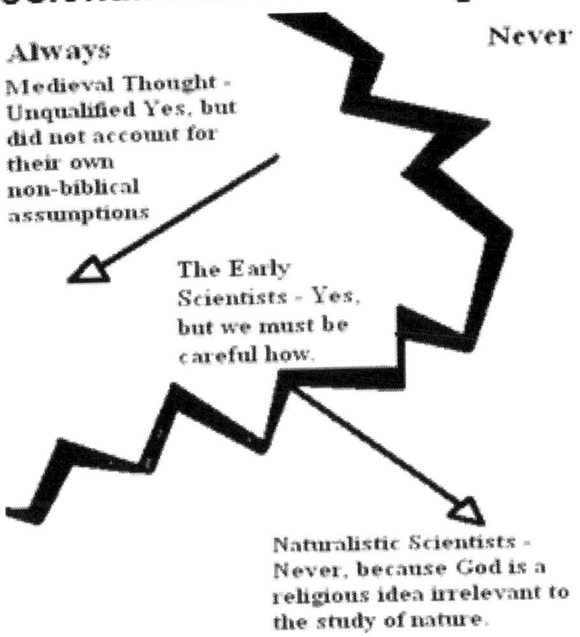


*Uniformitarianism* is the assumption that the slow geological processes often seen at present are *always* how they worked in the past. If big disruptions of normal geological processes took place in a global catastrophe, like Noah's Flood, then this would be a misleading rule for explaining fossil layers.

While a few fossil forms, like dinosaur nests and footprints, are sometimes difficult to explain by a yearlong water cataclysm, it is not impossible to do so. The vast majority of fossils are impossible to explain without a huge water catastrophe of some sort. Even the few that pose difficulties are explainable in global catastrophic terms by unique local conditions. [17] Nevertheless, Lyell and his allies pulled off a geological coup in seizing control of the Royal Geological Society. The ideological wave swell moved their way, and they wanted it to. This is largely because a vast amount time would be required by any naturalistic theory of either earth or life origins.

Only two realistic options exist for a first cause. Either random process worked in a "steady state" universe, where matter and energy were eternal or an intelligent designer created a finite cosmos. An evolving universe that created itself is an incoherent idea, popular as it might seem in a Postmodernist world that rejects reason. It is like me claiming to be my own father, my own mother, and my own grand-pa. Rational problems exist not with a well-reasoned supernaturalism, but for those who claim that nature created nature, in the beginning. *The problem for them is that anything exists at all.* The burden of proof is not on those who propose what is self-evident; that a functioning cosmos exists, which operates by orderly principles, even at its most chaotic. The burden of proof is on those who propose mechanics without a mechanical inventor.

Remember that Lyell's popularization of Uniformitarianism happened a full generation before Charles Darwin's book. Evolutionary hypotheses were legion at the time, but none of them passed the plausibility test. The best so far, that of Lamarck, proposed that evolutionary changes in lifeforms accumulated over time. Giraffes evolved from short-necked ancestors forced to stretch their necks to reach tree leaves in an alleged sparse ground vegetation environment. What is amazing is that Lamarck's idea was a serious contender. People who lose their legs do not pass on their lack of legs on to their children.

What would have happened to all those short-necked giraffe generations whose necks weren't long enough to reach the branches? They would die without reproducing. If they could reach some leaves, they would lose further motivation to stretch their necks. I remember learning about Lamarck in junior high school as a serious forerunner of Darwin, complete with scientific drawings of Lamarck's giraffes. This reveals a high degree of *desire* for a materialistic view of origins. Why was the intellectual culture so eager for an origins theory to fit the religious philosophy of Agnosticism? Was Deism, with its unknowable god that unsatisfying?

I can imagine some complaining at this point, that since acquired characteristics, like severed legs, do not pass on genetically to offspring; then the claims of Adam's sin nature being passed on to all humanity also fall apart. *That would be true, if genetics was how sin passed on.* The Curse affected all creation, according to Romans 8:20-23, which includes matter itself. Our bodies are made of curse matter, affected by death and decay. They are not evil of themselves, but the Curse affects them, quite apart from the sins that we choose to commit. We use the terms of inheritance metaphorically and legally in speaking of inheriting Adam's fallen nature. Jesus avoided the legal Curse by being virgin born, but he still experienced the temptations of a man in a body made of fallen matter.

Getting back to the desperation of an early 19th century intellectual culture in search of a materialistic model for origins; let me be clear about what I am not saying. I am not saying that evolutionists are automatically atheists or agnostics. That is dumb, and it is not the point. I am not even saying that men like Lyell always sought this out as a conscious motive. That goes beyond what is knowable. What I am saying is that *every moral system requires its own cosmology*. Once a moral system gains a large enough following, it seeks to construct one if it does not yet exist. It makes allies even of those who do not share its goals to do this.

The mind demands plausibility in its inward parts; a reflection of a desire for truth that comes from God's image in us, even after men reject truth or do not yet know it. Deism could not satisfy because it was logically inconsistent. It wanted things both ways. Deism also came from a time still sane enough that people admitted the inference of design. Just as an individual rationalizes out the plausibility of a lie before telling it, so civilizations seem to do the same; except individuals are not quite as consistent about it as societies are. An otherwise firm believer in Christ will accept beliefs built from another person's assumptions, premises that Christian would never assume himself. An Atheist might be the most caring, altruistic person around, though his worldview assumptions do not push that direction. Individual people make exceptions. Mobs and nations are far more predictable.

Patterns in Bible prophecy makes certain background ideas stand out bold relief.

Uniformitarians voiced in geological words the assumptions that the Apostle Peter prophesied would undergird the worldview of mockers in the last days.

> **3 First of all you must understand this, that scoffers will come in the last days with scoffing, following their own passions 4 and saying, "Where is the promise of his coming? For ever since the fathers fell asleep, *all things have continued as they were from the beginning of creation.*" 5 They deliberately ignore this fact, that by the word of God heavens existed long ago, and an earth formed out of water and by means of water, 6 through which the world that then existed was deluged with water and perished. 2 *Peter* 3:3-6 (RSV)**

Pure Uniformitarianism dominated geological science, until roughly the 1960s. By then, overwhelming evidence of plate tectonics—the idea that continents float on plate-like slabs of the earth's crust—made room again for catastrophism. Uniformitarian faith-assumptions also undergird the complex web of factors used to determine which radioisotope dates are valid, from what is always a spread of readings on any given rock. [18] (Though it should be noted that most invalid dates are thought by geologists "too old," rather than too young; frequent incidents of freshly cooled volcanic rock yield dates of millions of years. Melting the rock resets the clock, so to speak. To study this issue in more detail, check out the reading list in my bibliography at the end of this chapter.)

What makes Peter's prophecy relevant is that many thinkers in the early 19th century were indeed "following their passions." We saw how an emotional and ideological thirst for a materialistic creation myth occurred long before Darwin or Lyell wrongly supplied one. People always find what they want, if they look hard enough, and systematically ignore reasonable obstacles. This ideological demand was, and often still is, every bit as passionate as the desire that drives Bible believers to defend their faith. It was not mounting scientific evidence that lay at the foundations of Molecule-to-Man Evolution, but this desire. [19]

After more than 150 years, the search for evolutionary transitional fossils has come up empty handed. Each possible "missing link" has proved either fraudulent or insufficient by further research. [20] When a scientifically literate culture still holds molecule-to-man evolution even after finding that DNA carries a code, which is a self-replicating, error-correcting *language* built into each living cell; I suspect even our best thinkers still "follow their passions" on some level. Only an intelligent mind can create language codes, much less self-correcting and self-replicating ones. [21]

This is not to say that all or even most scientists are consciously involved in such a passionate crusade. By now, things have settled into an entrenched establishment in scientific circles. Most researchers are just trying to do their jobs based on the information their instructors gave them. Like most people, scientists often do not think of the faith-assumption biases that shaped their common beliefs and questions about the natural world.

This brings us to an important point. Peter's prophecy is not about science. It is about cultural attitude. The word *culture* comes from the word *cult*—not *cult* as in "a weird sect"—but as in *that which forms a people's view of what is real*. Today's dominant worldview rests on certain "articles of faith." It is a myth to think Bible-oriented Christians have a blind prejudice from their religion, while materialistic scientists are unbiased seekers of truth. There is no such thing as an unbiased observer. Because every person must start from assumptions held by faith, all have a bias of one form or another. It is not a question of whether science or religion is biased.

The question should be; *which bias makes the most sense in the big picture? Which bias coherently fits reality as viewed from across the spectrum of all forms of coherent reasoning?* One bias may fit some scientific forms of reasoning well enough, yet still be statistically absurd. It may also undervalue history, and ignore Divine revelation. Another bias might focus exclusively on Divine revelation, but scorn scientific, mathematical, and historical methods. Yet others might venerate historical records, but have a naïve ignorance of how records can be gamed. Still another might idolize mathematics as nature's "Holy Grail," yet go blind to the limits imposed by Quantum Mechanics; that nature does not permit infinite halving of quantities into endlessly smaller halves.

Another bias might do the same with Divine revelation. It would hold that moral reasoning is not just a matter of personal opinion—that evil ideas lead to evil actions. This idea might be applied realistically or not so much. Still, even if good ideas do not always prevent evil, they tend to decrease its likelihood.

Molecule-to-man Evolution "fits some narrow scientific forms of reasoning well enough," yet it ignores others, being statistically absurd. It also "undervalues historical record, and ignores Divine revelation." A straightforward faith in the God of the Bible need not "focus *exclusively* on Divine revelation, but *scorn* scientific, mathematical, and historical methods" as unimportant. Such a faith is free to, "coherently fit reality as viewed from across the spectrum of all forms of reasoning." The fact that some Christians foolishly do scorn such things does not imply that they need to do so for their system of belief to stand up. They might think they do, but they are wrong. Such Christians should take time to become educated on the issues.

**Some Different Tool Sets for the Mind**
**(Not an exhaustive list)**

- ***The Legal-Historic Method*** **(for history knowledge from documents or testimonies)**
- ***Mathematical Methods*** **(for manipulating & comparing information that can be expressed as various quantities & variables**
- ***The Scientific Method*** **(for discovering the mechanics of nature)**
- ***The Divine Revelation of Scripture*** **(for the information only God can give us)**
- ***Hermeneutical Methods*** **(for interpreting various forms of written texts)**

It was not the materialistic bias that set us on the road to our great level of technology. All that built from the foundations of men like Newton, Bacon, Des Cartes, Kelvin, Pasteur (who rejected evolution), Kepler, and Faraday—men in the hard sciences who operated mostly out of a Judeo-Christian worldview. The materialists mostly came later.

As an example of how ideological materialism has held science back, consider Gregor Mendel. Mendel discovered genetics (as a theory) in the time of Darwin, but an academic world in search of a materialistic "first cause" ignored him. Genetics implied some form of information processing system at work in the heredity of living things. Only intelligence can devise information. At the time of Darwin, this was an extremely unpopular idea in an academic world that felt it had finally sewed up a fully materialistic view of science. For the next hundred years, the evidence found by research into the mechanics of life supported Mendel's view and not those who had hoped on Darwin.

The proof for a genetic *code* had to be devastating to turn a reluctant scientific establishment toward the work of Mendel, an Augustinian monk. Even now, those committed to exclusively materialistic views of science look for ways to escape the implications. One approach is to focus on the fact that the DNA "codes" each stand for one of four *molecules*, adenine, guanine, thymine, and cytosine. These are not literal letters, but they do function as such in the mechanics of DNA information processing. Though they are molecules, the fact that *the sequences in which they line up* in the long helical strand of DNA form the set of instructions to other molecules; *not the chemical properties of these four molecules themselves*, also makes it a *code* in the normal sense of the word. [22] This objection is conceptual slight-of-hand—the very thing those who make it accuse Intelligent Design scientists of.

Another tactic is to redefine the word *information* to mean something that includes certain phenomena that do not have an intelligent origin. This, too, is slight-of-hand. The sheer amount of technical language needed for the study of genetics makes good camouflage. Most geneticists do not practice such dishonest tactics—academic ideologues do. They try to erase disfavored words to eliminate the *politically* incorrect concepts those words carry. They hope to do this without erasing the benefits that science brought, using the words that fell out of favor. Contrary to popular stereotypes, men and women in the professional hard sciences drive today's so-called "Young-earth" Creationism; and a more secular approach to created origins called "Intelligent Design." [23]

The academic world is often much more political now, than it was 14 years ago. Attempts to weed out well-qualified people from their professions, who hold these views based on the evidence, are proof of the weakness of the dominant worldview. [24] Any ideological system, religious or academic, that rules the minds of men by fear, uses the last resort of the incompetent. As Christians, we are not in a battle between faith and reason, but between two opposite and mutually exclusive faiths.

Materialists got the jump on using science as an ideological weapon, during the 19th century. They got away with it, in part, because Bible-oriented Christians either abandoned intellectual and artistic disciplines; or had no ample apologetic to deal with systemic attacks to the Faith in those environments. The retreat from large parts of the academic world, and from many of the arts, imitated Kierkegaard's philosophical distrust of the value of reason. There were notable exceptions to this, but that was the trend. This often happened in an unwitting pretext of avoiding worldly philosophy. Compared to today, however, colleges back then were tame, and forced students to work hard.

**The Pyramid of How Evolutionary Philosophy Interprets Reality**

**Conclusions & Interpretation**

1- The universe is all there is and all there ever will be.
2- Life must have evolved from simple to complex forms.
3- Everything is meaningless of itself. There are no absolute morals from God.

**Artifacts, Records & Experiments**

1- Fossils of lots of dead things in stone layers & artifacts of men from long ago.
2- (Automatically rules out) ancient records of origins or of contact with an intelligent designer.
3- Light from objects in space billions of light-years away. Stretched space & gravity dilated time. Radio-active isotopes decay into non-radiogenic elements.

**Foundational Faith-Assumptions**

1- Geologic processes in the present are always the key to understanding how they worked in the distant past.
2- Only the philosophy of materialism is rational - nothing supernatural can really happen. Origins must be explained by chance processes undirected by intelligent design.
3- God, if he exists, is unknown and unknowable, bound by natural processes and irrelevant to the study of natural origins.
4- Man can be completely objective if he follows the philosophy of materialistic Rationalism (Naturalism). Truth is totally relative.

*A map of a worldview governed by Molecule-to-man Evolution*

It is utterly irrational to suppose here that "the truth" can rest somewhere in between the two opposing camps in a Hegel-like "synthesis." Science must always be open to falsification by new data. When scientific institutions overrun by a faith-based scientism do not allow that to happen; Molecule-to-man Evolution is enshrined as dogma. Academic establishments stifle reasonable questions from qualified scholars who challenge it based on new data.

Both Molecule-to-man evolutionist and creationist views are religious because they build conclusions from starting assumptions beyond the ability of science to verify. Both systems try to answer religious questions like, *where do we come from? Why are we here? What is our destiny? And, what is the nature of good and evil?* Faith in a personal God does not make a belief system religious by itself. Many religions deny the existence of a personal god—Buddhism, for example. What makes a belief system religious is its attempt to answer the big questions through functionally faith-based dogma.

The response to evolutionary thought in most churches, from the mid-19th century until now, with very few exceptions, was inadequate at most every level. This, too, began as a worldview blind spot. As time went on, during and not long after the Great Revivals, it superficially seemed to many believers that biblical faith had regained lost ground. Compared to the prior two centuries, however, middle 19th century Evangelicals had lost interest in things like geology. This spread to other sciences and arts, as well. The superstructure had begun to collapse over a weakened intellectual foundation. The battle is spiritual; but the battlefield is intellectual and emotional. One is a gateway to the other.

**The Pyramid of How Modern Biblical Creationism Interprets Reality**

**Conclusions & Interpretation**

1- Record of fulfilled prophecy & redundant coded design in the Bible qualify it as best revelation candidate.
2- God has given us meaning & values.
3- God created things fully functional & Conditions during creation were unique.

**Artifacts, Records & Experiments**

1- Fossils of lots of dead things in stone layers & artifacts of men from long ago.
2- ( Provisionally accepts ) ancient records of origins or of contact with an intelligent designer.
3- Light from objects in space billions of light-years away. Stretched space & gravity dilated time. Radio-active isotopes decay into non-radiogenic elements.

**Foundational Faith-Assumptions**

1- Global catastrophes have interrupted normal geological processes because God has judged past societies for sin.
2- Order and design in nature demand a creator-designer. To create nature, this designer must be above the natural realm like an artist is beyond his painting - thus 'super-natural'.
3- Since we are beings that communicate with words, it is rational to suppose that the creator also communicates through words. We assume the creator has communicated and we look for records that show evidence of extra-temporal handiwork.

*There is much more detail to the creationist position than this pyramid can show. The popular stereotype of Creationism as a position that ignores artifact evidence and experimental science is without merit. The conflict is not between faith and reason; but between the reasoning of two different faith systems. There are scientists from every field in today's "Young Earth" Creation Movement—even experts on radiometric geologic dating methods.*

For many decades, the tools did not exist for believers to respond coherently to the worldview shift. Even some of the errors about Genesis, like the Gap Theory, Bible believing Christians embraced as honest attempts to make sense of things. Darwinism seemed at the prow of an intellectual juggernaut. Universities gave themselves to it. Evolutionary thought fit the increasingly popular materialistic worldview of most academics.

In the late 19th century, too many Bible-believing Christians in Britain and America slowly turned Kierkegaard's distrust of the intellectual side of Christian faith into something else. They embraced an irrational spiritual pride, as if the truth claims of evolutionary scientists just did not matter. At first, they probably did not seem to matter much. Christian ethics so fit common sense that most believers felt sure common sense would always supply a social tether to the truth that pastors and evangelists could appeal to easily. Late 19th century people could not picture the scale of today's Bible illiteracy. This form of spiritual pride showed itself in two ways; either by ignoring science totally or by imagining that evolutionary thought was so inconsequential that Christians could allow it to guide them in how they interpreted Genesis.

As time went on, however, church responses of ignoring evolutionary science and mixing it with the Bible both showed the same arrogance. The first seemed to imagine that churches in a technological civilization had no duty to express biblical ideas in approachable ways to those with a scientifically literate worldview; that the "intellectual pride" was always one-sided. This was a form of spiritual isolationism. The second response made an equally prideful, and irrational, attempt to mix evolutionary opinions with biblical belief. It assumed the new worldview so trivial that Christians could blend the two with little or no analysis.

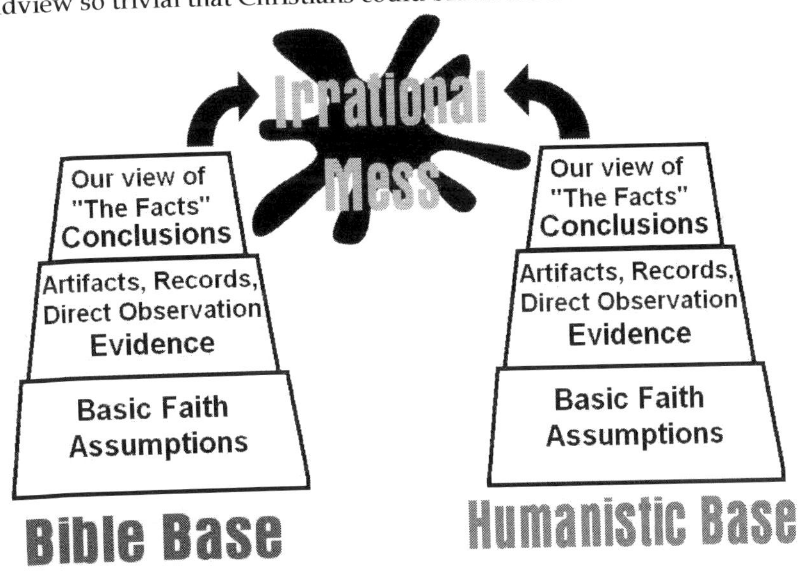


Both responses ignored a crucial fact; that the faith-assumptions that produced Molecule-to-man Evolution are mutually exclusive to those that produce Biblical Christianity. They cannot both be true. These two assumption sets lead any scientific study of the same evidence in opposite directions. The study of origins is primarily a *historical method* study, to which science can only lend assistance—not define.

The same is true of these differing assumptions in a theological study of the same evidence. Efforts to match Genesis with Molecule-to-Man Evolution, or its speculative claims, only yield hybrid ideas like Theistic Evolution, Progressive Creationism, the Gap Theory, and the Day-Age Theory. None of these fit either the scientific or the scriptural facts. These hybrids satisfy only the most superficial review. They redefine the biblical account in some way to fit Molecule-to-Man Evolutionary assumptions. Logically, they each reflect the previous diagram. They also fall into the "God of the Gaps" fallacy, except that they do not actually give us any useful knowledge about the "gaps."

Such compromises came partly because Christians did not yet see a difference between hard sciences, like physics and chemistry; and "historical sciences," like uniformitarian geology and evolutionary biology, which demand an interpretive bias shift. The soft "historical sciences" assumed that scientists could interpret rock layers and fossils with the same confidence possible in interpreting a written document. Forensic evidence, however, does not tell us anything without a grid of assumptions to interpret it through.

Another reason for compromising normal interpretation rules in early Genesis came with a growing view among Evangelical Christians in the 19th to mid-20th centuries; that callings for believers in the arts and sciences had no eternal bearing. They had accepted a Christianized form of utilitarianism, which valued people and their service only by their instant usefulness to direct evangelism. Reductionism now entered the church.

The issue of origins is not merely a sideshow about how God might have created things. How we interpret the past guides our explanation of the origin of sin and death—the very reason Christ had to come and die for the human race. The idea that the "death" resulting from sin was only "spiritual" explicitly rejects the clear words of Romans 8.

> **20 For *the creation was subjected to futility,* not of its own will, but because of Him who subjected it, in hope 21 that the creation itself will also be set free from its slavery to corruption into the freedom of the glory of the children of God. 22 For we know that *the whole creation groans and suffers* the pains of childbirth together until now. 23 And not only this, but also we ourselves, having the first fruits of the Spirit, even we ourselves groan within ourselves, waiting eagerly for our adoption as sons, *the redemption of our body. Romans* 8:20-23 (NASB)**

Redemption is not just spiritual. This passage clarifies material creation four times. If the original cause of death in the real world was not sin, then there is no reason to think that Christ's death in the real world has any unique meaning. If the problem is fictional, then there is no reason for the solution to be anything more than a fiction either. The issue of origins ties into everything a Christian believes. Every Bible doctrine finds its foundation in the first eleven chapters of Genesis. Those chapters define the Christian worldview.

There is no good reason to accept evolutionary ideas uncritically when ideology sets the mold for interpreting evidence. This is something much of the church has regrettably done in the last 150 years. There is another reason that this is more than just an abstract theology debate. In the 20th century, Darwinism became a pillar for two of the bloodiest political plagues in history, the Communist Purges and the Nazi Holocaust.

## MATERIALIST FAITH-ASSUMPTIONS IN LAW AND GOVERNMENT: MARXISM AND SOCIOLOGICAL LAW

Perhaps the last discipline to fully shift over to Enlightenment faith-assumptions, except in France, was Law. Likely, the Terror of the French Revolution helped forces in the English-speaking countries to step back from that precipice. Of course, the worldview shift happened at differing rates in different locations. We are again tumbling over the edge in America. The Russian Revolution of 1917-18 showed what Enlightenment assumptions in law and government worked through rejection of biblical moral absolutes. The American Revolution, though not perfect, reflects the tempering influence of those absolutes. Law and Government in the U.S.A. no longer have that protection, however. We seem well past the crossroads against which John Adams warned.

> *We have no government armed with power capable of contending with human passions unbridled by morality and religion. Avarice, ambition, revenge, or*

*gallantry, would break the strongest cords of our Constitution as a whale goes through a net.* ***Our Constitution was made only for a moral and religious people. It Is wholly inadequate to the government of any other***. John Adams [25]

One of Hegel's students was a brilliant, if tousled, hairball of a man named Karl Marx. Marx saw with great bitterness the apathy of institutional churches in the face of the labor abuses in the Industrial Revolution. He noted that the early church in Acts had "shared all things in common." Marx dreamed of making a utopian society where nobody owned anything or anybody, but shared the goods of life in harmony. He called this system ***Communism***. To Marx, the church was a mere spiritual propaganda arm for the rich and powerful. He quoted the Marquis de Sade in calling religion an *"opiate for the people"* that kept them from recognizing their misery and revolting. [26]

In this sense, his whole theory of Communism was a Christian heresy and a substitute gospel. Marx's bitterness against the church became bitterness against God. He failed to see that when the church acted this way it was not because of God's principles, but because of man's rejection of God's principles even in a religious environment.

The trend toward socialistic ideas in law and government is a direct result of Enlightenment starting assumptions in this realm. Beneath the political ideologies of Communism and ***Socialism***, a broader trend toward sociological law lurked. Schaeffer defined *sociological law* as *law based on social convenience* rather than moral principles. It took another century for it catch on in the United States. Jurists like Oliver Wendell Holmes Jr. pioneered it, at the turn of the 19th to 20th centuries. It became the leading force in American jurisprudence by the early 1960s.

Holmes, an ardent Darwinist, believed law should build from whatever worked best in the current social situation. He once said, *"I see no reason for attributing to man a significance different in kind from that which belongs to a baboon or a grain of sand."* [27] That might look like an off-the-cuff remark, subject to my taking it out of context. Here is something a little more substantial.

> *When twenty years ago a vague terror went over the earth and the word* socialism *began to be heard, I thought and still think that fear was translated into doctrines that had no proper place in the Constitution or the common law. Judges are apt to be naif* (naive), *simple-minded men, and they need something of Mephistopheles* (the name of Satan in the classic novel *Faust*). ***We too need education in the obvious—to learn to transcend our own convictions and to leave room for much that we hold dear to be done away with short of revolution by the orderly change of law***. Justice Oliver Wendell Holmes Jr. [28]

In other words, there was no unique significance to humanity given by the Creator for us to base sensible laws on. Therefore, law was merely a tool for social existence that we could make up for our own convenience as we went along.

The *Roe vs. Wade* decision of in 1973, which legalized abortion on demand; and the 2015 "discovery" of a constitutional right to homosexual marriage by the U.S. Supreme Court, illustrate sociological law in action. The 1973 decision declared the unborn child a non-person in a ruling that was both legally and medically arbitrary. It was legally arbitrary because the *Constitution of the United States* gives no absolute right over our own bodies, only limited rights. For example, it is illegal to commit suicide, and to aid and abet the suicide of another. Even if there were such an absolute legal right, a serious medical obstacle blocks such an attempt to blur the limits of "my body," and the body of another, in the context of pregnancy. The science is in, and it would be absolute in a legal system based on reason.

All scientific evidence points to life beginning at conception. An entire human chromosome base pair exists at conception, which contains and controls the growth and make up of an individual throughout life, womb to tomb. It is self-evident that mother, and unborn child, are separate individuals; the same forensics used to differentiate individuals outside the womb in a court of law shows this. Each has a separate blood supply, often with divergent blood types. Both have different DNA, the mother from both her parents and the child from the mother and its father. Even early embryos feel pain and react to stimuli, showing a level of consciousness. When an abortionist tears them limb from limb or chemically burns them alive by saline injection, sonograms show the unborn writhing in agony and struggling for life.

Left alone, the unborn are born as babies, being fully human from the get-go. They are merely at an earlier, less visible stage of development.

Few seriously question whether life begins at conception any more. The argument now is about when "personhood" happens—an entirely arbitrary legal fiction. Either way, the nonsense comes from the minds of those who have chosen to ignore genuine science based on observation, as well as the sanctity of human life in God's image. They want the license to kill unborn children for reasons of personal and sociological convenience. This is sociological law at its essence. We can expect more frightening examples in the future; law based not on moral principle, but upon whatever political and media elites think is socially convenient.

We are already in the "brave new world" of lurid science fiction with the legal practice of "partial birth" abortion, embryonic stem cell harvesting, and the specter of cloned human chimeras. The "Affordable Health Care Act" or "Obamacare" is a labyrinthine law that uses over 2000 pages of legalese to create another bloated bureaucracy with little or no limit to its powers; some over life and death.

Sociological law, guided by fallen humanity's corrupt sense of social convenience, has ultimately ended in only one kind of place; the guillotines of Robespierre, the purges of Stalin, the death camps of Hitler, and the killing fields of Pol Pot. Ironically, each of these examples of tyranny arose out of a distorted concept of "civil liberty." Communism promised equality, but some always proved "more equal than others." Nazism promised freedom for Germans from those who supposedly oppressed their economy—the Jews. Pol Pot wanted an agrarian utopia of absolute equality, where nobody threatened the collective with "harmful ideas." That would be teachers, people of faith, and people in cities who wore glasses.

In each case, the mainstream was mostly blind to what they were electing or supporting. In each case, the tyrants were moral relativists in how they lived, but enacted arbitrary absolutes once in power. Can we expect Post-Christian America's bizarre ideologies, disconnected from the moral absolutes that gave genuine equality under the law its meaning, to be any different? Now, powerful ideologues have redefined marriage; inventing a right for homosexuals and transgendered people never to face moral and intellectual reasoning on the nature of marriage, which might offend them. The bar for "offensive" speech and thought is now in freefall, and the thought police are coming.

Marriage is not a right. You don't need a license to exercise a right. Marriage is a privilege that reinforces society at its basic unit. It is a family ideal that self-evidently reflects human biological reproduction, anatomy, and a sexual ethic of love and commitment within that framework. Infertile couples can potentially provide children with male and female role models, as can older couples past childbearing age. *Male* and *female* are not arbitrary distinctions. They reflect an objective nature that has form and function. Nobody invented traditional marriage as a form of cruelty toward people with a homosexual orientation. Nor do biblical Christians maintain their convictions and concerns about the radical redefinition of marriage out of hatred for Gays.

Not every loving relationship is a potential marriage, nor should it be. Marriage preceded the state. The state has extremely limited legitimate concerns in regulating it for the protection of children, but it has no right to redefine it. In doing so, the courts have transformed marriage into something else. The state has made our society into a radical social experiment; granting unprecedented powers to the experimenters over those experimented on—mainly our children. Such rulings, in the end, subject the Constitution to unbounded sociological redefinition in a society that recognizes no historical context or original intent in its meaning. This is the mechanical endgame of sociological law. *When words can mean anything, they ultimately mean nothing.*

As harsh as that might sound to some; liberty also dies for all people, equally, in a reductionist culture convinced by its own deterministic assumptions that freedom of will is *nothing more* than a complex illusion.

## BIBLIOGRAPHY

1. Wiker, Benjamin, ***Moral Darwinism: How We Became Hedonists***, pp. 170-177, IVP, (2002)
2. Schaeffer, Francis A. ***How Should We Then Live? The Rise and Decline of Western Thought and Culture***, pp.166-169, 1976, Fleming H. Revell Co. Old Tappan, NJ.
3. Dr. Miriam Grossman MD, UCLA, ***Unprotected***, Chapter 1, Penguin Sentinel, 2006, 2007
4. Pearcy, Nancy R. & Thaxton, Charles B. ***The Soul of Science***, p. 42 & p. 138, Crossway Books (1994), Wheaton, Ill.
5. Op cit. Schaeffer, Francis A., pp.146-147
6. Ibid. pp. 162-163
7. Young, Edward J., in ***Baker's Dictionary of Theology***; under ***Criticism, Old Testament***; pp. 150-152; Baker Book House (1960).
8. Harrison, R.K., ***Introduction to the Old Testament***, p. 1111; Wm. B. Eerdmans (1969)
9. Evans, C. Stephan, ***Kierkegaard's Christian Ethics of Love***, in ***Cornerstone*** magazine, Vol. 28, Issue 116, pp. 29-31 (1999)
10. Ibid. p. 31
11. Op cit. Schaeffer, Francis A., pp.163-164
12. *Three good sources that deal with this issue in varying aspects are:* Josh McDowell's ***Evidence that Demands a Verdict*** (1972) and ***Daniel in the Critic's Den*** (1979) both from Campus Crusade for Christ Books, also ***Jesus Under Fire*** (1995), edited by Michael J. Wilkins and J.P. Moreland, Zondervan, which is a collection of essays by scholars and text critics that emphasize the evidence for divine inspiration and biblical historic accuracy.
13. Blomberg, Craig L., ***Where Do We Start Studying Jesus?*** in ***Jesus Under Fire***, pp. 19-23 & 28-36, edited by Michael J. Wilkins and J.P. Moreland, Zondervan (1995)
14. Montgomery, John Warwick. ***History and Christianity***, p. 29; Inter-Varsity Press, (1971)
15. Op cit. Schaeffer, Francis A, pp.175-176
16. Terry Mortenson Ph.D., ***The Great Turning Point***, *Contemporary Reactions to the Scriptural Geologists*, pp. 215-237, (2004), Master Books
17. McIntosh, Andy C., Edmonson, Tom, and Taylor, Steven, ***Flood Models: The Need for an Integrated Approach***; in ***Creation Ex Nihilo Technical Journal***, vol. 14 no. 1 (2000), pp. 56-58
18. Woodmorappe, John, ***The Mythology of Modern Dating Methods***, ICR Books (1999) - *This is an excellent in-depth analysis of the statistical and ideological pitfalls involved with the reasoning used in modern isotope dating methods by an expert in the field.*
19. Op cit. Schaeffer, Francis A., pp.146-147. See also, Pearcy, Nancy R. & Thaxton, Charles B. ***The Soul of Science***, pp. 105-117, Crossway Books (1994), Wheaton, Ill.
20. *Two excellent works (among many others) reveal the insufficiency of proposed evolutionary transitional fossils in an easy to understand way.* ***Evolution: The Fossils Still Say No!*** *by biochemist* Dr. Duane T. Gish (1995 - ICR Books) *deals with the lack of transitional forms in the fossil record in general. The same problem with human fossil transitions is covered exhaustively in* Marvin L.Lubenow's ***Bones of Contention***, (1992 – Baker Books)
21. *For more reading on this issue from the point of view of secular scientists who are grappling with this issue without advocating Creationism, see* Michael Denton's ***Evolution: A Theory in Crisis*** (Adler and Adler – 1986) and M.J. Behe's ***Darwin's Black Box: The Biochemical Challenge to Evolution*** (The Free Press – 1996). *For a biblical and scientific perspective see*, ***The Creator Beyond Time and Space***, by

Dr. Mark Eastman M.D., and Chuck Missler; (The Word for Today Publishers) *and for cosmological issues read* ***Starlight and Time***, by Dr. Russ Humphreys (Master Books).

22. Patrick Lockerby, ***When is a Code Not a Code?*** *The Chatter Box*, http://www.science20.com/
23. ***TJ (Technical Journal)*** *formerly called* ***Creation Ex Nihilo Technical Journal*** *is a science journal written by scientists for scientists and those interested in the sciences. The papers it publishes are all peer-reviewed by men and women of science in the appropriate fields.*
24. Ben Stein, ***Expelled: No Intelligence Allowed***, This documentary masterfully exposes the extent to which scientifically well-qualified people are being purged from their jobs in academies and media, some based only on a single act of allowing an Intelligent Design scientist make their case. Stein, a Jew, was shocked by what he discovered, and turned his considerable genius to work on this well-researched video.
25. October 11, 1798, A letter to the officers of the *First Brigade of the Third Division of the Militia of Massachusetts.* Charles Francis Adams, ed., *The Works of John Adams, Second President of the United States: with a Life of the Author, Notes, and Illustration* (Boston: Little, Brown, & Co., 1854), Vol. IX, 228-229.
26. Marquis de Sade, ***Juliette***, (1797) Wikipedia writes, "***Juliette*** is a novel written by the Marquis de Sade and published 1797–1801, accompanying Sade's Nouvelle Justine. While Justine, Juliette's sister, was a virtuous woman who consequently encountered nothing but despair and abuse, Juliette is an amoral nymphomaniac murderer who is successful and happy. The full title of the novel in the original French is *Histoire de Juliette ou les Prospérités du vice*, and the English title is *Juliette, or Vice Amply Rewarded* (versus *Justine; or Good Conduct Well-Chastised*, considered to be the prequel of *Juliette*). As many other of his works, *Juliette* follows a pattern of violently pornographic scenes followed by long treatises on a broad range of philosophical topics, including theology, morality, aesthetics, naturalism, and also Sade's dark, fatalistic view of world metaphysics."
27. Colson, Charles and Pearcey, Nancy, ***How Now Shall We Live?***, p.117, (Tyndale House 1999)
28. Justice Oliver Wendell Holmes Jr., speech at Harvard Law School Association of New York, New York City, February 15, 1913.—***Speeches by Oliver Wendell Holmes***, p. 101 (1934)

# 21

# Church Reactions to Shifting Foundations: Spiritual Outreach and Spiritual Isolationism

## Evangelical Outreaches: Effects of the Great 19th Century Revivals and Missionary Expansion

The 19th century church reactions to the worldview shift discussed in the last chapter, except for the Liberal one of compliance, produced two trends. I call them *spiritual isolationism*, and *spiritual outreach*. While much more than mere reaction happened in churches of that time, most of it fits those categories in some way. In a swiftly changing world, many Christians seemed overwhelmed by a sense that they needed to catch-up. As in other eras of history, churches sometimes responded well, and at others, shot themselves in the foot.

When churches responded well, they did so generally in some form of outreach, whether missionary, evangelistic, or by social services to the needy. When churches did not do so, it usually took the form of isolationism. This reflected a refusal to deal with new situations in realistic and/or loving ways. Two inverse forces accurately described Christianity in the 19th century. The spread of the gospel from the West reached high tide, winning souls through the "superstructure" of evangelistic and missionary activity. At the same time, ideological termites ate out the worldview foundation of a biblical Christianity with little hindrance. This made a great collapse imminent in the next century.

Church historians rightly view the 19th century as the culmination of a great age of Christian expansion. It began slowly and painfully with the Reformation, gained speed in the Colonial Era, and started to climax during the First Great Awakening and Wesleyan Revivals. The 19th century intensified this growth, and even gave the illusion to Anglo-American churches that it could go on forever. As with the Church at Philadelphia (Rev. 3:7-13), God put a door in front of English and American Evangelicals, "that no man could shut." The fact that the foundations were also in trouble should not detract from our esteem of all that God accomplished during this period. In some ways, most Christians at the time were not yet fully equipped to see the trouble in the basement for what it was.

In the first decade of the 19th century, a new big revival lit up the American Appalachian frontier. Historians often call it the 2nd Great Awakening. By now, the Calvinistic Puritan roots in New England had decayed into its own type of formalism. The "Idea Pendulum," once again, went too far. Too many Northeastern Calvinists behaved as if predestination of both the elect and the damned made evangelism a trivial pursuit. Some notable Calvinists, like Timothy Dwight, however, prayed for revival. Human choice seemed to lose meaning in what had become a form of unintended Spiritual Determinism.

Likely, this was why the 2nd Awakening embraced more Arminian leaders. It arose, in part, as a reaction to a distorted version of Calvinism. Though it brought massive conversions and motivated sweeping social reforms, not the least of which was the abolition of slavery in America; it also carried in itself the seeds of its own unraveling, even more than had the 1st Awakening. The "Idea Pendulum's" reverse swing hurtled past even Arminian territory, to new extremes and follies. For all too many converts, that arc would end in a poisoned wasteland of spiritual and intellectual delusion. It is important to remember that Scripture has passages that, when taken as isolates, seem in some places to favor Calvinism, and in others, Arminianism. It is indeed possible to warp the Faith by obsessing on either one over the other.

It is also important to remember that Scripture is not a collection of isolated sayings, except in some of the Wisdom Books, like Proverbs. Christians split the Bible into verses only in the Middle Ages, for ease of reference, not because God meant for us to interpret each verse as an isolated saying. The authors, including God, intended us to understand most of its books as literary wholes.

While the Bible teaches an individual predestination of the elect, it does not teach such a selective predestination of the damned. The closest thing in Scripture to resemble that would be Romans 9 and Jude 1:4. Romans 9 concerns God's sovereign right to elect Israel as a nation. It uses individuals as examples to illustrate that point.

Jude 1:4 reads; **"For certain men have crept in unnoticed, *who long ago were marked out for this condemnation*, ungodly men, who turn the grace of our God into lewdness and deny the only Lord God and our Lord Jesus Christ."** Jude does not elaborate on the sense in which such people were "marked out long ago." Scripture books from every stage of the Bible's development go to great lengths describing the behaviors and attitudes *that mark such people*. They give us warning, and remind us that God knows who those people are beforehand. They also tell us that He has prepared a place of judgement for those who fit those profiles.

Those who might object that "if the elect are predestined, then so must be the damned," forget that we deal with a God who lives in Eternity. God communicates to peoples that live in linear time. The biblically balanced idea here is that human choice does not supersede God's sovereignty in our salvation. God, in His sovereignty, is nonetheless free to mark out a domain for real human choices and responsibility to have meaning. To forget that God has done this is to oversimplify His sovereignty, and to create a spiritual form of determinism. That is what the Calvinist churches in the Northeast had largely done, by the dawn of the 19th century. Likewise, the seeds of the 2nd Great Awakening's end came through an oversimplification of its Arminian base.

The 2nd Great Awakening happened in two stages. The Eastern Phase came as a revival in colleges, like Williams, Yale, Princeton, and Hampton-Sydney College. This produced evangelists like James McGready and Christian academics like Timothy Dwight. Dwight was the grandson of Jonathan Edwards. The Western Phase happened mostly when the college men went west over the Appalachians. During the Eastern Phase, a prayer meeting in a barn near Williams College in Massachusetts gave birth to mission movements out West, and overseas. Historians call it the Haystack Prayer Meeting. One of its participants, Adoniram Judson, eventually went to the Far East to help the well-known British missionary, William Carey.

Moderate Calvinist James McGready (from Hampton-Sydney College) went west, into the wilds of Kentucky—a place where outlaws escaped to. At one point, the majority living there had a criminal past of some sort. McGready's initial claim to fame was that he had a face so ugly that it attracted attention (in his own words, and those of many who saw him). When one frontiersman saw him, and heard he was a preacher, he remarked, "Anyone that ugly must have something to say." The joker came to the meeting, and went home a Christian.[1] McGready influenced Barton Stone, who led the Cane Ridge Revival, also in Kentucky, where an estimated 23,000 converts came to Christ.

The frontier revival left lasting cultural icons, like big tent traveling evangelists—an American ***archetype*** that has faded to a stereotype. It also gave us "the anxious seat," where people needing prayer could often be trapped for hours by fiery evangelists with even more fiery prayers. The wildfire that Jonathan Edwards said had killed the 1st Great Awakening was even more a characteristic of the second. Even so, the 2nd Awakening launched other cultural norms, like the altar call, used effectively in mass-evangelism right up to the works of Billy Graham and Greg Laurie. Authentic fiery prayer would be refreshing, too. This revival also followed the pattern of genuine moves of the Holy Spirit. God moves, but Satan seeks to corrupt the results with varying degrees of success.

If the reader notices a change in my narrative tone here, it is not out of sarcasm for revivals. It is certainly not for men like Billy Graham and Greg Laurie, who have done so much to bless so many, especially me. It is because the growing stress on revival *methods* led to something so harmful in American Evangelicalism. This undue focus on method came as a logical result of an increasingly distorted form of Arminianism capturing the American psyche. I do not mean all Arminianism, but extreme versions of it that opened doors to bad things. This would end toxically for much of the 2nd Great Awakening, and for an American worldview that, even at this early stage, showed signs that big results had started to overshadow truth.

This focus on method began well enough, even as part of a biblical cure for the dead orthodoxy in that generation of Calvinists. Such spiritual lethargy demanded that somebody shout; "Just do something!" That does not imply that doing *just anything* was helpful, only that a clear need existed for westward facing evangelism, for which ample gifted people should have been available. No sense of urgency happened where there should have been some. God had no problem using human methods to good advantage when it suited Him, in Scripture. Even the composition of the Bible itself reflected God's use of human beings with human methods to work His Divine will. None of this was a problem, of itself. God preceded and providentially arranged such things. The problem came with an *undue* focus on human method driven by something lurking inside an early American worldview blind spot.

The idea took hold that if evangelists followed a sound method, it should always lead to successful results in a big way. That assumption led to the idea that big numbers always meant success. This opened the door to a Christianized form of Utilitarianism even before materialist Jeremy Bentham's corpse became a museum sideshow. One type of this swayed the application of otherwise biblical truths in American evangelism, but had little long-term intrusion on doctrine, until the 20th century. A more lethal form of Utilitarianism killed some late 2nd Awakening revivals. It had facets of both Rationalism and Romanticism doctrinally intact, and in control. This reduced and redefined the idea of Christianity to a "spiritual science," when carried to its logical conclusion.

Thus were born the first major homegrown American cults.

A Romantic version of Utilitarianism helped shape the hyper-individualist belief system called ***Transcendentalism*** by its founders. This ethic straddled the border between being an ideology and a religion. It idolized the American ideals of self-reliance, solitude, and simple living. Henry David Thoreau built a transcendentalist retreat in Massachusetts at Walden Pond, on Ralph Waldo Emerson's land. Later, they formed a commune. Transcendentalists rejected not only formalistic Calvinism, but also Original Sin and the idea of a personal God. This view had a vague pantheistic "divinity" pervading all of nature.

Core beliefs of transcendentalists also included the moral goodness of people and of nature. They believed society had warped humanity, mostly by religious doctrine and political parties. Here we see Rousseau speaking from the grave with a thin veneer of religion. They also failed to notice that nature is as cruel as it is kind, that horrors come with denying Original Sin. Without it, we cannot even logically argue God's goodness.

This, of course, does not mean that people cannot make emotional arguments for God's goodness without Original Sin; only that they do not stand up to examination of either Scripture or the natural world. Without a Curse event, nature, as it operates today, would logically reflect the character of its creator. Since nature is self-evidently both kind and cruel, then so, by inference, would be God. Original Sin teaches that God cursed all creation (not just Adam and Eve) in response to sin (Rom. 8:20-22). Because all creation is cursed, cruelties in nature, like natural disasters and monstrous behavior changes in animals, do not reflect the Creator's character by logical necessity. The Curse, while a judicial penalty, also tweaked creation so that sinful people could survive in it for a time. Physical changes occurred, the net effect giving God time to enact His redemptive plan.

Had creation remained in its original good state, its reflection of God's holiness would not have gone well environmentally for us sinners. Romans 8:20 also says that God subjected all creation to futility *in hope*.

Another commune of similar beliefs to the Transcendentalists, but more radical lifestyle, grew in Oneida, in western New York. John Humphrey Noyes (1811-1886) led the Oneida Sect, whose main teachings were "Complex Marriage" and "Perfectionism." "Complex Marriage" meant that every woman in the commune was married to every man there. It seemed that only by ditching monogamy could Noyes maintain the delusion of Perfectionism for more than a few seconds. Both communes, and other groups like them, often expressed their ideas in redefined biblical terminology. [2]

Terms from the rationalist end of the Enlightenment mixed with those of the late 2nd Great Awakening into the "Christian Science" of Mary Baker Eddy. As the term *Holy Roman Empire* described something neither holy, Roman, nor an empire; Christian Science was neither theologically Christian nor *science* in its method. We see in Eddy's teachings the same tension between matter and spirit as in the Greek heresies of the first four centuries, except here, matter is not even real. As the world around her veered again toward materialism, she, and several others in the wake of the 2nd Great Awakening, pitched hard toward this "spiritual mind science" worldview.

Eddy seemed unaware that her naïve use of mismatched terms from materialistic Rationalism to expand Scripture also brought in Rationalism's thought forms. She just did it differently than Liberal theology. For her, the spiritual world became as deterministic as any materialist one. Rejecting the Doctrine of God's Sovereignty as much as any materialist would, Eddy had only the dubious safety of her method to fall back on. If a sick person did not get well using Christian Science, the sick person was at fault. If they did, then Christian Science took the bows. [3] To one degree or another, less extreme forms of this have pervaded American faith healing to this day. The Mind-Science worldview would later penetrate some branches of Pentecostalism.

Around 1835, the region of Western New York and Ohio was nicknamed *The Burned-Over District* by Charles Finney. The revivals swept over the area like wildfires, year after year. At first half-humorous, this name came to illustrate the ashen legacy of a heresy that eventually burrowed deep into the 2nd Awakening; one that would most destroy its work—the ***Doctrine of Perfectionism***. Constant focus on evangelism, with so little on teaching, formed a setting where false teachers easily redefined key persons and concepts in the Faith. This world shaped the ideas of Joseph Smith, founder of Mormonism. Smith, and his crony, Brigham Young, built a theology that resembled a recycled Gnosticism voiced in early American garbled "King James-ish."

Smith also had interesting ideas on redefining marriage, except he was less "complex" about it than Noyes was. The Mormons revived plain old polygamy. This became odious to the surrounding community, which forced Smith and his followers to migrate west. Smith died in a gunfight in Missouri, leaving Brigham Young to lead the Mormons to their "promised land" of Utah. When the Utah Territory wanted statehood, toward the turn of the 20th century however, they had to get rid of polygamy as a condition. Mormon leaders soon received a convenient "revelation" to do just that.

One of the sayings attributed to both Smith and Brigham Young is that, *"As man is, God once was; and as God is, man may become."* [4] This is not the Judeo-Christian God of the

Bible, of whom Isaiah testified: "'**You are My witnesses,' says the LORD, 'And My servant whom I have chosen, That you may know and believe Me, And understand that I am He.** ***Before Me there was no God formed, Nor shall there be after Me.*** **I, even I, am the LORD, And besides Me there is no savior. I have declared and saved, I have proclaimed, And there was no foreign god among you; Therefore you are My witnesses,' Says the LORD, 'that I am God.'**" (Isaiah 43:10-12) The Mormon deity more resembles a Gnostic emanation.

We saw that the Gnostics believed the material world was made only by an emanation of an emanation of a long string of emanated god-copies. They saw the Old Testament God as an inferior being to the "Father of Jesus Christ." Mormon theology actually went a step further. It demoted Christ to the first son of a god who was merely the god of Planet Earth, and not the Creator of all things. Mormon theology is not monotheistic or Trinitarian, except by appearance from Planet Earth. In the universal "big picture," Mormonism is polytheistic because each planet has its own god.

Perhaps the most important figure in the late 2nd Great Awakening also worked the Burned-Over District, and gave it its name; a converted lawyer named Charles Grandison Finney. A prolific tract writer and speaker, Finney's revival meetings in the 1830s through 50s brought so many professions of faith in the Midwest, and New York City, that crime dropped visibly there. Newspaper clippings show that police actually complained of their own idleness for a short time. [5]

Unfortunately, Finney's poor grasp of biblical theology made him a bad teacher for those converted under his preaching. This showed in his denial of imputed righteousness and sin—the very basis of Paul's theology on Christ's sacrifice (Rom 3-5, 11:6, Heb. 9:13-14, 10:14). Finney made total sanctification into the requirement for justification! [6] If we could totally sanctify ourselves, why did Christ even need to die?

Charles Finney had a notoriously headstrong personality, qualities that show in testimonies from his friends, and in his works, *Lectures on Systematic Theology* and *Lectures on Revivals of Religion*. His friend, A. T. Pierson, described him as "*...a born reformer, impassioned to the borders of impetuosity, positive to the borders of bigotry and original to the borders of heresy.*" [7] Finney's use of language was hyper-absolutist, whether cultivated as an evangelistic method or the product of a personality so domineering that he jumped to conclusions and stuck to them no matter what; is hard to say. I do not mean simply that Finney taught moral absolutes—that is necessary. I mean that he often overstated his case, and habitually spoke in absolute *either/or* terms, even when scriptural *and/both* options existed.

Though a gifted exhorter and evangelist, Finney was so poor a Bible expositor that he seemed unaware how the worldly philosophies he condemned had shaped key parts of his own thinking. This showed when he tried to treat recent legal ideas and Mosaic ones as if they were the same. Imputation of guilt or innocence has no place in American law, but it did in ancient Jewish legal thought—hence, his resistance to the idea as silly. We shall soon see that Charles never applied himself to the study of theology.

Sadly, Finney's timely reaction to a distorted form of Calvinism became *reactionary*, and prone to serious errors of its own. Finney's personality also had a way of adding rocket fuel to the "Idea Pendulum." The most destructive of these errors was his advocacy of the Doctrine of Perfectionism. Originally, John Wesley had used the term *Perfectionism* to describe the Christian's *journey* in this life *toward* holiness and perfect love—what we might call a belief in *sanctification*.

The idea that a truly converted person increases in holiness, meaningfully in this life and perfectly in the next, is biblical. Certainly, a "carnal Christianity," where "faith" consists only of mental assent, with no desire to bring forth "fruit worthy of repentance," is not.

By Finney's generation, however, the word *Perfectionism* described a gross distortion of Wesley's view. Early to mid-19th century forms of Perfectionism rested on an over-simplified grasp of 1 John 3:8-9; **"He that committeth sin is of the devil; for the devil sinneth from the beginning. For this purpose the Son of God was manifested, that he might destroy the works of the devil. Whosoever is born of God doth not commit sin; for his seed remaineth in him: and he cannot sin, because he is born of God."** I have cited this in the King James because this is how it read to Finney in both that version, and in the earlier Geneva Bible. The Greek aorist tense does not exist in English. The verbs translated "committeth sin," "commit sin," and "cannot sin" are in the aorist tense in Greek.

This translation makes the passage appear hyper-absolutist to an English-speaking mind, if these two verses are taken as isolates; that is, *as isolated sayings*, instead of part of the reasoning flow in an epistle. The Greek aorist tense describes a verb where *the verb's action begins at a point of time, and continues onward in a progression*. In English, having no aorist tense, a direct translation of this passage, with no explanation, can be misleading. It gives the simple impression that once a person is "born of God" they do not ever commit sins again because they no longer can—ever. The entire text of 1 John shows the error here—it speaks earlier of believers confessing their sins. In frontier revivals, filled sometimes by poorly socialized and under-educated people, this was a spiritual land mine waiting for someone to step on it.

That person was Charles Grandison Finney.

Though well educated in law and philosophy, Finney's strong-willed personality brought him quickly to loggerheads with the man who tried to disciple him in the Faith. George Washington Gale was a moderate Calvinist Presbyterian who often agreed with Finney's assessment of the problems of their times. Gale cautioned Charles to deepen his knowledge of theology before launching into ministry, however. This was wise counsel. Finney's response comes best in his own *Lectures on Systematic Theology*.

> *To a great extent, the truths of the blessed gospel have been hidden under a false philosophy. In my early inquiries on the subject of religion, I found myself wholly unable to understand either the oral or written instructions of uninspired religious teachers. They seemed to me to resolve all religion into states either of the intellect or of the sensibility, which my consciousness assured me were wholly passive or involuntary. When I sought for definitions and explanations, I felt assured that they did not well understand themselves. I was struck with the fact that they so seldom defined, even to themselves, their own positions. Among the words of most frequent use, I could find scarcely a single term intelligibly defined. I inquired in what sense the terms "regeneration," "faith," "repentance," "love," etc., were used, but could obtain no answer, at which it did not appear to me that both reason and revelation revolted. The doctrines of a nature, sinful per se, of a necessitated will, of inability, and of physical regeneration, and physical Divine influence in regeneration, with their kindred and resulting dogmas, embarrassed and even confounded me at every step. I often said to myself, "If these things are really taught in the Bible, I must be an infidel."* Charles Grandison Finney, ***Lectures on Systematic Theology***, Author's Preface

Finney's *Memoirs* elaborate.

> *The fact is that Brother Gale's education for the ministry* ***had been entirely defective****. He had imbibed a set of opinions, both theological and practical, that were a strait jacket to him. He could accomplish very little or nothing if he carried out his own principles.* ***I had the use of his library, and ransacked it thoroughly on all the questions of theology which came up for examination; and the more I examined the books, the more I was dissatisfied****. [****Memoirs****, 55.]*

Gale founded Knox College, the first institute of higher education to allow people of color and women to study alongside white males. He was hardly a theological dullard. It was even possible that Finney learned many of his Abolitionist convictions from Gale. In any event, Gale's library would have had books from a wide range of Christian teachers, ancient and recent. Finney's statement in his *Memoirs* (in bold italic) say more about Finney's teachability and heart than they do about Gale or his library.

Finney's support for the Doctrine of Perfectionism grew in part from his own absolutist use of language, visible above. It also was a logical outcome of his rejection of Original Sin; and of making sanctification the requirement for justification, instead of the reverse. When Finney wrote, "*The doctrines* ***of a nature, sinful per se****, of a* ***necessitated will****, of* ***inability****, and of physical regeneration… and resulting dogmas, embarrassed and even confounded me at every step,*" he spoke of the doctrine of Original Sin. That is, the *sin nature* resident in our *fallen flesh that affects the human will*. The word *physical* referred to *the nature of something* in the 1800s, not just to the *material*, as it does today. It implied a *change of nature*, not *materiality*.

This embarrassed Finney, it would seem, because he had come into the Faith with a worldly philosophy that minimized sin down to *a mere choice to do evil acts*. While that, in itself, is serious, the Bible's description of sin includes such choices, but also much more. It would seem that Charles Finney did not understand grace well.

Finney never abandoned his lawyer's methods. These came partly from an academic background culture in growing denial of Original Sin. The assumption that his intuitive grasp of a major problem in the Christianity of his day qualified him to write off so huge a teaching from historical Christianity; left him prey to Perfectionism. Finney assumed that if God commanded anything, it must be something all people could do, simply by choosing to do it. Imagine the quandary this left him in when he read Matthew 5:48, where Jesus said, **"Be ye therefore perfect, even as your Father which is in heaven is perfect."**

Finney was not the maniac that Noyes was—the perfectionist who led the Oneida Sect—though he and Noyes knew each other. Finney seemed to wrestle honestly with this, as I also did as a young believer. Yet, his making total sanctification into a precondition for justification had severe logical consequences. It meant that a person's slip into a sinful thought, no matter how brief, removed them for the duration of their lapse, from being a child of God. After the period of the revivals, Finney often lamented at how few people had remained faithful to his vision.

> *"I was often instrumental in bringing Christians under great conviction, and into a state of temporary repentance and faith. [But] falling short of urging them up to a point, where they would become so acquainted with Christ as to abide in Him, they would of course soon relapse into their former state."*
>
> *Finney's* ***Memoirs****,*
>
> *[cited by B. B. Warfield,* ***Studies in Perfectionism****, 2 vols. (New York: Oxford, 1932), 2:24]*

Keep in mind that Finney's definition of "abiding" was a perfectionistic one, driven by the blind spots just enumerated. It was not a balanced view of "abiding" where we stay connected to the "vine" of John 15 by faith. In biblical abiding, we walk with Christ in a progression of sanctification that comes from Him having justified us. This also explains why most everyone sees the term *perfectionism* in a negative way, today, and justly so!

Finney's lack of theological grounding contributed to many of his converts quickly falling away, with no assurance of their salvation. Too much reliance on a lawyer's methods of emotional manipulation seemed to serve him well as an evangelist in the short term. In the end, however, it left his theology prone to excesses of hyper-Arminianism, Pelagian "will worship," and distorted views of justification and sanctification. His over-emphasis on method may have begun in a genuine response to a "do-nothing" form of what he called hyper-Calvinism. Too often, however, it ended in a Christianized Utilitarianism, even if not as extreme as that of some of the other sects.

We would call the "Burned-Over District" in today's language, the "Burned-Out Zone." People can only handle being jerked-around so much. By now, the reader might be convinced that I despise Finney, and the idea of revival. Nothing could be farther from the truth. I look with empathy on Finney. I suspect his later dismal view of the results of his work came from his own faulty ideas, more than an actual lack of enduring conversions, despite there likely being many of those. Mostly, I pity him. Charles Grandison Finney began his work in a time of genuine spiritual revival, and ended it with a bag of manipulative methods for mere Revival*ism*.

If I hope for, and believe in, spiritual revival in our times, why have I written of revival in what might seem, superficially, a negative way? It is because I also believe that revival, *when* it comes, must come with more than just emotional zeal. It must come with a view of our first love for Christ that is deeper than a mere romantic second spiritual honeymoon. In Finney's day, most Americans still had a Judeo-Christian view of reality. That is not true anymore. This means that when a Spirit-led revival comes, *it will not likely look like something out of the 19th century*. It must divert much more attention to helping people unlearn a deep-rooted worldview as they learn a biblical one for the very first time, in a setting of stifling skepticism. This requires gifts of teaching far more focused on apologetics, addressing both personal sin and a person's view of reality itself.

Finney's demands were often unrealistic. They kept many people in an artificial state where they felt in continual need of conversion. With proper teaching, converts might have reached spiritual maturity in greater numbers, with deeper roots. Finney was a master at forcing sinners to face their personal sins—in that, he did a great service. He did other things right, too. He planned his meetings so that local churches followed up on the converts. That meant he had many more real conversions than he would otherwise have had, and more than he thought he had during his waning years, in the early 1870s.

Charles Finney was yet another example of God using a man in spite of some of the things he believed, rather than because of them. Many of his other positions had biblical support. Some even positively influenced American Evangelicalism, where he became a lasting icon; a fact perhaps as disturbing as it is hopeful. He not only won more souls than either he or his detractors thought, nobody can deny his good impact on the abolition of slavery.

One of Finney's disciples, Theodore Weld, wrote anti-slavery tracts. These had a powerful effect on a young woman who understood that Christian literature should not consist merely of commentaries, lectures, and tracts. She used Weld's booklets as source material for one of the greatest of all 19th century American novels. Harriet Beecher Stowe wrote *Uncle Tom's Cabin* as a fleshed-out story based on hers' and Weld's research. [8]

Finney was also one of the first modern evangelicals to popularize a ***Pre-Tribulation*** view of the Rapture of the Church in prophecy. Many of his views on this topic came out in contrast to the fanatical Pre-Tribulationism of the Millerite sect of the 1840s, which tried to set a date for the Rapture. The Millerites sat on top of their roofs in white sheets to wait for it on the forecasted day. Finney, far more sensibly, insisted with the Scriptures that no man could know the day or the hour of that event.

The Pre-Tribulation view is a subset of the Pre-Millennial school of prophecy. Pre-Millennialism sees the 1000-Year Kingdom in Revelation as a literal theocratic monarchy that Jesus Christ sets up on earth, after his Second Coming. (Rev. 20) We saw in Chapter 3 that Papias, student of the Apostle John, held a Pre-Millennial view. This did not specify when the Rapture would happen, relative to the Great Tribulation. While it left the question open, that did not make the Pre-Tribulation View into a modern novelty. Recovered writings of the 4th century church father, Ephraem of Nisibis, show that the Pre-Tribulation Rapture was not a product of Finney's era. [9] Many Evangelicals now hold this view. It remains a major position, despite an upswing of ***Preterism***, which is the idea that the fulfillment of Bible prophecy all came somehow before 70 AD.

If this is the Millennium, I'm disappointed.

Revivals underwent a subtle change of emphasis in the later 19th century. This also rode the "Idea Pendulum," but more correctively than in a reactionary way. Two things drove this change; rising Liberalism in the mainline denominations, and the violence of the Civil War, where revival-driven Abolitionism had played a key role. Several church splits in the United States occurred over the issue of slavery, and the events that led up to and followed the Civil War. The most famous of those splits, among the Baptists, produced the Southern Baptist denomination.

White Southern churches often responded to the claims of Finney, Weld, and other revivalists by pointing out that the New Testament nowhere forbade slavery. It actually taught slaves to render respectful obedient service to their masters. It is superficially true that the abolition of slavery was not on the New Testament agenda as such. The Scriptures still had much to say applicable to the subject, however. The Epistle of Paul to Philemon charged masters to rise above the brutality of what Roman law permitted. This got little or no notice in the American slave trade, and the industries that used it.

The Southern argument had serious weaknesses. In most respects, American slavery based on race had little comparison to slavery in the Roman world of the New Testament. For one, a slave in the early church might have pastoral authority over his master. Callistus, Pope of Rome, was the slave of a Christian official in Caesar's court who recognized his slave's pastoral authority. [10] No one could imagine such a situation in the segregated American South. Another glaring flaw marred Southern appeals to what the Bible explicitly taught (or did not) on slavery. Unlike 19th century America, nobody at the time of the New Testament's authorship lived in a place where most people saw their country as culturally Christian. The idea was unthinkable in the Roman world. Such a place did not yet exist.

While many negative aspects came of the Christendom church-state fusion, one positive result was that it allowed the idea of a Christian society to develop. Even in America, where churches backed voluntaryism and a secular government led the state, people still thought themselves part of a culturally Christian nation. Perhaps it was mechanically impossible to come to that place without some period of church-state fusion, with its many problems. We may never know. Yet, the idea of a Christian social order suggested that culture and business practices should reflect the love and ethics of Jesus. It simply seemed the right thing to do.

Slavery just did not do this. It grew morally indefensible to a growing number of Christians of all varieties, and to non-Christians, alike. Even those in the few churches that defended it, eventually came to feel profoundly ashamed over it. The Southern Baptist Convention of today, thankfully, has left its Anti-Abolitionism behind. Still, in the 1860s and 70s, the ruin after the Civil War soured many Evangelicals on social activism, not just those who split over Abolition. This war-weariness hit both North and South in different ways.

If Charles Finney typified the evangelism of the first half of the 19th century, the second bore the mark of two giants in the faith, one British, and the other, American. Evangelicals still study the works of Charles Haddon Spurgeon and Dwight L. Moody, today. Unlike Finney, Spurgeon and Moody did not use sensationalist methods. They also had much firmer theological grounding in the word as gifted pastor-teachers.

Spurgeon, Moody, and teachers like them, began to respond against the influx of Liberalism into British and American churches. They emphasized the gospel as the power of God to salvation for those who believed, with a straightforward understanding of the Bible. Yet, despite the spiritual power of the revivals that they led, and many conversions and disciples, the worldview shift now had strong momentum. Even with Spurgeon preaching to a record million, before radio, and Moody as a Midwest powerhouse, they still represented a shrinking force. God had started to give Western Civilization what it wanted, and what it wanted was not good. The collapse of the intellectual foundations of a biblical Christianity paused only briefly at the revivals of the late 19th century.

In the early part of that century, revivals had both won souls and drove social change, as the Clapham Sect and Finney's work had the abolition of slavery. However, because Liberalism had deserted a biblical view of man and God, it seemed to have only one hope for affecting the world positively for Christ; taking on moral social causes. The idea of a "social gospel" developed, which had nothing to do with eternal salvation. Instead, it had everything to do with making life in the here and now more positive. Better technology had raised the standard of living in the West, and promised more. Such technology came from science. We saw that *hope in science* is itself an effective religion—***Scientism.***

Liberal theology now married Scientism, and birthed Theological ***Modernism.***

A Liberal Christianity, where men evolved into better human beings, now seemed not only plausible, but also attractive, and do-able. Modernism and Logical Positivism, with a patina of religion, would seek to prove via a social gospel, that they could bring heaven to earth through science; and do a more efficient job of it than historic Christianity.

It was not that men like Spurgeon and Moody were against social activism in a righteous cause, far from it! They simply saw the great danger in making social activism into a gospel, and neglecting the gospel of salvation that saved men permanently. Thus, the tone of the revivals shifted more toward individual salvation in preparation for the last days. To many who came afterward in this stream, there seemed no point in "trying to salvage a social ship that was eventually doomed to sink anyway." Because of this, many outside the later evangelistic movements accused them of being insular and isolationist. In actuality, conversions still happened, and converts still went on to work toward social justice, and on the mission field. Only mainstream culture had pulled away.

Some isolationist trends did begin to dampen the revivals, under the pretext of preserving them, however. These tended to steer people away from callings in business, politics, and in the arts and sciences. Yet, the work of Spurgeon and Moody deserves remembrance as *outreach* in its best possible light. The Moody Bible Institute continues to put out various forms of teaching literature, radio, and video media. It also produces other useful material for both evangelism, and equipping believers, to this very day. Present-day Moody Church Pastor, Erwin Lutzer, is both a prominent Bible expositor and a historian who reaches millions with his sermons and books.

Charles Spurgeon pastored London's New Park Street Chapel, later to become the Metropolitan Tabernacle, for 38 years. Roughly, 10 million people heard him preach during his lifetime. As mentioned earlier, this broke records before radio and mass communication. Spurgeon also deserves attention for another reason. Throughout his ministry, he suffered bouts with profound and debilitating depression, when he would need to retire to Cornwall for rest and prayer. God never took this away from him. No method could predict these spells or their duration. Spurgeon's biblical grounding and life shouted, **"Not by might, nor by power, but by My Spirit, says the LORD."** (Zech. 4:6) This provided a far better model for evangelism and revival than that of Finney.

During such times, Spurgeon had to rely on the promises of God as the author and finisher of his faith, rather than his own sense of "sensitivity to the Spirit" or lack of it. Had he relied on his emotional state, methodology, or his success at winning souls, the three would have seemed in apparent conflict with each other. Finney appealed to the entrepreneurial American mindset in ways that are still dangerous for us today, if for different reasons. American self-sufficiency is great as an economic application of biblical principles on hard work; but toxic as a spiritual ethic on how to relate to God, His people, and ministry. America has sadly lost most of that independence.

Should the "Idea Pendulum" swing our independence back to us, as I hope, its increasingly violent arc forebodes a backlash we would do best not to indulge. Spurgeon's depth is perhaps not as pleasing at first glance as Finney's energy. Yet, ultimately, it is far more satisfying, kinder, and better equipped to deal with human reality.

The impression that evangelism and activism—light and salt—became completely divorced in the era of Spurgeon and Moody would be a false one. In England, William Booth gave an example of continued social activism almost unharmed by the influx of Liberalism—at least in that generation. Booth worked with the poor of London, comparing the bleak living conditions of urban industrial workers to the darkness of Africa; where missionaries, like David Livingston brought the light and love of the gospel. Booth likened both the spiritual and physical need in the cities to a terrible war that only the toughest soldiers could effectively fight. He formed the Salvation Army on that model.

Events on the mission field also paralleled those going on in the revivals. One, in fact, produced the other. The gospel of Christ first came to the African interior through Livingston, while China opened up before the prayer and preaching of men like Hudson Taylor. Churches popped up all over the colonial frontiers, from the American West, to India, to Africa, Australia, and the South Sea Islands. The work of mission evangelism represented a tremendous outflow of the Holy Spirit, evidenced by the ministry of men like A.N. Groves in India.

> *In the 1860 Revival in Tinevelly, South India, the main instrument of God used was a native evangelist called Aroolappen, a disciple of A.N. Groves. Aroolappen wrote of the beginning of the movement as follows: "From the 4th of May to the 7th the Holy Spirit was poured out openly and wonderfully. Some prophesied and rebuked the people"*
>
> Arthur Wallis, ***In the Day of Thy Power***, *Cityhill Press*

Notice that the Spirit immediately promoted an indigenous believer to press forward with the work of Groves. This brought massive numbers conversions, confirmed by various spiritual signs following. Unfortunately, was not always so. Though missionary advance into what we call the "Third World" was great at this time, prelates back home often insisted missionaries keep control of the new churches from native pastors. By the dawn of the 20th century, Liberal Theology in mission societies at home, and blurring Christianity with Western culture in the field, had weakened the work.

That leadership stayed so long with Anglo-American missionaries also bred distrust in native peoples. This control-oriented approach to missions damaged many a good work in the field. It frequently set the stage for the gains of the 19th century to be lost in the 20th, when colonialism met its end. Fortunately, the "Indigenous Church" mission movements, late in the next century, would recoup some of these losses.

## Evangelical Forms of Isolationism: The Retreat from Progress

We saw a trend in 19th century Evangelicalism to retreat from the arts and sciences in various ways, and later from politics. In some of the movements that grew mostly out of the old Anabaptist sects, an even more radical retreat from the modern world manifested. The Amish not only withdrew from the intellectual scene, they refused even to have anything to do with most forms of modern technology. While many among the Amish have a robust biblical spirituality, an isolationism guided their idea of what it meant for believers not to be, "of the world." This has crippled their ability to reach people beyond their own communities on many levels, and currently devastates their young.

I remember vividly a conversation I had with an Amish gentleman in Chicago's Union Station in 1993. He and his wife waited to board a train for Pennsylvania, while my daughter and I headed to Boston. The light and love of the Holy Spirit simply glowed from this man's eyes, as he played with my young daughter and told her about the love of Jesus. I joined in the conversation, and we discussed many of the great truths we shared in common as Christians. Nevertheless, there was also a tension there. The man's wife sat silent, with a most disdainful frown on her face during the entire encounter. Occasionally, she rose up, and whispered tersely into her husband's ear.

For all the warmth that flowed from her husband, a secluded chill seemed to come from her, as if to cancel the refreshing calm this saintly gentleman had over our tiny corner of the station's tumult. While this is not a reflection against Amish women in general, there seemed to be a cultural gulf that this man felt spiritually compelled to bridge, which his wife seemed fearful of him bridging. I was a brother in Christ, yet I was an outsider, undoubtedly corrupted by the world with its tools and toys.

What does the Bible mean by "the world," when it warns us not to love the world or the things in the world? It often seems that Christians applied this truth differently in each new generation of church history. Rapid changes in Western culture that led up to the current "Post-Christian Era," have forced believers in all forms of Christianity, not just the Amish, to try to answer this question. I have seen many cycles of it in just the 37 years I have walked with Christ.

> **15 Do not love the world or anything in the world. If anyone loves the world, the love of the Father is not in him. 16 For everything in the world – the *cravings* of sinful man, the *lust* of his eyes and his *pride* in possessions – comes not from the Father but from the world. 17 The world and its desires pass away, but the man who does the will of God lives forever. *1 John* 2:15-17 NIV**

The word for *world* used in 1 John Chapter 2 has a two-fold meaning, discerned from the context in which it is used. When John had used the same word in his Gospel, he had said, **"For God so loved the *world*..."** thus showing the context there as the world of humankind. In the Gospel of John, 3:16, he used *world* in the sense of a planet full of souls that needed saving from eternal damnation. Romans 8 also talks about how nature itself will find redemption with the children of God, so Scripture also views the created world positively. Because of this, Christians can know that there is nothing wrong with enjoying the mountains, ocean, woods, or any other aspect of God's creation in the world.

In 1 John 2:15-17, the usage of *world* is different. Here it portrays *a system of thinking* or something closer to what we have called a *worldview*. It does not refer to people, the natural world, or even always to human culture and its necessary artifacts. **"The world and the things that are in the world,"** speaks of a way of looking at reality, and the consequences that view produces in the real world. Any system of thought and living that refuses to allow Christ His rightful place in our social existence is "the world." Enjoyment of simple pleasures, through created things, is not the issue here. Being addicted to these same things, and building one's life and worldview on the shifting sand of their supply and demand, is.

We are in love with the world when the things and pleasures of this life become the basis for existence and happiness. We are also in love with the world if we place God into a religious compartment, off to one side, so that He has little or no bearing on how we live in the real world. This cuts to the core of the Christian life because; **"...everything in the world – the *cravings* of sinful man, the *lust* of his eyes and his *pride* in possessions – comes not from the Father but from the world."** Notice that John breaks **"everything in the world"** down into three categories, where each is an *internal attitude* toward outward things, rather than the outward things themselves. The gold in the land of Havilah was good. Man just came to use it in sinful ways. (Gen. 2:11-12)

I see the struggle of churches that still take the Bible seriously to define *worldliness*, during the last two centuries, has often made two extremes. Neither has honored God terribly well. The first was to confuse human culture, and its effects, with "the world," instead of viewing the world system as something that infects human culture. This is sort of like confusing the patient with the disease. The arts, sciences, and politics were labeled as *worldly*, and thus not worthy of Christian patronage. This only accelerated the consumption of culture by the infection of what really was the world system. I have already discussed this trend, so I will not beat it to death here.

The Bible shows a view of humanity, individually and collectively in society, where God made Man in His own image. God likes to create things, and to bring them into harmony with Himself. Since this is so, human beings will also rightly display that property in various ways. While sin frustrates human attempts to create by infecting the process through the world system, that does not make Man's artistic nature itself "worldly." Nor do human attempts to understand the world through science become worldly, simply because ideology can pollute that method. *Culture* is not necessarily *the world*.

We need to realize that wherever human beings live together in one place there will be culture—systems of art, science, politics, education, and worship. None of these things will ever perfectly reflect a God-centered view of life this side of eternity, even in Bible-centered Christian circles. Revival can make things better, and indifference will make them worse, but being human is not the same as being sinful, even if sin has tainted all that is human. God did not make Adam sinful in the beginning, but He did make him human.

The second extreme about worldliness seemed to take the over-simplistic view that since culture is not in itself the *world*, then all aspects of any given culture are okay to pursue. This naïve approach pretends that all cultures are equally good and equally corrupt in any given point of the human condition. It ignores how ideas have consequences. This was more evident in churches affected by Liberalism, but it marked the development even of movements that rejected Liberal theology.

This extreme ignores the reality that while human culture is not of itself "the world," the world system always infects human culture to many degrees in our fallen environment. Arts and entertainment have a valid place in culture, but it is easy to see that the world system gravely infects much of today's art and entertainment. Science and education are essential; but that does not make the ideological assumptions driving these institutions in today's popular culture harmless or logically sound.

Most Protestant forms of spiritual isolationism appear to have grown out of a warped view of worldliness, or from misapplication of Scriptures on how believers should deal with it. All branches of Christianity at this time seemed to have an emotional need to withdraw in the face of new ideas, even in the midst of trying to reach out. Yet, the Bible teaches us that there is still a way to be **"in the world, but not of it."** Only by interacting with non-believers in loving and gifted ways that show the Spirit's power in all facets of culture, can we hope to reach a Post-Christian world.

The challenge is to do this without compromising faith, truth, or lifestyle.

## A Roman Reaction: Vatican 1, Papal Infallibility, and Catholic Forms of Spiritual Isolationism

It was not only among Evangelicals that reaction to the growing new worldview could be seen. Bruce Shelly's book, *Church History in Plain Language*, called the Vatican response to the secularization of culture the 19th century, *"The Restoration of Fortresses."* [11]

The Italian Revolution, led by Giuseppe Garibaldi and King Victor Emanuel, ended the Papal States in 1861. In 1870, it toppled the Pope's temporal authority as monarch of Rome. The revolutionaries opened the prison of the last inquisitions, and the "Congregation for the Doctrine of the Faith" replaced that institution in a curbed form. This essentially became the office of the papal censor. [12] Pope Pius IX had executed many protesters during the revolution. Some sources record that he still held about 8000 prisoners under draconian conditions at the fall of his government. [13]

For the Papacy, this was the ultimate indignity. It marked the end of the last tattered remnant of the Christendom illusion of Roman Imperial rule over a "Christian" Europe. Pius IX reacted with the paranoia, and insulted arrogance, of any deposed tyrant. He bemoaned that he was now a prisoner of the Vatican. Yet, Roman Catholicism, as a religious paradigm, needed to adapt to Europe's new governmental order or else it would perish. The idea of a Papal Caesar had become a huge liability. If the Papacy could part with it, but still retain a shell of its imagined splendor, then so much the better. That was what the Council of Vatican 1 was chiefly about.

By 1870, there seemed to be a sense of inadequacy in the "high churches" like the Anglican and Roman Catholic, where Christendom defined the church and its government. In England, the growing influence of the 19th century revivals, mainly among the middle and lower classes, spiritually squeezed the landed gentry out of the picture; the group that identified more with the "high church" and its emphasis on traditional liturgy. For some, the new view of the church that spread through the revivals seemed like the dismantling of the church and of Christendom itself. This marked a period when serious talk of reunification with Rome began by a few in the Church of England, called the Oxford Movement.

This rumbling in the Anglican Church came only a couple decades before Vatican 1. It resulted in a high-ranking Anglican bishop carrying this concern to its logical conclusion. He announced his radical decision to return to Rome. This made him the renowned example of modern Roman Catholic apologists for "the sincere Protestant returning home from the 'dead end' of the Reformation." The Vatican soon promoted him to high office, and Anglicans remember the name of John Cardinal Newman with mixed reviews to this day. The issue here was what we might call "core Christianity." Do we find the core of the Faith in Scripture, or in church systems and traditions that developed centuries later?

To us, the answer is obvious, but men like Newman might have framed the question thusly; "is core Christianity found in an obscure early era, or in where God led the church for the bulk of its history?" Of course, it did not occur to them that the revivals might be God's current work in the church.

Even so, we should not assume that Newman represented the totally isolationist kind of spirituality of Pius IX's later years. (Only a few followed Newman completely into Romanism.) Even Pius IX started out as a moderate, of sorts, who wanted some level of dialogue with the Italian secularists. The "high church" party in England also began outreaches to the poor and disenfranchised, which paralleled meaningful grassroots Catholic efforts. Such works came about not merely to compete for souls against the Evangelical revivals. They were an outworking of Christian charity in the social arena; even in their hope to re-establish what high church advocates thought was ancient Christianity. They were not without salt.

It is clear that the "high church" version of "ancient" Christianity was more traditional and accreted, than biblical and restorative. Still, most of them were men of good conscience, who operated from what they really believed was right, good, and necessary for social order. What everyone, even the revivalists, underestimated, was just how much the social order was changing; and how far that change had already advanced in the academies, both religious and secular. Much of what men like Newman felt were essentials in the faith were merely issues of liturgy and ritual—things that did not truly reach to the core of where people were in spiritual real life.

Despite his radical shift in loyalty, Newman stayed a moderate, as a Roman Catholic. He found the forceful way that the council pushed the issue of Papal Infallibility disturbing, and sensed that the issue was untimely.[14] The conduct of the discussion and vote troubled many others who attended Vatican 1.

The council had a more representative, international involvement than did the Council of Trent. Nevertheless, conditions forced on the voting bishops often proved censorious and high-handed. The Pope did not allow any discussion in small groups or notes about the doctrines under consideration. This made it hard for bishops to study the issues and form reasoned positions. Coercion even existed, where some participants felt the need to flee Rome rather than take part in the vote. Others who opposed this doctrine abstained from voting, either "out of respect for the Pontiff," or to "maintain church unity."[15]

But unity at what cost?

The idea of Papal Infallibility had been developing for a long time. It doubtless was the logical conclusion of Hildebrand's vision for the Papacy, 800 years before. By the time it finally came up for vote as a dogma, however, the very political and religious culture it might have fit had vanished into the mists of history. Pope Pius IX saw temporal power slipping like water through his fingers, and needed desperately to bolster his standing in the only arena left to him; spiritual headship over the world's Roman Catholics. This probably should have been his only concern all along.

Pius IX did not need to behave with the petulance and insecurity those that knew him often observed. The world's Roman Catholics flocked to him with great sympathy for his political woes, many unaware of the darker side of his Papacy. In the reactionary climate imposed over Vatican 1, most who opposed Infallibility deserted the sinking ship like frightened rats. Only a tiny minority around the eminent church historians, Bishop Josef Hefele and J.H. Ignaz von Dollinger, dared to voice their opposition openly. Von Dollinger was aware of the Pope's intent to ramrod infallibility through the council well before hand, and had written to warn against it.

> *None of the ancient confessions of faith, no catechism, none of the patristic* (church fathers') *writings composed for the instruction of the people, contain a syllable about the Pope, still less any hint that all certainty of faith and doctrine depends upon him…*
>
> *For the first thousand years of Church history not a question of doctrine was finally decided by the Pope. …Even the controversy about Christ kindled by Paul of Samosata, which occupied the whole Eastern Church for a long time, and necessitated the assembling of several Councils, was terminated without the Pope taking any part in it. …In three controversies during this early period the Roman Church took an active part – the question about Easter, about heretical baptism, and about the penitential discipline. In all three the Popes were unable to carry out their own will and view and practice, and the other churches maintained their different usage. …Pope Victor's attempt to compel the churches of Asia Minor to adopt the Roman usage, by excluding them from his communion, proved a failure.*
>
> *J.H. Ignaz von Dollinger,* ***The Pope and The Council****, (1869) pp. 52-55*

Dollinger tried not to form a schism over this issue, but it happened anyway, after the Pope excommunicated him. The dissenters, who called themselves the "Old Catholics," centered on the Jansenist congregation in Utrecht. They spread from there into Germany, Austria, Switzerland, and to some degree into the English speaking countries.

Many Protestants misunderstand what the Doctrine of Infallibility means, though they are right to oppose it. It is not a declaration that the Pope is sinless and perfect, nor is it a claim that the Pope is always correct about everything he says in the church. One could rightly define *Infallibility* as a supernatural shield against error that rests upon the Pope, only when he speaks ***ex cathedra*** or "from the chair" about faith and morals; in a way that explains, *"the revelation or deposit of faith delivered through the Apostles."*[16] What this means exactly is still open to some debate even among committed Roman Catholic scholars. The danger of it is that, ultimately, it can mean almost anything a pope with a strong enough following wants it to mean, but only under a creative set of conditions.

Popes have appealed to Infallibility only a few times since its inauguration in 1870. On the one hand, it sounds impressive. On the other, popes must be very careful not to use it lightly, where future evidence and events could objectively prove them wrong. To my knowledge, popes have only invoked Infallibility under two kinds of conditions. The first is to shore up a biblically unsupportable and logically unprovable teaching. The second is to stress ethics that have been historically indisputable parts of mainstream Christian belief all along. As a case of the first use of Infallibility, we have the ***Assumption*** and ***Immaculate Conception of Mary*** declared as dogmas during the 1950s. An example of the second use is in Pope John Paul II's encyclicals against abortion and euthanasia.

Papal Infallibility is the sort of idea that religious men promote after they have painted themselves into a corner. It comes by more than just living in an insular world that has passed away everywhere else. They had allowed biblical truths to distort and shift that Christians should not tamper with, while holding on to forms that were, at best, short-term measures, as if they were core matters of the Faith.

The Papacy's retreat into its cocoon of Infallibility only held off Liberalism a couple generations longer than in mainline Protestantism. It did so merely by shallow authoritarianism. Large numbers of lay people and parish priests at the grassroots accepted Liberalism; and its offspring, Neo-Orthodoxy in their Roman Catholic forms, long before such ideas ever became partially tolerated in Rome. The late 19th century Popes often behaved as besieged, offended monarchs in their Vatican fortress. Only the 1929 concordat with Benito Mussolini gave the Papacy political control of the Vatican again. It would take some decades for the popes learn how best to use this to advantage.

Roman Catholicism grew in this period at the grassroots, often outside Catholic countries, which now showed advanced spiritual decline.

## Another Catholic Response: Social Activism and Outreach

It would be unfair to say that Roman Catholics of the 19th century had a thoroughly isolationist style, just because the Papacy seemed to. Despite the polemic tone set by Rome, many Catholics made sincere and effective attempts to respond to the social ills of their day. As European immigrants swelled to the shores of the United States, Irish and Italian Catholics made up sizable blocs in America's big cities; chiefly in places like Boston, Baltimore, New York, and Chicago. Many took menial jobs in factories and transportation, under harsh conditions at low wages.

American Catholicism often grew in ways that late 19th and early 20th century popes found alarming. Here were Catholics loyal to Rome in spirit, but which had also embraced American Protestant ideals, like separation of church and state (by its original definition) and voluntaryism. Yet Pius IX and his successors denounced such ideas as bad for the Roman Church, if not heretical. Nevertheless, this was among the few places in the world where Catholic numbers actually multiplied.

Case in point, the work of my great, great grandfather, Terence V. Powderly; the son of an Irish immigrant, who went on to become a *de facto* Secretary of Labor and Immigration under President Theodore Roosevelt. He formed the first effective labor union, the lay Catholic *Knights of Labor,* in the 1880s. The Knights crusaded for fair working conditions at a time when the Industrial Revolution monopolies were at their height, and pay and benefits for workers at an all-time low. Powderly became instrumental in the design of Ellis Island. There, my Eastern European immigrant great grandparents on my mother's side of the family came ashore in 1902.

Terrence V. Powderly, cited by Shelley and other church history sources, became one of a meaningful minority of labor leaders to work from a Christian, rather than Marxist, base. Others included labor activists like Henry Cardinal Manning, in England, who had support from revivalist Charles Haddon Spurgeon. [17]

While this certainly does not qualify as a direct movement of the Holy Spirit that saved souls, it was an example of Christian ethics worked out for the benefit of the oppressed in this world; a "salting effect" Jesus said the church should exhibit. Powderly almost found himself excommunicated by Pope Leo XIII for his trouble. He did the unthinkable by admitting Protestants into the Knights. Only sponsorship from the Archbishop of Baltimore, James Cardinal Gibbons secured him from that fate. [18]

My ancestor and I are, no doubt, light-years apart theologically. Yet, we both seem to share a conviction that the most important things are often those that happen among the ordinary people of the church; rather than in intellectual ivory towers and cloisters far away from the concerns of daily life. We also would seem to share a distrust of religious and political forces that emphasize form over substance in issues of faith and practice. We also have a common leaning towards "favoring the underdog," as my father once put it, when discussing Terence's life and times.

Many in Rome feared that American Catholicism was becoming too American at this time. In 1899, Pope Leo XIII wrote a letter of warning to Catholics in the United States against this very thing. [19] Nevertheless, in far off places, like America, a Catholicism largely freed of its church-state shackles, took on a new vigor. With it came social outreaches in labor, medicine, and the mission field that have carried it as a religious force to be reckoned with to this very day.

## BIBLIOGRAPHY


1. J. Edwin Orr, ***The Role of Prayer in Spiritual Awakening***, DVD of talk by J. Edwin Orr, a Baptist church historian specializing in the study of revivals.
2. ***America and the Utopian Dream***, Yale University On-line Library, *http://brbl-archive.library.yale.edu/exhibitions/utopia/uc10.html*
3. Rosalie E. Dunbar, News editor for the Christian Science magazines, ***Calvinism, Christian Science, and God's Elect—A Christian Science Perspective /Christian Science Monitor***, March 30, 2010, see also Eddy, Mary Baker G., ***Science and Health***, Pg. 12-23, (1875)
4. Joseph Smith, Jr., ***King Follett Discourse, Journal of Discourses***, v. 6, pp. 3-4, also in ***Teachings of the Prophet of Joseph Smith***, pp. 345-346, Brigham Young, ***Journal of Discourses***, v. 7, p. 333
5. ***Harper's New Monthly Magazine***, Volume 52, *Editor's Literary Record* December 1875 to May 1876, Harper & Brothers Publishers, 1876, see also, Op cit. J. Edwin Orr DVD
6. Charles G. Finney, ***Lectures on Systematic Theology***, pp. 362, 368-369,
7. A. T. Pierson, ***Evangelistic Work***, 1892, p. 140, (quoted by P. Cook)
8. Shelley, Bruce L. ***Church History in Plain Language*** (2nd Edition), pp. 389-390, 1995, Word Publishing, Dallas, Tx.
9. Alexander, Paul J. ***The Byzantine Apocalyptic Tradition***, quotes Ephraem on p. 210, University of California Press, Berkely (1985). See also, Ephraem of Nisibis, ***The Book of the Cave of Treasures***, (circa 370 AD)
10. ***Catholic Encyclopedia***, *Pope Callistus I, C, http://www.newadvent.org/cathen/03183d.htm*
11. Op cit. Shelley, Bruce L., pp. 353-363
12. Hunt, Dave. ***A Woman Rides the Beast***, p. 131, Harvest House Publishers (1994)
13. Arribavene, Count Charles. ***Italy Under Victor Emmanuel***, vol. II, p. 366 & p. 389, London (1862)
14. Connolly, John R. ***John Henry Newman: A View of Catholic Faith for the New Millennium***, p. 10, Lanham, Maryland: Rowman & Littlefield (2005)
15. Hasler, August Bernhard. ***How the Pope Became Infallible***, p. 14, p. 64, pp. 66-69, pp. 71-72, p. 78, p. 80, pp. 93-94, pp. 97-98 & pp. 126-133; Doubleday & Co. Inc. (1981
16. ***Vatican 1*** (1870)
17. Op cit. Shelley, Bruce L., pp. 410-411
18. Powderly, Terence V. ***The Path I Trod*** (his autobiography), pp. 317-382, ***Ecclesiastical Opposition***, Columbia University Press, compiled and copyrighted in 1940.
19. Pope Leo XIII. ***Testem Benevolentiae*** (1899)

# 22

# CHRISTIANITY IN THE 20TH CENTURY: PART 1

## THE WELCH REVIVAL OF 1904 AND AZUSA STREET

From a worldview perspective, we might view the Welch Revival of 1904 as the last of the great 19th century movements, due to its style and structure. It was the last major revival before the advent of radio, and last to move in a Western grassroots culture still mainly Christian in its worldview. Because of this, it was also the last revival free to give undivided focus to individual repentance from personal sin. No major need existed yet at the grassroots to divert time and energy for unlearning a Post-Christian worldview. That coming need was closer than it appeared, however, and would take Christianity by storm.

God's primary vessel in this move of the Holy Spirit was a preacher named Evan Roberts. Yet revival in Wales was not the story of Roberts, as it much became the story of Finney in America. The Welch Revival had learned much from the mistakes of its predecessors. Church historian, J. Edwin Orr, who specialized in the study of revivals, poured over the local Welch and English newspapers of those years. He found some remarkable documentation about the products of the Welch movement.

As in other historic revivals, the one in Wales also produced an emphasis on simple apostolic faith, as revealed in the New Testament; and moved away from complex religious structuralism. Spontaneous preaching was common, often followed by supernatural spiritual works and healings. God's presence and guidance dramatically changed people's lives.

News reports spoke of how local pubs and breweries simply went out of business for lack of clientele during this revival. This was not necessarily due to a severe prohibition from the pulpit. Even strongly Bible-centered churches in England and Wales rarely preached total abstinence as a doctrine. Instead, so many people drank the living water of the Holy Spirit that no desire remained for artificial stimulation from distilled beverages. Anybody who has traveled to the British Isles knows that the pub is one of the main focal points of social activity in that culture. "Hoisting one with the mates" seems to be an icon for friendship and fellowship that has endured long centuries. When not taken to the point of drunkenness, it even found a place in European Church culture.

Early English Reformation leaders met in a pub for Bible study. God seemed to be trying to make a point in the Revival of Wales that perhaps, by this time, needed making more strongly. There is a big gulf between the warm fuzzy kinship between friends over a pint in moderation, and the "*koinonaeia*" fellowship of brothers and sisters united by the living water of God's Spirit. One may not necessarily negate the other. Yet, in a world where strong drink was getting stronger, and weak men, weaker, wisdom and love often demanded that Christians abstain. The consciences of new converts with pasts marked by drunkenness can be easily confused, and turned back to a bondage the Lord died to set them free them from. This should be common sense, whether God gives one personal liberty or not.

Another strange thing Orr found in the Welch newspapers of 1904-1906was that productivity in the local coalmines declined drastically. These reports puzzled him at first because one would have expected conversion to enhance the work ethic of miners rather than the opposite. Actually, it did. The miners wanted to be more diligent in their work than ever. Unfortunately, the mules that hauled coal up out of the tunnels did not understand the commands of their masters any longer. The commands no longer came with the accustomed profanity that used to lace every *blankety-blank* word. [1]

No other revival since has spread proportionally as far, and as fast around the world through mission activity, as the one from Wales. Not even the "Jesus Movement" of the late 1960s and 70s, which birthed ministries like Calvary Chapel, and Jesus People USA, had such proportional growth even with radio and some TV. Of course, to be fair, the Jesus Movement had to help converts not only to see and repent from personal sins, but also to unlearn an entrenched false view of reality. It also helped to re-build the ravaged intellectual foundations of Biblical Christianity; often it seemed without realizing it.

Many Christians complain today that "so-called revivals" of the late 20th century failed to yield the social changes that revivals did before 1904. People who say this are usually trying to admonish today's Christians for lack of commitment or spiritual depth—certainly areas where we often have serious weaknesses. Almost nobody with such complaints asks how conditions in the 19th century differed from the 21st, and what those differences meant practically. Nor do they usually ask if it is reasonable or even useful for revivals today to look like they did in the 19th century. Of course, a revival would need to reveal sin and call for repentance, and steer people toward Bible literacy, deeper communion with God, and church community. I am talking about how that happens in an Information Age culture, and the obstacles that culture presents.

Before the 1900s, even unbelievers in Europe and America saw reality in terms not hostile to a Christian worldview. Culture still reinforced a biblical view of sex, family, and basic social relationships. More social "road signs" pointed to moral sanity for both believers and unbelievers alike. This does not mean people and nations always obeyed those road signs, just that everybody understood sin and redemption because it meshed with their view of reality. Today, Biblical Christianity is more like it was during the first few centuries of church history, with one huge difference. The background culture views it not as something new and untried, but with a "been there, done that, let's move on to something else" attitude. Often, it is a "let's move on to *anything* else!" attitude.

Not only does the general culture not reinforce a biblical worldview, it actively works against it at almost every level. Individual lifestyles changed dramatically in the early church, but Christianity did not create lasting social changes until the dawn of the 4th century. While I have rightly commented on the weaknesses of Christendom, it did help set the stage for a Christian background culture to thrive in Europe. This enabled more systematic appeal to people's consciences through much of Western history whenever the Holy Spirit moved. The fusion of church and state dragged the church down; but it also, for a long time, lifted the culture up in ways that supported the ability of individual Christians to spread the gospel on a wider scale.

We still enjoy a little of that momentum, though it is fast losing steam—faster than I had imagined, in the 14 years since the first edition of this book. Leave it to God to bring good even out of what amounted to the corruption of His church! Even so, a compromised church becomes totally "without salt" in time. God must renew it, often at the expense of whatever advantages seemed to come as a side effect of the process that corrupted it. By the turn of the 20th century, the world was becoming a much smaller place. Christianity, as a widespread cultural worldview that took the Bible seriously as absolute truth, was in serious decline. Not even the work in Wales would change that.

Two years after the dawn of the Welch Revival, another spiritual event took place in a tiny corner of Los Angeles California. It would soon send ripples of both revival and reaction across, first the United States, and then the globe. Newspapers reported that a new fanatic sect had appeared at the Azusa St. Mission. People in it babbled in tongues and fell all over themselves in a strange religious frenzy. The diary of Frank Bartleman gives a more fair account of the dawn of modern Pentecostalism. Bartleman was an itinerant minister and journalist who documented what he observed with a prayerful heart. 2 His intimate knowledge of the people and events at Azusa Street revealed a tie between that movement and the more broad-based Welch Revival. Bartleman and Evan Roberts exchanged mail several times. Roberts always spoke with warmth and encouragement toward the people at Azusa.

Like the Anabaptists and the Great Awakenings, the Azusa Street "Pentecost" produced a mixture of teachings and events, some biblical, others dubious. It would seem that any sudden move of the Holy Spirit causes immediate reactions in the lives of the different people touched by it. It depends on what kind of heart they have. Some make a thoughtful, biblical response, while others dance in the wildfires of an immature fanaticism that carries them away. Still others easily follow demonic counterfeits in the spiritual warfare equivalent of a melee. The last becomes more likely whenever leaders in the movement fail to cultivate deep study and application of God's word.

Another pattern also emerges—some people deviate at first, but then learn more cogently from Scripture what God wants for them. They act in all sincerity, yet make their fair share of mistakes along the way. These dynamics describe the onset of Pentecostalism very well. At times, the bigger historical picture of what God does in these puzzling, sometimes disturbing, encounters are unknowable until years later. Sometimes, nobody has a clue until after the original participants are dead.

Pentecostalism grew from roots in the 19th century Methodist and Holiness churches that sprang out of the Wesleyan Revivals, and 2nd Great Awakening. The Holiness Movement built on Wesley's teaching of a "second blessing" after justification. This they linked to *sanctification*, but sometimes with a mistaken view that it happened suddenly, instead of as a process. They also stressed divine healing. Some of the original Holiness preachers of the 19th century advocated a form of Perfectionism; that it was possible through this "second blessing" for believers to achieve sinless perfection in this life. Most abandoned that extreme out of embarrassment before too long, but rightly still insisted that holiness was possible.

Unlike the later Pentecostals, Holiness teachers did not associate the second blessing with the gift of tongues, but with empowerment by the Spirit to live a holy life. When kept away from the pipe dream of Perfectionism, this was a good and proper biblical emphasis. Yet, many in the ranks of the Holiness Movement sensed that something was still missing. Even those who felt sure they had received this second blessing found that they had not really attained the great level of super-holiness they had expected.

Holiness believers struggled with the tug of the flesh along with the rest of us. Though likely few of them would have ever admitted it, a reading of their personal writings leaves one with the sense that they were often a frustrated people. One can hardly fault them, we all "groan within ourselves" together, as we wait for the redemption of our bodies. (Rom. 8:23) Having an "earnest" or a "deposit" of our full inheritance, the Holy Spirit dwelling in our clay vessels, gives us a taste of the power to come. (Eph. 1:14) Yet we are still often frustrated and limited by our flesh on many levels. (Rom. 7:14-25)

The theological foundation of what happened at Azusa Street came through the teachings of two men; Charles Parham, a white Methodist pastor in the Holiness Movement, and a southern black preacher named William J. Seymour, who studied under Parham. Parham spearheaded two schools. Students affectionately called the first, at Topeka Kansas, "Stone's Folly." Seymour studied at the second, later academy in Houston, where Parham permitted him to listen from outside the classroom door, because of segregation laws. There was no tuition at either school. Students were required to live by faith for their own support. It was in 1901 that one of Parham's female students was first "baptized in the Holy Spirit" in the 20th century Pentecostal sense, and "gave evidence" by speaking in tongues.

Parham's major teachings centered on five points; justification by faith, a second blessing of sanctification, divine healing, the pre-Millennial second coming of Christ, and the "third blessing" of the baptism of the Holy Spirit, evidenced by speaking in tongues. Later Pentecostal teachers merged the "second" and "third" blessings into a more inclusive "second blessing" of the baptism of the Spirit. These "blessing" categories were quite artificial. Yet, the stress laid on believers experiencing the Holy Spirit's power for sanctifying and gifting works beyond justification is biblical. Regardless of how one parses it out in a formal theology, God does not justify us without further sanctifying and gifting us for service.

Believers cannot simply do the works of God on their own, with a mere intellectual assent to the truths of the Bible—even a sincere one. History, Scripture, and personal experience all show that mere intellectual belief is not enough to live out an effective relationship with God. This can be so even when people make honest human effort to obey the Bible. On the other hand, empowerment by the Holy Spirit is not a panacea that removes struggles with the flesh for those who have God's gift in "jars of clay." Pentecostals were wrong about some details, like needing tongues as evidence of Spirit baptism. Still, their focus on believer's experiencing the Holy Spirit's power in life was necessary.

William Seymour moved on to California. There he became the vessel that sparked Pentecostalism as more than just an isolated anomaly in American religion. He had studied carefully under Parham at Houston, but Seymour never had the baptism until the Azusa Street event in 1906.

Parham did not come to Los Angeles, except to visit later. Then he had a sharp falling out with Seymour over the black pastor's reluctance to expel some people from the movement that Parham thought were practicing the occult. He also opposed the racially mixed nature of the fellowship. However, neither Parham nor Seymour seemed capable of exercising much in the line of a biblical model for pastoral leadership. Since Parham resisted all attempts at church organization, his earlier Midwest works flew off in different directions. Regrettably, this also happened to the Pentecostal Movement on a larger scale. It came mainly through a teaching commonly called the "Oneness Doctrine."

"Oneness Pentecostalism" revived the old Monarchian heresy, at first, perhaps, not on purpose. I suspect this because I went through a brief phase of similar ideas on the Trinity as a young believer, in my early 20s. I had never read either Monarchian or "Oneness" works. Of course, careful reasoning and good teaching, coupled with growth in spiritual gifts, soon revealed the spiritual and rational flaws of my position. The Oneness Doctrine got so far splitting Pentecostalism, in part, because a Kierkegaard-like distrust of reason had quietly lodged in so much of grassroots American Revivalism. This fostered a shrinking value for an essential part of biblical theology—logic.

Oneness teachers insisted that the only "true" baptisms happened "in Jesus' name only," instead of the **"Father, Son, and Holy Spirit."** Unfortunately, for those who have a problem with the Trinitarian formula, it comes from Mathew 28:19 in the Lord's own words. Acts 10:48 mentions Peter ordering the household of Cornelius baptized, **"in the name of the Lord;"** either as brevity in a historical narrative or because either formula is acceptable. Satan used this inept, meaningless dispute to hurt the integrity of the Pentecostal Movement quite successfully. He just exploited a serious spiritual worldview blind spot, as he so often does.

Many of the original movers and shakers of Pentecostalism seemed to come to bad ends. Fragmentation and breakdown follows any fondness for focusing too much on experience and not enough on expositional Bible teaching. I am not making a judgment of their intentions or even of their salvation, just the cause-and-effect ministry fruit.

Missionaries went out convinced that they would expound on "the wonderful works of God" in distant lands, using the gift of tongues they had never learned. They assumed that if they disengaged human intellect, the Holy Spirit would then be free to work unimpeded. That ignored how the Holy Spirit most often worked though people in the Bible. It also fell flat with embarrassing speed as a mission method. Some isolated incidents of people speaking in unknown tongues being overheard by speakers of that language, have been documented in the last two centuries; but these hardly represented another Pentecost. [3] We can say positively that much of the Pentecostal Movement learned from its mistakes. Serious missionary works followed that bore fruit.

The real tragedy in first generation Pentecostalism was what happened to some of its leaders, who seemed to follow the Spirit for many years, only to go astray later. As a black pastor, and a kindly man who always erred on the side of God's love, William Seymour's heart must have broken to see Charles Parham, his mentor, fall away from the truth; and embrace the racist ideology of the Ku Klux Klan. [4] This was especially tragic, for Frank Bartleman had captured the real spirit of Azusa Street, when he had exclaimed, *"The color line was washed away by the Blood!"* Yet, even prayerful men like Bartleman, in later years, embraced the Oneness Teaching, which so divided the movement.

Church history seems to show repeatedly that God still works through His people, in spite of their human foibles; and sometimes even in spite of their downright defections from truth. Were some such men hell-bound apostates? Likely, some were. Did some simply lack critical thinking skills? Likely so. Were they "never really saved to begin with" or did they so consciously reject God's grace from a place of such intimate knowledge that they not only fell from truth, but also from grace? That is unknowable. Both possibilities are equally disturbing in their implications and horror.

The idea that God used men like Parham and Bartleman anyway in no way justifies their defections. It in no way denies that they did great damage. It only reassures us that the "gates of hell," in the end, will not defeat the ultimate good plans Christ has for His church.

Biblical streamlining came to the Pentecostal Movement in time to save it from oblivion, however. From the Trinitarian side came several non-heretical denominations, like the Assemblies of God, the Church of God, and later, the Foursquare Church. The United Pentecostal Church arose out of the Oneness party, and has serious problems in its theology. Nevertheless, it is often a way station on people's journey to finding the biblical Jesus, even if they must eventually move on from it. Logical consistency in doctrine, while extremely important, is not always the final guarantor of life in Christ. Nevertheless, the absence of such consistency makes a lasting spiritual work much less likely.

## Fundamentalism versus Pentecostalism: The Battle between Two Different Essentials of Biblical Faith

The term *Fundamentalist*, and Fundamentalism in general, has become a word for any intolerant, extremist religion, of any kind. This word did not always have such a negative connotation or such universal application. Present-day use of it robotically slanders the Christian belief system it originally identified; and doubtless, the redefinition is permanent, as most widespread shifts of word-meaning are.

Evangelical Christian Fundamentalism reacted to the Liberalism that, by the late 19th and early 20th century, ruled older Protestant denominations. As such, Fundamentalism grew from the kind of revivalism typified by Moody and Spurgeon; moderating that of Finney, though it also had roots in the Welch Revival. It came as a vital biblical response desperately needed in 20th century churches—both those that accepted it and those that did not. It began its search for truth in Scripture from foundations opposite to the materialistic faith-assumptions of Liberal Theology. This triggered several unavoidable church splits.

The crisis of World War I delayed these schisms, but they were the only logical response to the "unequally yoked" leadership in many of the mainline denominations. The name

"Fundamentalism" came from a series of 12 small books, published between 1910 and 1915, titled, *The Fundamentals.* A wealthy Christian oilman in Southern California, named Lyman Stewart, authored them. Stewart was convinced it was time somebody gave an intelligent defense of biblical truths against the relentless onslaught of so-called "Higher Criticism." In this, he had the professional and spiritual aid of Moody Church pastor, Amzi Dixon. Support and peer review came from a committee that included the eminent evangelist and teacher, R. A. Torrey.

By 1920, moderates and conservatives in the Northern Baptist Convention began to call themselves *Fundamentalists,* after Stewart's books. They believed, with good reason, that Liberal modernists had surrendered the very basics of the Christian faith. Seminaries denied the depravity and Fall of man, salvation by grace through faith, Christ's substitutionary death for sin, the Resurrection, Virgin Birth, and visible Second Coming, and more. Presbyterians went through the same thing as the Baptists. Fundamentalist Presbyterians eventually had to form their own independent denominations, the Orthodox Presbyterian, and Bible Presbyterian churches, versus the Liberal United Presbyterian Church.

If God objectively existed, and had revealed His mind by intelligible statements that people could understand in normal ways; through the teachings of Christ, the Apostles, and the Old Testament Prophets, then the issues at stake here for the churches really were fundamental. These were not just a bunch of dry, stuffy doctrines that had lost their relevance in the modern world. They signified accurate Divine descriptions of humanity's most basic need, and God's age-long plan to meet it. Taught in intelligent and loving ways that dealt with what the Liberal skeptics said; these truths applied to the human condition better than the romantic theories of man's evolving "goodness," Modernism offered. Today's broken culture demonstrates this better than I can.

This will yet prove the face-off between popular perception, driven by intellectual dishonesty, and substance in the spiritual, historical, and moral realms. *Dishonesty* is not too strong a term. I am applying it *to a system of reasoning* that, without real evidence, rejected a logical, biblical supernaturalism out of hand based on ideological desire. I do not mean that everyone in the academic world of the last three centuries was knowingly dishonest or involved in some huge conspiracy of Materialism. That is silly, and does not fit the facts. Conspiracy is rarely a good historical explanation for major change. They happen, but usually only in ways that exploit bigger, uncontrolled forces, which already push events the way the conspirators want.

Conspiratorial control, like most other forms of human control, is an illusion.

What I mean is that a worldview shift happened. It began in late 17th century academics; driven by starting assumptions people did not question well enough, partly due to worldview blind spots that maybe seemed reasonable at the time, but also partly due to ideological preference. In either case, this shift is still long overdue for critical academic re-evaluation in our day. Fundamentalism began as an artless first attempt.

The strength of Fundamentalism rested in two things; its view that the Bible was the church's highest authority, and its rational approach to interpreting Scripture in a way that stressed the logical law of non-contradiction. A thing could not be both true and untrue at the same time, in the same sense, and in the same context. Several books of the Bible made the claim, in one way or another, to be God's word. The history of their influence and fulfilled prophecy is well established. God will not contradict Himself in them. It is reasonable to assume their inherent authority. It behooves us, then, as His children, to interpret Scripture so as not to force artificial internal contradictions.

By studying the Bible systematically, with a reasoning reverence for its teachings, book by book, verse by verse; God reveals to us how He wants us to worship Him, and how we can be saved. This sheer straightforwardness appealed to those who culturally valued straight-talking simplicity, and rightly so. Its blind spot lay in the shadow of its greatest strength, however. Many Fundamentalist believers, despite their desire not to bring their own ideas to the text, often seemed to be the most unaware of it when they did just that. This sometimes produced an unconsciously provincial view of Scripture, and of some of its teachings. People did not always think the historical context of the Bible important to its interpretation. Cultural preferences with surface resemblance to a biblical verse sometimes took on undue weight, like length of hair or use of cosmetics.

Some Fundamentalists reacted critically not only to Liberalism, but also to Pentecostalism. Here they saw another violation of a reverently rational view of Scripture. By *rational* I do not mean "materialistically rational," as in Liberalism; but rather the truer sense in which *rational* means *systematic, sensible,* and *logical*. Often Fundamentalist criticism of the Pentecostal Movement had some merit. As time went on, however, certain elements in Fundamentalism began to grow more caustic and careless in their approach. A kind of "critical spirit" based on suspicion, not on real discernment, began to show. Some created arbitrary, even linguistically artificial, forms of interpretation that they used only on passages or Greek words that dealt with Pentecostal things, like spiritual gifts.

Fundamentalists who indulged these methods (not all did) designed them for one thing. As a starting assumption (*a priori*), they barred the idea that believers today could have anything like the tongues, prophecy, and healing miracles of the New Testament. An early example of this doctrinal artificiality was the claim that "the perfect," in 1 Corinthians 13:10, referred to the finished New Testament canon. This verse teaches that, at a future time; **"when that which is perfect is come, then that which is in part will be done away."** (KJV) The claim identified, **"that which is perfect,"** not as Christ at His return, but as the completed canon of the New Testament. They argued that because *perfect* is in the Greek neuter gender in the text, not the masculine, it could not refer to Christ.

In this early Fundamentalist view, **"that which is in part,"** was the spiritual gifts, like tongues and prophecy. This view overlooked a more natural interpretation; that the "perfect" referred to a state of resurrected perfection for all believers (regardless of gender) at the Second Coming of Christ—something Paul went on to define in Chapter 15. The text in Chapter 13 compares the present state of believers with what we will experience when this perfection comes. **"For now we see through a glass, darkly; but then face to face: now I know in part; but then shall I know even as also I am known."** (1 Cor. 13:12) No matter how well we know the Bible, we still do not see Jesus face-to-face. We do not know Him *as He knows us.*

The angle taken by these Fundamentalists ceased to address the original point—disorder and division in the church. It made the matter about spiritual gifts. The terminology of the debate even changed, by the end of the 20th century. ***Continualists*** held that Spiritual gifts *continued* in at least some recognizable form, while ***Cessationists*** said they *ceased* with a finished New Testament canon. Not all Continualists were Pentecostal, or even Charismatic, which we will cover in the next chapter. A growing number of teachers simply did not find enough solid biblical proof to exclude the possibility of gifts like tongues, miracles, and prophecy. They decided that God should be free to move either way. It did not seem that Fundamentalist Cessationists took Paul's approach, which gave room for the Spirit, yet provided structure. (1 Cor. 14:6-40)

> **39 Therefore, brethren, desire earnestly to prophesy, and do not forbid to speak with tongues. 40 Let all things be done decently and in order.**
>
> **1 Corinthians 14:39-40 (NKJV)**

A later effort to get rid of Pentecostal-like gifts made non-natural distinctions between "supernatural sign" gifts, and "endowments," like teaching, helps, and administration.

Cessationists appealed to the different Greek words used for spiritual gifts in the New Testament, but these, too, proved artificial. The *charisma* "sign" gifts were supposed to be different from the "ordinary" *dorea* and *merismos* ones. The problem is that Romans 12:6-8 uses *charisma* to describe "endowments," like teaching, serving, giving, and exhorting. *Merismos* simply means generic "distributions," in this case, of spiritual abilities. *Dorea* is simply a generic word for *gift*.

Expository dictionaries and Greek lexicons give no hint that these New Testament words for spiritual gifts form such convenient categories. Clearly, some Fundamentalists, in an otherwise legitimate desire for orderly churches, went too far. This helped to set in stone a disagreement about whether or not all the spiritual gifts are alive and active for Christians today. The dispute characterized much of 20th century American Evangelical Christianity, and extends to the present day.

I do not mean that if we are simply open to the spiritual gifts, it solves the apparent difficulties in this dispute, especially in American Christianity. Recent history and 37 years of experience have sadly convinced me that no Continualist movement has borne, *on any large scale*, holier, stronger, and more loving churches than found among Cessationists. Individuals and local fellowships can, and do, shine. I have encountered Continualist fellowships that excel in love and spiritual power, but I have also seen many Cessationist fellowships do the same. The reverse has also been true, all too often, in both camps. The fruit of the Spirit is love—that is the proof. (Gal. 5:22-23)

There is a difference between operating our spiritual gifts, and conforming to the cultural expectations of modern American Pentecostalism and its stepchildren. The cultural expectations often do not help a biblical case for modern use of what some have called "sign gifts." Generations of functionally Existentialist, and now Postmodern, people have since entered the Faith. This brought Kierkegaard's "war between faith and reason" into the Christianese of 20th century American churches, in waves. There seems to be a growing delusion among many believers that there are "Word Christians" and "Spirit Christians," and that the two are in conflict. I have even heard people use those two terms for it.

I see two main reasons for this tension. One is unrealistic expectations, driven by Late American Worldview assumptions about spiritual power and relationship, which people unknowingly read into Bible texts. The other is that *it may not always be realistic to expect miraculous spiritual gifts to look exactly as they did in the 1st century*. I have come to find it hard to believe that such assumptions have had no effect on how American church ideas about "spiritual power" and a "personal relationship with God" have developed.

I do not doubt in power from the Spirit or in having a personal relationship with God by a fully biblical definition. I question some apparent American cultural assumptions pulled into those ideas, which show a distorting effect. *By "Late American Worldview," I do not mean Founding Fathers stuff; but the worldview of 20th and 21st century Americans, mostly—but not exclusively—since World War 2.* For generations, we have lived with expectations that we can flip a switch and light will happen, turn a faucet and have clean water, and pick up a telephone for intimate two-way conversation with someone thousands of miles away. It is expected. The only pre-20th century aspect of this worldview builds from unconscious 19th century Utilitarianism and hyper-Individualism; the knee-jerk sense that the question of "does it work?" trumps that of "is it true?"

It does not logically follow that if the gifts continue today, they must appear *exactly* as they did during the foundational era. *They will still be consistent with the biblical pattern, but consistence is only about non-contradiction of that pattern, it is not the same as uniformity.* We allow for this diversity easily when we talk of the gift of teaching. Individual styles self-evidently differ. It is also reasonable to allow for diversity when considering the historical and geographic part of the church where we exist. The builder's work in the superstructure is not the same as it is when pouring the foundation, even if the same skill sets are required in some way. (That's true even if there's a "cement pond" on the roof, as Granny might say.)

Most pastors I know recognize the difference between a gift and an office. The foundational office of Apostle no longer exists because the requirement for it is no longer possible; that of being a historically verifiable witness of the risen Christ. (Acts 1:21-21) Yet some aspects of apostleship continue in cross-cultural missionaries, even if the office does not, and miracles on the level of Peter and Paul's happen with extreme rarity.

Ironically, yet another weakness in both Fundamentalism and Pentecostalism is curled inside both of their biggest strengths. Both of the extremes in these two parties, at least on the spiritual gifts issue, appeared to react to the same worldview assumptions, just in wildly opposite ways. Continualists tended to respond by focusing on direct spiritual power. They also stressed intuitive, voice-to-voice relationship with God, sometimes to extremes. This reflects the cultural assumption that "the Spirit only works intuitively, not rationally." (*Face-to-face* also normally implies *voice-to-voice*; there were no telephones when Paul wrote, and throughout most of church history—see 1 Corinthians 13:9-12. I am a Continualist, who was once a Cessationist, so please bear with me here.)

Fundamentalist Cessationists seemed to respond to American assumptions about power along the pattern of the proverb, "knowledge is power." This meant precision knowledge of the Bible; sometimes even to the point of parsing artificial distinctions that make Scripture say more than it actually does. *Driven by Late American assumptions on power and relationship, both camps have drifted toward trying to squeeze out of God what only a "face-to-face relationship" can ultimately give. They just squeeze in different places.*

We will have that "face-to-face" with God someday; but 1 Corinthians 13:8-13 effectively says, "Not yet, normally speaking." We can know that we are God's adopted children by the promises of God, and "have the mind of Christ" from Scripture. We can also experience spiritual gifts and a deep intimacy with God through prayer. God is always free on His end to work in any manner He wants, in the here and now.

He does speak to His children in ways we can "hear," and we need to learn to "listen."

Nevertheless, it is good to be aware of American worldview expectations, assumptions, and the blind spots they can cause; even for those who reject the overt doctrines arising from them. We cannot package things like spiritual intimacy, spiritual power, and church growth for mass-market style distribution, in five simple steps. It matters little if we package them as steps of spiritual experience or of spiritual discipline attainment.

Pentecostals did not have a "face-to-face" relationship with God. Formulaic methods for developing intuitive sensitivity to the Spirit do not provide that—not even arguably scriptural ones. (1 Cor. 13:12) Neither could Fundamentalists build a "face-to-face" relationship from precision knowledge of the Bible. That would be as if I said that you, the reader, had a face-to-face relationship with me, simply by reading my books, and interacting with posts I have made on a blog or Facebook. We might develop a good relationship on-line. Yet, that is not the same as a face-to-face relationship, where you see and interact with me directly, as I am.

Knowing the truths of Scripture, without actually experiencing them in one's life, can be just as much of a trap for churches as rushing people through a rat maze of subjective impressions that "verify" the Holy Spirit. An intellectually consistent understanding of Scripture is an essential and marvelous tool. Yet, a faith of mere intellectual assent to Bible truths cannot move people by its sincerity and logic alone. Still, it is unfair to brand most Cessationist Fundamentalists by dead intellectual faith. It is, likewise, unfair to stigmatize all Continualists as addicts to subjective emotional wildfire. Why do I say this?

I say it because Pentecostals and Fundamentalists each typified a necessary aspect of New Testament faith. I say it also because their unfortunate stereotypes contain a germ of truth. Throughout much of the 20th century, there often seemed to be no way to bridge this impasse. In Fundamentalism is the ideal of a consistently rational belief system set in the Bible's *objective* content; a standard outside of ourselves to sanity check our internal experiences by. In Pentecostalism, lies the ideal of a *subjective* experience of power from the Holy Spirit that, when realized, equips us beyond human limits as living instruments of Christ. Christians need both ideals.

We shall see in the latter part of the 20th century a growing conviction that the two need not be mutually exclusive. While some might complain that putting the two together is nothing more than a "Hegel-style synthesis," remember that Hegel's style of logic can sometimes find a balancing application; just not as the foundational axiom of all truth. Putting Hegel aside, *power from the Holy Spirit and interpreting the Bible rationally and inductively, are not ideas in natural conflict with one another.* The Holy Spirit, after all, breathed life into the inspiration of the Scriptures. He organized them into a pattern so that believers can understand them.

As for the long-term impact of the best in Fundamentalism, it started to reaffirm for the 20th century a rational approach to God's word. This approach began from presuppositions that assumed the integrity of the Bible revelation, rather than its fraudulence. That does not mean everything done in Fundamentalism has been rational and sensible. The outset of this battle often found them clumsy, and ill prepared to defend their belief system. Nowhere was this more evident than at the Scopes Monkey Trial in 1925. In Tennessee, legislators tried to keep the teaching of human evolution, but not evolution itself, out of the public schools by passing a law.

Further research has long since invalidated every point of scientific evidence raised by the Darwinist defense. "Nebraska Man" turned out to be the tooth of an extinct pig, and "Piltdown Man" later proved a hoax. When the prosecutor, William Jennings Bryan, allowed himself to be put on the stand as an expert on the Bible, (which he was not), it played right into the defense's plans. [5] The defense never actually intended to win the case. Scopes' lawyer, the infamous Clarence Darrow, wanted only to gain public sympathy for evolutionary dogma in schools by a pre-arranged media circus. [6] Before the prosecutor could counter, and question the defense to reveal the ideological, rather than scientific, nature of the issues, the defense changed the plea to guilty; and ended the farce.

The same simplistic attempt to push religious social convictions from the top down onto a culture unconvinced by them came in the fiasco of Prohibition. Fundamentalists did not drive the Volstead Act, however. The 18th Amendment, which outlawed the manufacture and sale of alcoholic beverages in the U.S., began with the temperance societies. These grew out of the 2nd Great Awakening, a hundred years before. Laws based on spiritual conviction are not necessarily always wise laws. It depends on the issue, and if the legislation logically deals with its own consequences. Stamping out drunkenness at the price of creating massive organized crime and violence is foolish.

After winning a couple battles that lost them the war, Fundamentalism stood in a cultural position where the very tools it used to reassert a positive central place for the Bible in church life were now suspect. They had a century of intellectual opposition to catch up on. Like people out of shape for a triathlon, Fundamentalism required time to get its spiritual and intellectual muscles up to speed. It had to overtake, and then compete with a Modernism dominating many Protestant churches, and the culture at large.

Even with their emphasis on rational Bible study, Fundamentalists still began from a culturally stunted position. They did not represent their ideas in the arts; and education, media, and the sciences resisted most attempts for them to do so there. They could not often relate the importance of what the Bible taught to things in the real world that had to do with those realms. Yet, in a technological civilization, these very realms seemed like the bulk of reality. What political representation they had at the time was often sincere, but incompetent. By this time, the Great Revivals were only a memory.

Demonic evils, like Communism, Nazism, and Fascism, made Fundamentalist concerns over Liberalism seem petty and out of touch. They weren't, but it could seem that way. In many people's minds, the intellectual foundations of biblical Christianity had been demolished; even those who wanted desperately to believe.

Fortunately again, God favors faithful hearted underdogs, in spite of their messes.

## Neo-Orthodoxy: Modern Existentialism Couched in Christian Terminology, "Christianized" Pantheism, and Postmodernism

We touched on one aspect of the distrust between Fundamentalists and Pentecostals. Pentecostal focus on experiencing the Spirit sometimes looked from the outside like a form of modern ***Existentialism*** in action. It even, at times, became a way for that philosophy to enter the church. As the 20th century went on, generations of effectively existentialist people entered the Faith. This expressed Kierkegaard's "war between faith and reason" into American churches, in waves, even though most such people had no idea what *existential* meant or who Kierkegaard was. People converted into the Faith culturally primed to expect a non-reason experience. While we need to experience the Holy Spirit, the cultural assumption that doing so means setting aside reason creates a warped view of the that Spirit. It also creates the sort of instability false teachers easily exploit.

Secular Existentialism believes in the total autonomy of human choice; that free will acts against a reality outside the human mind that is indifferent to human existence, and meaningless of itself. Human experience arbitrarily assigns meaning to the universe, according to this view. This, too, was an outgrowth from Soren Kierkegaard's feeling that analytical thought leads to despair. Hope came only through a *"leap of faith"* outside the bounds of reason, to an optimism that ignores intellect. Certainly one can understand the concern about how easily this might infiltrate a movement like Pentecostalism.

A huge difference lay between existentialist experiences and the biblical experience of spiritual gifts, however. Pentecostalism did not deny a higher truth from God. It sought its experience with God within a biblical framework, even when it misunderstood the details of that framework. Existentialism denied that framework, and made man the measure of all things. The first major wave of its philosophical subversion of 20th century Christianity did not come through Pentecostalism, though some later ones used that door. It came through a movement that built its view of the Bible from 19th century Liberalism, yet irrationally clung to Scripture as "religious truth," anyway. Church history calls this ***Neo-Orthodoxy***, or the "New Orthodoxy."

Theology and irrationality seemed compatible for the first time during the 20th century. In all the centuries before it, Christian theology had been the mother of reason. Existentialism is also a belief where objective reasoning about a material world is, in the end, meaningless. The material world has proved to be absurd in this view, therefore so are any ultimate truth claims that appeal to that realm. Thus, meaning and values come only by making a leap of faith into an experience that rejects the restraints of reason in some way. This idea came of age as a secular philosophy in the early 20th century with the French existentialists Jean-Paul Sartre and Albert Camus.

In secular Existentialism, it did not matter what the defining experience of one's life finally was; as long as it broke free of reason's tyranny, and granted an epiphany of meaning to an otherwise purposeless existence. Existentialism largely died out as a formal philosophy by turn of the 3rd millennium. It still entered the worldview of grassroots culture via the arts and entertainment media throughout much of the 20th century. This indirectly defined how most people saw truth and reality, who came of age in the 1960s, 70s, and 80s.

Before that, modern art began to depict human figures in a more fragmented way. It also began to emphasize the themes that "all is random," and "hope can only be found in a romantic emotional experience apart from reason." Yet, even as many artists made such statements, their art itself betrayed an underlying order to things.

Francis Schaeffer described how modern painter, Jackson Pollock (1912-1956), tried to paint the idea that the universe is random and futile. Pollock hung paint cans with holes in their bottoms by strings, from a moving lattice. This allowed the paint to drip randomly on a canvass underneath. [7] Yet, his art betrayed him. When one looks at this work, one sees that the paint dribbled out in elliptical patterns that signified the laws of motion described by the lattice's movement. There was order in the universe after all.

**Common Existential Assumptions Expressed in Christian Terminology**

**Perceptions about Spirituality**
1- Scriptural reasoning & the Holy Spirit's leading are often in conflict.
2- We must choose between being a 'doctrine' Christian or a 'Spirit' Christian.
3- 'Doctrine' & 'Spirit' Christians are in conflict. Intellect cannot be spiritual.

**Observations, Evidence and Artifacts**
1- Knowledge can make people arrogant. 1Co. 8:1
2- Members of the world's intellectual elites rarely embrace a Bible-based belief system. 1Co. 1:26
3- The dominant philosophies in education today are either materialistic or pantheistic. The media, arts & entertainment usually reinforce such philosophies and thus have an anti-Biblical bias built in to them.

**Foundational Cultural Faith-Assumptions**
1- Reason & intellect are automatically at war with faith & the leading of the Holy Spirit.
2- Science disproves faith - one can only have hope through denying what reason says.
3- Faith is a form of positive energy we can harness, while reason is cold, dead and negative.
4- Faith is emotional, while reason is always intellectual & cold.
5- Reason can't be applied to matters of faith & values.

Movies made these kinds of statements even more powerfully, not only because of the spectacle, but because film reached more people than the fine arts did. Schaeffer also gives a list and description of how movies proclaimed this kind of message throughout the 1960s and 1970s. In one title, *Blow-Up*, the trailer for the film poster read, *"Murder without guilt, love without meaning."* [8] Heroes often vanished, replaced either by an anti-hero who has an existential experience that drives him to authenticate his existence by making a dramatic choice; or simply a character that becomes the focal point of the movie, who meanders through his or her meaningless "reality" into madness. *Blade Runner* is a later example of the anti-hero, and Stanley Kubrick's film version of the novel *A Clockwork Orange* describes the second type of focal character.

Existentialism involved a split view of reality. The material world was meaningless as far as objective truth went, merely objectively factual in terms of physical events. The realm of "values" and meaning existed on another level, which had no connection to the material world of cause and effect. This involved erasing the idea of moral absolutes for the individual. Academics supported this by assuming that Hegel's view of logic was the ultimate truth of how things really are. In Existentialism, individuals created their own values and meaning regardless of facts or any ethic based on moral absolutes. Philosopher Nancy Pearcey calls this the "Fact-Value Split" in her landmark book, *Total Truth: Liberating Christianity from Its Cultural Captivity.* [9]

I have mapped it out similarly as the removal of meaning from the world of matter.

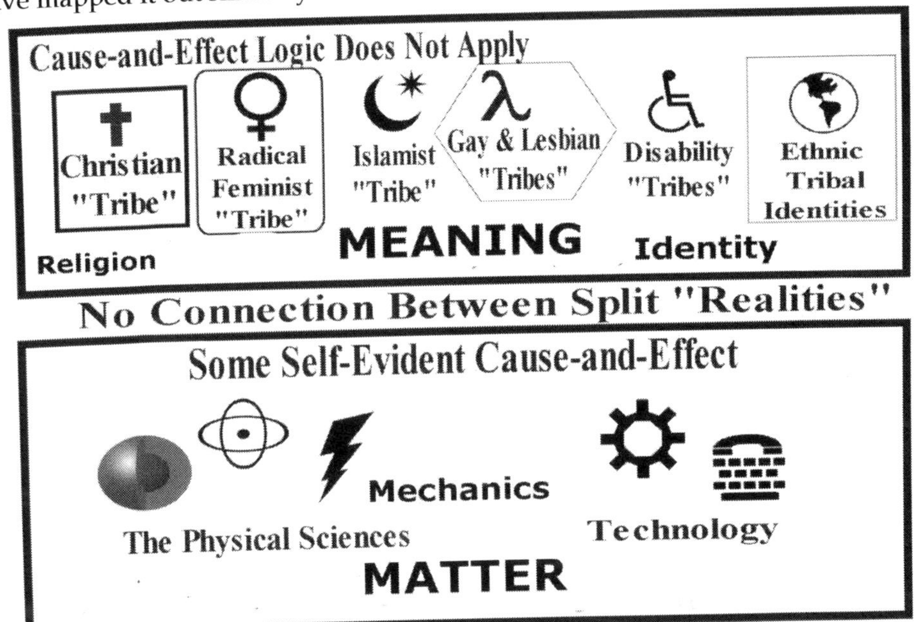


In the generations since the Baby Boomers, it has become apparent that individuals creating their own morality make for an unstable society. This should really have been self-evident from a common sense perspective, but people really fell in love with themselves, and with the idea that they could invent their own truth. I remember doing so, before my conversion to Christ, in 1978. That instability forced the rebirth of "tribes," where social, religious, or ethnic identity became the arbiter of truth, instead of the individual. Moral absolutes based on a transcendent ethic, such as from the Bible, or rooted in objectively evident aspects of the human condition, though still the most viable alternatives to chaos; had already met with rejection at the cultural level.

"Tribes" are also unstable as the final say in truth and morality, however. They lead to the balkanization of civilization into hardened groups that have no motive to seek common ground with each other. The death of objective truth means in the end that people do not see a truth out there worth discovering. They do not even ask if what their own "tribe" says and does is true or right. Societies who buy into this sort of worldview lose their motivation to discover things because nothing is really worth knowing. Finding objective "common ground" with different groups therefore becomes unthinkable, not in the sense that nobody wants peaceful coexistence; but in the sense that nobody thinks common ground is possible. This is the inevitable endgame for the worldview of ***Postmodernism***.

The irony here is that this is the mechanical result of society engineering an artificial set of standards designed to make people accept each other. Yet, if we pretend that everyone's beliefs are true in public, then nobody's are. Ideas, cultures, lifestyles, even people lose their inherent value in such a way of thinking. This system assumes that people are what they *do* and *believe*; so that the only way to grant everyone dignity is to publically affirm every idea and lifestyle, no matter how ludicrous or self-destructive. Take away our creation in the image of God, as the basis for human dignity, and this sallow counterfeit is all that remains possible.

In Existentialism, the individual sought authentication, but in Postmodernism, only the diktat of the tribe has meaning. **"While they promise them liberty, they themselves are slaves of corruption; for by whom a person is overcome, by him also he is brought into bondage."** (2 Peter 2:19 NKJV)

Modernism imagined that it was being objectively accurate and truthful. Postmodernism showed Modernism that it was not by turning Modernism's skepticism against modernist truth claims. Postmodernism is, in fact, the natural outgrowth of Modernism. They both rest on the faith-assumption that *faith-assumptions themselves are not real*. Modernism does this by imagining it builds from objective evidence without any grid of assumptions for interpreting that evidence. Postmodernism does it by rejecting the possibility of objectivity, period (now, shut up and watch the TV). Of course, Postmodernism expects us arbitrarily to treat its diktats as objective. In both cases, the *foundational assumption is that there are no foundational assumptions*.

"Gee Obi Wan, are you absolutely sure?"

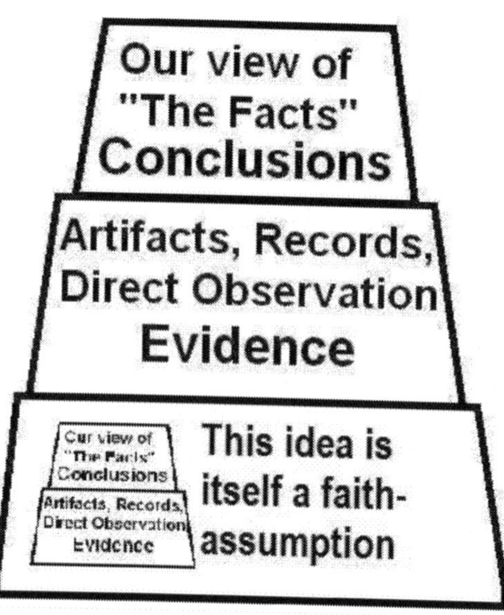


Either version of this, however, is itself a faith-assumption. Confused yet?

Postmodern people in the West now see reality in a split, existential way, even if they have never heard of the word *existential*. [10] People today exist with a fractured double view of reality. On the lower level, reason (force-marched by materialistic faith-assumptions) has led to the conclusion that we are nothing but meaningless biochemical machines; evolved accidents, and that *real choice* is an illusion. On a detached upper plane, effectively existential generations, at the same time, imagine themselves "free" to build their own arbitrary meaning and morals—their own *reality*. It is needless for these individualized or tribal "realities" to correspond to each other on a social level, or that they connect to any system of reason or ethics. They each build from an irrational "leap of faith," and assume all others do the same. It is an Information Age "Tower of Babel."

This is not the faith of biblical Christianity, which has a reasoned basis.

Of course, few ever consciously become aware of this dynamic. Many pull it into their Christianity with them, however, when they convert. In today's cultural mindset, it is possible for everybody to have contradictory concepts of religion and God, and yet, to have them all be "true." This all rests on the assumption that nobody can really know anything at all about God in the real world. It brings to mind a story I heard years ago, on the radio commentary, *Breakpoint*.

A Christian girl went to college, and got into a conversation with her new roommate about issues of faith. She found her roommate remarkably open, and supportive of her biblical ideas. The two girls later met with some other college ladies at a café. There, the Christian discovered that her roommate seemed just as willing to agree with the Buddhist girl, the agnostic humanist, the Muslim, the Neo-Pagan Wiccan, and the New Age Spiritist. In the end, the roommate said that everybody was really saying the same thing. All the other girls nodded in eager agreement.

This story does not describe a tolerance that respects the individual right to differ, which I think all of us would agree is a good thing. Rather, it is the actual thrusting of all things moral, philosophical, and religious into a faerie realm, *where nothing really matters*.

In such a realm, cause-and-effect reality and the law of non-contradiction become meaningless. Nothing in this kind of "personal faith" ever touches the real world in a way that can affect anybody else or stand up to evidential reasoning. If this is so, then faith and morals do not really belong in the marketplace of public discussion at all. The only tattered remnant of moral sanity such a belief system offers is the tepid hope that some "nice people" will always be around. But who defines "nice," and how?

This dystopian society burdens us not only to respect another person's *right* to believe absurd ideas. It demands that we *publicly affirm those absurd ideas ourselves*. To question the rationality and morality of any worldview or lifestyle might violate the emotional comfort zone of those who hold that view. It might *make someone* do something violent. This is the essence of ***dystopia***—making unjust rules to try to ensure an equal outcome; as opposed to having fair laws, which we all know can never ensure equal results in the real world.

In the naïve cocoon of such a society, conditioned (rather than educated) people treat even civil attempts to persuade through intellectual and moral means as evil. In this view, different cultures must remain pure, no matter what, rather than truly interact and risk assimilation. People groups cannot share good ideas or grow beyond bad ones.

This mindset treats Christian evangelism, and apologetics based on reason, as if they were forms of coercion. The scenario also has a maddening tendency to work only one way. It is quite all right for people to question a worldview that believes in moral absolutes, but the reverse is abominable and intolerant. Once society equates civil moral reasoning with political intimidation, Christians have no other way to obey the Great Commission. Not only that, everyone else ultimately loses their right to challenge any bad idea through reason and appeals to conscience.

Under the pretext of preventing bullying, the bullies destroy the exercise of legitimate free speech. People can no longer discuss a whole array of important moral and spiritual issues within a relativistic value system. This system leaves them wringing their hands at the "unexplainable insanity" of kids who shoot their classmates, and fanatics who fly jets into skyscrapers. Yet, an honest look at the moral and spiritual worldview backgrounds of the offenders often makes the motivation behind such incidents clear. Comparing the moral and rational strengths of different worldviews not only makes such crimes more explainable, but also more preventable.

Our society began to see the mechanics of what I have just described take its current form in the 1960s; when this split view of reality that incubated in academics broke through, and took seed in the grassroots culture of the English-speaking world. That generation saw

Existentialism flower, and ripen to decay as Postmodernism. At the time, it did not matter what kind of existential experience people placed hope in, as long as it seemed to work superficially for the individual. The person who found meaning in an acid trip was essentially on the same level as the artist who hoped in the existence of art; or the religionist who experienced ecstasy with no intellectual content, or the scientist who dreamed of seeing the next quantum leap in human evolution.

Unfortunately, people now saw the Christian faith in this domain, alongside UFOs, Mother Earth, and peyote buttons. People and methods operating inside churches often reinforced this view. Theological Liberalism was the Materialism of the Enlightenment voiced in Christian words. Likewise, its stepchild, Neo-Orthodoxy, became Existentialism in God-speak. This "new orthodoxy" claimed to revive a respect for the Bible, while it accepted Liberal claims about Scripture being largely the work of pious fraud. I can think of few concepts more irrational than that! A Neo-Orthodox theologian, to one degree or another, believes that the Bible is full of historic and scientific errors about nature; and yet somehow that a kind of "spiritual truth" still glows through it anyway.

This left us with the subjective snag of how to know whether any given Bible passage is a product of the "glowing spiritual truth" or human fraudulence. However, Neo-Orthodoxy came across to the unwary as a return of sorts to the Bible. Its methods managed to influence even conservative Christian institutions in ways pure Liberalism never could. For one, many Bible-believers throughout the 20th century still had an almost subliminal cultural distrust of things related to science. Neo-Orthodoxy seemed neatly to sidestep the kinds of issues raised by those realms by dismissing them as unimportant.

In fact, Neo-Orthodoxy is not a theological view with thesis points, like Calvinism or even Pentecostalism, at all. Instead, it is an interpretive method, which brings the world's Existentialism into the church using re-defined Christian words. It results in a variety of conclusions on any topic to which it is applied. Some of these would even seem charmingly orthodox, if one could be sure the definitions of the words used were the same ones historically known. As slippery as all this is, some genuine lovers of Jesus in the 20th century had limited amounts of this Neo-Orthodox view in their thinking. Yet each time someone applied it, the effect was spiritually and intellectually corrosive to any system of evidential biblical faith, in direct proportion.

Within the Neo-Orthodox model, it seemed possible for teachers, who claimed to follow Karl Barth, to have respect for biblical morality and spirituality in religion; yet concede the scholarly issues over to the Liberals. Barth lived in Germany and Switzerland during the rise of Adolf Hitler. He rejected his portrayal as "Father of Neo-Orthodoxy" by some of his contemporaries. Barth claimed rather to teach that paradoxes exist in God's relationship to humanity—which is a biblically realistic claim. He openly rejected theological Liberalism, which I assume includes its claims against inerrancy.

Even if Barth did commit the intellectual suicide of Neo-Orthodoxy—which I have come to doubt—we should not doubt the man's bottom line faith. Even some otherwise good Christian thinkers of the early middle 20th century suffered partly from Neo-Orthodox influences. Many felt lost in the philosophical rubble Modernism had made of what used to be Bible-centered universities. Barth stood with Dietrich Bonhoeffer in signing the 1934 *Barman Declaration*; a courageous refusal of Hitler's attempt to make the church into a propaganda arm of National Socialism. Not many other pastors in Germany at the time showed as much courage or biblical conviction.

Nevertheless, even had Barth been the "Father of Neo-Orthodoxy," we could not simply say that because of his bravery; his having an alleged Neo-Orthodox dualism in his theology really did not matter, either. The next generation of Christian thinkers had a severely eroded foundation to build on at a time when big storms were on the horizon.

Nazism was more than just a political movement. It came rife with twisted messianic overtones and various kinds of occult spiritualism. Its ability to saturate so much of German culture came in part from social backlash against the moral ruin and wishy-washy-ness of German Liberalism. Even many conservative church leaders went along with Hitler because they thought he would clean up the streets and the brothels. The depth of their miscalculation only occurred to them, as sanctioned gang violence from the Brown-shirts and then the SS made clear the true nature of the new order. This, of course, does not excuse the majority of church leaders in Germany for their blindness and apathy.

The proverbial writing was on the wall many years earlier with the Nazi and Communist acceptance of Social Darwinism as a political philosophy; and the anti-Semitism that Hitler never even bothered to hide. ***Social Darwinism*** is the idea that certain people groups are more evolved and less beast-like than others are. Before World War II, the deciding factor that made people "more evolved" was racial. Since the fall of Hitler, the deciding factor in Social Darwinist ideologies has shifted from the racial to the philosophic and religious. "Highly evolved" people are those who accept a pantheistic view of God and humanity. Evolutionary throwbacks are those who cannot or will not accept such a thing.

The same spiritual saltlessness in the Liberal church that shaped Neo-Orthodoxy had also let the social evils fester in Germany that Nazism falsely claimed to cure. Ultra-rightwing, white supremacists claim to have such similar "cures" today. I do not mean that Neo-Orthodox theologians leaned toward Nazism. None that I know of did, and many opposed it in strong terms. What I mean is that the assumptions of Liberalism produced conditions that allowed both to happen. One reason people found Hitler so believable at the time, and came to think that Nazism had real answers for them; was because experience had convinced them that dead churches and Democracy clearly did not.

Even if the alleged Neo-Orthodoxy affected Karl Barth's theology, he reached a place of ethical stamina to stand against the Nazis. His respect for the Bible's morality held, in spite of any alleged belief that the Scriptures were inaccurate in history and nature. Is such a thing possible? Individuals can make decisions contrary to their own underlying assumptions—people do it all the time. Even so, with a fractured worldview foundation, such an individual's moral stamina cannot be so culturally contagious. The remnant of faithful German Christians from both Catholic and Protestant denominations suffered the "trampling under the foot of men."

Churches, as institutions of culture and religion, had lost their power to use moral and intellectual reason credibly to express a biblical worldview. One could not give to people what one no longer had. Reinhold Niebuhr was a theologian more deserving of the title "Father of Neo-Orthodoxy." He rejected the naïve view of human nature's goodness put forth by Liberal Theology's Social Gospel; but equally rejected the inerrancy and plenary inspiration of the Bible. He called himself a *Christian Realist*, but his "realism" did not account for the materialistic faith-assumptions driving the mainstream biblical scholarship of his day. Niebuhr's "realism" had more in common with materialistic Rationalism than with a biblical worldview.

Another tendency that came from Neo-Orthodox-style approaches to Scripture was the open acceptance of Pantheism. Recall that ***Pantheism*** is the idea that everything in the universe added up together equals God; in the form of an impersonal force, that permeates nature. This type of Neo-Orthodoxy denied that the content of the Bible told us anything useful about moral absolutes, history, and God. Those with this view saw Scripture as useful only for creating a Christianese existential emotional experience. Yet, if the content of what Scripture says about God and Christ is unimportant, then how does one reach a place of knowing anything about who and what God is?

By the 1960s, this school of theology simply threw up its hands with Nietzsche, and announced, *"God is dead."* The majority of Americans were shocked to hear the news reports of this coming from church leaders and theologians. I remember my mother's reaction to the news report. Yet, for most people by this time, effectively convinced that reason led only to despair and emptiness, any certain content about God was as extinct as the dinosaurs. This was as true of most shocked news report listeners as it was of the theologians who said, "God is dead."

Francis Schaeffer pointed out brilliantly that, because of this, the Neo-Orthodox believer ultimately has only the word *God* left, with no meaning behind it. When stripped of its historical Judeo-Christian significance, the word *God* can signify any meaning, whether seemingly gentle, or manipulative and malevolent. [11] Biblical statements as moral absolutes also become extinct in this view of faith. It leaves people only with token religious catchphrases with no sure definition, and a god that is nothing more than an impersonal "higher power." Such a god can have no more power and reality than the psychological effect of positive thinking.

There will always be things made somewhat better by positive thinking. That is not power, grace, and love from a Creator and Redeemer God who is objectively real, whether people think positively about Him or not. We need a God at least as real as the world He created. Only that God is worth worshipping.

Schaeffer also foresaw something else; that dishonest spiritual and political forces would redefine religious words from our biblical past into tools for religious and social manipulation, more and more. [12] It becomes much easier, then, for those with any spiritual and political agenda to sway even traditional and orthodox people into just about anything. Evil becomes good, light becomes darkness, and non-God becomes god.

That is where a frighteningly large segment of Christian religion has been for over 65 years.

## BIBLIOGRAPHY


1. Orr, J.Edwin. ***The Role of Prayer in Spiritual Awakening*** (video), Inspirational Media (1977)
2. Bartleman, Frank and intro by Synan, Vinson. ***Azusa Street: The Roots of Modern-day Pentecost***, Logos International (1980)
3. Wallis, Arthur. ***In The Day Of Thy Power***, pp. 75-77, Cityhill Press (1956)
4. Synan, Vinson. ***The Holiness-Pentecostal Movement in the United States***, p. 109, Eerdmans (1971) *Author's note: Synan is a Pentecostal writer.* See also, Cecil M. Roebeck Jr., ***THE PAST: Historical Roots of Racial Unity and Division in American Pentecostalism***, pp. 15-15, Fuller Theological Seminary, (Note: Roebeck is an *Assemblies of God* Pentecostal, who wrote this paper to fairly chronical the sometimes puzzling history of race relations in Pentecostalism. It is well researched and documented, available at *http://www.pctii.org/cyberj/cyberj14/Robeck.pdf*)
5. Cornelius, R.M. and Morris, John D. ***Scopes: Creation on Trial***, p.12, Master Books (1999)
6. Ibid. p. 13
7. Schaeffer, Francis A. ***How Should We Then Live? The Rise and Decline of Western Thought and Culture***, pp.190 & 195 & 197, Fleming H. Revell Co. Old Tappan, NJ. (1976)
8. Ibid. pp. 201-204
9. Nancy Pearcey, ***Total Truth: Liberating Christianity from Its Cultural Captivity***, (2004) Crossway
10. Op. cit. Schaeffer, p. 169
11. Op. cit. Schaeffer, pp. 176-181
12. Op. cit. Schaeffer, p. 178


For a deeper look at the biblical arguments on spiritual gifts and their abuse, I recommend the reader check out Chuck Smith's book, *Charisma vs. Charismania*.

23

# Christianity in the 20th Century: Part 2

## The Ecumenical Movement and Vatican 2: All the Kings Horses and All the Kings Men

There is a cry within many churches today—a lamentation over the sins and divisions of the past—sort of. Emotional fatigue engulfs many believers over the biblical and historical issues that split the visible church—all the bitterness, bickering, even wars; after 2000 years of bloody history's weight, who can blame them? But is the church uniting under one roof really just a matter of forgiving and forgetting? Certainly, relational unity between individual believers is. No doubt, that much needs to happen in spirit.

In an environment where Jesus warned that, "wheat and tares" existed, is it just enmity that prevents diverse Christian churches from coming under a single leadership system? Is that really what unity should be all about in the first place? If so, under whose banner do we organize? Can we realistically just say, "Let's organize under Jesus!" and leave it at that? Yet, how can we expect that the attempt will not create another new, and perhaps more terrible religious monstrosity than those we have already seen? Is it faithless to ask such questions in the face of Jesus' prayer for Christian unity in John 17? Yet, how can we be so naïve as to not ask them in the face of our own history? Is such an asking really a face-off between Jesus and History anyway?

What if there is a beneficial side to a non-hostile, benevolent, Christian diversity?

We are all spiritually and emotionally tired of church disunity. Most everybody is sick of the petty bickering, and hateful demonization of other Christians, heard sometimes inside the walls of church. Nevertheless, tired people are apt to make many careless mistakes, and to misread the signs of the times in disastrous ways. Even alert people often tend only to see what they want to see, and have blind spots they cannot see.

The Ecumenical Movement grew from 19th century cooperation between diverse mission societies, during the Great Revivals. We can trace the development of the World Council of Churches, and the National Council of Churches, from these earlier mission alliances. Liberal Theology and Neo-Orthodoxy infiltrated many of these groups in the early 20th century. This affected how they later understood "missions." It also made them less a means for spreading the historic Christian gospel, and more instruments of a nearly secular social renewal.

The materialistic assumptions of Liberalism prevented its hosts from taking the Bible seriously as an account of real historical events. Now, the same "unequally yoked" leadership model in the mainline denominations spread to the ecumenical councils. As time went on, Modernism absorbed more and more of the decision-making structures in these organizations. The current World Council is completely left wing by any reasoned meaning of the term. Consequently, Christians who took the Bible seriously did not entangle themselves in this movement; or if they did, they found their ministries limited by a system hostile to their biblical convictions. Weariness, and sincere desire for inter-denominational dialogue, makes this a reality many do not want to see.

Please understand, I am not saying that the desire for inter-denominational dialog is bad or that we should not seek after it, only that we must do so with our eyes open. Part of the problem is that the word ***ecumenical***, in today's sense, conjures up two entirely different pictures for people. Many are not even aware that this word now conveys two entirely different ideas. The first view of Ecumenicalism is that of believers from many denominations treating each other with mutual respect and dignity. They pray together for much the same things, and recognize that they all serve the same Lord. This is really a renewal of denominationalism in its positive sense, as opposed to sectarianism.

Bible-oriented believers, including me, can get behind ecumenical visions of this pattern because they do not require us to check our minds at the door; and to submit to ideas and parties we believe anti-biblical in philosophy. We can cultivate relationships with individuals in other camps without accepting all their doctrinal positions or church practices. This view of Ecumenicalism does not require us to compromise biblical issues for fear of further division. Rather than seeing other Christian ministries as tragic fragments of a once united church, this view rejoices in the distinctiveness of each movement. It recognizes that God might have designed each to minister to certain kinds of people that were not reachable any other way.

Of course, there are biblically reasonable limits to how far this view can stretch. Certain foundational distinctives apply to all genuine Christians, which earlier chapters in this book have covered. The Ecumenicalism above demands no administrative merger of church government, just loyalty to basic biblical orthodoxy.

The second view of Ecumenicalism is another creature entirely. It sees the first form only as a tactical step toward merging all Christian religious systems into one political-religious entity. This ambitious strategy assumes that, ultimately, it is not enough to have the first kind of ecumenical teamwork because it has no human way to control it. A system where local churches can freely stand on the Bible against unscriptural ideologies or immorality limits any global religion. Gluing Humpty-Dumpty together from thousands of shards, this second view insists that *"all the King's horses and all the King's men"* commit to merging into some global church government form.

Such a global religious system, by necessity of political mechanics, would need to place its own authority over that of God's word, even if, at first, it did not intend that. Such a system is just too big and top-heavy for a New Testament church. History has already proven that on a smaller scale. That assumes such a system even begins with good intentions. With totalitarian control now well within technological means, a "New Christendom" (or worse, a "New Islamic Caliphate"); where a global government and religious government reflect each other, is more nightmare than dream-come-true. Nor does Secularism offer any hope for sanity. It, too, functions as an unaccountable religious philosophy when given free reign. Just ask anyone not in power inside North Korea.

Some people who are "Ecumenical" in their outlook might believe in various mixtures of these two views; but it is important to understand that there are actually two very different pictures out there, when it comes to this thing called the Ecumenical Movement. The first is beneficial when we approach it with eyes open. The second is the embryo of another religious monster.

This is not to say that all "organizational mergers" are necessarily bad of themselves. Genuinely like-minded spiritual groups benefit from pooling resources. Yet, not all churches are genuinely like-minded. Not all equally share a biblical worldview. The first ecumenical form gives potential for spiritual unity based on love, amid a true Holy Spirit-led diversity. The second demands a unity based on an existential leap, which effectively portrays Scripture as unknowable. It replaces the Bible's authority with yet another system of human political engineering.

The leavening of so many modern churches with a Neo-Orthodox existentialist view of faith makes much of the ecumenical process even more disturbing than that. At a time when walls are coming down, and inter-faith discussion is common, the very words key to the conversation are often being redefined. Political and ideological agendas have infiltrated the process to the point that, amidst all the warm fuzziness; the very meaning of what people say is growing less and less certain. What kind of "unity" will this leave us with in the end?

If two groups in a hypothetical ecumenical union use the word *salvation* in the same context, but privately define it in conflicting ways, how is that real unity? If one group defines it as *biblical justification before God as the free gift of eternal life,* while the other defines it as *a religious term for psychologically healthy self-esteem,* are the two groups really united in spirit? Worse, imagine that both groups exist under a new religious authority that demands they make no waves within the system; and assumes that both groups are spiritually united in the basics, when in fact they are not. This is a recipe for superficiality. Biblical faith must ultimately die to preserve the religious system. Built-in social mechanics makes it inevitable.

Events set the stage to fold this sort of complexity into the dough, in the 1960s, with the results of Vatican II. It seemed that after long last, the Roman Papacy wanted seriously to talk of unity. There seemed to be a realization that those who had left Rome's fold during the Reformation had done so for some good reasons. I do not question the sincerity and human warmth of Pope John XXIII, nor of his spiritual successors, Paul VI, John Paul I, and John Paul II; concerning their desire to see better understanding between most other Christian churches. Yet, in parts of Vatican II, one can see, again, the illogical existential leap of Neo-Orthodoxy in action.

The papal "fortress" had resisted every attack by pure Liberalism. Yet, Neo-Orthodoxy passed almost unseen, right through the front gates, dressed in the clerical garbs of traditional Roman Catholic terminology. The same assumptions that felled the major Protestant denominations, now passed into Rome. It just took the same time as it did a young seminary brother to rise through the priestly ranks, to the College of Cardinals and the Papacy. A Catholic form of Neo-Orthodoxy did not drive every idea at Vatican II; but enough existed in the mix to make the following, admittedly over-brief, analysis fair.

Recall that in a Neo-Orthodox, existentialist worldview, the realm of reason and doctrine led to despair and deadness. Any hope in faith originated in a realm apart from reason. On the hopeless level of reason, the 2nd Vatican Council's written reaffirmation of *all* the canons of the Council of Trent damned Reformation-based teachers to hell. [1] That is what the canons of Trent say and Vatican 2 says it holds to those canons. Also, on the level of reasoned content, is the continued acceptance of Vatican I and Papal Infallibility. [2] The latter position, as far as cause-and-effect rationality goes, burns Rome's theological bridges behind her. The Vatican cannot logically retrace its *doctrinal* steps by admitting where the Papacy went wrong in its side of the divisions.

Yet, despite this intellectual reaffirmation, a leap of non-reason now makes Protestant leaders into "separated brethren;" while upholding the canons that the Council of Trent said would damn them to hell. I have listened to otherwise brilliant Roman Catholic thinkers try to bridge this chasm in the logical law of non-contradiction, and have yet to hear a satisfying answer. It is not that they do not want an answer. It is just that working from a position based on reason, which insists on building completely from the foundation of Trent and Vatican I; it is impossible to conclude that Protestants are "separated brethren."

If the Trent canons are correct (Infallibility virtually demands Roman Catholics believe that they are), then anybody with an assurance of salvation, who rejects purgatory, and who teaches justification in the Reformation sense is damned. The only way to secure "separated brethren" status for Protestants, while building from this foundation; is to do so arbitrarily, as an irrational leap into a realm where the rules of logic no longer apply. Such a realm captures and disables even the sincere. The inevitable result is that words will only mean whatever anyone using them wants them to mean. Objective truth eventually dies in such a place, even among those who most zealously defend it.

I grew up in the Catholic Church of the decade between 1966 and 1976, when sweeping reforms happened. I remember seeing the Mass done in Latin as a child; and then the sudden change, just when I had become an altar boy, of having to learn to do it in English. This was a great improvement for Roman Catholics that indirectly boosted interest in hearing biblical truths even from outside the Roman system. It was not so much the intentions of Vatican II, and the Ecumenical Movement, that posed the real problem; but existentialist shortcuts that left people with a fragmented sense of truth and reality. That included a realistic view of God as a person, who has communicable ideas revealed in Scripture, which are knowable to us through language.

For example, I remember the nuns, and other early Sunday school teachers, teaching that Genesis portrayed Adam and Eve as real people in real history. The reason they gave for why we should believe this was that the Church said so. These church ladies, who handled my early education in the Catholic Faith, represented a non-fragmented approach to truth; seen through traditional Roman Catholic lenses. Then suddenly—so suddenly that I can pinpoint the year, and the grade of school I was in, (6th Grade, 1970)—much of what the church had taught me changed.

Just before my Confirmation, seminary brothers from the diocese took over the Confraternity of Christian Doctrine (CCD) at our parish, in southeast Massachusetts. As a 6th grader, I was inquisitive, and had a special interest in life science that showed in a fascination for dinosaurs and the theory of Evolution. I already read at a college level, which meant I had well developed ideas for my age. They were not often good ideas, but they had a high level of complexity. Consequently, I had a problem with what the church ladies had taught me earlier. I wanted to revisit the issue, since the seminary brothers seemed more approachable than the churchwoman I had questioned the year before.

I did not know it at the time, but the answers I got from the seminary students were standard Neo-Orthodoxy. I remember one of the brothers resembled Art Garfunkel and the other looked like "the Fonz," although "Happy Days" would not debut for several years yet. "Brother the Fonz" assured me that the Genesis account never really happened in the real world. It was just a story somebody had written to show that God made everything. "Brother Garfunkel" nodded his head. God had inspired someone to write Genesis this way, according to Brothers "the Fonz" and "Garfunkel;" because older people, like the ladies that had supervised my earlier church education, cannot "relate to" modern scientific concepts like evolution.

I wondered, however, if I had come to Brothers "the Fonz" and "Garfunkel" with the same question as a "little old lady;" would they have told me "modernist ideas like evolution are tolerated because scientists and students today have no other way to relate?" Even as a 6th grader, I suspected something wrong, not only with the blind authoritarian approach of the ladies, but also with the sidestepping of the seminary students. Thus began my rejection of the Roman Catholic system as a teen-ager, though haircuts and other pre-teen quirks also fell into the mix.

Sad to say this situation did not improved with time. Formerly excommunicated Catholic evolutionary pantheist, Teilhard de Chardin, became one of Pope John Paul II's favorite authors. That Pope's refusal even to speak with scientists from the Institute for Creation Research before issuing his encyclical on Molecule-to-Man Evolution; revealed much. [3] At least on some levels, the Neo-Orthodox split view of reality had found a new and powerful sponsor in the Vatican.

When unhealthy worldview influences drive the formal Ecumenical Movement, is it realistic for people to expect it will create a kind of unity worth having? Certainly, a unity based on *agape* love among individual believers from differing movements should be cultivated; if it does not involve compromising biblical truth. This is the spirit of Jesus' prayer in John 17, as best as we can probably apply it in our current historic situation. When political ambition, fear of the Bible dividing people, or emotional exhaustion from unresolved issues pollutes a desire for unity, something disturbing happens. The Neo-Orthodox idea that intellectual content is unimportant to faith creates a false comfort zone. The only way, ultimately, to sustain this comfort is at the price of abandoning the very things that really are knowable about God from Scripture.

This does not happen all at once, but over time. Nor does it always happen completely. Still, a played down redefinition of words in any dialogue conjures only an illusion of communication. Ironically, the very Existentialism that promised an "experience with God" without taking the Bible seriously; produced a "god" no longer functionally real, in the sense of Him being a knowable person outside of our own heads. When all beliefs become "equally true," then none of them is. If the price of "unity" is downgrading God to the unknowable in any of these ways, then the price is far too high. The specter of the Book of Revelation's future "religious whore of Babylon" haunts such a path. (Rev. 17-18)

## BILLY GRAHAM AND MODERN EVANGELISM: REACHING OVER THE WALLS

Billy Graham, the classic evangelist of the late 20th century, best pictures the positive form of Ecumenicalism. Graham's preaching was the first product of a more-or-less Fundamentalist view to find wide acceptance. His early ministry came in the late 1940s through mid-1960s, when Americans mostly still had a memory of Christian worldview and ethics. Yet, Graham refused to gloss over the sins of 19th and early 20th century America, rather than idealize that era for Evangelicals. He ordered racial segregation barriers taken down during his crusades in the American South. The bulk of his ministry coincided with the Jesus Movement Revival, and its resulting churches, which Graham often worked with from the 1970s on.

Billy Graham presented the sin problem in down-to-earth terms, and yet he did not demonize people in the process. While he never avoided a frank portrayal of the moral problems in our culture, he did not allow any one social issue to sidetrack him from his purpose of winning souls. His reach across the many walls has been long and steady, from those of denominations, to those of the Generation Gap, and even those of the Iron Curtain.

Aside from his flair for diplomacy, television gave Graham a pipeline into the homes of people who would never go out to see a travelling preacher. Even before the proliferation of television, Graham reached many thousands; in old style tent and stadium crusades reminiscent of the revivalists from the 19th century. The tube multiplied his reach to untold millions across the globe. Yet, even though he first make effective use of TV for Christ, it is hard today to think of Graham as a "televangelist," because of what that word has come to mean. Many imitators have tried to equal his success without matching his integrity, and fiscal accountability.

Billy Graham brought aspects of revival again to times not always characterized by what students of church history would call revival. Historic revivals drew swarms of deep conversions, which quickly filled local churches of many denominations. Graham applied one of Finney's best methods by canvassing local churches of all interested persuasions. He then helped those churches train new believer ministries, and pointed converts who came forward at his altar calls to them for discipleship. Usually those churches supplied the new believer counselors used at Graham's altar calls.

By the early 21st century, most neighborhoods in the United States and in many other places had somebody who had first experienced salvation listening to Billy Graham. His ministry demonstrates that the gospel is truly the **"power of God for salvation to those that believe."** (Rom. 1:16) Certainly, Graham set the matrix for the evangelistic model of the late 20th century and beyond. His son, Franklin Graham, continues his father's work through the ministry of Samaritan's Purse, which brings material relief and the gospel to war torn parts of the world. The extended Graham's family also continues in fruitful ministry. Billy at the time of this writing is 97 years old.

Evangelist Greg Laurie's Harvest Crusades also carries on the legacy of Graham. Pastor Greg, and other Harvest and Calvary Chapel pastors and evangelists, often trained at Graham's retreat "the Cove."

## THE CHARISMATIC RENEWAL

The Charismatic Renewal also reached over denominational walls in the second half of the 20th century. Theologians sometimes called this *Neo-Pentecostalism*, but the term *Charismatic* stuck. The older Pentecostal Movement had appealed to disaffected black and poorer white people at the turn of the century. The Charismatic Movement, likewise, ramped up in the 1960s during a generation dissatisfied by the deadness in much of formal Christian religion.

The movement spread from traditional Pentecostal churches into many other denominations in just a few years. It even won many Lutherans, Anglicans, and Roman Catholics. Many who received the "baptism of the Holy Spirit" chose to remain in their old churches. Most of the mainline denominations tolerated them in a way that would have been unthinkable only a decade before.

Theologically, the Charismatic Movement stressed the same ideas and experiences the older Pentecostalism had; but, at first, without much of the fragmentation that followed. Things unfolded this way partly because believers in the new Pentecostal experience were often better educated at the outset than those of the older one. They were not as apt to get embroiled so quickly in artificially induced doctrinal contradictions like the Oneness dispute. Unfortunately, it also had something to do with the fact that, by this time, a Neo-Orthodox view of faith had often badly de-emphasized doctrine. Fewer believers bothered to pay close enough attention to what the Scriptures said, even with eyes that misread its words.

The earlier Pentecostalism had hoped to cross over denominational barriers, but often could not do so. There was a two-fold reason for this, as well. One involved racial and religious prejudice, and the other was that many biblically informed believers still cared about doctrinal content. Those who cared about doctrine would not embrace a movement that often seemed like it could not intelligibly agree on what it believed. The Charismatic Renewal did not have to face this obstacle as much. Of course, this only fed into the false perception that reason and doctrine divided, while experience apart from analysis healed.

Two things contributed to the falling down of the walls. One was a truly biblical desire of people to experience the power of God in their lives at a time when many churches were in decline; and Christianity seemed less and less relevant to the real world. This was a real conviction that dead, authoritarian orthodoxy could not reach a new generation asking relevant questions. The other factor was the Neo-Orthodox de-emphasis of doctrine mentioned above. This had seeped in to many of the denominations that welcomed the Charismatic Movement long before the Charismatics came.

In fairness, the Charismatic Movement did not create this cavalier attitude about doctrine. It was often already there, and entered the movement through people who already had it. The problem in the movement was that it often failed to filter it out. This is the danger when a spiritual movement emphasizes experience over content. It seems to bring people together, but often does so by sidestepping the rationality vital to historic Christian theology. It creates a blind spot that makes the Holy Spirit's correction sound like something it is not—an attack. Couple that with Christians who phrase things as attacks, or who have unrealistic expectations, and we find exactly what we see today.

One cannot deduce reasonably that accepting present-day charismatic gifts by itself causes a loose attitude about biblical doctrine or vice versa.

Dr. John MacArthur recently made a startling claim, unlike his normally logical Bible exposition. He suggested that *any* acceptance of present-day supernatural gifts, even Calvary Chapel-styled Continualism; "enables" the silly and distorted extremes we so often see on much of Christian television. This is a logical fallacy; it is like saying that any teaching of *salvation by grace alone through faith* enables *dead faith without works*. It is not the same topic, but the logic is the same. The biblical teaching of salvation by grace alone does not enable distorted versions of itself in the sense of making them inevitable; any more than the continuation of spiritual gifts enables and makes inevitable distorted teachings about spiritual gifts. By that logic, nobody could ever teach anything from the Bible, in fear that somebody else could then come and present a distorted version of it.

As an explanation for why many Continualist teachers seemed to get strange, it falls flat. It does not explain the facts because it does not ask enough questions of the worldview environment that has characterized post-World War 2 America; and the parts of the globe it so deeply influences. The underlying nature of Late American Worldview assumptions about spiritual power and relationship offers a far better explanation for the phenomenon of distorted teachings on spiritual gifts. Claiming that the origin of Pentecostalism was biblically rocky also falls flat—so was the origin of the Radical Reformation; the modern source for many biblically straightforward teachings shared by anyone who believes in Believer's Baptism as opposed to Infant Baptism.

Filtering out the chaff from the wheat takes time, and sometimes fails.

Though existential thought now shaped much of American culture, it is careless to write off the Charismatic Renewal as mere Existentialism in Christian garb. That would be a form of reductionism; an explanation that reduces the phenomenon to something less than what it really is. Many have tried to do this sort of thing under the pretext of limiting the discussion only to things explicitly written in Scripture. Yet, each attempt has been unfair and overly simplistic. *We are using Scripture to analyze a present-day phenomenon; not playing a game that isolates the conversation only to biblical terminology.* We need to build *from* Scripture *to* what is happening. That means we need to understand the terms of the thought environment that has created the situation. Paul cited Greek poets on Mars Hill, not Jewish scribes. (Acts 17)

The New Testament, read without prejudiced assumptions, allows for the continuance of tongues, prophecy, and healing until Christ resurrects us. Still, we would be negligent to deny that, too often, lack of biblical teaching on properly using the gifts of the Spirit in the church has enabled waves of extremes. *This is not a product of teaching that the gifts continue, but of doing so without emphasizing what the Bible says about how we should use them.* (1 Cor. 14) That lack of emphasis stems from inadequate analysis of the text. People sometimes would "catch the fire" and never settle into a place of obedience and study of God's word. Not everything that went on in the name of the Holy Spirit truly bore the marks of that Spirit.

As in movements of the past, the Charismatic Renewal also produced a mixed bag of results, some powerful and promising, others divisive and truth diluting. Good churches matured out of it, as well as some shaky fringe elements.

## Children of the Jesus Movement: Calvary Chapel, L'Abri, and Kindred Forces Rebuilding Christian Worldview Foundations

Many Christians had seen a renewal of faith that helped them through the terrible years of the Great Depression and World War II. The immediate post-war prosperity however, often saw the minds and hearts of that generation suddenly turned to other things. The "Generation that Saved the World" deserved some earthly respite, but they were not immune to temptation more than any other generation. If that temptation came wrapped in a desire and unique ability to provide for their children and grandchildren, then we should look back on them with both gratitude and mercy.

Culturally speaking, people that came of age in the 1930s, 40s, and 50s existed with Christian values they had inherited from earlier times; yet often without a believable Bible-based intellectual foundation to match. "Intellectual foundations" are not just for intellectuals. Everybody needs confidence that their ethics fit the real world, no matter what they are. Unless the God of the Bible is the God of reality, any further talk of sin and salvation becomes a waste of time and energy.

Intellectual foundations, whether understood in complex terms or simple, are one of the main supports for confidence in any worldview. Knock out a worldview's intellectual base, and its authority base will crumble; then its ethics and confidence in its spiritual and moral values will fall. It is only a matter of time and pressure. The value system, and its benefits, may hold the tottering superstructure together for a time—until a strong wind comes along or the beams rot.

Perhaps one might also think of the generally Christian Western worldview like an automobile. The spiritual, volitional, and intellectual drive is what turns the transmission and axle. Lose the intellectual mechanism, and the spiritual power is either blocked or not processed properly. The willpower engine stalls, but the car rolls on for some ways, depending on whether the grade of the road is steep or shallow, uphill or down; as long as its path demands no great change of direction. As Schaeffer concisely put it, the values of those who matured in the 30s, 40s, and 50s often ran on *"cultural inertia."* [4]

This expressed during the 60s and 70s by a general tendency for parents to be able to tell their children what was morally right; but without a convincing intellectual foundation for holding up those values. They could give pragmatic reasons not to sleep around and do drugs, like the risk of unwanted pregnancy or that brain damage could mess up an education. Yet such reasons never got to the spiritual and intellectual bottom line. Contraceptives were getting more available. Kids knew of brilliant musicians, artists, and college professors who advocated the drug ***counter-culture***. Though a generalization, social historians called this the *Generation Gap.*

By the early 1970s, youthful idealism that had flamed high against Materialism during the 60s, now slumped to mere sex, drugs, and rock n' roll. Young people had dropped out of a tarnished Judeo-Christian worldview "establishment" that seemed to value only affluence and the *status quo*. They had tried to find existential answers in psychedelic drugs, sexual liberation, pantheistic religious experiences, and leftist ideology; but now found that this, too, was a dead end—one that led to hypocrisy far worse than thought to exist in their parent's generation. Most eventually closed their eyes to it.

This left many parents also questioning the relevance of their own values. It was not that one generation was hypocritical and the other was not. Both generations had their share of genuine and superficial people alike. Yet something menacing had long been growing beneath the cultural surface. It now broke through, at a time when all kinds of Christian churches in particular, and Western social institutions in general, were not prepared. The rift between generations, now seemed like a yawning chasm, bigger than the Grand Canyon, larger than it had ever been before or since. There was a reason for this, deeper than normal teen hormones or hard-working parents that felt unappreciated.

Biblically and traditionally orthodox churches often seemed to show the stuffiness and self-righteousness that hippies assigned to them. I remember going to a church with my grandmother, and some of my friends, during this period. An usher stopped one of the girls with us at the door, and told her that she could not enter because she was wearing sandals. We were not hippies by any stretch of the imagination (not yet anyway). In fact, we did not even have the temerity to mention that Jesus had worn sandals. We didn't think of it until later.

On both sides of the country, teen-agers experienced the same kind of thing. Deacons told young men they could not attend services without a "proper haircut and shoes," while girls had to wear dresses or skirts—no denim! Yet the generation of the 1960-70s rarely heard believable reasons why God should care about these meaningless things; let alone, more important questions of faith, worldview, and morality. The ideologies of Rousseau, and his intellectual offspring, had total dominance in the universities. Young people everywhere asked the rhetorical question in the rock opera *Hair*:

*My hair like Jesus wore it*
*Hallellujah! I adore it!*
*Hallellujah! Mary loved her son*
*Why don't my mother love me?*

Whether the perception was fair or not, in the minds of almost an entire generation, churches had sided with form over substance in the battle for love and truth. Some of them still do. Other churches, in desperation, superficially tried to "get hip" with an array of music and worship service gimmicks. These ranged from the relatively sincere to the neurotic and obnoxious. Neither traditionalists nor progressives seemed to catch on that the worldview shift, which had begun among 18th century intellectuals; had finally percolated into the grassroots, and gone to seed. No larger exodus from Christianity, and other traditional Western values, swept one generation in Western history.

The situation in churches was just the tip of the iceberg. Relativist academics changed the name of ethics classes in universities and high schools to "Values Clarification" classes, during the 1970s. *This act of social engineering removed an entire category of thought from the minds of the following generations.* The term *ethics* implies *moral absolutes.* Calling morality *values* implies that morals are a mere matter of *personal preference*. Using the word *values* has that suggestion effect *even on the minds of people who reject moral relativism, who want to restore belief in moral absolutes.* I may value red over blue, but is valuing marital fidelity over adultery simply a matter of opinion, as the word suggests?

One cannot speak of "journalistic ethics" without implying that there is an objective truth out there worth finding; that some methods offer greater likelihood of reaching that truth with integrity than others do. If I spoke of *journalistic values*, the term would be meaningless. There is no point to journalism if all we watch and read is the personal preference of the journalist. Today, the line between hard news and editorial has dissolved.

Control the terminology of the debate, and you leverage its outcome.

History has just proven my point this year in the Supreme Court, and not for our better.

Supplanting *ethics* with *values* is just one way that capable language, used tactically against the Faith, helped tip a morally Judeo-Christian people so quickly. Today, even Christians sometimes feel a twinge of guilt for saying that moral absolutes exist in human sexuality. I am not trying to make people feel stupid by pointing this out—especially those who, like I do, believe in traditional values. *It happened on my watch, too!*

I hope to sensitize us, especially teachers of the word, to how language is a tool. Using it tactically has a powerful effect for good or evil. This is not a mere "wrangling about words." Nor am I scolding those who have used the term *values* as if it meant *morals*—done it, myself. Still, it would do great service to see a rebirth in the use of the word *ethics*, with a high profile explanation of all it implies. The moral realities still exist.

People build values from many things; convenience, sensory pleasures, intellectual stimulation, family history, divinely revealed moral absolutes, greed, and an infinite variety of objects both good and evil. Revealing the difference between *values* and *morals* shines light into a realm of applicable *biblical* ideas almost closed off to the thinking of three generations. Christians who have a nagging feeling that their attempts to stand for biblical truth only "force their values onto others;" do so because they do not see the category difference between *biblical ethics* and *personal values* clearly. Nor does it take many big words to re-open those doors, though we should not dismiss learning new words because they carry ideas. This is worth discussing because of how many spiritual, moral, and social issues lay downstream of it.

Just when it seemed like the churches of the late 1960s and early 70s had lost an entire generation for Christ, the tide began to turn. God broke the hearts of a precious few in pastoral circles with the conviction that the sin laid not so much in the communes as in the pews. Two of those pastors have already been quoted in this book extensively because both have deeply influenced my thinking and spiritual growth. Both have since gone home to be with the Lord. I never had the privilege of meeting Francis A. Schaeffer in person, but his books helped me discover reality out of the swirling intellectual storms of my youth. The other man, who mentored the men who spiritually mentored me, and who I met only briefly on a couple occasions; was Chuck Smith, founding pastor of the Calvary Chapel movement.

Smith, Schaeffer, and others like them, were part of a growing church trend that began to welcome hippies into their congregations to talk *with* them instead of *at* them. History has called this phenomenon the Jesus Movement.

If any move of the Christian faith in the last two centuries seemed, at first, least likely to go anywhere serious, the Jesus Movement was it. At its start, young Bible teachers, barely more than babies in the faith themselves, became excited about the love of Jesus they shared indiscriminately with their friends. The Spirit-led enthusiasm was contagious. Many pastors thought this was just another desperate rash of worship service gimmicks, and reacted to it with harsh polemics. Others showed more wisdom, and took a gracious "wait and see" approach. The most discerning pastors of all recognized the great potential, but also the looming spiritual dangers.

Francis and Edith Schaeffer started a Christian commune in Switzerland, L'Abri Fellowship; concerned that the young multitudes would simply *"drop out and turn on with Jesus"* as just another *"existential leap into non-reason."* Indeed, some seemed to do just that. Some cults that denied the central teachings of Christianity, like Moses David's "Children of God," also began in the Jesus Movement. Instead of pitting the Bible against human reasoning skills, as so many had done over the previous decades; Schaeffer concentrated on a regimen of Bible teaching and Christian philosophy based on that teaching. He designed this to show that the historic Christian faith had the only consistent answers for the worldview questions young people were asking at that time.

Some Christians complained that his work was "too intellectual." Yet it came at the dawn of an era when young Christians were often in greater danger of being anti-intellectual, and giving up on a sensible understanding of Scripture in favor of existential fairy tales; than of having a mere "intellectual faith." These kids were searching. Schaeffer tempered his intellectualism with vast reservoirs of *agape* love.

In Southern California, Chuck Smith dealt with the same kind of problems, but in a way more suited to his unique style of ministry. Coming from a Pentecostal background, Pastor Chuck understood the importance of the experiential side of Christianity. Yet he never allowed that to come at the expense of a balanced and reasonable understanding of Scripture. Exposed to spiritual abuses in Pentecostalism during his childhood, Chuck Smith saw serious need for expositional teaching in the Jesus Movement. One of the great successes of Calvary Chapel is its ability to emphasize the need for an experience with

God, through the Holy Spirit; and in harmony with a logical, defensible, obedient, and systematic understanding of the Bible.

Chuck Smith taught the Scriptures simply, book by book, verse by verse, in this way for over five decades, until the Lord took him home in 2013. Following his model, Calvary Chapels often fostered an environment where believers could practice the gifts of the Spirit; but without the divisive bad doctrines and behavior extremes. Some Continualists have criticized Calvary Chapel for "quenching the Spirit" because they do not often hear people speaking in tongues aloud in Calvary services. Yet, isn't it possible that the Holy Spirit sometimes leads us *not* to speak in tongues; that there is a time and a season for everything under heaven?

I do not mean that those gifts have ceased, just that even the Apostle Paul, who according to 1 Corinthians 14:18 spoke in tongues more than anybody did; would rather have spoken five words plainly in the church service, than ten thousand words in an unknown tongue. I'm not saying that it's against God's will for people to speak in tongues anymore, just that it is possible to lay too much weight on it. Can it be that in the sincerest desire to shed tradition and follow the Spirit, a human tug remains. We form new traditions, which we elevate too high, until we must shed them, too, lest they eclipse God's bigger picture. Of course, being unduly locked into tradition can work in many ways—often in ones we least expect. Traditions are not always bad. We just have the human tendency sometimes to make idols out of them, which then slowly bend us away from God's word.

The Jesus Movement reached what was then the young, post-World War II "Baby-boomers," born between 1946 and 1966. It was perhaps the first move of the Holy Spirit to focus, not on people at a geographic location; but on an age group layer within Western civilization in general. Indeed, it aimed for the very first generation to be existential, and post-Christian in their worldview.

God's Spirit transformed marijuana smoking surfer-dudes and misfits such as Skip Heitzig, Mike MacIntosh, and Greg Laurie into Christian disciples, taught in the Scriptures by Chuck Smith. They have since come to spiritual maturity, to mentor others in the same way. God snatched violent personalities like Vietnam veteran and martial arts expert, Raul Ries, from the very brink of murder and suicide; and transformed them into loving servants of the Prince of Peace. Raul today pastors Calvary Chapel of Golden Springs in Southern California.

As Jesus Movement outgrowths like Calvary Chapel, L'Abri, and Jesus People USA matured, they came to appeal to far more than just the Baby-boomers. They came to attract many in the older generations, as well as "Generation X," and now the "Millennials." As college age kids from the 70s and 80s pressed on into adulthood; a much wider biblical revolution in church culture occurred that, at last, began to flex its muscles into the realm of the arts and sciences again. Though some Christians found the process disturbing, because many traditional molds were broken, the picture shows some promising results. If we remember that the Holy Spirit often brings things together from many elements, which seem out of contact with each other at first, hope is easier to come by.

Contemporary Christian music has its godly talent and gimmicks, but it now comes in all forms, and enters parts of culture long unexposed to biblical ideas of truth and reality. While music is not the same as gospel preaching and expositional teaching, it helps set a mood where people are often more receptive to the latter. It is also a proper reflection of the image of a creative God in man. It is art. Many Evangelicals seem to be shaking off the 200-year-long tie to Utilitarianism that has marked our churches. One can only hope that Christians will see this change for what it is.

Fictional literature seemed aimed in the same direction, until larger secular media groups bought most of the major Christian publishers. These now market most Christian fiction only to the largest demographic—female, age 18 through 45. While women readers are wonderful, the attempt to satisfy only that plurality stunts the art because more than one demographic needs fiction. The Internet and the rise of the Independent author may yet counterbalance this literary trend. Either way, cultural life in American Evangelicalism stirs in ways unthinkable fifty years ago.

The Creation Science Movement and Intelligent Design Theory have challenged the academic world. Highly qualified Scientists have come to doubt that the assumptions of mainstream Ideological Naturalism can explain what we now see in nature. Modern Biblical Creationism grew around rare elder Christian intellects in engineering and the sciences, like Henry Morris, John Whitcomb, Duane Gish, and A.E. Wilder-Smith. It attracted growing numbers of Christian college kids in the 1970s and 80s, who were hungry for the God of Reality. These men and women bravely searched out their own worldview foundations to find again both the word of God, and a compelling motive for discovery. They not only asked the right questions about the assumptions under their own beliefs, but those of their churches, and those beneath the dominant view of science.

Thousands followed callings in the sciences in the 1980s, 90s, and the first decade of the 2000s. Today, however, academic institutions devoted to ideologically naturalistic and postmodernist worldviews try to purge them out. Famed economist and political analyst, Ben Stein's documentary, *Expelled – No Intelligence Allowed* shows a chilling trend in America. "Big Education" uses the techniques of politics—lobbying, the courts, isolation, and defamation of character—not scientific arguments from evidence, to purge Intelligent Design scientists. Universities and the media have shut down the "free market place of ideas."

Government has only followed, reinforced, and exploited that trend. This goes far beyond anything the Tennessee Legislature did in 1925, only the sides have flipped. The fanaticism involved in stifling Information Age inquiry because it does not fit the ideological model developed by 19th and early 20th century educators; is deep indeed.

Creationist and Intelligent Design theorists are a minority in the scientific community. Yet, they are a significant one that not only have held their own; but also have gained much ground against both materialistic and pantheistic forms of Molecule-to-Man Evolutionism at the highest doctoral levels. The evolutionary educational establishment now sees them as a viable threat. Unable to win the debate based on its merits, they now seek to advance "science by consensus," or the idea that the majority paradigm must be the right one. This is the beginning of a slow death for science. History shows many instances where the majority paradigms in both science and religion proved wrong.

Academic freedom is once again at stake. If we do not start thinking tactically as Christians, as if we really are in a spiritual war on a battlefield of ideas; we will not serve God effectively and doom our children to the consequences. Scripture gives us the enemy's unchanging *strategy* and God's armor. Strategy, however, is not the same as *tactics*. Tactics are about how that enemy is forwarding his strategic goals *on this particular battlefield, in this particular time and place in history*. That means we must learn not only to reason *in* the Scripture, but *from* it into the stream of whatever the enemy is throwing at us right now.

This book is too short to do the subject of religious and academic freedom justice, other than as an introduction that directs the reader to further research and action. The hopeful side of this is that it shows at least some forms of late 20th century American Bible-centered Christianity acted as both salt and light. In some ways, this accomplished more than we think. The revival in the 60s and 70s had to expend energy, not only to evangelize, but after conversion, for people to unlearn a post-Christian worldview. It also had to discover that revival must to do this extra work for the first time in the Western world since Christianity originally met our savage forebears.

It is true that independent ministries from the Jesus Movement had crisis points that might not have come to more centralized and traditional bodies. However, in more centralized institutions, the Holy Spirit would not have had the freedom to move as far. During the early 80s, in Calvary Chapel, a parting of the ways came between Chuck Smith and the Vineyard Fellowships once part of the Calvary fold. This arose over a dispute on the main emphasis of the teaching ministry in the church—spiritual experiences or expositional Bible study; a division mirrored in many movements of recent church history. Chuck Smith believed we had no way to understand our spiritual experiences, and relate them to God's person and will, without a main emphasis on expositional Bible teaching. History has, and will continue to prove him right about that.

Spiritual spontaneity has many places in church life, particularly in worship. It could never exist as the foundational standard. Too many unhealthy spiritual influences try to deflect God's people into an unstable orbit around something other than Christ, and the word of God. In addition, God could not have effective lordship over the intellectual side of man if people habitually sidestepped the intellectual in the name of spirituality. Christian teachers, at least, need to be equipped at some stage to deal deeply with the intellectual issues. The war is spiritual, but much of the battlefield is intellectual. The spiritual and intellectual cannot march in opposite directions.

The fellowships and ministries that arose out of the Jesus Movement have seen phenomenal growth in the past 45 years, not only in terms of numbers, but in spiritual depth as well. Counter-culture origins may have prepared them to exist as a Christian counter-culture in a Post-Christian mainstream. Calvary Chapel alone grew from one small church in 1968 to over a thousand fellowships worldwide, with more added every year. Many of these churches draw memberships that number in the thousands. That is actually comparable to the expansion of the 1st century church!

This is not automatically a signature of success, however. Rather than end on such a proud note, it behooves those of us who understand the dynamics of church history to pray diligently and in the holy fear of God. While God's desire is for us, the trend of human choice in church history is against us. We must pray that such movements remain humble, with hearts sensitive to the Spirit, and minds building from the Word, through the church, and into the world.

The disciples made during the Jesus Movement now hand their torches down to a new generation, in a new millennium, in an increasingly hostile Post-Christian age.

## BIBLIOGRAPHY

1. See ***Council of Trent***, Canons 11, 12, 15, 24, 25 & 30 cited in Ch. 16 of this book.
2. Flannery, Austin O.P., gen. ed., ***Vatican Council II: The Conciliar and Post Conciliar Documents*** (revised edition) vol. 1, p. 412; Costello Publishing (1988)
3. Morris, Henry M. ***Evolution and the Pope***, in ***Vital Articles on Science/creation, Acts and Facts*** Dec. 1996, found at the ICR web site **http://www.icr.org/**
4. Schaeffer, Francis A. ***How Should We Then Live? The Rise and Decline of Western Thought and Culture***, pp. 216-217 & 205-206, Fleming H. Revell Co. Old Tappan, NJ. (1976)

# 24

# A Christian Worldview for the 3rd Millennium

## The Prophetic Outlook for Christianity: "Great Falling Away" versus "Latter Rain"

Where are we as Christians going today?

The approach of many detailed prophecies, from Daniel 9-12 to Ezekiel 38 and 39, and Jesus' Olivet Discourse in Matthew 24, suggest we live near the end of the age. Israel is again a nation within its historic homeland, as predicted. The alignment of the Gentile nations fits the end-time pattern revealed by the Prophet Ezekiel; if one understands which modern peoples stem from the tribes named in his vision 2600 years ago. (Ez. 38 & 39) Advances in computers and the trend toward globalization make the worldwide economic tyranny foreshadowed in the Book of Revelation seem close to home, indeed. (Rev. 13:11-18)

What does that mean for Christians who may live to see the Rapture of the Church or, at least, a light at the end of the historic tunnel?

Two major pictures of the church in the last days emerge, as one surveys different conclusions from thoughtful students of Bible prophecy. In one picture the church receives an abundant "latter rain" of the Holy Spirit during the times leading up to Christ's Second Coming. This "final revival" unites and empowers believers with supernatural signs, and wonders that at least approach in some ways those of the Apostolic Era. [1] The second picture, on the other hand, describes a slow weakening of the church, where "deceivers wax worse and worse, deceiving and being deceived." Christ returns for a tiny remnant, wondering if he will even "find faith alive upon the earth." [2] Both pictures come from prophetic Scripture. Both have applications to the Church Age.

I have observed often that those who follow a more-or-less Fundamentalist Cessationist orientation tend to hold the "Great Falling Away" view. Those with a Continualist persuasion usually seem to gravitate toward the "Latter Rain" scenario. In talking to believers in both these camps about the future, I often find that each holds their view as if it were mutually exclusive to the other. Every new "wind of doctrine" and experience to come down the pike is a sure sign of "latter rain" to one party. The other rejects anything that might resemble revival because they are certain only a weak remnant of the church can be faithful in the end. However, since both pictures appear in prophecies that apply to the Church Age, *are both positions truly mutually exclusive?*

I have found a close study of the Book of Revelation's prophetic seven letters to the churches, in Chapters 2-3, extremely helpful for understanding the church in the last days. Several overlapping models exist for interpreting the seven letters. The one most helpful, in this instance, is to view them as a thumbnail sketch of the kinds of church systems that will exist at the time of Christ's return. This does not make the other views wrong. That is the neat thing about Bible prophecy—it has layers of pattern and multiple dimensions of meaning, though they cannot mean just anything.

Jesus, who dictated the seven letters to John, rebuked five of the churches for serious spiritual and moral problems. The Lord also commended three of these chastised churches in varying degrees for the things they did right. Two, however, Sardis and Laodicea, received no commendation as churches at all, although he mentioned that Sardis had a few individuals who had not stained their white robes. Two of the seven churches, the persecuted Church of Smyrna, and the fellowship of brotherly love that held to the word,

Philadelphia, Christ did not rebuke at all, but commended. In the last four letters, to Thyatira, Sardis, Philadelphia, and Laodicea, Jesus made direct references to his Second Coming, and to how those churches will fare at that time. Thus, at least these four kinds of church (and probably the other three also) will exist together when the Lord returns.

It can be an exercise in over-generalization to match these prophetic church descriptions up to exact denominations and movements. Yet, the pattern describes a situation where different models for real churches exist in the last days. Possibly all kinds of church can exist in any given system, but sometimes, only one of these prophetic models dominates the movement. One of the church models—Philadelphia—fits the "Latter Rain" description, but not as a super-church led by super-apostles. This church is said to have only **"a little strength,"** but it is given **"an open door that no man can close"** to spread the gospel. Sounds like powerful revival in the last days to me, though not one that reaches the entire church or demands the re-establishment of apostles.

Just how much of the universal church a Philadelphian revival influences may be up to us, in some ways. At the very least, it would seem that the periodic revivals since the Reformation Era conform to this pattern; with possibly more to come, until Christ returns. This makes it a terrible mistake for today's believers to write off the possibility of large revivals, no matter how bad society and the church gets. A pattern has been "situation normal" throughout church history. New moves of the Holy Spirit periodically come. These approach Bible truth with new applications, and sometimes discard old ones that no longer function. "Latter rain" is a real possibility, and not to be discounted.

The rest of the churches described by the seven letters (except for persecuted Smyrna) conform to the "Great Falling Away" model. Post-Christian philosophies and lifestyles dilute churches increasingly of their truth, faith, and effectiveness. Christ returns in the end only for a tiny remnant. This model does not only apply to the "dead orthodoxy" stereotype of the dry stuffy "relic church" where "nothing is manifesting." Sardis had a reputation for being alive, but Christ called that church dead.

One does not get a reputation for life unless something that mimics life happens regularly. Postmodern views of faith and reality psyche people up with vivid, emotional, non-reason experiences of many forms. Other churches will give in to philosophies of the age that perhaps we have not seen yet. It is dangerous to follow every new doctrine and feel-good experience as if it were Montanus' "new wind of the Spirit."

While **"God's ways are not our ways"** and **"God's thoughts are higher than our thoughts,"** He still speaks to us with words in Scripture containing understandable ideas, which can apply in whatever current situation we find ourselves. God's Spirit is not always going to move in ways that "bypass our intellect." Even when He does, there will still be a reason for it eventually relatable to Scripture. I'm not saying those reasons will always be apparent at first, merely that we should look for them, as we rationally check what is happening by the word. Nor am I saying the intellectual should rule over the spiritual. We must yield all our human faculties to the Holy Spirit.

Scripture and history repeatedly show that a **"zeal for God"** that is **"not according to knowledge"** does more damage than good. In a world where the border in people's minds between fantasy and reality is getting thin and eroded, we need to have a Christianity that fits reality at the bottom line. I do not mean a "reality" that conforms to materialistic faith-assumptions, or to pantheistic, modernist, or postmodernist ones. I do not mean a reality culture-crafted by the world, just one that fits what careful observers really can see. Christians must be able to **"contend earnestly for the faith which was once for all delivered to the saints;"** even in a postmodernist culture that no longer cares if a belief system stands up to reason. (Jude 1:3b NKJV)

God cares and if He has His way in our hearts regarding the truth, so will we.

This is not because people need to have everything figured out before they can believe. Nobody starts into any belief system from such a place, no matter how skeptical they think they are. Rather, God expressed His revelation in Scripture in propositional statements that are either true or false in the real world. Reason is a fundamental necessity for any belief system that assumes objective truth exists; and that ideas and behaviors have cause and effect relationships. Christianity demands both Divine and human reason. It cannot exist in a Bible-centered form without it. This, of course, assumes that our reasoning begins from biblically faithful starting assumptions—like Hebrews 11:6.

> **And without faith it is impossible to please him; for any one who comes to God *must believe that he exists* and that *he rewards those who search for him.***
>
> ***Hebrews* 11:6 (NEB)**

Because of the historic patterns observed; both the genuine move of God's Spirit and existential delusions will likely occur at the same time, and in close proximity to each other—sometimes even within the same visible movements. There is also the overtly demonic element. We are in a real spiritual war where infiltration and misinformation is an enemy tactic always seeking new, deceptively "safe" looking fronts. That is why we need church cultures open to the Spirit, yet discerning in love, according to the standards of Scripture. We will imperfectly execute our efforts to discern spiritual experiences biblically. Yet, we cannot give up on either discerning or having an experience with God's Spirit, without producing a lopsided view of the Christian life and message.

Consequently, many of the trends in today's churches have the potential of going either way toward "latter rain" or "great apostasy," depending on how we handle them.

## Mega-Churches: Philadelphia or Laodicea?

Historians call a major trend in American Christianity, today, the *mega-church.* This is the tendency for fellowships in densely populated areas to grow rapidly to large size, often in less than ten years. These fellowships become umbrella organizations for meeting a range of regional needs through a network of smaller ministries, each knit together by a large local church. Many have their own K-12 school, rescue mission, library, café, and bookstore; some even have bowling alleys, right there at the church building, which is really more of a church complex. This has many practical advantages, and a few potential liabilities.

The mega-church trend was an outgrowth of the biblical Christian worldview becoming, at best, a ***counter-culture*** instead of the mainstream in Western civilization. American and European society slides farther away from a biblical view of life and reality. Powerful political and academic elites seek to engineer this slide, or at least exploit it. Public schools, for example, often turn into detrimental experiments, with our children as guinea pigs.

We face a perfect storm. Hedonistic entertainment media is inescapable—even when we "turn it off," our children have regular influential contact with those who do not. Ideological Naturalism and Postmodernism control public education with the force of a hyper-secularist state cult. This leaves our children gripped by technologically magnified levels of suggestion unique in human history. We live daily in a situation far worse than the most hideous nightmares of Pilgrim separatist, John Robinson.

Compare Robinson's concern over formalistic state churches degrading the morals of the Pilgrim children, to our situation. We face an education system and media barrage that indoctrinates children into self-destructive, anti-Christian ideologies, some of which promote sexual perversion as healthy—even against common sense and science. Today, no "New World" exists to which Christians may flee. Alert Christians began to create alternative institutions. It is only convenient if those alternatives are centrally located.

The mega-church trend, in itself, need not result in a wholesale loss of intimacy in small groups. The very basis for success is when the parent church emphasizes small home fellowships throughout the week or "cell groups" as some call them. This reflects in some ways the large early churches at Jerusalem and Antioch, in the Book of Acts, only on a more sophisticated, economically prosperous scale. One thinks of such fellowships as the enormous Calvary Chapel of Costa Mesa or Willow Creek Community Church, near Chicago. Though not free of blind spots (nothing is), mega-churches have potential to offer firm platforms for a Christian worldview to build active counter-cultures not easy to marginalize.

Mega-churches often have varied services, each designed to reach out to Traditional, Contemporary, and Postmodern tastes. By *Postmodern* here, I do not necessarily mean Postmodern*ism*, which denies absolute truth. Rather, "Postmodern" is a form of teaching designed to reach people raised in a completely Postmodern culture—usually those who reached adulthood in the late 1990s and since. Pastors with Postmodern teaching styles give sermons designed to stir people into asking the right questions of Scripture, instead of trying to answer everything from the pulpit. Done well, this approach trains people to reason from the Scripture. Done poorly, and it falls into a Christianized Postmodernism characterized by loss of certainty, and no sense of urgency.

Each approach has its strengths and weaknesses. Worship leaders designed the "Contemporary" style of worship to appeal to "Baby-Boomers" who came of age in the 1960s, 70s, and early 80s. "Traditional" services worship with the old hymns and traditional sermons. Nevertheless, no spiritual trend is without dangers. Taking this method to extremes encourages a "smorgasbord" approach to worship and teaching. This can be disastrous in an American worldview focused on "what works" more than on "what is true." The speed of living today often reduces human relationships to what I call "relationship-lites." Relationship-lites seem to have the "flavor and texture" of interpersonal relationships; but without requiring the time and attention actual human relationships need. Larger numbers force faster paced ministry.

The mega-church clearly has an emphasis on ministering to as many different kinds of people as possible in one community. These all have a wide variety of different needs as well as personal tastes. This is a well-intended emphasis. Yet, it is possible to adjust ones ministry approach to the prevailing pattern of the culture too much. We live in a fast food, fast-paced world where people feel they must pack their schedule far past any reasonable limit. Marriage and family relationships among Christians disintegrate at almost the same rates found in secular society. People are not taking the time to know and love one another at an adequate depth of commitment. The outcome is that natural affection, and its enjoyment, withers unnourished.

In the face of all this, should churches tailor their teaching methods down to a level of mere 15-minute sound bites? Can we pass on something as rich and as deep as God's word effectively that way? What happens when even Bible translation accommodates this situation; rendering translations intended for adults that read at a 6th grade level in the name of making the Scriptures more accessible? Why are we finding Christians less, rather than more, interested in Bible study, on average, than a generation ago? Could it be that most of us are no longer in the 6th grade? Yet, could it also be that literacy skills collapse because of a shift in how our society processes information? On top of all the worldview shifts previously covered, do we now face an intellectual collapse driven by icon-based thinking from video and the personal computer? Is "magical thinking" back?

It seems that Christians have faced this situation before, on a less sophisticated scale, but severe historical illiteracy keeps us in the dark. Is it really "condescending" to point this out after three generations of deliberate dumbing-down in our education system?

The computer term *user-friendly* has come to be associated with the mega-church by experts on current social trends, who modified it to ***seeker-friendly***. Originally, this described the way mega-churches attracted people; using a winsome and approachable method of presenting the gospel, and teaching the Bible. As a concept, it grew from the Jesus Movement method of talking *with* rather than *at* young people. (Most mega-churches grew out of ministries to the young during the 70s and 80s). Unfortunately, the term *seeker-friendly*, like *Fundamentalist*, has taken on some negative connotations as time went on. Equally unfortunate is that this term actually deserves the stigma.

Many ministries that desire growth have tried, with varying degrees of success, to imitate what they perceive to be the "Calvary Chapel" or "Willow Creek" method of contemporary music and winsome teaching style. Charles Finney's archetypal over-focus on method has resonated with American worldview self-sufficiency. "If we only use the right methods of evangelism and church growth, then we will flourish." "Build it, and they will come." It often seems burned into our psyche with a hot iron. Social engineering is "in."

When the focus falls off of the work of God, and our being yielded to Him in the ministry; there comes a tendency to artificially culture-craft our teaching and worship styles to whatever currently makes people feel either comfortable or motivated.

We want people to be comfortable enough in our churches that they can learn and grow, but it is possible to make them too comfortable. There is such a thing as making people so comfortable that they will **"not endure sound teaching"** when it deeply convicts their hearts of sin or challenges their minds to a deeper grasp of biblical truth. We want Christians motivated by godly things. Yet, it is also possible to motivate by manipulation, and leave a 21st century "Burned-Over District" in people's hearts. The technology to do this is both all around us as a humming background noise; and terrifying, once we understand it, to the point of deer-in-headlights immobilization. The American Dream can easily be a nightmare.

I am not saying that this is where mega-churches need end up because of their built-in mechanics. Nor is it reasonable to conclude that all mega-churches necessarily move in the same cultural and spiritual direction. I confess it disturbs me to see so many churches with a pastor-teacher no one can interact with piping video sermons, each Sunday, to multiple congregations from another city. I am not trying to pass judgment on every fellowship that does this. Nor am I saying that there might not be good reasons for it, sometimes. It disturbs me because "relationship reductionism" already so deeply undermines American churches. It is the side effect of a machinegun-paced, multitasked, Information Age society. Given our culture, and human nature being what it is, this is a clear and present danger.

Another hazardous potential comes by the normal spiritual dangers in any affluent society. Mega-churches in Western culture are, by definition, affluent organizations. They own conference centers that used to be resort hotels, sponsor yearly trips to the Holy Lands, and pour vast sums of money into publishing, TV, and other influential media. None of these things is bad. Mega-churches can supply the financial and training needs of huge indigenous missions overseas, and influence even the mainstream culture by media. Yet, the gravity toward self-sufficiency instead of reliance on God looms. I also find it disturbing when I hear church staff and ministers use the jargon of secular corporations. Corporations are not evil, but neither are they church ministries. Words carry unintended ideas.

This is the dividing line between the churches of Philadelphia and Laodicea. The mega-church has the potential to reflect either prophetic model, depending on where its reliance ultimately rests. It can be a powerful instrument of God's love to people in need, who live in hostile cultures worldwide. It can feed the poor, and care for the sick, while it teaches the word of God to them. It can be a place where relationships that have suffered every kind of hurt are healed; abused wives, young husbands who never had a father figure, and men or women who struggle with homosexuality yet do not know how to deal with that biblically.

Nevertheless, God does not *need* the mega-church to do this today. He often works more deeply in people through smaller fellowships, driven at a less frenetic pace.

The mega-church also has the potential to become a padded resort for "bless-me club saints." It can be a fountain of psychobabble in thinly veiled Christianese, where Wal-Mart sized nurseries of spiritual babies cry for American Dreams of health and prosperity. It can be a self-affirmation fortress for those who do not want to deal with reality, and the needs of an outside world lost and headed for hell. It can also be an intellectually and spiritually glutted society of amateur Bible professors, who hear the word so well that they can write entire books on the subject; but who would not cross the street to help a homeless person or a victim of assault or rape. It can be the self-sufficient Laodicean church, which thinks it **"has need of nothing and does not know that it is wretched, poor, miserable, blind, and naked."** (Rev. 3:17)

By God's grace, our generation still has a chance to decide whether church history remembers the mega-church as a providential blessing or a mutated nightmare.

## THE EMERGENT CHURCH: POSTMODERNISM SHAPED LIKE 21ST CENTURY CHRISTIANITY—MORE... OR LESS...

I had not yet encountered the Emergent Church when I wrote the first edition of this book. A pattern had become evident, however. I watched for a major movement to express Postmodernism under some form of Christian identity. Liberalism had voiced the Enlightenment's Rationalism and Romanticism in 19th century Christianese, and Neo-Orthodoxy had expressed 20th century Existentialism; the next logical step, Postmodernism, must also find its host for the 21st.

By now, the "Idea Pendulum" seemed to swing at strobe-light speed. In reaction to the prior generation's Jesus Movement, which swelled non-denominational mega-churches with those seeking return to biblical orthodoxy; a new generation looked for "orthopraxy" or *right practice*. Yet it often seemed as if this new movement assumed that orthodoxy and orthopraxy opposed each other. Enough time had not elapsed to produce large-scale "dead orthodoxy" in churches that grew from the Jesus Movement. Rapid growth had made a machine-like form of ministry not only possible, but also seemingly necessary. Not that anyone wanted it, nor even that it habitually happened, just that it happened enough that people reacted.

In addition, some mega-churches had not deepened their teaching of the word. Some, in fact, had made mystical experiences or an almost therapy session model paramount. Unrealistic expectations of what it meant to have a "personal relationship with God" took hold from the worldview of Late American society. We might well call a Late American Worldview a *Late Western* one, given the influence the United States has in shaping ideas. Patterns of civilization decay sometimes make me feel like a spiritual forensic pathologist.

The Emergent Church is somewhat different from the previous Liberalism and Neo-Orthodoxy; it appears to move in a more grassroots upward direction. It also tends to avoid the use of Christianese jargon, which is somewhat refreshing. This does not necessarily commend it. Grassroots forces are no less corruptible than hierarchical ones in a cultural backdrop that rejects the reality of objective truth. It is also possible that, by now, "Christianese" is more useful for creating a "***straw man***" version of the "modern church" than it is as a vehicle for penetrating real ones. Some Emergent Church criticism of Evangelicalism, Fundamentalism, and Modernism has a sound base. What we should be asking, however, is, *what is the "Emergent" cure for these problems, both perceived and real?*

The Emergent Church arose in the late 1980s and 1990s, and reached "household word" status as a movement in the early 2000s. I first heard of it shortly after the 1st edition of this book came out, late in 2002. Its leaders seemed to have roots in the tail ends of the Jesus Movement, but to have reacted against the trend toward mega-church. Ian Mobsby, an Emergent leader in Britain, suggested that the movement is a synthesis of mystical and sacramental Christianity that reaffirms "Trinitarian Ecclesiology" against the kind of judgmental certainty, and Fundamentalism that grew after the Enlightenment. [3] Emergent "elder statesman," Brian McLaren, summed this approach up in the term, "generous orthodoxy."

I noticed this reaction habitually tried to deconstruct Reformation biblical thought and confuse it with Enlightenment rationalism. If any single word describes a major distinctive of the Emergent Church, *protest* is it. The target of its protest seems to be what leaders in the movement call "Modernism." I use the word in quotes because not all the objectionable distinctives they identify with their version of "Modernism" are unique to Modernism. Some are equally true of historic Christianity. I speak particularly of how Emergents disown the ideas of reasonable certainty, objective truth, and that analysis has value as a tool for discovering these things. Both the Judeo-Christian worldview and the modernist one predict objective truth and the possibility of reasonable certainty, if for different reasons.

The Judeo-Christian worldview assumes that Scripture gives us propositional truth. This is a concept that all Christians have shared for most of our 2000-year history. Modernism assumes that only human reason can arrive at materialistic axioms—self-evident truths which require no faith—although that has not proven so. Emergent leaders belittle not only Modernism; but also the use of analytical apologetics to answer modernist objections, as if using analytical methods made Christians hypocritically modernist. The objections all seemed to assume that what made Modernism truly *Modernism* was its attempt to use analytical methods to discover truth. This fallacy ignores the foundational assumptions of both Modernism and historic Christianity, as if they were unreal.

Once again, we face another version of the artificially devised fracture between "faith" and reason. Non-reason mystical experiences trump a biblically reasoned faith here; even one with rich experiences in the Holy Spirit. At the beginning of this book, I said, *"Whenever the world thought Christianity obsolete as a spiritual and intellectual force, Christians rose from the ashes. They reshaped both themselves, and their societies, by radical new applications of ancient and timeless Bible truths. They made comebacks by embracing in new ways the same scriptural principles that seemed so hopelessly outmoded to their critics. At such times, they did what appeared to be the very opposite of what conventional wisdom dictated, and history proved them right."*

Postmodernism gives the faith a few new tools, like a sharper ability to deconstruct worldview assumptions, and notice their presence in a belief system. Yet, Postmodernism, also, is a worldview that needs to be deconstructed and analyzed comparatively, according to Scripture; before we determine what redemptive elements it may possess. As any worldview before it, Postmodernism has parts that are redeemable, and others fit for nothing but rejection. In the Emergent Church, the level of influence that ideological Postmodernism has varies between fellowships. This book is not a complete analysis.

I can say this much; Postmodernism is as unfit to serve as the guide for understanding Scripture as Modernism was. We need to show sensitivity to generations raised without any biblical background or model. Yet, there is nothing "generous" or "orthodox" about taking people's equipment to understand God's word away from them. Analytical reasoning is an important part of that tool kit, nurtured in a Judeo-Christian worldview unafraid of truth. If people reject Christian faith because they do not like the clearly defined categories it sets, then they do so knowingly, at their own peril, and in the face of honest presentation. Refusing to indulge "superficial labels" is not the same as avoiding clear definitions. The first may be the opening part of a legitimate conversation. The second is just dishonest.

When I see mysticism pitted against analysis, circular authority structures squared off against hierarchical ones, and an aversion to categories that makes finding out where people stand like nailing Jell-O to the wall; I am rightfully suspicious. Scripture contains both narrated spiritual experiences, and epistles designed for analysis of truth. It contains both circular and hierarchical forms of submission to authority. (For example, compare Eph. 5:18-20 with 5: 22-24.) The Bible does not avoid calling something true or false.

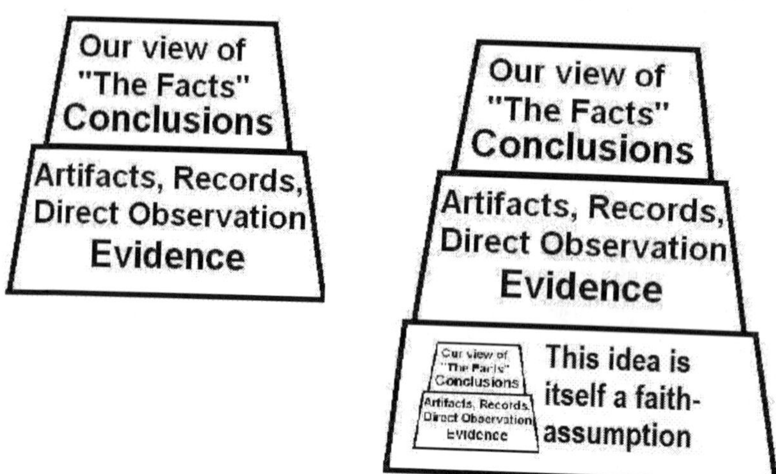


*The idea that "there are no foundational assumptions," whether in the Modernist sense that "superior axioms" erase their need or in the Postmodernist assumption that "none are possible," only creates another faith-assumption network that sits as a foundation for a view of reality*

A major school of Postmodernism that sways the Emergent Church, is ***Minimalism***; a form of radical text criticism that somehow broke out of its stall to become a fad in everything from architecture to art. Minimalists *over*simplify. They do this to text criticism past all common sense, using the tools of reason to violate reason. Perversely, in the name of finding objective proof, they use methods that assume objectivity is a fallacy. On the one hand, Minimalism insists that archaeological artifacts, not ancient texts, are the only objective window on history. After all, ancient texts each have a human point of view, and points of view distort objectivity—they say. On the other hand, they deny the reality and know-ability of objective truth. Which is it, guys?

Since perfect objectivity is humanly impossible because we all bring at least some assumptions to the text, Minimalists say nothing survives from the original author's mind. We bring it all to the text. Finding the truth about what happened in the past thus becomes unthinkable. History effectively dies. So does law.

The absurdity of Minimalism becomes immediately apparent if we simply replace the value of *objectivity* with some other human value—say, *selflessness*. Just because absolute perfect selflessness is humanly impossible does not mean substantial selflessness is not attainable or desirable.

Minimalism denies the reality of any biblically recorded event to which no extra-biblical source attests, despite the fact that most of ancient history is knowable only from single source accounts.

Postmodernism is also the easiest worldview to deconstruct at its foundation. Just ask Obi-Wan if he is still so sure that only Siths deal in absolutes.

## Indigenous Churches in the 3rd World: The Philadelphia to Smyrna Pipeline

The *3rd World* might be defined as those parts of the globe that are not the center of attention in a study of Western history concerned mostly with the "Old World" of Europe and the "New World" of America; but not so much the "3rd World" of everywhere else. This sounds arrogant, and it is, but that is how the division seems to fall. Actually, the term had more to do with convenience than arrogance. It began during the Cold War, as a political designation for countries not aligned with either NATO or the Warsaw Pact. It just happened that most of those were developing countries. Who knew?

One good work that became possible through the affluence of American churches was the financial sponsoring of native missionaries in 3rd World countries on a massive scale. I call this the *Philadelphia to Smyrna Pipeline* because many 3rd World brothers and sisters undergo intense persecution for their faith in places like India, China, Sudan, and Central Africa. Mega-churches in the West have been able to help carry heavy financial loads for indigenous gospel workers; though admittedly, we could do much more if we in the West consistently unstopped our "Laodicean clogs" in the pipeline.

By the mid-20th century, churches in the 3rd World often suffered from missionary movements that had effectively replaced the gospel with endless, ineffective relief efforts. Corrupt post-Colonial governments in their own countries also viewed Christian churches as a remnant of hated colonialism. Warlords often took much of the relief, leaving their peoples in just as much need.

Renewal in the late 20th century of a form of Christianity that took the Bible seriously again brought with it a new model. Indigenous pastors, like K.P. Yohannan, pioneered new models for missions in places like India and Africa. Yohannan came to the United States more than three decades ago, filled with idealistic visions of a country where authorities and thugs did not beat people up for their faith. With plentiful Bibles and other resources, Yohannan figured industrious Americans would eagerly help him raise support for in-country missionaries in India. The cheerful K.P. was somewhat disturbed by the sense of unreality he saw in the churches of our country, and who could blame him?

We, in the Western church, have little concept of where this planet really is spiritually. Our confused awareness of how our brothers and sisters actually live in the 3rd World, versus the imperial splendor that even our lower middle class enjoys, runs a close second. I largely have K.P. Yohannan to thank for this epiphany. His book, *Road to Reality,* put historical flesh on the danger in an affluent society of having an existential "personal faith experience" that does not touch the real world outside. He founded an organization called *Gospel for Asia* (www.gfa.org) as a conduit for concerned individual Christians in wealthy America to support individual missionaries in the 3rd World.

Visions like Gospel for Asia, and the *World Christian Movement,* are part of a major paradigm shift that sees the gospel as ***trans-cultural***, that is; best spread to a given people by those who are actually a part of that culture. Instead of trying to "westernize" non-western peoples, indigenous mission workers find ways to make the content of Scripture make sense to the cultures in which they already exist. They live at the same economic level as the people, rather than by Western standards.

Indigenous missionary evangelists also have the help of new Bible translations, sometimes in languages that never before had an alphabet. Ministries like Wycliffe Bible Translators produce these. Wycliffe's work requires learning the language, worldview, and culture of any given people for whom they translate the Bible. This makes it also a pioneer of this model. Franklin Graham, son of Billy Graham, leads Samaritan's Purse, which provides material relief, but does not do so at the expense of the gospel.

Even with this hopeful new trend in spreading the gospel to unreached peoples, the world's population has multiplied exponentially in the last century; much faster than the ability to evangelize can pace. Proportionally speaking, a smaller percentage of the global population have heard the gospel of Jesus today than was so a century ago. Cultures once saturated with the love and knowledge of God have now largely forsaken Him.

The day may come when missionaries from spiritually living churches in East Asia will come to a totalitarian United States. If so, will they be able to win an intellectually and morally bankrupt Neo-Pagan nation back to Christ?

## THE AMERICAN CHRISTIAN RESPONSE POST-9-11

Recent history shows just how totally dystopia has set in for American culture. In the decade and a half since ***Islamist*** terrorists turned two jetliners into oversized cruise missiles that toppled the World Trade Center towers, and part of the Pentagon, on 11-September of 2001; the American worldview has proven just how much it has already shifted—perhaps irreversibly.

I can remember commenting to my mother; "At least the Japanese had the decency to restrict themselves to military targets at Pearl Harbor." Our illusion of security died, and our blind faith that all worldviews are equally sound should have collapsed. The sight of Palestinians and other Islamic peoples cheering and dancing in the streets on TV should have done that much, but it did not. [4]

Fifteen years of media hype that terrorists "co-opted a peaceful religion," and are not "true Muslims," does not change the fact that their actions came from reasoning that makes sense in an Islamic worldview. Yet, we still behave as if that is irrelevant, even after continued terrorist attacks of smaller scale but unrelenting purpose. Muslim terrorism, and most American reactions to it; equally shows the power of suggestion used to condition people in totalitarian ways. Palestinian TV media uses repetition of ideas, as American media does. The only difference is the suggestive content, and the level of sophistication in method.

This is not a statement of race, but of the effect of ideas. I speak of cause-and-effect reasoning from what the Qur'an objectively says; and of how repetition of the ideas contained in multiculturalist Postmodernism—that all cultural ideas are equal—affect current American thought. There are decent sane Muslims, abominably mad Christians, and the reverse—that is not the point, and never was. Bad ideas have bad consequences, whether we talk of their effect on young white males in Germany of 1935, urban black males in America of 2015, or young Arab people who volunteer for suicide bombings. Other people within all these groups have spoken out against the bad ideas, so that eliminates the idea that the issue is racial.

To their credit, many Muslims do not apply their sacred writings in the way that terrorists do. This is not the same as saying that all worldviews equally foster values of intellectual and religious liberty, and adequately deal with the human condition. This is why America's attempts to transplant American style democracy to the 3rd world have been such an unmitigated failure. Islamic and Eastern worldview assumptions do not lead to conclusions of liberty and equality if we simply graft democracy onto them. It used to comfort us to believe that Islamist terrorism was the act of violent people co-opting a peaceful religion. It comforts many, now, to view religion itself as the problem. Both views are childish evasions of the fact that fanaticism and violence are not a uniquely religious, but a universally human problem.

These comfortably pluralistic, yet bigoted, illusions ignore both history and the way worldviews work in the real world. Sadly, we saw in Chapters 10 and 11 how a straightforward interpretation of the Qur'an and Hadiths make terrorist applications of them all too easy to grasp. We also saw in Chapter 18, and in the Communist genocides of the 20th century, that purging religion from public culture only makes the problem worse. Not all ideas are equal, and neither are all religions, when it comes to producing peaceful, morally sane societies. Christianity is also susceptible to these horrors; but only after the contortion of its basic teachings, their application, and/or fusing them with anti-biblical ideas in ways that mask the hypocrisy involved.

It is important to understand how Muslims define words in the Qur'anic text translated *oppression* and *tumult*.

> *Say to the Unbelievers, if (now) they desist (from Unbelief), their past would be forgiven them; but if they persist, the punishment of those before them is already (a matter of warning for them). And fight them on until there is no more* ***tumult*** *or* ***oppression****, and there prevail justice and faith in Allah altogether and everywhere; but if they cease, verily Allah doth see all that they do.* **Qur'an Sura 8:38-39**

Much of the Islamic world sincerely believes that Christians in general and Americans in particular "oppress" them simply because we are allied with Israel. Though the Qur'an encourages fighting most often when first attacked, Muslim scholars offer some creative interpretations of what an "attack" or an act of "oppression" is. When Christian and Jewish communities would not aid Mohammed in his military adventures, Mohammed took it as "oppression" and "tumult." The Prophet threatened that God would change them into apes. (Sura 2:64-65) Human nature being what it is; modern Islamist ideologues are even more creative in how they define an "attack."

While media and political leaders bemoan the "incomprehensible" motives of terrorists, an intellectually honest grasp of worldviews asks; "How much clearer can they be?"

Another scary thing to consider is the dynamics of population growth. Europe and America have bought in to secularist propaganda that we are in a terminal population explosion crisis. Nobody denies that the global population is increasing over all, but there is much evidence to support that it is a politically contrived "crisis." Overpopulation and lack of resources do not usually cause famines; political and economic mismanagement does. The average American family of 1.8 children is not near enough to maintain our current population levels. This endangers immediate future labor requirements to care for the elderly, as Baby-Boomers reach their senior years. It is even worse in Europe. The Islamic world, on the other hand, has a population base that is growing at an alarming rate, and spilling over into non-Islamic countries.

Historically, Islam is a "peaceful religion" where it is the minority religion. This is as it usually is in the United States and still in parts of Europe; and as it once was in Arabia, until Mohammed gained his power base at Medina and conquered Mecca. Yet, once an Islamic population in a given nation grows, or conditions seem right, something begins to change. History bears out that, at such a point, the Islamic population begins to think of that country as exclusively "Islamic" and to push harder for Islamic laws. They view any attempt to reverse this critical mass through talk of religious freedom or free expression of ideas as an "attack." As we see today in Dearborn Michigan, and in large parts of France, Britain, and Sweden, the sources of such "attacks" become open to violent retaliation.

This is why the nation of Israel is so offensive to many Arabs. They see it as a Jewish incursion into Islamic Palestine, even though they had no interest in the area before. If we couple this historic trend with the facts of population growth, it becomes apparent that by 2030; the Islamic world may well be able to dictate terms to us in ways that make our current ability to "oppress" them seem mild by comparison. It is already happening in Europe. Given our shrinking population, today's permissive sociological approach to abortion may even help in our own undoing. America performs millions of abortions each year.

In view of such an alarming analysis, what should the American and Christian response be to the Islamic worldview? Should we launch a 21st century version of the Crusades? Hardly—that only plays into the Islamist perception that we want to oppress them. It will lead more Muslims to believe that the Jihadists are right. (The terms *radical* and *moderate* are not meaningful to the Islamic worldview, as they are to the American one. We merely project our own ideas onto them by using such words.)

Should we indulge in the naïve fiction that Allah is merely another name for Jehovah God, and that terrorists are not "true believers" in Islam? Not if we want to survive the 21st century as a civilization. While national diplomacy may demand this approach sometimes, policies based on a denial of fact produce delusion and then destruction. That is what the Obama Administration's foreign policy has done; and it has destabilized the entire region, causing refugees to swarm into Europe.

Decisions made on inaccurate information create disaster in the real world.

The Bible teaches us to love our neighbor as ourselves, and to love our enemies. This confuses many people today, because they think that love is a feeling. They don't understand how to have feelings of affection for people that hate them. Islamic people are always our neighbors, and under current historic conditions, sometimes our enemies. Yet the Christian answer is not to forsake national defense, and try to have warm fuzzy feelings for terrorists. That shows a shallow understanding of the Bible's concept of love. Nor should we engage in a "holy war" beyond legitimate forms of national defense.

Paul's 1st Epistle to the Corinthians, Chapter 13, describes biblical love using action verbs. Love is something we *do* regardless of the emotions we *feel*. We might sum it up by saying, "Love does the right thing."

It is right to practice patience and kindness, to endure the weaknesses of others in humility, and try to understand people without justifying their sins. It is right to be as approachable as we reasonably can; even toward those who strongly disagree with us. It is right to defend the helpless, even with deadly force, though it is wrong to use violence easily. It is right to help those who need help—to give food to the hungry, and drink to the thirsty, and shelter to the destitute. Love does these things regardless of feelings against the people that benefit.

When Jesus told us to love our enemies, he was telling us to practice these behaviors in our relationships. I was gratified when so many American churches helped their Muslim neighbors in the wake of 9-11. They defended them against reactionary bigotry by helping them clean up angry graffiti on their homes and mosques, and by escorting them to stores in difficult neighborhoods. The food and medicine the United States military has brought to destitute Afghanis was likewise an example of a Bible-styled love emulated by national policy, despite whatever imperfections the system had.

None of these things makes worldview analysis wrong. The Christians who helped their Muslim neighbors did not do so because they had rosy illusions about the nature of Islam as a belief system. They did so because it was the right thing to do in the face of human need. The comparison of ideas for moral and practical value is necessary in the real world. It does not mean we hate the people who hold worldviews that have moral or rational problems from a Bible-based perspective.

Our response must reflect this kind of biblical love, unconfused with either our feelings or the current popular definitions of "love" and "tolerance" that do not stem from a realistic moral foundation. Biblical love does not negate a sound military policy in what Augustine of Hippo called a "just war." God gave Old Testament legal standards (which included some military rules of engagement) to the nation Israel for realistic national policy in a hostile, fallen world. The commands of Jesus, on the other hand, went to individuals, to guide them in their personal relationships. There is no real contradiction between the two, only historic misapplications.

Here is where the post-Christian worldview in American and European culture has consistently worked against itself. The leading relativistic view of "tolerance" keeps us from facing the Islamic worldview, and many others, realistically. We have indulged the fiction that all belief systems are equally valid—as opposed to *all men are created equal*. In doing so, we have opened ourselves up to being manipulated on a global scale.

Powerful leaders in Washington now view even the attempt to use rational worldview analysis as if it was a form of bigotry. This fits the "shooting ourselves in the foot" scenario I warned against in this book's first edition. Academic, media, and government leaders have not amply questioned postmodernist faith-assumptions in foreign (or any) policy. Rather, they have strengthened them against all reason, increasingly by force of law.

The problem for us is our public schools and colleges have taught for over three generations that morality is defined solely by whatever culture it developed in. They have denied even the possibility of an objective moral standard, whether revealed by God or self-evident in the human condition or both. People in America now see biblical divine absolutes as "just another set of culturally defined standards." Not even the self-evident attributes of human biology stand in the way of this assumption-base. Few imagined the implications of this shift. It means that our culture no longer has any moral or intellectual basis for believing American values of life and liberty are better than Islamist values of suicide "martyrdom," and mindless submission.

People will not die for something of neutral value.

This is also the problem with the redefined form of "tolerance" that is today's supreme value. Strip off the fresh paint job, and underneath it lays plain old *indifference*. There can be no genuine love where moral indifference rules, because indifference—not hate—is the opposite of love. Any person will hate anything or anyone that threatens their children, their homes, and their spouses. That is what it means when the Bible says, "God is a jealous God." This virtue allows men to put their lives on the line for their families, and for their nation. This virtue empowers mothers to do the almost miraculous in defense of their children. Postmodernism drains this virtue from our thought life, because common sense tells us that "all ideas are not equally good." It also tells us that when bad ideas network together to grip the worldview of an entire people, there is literally hell to pay."

Just ask those in Germany old enough to remember the Nazis.

This is the result of moral and cultural relativism.

The current view of "tolerance," as an absolute, cannot discuss and act on the merits and liabilities of different worldviews. It is not the same as genuine respect based on human dignity. The biblical view, by contrast, allows for sensible tolerance of people with non-Judeo-Christian opinions; without demanding we abandon our cultural foundations and morals. Tolerance, by its very nature, cannot ever be an absolute that overrides all other factors. Then we would need to tolerate evil. The pretense of today's false view of "tolerance" is impossible to maintain anyway. Any attempt to be "neutral" on such a scale only creates another worldview to add to the mix. Our own national rejection of God's word as an ethical absolute thus becomes an instrument of manipulation used by our enemies.

Jesus practiced genuine love, but did not allow his adversaries to manipulate him. Even when events led up to the Crucifixion, Jesus stayed completely aware of circumstances, and of his enemies' motives. Christians, who actually engage Muslims in a discussion of God, and other worldview topics, have found an interesting thing. Because Islamic governments shut down traditional western missionary activity, most work goes on over the radio or through the Internet. The neat thing about the Internet is that it allows relatively deep levels of two-way communication. Many Islamic people are happy to discuss faith and worldview issues with respectful and kindly Christians, who patiently answer their questions without pressure; and who take the time to get to know them.

Many who fear to speak openly are happy to explore the issues in private. In many Islamic nations, it is a capital crime to convert to Christ. The Qur'an does not depict a god who loves and redeems sinners, or teach that people can have a personal relationship with Allah. Many in the Islamic world have desperate questions and unmet human spiritual needs for which their own worldview has no satisfying answers. Mothers will not put up with the harvesting of their children as suicide bombers forever, despite the most effective religious propaganda. Christians can give them an alternative hope, if we will take the time and expense to learn how. My missionary friends have unprecedented numbers of hits on their websites from citizens of Islamic countries, who are unhappy with their leaders, and want to know more. [5]

As with many other historic examples of real social transformation, change must come from the inside out, and slowly, from the grassroots up. Governments may be closed, but individual people are often open. It is from individual people that terrorism draws its volunteers; and from individual people that transformative ideas begin to take root that eventually influences multitudes.

The hope is that Americans can rediscover the benefits of a Christian worldview that can face both military defense and ideological (including spiritual) outreach honestly. The dominant American perception, today, is that Christian missionary activity can only stir up more trouble; but that is self-defeating. Radical Islamic missionaries in America have no such illusions, as the exploits of "American Taliban" John Walker Lindh, "Jihad Jane" Coleen Larose, Zachary Adam Chesser, and a growing host of Western converts to Islamic Jihadism illustrate. Powerful ideological Postmodernist multiculturalists, even in the White House, have argued to keep Islamic terms, like *jihad*, out of intelligence briefs—even when they describe the common denominator! President Obama even agreed. [6]

Radical Islam is one of the fastest growing religions in the world—perversely, even in America post-9-11! I am not suggesting that the United States government actively finance Christian missionary activity. That would get ugly fast, aside from the internal controversy. Government can unofficially encourage things without direct involvement, however. It can also recognize the value of its own spiritual heritage, and discourage the growing trend of judicial tyranny against people of faith. Government can stop discouraging discussion about Christian sourced ideas that have repeatedly proven themselves to work.

The hope of an effective Christian evangelism in Islamic countries may not seem like much, to many people. Nor am I placing this hope out there as an official foreign policy alternative. Nevertheless, those who know their history can remember the transformation of the Roman Empire. They also can see that later departures from the New Testament drove the problems that arose in Christendom. Yet, when Christians returned to their foundations, things slowly improved. Respect for life wins over fanatical violence in the long-term, though good people often die to make that point.

## Pressure to Conform in the Post-Christian World: Thyatira Redux?

The cream of agnostic evolutionary Humanism that controls education faces a crisis it never expected. They are responding in two "last resort" style ways—pretending it is not happening, and "shooting the messengers." The technological ability to observe life at a molecular scale has caused a realization in a significant number of scientists. It is growing evident to a substantial minority that the most reasonable explanation for the irreducible complexity inside living cells; and the language system within our very DNA, is that someone intelligently designed them.

Language code systems require an intelligent source. What makes them work is a reasoned understanding that certain symbols (or in the case of DNA, nucleotide sequences) mean certain things, like blue eyes or black hair. There is no chemical reason why certain sequences code for these things. The language system imposed by the sequences direct the process, not the chemical reactions *per se*. [7] Amino acid sequences in DNA's helix structure are like letters in an alphabet. This makes the DNA molecule like a computer flash drive and the different nucleotide sequences like the software code on that drive.

***Irreducible complexity*** starts with the fact that the mechanism of each cell is incredibly complex. What makes it *irreducible* is that many aspects of the cell cannot arise from any simpler form without giving up its ability to work as a living organism. [6] It needs all its parts as they are. Millions of molecule-sized machines operate together in a complex web to make each cell function as a living system. In other words, the bridge between molecule and living organism is a lot longer and more treacherous than Stanley Miller imagined in the 1950s. Doctors Miller and Urey successfully generated statistically equal amounts of left and right-handed forms of the simplest amino acid in the laboratory; under conditions believed back then to mimic the "primitive atmosphere." They needed a complex trap to keep the amino acids from instant destruction by the main product of their experiment—corrosive tars.

Amino acids each come in two forms, which, on the molecular level, are mirror images of each other. Only the "left-handed" kind appears in living organisms. This type must be formed a statistically absurd 100 percent of the time for any naturalistic, design-free, amino acid-to-life theory to work. The news reports at the time failed to mention this. Amino acids are only the simplest of the chemical building blocks for life. The headlines about Miller's experiment claimed he "created life" in the laboratory. It was not even a fair exaggeration, then. Now, it is a source of embarrassment as a serious naturalistic case for life origins. [8]

The advent of a Creationism peopled by experts in relevant scientific fields has forced naturalistic education elites to run for cover. Something they do either by avoiding the topic or by suppressing the scientists who raise it. The rise of ***Information Theory*** from the development of the computer, and how it applies to the DNA code, has connected certain dots for some. Purely naturalistic cases for origins do not seem as realistic to educated people anymore. Appeals to the old "Monkey Trial" stereotypes now look like the *ad hominem* subterfuges they always were. In some ways, for those who are just learning about this, it is as if parts of science are beginning to switch sides in a long-standing debate.

Of course, nothing like that is really happening. People are just more aware of the role faith-held assumptions play in naturalistic science, as they play in every way of knowing things. The evidences for intelligent design appear virtually anywhere we choose to look. This does not mean that many people want to re-examine the God of the Bible as a realistic option, unfortunately. That should be on the table far more than it is. Naturalistic Bible scholarship should now be open to severe criticism; subjected to the same skepticism as conservative Christian scholarship has been for two hundred years. Even so, it means that a new battle for intellectual freedom has erupted in our culture that Christians should care about intensely. Science is just one of its fronts.

Our judicial and educational establishments buy a ***reductionist*** idea that "religion" is "belief in God," while non-religion means "no God." They thus have the uncomfortable dilemma of dealing with mounting science-related evidences that suggest the existence of God. Baseless questions arise like, *how can we let this kind of scientific outlook and its data, into public classrooms without "establishing a religion"?* They ignore how *they have already imposed a public religion by excluding such information and the viewpoints that logically follow it*. Several major religions, by faith, deny the existence of a personal God, Buddhism for example.

Any faith-held belief system that tries to answer the big questions of *meaning* involves *religion*. It may be a theistic one like Christianity, Judaism, or Islam, or it might be pantheistic like Hinduism or Buddhism, or Neo-Pagan, like Wicca, or humanistic like Scientology and any agnostic or atheistic set of beliefs; all start from dogmatic assumptions. Even if the answer offered is that "there is no answer," a person can only accept that answer by faith. It is unprovable, and not the only reasonable option out there. People still ultimately base God-less answers on subjective feelings, even if those feelings are a reaction to objective events, like the Religious Wars. It makes no difference if they have woven a consistent naturalistic rationale to back their view, any more than if they have woven a theistic one.

Science will never be able to tell us which god is the real God. *Science is not a method designed for discovering that kind of information*. It can however, testify to design being the most reasonable explanation for the natural world, in many cases. What will happen when discoveries in biology and physics continue to reveal the probability of intelligent design? Will political correctness try to tell us what science is? Will lawyers? We are beginning to see evidence that this establishment will not go down without a fight.

No establishment ever does, regardless of evidences that they should.

Some academics now suggest that even tenured scientists, who come out in favor of Creationist and Intelligent Design positions, should have their credentials revoked. American universities already informally exclude such scientists from many advancement opportunities. A leftist media often smears them by pretending they do not exist, or by mislabeling them. Why is this so? Qualified men and women raise compelling scientific doubts about the adequacy of the dominant *philosophical* model to deal sensibly with evidence we now see. When the debate stays on scientific issues, and not politics, evolutionary materialists do not fare so well.

The angriest attacks against scientists who question the dominant model often come from other Christians. Theologians that promote Molecule-to-Man Evolution as fact, and believers unwilling to deal with the presupposition-driven nature of the issue, find it awkward. They behave as if scientists fully solved the issue long ago, and no new data could ever warrant re-examining the assumptions of 19th century science. Some may still be honestly unaware of how much the current system builds from ideology, but the issues are becoming clearer. Not all believers respond well to the emerging picture. Like other cultural situations Christians have faced in history, pressure to conform has been huge.

With the angrier academic tone, what can Christians in the science and education worlds, unwilling to barter their worldview, expect? Watch Ben Stein's *Expelled: No Intelligence Allowed* for the increasingly frequent answer. Case in point—award-winning astronomer, Dr. Guillermo Gonzales; whom Iowa State University denied tenure to because of his work showing intelligent design also exists at the astronomical scale. The Discovery Institute's background page on Dr. Gonzalez, who is one of its fellows, reads:

> *He has published more peer-reviewed journal articles than all but one of the faculty members granted tenure this year at ISU – across the university as a whole, not just his department. In fact, Gonzalez has more peer-reviewed journal articles to his credit than all but five faculty members granted tenure at ISU since 2003. In addition, he exceeded his department's own tenure standards, which define "excellence" in terms of publications in refereed science journals, by more than 350%...In 2006, the year he was up for tenure, Gonzalez published more total articles than all other tenured ISU astronomers. Moreover, Dr. Gonzalez has more per-capita citations in science journals and per-capita scientific publications than any other tenured astronomer at ISU since 2001, the year he joined ISU. In other words, Gonzalez outperformed the very astronomers that voted against his tenure... Meanwhile, his work has*

*been featured in the world's most prestigious science journals,* ***Nature*** *in 2002 and* ***Science*** *in 2004. He co-authored a cover story for* ***Scientific American*** *in 2001, and he is co-author of a 2006 peer-reviewed Cambridge University Press textbook,* ***Observational Astronomy****. He is clearly impacting the next generation of scientists, as his ideas about the Galactic Habitable Zone have even been incorporated into two astronomy textbooks by other authors.*

***Discoveryinstitute.org,***

*http://www.evolutionnews.org/2013/07/statement_from_074251.html*

Gonzales did not use his classroom as a platform. He published a book, *The Privileged Planet*. This well researched work confronts ideological assumptions in astronomy that overlook abundant evidence that the Earth and its solar system inhabit a unique region of space. This region not only has an array of improbable qualities that allow life to exist; it gives us a rare ability to make scientific observations of distant objects, which we would not have if our solar system were inside, instead of between, our galaxy's spiral arms.

Ben Stein verifies that this political tactic is no isolated incident. Academics often blacklist scientists in the United States for doubting the party line of materialistic ideology that hides inside science education. Nor could Discovery Institute get away with making this stuff up. Powerful opponents look for ways to discredit this institute simply for its open Intelligent Design stance.

This conflict has more dimensions to it than just creation versus evolution, though that deals with the essential worldview foundations. Historically, when a dominant political, religious, or scientific establishment seems to run out of persuasive arguments based on reason, things get ugly. In the real world, popular science is often anything but objective. The same political games go on in science as anywhere else. Consider how the news media handles science related issues.

Major TV networks warped the story of psychologist Dr. James Dobson's meeting with condemned mass-murderer and rapist, Ted Bundy, before Bundy's execution. During his last months on death row, Bundy apparently came to a saving faith in Jesus Christ. He recognized that he had to die for his crimes, and called on Dr. Dobson. Bundy said that he wanted people to know how much of a negative impact pornography had on his sexual development. Without blaming porn for his choices, He related how it had reinforced a fantasy life that he eventually acted out in rape and murder. Bundy insisted that he still made the choices in the end, not that "porn made me do it." As a man thinks, so he becomes.

When the national news of at least two networks covered Dobson's visit, the good doctor found himself stripped of his credentials by the media! Both reports I watched referred to him as, "*televangelist James Dobson.*" The newscasters on both networks then introduced another psychologist, by credentials similar to those of Dr. Dobson. Dobson was associate professor of pediatrics at the University Of Southern California School Of Medicine, and a PhD in child developmental psychology before founding *Focus on the Family*. The other psychologist refuted everything Dobson said about what has since become a well-recognized connection between pornography and violent sex crime.

In Aldous Huxley's *Brave New World*, one of the standards his fictional totalitarian regime used to control the thinking of the masses was; "*several thousand repetitions equal one truth.*" See if that does not feel eerily familiar, the next time you watch TV. That is the hope of dying, prostituted establishments that resort to *ad hominem* name-calling to maintain power. Keep people distracted long enough with non-issues to set up political barriers against facing the real ones. Politically correct education policies do not teach children *how* to think, but tell them *what* to think. Historically, this tactic can only hold off the inevitable for so long in a free society. The only resort after that is unjust suppression of dissenting ideas, and evidence. Everyone knows this. Nobody wants to face it. But, it is here.

Why the big stink over academics? The issue is not scientific, but political, and ultimately, spiritual.

American courts, and the Obama Administration, seem committed to a judicial redefinition of the 1st Amendment. This redefinition, an idea of only recent decades, seems intended to purge any signs of Christian culture from public life, however minor. The media, courts, and Federal Government have come to the same place as the Roman Emperors Decius, Valerian, and Diocletian. The issue is not the right to worship Jesus. It never is, and never was. *Freedom of worship* is a bait and switch tactic that only a dumbed-down society can mistake for *freedom of religion.* [9] Christians can and often do "worship Jesus" in ways that don't actually treat him as a real person or affect how they approach the problems of real life. They "worship Jesus" inside their church walls for two hours, every week, and nobody will ever bother them.

The issue is whether the Bible's God is the God of the real world or just of our private existential religious fantasies. The issue will be whether we can actually teach our children a worldview that treats God as a functionally real person. That means one who has knowable ideas that He has communicated for us to obey in the real world. The issue will be whether we can really follow the evidence where it leads in the realms of science, history, family ethics, and education; or knuckle under to the machineries of a totally secularist worldview. If the God of the Bible is seen as a real possibility again, then so is accountability to Him. *Yet, in the present age, in this life, our submission to that is voluntary.*

***Secularism***, as an ideology, pretends to be neutral on religious issues. Actually, it suppresses vital information, at best, by trivializing it. The history of the 18th through 21st centuries show Secularism has a humanistic religion to establish. This religion is anything but fair or free of fanaticism. It can be horrifically arbitrary, as well. That a secularist American society destroys its own constitutional rights based on a warped view of "civil liberty" is the most diabolical irony of all.

That is where we are right now, not where we might be in the future.

In Postmodernism's rejection of objective truth comes the suggestion that "truth claims" are mere political tools to gain and keep power over people. A worldview that assumes such a thing sanctions the very evil it claims to expose. Once society takes claims to truth from the realm of objective evidence, and from an ethic of moral absolutes; then no motivation remains plausible except gaining or keeping political power. People who accept the assumptions of Postmodernism still make truth claims. Each "tribe," whether ethnic, political, religious, or social, still has its own truth claims. Removing those claims from reason and provability also removes any motive for finding common ground.

It also leads to the justification of manipulative social engineering and bullying. It means that media, political, and, eventually, physical "might makes right." No other outcome is possible in this mindset because the assumptions of Postmodernism rule out other motivations from the start. Not all ideas fit reality equally well, no matter how much a powerful "***politically correct***" worldview demands we all pretend they do.

Many structurally postmodernist political and social "tribes" exist today. We saw one in today's politico-religious Islamism, where "truth" is whatever furthers the cause of Islam. In the West, a postmodernist social "tribe" grew out of the Sexual Revolution. This group demanded that thousands of years of legal and social family law precedent be overturned. It has successfully convinced a narrow majority of one Supreme Court justice to redefine marriage in the United States. The Gay Movement has swayed Western Civilization to affirm homosexual behavior, and a Gay/Lesbian worldview, as a healthy norm. Its assumptions and methods show the fallacies of postmodernism in action.

First, some background.

The terms *Gay* and *homosexual* are not synonymous—at least not at this stage, anymore. A *homosexual* is one who practices homosexuality. *Gay* is a subculture centered on the desire and practice of homosexuality. The terms are closely related, but they are not the same thing. Not all homosexuals identify with the Gay subculture, nor is it simply about "closets."

The male and female aspects of human nature are physically self-evident, except in cases of rare genetic disorders. Family law should reinforce the norm, not its exception. One must do intellectual gymnastics from deterministic assumptions to believe that gender is a purely relative continuum, with no absolutes of maleness and femaleness. The idea that these designations have no fixed social, moral, and biological meaning is self-evidently ludicrous. This does not deny that physical biochemical factors might not affect some personal struggles. It merely denies determinist assumptions about those factors, and relativistic assumptions based on logical fallacies. *Male* and *female* are not arbitrary categories. They objectively exist, even if imperfectly, in a fallen world.

An *imperfect* norm is not the same as an *arbitrary* one.

Until recently, family law upheld maleness and femaleness as healthy and meaningful family norms. They also accepted reality—that the ideal does not always exist for some families, nor is it always possible. Single parenthood was always a fact of life. Marriage laws that limited marriage to between a man and a woman were not arbitrary. Nor were they religiously motivated. Lawmakers over the centuries did not institutionalize one-man, one-woman marriage as a way of sticking it to homosexuals. It developed legally because thousands of years of human experience showed that, ideally, children do best with morally sane male and female adult role models. Social sciences prove this repeatedly, the caveat being that male and female partners be morally sane individuals. Law favored the ideal of what is generally true of humanity, not the exception. [10]

Marriage law is primarily about the stability of children, not the happiness of couples.

Nobody denies that people have often treated homosexuals badly throughout history. It is even understandable why Gays should want to form their own subculture. Likeminded people do that sort of thing. Nor is there any question that Christians ought to treat Gays, Lesbians, and Transgendered people with human dignity. God created their humanity, as He did all other people's, in His own image, even He did not create their sin (or ours). There is a difference between what we are and what we do. In the first edition of this book, I barely mentioned the Gay Movement because, at that time, it did not seem as central to how worldviews had affected church history. I saw a potential for that to change in the way that it has, but it had not yet done so enough to focus on it. Human sexuality, of itself, is part of God's creating us in His image.

> **So God created man in His own image; in the image of God He created him; *male and female* He created them. *Genesis* 1:27 (NKJV)**

Every aspect of the human condition, as it exists in today's fallen world, is a result of either Creation or of the Curse. The idea of a "relative gender continuum" does not fit reality if we consider all of the facts, instead of focusing on exceptional cases. God's word tells us the male and female pattern is the created one, and plainly His desire for human sexuality. Biology also tells us this, apart from any religion, because that is what functions reproductively and best, in terms of family psychology. When the church compromises on this, it reflects the same condition as existed at Thyatira. This is so whether by heterosexual promiscuity or by homosexual breaking of God's natural design for sex.

> **"And to the angel of the church in Thyatira write, 'These things says the Son of God, who has eyes like a flame of fire, and His feet like fine brass: *I know your works, love, service, faith, and your patience; and as for your works, the last are more than the first.* Nevertheless I have a few things against you, because you**

**allow that woman Jezebel, who calls herself a prophetess, to *teach and seduce My servants to commit sexual immorality* and eat things sacrificed to idols.'"**

***Revelation* 2: 18-20 (NKJV)**

Thyatira was a loving, serving, patient church that had faith, and these good things were increasing. Why would Christ have such a problem with that? It goes to how serious sexual sin is. Sin, and its damage, has warped human sexuality in every conceivable way, since the Fall. This is true whether it happens by a person's own choices or through the choices of others. People inflict lasting damage on others through childhood sexual abuse and rape. Diseases also result from the Curse, with no link to an individual's choices or conduct; rare genetic disorders, such as pseudo-hermaphroditism, that we are only beginning to understand. We should never confuse Hermaphroditism and Pseudo-hermaphroditism with homosexuality. They do not even correspond well to transgenderism, except in some childhood and teen cases. [11]

One troubling aspect of the rush to make laws here is the lack of a firm definition of what a *sexual orientation* even is, or what causes one. The idea that choice has no part of it is growing less believable, as science reveals that deterministic models do not explain human behavior very well. That does not mean other factors besides choice are not sometimes involved, too. It only means such factors *affect* homosexuality, they don't *determine* it. The pro-Gay American Psychological Association's definition of a *sexual orientation* is telling.

> *Sexual orientation is commonly discussed* ***as if it were*** *solely a characteristic of an individual, like biological sex, gender identity or age.* ***This perspective is incomplete because sexual orientation is defined in terms of relationships with others. People express their sexual orientation through behaviors with others,*** *including such simple actions as holding hands or kissing. Thus, sexual orientation* ***is closely tied to the intimate personal relationships that meet deeply felt needs*** *for love, attachment and intimacy. In addition to sexual behaviors, these bonds include nonsexual physical affection between partners, shared goals and values, mutual support, and ongoing commitment.* ***Therefore, sexual orientation is not merely a personal characteristic within an individual.*** *Rather, one's sexual orientation defines the group of people in which one is likely to find the satisfying and fulfilling romantic relationships that are an essential component of personal identity for many people.*

***Sexual Orientation & Homosexuality, What is a Sexual Orientation?***

*http://www.apa.org/topics/lgbt/orientation.aspx*

*Orientation* simply means *directionality*. In the case of sexual orientation, it means the directionality of a person's sexual desires. It is *descriptive*, not *a cause*. Deterministic assumptions, and psychological classifications, rarely touch on causes they merely describe effects. Technical terms often make it sound like "sexual orientation" *causes*, rather than *describes*, the direction of desires that lead to behavior. Put simply, a man saying he has sex with other men because of his sexual orientation is linguistically the same as him saying that he has sex with men because that is the direction of his desires.

Gay activists pushed the term *orientation* to replace *preference* in the 1970s because *preference* implied that choice played some role in the process. This was an attempt to shape public thought, not the result of scientific discovery proving such a thing. [12]

Sexual orientation is a subjective experience, not an objective property. Even those who experience solely homosexual orientation need their partner to simulate the opposite sex somehow, if only in mechanics. This is necessary because sexual organs have an *objective form and function*. Homosexual orientation may have some non-volitional aspects that make some people more tempted toward it than others are, even to extreme degrees;

but that is true of all forms of temptation. *People do not often choose which sins tempt them, and which repel them. They do choose whether to see it as God sees it or to invent another explanation for the behavior (or to follow ready-made ones supplied by a sub-culture).* The history of the concept of sexual orientation goes only to the early 20th century, but follows a worldview dynamic old as the Tower of Babel. Invention follows desire, in building models presented as proofs.

> **And the Lord said, See, they are all one people and have all one language; and this is only the start of what they may do: and now it will not be possible to keep them from any purpose of theirs.** ***Genesis*** **11:6 (BBE)**

In the model floated over the last 30 years, we see a departure from a *behavior-based* definition of homosexuality in favor of an *orientation-based* one. The Bible uses a behavior-based definition, and if we are wise, so will we. Use of the word *orientation* in this way assumes that sexual desire leanings are an objective trait rather than a subjective experience. Show me a person's orientation without their behaviors, and I'll show you mine by my behaviors. Using words tactically has won the Gay Movement its new ground. Christian apathy, and unwise acceptance of deterministic and reductionist terminology, with little analysis until late in the game; lost us much of ours. The price is high and getting higher.

Laws can only justly govern behavior. Motive requires proof beyond reasonable doubt. Right now, many Gay activists, and much of the media, assume Christian photographers, wedding cake bakers, artistic designers, and florists refuse to use their talents in homosexual wedding ceremonies out of hatred. Powerfully backed by the ACLU, heavily financed Gay activists drive artistic Christian small business owners from their livelihoods. These artists politely refuse to agree with something that biblical Christians have always believed is wrong. This happens today with growing frequency.

The Gay Movement's stand does not truly compare to the Civil Rights Movement's position against some churches that wrongly opposed inter-racial marriage. Christians led the fight against racial discrimination, and Genesis teaches that all people are of one blood. Churches that opposed inter-racial marriage did so for worldly cultural reasons, not biblical ones. Skin color is an objective property. It is not a behavior pattern driven by subjective experiences shared by a small minority, which may have involuntary contributing factors.

The comparison of this with civil rights for blacks is an "apples and roundish rocks" one, *except for the anger.* As with all the other bad ideas Postmodernism fosters, this, too, shows a pattern. Enough people have left a solely homosexual lifestyle to make the claim that sexual orientation is an unalterable trait extremely suspect. [13]

In fact, many studies into human sexuality suffer in one degree or another from the broader worldview assumptions mentioned in Chapters 18, 20, and 22 of this book. Dr. Thomas Landess, former Academic Dean at the University of Dallas, and former Policy Analyst at the U.S. Department of Education, put it this way in his analysis article, *The Evelyn Hooker Study and the Normalization of Homosexuality*:

> *This unquestioning acceptance of "authorities" on the basis of professional reputation or political correctness threatens the integrity of our legal system. Judges must take greater responsibility for assessing the soundness and accuracy of testimony by so-called experts; yet, paradoxically, such a task is manifestly beyond the competence of the court.* ***This dilemma is the consequence of the politicizing of the scientific community over the past several decades, particularly in questions of sexuality. The recent exposure of Kinsey's errors indicates just how long researchers have been careless or deliberately misleading in approaching sexual questions.*** *And the widespread acclamation of recent, flawed studies "proving" that homosexuality is inherited genetically is evidence that the problem has only worsened over the years.* [14]

Of course, counter-experts, and counter-counter-experts will refute Landess, and refute the refuters of Landess. Enough "Ex-Gays" give up and return to their old lifestyle that there are now many Ex-Ex-Gays. This is exactly what one would expect if we were dealing with suggestive ideas more than with biology. Sin tempts. This is also the problem with the assumption that the scientific method is the best way to study all aspects of the human condition. That method can't yield results with the same confidence as one finds in physics or chemistry. Human beings are more complex than atoms.

The Bible depicts people who return in despair to their sin. They do not destroy the faithfulness of God's word by giving up on it. Many repentant homosexuals remain, who do not give up—as is true of people that have turned from any other sin. Their reality is still meaningful. Homosexuals who have left the lifestyle are likely the first class of political "nonpersons" in mainstream American history. *Nonpersons* are not just an excluded class of people, but *people whom the mainstream denies even exist*. I've watched these men and women booed and harassed in the capitol roundhouse at Santa Fe, New Mexico, when one testified before the legislature. I know several personally.

The Christian businesses under attack today have no problem serving Gay customers in a general way. Some even have historically had good relations with their Gay customers, knowing those customers were Gay. These business owners only insist that they have a religious right not to use their artistic talents to affirm a message they oppose. That is plain old free speech. Christians are not refusing to serve Gays in restaurants, or grocery stores, or in any basic service. This doesn't fit bigotry or "homophobia"—accusations used to silence sensible discussion that includes both sides since the 1980s. It is only businesses that require artistic participation and affirmation of a message or practice where Christians, by conscience, must say, "no."

A *phobia* is an *irrational fear*. I'm not sure *homophobia* fits that bill anymore—not when a Christian baker in Oregon is fined $135,000 for politely declining to bake a wedding cake for a Lesbian couple that most bakers would be willing bake. The same thing happened to a Christian wedding photographer in New Mexico, to the tune of $7000. I'm not so sure the chill of fear is so irrational when businesses routinely fire people for simply expressing their point of view, civilly, off the job. Surely, there is nothing scary when a Christian florist, who has had friendly relations with her Gay customer for years, kindly and politely, draws the line at doing his wedding, based on her religious convictions; only to have high financed activist groups slap her with a crippling lawsuit. How insane is it when the pro-LGBT mayor of Houston subpoenas sermon notes from local pastors who spoke against a now repealed local law mandating that public lady's rooms be open to men who self-identify as women? [15] I could fill pages documenting this stuff.

What I write here is not out of fear or hatred. It is simply about why biblical Christians cannot affirm homosexual lifestyles. It is also about logical consequences and common sense. This is a moral issue, not a primarily political one. Nor is what I am saying *intolerance* by any reasonable definition. *Tolerance* is *peaceful coexistence with people I disagree with, and the affirmation of their human dignity*. Tolerance does not guarantee my opinions will never offend anyone. It just means that I am not looking to do so, only to explain a biblical Christian position on sexual ethics that fits human reality better than the "new normal" does.

Freedom of religion is the liberty to live out our beliefs in the real world. It does not mean we can or should force other people to share our views, but it does mean we have a right to express them, and live by them, publically in a civil manner. Mere "freedom of worship" places Christians into a cultural and intellectual ghetto. It coerces us to live as if the God of the Bible is not the God of reality. The Bible does not give us wiggle room on whether we can call homosexual behavior a sin or not.

**We know that the law is not meant for a righteous person, but for the lawless and rebellious, for the ungodly and sinful, for the unholy and irreverent, for those who kill their fathers and mothers, for murderers, for the sexually immoral *and homosexuals... for whatever else is contrary to sound teaching based on the glorious gospel of the blessed God* that was entrusted to me.**

***1 Timothy* 1:9-11 (HCSB)**

**Do you not know that the unrighteous will not inherit the kingdom of God? Do not be deceived. Neither fornicators, nor idolaters, nor adulterers, *nor homosexuals,* nor sodomites... *1 Corinthians* 6:9 (NKJV)**

**"You shall not lie with a male as with a woman. It is an abomination."**

**Leviticus 18:22 (NKJV)**

The Greek word *arsenokoitai*, translated *homosexuals*, describes the act and relationship; *arseno* being *male*, and *koitai* being the Greek root word for the Latin *coitus*—sexual intercourse. Many books have covered in detail the straightforward interpretive issues here. It would make this book too long for me to cover the matter in more detail. [16] The point is a Bible-based sexual ethic rules out the practice of homosexuality. A person who wants to practice one cannot practice the other. Nor can Gay activists expect that Christians will rewrite the Bible to suit them when we cannot do so, rightfully, to suit ourselves, whenever we struggle with what it says. Everyone who handles the Bible honestly, struggles with it.

Under the pretext of preventing bullying from a people not generally given to such behavior, bullies now destroy the exercise of legitimate and civil free speech. I do not say that Gay people are bullies; only that *this kind of tactic*, now used by powerful Gay activists, is nothing less than bullying. The first claim unfairly overgeneralizes. The second is true of any use of such a tactic, by anyone. It also shows the tyrannical outcome of moral relativism, even when tyranny is not the root intention.

People can no longer discuss a whole array of important moral, social, and spiritual issues within the relativistic value system of Postmodernism. Gay ideology is but one example currently in the news. *Once society accepts the idea that people have a right never to have their worldviews or lifestyles challenged by civil intellectual and moral reasoning; that pseudo-right can only be enforced by taking away everyone's genuine rights—freedom of speech, freedom of religion, freedom of association.* Nobody has the right to insulation from other civilly expressed viewpoints that might offend their own. Christians do not. They never have. Human rights die when society accepts this idea. It is mechanically impossible to have things both ways.

In 2000 years, the church has come full circle, except for the weight of history that it must bear. Even when we get "abundant showers of latter rain," it does not always have quite the same spiritual agriculture effect on the world as the "early rain" in the 1st century. Hard, dry soil is either resistant to moisture or it erodes too easily. The Post-Christian world is often saying, "been there, done that, and don't want to do it again." This does not mean that many individuals will not respond to the love of God, and follow Christ. It may mean that Christianity has had its day as the dominant cultural paradigm; that the church, as a political-religious institution, sometimes abused its opportunities and lost them.

It may not mean that.

It does not mean that new opportunities will not arise. Nor does it mean that God does not meet each of us where we are. He accepts us each as we are, when we come to Him on His terms, but He loves us all too much to leave us that way. Voltaire and Bentham were certain that Christianity would be dead within 30 years of their generation. A mere 30 years after Voltaire's death, a Bible society was printing Bibles in what used to be his house. The basic need of the human soul has not changed. Neither has God's revealed answer for it.

Changing our environment or biochemistry cannot change that.

Sin is real. It rots the human condition like a cancer, so entirely that we cannot possibly overcome it by our own devices, even when we mean well, and want to make the world better. Jesus died to pay for the sin of humankind, and rose from the dead to offer the gift of salvation to all who will come to him. Yet, we must come to him as broken individuals, and ask him into our lives with the trust of small children. In relation to God, that is what we are. Jesus will also return visibly someday to restore the creation He has redeemed. That is the gospel in a nutshell.

Though the Christian faith has been through many transitions, another thing has not, and will not ever change while the current world lasts. Jesus said, **"All that the Father gives Me will come to Me, and the one who comes to Me I will by no means cast out."** (John 6:37 NKJV) As long as people still genuinely follow Jesus, the church—in whatever form—is alive and has a mission to perform; and **"the gates of hell will not prevail against it."**

## BIBLIOGRAPHY


1. Hosea 6:1-3; Jeremiah 3:1-5; Joel 2:21-32; Acts 2:17-22; Zechariah 10:1-4; Haggai 2:6-9
2. 2 Timothy 3:13 & 3:1-5; Luke 18:8-9; 1 Timothy 4:1-3; 2 Peter 2:1-3; 1 John 2:18-19; Jude 1:3-4
3. Ian Mobsby, ***Emerging & Fresh Expressions of Church***, (London: Moot Community Publishing), 28-29. See also, Ian Mobsby, ***The Becoming of G-d***, (Cambridge: YTC Press, 2008), 98-101.
4. ***The Times***, Sept. 11, 2001, *Attacks Celebrated in West Bank*; see also, ***AFP***—Ain-al-Heleh, Lebanon, Sept. 11, 2001, *Palestinians in Lebanon Celebrate Anti-US Attacks*; see also, ***Reuters***, Joseph Logan, Sept. 12, 2001, Beirut—*Palestinians Celebrate Attacks with Gunfire*; see also, ***Fox News***, Sept. 12, 2001, *Arafat Horrified by Attacks, but Thousands of Palestinians Celebrate; Rest of World Outraged*; see also, **AP** Jerusalem, Sept. 12 2001, *AP Protests Threats to Freelance Cameraman Who Filmed Palestinian Rally*; see also, **Middle East Newsline**, Sept. 13, 2001, Ramallah—*Palestinian Authority has Muzzled Coverage of Palestinian Celebrations*; see also, ***Jerusalem Post/AP***, Sept. 13, 2001, *Israel to AP: Release Film of Palestinian Celebrations*; see also, ***AP***, Sept. 14, 2001, *Bin Laden Poster Seen at Gaza Rally*; see also, ***Opinions and Attitudes to Peace Process, Governance, Security, and Service Provision in the West Bank and Gaza Strip***, FAFO/AIS poll, 19-Nov to 10-Dec-2005, *Table 2.22(2) - Support to Al Qaeda's actions like bombings in USA and Europe* shows a 65% support among Muslim Palestinians
5. **www.aboutisa.com** – *Note: "Isa" is the Arab pronunciation of Jesus.* See also, **answering-islam.org**
6. Eastman, Mark M.D. and Missler, Chuck. ***The Creator Beyond Time and Space***, pp. 35-36, The Word for Today (1996)
7. Rowan Scarborough, ***Obama's Scrub of Muslim Terms in Question***, Washington Times, April 25, 2013, *http://www.washingtontimes.com/news/2013/apr/25/obamas-cleansing-of-islamic-terms-suppresses-commo/?page=all*
8. For more reading on ***Irreducible complexity*** from the point of view of secular scientists who are grappling with this issue without advocating biblical Creationism, see Michael Denton's ***Evolution: A Theory in Crisis*** (Adler and Adler – 1986) and M.J. Behe's ***Darwin's Black Box: The Biochemical Challenge to Evolution*** (The Free Press – 1996). For a biblical and scientific perspective see, ***The Creator Beyond Time and Space***, by Dr. Mark Eastman M.D., and Chuck Missler; (The Word for Today Publishers – 1996)
9. Shapiro, Robert. ***Origins – A Skeptics Guide to the Creation of Life on Earth***, pp. 105-128; (1986)
10. Sarah Torre, ***Watering Down Religious Freedom to 'Freedom of Worship,'*** The Heritage Foundation, *http://www.heritage.org/research/commentary/2014/9/watering-down-religious-freedom-to-freedom-to-worship*, See also, Alliance Defending Freedom, *http://www.alliancedefendingfreedom.org/Home/Detail/7924?referral=I2015GENB0*
11. Girgis, Sherif, Ryan T. Anderson, & Robert P. George, ***What Is Marriage? Man and Woman: A Defense***, Encounter Books, 2012, (Argues from Natural Law for the conjugal view of legal marriage.); See also, Lee Patrick & Robert P. George, ***Conjugal Union: What Marriage Is and Why It Matters***, Cambridge University Press, 2014; See also, Daniel Heimbach, ***Why Not Same***

***Sex Marriage? A Manual for Defending Marriage Against Radical Deconstruction***, Trusted Books, 2014, See also, Robert P. George & Jean Bethke Elshtain, editors, ***The Meaning of Marriage: Family, State, Market, and Morals***, Spence 2006, Dallas, TX.

12. E Urban M, Rabe-Jabłońska J, ***Transsexualism or Delusions of Sex Change? Avoiding Misdiagnosis***, *Psychiatra Polska* (Polish Psychiatric Journal), 2010 Sep-Oct, 44(5):723-33. See also, Borras L. (Department of Psychiatry, University Hospitals of Geneva, Switzerland), Huguelet P, Eytan A, ***Delusional "Pseudotranssexualism" in Schizophrenia***, *Psychiatry*, 2007 Summer;70(2):175-9, Note: *The point here is not that transgenderism is caused by schizophrenia, but that much transgenderism does not correlate strongly to objective, genetic causes like pseudo-hermaphroditism; although childhood, puberty, and teen correlations seem like reasonable possibilities sometimes for cases in that age group. The author does not pretend to be an expert, but one does not need to be to have reasonable concerns over the effect normalization of transgenderism will have in the rigor of diagnostic and ethical questions asked within a setting that makes deterministic assumptions about human sexuality.*
13. Judith Reisman, Edward W. Eichel, J. Gordon Muir, J.H. Court, ***Kinsey, Sex, and Fraud: The Indoctrination of a People***, (1990 ) See also, *http://ex-gaytruth.com/ex-gay-testimonies/*
14. Paglia, Camille, ***Vamps and Tramps***, 1994, New York Vintage Press. Pgs 70-71. Note: *Lesbian author and activist Camille Paglia writes;* ***"...nature exists whether academics like it or not, and in nature procreation is the single relentless rule. That is the norm... Our sexual bodies were designed for reproduction...*** **no one is born gay.** ***The idea is ridiculous... homosexuality is an adaptation, not an inborn trait."*** *From this, Paglia somehow draws the conclusion that,* ***"We have not only the right but the obligation to defy nature's tyranny."*** (Compare to Rom. 1:18-32)
15. Sharon Kass, ***Conservative's Ex-Gay Phobia***, *http://www.wnd.com/2010/08/193745/*; See also, E.M. Pattison and M.L. Pattison, ***"'Ex-Gays': Religiously Mediated Change in Homosexuals," American Journal of Psychiatry***, Vol. 137, pp. 1553-1562, 1980; See also, *http://pfox-exgays.blogspot.com/2015/03/setting-record-straight-on-science.html.*
16. ***Washington Post***, *www.washingtonpost.com/posteverything/wp/2015/05/12/im-a-florist-but-i-refused-to-do-flowers-for-my-gay-friends-wedding/*; See also, Jordan Lorence, ***National Review***, Supreme Court Turns Down Elane Photography Case, *http://www.nationalreview.com/bench-memos/375210/supreme-court-turns-down-elane-photography-case-jordan-lorence*; See also, Michael Muskal, ***Los Angeles Times***, Former Oregon Bakery Owners Must Pay $135,000 For Denying Lesbians Wedding Cake, *http://www.latimes.com/nation/la-na-oregon-bakery-wedding-cake-20150703-story.html*; See also, Peter LaBarbara, ***Whistleblower Magazine***, "Gay Power" vs. Religious Liberty, *http://www.wnd.com/2013/11/gay-power-vs-religious-liberty/*; See also, Matt Bonesteele, ***Washington Post***, Craig James Sues Fox Sports, Alleging Religious Discrimination, *http://www.washingtonpost.com/news/early-lead/wp/2015/08/04/craig-james-sues-fox-sports-alleging-religious-discrimination/*, See also, Alexa Ura, ***The Texas Tribune***, Bathroom Fears Flush Houston Discrimination Ordinance, Nov. 3, 2015 (I can fill pages, but this is a wide enough spread to prove my point-KGP)
17. Kevin DeYoung, ***What Does the Bible Really Teach about Homosexuality?***, p. 44, p. 65-66, pp. 39-47, 59-67, Crossway, Wheaton Ill. (2015); See also, Thomas E. Schmidt, ***Straight and Narrow: Compassion and Clarity in the Homosexuality Debate***, Inter-Varsity Press, 1995; See also, Robert A.J. Gagnon, ***The Bible and Homosexual Practice: Texts and Hermeneutics***, Abingdon Press, 2001

# CONCLUSION

## EPISTEMOLOGICAL BREAKDOWN

What comes upon a civilization two generations or so after moral breakdown? We saw that chucking moral absolutes means chucking objective truth in more than the realm of morality. While *truth* and *degree of precision* are two different things, *accuracy* is a form of truth. Our society politicizes science as an institution, along with journalism, law, religion, and most everything else. Accuracy and objectivity are only the first in a long line of casualties from this. People now habitually equate point-of-view to mere spin. This brings us to where we have no way of knowing if information we get from the academy, newsroom, government, and religious institutions is even true or useful. This comes in the Information Age, when more information bombards us than ever imagined.

This is a "perfect storm" scenario. Cultural mechanics pushes even sincere Christians to the terrifying borders of being **"always learning and never able to come to the knowledge of the truth."** (2 Tim. 3:7) I say *terrifying* because that verse describes the apostates in the churches of the last days. (2 Tim. 3:1-9) We communicate truth via information, and our way of life. Uncertainty about truth destroys hope, and then fidelity.

It used to be said that, "talk is cheap." Now, it seems that knowledge itself is. If we can't be certain about knowledge, then what value is there in knowing things? People believe this especially true about spiritual, historical, and philosophical knowledge. The devaluation has bled into many other subjects, as well. Politics was once the realm of *polity*—civil leadership and discourse. Lack of integrity in this institution causes people, now, to view it with disgust. As postmodernist journalism, academics, and law reveal their lack of integrity; the prostitution of one social institution after another on such a massive scale fades into background noise. Science, as an institution, is not immune, and neither is religion. A stifling sense of either helplessness or indifference grips people today.

Feelings of futility tug at me, too. Those who do not sense that tug are not paying attention. Not paying attention to it is a form of giving in to it.

If nothing seems worth knowing, nobody is motivated to discover truth, especially when told in a million different ways that truth is an illusion. Truth undiscovered is truth unapplied. This disconnects people from one another, and within themselves. It stems from long disconnection from God. The Bible now seems irrelevant to many, when, in reality, it best describes what we see all around us, if in terms most would rather not think about.

We hear of far-reaching decisions made by influential social institutions that, if made by an individual, would identify that person as insane. If someone tried to keep from going bankrupt by spending more than they earned or had saved, it would be pathological. When a person pays millions of dollars for a sealed box, without knowing what is inside, that person is either a fool, insane, or both. When the Speaker of the House of Representatives says, "We need to pass this bill so we can find out what it says," and people think that is fine; we are dealing with something past mere corruption. When a Supreme Court majority thinks it can ignore what a document *says* to get at what it *means*, and half the nation cheers, it shows a serious large-scale disconnect from reality.

When church leaders think that Christian churches can reform by distancing themselves from their biblical foundations, it is delusion. When a civilization behaves regularly as if ideas have no consequences, it is social insanity. When a society classifies a concern born out of love as "hate," it will suffer the results. What kind of society considers the murder and dismemberment of infants a "right," and the source of a medical commodity? When a culture effectively takes the substance of *moral indifference* and packages it as "tolerance;"

that indifference becomes valued over truth, and genuine love withers away. The results may not be instant, but they are approaching, and they will not be good for the human condition. Reality always catches up.

Isaiah the Prophet understood this well.

> **Woe to those who call evil good, and good evil; Who put darkness for light, and light for darkness; Who put bitter for sweet, and sweet for bitter! Woe to those who are wise in their own eyes, And prudent in their own sight!**
>
> ***Isaiah* 5:20-21 (NKJV)**

Were I to give this civilization-scale insanity a technical term, I would call it *epistemological breakdown*. (I know, "not another technical term!") Since it seems a majority in our culture now deny objective truth exists, and with it, by extension, absolute truth, such as the moral absolutes of the Bible; the idea of a truth outside our subjective social experiences now seems unthinkable to many. They are convinced of this by repetitive media suggestion, rather than by reasoning it out, however. We see a breakdown in the ability and motivation *to know*, because integrity has broken down already in the institutions that handle and pass on knowledge. My pastor, Robert Hall, put it this way, "Sin makes you stupid!"

With our society's motive to discover truth withering, the value of knowledge itself has come into question—except as a tool for manipulating others. This reinforces what many have called the "dumbing down" of our culture. Fewer people can "connect the dots," so to speak. This has powerfully bad implications for any Bible believing church, as we already saw. Not only will Christians face fierce opposition from outside; they must take on the additional burden of educating not only the uneducated, but the mis-educated, who come to the church unaware that much of what they think they know, they really don't.

*Epistemology* is the *mechanics of how we know stuff*, and the mechanics is broken. The Bible is also a literary information system that urges people to learn in all aspects of life, starting with the ability to read enjoyably. Our church culture needs to reflect and reward that ideal, without alienating those whose gifts are not in the knowledge and analysis area. Too often, we seem to fear that we can't do the former without doing the latter.

We need nothing except Scripture for our highest authority, foundation, and gospel. Salvation is "Jesus plus nothing." That does not mean we do not need to relate what the Bible says to other aspects of the real world. We need history and philosophical reasoning skills to do that effectively; and should not fear such gifts when they build from the foundation of Scripture, into the flow of what reality throws at us. The life of the Apostle Peter shows this. A coarse, bull-headed fisherman, when Jesus found him, Peter grew. In his last letter, 2 Peter, he commended the Apostle Paul's writings, even though he called them in some places "hard to understand." (2 Pet. 3:15-16) Peter also used some of the most complex science terms of his day, "the elements (*atomos*) will melt with fervent heat." (2 Pet. 3:10)

As society embraces moral and cultural relativism more and more, it further marginalizes biblical Christianity. Churches feel pressure to cave-in to the "new normal" to "stay relevant." Nor can believers support specialized parachurch ministries as well in financial hard times. Political tyranny eventually shuts them down altogether. We already see Christian artists, like photographers, florists, and bakers forced from their livelihoods by demands that they affirm social messages against God's word. Parachurch organizations are a distinctive of affluent societies with affluent churches. When wealth vanishes, the decrease of parachurch ministries must soon follow. This is a shame, but we must face probability that it is coming.

This means local churches must raise-up their own homegrown people who have specialized gifts, and share them with other fellowships less endowed. It will mean thinking differently about priorities; how seemingly less important things can enable or disable those things most important. It will mean valuing different things, like substance over sound systems. It also means that, like the monasteries of old, we must make our churches refuges of general learning and literacy for those whom God accordingly gifts. How each church does this, and to what degree, will of course, vary, but the need already exists.

Those who convert to the Faith today, do so from an increasingly disabled place. What I mean by that, is they come from a culture less and less informed by Bible literacy; and more and more by technologically reinforced conditioning into worldviews openly hostile to the Faith. This conditioning is hostile not only to Scriptural ethics and doctrine, but to a view of reality consistent with the Bible's revelation, itself. They often come to the Faith with a background less informed by a love of literacy, too. This is not as it was during the 19th century revivals. Back then, converts knew almost instantly what to do with their faith because even unbelievers had a Judeo-Christian worldview. Today, incredible thought and energy must go into unlearning an entrenched worldview, as biblical thinking ramps up in the discipleship process. Or, at least, it needs to when, too often, it doesn't.

I love the Calvary Chapel philosophy of "putting the cookies on the lower shelf," where even the children can get at them. This came from a healthy conviction that we want to make the word of God, and the things of the Faith, as accessible as possible to people. This strength, as all strengths, has a shadow, however; where it is not hard to imagine a blind spot might lay, especially in a day when the world is dumbing people down so radically. Good as this strength is, we must now be much more careful how we use it. Words have meaning. Erase too many of them from common usage, and *meaning goes away*, too. If a boot camp drill sergeant makes boot camp too easy, soldiers go off to war ill prepared for battle in a foreign landscape.

Of course, God can and does restore forgotten essentials. We saw that, too. This does not mean we need not consider the cost of losing such things. Preservation is always less costly than rebuilding from scratch. My study of worldviews in church history is in part a tactical analysis, and in whole intended as an aid for growing leaders who must navigate not only personal Bible application; but also social, cultural, and whatever other applications become needed, as the world throws things at us in the last days. Remember the words of my pastor's wife; "Our weaknesses hide in our strengths."

My adaptation of her words is also worth revisiting. "Our biggest blind spots hide in the shadows of our greatest strengths." Satan—as any military commander—will exploit those blind spots to their fullest, if allowed to do so. This does not just mean the shadow of our natural strengths, but even those spiritual gifts God gives to us. The reason it includes those is that Satan wants to make a mockery of whatever God does in any given generation. That means he is going to aim his attention at the things we are doing right, in order to discredit those very things. That, too, is a pattern in church history. It is one reason so many Christians find it a discouraging study. Unrealistic expectations drive such discouragement.

Historical tactical analysis should never foment what I have often heard termed "a critical spirit," where spectators in pews watch and comment from the sidelines. It can do that, if misused. Rather, it is designed to play its small part as an organ in the body of Christ; a salt to provoke a thirst for something our generation is dreadfully in need of—historical perspective that contributes to healthy Bible application in the face of unfolding events.

I hope Jesus returns sometime before I finish typing this sentence. If He does not come quite that quickly, we need to give thought to some things that Americans have never needed to consider before. *Have we reached the same place as the Prophet Jeremiah – where we can no longer be both "prophets" and patriots, as Christians; but must choose one over the other?*

What does it mean to be "salt of the earth"? Is it just about being politically involved? It certainly includes that, and shame on any Christian who has not voted as an American. Still, I'm asking if it is *only* that, or even *mainly* that? What happens as the new American Dystopia engineers elections that are less and less meaningful in terms of real choices; and more and more an entertainment ritual to give people an illusion of political liberty? Where do we invest our talents best to win hearts and minds in a world where people shut off their minds and let their hearts grow cold? Will our investment show the large-scale returns that we in American Evangelicalism often seem used to? I don't have the answers to any of these questions, but I know answers exist. They are worth seeking, even at this late date. Should we not pray that God rewarm hearts in a manner that jump-starts minds?

God bless you, the reader, and thank you for your kind attention and patience. I pray this work was useful to you in whatever ministry or vocation of life God places you in.

K.G. Powderly Jr.

# More Than a Glossary

***agape*** **–** The Greek word translated *love* or *charity* in 1 Corinthians 13, which describes and defines it as an unselfish love that loves even when it hurts the self. Often characterized as *God's unique form of love*, because that is the love shown by Christ in dying for us on the cross. However, 1 John warns us not to *agape* the world or the things of the world, which implies that it is possible to practice *agape* love in the wrong way. Loving without concern for oneself is probably the best definition of *agape*. Christ unselfishly died for us without concern for himself. An addict shows no concern for the consequences to self by giving himself over to the thing that he is addicted to, even though he knows it will destroy him. Christ exemplifies proper *agape* love, the addict, an improper form of it.

***Agnosticism*** **–** The idea that it is impossible to know if there is a God or not. As a philosophy, it is a generation down the road from Deism, which assumes the existence of a creator but says we cannot know him or anything about him, except by inference from nature. Agnosticism does not absolutely deny the existence of God but it places him in the realm of the unknowable and assumes that God is irrelevant to any study about things that take place in the real world. The word comes from the negative of the Greek word for *knowledge – gnosis,* which uses the prefix 'a' to form the opposite of that meaning – *no knowledge* – in this case no knowledge of God. See ***Deism***, ***Gnostic*** and ***Gnosticism***.

***alchemy*** **–** A medieval philosophy of magic that centered on theories of how to transform base metals into gold, and how to mix substances in such a way as to produce the *panacea,* which would cure all diseases, and the elixir of youth that would grant physical immortality. Alchemy concerned itself with any transformation of substances for magical purposes. People believed that eventually the study of alchemy would produce the ultimate cure for all problems. Ironically, medieval alchemists were among the forerunners of modern scientists, except most scientists no longer believe in the alchemist's dream. *Popular science* or *Scientism,* however, still buys into a version of the alchemist's dream, except it has replaced *alchemy* with *science*. It is the idea that science will solve all the basic problems of the human condition. Alchemy first appeared in a Christian guise through the doctrine of Transubstantiation; the idea that a special priestly power is needed to *transform* the *substance* of common wafers and wine into the grace sustaining body and blood of Christ. See ***Transubstantiation***.

***allegorism*** **–** A tendency to lean primarily on allegory as a literary device, or as an interpretive tool for a body of literature, whether that body of literature resembles allegory or not.

***allegory*** **–** A symbolic performance or story where words and names represent other deeper truths than their literal and normal definitions. A good example of allegory in Scripture is where Paul uses the story of Hagar and Ishmael to represent the physical attempt to be saved by keeping the Law versus Isaac, who represented the children of promise that walk in the Spirit. See Galatians 4:22-31

***Anabaptists*** **–** Often considered as another name for the Radical Reformers of the 1500s or as the largest movement among those reformers. Their primary belief was that baptism should come only after a person had believed and converted to the Christian faith as a conscious educated choice. They correctly rejected infant baptism as unbiblical, and were given the misnomer of Anabaptist (re-baptizer) because the Catholic Church and the mainstream reformers practiced infant baptism as a European cultural institution of the Christian Era. The Anabaptists were biblically sound on many issues, but often overly *sectarian* and unrealistic in their approach to civil government. They did not believe Christians should serve in government or the military—which would have limited the extension of Jesus' teaching that we should be the "salt of the earth" by restricting genuine biblical influence from Christians in military and government circles against corruption.

***anathema*** **–** The Greek word for *accursed*. Paul the Apostle uttered an *anathema* against those who would teach a different gospel from that of the Apostles. Such strong language implies there is much at stake in having a biblically correct understanding of the gospel message. This is true even though, ultimately, Christ's work, not our human ability to understand it, saves us. According to Romans, the gospel is **"the power of God that leads to salvation for those who believe."** A false gospel is a set of bad directions on how to be saved from eternal damnation—the natural conclusion of human life in a fallen state. Giving somebody a false roadmap to salvation is like prescribing a slow-acting poison to a sick person under the guise of offering a cure. Later in church history, bishops and popes used the term *anathema* increasingly against people for less essential and even abusive purposes, even as a curse on those who seemed to threaten the papal religious and political power base. One must carefully consider the motives of people who used this term in history wherever it appears.

***antichrist*** **–** Any spirit, teaching, influence, person, or philosophy that offers a substitute for Christ as a means to salvation or tries to stand in the place of Christ in the life of the church. Christians use this term most commonly to describe the Antichrist of the last days, but not to the exclusion of other "antichrists" throughout history.

***Antinomian*** **–** Literally, "against law." A form of early Gnosticism known for being against any law or moral regulation in the church. *Antinomians* had a distorted view of Paul's teachings on justification by faith alone in that they believed intellectual assent to the gospel was all that was required for salvation, and that it did not matter what people did outwardly with that knowledge. See ***Gnostic*** and ***Gnosticism***.

***anti-pope*** **–** A false claimant to the Roman Papacy or one declared false for political or religious convenience, after the fact.

***antithesis*** **–** The opposite statement of any *thesis*. If Jesus made the *thesis* statement that **"no man comes to the Father but by Me,"** then the *antithesis* of that would be the idea that there are other ways to the Father besides Jesus. See ***thesis***.

***Apocrypha*** **–** Usually understood as the books added to the Roman Catholic Bible during the Council of Trent. The Apocrypha consists of the books of *1 Esdras, 2 Esdras, Tobit, Judith*, an addition to *Esther* (Vulgate Esther 10:4 – 16:24), *Wisdom, Ecclesiasticus* (also known as *Sirach*), *Baruch* and the *Epistle of Jeremy* or *"Jeremiah"* (in Geneva Bible—all part of Vulgate *Baruch*), *Song of the Three Children* (Vulgate Daniel 3:24–90), *Song of Susanna* (Vulgate Daniel 13), *Bel and the Dragon* (Vulgate Daniel 14), *Prayer of Manasses* (follows 2 Chronicles in Geneva Bible), *1 Maccabees, and 2 Maccabees*. In a general sense, the word *apocrypha* can also refer to any period writing where the Divine inspiration is questionable, but which is not heretical in nature.

***apologist*** **–** One who forms a reasoned intellectual defense for a religion, belief system, ideology, or philosophy. In the Christian sense, an apologist systematically defends the faith through sound intellectual and spiritual methods much as a defense lawyer defends a client.

***apostolic succession*** **–** In general, the effort to trace a bishop's office back through history, man-to-man, to one of the Apostles. Originally used as a sort of spiritual pedigree for Christian teachers in the early centuries, it eventually developed into an elaborate formal system that focused on the religious politics of official succession, while virtually ignoring whether potential ecclesiastical candidates had lifestyles that were apostolic in character. The

Roman Catholic claim that the Pope is the direct successor of Peter is the most well known example, though Eastern Orthodoxy also has equal historic claims under this kind of system.

***archetype*** **–** A term borrowed from the race memory psychology of Karl Jung that is useful in a more general way, even to those who reject Jung's theories and philosophy (as I do). An *archetype* is an original model of an idea, image, or cultural theme that keeps popping up in different ways throughout history. It is like a prototype for a trend or pattern in human thought or culture. *Archetypes* often appear in Bible prophecy—*Jezebel* for the false prophetess in the church of Thyatira, in Revelation 3, for example, or the *dragon* for demonic forms of evil. Many common *archetype* images trace back into prehistory, and seem embedded in all human cultures. Jung observed this, though he developed many unbiblical theories about the true nature of such *archetype* themes and images, which denied their origins in man's broken relationship with God. The best explanations for them tie in with man's broken relationship with God, and the Genesis account of the origins of evil in human society.

***ascetic*** **–** Any ideology or person that believes physical pleasures are inherently evil in any circumstance. An ascetic person takes the idea of self-denial to bizarre and unbiblical extremes that reject legitimate God-ordained pleasures and natural desires, like married sex, and enjoying the fruit of one's labor. While Christians must **"deny ourselves, pick up the cross and follow"** Jesus, Colossians 2:16-23 warns against worshipping our own will power or getting sucked in to the idea that certain diets, or refraining from marriage, will contribute to our salvation or spirituality. While we should not live for eating or for sexual appetites, the Bible teaches a balanced worldview, where there is a place for the physical. Asceticism entered Christianity from the Greek pagan worldview, which had no effective way to balance the spiritual with the physical. See ***Docetic*** and ***Semi-Docetic***.

***Assumption of Mary*** and ***Immaculate Conception of Mary*****–** The Roman Catholic teachings that God took Mary bodily into heaven, and that she was conceived by the Spirit, as Jesus was.

***Baptismal Regeneration*** **–** The teaching that the ritual of baptism triggers spiritual regeneration, salvation, and power from the Holy Spirit. One must introduce needless complexity into theology to sustain this belief, since the Bible depicts people saved without baptism, like the thief on the cross. Scripture also shows power from the Holy Spirit coming upon believers before baptism, as in Acts 10, where Cornelius' household received the Spirit before being water baptized. Paul's epistles repeatedly say that salvation comes through believing the gospel message, not through being water baptized. Baptism should follow conversion, as an act of obedience to Christ.

***bishop*** **–** Originally the primary teaching elder of a 1st century local church, similar to a modern church pastor. From the Greek *episkopos*, which means *overseer*, and from which we get the words *Episcopal* and *Episcopalian*. Eventually, the term came to refer to a high-ranking church officer that had oversight over many churches in either a large metropolitan area or region called a *diocese*.

***born again*** **–** A common term for Christian spiritual rebirth or conversion, originating in John 3:3, where Jesus told the sincerely searching Jewish religious leader Nicodemus that he had to be born again in order to see the kingdom of God. People often use this term today in figures of speech that have little or nothing to do with its original meaning. People use it legitimately in Christian circles as another term for eternal salvation, spiritual regeneration, or the point at which one believes the gospel for the first time, and invites Jesus to become Lord of one's life.

***bull*** **–** An official document issued by the Roman Pope and closed with a seal called a *bulla*.

***Byzantine*** **–** Anything having to do with the Eastern Roman Empire, after Constantine made Byzantium his main capitol, and changed its name to Constantinople (modern Istanbul, Turkey), can be called *Byzantine*. Art from the Eastern Empire after Constantine's time is called *Byzantine* art. The word is also an adjective describing any complex, compartmentalized, and corrupt government or religious system. For a time, the Eastern Orthodox Church merged so much with the imperial state that it took on its penchant for elaborate political intrigues.

***Canon*** **–** The official list of inspired books in either the Old or New Testament. A *canon* is also a rule or list of laws in a given church system. In medieval times, it was also a term for a church legal scholar.

***Catastrophism*** – The scientific belief that most of the fossil record is explained better by brief and intense catastrophes, rather than by the gradual processes that are the norm today.

***Catholic*** **–** Originally a term for the *universal* church; later, a term for Orthodox churches, and later still, a term for the more exclusive Roman Catholic Church.

***cause and effect*** **–** The idea that everything happens for a reason, but more specifically, the formula that causes lead to effects, and effects always have a cause. The mechanics of cause and effect was a basic part of Tomas Aquinas' argument for the existence of God as the First Cause. It later became a leading premise that led to experimental science as a method. One of the main implications of this idea is that a cause is always greater than its effect, which means that nature needs a cause greater than it is, and therefore could not be eternal or spontaneously generate itself.

***Cessationist*** **–** A Christian who believes that overtly supernatural spiritual gifts ceased with the writing of the New Testament, sometime around the end of the 1st century.

***Chilaism*** **–** An old version of Pre-Millennialism often put down by the theologians of Saint Augustine's era (late 4th to 5th century AD) as a heresy, but which actually had a fairly straightforward understanding of the biblical teaching on the Millennium found in Revelation 20. The reason many theologians of Augustine's era had problems with it was Greek faith-assumptions and philosophy had unduly affected their own thinking. See ***Pre-Millennialism***.

***Christendom*** **–** A combination of the words *Christianity* and *kingdom* that describes the model of church and state in medieval society, which started with Charlemagne, and drew its pattern from the Roman church-state of Constantine and Justinian. *Christendom* was the system of state sponsored churches in both the East and West. As such, the meaning of the word slowly morphed into another term for the collective Christian denominations and sects of the globe, but that is not its precise historical definition.

***Christian Humanist*** **–** Not to be confused with today's "Secular Humanists," the Christian Humanists were originally believers who studied human issues like art, science, and ancient languages to try to build from a Christian theology what eventually was called "the humanities" in education circles. They paralleled the Renaissance Humanists in their interest in art, history, and culture, but did so usually from a biblically sound intellectual base. Christian Humanists like Reuchlin and Erasmus were the forerunners of Reformers like Luther, Melanchthon, and Zwingli; though eventually Roman Catholicism also embraced Christian Humanist ideas, and adapted them to their own ends, through the work of Ignatius Loyola and his Jesuit Order.

***Christology*** **–** The study of the nature of Christ.

***Church Canon*** **–** The volumes of Roman Catholic Church law; also a term (in lower case letters) for a medieval scholar, expert on that law—for example, Peter Abelard.

***closed system*** – Either a natural or artificial system that cannot be disturbed or altered from forces outside of itself. The *closed system* is an almost completely theoretical idea, since science has not found any truly closed systems in nature, only those that are relatively closed. Hypothetically, we could set up an engine with its own self-contained air supply, an ability to recycle fuel and oxygen from waste, and a complex self-repair feature; seal it in a vacuum chamber, and leave it to run with no input or interruption from outside the chamber. Such a device would be a *closed system*, though it would not be an absolutely *closed system* because matter-penetrating neutrinos, electromagnetic fields, and gravity from the earth and countless other forces still affect it. Philosophers like Voltaire and Hume, and modern pop-scientists like Carl Sagan, assumed that the natural universe is a *closed system* that has no outside, with no God beyond the system greater than that system who can interfere with operations inside "the box" from outside. See ***open system***, ***Naturalism***, ***Rationalism***, and ***Materialism***.

***College of Cardinals*** – The church rank of *Cardinal* began to develop among the bishops of churches, mainly in the Papal States, late in the 1st Millennium, when it became increasingly clear that the system of emperors, kings, and dukes selecting bishops and popes was detrimental to the church. (See ***lay investiture***.) When the Cluny educated reformer, Bruno of Toul became Pope Leo IX in 1049, he empowered the *College of Cardinals* into a system for churchmen to elect popes and other high ecclesiastic officers. There are 3 ranks of Cardinals, the most common being Cardinal Archbishops and bishops. Less common are Cardinal Priests, and Monsignors. Deacons of the local Church of Rome, in the Vatican, are Cardinal Deacons, and often act as the Pope's immediate advisors.

***Communism*** – That form of extreme Socialism that believes total revolution and a "dictatorship of the proletariat (or worker)" is essential to humanity's further evolutionary development, which is seen only in terms of economic class struggle. See ***Socialism***.

***Confessors*** – Those Christians who suffered persecution and torture short of death during the 3 Universal Persecutions, in the middle 3rd and early 4th centuries; can also be applied to such believers from earlier local persecutions. People eventually believed that Confessors had power from God to absolve sins. The Roman Catholic Sacrament of Penance developed from this belief.

***Congregational*** – Describes both a range of denominations, and a generic church leadership system, where the congregation elects its pastor and elders. This model arose mainly during the Colonial Era in what was to become the eastern United States. It is largely a reflection of part of the developing American political philosophy, expressed in Christian terms. The strength in a congregational system is that gifted Christians in the congregation may potentially have more freedom to use their gifts, though this is not necessarily the case very often. The weakness is that the pastor and even the elders can be so politically beholden to powerful congregation members that they are not free to follow God's leading, and teach the word, if enough vocal members of the congregation oppose them. There are no biblical examples of congregational leadership in the New Testament, and no compelling biblical case can be made for it, though several can be made against it. See ***Presbyterian*** and ***Episcopalian***.

***Continualist*** – Any Christian who believes that overtly supernatural spiritual gifts like prophecy, miracles, healings, and tongues still continue in some form today, and will continue to do so until the resurrection of believers at the end of the age. See ***Cessationist***.

***counter-culture*** – A culture created by a significantly sized minority group that has become alienated by the practices and policies of the mainstream culture, and offers an alternative life-style or worldview. Originally used to describe alienated young people in the 1960s, but increasingly applicable to biblical Christians who have been alienated from mainstream Western culture by growing immorality in schools, government, entertainment, and the workplace. *Counter-cultures* are different from sub-cultures in that they offer a dynamic alternative to the mainstream, as distinct from just being in a social and intellectual ghetto.

***Counter-Reformation*** – A movement in the Roman Catholic Church of the late 16th and early 17th centuries that tried to reform the clergy of gross moral corruption and administrative abuses. It came in response to the Protestant Reformation as a force that attempted to "clean Rome's house" from the inside, while it continued to suppress the Protestant reformers outside. Though it succeeded in restoring some ethical vigor to Roman Catholic leaders, it did not address the strong probability of doctrinal corruption in a religious environment that had so long fostered moral and administrative abuse. It assumed that God would miraculously prevent the Roman Church from falling doctrinally as it had fallen morally, philosophically, and administratively. Consequently, Protestants usually feel that the Counter-Reformation, while improving some conditions, did not go far enough to make returning to Rome a spiritually and biblically feasible option for Reformation-based believers.

***creed*** – A formal statement of the essential articles of the Christian faith, such as the Apostle's Creed and the Nicene Creed. Creeds were often a quick formalized way for people to summarize their core beliefs at early church councils that had to explore the implications of Christian essentials like the deity and humanity of Christ or the nature of the Holy Spirit. They eventually became an integral part of Roman Catholic, Eastern Orthodox, and many Protestant religious services.

***deacons*** – Originally a group of 7 servants in the Book of Acts appointed to look after the practical ministries of the church like caring for widows, orphans and the sick. The office of deacon eventually evolved into a powerful position from which metropolitan churches usually chose their bishop candidates. In modern times, the office of deacon has many forms, some resembling the political powerhouse model, and others the servant ministry worker. Certainly, the latter is the proper biblical pattern.

***definitive (definition)*** and ***connotative (connotation) meaning*** – Word meanings are a mixture of *definition* and *connotation*. *Definition* (sometimes called *denotative* meaning) is like a dictionary definition. *Connotation* is the mood or emotion evoked by the word, which can be positive or negative. Many words mean the same thing in terms of definition, but have differing connotations.

***Deism*** – A belief system that claims to build only upon reason, which accepts the existence of God as creator by deduction from evidence for design found in nature. Because the world of human religion is so chaotic however, *deists* assume that God must have abandoned His creation to run on its own, with no revelatory guidance to humanity. While this may sound reasonable to many people, there are some unseen ideas built in to this assumption that are not so reasonable. It presumes, by faith, that the chaos in human religion is the result of no genuine divine revelation, rather than a byproduct of the universally observed human tendency toward self-protection, self-glorification, arrogance, and other sins. It assumes that "reasonable people" have such an immunity to these qualities that they would universally be capable of doing what is right with such a divine revelation, were they to encounter one. The naiveté involved in these assumptions about humanity is staggering. Deism is not a formal religion that has churches or sects, but rather a way of approaching the idea of God, which came into vogue during the 1700s in intellectual circles both religious and secular.

***demiurge*** – Derived from the Greek word for *craftsman*, it became a popular Gnostic conception of God. It was usually associated with the original Being that created several lesser gods or a series of emanations, one of which eventually co-mingled with pre-existing formless matter to create the material universe. Since the Gnostics envisioned a creator who created other lesser creators that then made the cosmos, the *demiurge* was a term sometimes used for these lesser creators or emanations as well. Each major Gnostic teacher had his or her own peculiar version of how creation happened. See also ***emanation*, *Gnosticism*** and ***Gnostic***.

***denomination*** and ***denominational*** – A *denomination* is a Christian religious system centered on a unique doctrinal and/or church leadership philosophy that falls within the scope of general biblical orthodoxy. I have followed several historical sources that use this term in a more specific sense than commonly used by current American culture. The adjective *denominational* usually refers to Reformation-based church systems that do not see themselves exclusively as the only true Christian church. For example, Baptists do not deny the genuine biblical Christianity of Orthodox Presbyterians as a rule, and Pentecostal Holiness churches do not teach that the Assemblies of God are a false religion. Unfortunately, accepting the members of other denominations as "genuinely saved" is not always the same as treating them fairly in debates over secondary issues, where an objective and prayerful interpretation of Scripture allows for a range of perspectives. Debate is not always a bad thing when handled with an attitude of biblical love, and an equal commitment to truth and fairness, with sensitivity to the Holy Spirit. The fact that historic doctrinal debates have sometimes gotten out of hand has colored the term *denominational* negatively. Many people today assume that it automatically implies a *sectarian* or divisive church atmosphere. This negative undertone developed mostly in the last century. It has caused many independent Bible oriented churches to distance themselves from this word by calling themselves "***non-denominational***," by which they mean, "non-sectarian." Many such churches have been so successful that they have spread new fellowships across the country, and even the globe, while maintaining affiliation with each other for spiritual and practical reasons. As this situation moves into its fourth generation, many find their "non-denominational" churches have become *denominations* in everything but name; "tragic victims" of God's blessing, growth, and provision. While there are always built-in dangers to growth, there are also built-in dangers to staying small and disconnected in a culture that systematically tries to marginalize Christian belief systems. Prayerful, Bible-based, independent church leaders should not let the "fear of becoming a denomination" stop them from starting new churches and establishing a few ministry distinctives, while networking with affiliated congregations. Good Bible-based organization is not the same as departing from the Spirit.

***determinism*** – The idea that something other than a person's will is responsible for that person's behavior; that people's behavior is *determined* by something outside the person. *Determinism* most often takes the form of the materialistic assumption that some scientifically measurable process, which has nothing to do with the soul and the spirit, pre-determines human behavior and choice. Academics have proposed various processes, and mixtures of processes, but they usually boil down to two main categories; chemical processes or environmental ones, or "nature versus nurture." A *chemical determinist* believes that people act as they do only because of chemicals in their brains. There is some truth to this—various glands bio-chemically generate chemicals that effect our emotions, and the process of thinking involves neurons that fire off chemical messages to the brain, which is itself a complex web of specialized neuron cells. A major form of chemical determinism is *genetic determinism*; the idea that our genes so heavily affect our development, that even our choices and lifestyles are as predetermined as our eye color. This form of *Determinism* is popular in the Gay Movement, though every attempt to find a "Gay gene" has quickly failed scientific peer review (when other, more objective scientists try to reproduce experimental results under the same conditions). There is a sense however, in which what Ephesians 2 calls, **"the desires of the flesh and of the mind"** are bound up with chemical processes in the body, some of which may involve genetic inputs. Chemical and *genetic determinism* however, (by faith) deny any spiritual element, which is more than emotion, will, and intellect. The presence of chemical processes at work in our thinking and feeling does not prove or imply that what makes us human and spiritual is closed off to all but chemical processes—or environmental ones. That would be a *closed system*, and human beings are anything but closed systems. *Environmental determinism* gave birth to the idea that our ethnic or family environment determines who we are, and how we act; and that nothing outside the system should interfere. *Economic environmental determinism* spawned the disastrous social manipulations of Marxism, and the idea that poverty always leads to crime (it didn't so as much in the Great Depression, when most poor people still operated by a basically Christian moral code). Of course, the environment people grow up in weighs down the choices they make in certain directions. Conditioning can horrifically reinforce behavior, and atrophy our willpower to choose in specified directions. For example, sexually abused children grow up more often to become sexual predators of children than do those raised in a healthy family environment; *more often*, but not always, and *not even most of the time*. Choice can still override extreme environmental and chemical predisposition, *as long as people believe that real choice is possible*. A Christian worldview believes that real choice is possible, and that God will strengthen us in our faith to make right choices along a growth curve. *A worldview colored by determinism denies the possibility of real choice*. It looks only toward cultural, genetic, or bio-chemical, and now, sexual "orientation." Yet anything called an *orientation* is descriptive, not causal. It describes a visible effect on behavior, not its cause. Most academics today believe in a mixture of chemical and environmental determinism, but this still arbitrarily leaves out the spiritual factor, and the real human ability to choose against one's own inclinations. This factor is at the root of the current social inability to deal with juvenile delinquency and violence. The scientific facts do not produce deterministic theories. Materialistic determinism is assumed by faith, sometimes consciously, but most often by accepting a system of reason that has that assumption built into it. The assumption of Materialism then exerts control over data interpretation before the data is gathered. A form of *spiritual determinism* also exists in extreme forms of Calvinism, which emphasize the sovereignty of God to the point of denying a human ability to exercise real choice.

***Diatessaron*** – The first known harmony of the 4 Gospels, arranged by Tatian.

***diet*** – Not an eating regimen, but a legislative body similar to a congress or parliament.

***Diocese*** – The region of a bishop's "see" or oversight comprised of many parishes, or local churches. In highly populated areas, several diocese came together under an *archdiocese*, which an archbishop supervised.

***Docetic*** and ***Docetism*** – In the central sense; the teaching that Christ never came in a physical form or never had a real human body, but only the appearance or apparition of one. The word *docetic* comes from the Greek *dokei*, which means *in the appearance of*. As one of the earliest errors to show up in the church, John the Apostle warned against it in 1 John 4:2-3. The first known teacher of this heresy was Cerinthus, a student of Philo at Alexandria. (See Chapter 3) At its essence, *Docetism* takes Greek worldview assumptions about the alleged inherently evil nature of physical matter, and expresses them in Jewish and Christian words. In this view, a holy God could not create a material reality; and so creation came through the agency of secondary beings, often called *emanations*. *Docetism* was the most effective and lasting form of Gnostic teaching because it usually encouraged ascetic values that sometimes superficially resembled a Christian denial of self. See ***ascetic, Gnostic, emanation,*** and ***demiurge***.

***Doctrine of Abrogation*** – The Islamic doctrine on divine inspiration that teaches Mohammed's later sayings in the Qur'an and Hadiths have more weight than his earlier ones. Since the Qur'an (also spelled *Koran*) is not written in chronological order—even within its *sura* /chapter divisions—Islamic religious leaders study not only the verses, but the historic traditions that reveal what period of Mohammed's life each verse was written in. Abrogation frequently goes so far as to cancel out the teaching of an earlier verse when a later verse contradicts it. Islam freely admits there are many such contradictions, which frequently makes for an overly convenient sense of divine ethics. Unfortunately, many of Mohammed's earlier verses are idealistic, while his later ones are more hostile and warlike.

***Doctrine of Justification by Faith*** – The biblical, Augustinian, and Reformation based teaching that man is justified before God because of faith in the shed blood of Christ as sufficient to pay for sin, and not by good human works or by religious ceremonies. It also rejects the idea that justification before God comes by any combination of faith, works, and sacramental ritual.

***Doctrine of Perfectionism*** – The early 19th century American religious teaching that Christians can achieve sinless perfection on earth, in this life, through rigorous spiritual discipline. Perfectionism assumed that all commands of God must be do-able by human choice and effort. It arose as the understanding and acceptance of Original Sin and the Curse came under fire by some 2nd Great Awakening revivalists, like Charles Grandison Finney, and John Humphrey Noyes. Though John Wesley and Francis Asbury had used the term *perfectionism*, they had emphasized it as process-driven, enabled by Justification by grace through faith. They did not teach that believers completed the process in this life. Wesley and Asbury, who knew each other, gave a definition of *perfectionism* closer to what we might call *sanctification*, with perhaps a few subtle distinctions. Finney ran roughshod over the intellectual safeguards in Wesley's writings, and Noyes just plain gave Perfectionism a bad name. We use the term today to describe a pathological behavior that demands the impossible from self and others.

***Doctrine of Purgatory*** – The Roman Catholic teaching that temporal punishment for post-conversion sins, which are not worked off by penance on earth, must be purged in a kind of temporary hell-like fire, before the believer can go to eternal heaven.

***Doctrine of the Fall*** – Often called ***Original Sin***, the Fall is the biblical teaching that man has had a sinful nature ever since Adam chose freely to sin in Eden. The entire human race inherited Adam's acquired deficiency not genetically, but through God's Curse on Creation in the wake of the Fall. (Most of the curses in Gen. 3 are material changes.) Human nature became sinful by the Fall, not because God created the first man and woman that way. The *Doctrine of the Fall* also includes the teaching that God cursed nature to reflect the new spiritual condition of its fallen caretakers. (Gen. 3:17-19) He did not do this out of spite, but to protect the humans from eternal life in a sinful state, which would amount to hell and a nature of infinitely growing malice, like that of Satan. (Gen. 3:22-24) The Curse involved both environmental and biochemical changes to matter itself, by logical implication, because a Nature that fully reflected God's goodness would also reflect His holiness, making it impossible for fallen humans to survive there. Erosion, disease, death, and decay entered the natural world because of man's sin, though not often in proportion to each individual's sin. Rain falls equally on the relatively just and unjust. As fallen humanity retains a marred image of God, and some ability to do right things, fallen nature retains some of the grandeur and design from God's handiwork. In terms of his basic nature however, man is totally depraved. This does not mean that fallen people cannot really desire to do good, or to do things that, when viewed in isolation, are right as opposed to wrong. It means that sin has infected every aspect of the human condition; that even the right things man manages to do in his fallen state eventually turn to futility and corruption. This happens through self-centered motives and the slow distortion of the conscience that pride always exerts to varying degrees. While God still accomplishes His long-term will even in a fallen world, by virtue of His redemptive plan, events and processes in Nature no longer fully reflect God's good character; but the futility and mixed drives of the human psyche. (Rom. 8:20-23) Nature is both kind and cruel; just like humanity. Sometimes even the kindness of man and Nature are really a more subtle form of cruelty. At other times, often (but not always) where God's redemptive plan is most evident, the face of human or natural cruelty inspires acts of great kindness and courage. There are sunny days at the beach and catastrophic upheavals that kill on a grand scale, and pollute the environment even more than humanity often does. Nature has fuzzy mother bears nurturing cute bear cubs, and spider wasps that lay their eggs down the throat of living ground spiders so their larvae can eat their way out of the living host like the creature in the movie *Alien* (a behavioral adaptation). Because of the Fall, we can no longer consistently discern God's personal character from Nature; only his power, eternal attributes, and intelligent design abilities. (Rom. 1:19-23) Were we to assume that nature *as it is now* reflects God's character, we could only draw the logical conclusion that God is an amoral trickster, who tantalizes us one minute with profound beauty, and crushes us the next with cruel agonies that torment the relatively just and wicked alike. To know God's character, we must look to His word. In it, we find that Jesus is the core of God's redemptive plan, which can only be fully appreciated when we understand the deep and terrible scope of the Fall, in both ourselves and the natural universe. Though we can receive the gift of salvation without such an understanding, the sense of relevance that redemption has to our situation in history, and to our personal spiritual growth, requires a full understanding. If we don't know how Nature and humanity are broken, we will not be able to participate as efficiently in God's redemptive plan that promises restoration. See Genesis Ch. 3 and Romans Chs. 1-8.

***Doctrine of the Remnant*** – The observation that usually only a small remnant of people truly come to God, or remain faithful to Him, in any given historic situation. Jesus made this observation when he said, **"Enter by the narrow gate; for the gate is wide, and the way is broad that leads to destruction, and many are those who enter by it. For the gate is small, and the way is narrow that leads to life, and few are those who find it."** (Matt. 7:13-14 NAS)

***Doctrine of the Trinity*** – The teaching that God consists of the Father, the Son, and the Holy Spirit, who exist as distinct persons that share the single Divine nature called the Godhead. Early Church Fathers arrived at this teaching because a variety of Bible passages each called the Father, Jesus, and the Holy Spirit "God" in various ways, while other passages showed the Father speaking from heaven to Jesus, and the disciples, on the earth. In Acts 5, Ananias and Saphira lied to the Peter. The Apostle asked the couple why they had lied to the Holy Spirit, and said that in doing this they were lying not to men but to God. This equated the Holy Spirit with God. While the Bible does not contain the word *Trinity*, the only rational way to understand what it teaches on the nature of God, without ignoring or selectively downplaying some of the relevant passages on the subject, is that somehow God is one and yet consists of three persons. This is not a violation of Hebrew Monotheism as is often claimed. When the Old Testament says that the Lord God is "one," it uses the same word found in Genesis 2, where it says that a man and his wife are "one flesh." Since married couples are not surgically grafted on to each other, and retain their individual personhood, it is not a violation of God's oneness to think in terms of His existence as 3 persons.

***dominion*** – In the late medieval sense, *dominion* is what we today would call *authority*. It implies the lawful right to manage a certain domain. Human authority derives from God both directly and indirectly, according to the Bible. Exactly how this authority goes from God to His human vassals is a subject that is not always so clear, though the Bible does give principles, commands, and guidelines that we can practically apply.

***Donatism*** **–** The sect that followed a bishop, Donatus, in the 4th century, which believed Catholic churches had been too lenient on the lapsed. Donatists refused to recognize the ordination of church leaders by bishops that had surrendered even old and tattered copies of the Scriptures for burning by Roman authorities that persecuted the church. The Donatist church was also extremely superstitious about the relics and preserved body parts of the martyrs. They were the cult of the martyrs taken to extremes.

***dualistic*** and ***dualism*** **–** Defined philosophically as the assumption that reality has two basic components, usually *soul* and *matter*. In theology, it is often defined as the belief that the universe is ruled by two opposite and basically equal forces of good and evil (not really the biblical view, since Satan is a created being nowhere near God's equal). While the words *dualism* and *dualistic* have many applications, I used them mainly in a modern philosophic application; where *reason* is associated with *knowledge of material things*; and *spirit* or *soul* implies *spiritual experiences and values*. (I realize there is a biblical difference between the soul and spirit, but most philosophies tend to blur the two.) My use of these terms describe a view where the two compartments of *reason* and *spiritual values* are so totally separated that they rarely interact with each other in any meaningful sense. This unconsciously turns a convenient distinction of categories into a fragmented concept of reality. When this kind of view takes a christianized form, it can manifest in several ways, and to varying degrees. One way is as a perceived on-going conflict between Bible-based reason and the leading of the Holy Spirit; things that should not be in true conflict, if the God of the Bible is objectively real. Another completely different manifestation is when believers have extremely vivid internal faith experiences that make them feel positive and spiritual; but do not touch the practicalities of how they behave in the external world toward their fellow man. An example of this is the current over-emphasis of individual internal relationship with God *at the expense of* Christian community in an external local church. We need an individual personal relationship with God, but we can't de-emphasize the externals of Christian living in order to make space for more emphasis on the personal relationship. In medieval times, "the church" had set itself up as the sovereign arbiter of salvation; to the point where the biblical truth was lost that trusting the gospel message about Christ's work saves individuals, and enables them to have a personal relationship with God. Today the pendulum has swung so far in the opposite direction that even many believers view the church as irrelevant to salvation, and the individual Christian life. A third possible example of existential dualism in Christian form is the pseudo-spiritual impression that the intellectual, artistic, and scientific disciplines have no significant value as Christian callings simply because they are not necessary for individual salvation. This last example sees a functional disconnect between the work of God in election, and the work of man in providing a church culture that can deal biblically with questions across a whole spectrum of real world issues. It places too high a wall between the secular and spiritual in a culture where the secular is already gobbling up areas of social existence where biblical ideas used to be welcomed. While Christians must prioritize the spread of the gospel in church ministry; that is not the same as declaring the so-called "secular" callings "unimportant" or without spiritual value in the church. We do not win Souls in a cultural vacuum, where only God, the sinner, and the Bible exist. See ***Existentialism*** and ***existential***.

***dystopia*** **–** A dysfunctional utopia—a society that thinks it has found the perfect answers to human problems, but lives in denial of its own dysfunctional nature; also a form of modern fiction set in such societies (for example, *Brave New World*, *1984*, and *The Hunger Games*). In historic reality, all attempts at utopia have produced only dystopia—like the one Americans currently live in. See ***utopia*** and ***Doctrine of the Fall***.

***Ebionites*** – An early cult that arose among the Jewish Church that believed Messiah was only a man, and Gentiles must proselytize into Judaism before they can be saved. Ebionites considered the Apostle Paul a heretic, and accepted only the writings of Peter, John, Matthew, James, and Jude.

***ecumenical*** – That which pertains to the whole church world-wide. It is often used as another term for *universal* or *catholic* (in its original sense), as in the first 7 *ecumenical* councils. In the modern sense, it describes a movement that is trying to bring all branches of Christianity back together either organizationally or else simply in a spirit of cooperation.

***elders*** – See ***presbyters***.

***emanation*** – A Gnostic term for a secondary god or angelic being that either had sexual union with pre-existing formless matter to create the physical world or grew far enough away from the original proto-god to think that creating a material world would be a good idea. See ***Gnosticism*** and ***demiurge***.

***Empiricism*** – The assumption that we can know things only by direct sensory experience and the epistemology build on that assumption. See ***epistemology***.

***Enlightenment, the*** – That period in the history of Western thought and culture that followed the 17th century Religious Wars, and sought to impose a new form of ideologically Epicurean Materialism onto academics to replace Judeo-Christian thought and influence. Not to be confused with the rise of science, which preceded it—something present-day ***Modernist***, ***Positivist***, and ***Postmodernist*** ideologues seek to do. See the above words.

***Epicureanism*** and ***Epicureans*** – A Greek philosophy started by Epicurus, which sought escape from pain and emotional disturbance. Generations later, Epicureanism fell into Hedonism; the assumption that if people are helplessly mired in the material world, then fighting material pleasures is useless. Epicurus also rejected the idea that the gods interact with men. He was the forerunner of modern Materialism in both its philosophical and practical forms.

***Episcopalian*** and ***episcopal*** – Normally considered a church system governed by a pastor, regional bishop, national archbishop, or pope, such as the Church of England or Roman Catholicism. Some independent Bible oriented churches are *episcopalian* in their small-scale local structure. Their pastors are seen as men called by God to lead the local church, and should be free to do so within objective biblical guidelines. This is the strength of an *episcopalian* leadership system; the Spirit-anointed leader is potentially free to follow God's guidance without too many political considerations. That does not mean such potential always became actual in historic *episcopal*-based systems. The weakness of an *episcopal* system is that it is usually dependent on the spiritual and biblical integrity of the pastor or bishop. It's a fantastic church leadership model when the pastors are walking in the Spirit, and committed to teaching the word of God. It becomes a miserable tyranny if those pastors should ever divert from the leading of the Spirit and the Bible. There are many examples of both the strength and weakness of the *episcopal* leadership system in history; and a strong biblical case can be made for it as a primary church leadership model. *Episcopalian* is also the formal name of an American denomination that broke with the Church of England during the Revolutionary War; George Washington belonged to it. See ***Presbyterian*** and ***Congregational***.

***epistemology*** and ***epistemological*** – The study of the nature and origin of knowledge, and the mechanics of how people and cultures know things.

***etymology*** **–** The study of word origins, that of their components (if it's a compound word), and how their meanings have changed throughout history. Every single word of every single language has its own history. This means that the idea of a word-for-word translation is a myth even if an essentially literal translation is not. It also means that all translations, though adequate, still have their strengths and weaknesses.

***Eucharist*** – The term Eucharist comes from the Greek word, *eucharistos*, which means *thanksgiving*. It eventually developed into another term for communion, and later still into that portion of the Catholic and Orthodox Mass where communion is taken. As time passed, the word became a synonym for the communion elements of bread and wine, after the priest blessed them—though the proper word for that in Roman Catholic terminology is the *host*.

***ex cathedra*** **–** When the Pope proclaims something *"from the chair"* of Saint Peter that is supposed to be infallible. Not every papal proclamation is *ex cathedra* – actually, there has been only a small handful since this idea became Roman Catholic dogma in 1870.

***excommunication*** **–** In its biblical sense, a term for the practice of putting an unrepentantly sinning local church member out of the church, like Paul admonished the Corinthian church leaders to do in 1 Corinthian 5. Medieval church leaders later distorted *excommunication* into a political power tool, where popes could excommunicate people for virtually any reason.

***Existentialism*** and ***existential*** **–** The 19th and 20th century philosophy that centered on the individual as being isolated within an external universe that was meaningless of itself; and totally indifferent to the individual's existence. In its secular form, *Existentialism* regarded a personal God as unknowable, and human existence as unexplainable, thus making the individual person totally autonomous and responsible for creating their own ethics or religion; and then living with the consequences. It resulted in the perception that reason had little value, since reason only rambled on about an observed physical reality that was absurd and meaningless. One can only find hope, meaning, ethics, and values in *Existentialism* by making a leap outside of reason, to an arbitrary emotional experience that does not have to make sense in the external world. In *Religious Existentialism*, God is equally unknowable in terms of intellectual content or true information, but can be touched emotionally in different ways, depending on individual cultural preference. This is why the statement, *"That's true for you, but not for me,"* seems to make sense in today's culture, when used about basic ethical realities. Of course, the "sense" of this breaks down immediately when taken to its logical conclusion by a person who feels right about keying another person's car, or murdering someone because they do not share the same values. *Existentialism* does not fit reality. *Religious Existentialism* has made huge inroads into the church through many vehicles, the first of which was Neo-Orthodoxy, and the most current are a multitude of movements that emphasize ecstatic spiritual experiences over a working understanding of the mind of God in the Bible. The current worldview of ***Post-Modernism*** is functionally *existential*, though *Existentialism* as a formal philosophy has largely died out. See ***dualism*** and ***Neo-Orthodoxy***.

***extreme unction*** **–** The Roman Catholic sacrament of last rites, where priests anoint a dying Catholic with oil and pray for their soul.

***feudalism*** **–** A government or economic system composed of semi-independent land barons that owned not only the lands but the serfs or peasants that worked the lands.

***Five-point Calvinism*** **–** A formulaic distillation of what later Calvinists believed were the 5 main points taught by Calvin, memorized by the mnemonic acronym **TULIP**:

Total Depravity
Unconditional Election
Limited Atonement (also known as Particular Atonement)
Irresistible Grace

Perseverance of the Saints (also known as Once Saved Always Saved)

As many such distillations from other belief systems, including Arminian ones, most of these particulars prove to be oversimplifications on close examination. Calvinists did not develop the "5 Points" until after Arminius' time, let alone Calvin's, who was dead before Arminius.

***geocentric*** **–** An Earth-centered cosmology. The Bible often describes things from a geocentric point of view, ~~but~~ that is not the same as teaching that the earth is the center of the solar system; any more than the weatherman claims the sun orbits the earth simply because he tells us when the sun will rise locally. The Greek philosopher Aristotle taught that the earth was the center of the universe. See ***heliocentric*** and ***phenomenological language***.

***Gnostics*** and ***Gnosticism*** – An early 1st millennium belief system that took Greek and Oriental mystical assumptions about reality and expressed them in Jewish and Christian terminology. One of the basic assumptions of Gnosticism was that matter is evil and spirit is good. Because of this, Gnostics did not accept that Jesus came as a physical human or that he was physically raised from the dead, or that believers will experience a physical resurrection. They also did not believe that God directly created the material universe. See ***emanation, demiurge, Antinomian*** and ***Docetic***.

***God-breathed*** – A direct translation of the Greek word *theopneustos*, which is the term 2 Timothy 3:16 uses for the unique form of divine inspiration found in all genuine Judeo-Christian Scripture.

***God-fearers*** **–** Groups of 1st century Gentiles that had close ties to Jewish communities and believed in the God of the Jews, but for various reasons did not become circumcised Jews themselves.

***Godhead*** **–** The theological term for the Trinitarian relationship of God, as Father, Son, and Holy Spirit—one *what*, consisting of three *whos* or *persons* within the *Godhead.*

***Gothic*** – Having to do with a Germanic tribe known as the Goths, but usually a form of architecture that developed in Franko-Gothic medieval European lands during the late 1st and early 2nd Millenniums. Gothic cathedrals were characterized by tall spires and arches that seemed to soar heavenward, but often caved in because they were top-heavy.

***grassroots*** **–** A term for the common people in a given society—the workers, farmers, merchants, and craftsmen that are the backbone of any civilization; often used to describe the "average person" or the laity in the church.

***Great Schism*** **–** The word *schism* means to split or to form factions or divisions. The Great Schism refers to the division of the Roman Catholic Church between competing Popes during the 14th and 15th centuries, ending with the election of Pope Martin V at Constance.

***Great Tribulation*** – A common term for the global end-time judgments described in the Book of Revelation; synonymous to the 70th week of Daniel 9:24-27.

***Hadiths*** **–** Early Muslim commentaries and histories of the life and conquests of Mohammed; considered holy writings on par with the *Qur'an*, or perhaps second only to it.

***hagiographer*** – A medieval sacred story teller that popularized the exploits of both real and fictitious saints.

***hedonism; hedonistic*** – The effective worship of pleasure over or instead of God

***heliocentric*** **–** A cosmology with the Sun at the center of the solar system. Early heliocentric cosmologies like those of Pythagoras and the Neo-Platonism of Copernicus placed the Sun at the center of the universe.

***Hellenized*** **–** To be heavily affected by or spawned within Greek culture.

***Hermeneutics*** **–** The science of text interpretation.

***Historiography*** **–** The mechanics of how we know history.

***hyperdoulia*** and ***doulia*** **–** That form of veneration in Roman Catholic and Eastern Orthodox theology that was aimed at icons and saints but was considered technically distinct from *worship*, though the emotions and heart attitude was the same. See ***latreia***.

***Iconoclasts*** – Byzantine Christians that believed icons had become idols and advocated getting rid of them.

***Incarnation*** **–** The act of God becoming flesh in Jesus Christ—for a spiritual being to take on fleshly form.

***inductive reasoning*** and ***Inductive Bible Study*** **–** In the context of reasoning from Scripture, the inductive method draws systematic and generally applicable conclusions from the particular revelations found in the Bible. It rests mainly on the assumption that words have understandable meanings in a given historic, literary, and cultural context; and that we can discover these meanings. Because we are dealing with the word of God, it also assumes that the words of Scripture will convey applicable principles that are meaningful and authoritative in any comparable human context, even if the ancient particulars no longer exist. For example, New Testament teachings in Ephesians 6 about slaves and masters have applicability to modern employer-employee relationships even though the employee is not a slave. The most important aspect of inductive reasoning from Scripture is the emphasis on observing what is objectively recorded in the text, and letting it shape our ideas; or as Paul once put it, **"comparing Scripture with Scripture."** Another person said it this way; "The Bible is the best commentary on itself." Of course, people must use some deductive reasoning to reconstruct history, and the Bible does not exist within a closed intellectual system. People need to be at least moderately literate, and have some grasp of history to understand much of it properly. However, the inductive method allows us to draw foundational assumptions about truth and reality from Scripture with a minimum potential for reading our own desires, worldviews, and ideas into the text either accidentally or deliberately. In a more general context, inductive reasoning moves from the *particular* to the *universal*.

***indulgence*** **–** The papal practice of granting an exemption to a Catholic from temporal punishment either on earth or in purgatory for sins committed after baptism. The idea is based on the belief that the Roman Pope has the authority to manage the grace of God on earth, and has access to a vast reservoir of merit built up from the works of the saints and martyrs. During late medieval times, this concept was grossly abused; church officials would essentially sell indulgences for monetary donations. They ruthlessly fleeced believers to finance crusades and ornate building projects like Saint Peter's Basilica. The sale of indulgences was one of the main papal abuses that hastened the Reformation.

***Information Theory*** **–** A theory of information that arose from the computer revolution, and the development of software. Growing from the science of cryptology, and advanced computer theory, *Information Theory* deals with coded systems like language, binary code, and the nature of information. With the discovery that the DNA molecule conveys meaningful information at a sending and receiving end, it implies that information is a fundamental entity of reality, like matter, and energy. It demonstrates that coded information systems do not arise spontaneously by chance—they require intelligent design to convey information that means something to both the sender and receiver. People identify Information in Nature in several ways. It has distinct properties like syntax, semantics, and words, symbols, and/or sequences that are non-random, and associated with distinct meanings and instructions. The "DNA code" is a complex non-random information system;

as opposed to a crystalline lattice, which is a repetition of identical molecular structures with no information carrying properties. Evolutionists are working hard to obscure the rather obvious implications of this for philosophic reasons, but many biochemists are beginning to allow the evidence to lead them where it will; into the camps of "Intelligent Design Theory" and even Creationism. For a more detailed look at this exciting scientific frontier, I recommend the following books: *In the Beginning was Information* by Werner Gitt Ph.D., and *Darwin's Black Box: The Biochemical Challenge to Evolution* by biochemist Michael Behe.

***interdict*** – A political power tool that grew out of the medieval papal distortion of *excommunication*. An *interdict* essentially excommunicated an entire nation except for the sacraments of baptism and extreme unction. This form of political coercion was extremely effective in a society based on the Christendom model, where one had to be in communion with the church to function in just about any national or international social institution. It only lost its deterrent effect as popes abused it for centuries on end until kings and princes got frustrated to the point where the risk of eternal damnation actually seemed preferable to obscenely high church taxes and other forms of corrupt ecclesiastical power grabs.

***irreducible complexity*** – The scientific observation (first systematically defined by biochemist Michael Behe) that one-celled living systems are more intricate than major cities. They have molecular machines that work together in a complex way *impossible to simplify without destroying the cell's ability to function as a living organism*. A modified version of this exists for viruses, which require cellular host organisms to thrive anyway and could not develop and reproduce on their own without them. The implication is that life had to be intelligently created, complex in a balanced micro and macro ecosystem, from the start. Amino acids, proteins and other biochemical building blocks for life require the information coded on DNA in order to arrange into living systems. DNA needs these building blocks to exist already in living systems in order to replicate itself. Neither component could possibly arise spontaneously without the other. Both must be fully formed and functional for life to exist even for a moment. This is horrendous for anybody that is looking for a chain of evolution from molecule to virus to cell and beyond, but is exactly what Creationist and Intelligent Design theories would predict.

***Islamist*** – A political position favoring the imposition of Islam by any means necessary, as distinct from the word *Islamic*, which simply describes the Muslim religion.

***jihad*** – The Islamic concept of holy war.

***Judaizers*** – Jewish Christian forerunners of the Ebionites that tried to pressure the Apostles to make keeping the Jewish Law a requirement for salvation. See ***Ebionites***

***Just War Theory*** – A theory developed by Augustine of Hippo in City of God and other writings that described rules of engagement and conditions under which a war may justly be fought, for example national self-defense, or defending the weak. It specified that prisoners should not be abused.

***Koinae Greek*** – The common market place Greek of the 1st century, in which most of the New Testament was originally written. (Matthew may have been written in Aramaic, but was quickly translated to Greek within the Apostle's lifetime, possibly by Matthew himself.)

***laity*** – Those in the church who are not clergy. The so-called 'common people' in the pews.

***Latin Vulgate*** – An early authorized Latin Bible developed mainly from the translation of Jerome.

***latreia*** – That form of worship reserved only for God according to Roman Catholic and Eastern Orthodox theology. See ***hyperdoulia***.

***lay investiture*** **–** The practice of laity nobles and kings appointing bishops for their districts, as opposed to churchmen ordaining bishops trained for church service.

***legal-historic method*** **–** A method of knowing the past that involves recording, and harmonizing many testimonies. It is ultimately our only way to know that history even happened. This method of evidence is used in courts of law. It is based on Aristotle's Dictum that the benefit of the doubt must be given to any document or testimony that tells a history; and not the philosophy of the critic who reads the document or hears the testimony.

***Liberal Theology*** **–** At its essence, Christian Liberalism is the expression of popular 18th and 19th century materialistic Rationalism and Romanticism in Christian theological words. Once biblical history and theology was undermined in this way, just about anything could be made to seem tolerable.

***Logical Positivism*** **–** See ***Positivism***.

***Logos Theology*** **–** An early Orthodox theology developed by Justin Martyr mainly from the writings of John that emphasized Jesus as the living word of God.

***Machiavellian*** **–** An adjective used to describe a complex and manipulative political system devised to exploit people as "assets" or "resources" without thought to their humanity, and no consideration of the moral implications of such a system. The word arose from the name of Nicolo Machiavelli, whose book *The Prince* was a political manual for how to effectively manipulate henchmen and social institutions for personal and national power gain. Even Scripture (mainly in Proverbs) recognizes that legitimate political and military systems sometimes must take a buffered "Machiavellian approach" in order to get things done efficiently in a fallen world. A good general must use his soldiers as potentially expendable assets, and an effective politician must be shrewd in order to survive in a political environment even if they both reject Machiavelli's self-serving personal philosophy of "the end justifies the means." One hopes that such generals and politicians do not completely forget the humanity of their assets, and have a sound ethical compass, which is still sometimes the case in Western societies even in today's world of shrinking moral consensus. The departure of the Christian worldview as a mainstream voice in culture makes this positive buffering increasingly less likely, however. A biblical example of a Machiavellian political move was how King David arranged for the murder of Uriah the Hittite in battle to cover the fact that David had slept with Uriah's wife, and gotten her pregnant. This was not a morally acceptable application of such political theory however; it merely illustrates the term.

***machine of the cosmos*** **–** A description of the entire working universe that emphasizes the mechanics found in nature on both the microscopic and telescopic scales.

***Marcionism*** **–** An early church heresy that followed the teachings of Marcion, who believed that the God of the Old Testament and the God of Jesus were two different beings and which rejected the mainly Jewish oriented apostolic writers like James, Jude, John and Peter.

***martyr*** **–** The Christian definition of a martyr originally meant a witness to the power of Christ evidenced by a radical change of lifestyle and thinking. Later, because so many Christians died for their faith in the early centuries, the definition shifted to specify those who died for the Faith. At no time in history did Christian martyrs, as martyrs, ever call for the death of those opposed to Christianity, or murder opponents as an "act of martyrdom."

***Mass*** **–** The recognized term for Roman Catholic and Eastern Orthodox liturgical religious services.

***materialist*** and ***Materialism*** **–** The philosophic faith-assumption that only matter and the energies of its various chemical conversion processes are real and that everything, including the soul and spirit must be explained by a material process. Materialism is a faith-assumption and not a scientifically proven absolute that needs to guide science as a discipline. Because many scientists in the 19th and 20th centuries were philosophic materialists, there was a tendency for the more zealous evangelists of that philosophy to use science as an evangelistic tool, and to create the popular impression that their philosophy was an essential aspect of science. Nevertheless, those who developed the scientific method—men like Newton, Keppler, Pascal, and Francis Bacon—were not philosophic materialists, and even warned against approaching science exclusively in those terms. Science and technology advances were already moving forward on their own power, as it were, before Materialism became a dominant philosophy among scientists—so it is wrong to claim that philosophical Materialism gave science what it needed to produce remarkable technology. This definition of Materialism should not to be confused with the common use of the term today as meaning "greedy for possessions." There have been philosophical materialists in history who were also, for various reasons, extremely altruistic and generous. However, it is often true that a general culture colored by the philosophy of Materialism will tend toward an atmosphere of greed over material possessions, and neglect of spiritual and moral values.

***Mechanistic Philosophy*** or ***Mechanist*** – A philosophy of science, developed in the flow of Newtonian physics, which emphasized the machine-like nature of the universe.

***mendicant*** – A person or group that makes their living by begging or receiving religious *alms* (not to be confused with *tithes*).

***Merovingian Dynasty*** – The dynasty of Frankish chieftain, Chlodovacar or "King Clovis," who became the first Germanic chieftain to convert to Orthodox Catholic Christianity in 496 AD, named for his grandfather, Merovech. The Franks later became the main people group to meld together into those we know as the French.

***Methodological Naturalism*** – Originally the methodology of science that recognized science's limitation to knowledge concerning the natural world, as it currently operates. It morphed over time to an Ideological Naturalism, which adopted materialistic faith-assumptions, and denied the reality of anything beyond the natural. See ***Materialism*** and ***Rationalism***.

***metonymy*** – A word used in a non-literal figure of speech where that word brings to mind another more abstract concept than its literal definition. For example, when Jesus said, **"I am the *door* of the sheep"** the word *door* is a *metonymy* in a figurative expression. Jesus is communicating the abstract idea that he is the method by which humans can enter God's presence as members of God's community (symbolized by the metonymy of a flock of *sheep*).

***Millennial Kingdom*** – The 1000-year era described in Revelation 20 when Satan is bound, and Christ rules on earth from Jerusalem as king. After the Millennium, Satan is **"loosed for a short season"** before God brings final judgment and remakes the heavens and the earth, which will then be eternal.

***Minimalism*** - The view that all forms of interpretation merely read our own ideas back into the text. This form of radical text criticism somehow broke out of its stall to become a fad in everything from architecture to art. Minimalists *minimize*; they *over*simplify text criticism, and use the tools of reason to violate reason. See ***Postmodernism*** and ***Empiricism***.

***modernist*** and ***Modernism*** – A movement in Christian churches that tried to redefine faith and biblical teaching to fit with modern philosophic concepts like Materialism and Existentialism. Such forces often operated without a clear notion of the difference between scientific fact and popular science-exploiting philosophies that are heavily driven by arbitrary faith-assumptions expressed in technical language. Modernists had a great emotional attachment to reason, yet often did not employ sound reasoning skills. As such, modernists often thought they were simply following proven science that could not be logically argued against, when in fact they were responding largely to a philosophical preference. Modernism is in decline and the churches and denominations that have succumbed to it most are now facing a massive loss of membership as churchgoers increasingly embrace either a revitalized biblical worldview or pantheistic New Age occultism. The term *Modernism* can also be used in a more general way to describe the philosophic flow of the era from the 18th through early 20th centuries, when Western intellectuals had a love affair with materialistically based reason and felt that science would eventually solve all of our social problems. Most thinking people today know better. See ***Materialism***, ***Rationalism***, ***Liberal Theology***, ***determinism***, and ***Existentialism***.

***Monarchianism*** – Having to do with any teaching on the Christian God's nature that emphasizes God's oneness to the effective exclusion of the Trinity.

***Monophysite Heresy*** – The teaching developed in the 5th century that said the divine nature of God swallowed up the human nature of Jesus as "an ocean swallows a drop of honey," to combine into a unique nature of "Christ"—eventually seen as a single divine nature.

***Naturalistic Law*** – A theory of jurisprudence and law that looks to nature rather than Divine law for a primary model of human social and legal co-existence; not to be confused with Natural Law by either its legal or scientific definitions.

***Neo-Orthodoxy*** – An approach to Christian truths that embraces the assumptions of 20th century Existentialism; that Liberalism is correct in the scholarly realm, but that we can still have religious truth in an "upper-story" realm by a leap of faith apart from reason.

***Neo-Platonic*** – Describes a revived following of Plato's philosophy around the time of Saint Augustine, that was again revived in the Middle Ages, and characterized by ideas that included a sun-centered universe, and an original creation of interrelated master geometric forms for all things, from which current objects are derived.

***Nicene Creed*** – The Trinitarian creed that eventually arose out of the 1st Ecumenical Council of Nicea, which became the basis for all orthodox Christian creeds since.

***non-denominational*** – See ***denomination***.

***nuncio*** – An official papal emissary similar to an ambassador.

***objective*** – An object or idea based in something visible and outside of our own minds, will, and emotions. The Bible is an *objective* standard of truth because it is a record of Divine interaction in the external world, which we can handle, read, and obey. See ***subjective***.

***Occam's Razor*** – An elegant intellectual rule of thumb that says the simplest explanation for any given phenomenon that uses the least number of assumptions is usually correct.

***Omnipotent*** – All-powerful.

***open system*** - Either a natural or artificial system that can be disturbed, added to, subtracted from, or altered from forces outside of itself. An auto engine is an *open system* because a mechanic can replace parts, and users can add gas and oil. Isaac Newton assumed that the universe was an *open system* in the sense that God was outside of it (as well as omnipresent throughout), and could intervene in it as he saw fit. That is also the biblical view. An insertion by God of new information, energy, or matter from outside the *open system* universe would be what the Bible calls a *miracle*. Every observed natural system is an *open system*, and science has never found an absolutely closed one—only ones relatively closed. Nevertheless, currently dominant materialistic science philosophy assumes that the universe is an absolutely *closed system*, with nothing beyond. Experimental science does not prove or imply this—it is an arbitrary assumption based on ideology. A growing number of scientists are beginning to assume an open system universe again, with respect to its Designer, because materialistic assumptions have proven inadequate to explain many of the things our technology now allows us to observe directly.

***Orthodox and orthodoxy*** – These words were coined by Irenaeus in the late 2nd century to generically describe those who thought in a rationally honest and scriptural way about the things of God; and who did not allow Greek worldview assumptions to affect their view of the nature of Christ. It later became part the official title for eastern churches like the Eastern Orthodox or Russian Orthodox Church. Roman Catholicism is also an Orthodox Church in this sense because it accepts the formulations of the first 5 general church councils on the nature of Christ and the Trinity. *Orthodoxy* in its generic sense also describes Protestant biblical theology, defined as agreement with the first 5 general church councils, and a doctrine of salvation drawn directly from Paul's Epistles to the Romans and Galatians in a way that takes into account all other relevant Bible passages on the subject. Formal Orthodoxy refers to either the Eastern Orthodox or Roman Catholic Churches; indicated by the upper case *O*. General orthodoxy or biblical orthodoxy leaves the *o* in the lower case, since it refers to a way of thought rather than to a formal institution.

***Pantheism*** – The belief that all natural forces embody God, and the worship of all such forces and their assigned gods together as "God;" for example, Nature Worship, and the worship of "Mother Earth." I have actually used one of the most common forms of Pantheism as its main definition in this work because that seems to be the one gaining the most ground. This is the idea that God equals the sum of all natural forces; or that God equals Nature in its most inclusive sense, or that God is a spiritual energy that permeates nature like the Force in *Star Wars*. All of these variations on the theme of *Pantheism* depict God as impersonal and natural force-like, and not as a being who has ideas that he can express in words.

***paradigm*** – The controlling part of any worldview model. For example, evolution is a philosophic *paradigm* because academics assumed it is true in a way that controls how many scientists and educators think about other subjects that have nothing to do with biological evolution, and have no experimental validation pointing toward an evolutionary process. It has swallowed up physics, education, the arts, religion, and just about everything we think about in some way or another, despite the fact that it is failing many important scientific challenges in its original realm of biology. When a paradigm loses control over the worldview of enough people—as the Christian paradigm did in the 19th century, and the evolutionary paradigm may be doing now; another controlling model sweeps in to take its place. When this happens, people commonly call it a "paradigm shift." Though generally unpopular now among elite academic establishments, "Intelligent Design" is beginning to supplant evolution as a scientific paradigm because it has more explanatory power on many levels. This may be the start of a major paradigm shift. Sometimes because the term *paradigm* is over-used in New Age circles, Christians fear that it has a built-in New Age or occult connotation, and unfairly shun it. It does not have any such thing. It is a generic term for *the controlling part of a model*, or another term for a model itself. The model can be of any idea system or worldview.

***particular*** – An object—any object—that is virtually meaningless by itself, and derives its meaning from a universal. See ***Universal***, and ***inductive reasoning and Inductive Bible Study***

***Pax Romana*** – The peace of Rome enforced by Roman military might and guaranteed by Roman law.

***Pelagianism*** **–** A heresy originating with a Celtic monk named Pelagius, who denied the Doctrine of the Fall (or Original Sin), and taught that death was not the result of sin; that every man was born good until he chose to sin as an individual. Aside from its disregard of God's word, Pelagianism created a philosophical problem because it had no adequate way to explain how a righteous and loving God could create a cosmos already filled with death, pain, disease, and violence as built-in components and then call it "good." See ***Doctrine of the Fall***.

***phenomenological language*** **–** A form of language use that describes how a phenomenon appears to happen without addressing its actual mechanics, yet without violating the literal discussion of that phenomenon; for example, when the weatherman says that the sun will rise at 7:00 AM. The weatherman is not claiming the sun rises and circles the earth, but that the local geographic coordinates will pass under the night-day meridian at 7:00 AM. He is still describing a literal sunrise, but according to its appearance, not its mechanics.

***philology*** **-** The study of the structure, historical development, and relationships of a language or languages, and of the language conventions used. For example, educated people did not clearly recognize ***phenomenological language*** for what it was during the Galileo Conflict because *philology* had not yet advanced to where it had defined the term or studied it as a language convention. See ***etymology*** and ***hermeneutics***.

***Platonism*** **–** The philosophy of Plato. See ***Neo-Platonic***.

***plenary indulgence*** **–** A Roman Catholic papal indulgence that wipes the slate for all temporal sins committed after baptism. See ***indulgence***.

***polemicist*** **–** One who refutes doctrinal errors within the church that arise from those who are otherwise considered orthodox, as opposed to an *apologist* which defends the faith against ideologies that arise from outside the church or from fundamentally non-orthodox sources. For most of church history, the work of the polemicist was generally seen as a valid service to the church. Today polemics are viewed in an almost universally negative light, which might be a sign that believers are adopting an overly naïve and unbalanced view of the church in reaction to past polemicists that sometimes went too far into a witch-hunt approach. See ***apologist***.

***Politically Correct*** **–** A radical Leftist idea based on the assumption that politics should drive morality, rather than the other way around. It has infected American thought and culture in direct proportion to the degree that culture embraces moral and cultural relativism. Political Correctness enshrines a redefined version of the word "tolerance" as its highest moral priority. Unfortunately, the "tolerance" it enshrines is not the word as originally defined—*the ability to extend human dignity even to those with whom you sharply disagree in a "live and let live" way*. The new definition is that of *moral indifference*, and extends not only to people, but also to the ideas, worldviews, and lifestyles of people. *Politically Correct "tolerance" demands we effectively accept that all ideas and lifestyles are equally good, which demands we bow to moral relativism; an idea based on a logical fallacy*. Political Correctness is in fact an instrument of intolerance; a shabby and ugly counterfeit of genuine tolerance based on respect and human dignity.

***Polytheistic*** or ***Polytheism*** **–** Any religion that worships many gods.

***Pontifex Maximus*** **–** Originally the pagan high priest of the Roman Imperial Cult, modeled after the priestly worship of the Babylonian god-king, whose priests the Romans had found in exile at the Greek city of Pergamum. The term *pontifex* originally carried the idea of *bridge-builder* because such priests were supposed to build spiritual bridges and become mediators between men and the gods. We get our word *pontoon*, which is a type of floating bridge support, from the same root. The Latin word *maximus* simply means *chief* or *most high*—we get the English, *maximum* or "*maxed-out,*" from this word. In the 4th century, the title *Pontifex Maximus* had such strong pagan religious connotations that the Christian Western Emperor Gratian refused to use it any longer. Before that time, the Roman Emperor was considered high priest of the Imperial Cult, which worshipped the idea of Rome, and the emperor as a god. After Gratian renounced the title, Damasus, Pope of Rome worked to be elected to that position. However, only in the next century did Roman Popes really emphasize it, after Leo the Great magnified the title to reflect the civil power that the dying Roman government at Ravenna had given him. It has since become a title synonymous to the Roman Catholic Pope.

***Pope*** **–** Originally a title of affection that meant *papa* or *dear father* given by Christians to bishops of large metropolitan churches in cities that had political authority over major regions of the Roman Empire. Eventually the word developed into a synonym for *Patriarch,* that title often used for the bishops of eventually 5 major *sees* or regional pastoral seats. By the 5th century, there were Popes of Alexandria, Rome, Antioch, and Jerusalem, with the functionally equivalent office of the Patriarch of Constantinople, which because of the city's late use as a major capitol, never was really called by the title of *Pope*. Because Rome had the biggest region of jurisdiction and local turmoil had dissipated the political and religious power of the churches of Antioch, Jerusalem and Alexandria, soon only the Pope of Rome in the West and the Patriarch of Constantinople in the East were left as major ecclesiastical influences. When the empire crumbled in the West, the Roman government gave Pope Leo the Great civil authority and compelled all Western churches to submit to his see. This situation developed into the Roman Catholic Church and its papacy, as we know it today.

***Positivism, Logical Positivism,*** and ***positivist*****–** A philosophy that says human sense perception is the only allowable basis for knowledge. Auguste Comte developed *Positivism* into a philosophy of history, epistemology, ethics, and science in the early 19th century using the faith-assumptions of materialistic Rationalism as an intellectual base. Philosophic *Positivism* was supposed to eventually replace theology and metaphysics as a system for knowing reality, but ultimately succeeded only in miring the search for scientific truth in a dogmatic Materialism. While the Positivist system of epistemology is useful in certain hard sciences like chemistry, it is hardly capable as a universal system of knowledge for all areas of reality. Historians now reject it. See ***Materialism, Rationalism, epistemology, the Enlightenment,*** and ***Modernism***.

***Postmodernism*** and ***Postmodern Era*** **–** The currently dominant worldview, which claims, "all truth is relative" to ethnic, religious, social, and political "tribes;" that all we can really have are "truth claims." The Postmodern Era began roughly from the late 20th century, on. It is characterized by a decreasing value placed on reason and analytical thinking, and any system of moral or spiritual absolutes that can be proposed or debated in a rational way. Postmodern people often see reasoning systems correctly as useful tools in the sciences and technology, but incorrectly as useless in the realms of ethics, religion, spirituality, and interpersonal relationships. Because postmodernist assumptions underestimate *cause and effect* in morality and business ethics, we see a rise in abuse, and loss of fidelity and responsibility in family, business, academic, and political relationships. With the dominance of Postmodernist "Living Document" approaches to constitutional law, the Constitution has now become a plaything in the hands of whoever has the power to redefine its terms, without connection to its original intent. In Postmodernism's rejection of objective truth comes the implication that "truth claims" are mere political tools designed to gain and sustain power. Once society removes claims to truth from the realm of objective evidence, and an ethic of moral absolutes; then no motivation except gaining or keeping political power remains plausible.

***Preterism*** **–** The belief that Bible prophecy, particularly Matthew 24 and Revelation, was fulfilled before 70 AD.

***Pre-millennial or Pre-Millennialism*** – A major school of biblical prophetic interpretation that sees the visible Second Coming of Christ as happening before the Millennial Age, which is how the Book of Revelation sequences it. Pre-millennial adherents are often the most literal and natural in their general interpretations of Scripture (which does not mean they don't recognize obvious figures of speech for what they are). This author's prophetic view falls within the Pre-Millennial camp.

***Pre-Tribulation Rapture*** – The view that Christ will take his church out of the world some time before the beginning of the Tribulation Period described in Revelation.

***Presbyterian*** – Both a range of denominations, and a generic church leadership system, that emphasizes the role of a council of elders or *presbyters* as the highest human church authority, rather than the pastor or bishop. Pastors in *presbyterian* styled churches are at best the executive elder on a board of elders or at worst a hireling of the elder board. A biblical case for a *presbyterian* church leadership structure can be made from New Testament Scripture as can a case for an *episcopalian* system. The strength of a *presbyterian* system is in Spirit-led consensus among recognized elders to sanity-check each other. See ***presbyters***, ***Episcopalian*** and ***Congregational***.

***presbyters*** – Originally, a Greek derived word that described early church *elders*, it eventually developed, beginning around the time of Cyprian (middle 3rd century), into a standing priesthood. From there, it became the word for Eastern Orthodox and Roman Catholic *priests*. During the Reformation, the word was returned to its most basic meaning of *elder*, as it has been defined within Reformation-based churches ever since.

***presupposition*** – An idea or belief assumed in advance of any evidential investigation, or taken for granted in a way that often goes without saying during a given investigation; also a term for a foundational assumption or starting assumption or, as I have often put it, a *faith-assumption*. All investigations and belief systems begin from a set of presuppositions because nobody can begin to reason in any area without assuming some things are already true. Good presuppositions will lead an investigation to a sound interpretation of evidence. Faulty presuppositions will skew the interpretation of evidence in inaccurate directions. A mixture of good and faulty presuppositions (which is often what happens) will lead to an interpretation of evidence that is partially sound, but may have serious flaws at several points—hopefully for the investigator, not key ones. People can only discriminate sound presuppositions from unsound ones by how well they seem to fit reality over the long term. It is an inexact science, which is why we need more exact ways of knowing wherever possible. Since presuppositions usually are made about ideas that can neither be proven or disproven, they are usually guided by such things as worldview, political ideology, culture, and religion in ways unavoidable at the bottom line. That does not mean a certain amount of objectivity is not possible, only that it is impossible to be totally objective in our scientific, historic, or forensic investigative methods.

***priest*** - one who makes sacrifice and mediation possible between men and divinity, as in the Old Testament Aaronic Priesthood. The word can also be used for religious or shamanistic offices in pagan religions. The word eventually became synonymous in early Roman Orthodoxy with the *presbyter*, who was the early church officer most often charged with the service of communion.

***priestly concubinage*** – The practice of late 1st millennium Roman Catholic and Eastern Orthodox bishops and high-level priests that kept harems of wives, mistresses and concubines. The Cluniac Reform Movement of the early 11th century shifted the Western Church from this extreme to that of required celibacy vows for the priesthood.

***Protestant*** – That group of Christian church denominations that came in the wake of the *Reformation*, and which originally recognized fidelity to Scripture as more important than apostolic succession from either Roman Catholic or Eastern Orthodox lines. The Roman Catholic Church excommunicated Protestant teachers; hence, the latter do not accept the authority of the Pope of Rome as Christ's Vicar on earth. The name originated from a letter of protest called the *Protestatio*, which signaled for many the formal break with Rome. By this definition, today's independent churches, like Calvary Chapel, would be classified *Protestant*.

***Qu'ran*** or ***Koran*** – The Islamic holy book written over 23 years by Mohammed and arranged as sayings with no thought to chapter themes or chronological order.

***Radical Secularism*** – Any ideology that seeks to remove Christian ideas from Judeo-Christian influenced Western societies. When we can't even say "Merry Christmas" anymore, we are living in a ***dystopia*** governed by some form of *Radical Secularism*.

***Rapture*** – Taken from a Latin word, which means *to be quickly snatched away*, the *Rapture* is a common modern Evangelical term for when Christ comes to suddenly take those who are genuinely regenerated believers off the earth to meet him in the air. (See 1 Cor. 15 and 1 Thess. 4 and 5.) Within the Pre-Millennial prophetic understanding (which is the only school that takes Bible prophecy in such precise terms), there are three basic beliefs about when the Rapture will happen relative to the visible Second Coming of Christ. One view is the Post-Tribulation Rapture, which obviously places the event after the Great Tribulation global judgments. Another is the Mid-Tribulation view that associates the Rapture with the taking up of the Two Witnesses described in Rev. 11. The 3rd view and the one I personally believe best accounts for all the relevant Scriptures, is the Pre-Tribulation interpretation. This model usually depicts the Rapture as happening immediately before the Great Tribulation, though the relevant Scriptures allow for a Rapture that happens considerably before the Tribulation, so long as the end of the Tribulation occurs before the generation that witnessed the Rapture is completely gone. After the Rapture, God will work primarily through Israel as his main witness in that generation. While Israel became a nation again in 1948, it is possible that its full spiritual rebirth (or budding) will not come until God deals with them again as his primary instrument of revelation rather than the church. While I do not say that is necessarily how it will happen, the relevant Scriptures leave open that possibility. (See Luke 21 and Matthew 24.)

***Rationalism*** – In its broadest sense, the philosophical theory that human reason is the only valid basis for truth, as opposed to experimental observation, divine revelation, or authority. Most often, the term refers to a materialistic Rationalism that begins its search for truth from the faith-assumption that nothing exists beyond the universe, and therefore anything supernatural is automatically impossible. I have defined Rationalism generally in the latter terms because that is how it most often manifests in our culture.

***Reductionism*** and ***reductionist*** – A necessary tool in hard sciences, like physics and chemistry, which deal in extremely large quantities of atoms; social soft sciences often apply *reductionism* improperly to studies of the human condition. As a thought system, *Reductionism* seeks to *reduce things to their basic components*—a useful tool for engineers and chemists. *Reductionist* describes any person or formula given to using *Reductionism* over-much, or in the wrong way, or as an ideology, particularly in things pertaining to the human condition. In practice, this form *Reductionism* often leads to oversimplifying whatever process is under study, to the point where the interpretation of that process is no longer truly accurate. One can usually identify an ideologically reductionist concept by its use of words like *only* or *just*; the statement that, "man is *just* a series of biological DNA replication errors," for example. Not every *reductionist* formula is wrong. My assessment that "Liberal Theology is *only* an expression of the Enlightenment's materialistic Rationalism in theological words" is still accurate, even if I could say much more. Nevertheless, the systematic use of *reductionist* conclusions in the study of the human condition often leads to errors that people must correct later, often systematically, and at great cost. (See Ch. 20.) People and their ideas are not that simple.

***Reformation*** – The broad-based Christian reform movement associated with Luther, Zwingli, Calvin and other Protestant reformers beginning in the 16th century. The *Reformation* was characterized by a rejection of the papal system from being a necessary attribute of Christian faith, and an emphasis on the biblical Doctrine of Justification by Grace Alone through Faith, which produces good works as a result.

***Regenerated*** – The process, and those who go through it, that the Holy Spirit performs on the minds and hearts of believers in Christ, described in Tit. 3:3-7, Rom. 12:1-2, and Eph. 4:20-24.

***Roman Catholic, Romanist,*** and ***Romanism*** – Having to do with that form of Orthodox Catholicism that arose in the wake of Pope Leo the Great's consolidation of most of Western Christendom under Rome's see during the fall of the Western Roman Empire. *Romanism* is the teaching that submission to the Roman Pope is a basic article of the Christian faith that must be preserved at all costs. It also encompasses the acceptance of Transubstantiation, purgatory, penance, and the idea that Mary is a co-mediatrix and co-redemptrix with Christ.

***Romanticism*** – A philosophy beginning in the late 18th century, which emphasized the value of subjective experience over the classical submission to objective rational thought. *Romanticism* was a feelings-based view of reality that saw the human imagination as good without any moderation supplied by rational intellect and moral absolutes. Historians often consider Jean Jacques Rousseau the father of *Romanticism*, though other famous romantics were Johann Wolfgang von Goethe, David Hume, Ludwig von Beethoven, Johann Christoph Friedrich von Schiller, William Wordsworth, and Samuel Taylor Coleridge. Much of the secular thought of the 19th century arose out of a cooperative fusion of *Romanticism* with materialistic Rationalism; two streams of thought one would think incompatible, but which often balanced each other off in a perverse sort of way. Darwinism is a good example of Romanticism fused with materialistic Rationalism. Molecule-to-Man Evolution provided a materialistic theory of origins, while it tied humanity to the animal world in a way that appealed to romantics for whom Nature was the highest ideal. To read Darwin, and his immediate followers, is to read an imaginative and romantically laced account of a Materialist myth on origins. Such writings are as filled with leaps of fancy as with careful observations of the natural world. See ***subjective, objective, Materialism,*** and ***Rationalism***.

***Rosary*** – A beaded chain usually in sets of 10 beads apiece that usually contains a small crucifix and icon of the Virgin, used to recite repetitions of the *Lord's Prayer* and the *Hail Mary* in 10 repeated sets called decades. The *Rosary* is a common Roman Catholic prayer form used at wakes and funerals but not limited to those occasions.

***Sabellian*** *and* ***Sabellianism*** – A form of early Monarchian heresy started by a teacher named Sabellius, who taught that the Father, Son, and Holy Spirit are just three different roles the One God plays in different circumstances, rather than the three persons of the Godhead. See ***Monarchian***.

***Sacradotalism*** – The belief that God sends His grace mainly through sacramental rituals, which require the office of a special priestly caste or order to properly perform.

***sanctified*** and ***sanctification*** – The process by which the Holy Spirit conforms the justified believer in Christ into Christ's image during this life, which ends only when the Lord calls us home, and culminates with glorification at the believer's resurrection, when Christ returns.

***Scholastic Theology*** – A late medieval Roman Catholic theology centered on Scholastic teachers like Anselm, Thomas Aquinas, and William of Occam. It focused on the theological authority of Latin Church fathers like Jerome and the philosophical authority of Aristotle.

***Scientism*** – A functionally religious belief system that places its faith in science to solve the basic human problems and to answer life's "big questions." *Scientism* rests on the assumption of an Ideological Naturalism. See ***Methodological Naturalism***.

***sectarian*** – A view of the church where one considers their own local religious system or sect to be the "true church" exclusively to all other Christian religious systems regardless of similarities between the systems. See ***denominational***.

***Secular Humanism*** or ***Secularism*** – A belief system that adheres to a completely secular form of Humanism that denies the reality of divine revelation, and believes humanity is its own highest authority. Usually built, as an ideology, upon varied mixtures of Romanticism and materialistic Rationalism, *Secular Humanism* looks to science and human intellect alone to answer the big questions, and universally embraces evolution as the foundational guiding principle of all science. Generally, it is the intellectual foundation for the mainstream worldview of the West, today. See ***Romanticism***, ***Rationalism***, ***Modernism***, and ***Materialism***.

***see*** – A noun that describes the largest region of ecclesiastical oversight for bishops – usually used to for the episcopal jurisdiction of a pope or patriarch, but applicable to any regional bishop's sphere of responsibility.

***seeker-friendly*** – A term used to describe churches that make an extra effort to attract spiritual seekers, but sometimes in a way that is too accommodating to present culture and does not stress important but socially difficult biblical truths adequately or honestly.

***semi-Docetic*** – A description of early Orthodox and Catholic views that rejected the grosser *Docetic* heresies about the nature of Christ but accepted the same set of cultural assumptions that led to *Docetism* when they were applied to lesser subjects like married sex, holiness and the value of asceticism. See ***Docetic***, ***ascetic*** and ***Gnosticism***.

***Semi-Pelagianism*** – A moderated form of the Pelagian heresy that made God's grace a necessary part of salvation, but which said that humans had to take the first step toward God and contribute towards meriting God's grace. One should not confuse that with the biblical idea that receiving real grace will result in good works. Since grace means *unmerited favor*, speaking of "meriting grace" in any terms is an oxymoron.

***Septuagint*** – The first known translation of the Hebrew Scriptures, and earliest extant version of the Old Testament. When Greek King over Egypt, Ptolomy II Philadelphus, built the Great Library of Alexandria, he requested that all non-Greek subjects translate their early writings into Greek for the library. Seventy Jewish scribes living in Alexandria translated probably pre-Exile versions of the Mosaic Law, around 280 BC, and later, the Prophets, and Writings into Greek, around 250-30 BC. Historians call this body of texts the *Septuagint* (or LXX) because it is Latin for the number 70. I suspect they were pre-Babylonian Captivity texts because the pre-Exile "Paleo-Hebrew" of the prophets and the "Paleo-Semitic" of Moses' day more resembled Phoenician, than the post-Exile Hebrew we recognize. The Greek alphabet and much of the language also developed from Semitic Phoenician. If you were a Jew, asked by a Gentile king to translate Moses into Greek, would you use pre-Exile texts written in a language more similar to Greek; or post-Exile texts of Ezra's school, written in a form of Hebrew very distant from Greek? The differences between the Septuagint and Hebrew texts of the slightly later Dead Sea Scrolls (circa 200 BC to 135 AD), and the much later Masoretic Text (500-900 AD), can largely be explained by the Alexandrian scribes using pre-Exile texts. This also explains why Jesus and the New Testament writers had no problem calling both the Septuagint and the Hebrew versions "Scripture" without arguing over which was corrupted. The New Testament was written in a single generation, the Old, over at least 1600 years. That means inspired writers at key points in OT history, like Samuel, Solomon, and Ezra, likely updated the language, and added a few editorial explanations that future generations would not intuitively know. This explains the differences between the MT and LXX, why Jesus and the NT writers had no apparent problems with those differences, and why there are sometimes evidences of editorial insertion in OT books. This explanation is faithful to traditional views of inspiration, and makes better sense than the Liberal "JEPD" Documentary Hypothesis.

***Simony*** – The practice of buying or selling church offices; named for Simon the Sorcerer of Acts 8:18-24, who tried to buy the Holy Spirit from Peter.

***Social Darwinism*** – Darwin's theory of evolution as applied to social systems. *Social Darwinism* is the idea that some humans are more evolved than others are and therefore have a greater right to survive. Originally prevalent in the racism of the late 19th and early 20th centuries, the ugliness produced by Nazism and Communism has made racial and economic models of Social Darwinism unpopular. The current model in vogue is spiritual – the idea that evolved humans can accept pantheistic and non-rational existential forms of spirituality that deny divine absolutes in morality and culture. This mode of Social Darwinism is at the same time more subtle and more dangerous than the older forms because it is not often recognized for what it is. In time, the results will be at least as ugly as those of the older models turned out to be – only the standards for 'evolved humanity' will be far more fluid and arbitrary. Yet another form of Social Darwinism revolves around the scientifically disproved hypothesis of embryonic recapitulation – the idea that embryos retrace their evolutionary ancestry in the womb, from unicellular to multi-cellular, to primitive chordate, to fish-like and so on. This idea is now almost universally rejected among biologists, because embryonic features that superficially resemble gills at the alleged 'fish-like' stage have nothing whatever to do with respiration organs. The same is true with many of the other supposed 'evolutionary' replays in the womb. The Social Darwinist approach allows people to artificially justify abortion and fetal-destructive experiments under the pretense that embryos 'at an earlier evolutionary stage' are not really human. Yet all embryos at every stage are genetically human right from the start, and can easily be proved so at the bio-molecular level. If embryonic recapitulation were really true then the DNA should morph through a fish-stage or a chordate stage on the microscopic scale to match whatever superficial imaginary resemblance exists on the macro level. It does not. Only the most dishonest or behind-the-times scientists allow embryonic recapitulation to be propagated any more, though it is still a popular theme in Hollywood sci-fi and among abortion rights advocates.

***Socialism*** – Theoretically, a social system where the worker/producers have political power and the economic means to distribute the goods they produce. Obviously this covers a wide range of scenarios. Often people use *Socialism* as another name for *Communism*, but that is not precise. Communism is only the most extreme form of Socialism; though perversely, Socialism in all its forms tends toward the same kinds of human oppression and economic breakdown as Communism, only at slower and less extreme rates and methods. Though all Communism is Socialism, not all Socialism is necessarily Communism. See ***Communism***.

***Socratic Dialogue*** - A formal teaching method where a small group, guided by a teacher or mentor, discusses and discovers precise answers to universal questions.

***Sola Scriptura*** – The idea that only Scripture is the final authority in the church; and the final measuring stick for whether doctrines or ideas are apostolic in character.

***Stoicism*** and ***Stoic*** – These terms describe the ancient Greek philosophy that reacted against the sensual fatalism of the Epicureans by saying that the sage (or wise) could rise above the material, and control it. While there is much truth in the *Stoic* idea that people can rise above their physical impulses, the degree to which that is possible is insufficient to counteract our basic sinfulness. Those who seem particularly good at living above their physical drives inevitably fall into the labyrinth of spiritual arrogance—unless they are doing so under the power and guidance of the Holy Spirit, as regenerate Christians (and even that is not a guarantee against stumbling into spiritual pride). *Stoicism* arose as a philosophical reaction to the same basic worldview that produced the *Epicureans*—the assumption that material things are bad simply because they are material. It failed to see evil as a spiritual problem that originated in the human heart. Therefore, it arrived at the idea that asceticism was the answer to evil—that if people avoided material things and desires enough, they would lessen human evil in direct proportion. While this might seem to work on certain levels, it fails to address the true nature of human evil the way Jesus did:

> **For out of the heart proceed evil thoughts, murders, adulteries, fornications, thefts, false witness, blasphemies: These are the things which defile a man: but to eat with unwashen hands defileth not a man. *Matthew* 15:19-20 KJV**

See ***Epicurean*** and ***ascetic***.

***straw man*** or ***straw man argument*** – A dishonest form of argumentation that does not address the real point in dispute, but rather creates an oversimplified cartoon version of that point that anybody would find silly, and then knocks it down. A "*straw man*" is a caricature or parody of a real man. In the same sense, one can make a straw man and tape the face of the heavyweight champion on it, and anyone could knock it over. Put a man into the ring with the real heavyweight, however, and it is an entirely different story. People can reduce ideas in the same way to something less than what they really are, if they have a clever wit and are too lazy to actually learn the position they are arguing.

***subjective*** – That which exists only in a persons' mind or internal experience; and cannot be proved by a rational process using external evidences. In today's world, people generally treat the *subjective* as unreal, while at the same time they give *subjective* experiences undue value in the area of spirituality and moral guidance. There are proper *subjective* spiritual experiences in Christianity, like experiencing the inner witness of the Holy Spirit reassuring us as individuals that we are God's children (1 John 4:14 and 5:9-10) or in some of the gifts of the Holy Spirit, like praying in tongues. Different Christian groups tend to emphasize either the *objective* or the *subjective* aspects of Christianity, as if holding to one makes the other invalid. In reality, a biblical Christianity demands both. Believers require rational instruction in *objective* Scriptural truths as well as the *subjective* witness of God's Spirit within them, to give power to take those Bible truths and apply them to all areas of life. Because God has made us, and revealed Himself within an integrated reality, it should not surprise us that He expresses Himself in both *objective* and *subjective* ways. See ***objective***.

***Syncretism*** – The mixture of two religious belief systems without regard to their compatibility, such as mixing the worship of Yahweh with the Baal and Asherah cults or combining New Testament Christianity with moral relativism. *Syncretism* has a strong relationship to the next word in this glossary.

***synthesis*** – The combining a *thesis* and its opposing *antithesis* to form a new, and supposedly "higher," hybrid *synthesis* of ideas. This word's relation to the meanings of *synthetic* and *artificial* is not accidental. While some opposing ideas are so extreme that they need moderation, most opposing concepts are absolute; and combining them creates a misleading and artificial philosophical position that does not fit reality. An example of a valid *synthesis* would take opposing views like, "*Christians should study the Bible and avoid subjective spiritual experiences*" and "*Christians should put spiritual experiences first and not emphasize human reasoning about Scripture*" and examine the strengths and weaknesses of both points. The resulting *synthesis* might say, "*Christians need both objective analysis from studying the Bible, and the subjective experience of assurance and power from the Holy Spirit, to live it out in the real world.*" An invalid use of *synthesis* denies the existence of absolutes and seeks to combine or moderate opposing ideas indiscriminately. This is one of today's most basic worldview weaknesses. For example, our culture takes divine absolutes like *the sanctity of human life* on the one hand, and the idea that *humans are an exploitable resource* on the other, to create a synthesis that is totally artificial and arbitrary. The idea that unborn children are not actually *persons* until they are born is an example of this kind of arbitrary *synthesis*. So is the belief that science should harvest unborn children for valuable stem cells and organs for medical research. When the *thesis + antithesis = synthesis* method is used to deny moral absolutes, it becomes *moral relativism*; the idea of right and wrong fades to a putrid corpse-like gray. See ***thesis*** and ***antithesis***.

***Talmudic*** **–** Having to do with the Jewish *Talmud*; a body of ancient rabbinical religious laws in addition to the biblical Mosaic Law, designed to interpret the divine statutes given to Moses. The *Talmud* is divided into two bodies of literature called the *Mishnah* and the *Gemara*, and is considered the basis for Jewish religious authority in much the same way that Church Canon is the basis for religious authority in the Roman Catholic Church.

***teleology*** **-** The explanation of phenomena and objects by the purpose they serve rather than by speculations about what caused them. Of course, teleology can also be speculative if the purpose of a given object or phenomena is not obvious or apparent.

***Theocracy*** **–** A form of government formally controlled by a single religious system, like the Islamic Republic of Iran; not to be confused with having a state church. In a *theocracy*, an institutional church, mosque, or temple controls the state directly.

***thesis*** **–** A point of intellectual argument expressed as a propositional statement. We could make a simple hypothetical *thesis* that *A* is not the same as *non-A*. Somebody could then come along and argue the opposite; that "certain *non-A*'s are actually the same as *A*." To put this in useful terms, we could make the *thesis* that "*evil behavior is never good, and does not lead to happiness.*" The *antithesis* or opposite statement would be, "*evil behavior is always good because it's fun.*" Many of today's social engineers, which are often educated way beyond their intelligence, would then argue for a *synthesis* that might say, "*Some evil behavior is actually good in the long run, and some good behavior produces evil social conditions.*" If that last sounded right to you, you are a child of the 21st century who needs to think more clearly on the subject.

***trans-cultural*** **–** Describes an ability for a religion, philosophy, or ideology to transcend cultural boundaries and re-express themselves in terms that seem native to new cultures.

***transmutation of matter*** **–** The medieval alchemy idea that substances can be transformed into other substances if only one can figure out the magical or chemical formula. See ***alchemy***.

***Transubstantiation*** **–** The Roman Catholic doctrine governing how Christ's presence operates during the Eucharist or Holy Communion; it basically teaches that ordinary bread and wine are literally transformed into the body and blood of Christ through the divine authority vested on the priest, only in such a way that human sense or instruments cannot detect the change.

***Uniformitarian*** **–** Describes the assumptions that present processes in nature are *always* the key to understanding how they operated in the distant past; and that all existing forms developed by gradual changes. Generally, *Uniformitarianism* is the opposite of ***Catastrophism***.

***universal*** **–** In the context of inductive and deductive reasoning, a *universal* gives meaning to particulars. A chess piece, apart from the game board and the company of those who play chess, is just a meaningless figurine—a *particular*. The chessboard, the rules of chess, and people who like to play chess are the *universals* that give meaning to the chess piece. In the same way, God and His word are the universals that give meaning to all created things, including people. See ***inductive reasoning and Inductive Bible Study***, and ***particular***.

***Universalism*** **–** In its Christian form, the belief that all persons will be saved eventually through the redemption purchased by Christ. In its pagan form, *Universalism* usually takes on a pantheistic view of God or the gods. Both forms of *Universalism* ultimately promote the idea that "all roads lead to God." People often find this view naïvely comforting, but the words of Jesus or any of the other biblical writers do not supported it, and it even violates many human concepts of justice. *Universalism* is the ultimate spiritual narcotic; it keeps people from seeing that the stakes really are high in a fallen world, and that sin, left unattended, has eternal consequences spelled out unmistakably in Scripture.

***utilitarian*** **–** Relating to the philosophy of ***Utilitarianism***, which makes "practical usefulness" the bottom line for human value. In a utilitarian view, the aged and many handicapped people are a drain on society because they can be of no practical use in a culture that, ideally, should run like a well-oiled machine. Some Christians have adopted a sanitized version of Utilitarianism in that they reject the value of anything that does not directly further the spread of the gospel, like the arts or sciences. This "Christianized Utilitarianism" can sound most spiritual, but it eventually becomes a victim of its own shortsightedness; the gospel spreads more readily, and more deeply, among people culturally prepared for it across a wide range of subjects and disciplines. Christian Utilitarianism also violates the Reformation-based biblical work ethic that gives intrinsic value to all non-sinful professions in society.

***Utopia*** and ***Utopian*** **–** An idealized perfect society, named from Sir Thomas More's satirical novel, *Utopia*. *Utopian* describes any ideology or attempt to form a perfect society—a process that always involves unfair laws designed artificially to ensure supposedly fair outcomes. This always produces *dystopia*. Fair laws can never guarantee perfect outcomes, only define, and punish crimes. See ***dystopia***, ***Communism***, and ***Socialism***.

***Vicar of Christ*** **–** A term for the Roman Pope, which came into vogue during the Lay Investiture controversy; especially after Pope Gregory VII defined papal authority in its most far-reaching terms. A *vicar* is a deputy or substitute agent supposed to execute authority in his master's name—In this case, Christ. The problem with this concept is that Christ needs no substitute in the church. Necessary human authority in the church or elsewhere is always provisional, not ultimate. Even the Apostle's authority was provisional—Paul said, **"But though *we*, or an angel from heaven preach any other gospel unto you than that ye have received, let him be accursed." Galatians 1:8 KJV** The implication of saying "we" here is that even the Apostles were subject to the objective gospel revelation that eventually found its written form as the New Testament.

***voluntaryism*** **–** The idea that the state should not coerce people to join a particular church and should leave spiritual matters to the churches so that people can approach God on a voluntary basis; not to be confused with voluntarism. The original emphasis of this ideology was to protect churches from state interference. Socialists and Secular Humanists, who want to purge the state from the influence of Christian ideas on its history and development; have distorted voluntaryism today in ways that changed the American government into something fundamentally at odds with what the Founders designed. But such a purging only produces "politically correct" dogmas, and an effective state religious philosophy that violates its own supposed neutrality in things religious.

***worldview*** – The basic view of reality of any person or culture. Worldviews are distinguished from philosophies in that they usually are made up of unprovable cultural assumptions that people don't always know they are making or think about, but take for granted. Philosophies and religions then try to deal with the issues that arise from various worldview perceptions.

***worldview apologetics*** –A form of defending the Christian Faith that makes use of knowledge about ancient and modern worldview assumptions, within a biblical philosophical framework.

## Also by K.G. Powderly Jr.

*The Windows of Heaven* novels:

- **Dawn Apocalypse Rising** – Book 1 of *The Windows of Heaven*
- **The Paladin's Odyssey** – Book 2 of *The Windows of Heaven*
- **A Broken Paradise** – Book 3 of *The Windows of Heaven*
- **The Tides of Nemesis** – Book 4 of *The Windows of Heaven*
- **Gate of the Gods** – Book 5 of *The Windows of Heaven*

Made in the USA
Charleston, SC
10 January 2016